Introduction to **Statistics in Psychology**

Visit the *Introduction to Statistics in Psychology* 5th edition Companion Website at **www.pearsoned.co.uk/howitt** to find valuable **student** learning material including:

- Chapter overviews to introduce and give a feel for topics covered in the chapter
- Multiple-choice questions to test your understanding
- Additional datasets with exercises for further practice and self-testing
- A set of research scenarios and questions that enable you to check your understanding of when to use a particular statistical test or procedure
- An online glossary to explain key terms
- Interactive online flashcards that allow the reader to check definitions against the key terms during revision
- A guide to using Microsoft Excel to help you if you're doing statistical analyses using Excel
- A guide to statistical computations on the web for your reference
- Roadmaps to help you to select a test for analysis of data

Introduction to
Statistics in Psychology

Fifth Edition

Dennis Howitt Loughborough University
Duncan Cramer Loughborough University

Prentice Hall
is an imprint of

Harlow, England • London • New York • Boston • San Francisco • Toronto • Sydney • Singapore • Hong Kong
Tokyo • Seoul • Taipei • New Delhi • Cape Town • Madrid • Mexico City • Amsterdam • Munich • Paris • Milan

Pearson Education Limited
Edinburgh Gate
Harlow
Essex CM20 2JE
England

and Associated Companies throughout the world

Visit us on the World Wide Web at:
www.pearsoned.co.uk

First published 1997
Second edition published 2000
Revised second edition 2003
Third edition 2005
Fourth edition published 2008
Fifth edition published 2011

© Prentice Hall Europe 1997
© Pearson Education Limited 2000, 2011

ISBN: 978-0-273-73430-7

British Library Cataloguing-in-Publication Data
A catalogue record for this book is available from the British Library

Library of Congress Cataloging-in-Publication Data
Howitt, Dennis.
  Introduction to statistics in psychology / Dennis Howitt, Duncan Cramer. – 5th ed.
    p. cm.
  ISBN 978-0-273-73430-7 (pbk.)
1. Psychometrics.   I. Cramer, Duncan, 1948–   II. Title.
  BF39.H74 2011
  150.1′5195–dc22

                                2010032827

10 9 8 7 6 5 4 3 2 1
16 15 14 13 12 11

Typeset in 9.5/12pt Sabon by 35
Printed by Rotolito Lombarda, Italy

Brief contents

Contents

Part 2 Significance testing   97

Part 6   Advanced qualitative or nominal techniques   509

Supporting resources

Visit www.pearsoned.co.uk/howitt to find valuable online resources:

Companion Website for students

- Chapter overviews to introduce and give a feel for topics covered in the chapter
- Multiple-choice questions to test your understanding
- Additional datasets with exercises for further practice and self-testing
- A set of research scenarios and questions that enable you to check your understanding of when to use a particular statistical test or procedure
- An online glossary to explain key terms
- Interactive online flashcards that allow the reader to check definitions against the key terms during revision
- A guide to using Microsoft Excel to help you if you're doing statistical analyses using Excel
- A guide to statistical computations on the web for your reference
- Roadmaps to help you to select a test for analysis of data

For instructors

- PowerPoint slides that can be downloaded and used for presentations
- Testbank of question material

Also: The Companion Website provides the following features:

- Search tool to help locate specific items of content
- E-mail results and profile tools to send results of quizzes to instructors
- Online help and support to assist with website usage and troubleshooting

For more information please contact your local Pearson Education sales representative or visit **www.pearsoned.co.uk/howitt**

Guided tour

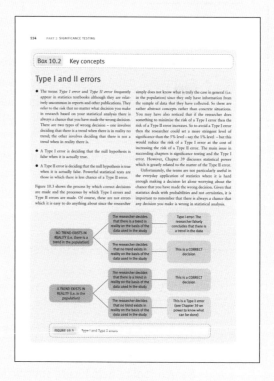

Clear overview

Introduces the chapter to give students a feel for the topics covered.

Key concepts

Offer a reminder of, and guidance on, important concepts and issues discussed in the text.

Focus on

Explores concepts and issues of importance.

The following shows a page reproduction containing Box 10.1 "Focus on" with the heading "Do correlations differ?", Section 10.4 "Pearson's correlation coefficient again", and Table 10.3 "A sample of 10 pairs of scores".

Screenshots, figures, graphs and tables

Are included throughout to clarify and further illustrate exploration and processes.

Calculation

Provides step-by-step instruction for working through a calculation.

Key points

Each chapter concludes with a set of key points to help summarise chapter coverage and serve as a useful reminder when revising a topic.

Computer analysis

Where relevant, you will see a link to the associated textbook, *Introduction to SPSS Statistics in Psychology: For version 19 and earlier* by the same authors. This book features step-by-step advice and instruction on analysing data using the computer package, SPSS Statistics.

Most chapters provide step-by-step instructions for carrying out the analysis on a computer.

Guided tour of the Companion Website

The website accompanying this book contains a range of resources to help you consolidate and test your understanding of concepts, tests and procedures. Go to **www.pearsoned.co.uk/howitt**

Homepage

Lists and links to the resources.

Multiple-choice questions

Allow you to check your knowledge for every chapter.

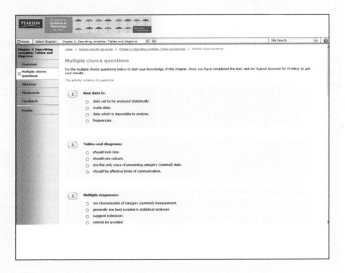

Roadmaps

Help guide you to the right test to
analyse a set of data.

Research scenarios and exercises

Allow you to check your knowledge of
which type of test or procedure to use in
different situations.

Datasets and exercises

Offer the opportunity
for you to practise
analyses with datasets.

Introduction

This fifth edition of *Introduction to Statistics in Psychology* enhances the student experience even further. There have been a a number of changes. Two new chapters have been added dealing with statistical power analysis and moderator variables. Significantly, this new edition has been produced in full colour enabling its visual impact to be improved. These changes are in keeping with the desire to have the most comprehensive yet user-friendly statistics book in the universe. We certainly know of no other single volume that covers so much at an accessible level for all students. One feature of the book which sets it apart from others aimed at students is that it continues to provide an accessible introduction to the wide range of statistics employed by professional researchers. Those who studied using the earlier editions may now be well into teaching and research careers of their own. We hope that these further enhancements may encourage them to keep *Introduction to Statistics in Psychology* permanently on their desks – open.

For this edition, we have added detail about how to go about carrying out data analyses using computers. There is nothing unusual about tying statistics textbooks to computer packages such as SPSS Statistics. Indeed, our *Introduction to SPSS Statistics in Psychology: For version 19 and earlier* is a good example of this approach. There is, however, a major drawback to using SPSS Statistics for computations – it simply is not sufficiently comprehensive to help with all of the statistical techniques that even students need to know about. It is very good at what it does, but there are times when additional help is needed. This is why we introduce students to other programs which will be helpful to them when necessary. One of the most important features of SPSS Statistics is that it is virtually universally available to students for little or no cost thanks to site licensing agreements. Unfortunately, this is not true of other commercial statistics software. For that reason we have suggested and recommended programs which are essentially free for the user. The web has a surprisingly large amount of such software to carry out a wide range of statistical routines. A few minutes using Google or some other search engine will often be surprisingly productive. Some of these programs are there to be downloaded but others, applets, are instantly available for calculations. We have added at the end of each chapter, advice on the use of software. We have not neglected SPSS Statistics and detailed step-by-step instructions are provided where SPSS Statistics will carry out the necessary task. For many users, these instructions will be all that they require though, of course, minutely detailed instruction books for using SPSS Statistics are readily available including our own *Introduction to SPSS Statistics in Psychology: For version 19 and earlier*.

The basic concept remains the same – a modular statistics package that is accessible throughout to a wide ability range of students. We have attempted to achieve this while being as rigorous as possible where rigor is crucial. Ultimately, this is a book for students, though its emphasis on statistics in practice means that it should be valuable to anyone seeking to familiarise themselves with the vast majority of common statistical techniques employed in modern psychology and related disciplines.

◼ Structure

This textbook is intended to cover most of the statistics that students need in a first-degree course in psychology and well beyond.

- Part 1 covers basic descriptive statistics from tables and diagrams through to the correlation coefficient and simple regression.

- Part 2 covers basic inferential statistics – significance testing. So the significance of the correlation coefficient, the *t*-tests and nonparametric testing are major features of Part 2.

- Part 3 covers the analysis of variance (ANOVA) up to the level at which the use of computers is recommended, not merely desirable. The most common and useful ANOVA designs are presented, including one-way related and unrelated ANOVAs, two-way unrelated ANOVAs, mixed designs and the analysis of covariance. The computation of appropriate significance levels for multiple comparisons is given special attention. MANOVA and discriminant (function) analysis are also included in Part 3.

- Part 4 covers more advanced correlational statistics such as partial correlation, multiple regression and factor analysis.

- Part 5 includes a miscellany of advanced techniques including meta-analysis, log-linear analysis, reliability and confidence intervals. Confidence intervals have been advocated increasingly in recent years as an alternative to conventional statistical significance testing. The new chapters on statistical power analysis and moderator variables are to be found in this section.

- Part 6 is concerned with the analysis of complex qualitative, nominal or category data. It features log-linear analysis together with two sorts of logistic regression – multinomial logistic regression and binomial logistic regression. Logistic regression can use score variables as independent variables, of course, but we have emphasised nominal or category independent variables.

◼ Package

The textbook is part of a package of materials for the teaching and learning of statistics as applied in psychological research. The package consists of the following four parts:

- This textbook, which provides an overview of the use of statistics in undergraduate laboratory work, practical work and final year projects.

- A computer book, *Introduction to SPSS Statistics in Psychology: For version 19 and earlier*, which explains how computations are easily carried out using a standard computer package. The student will learn to use SPSS Statistics for Windows. This is commonly available at universities and colleges throughout the world. It is now generally user friendly and solves many of the problems associated with the analysis of psychological data. Computer packages make it feasible to include more advanced statistical techniques than are normally included in statistics textbooks for psychology students.

- A research methods textbook, *Introduction to Research Methods in Psychology*, is available to supplement the other two texts.

- The companion website (see page xxiii) has been further improved with data sets and other new material.

In addition, Pearson Education now publish Dennis Howitt (2010), *An Introduction to Qualitative Research Methods in Psychology* which provides a comprehensive overview of qualitative methods in psychology and a practical introduction to their use.

These books offer a flexible and complete package to meet the needs of modern students at both the undergraduate and postgraduate level – and beyond. Research in psychology and related disciplines is increasingly varied and the modular approach of the three books allows instructors and readers to find their own route through the material. There is a close correspondence between the contents of the three books so far as quantitative methods are concerned. So in addition to the conceptual understanding provided by the statistics textbook, the SPSS Statistics book describes computer procedures in step-by-step detail – how data items are entered, how the analysis is run, how the output is understood and how the results are reported.

Another important feature of *Introduction to Research Methods in Psychology* is that both quantitative and qualitative methods are covered. Although statistical analysis is often not carried out on qualitative data, it is feasible to do statistical analyses of qualitative data and it may have enormous benefits. Appropriate techniques are drawn together in the statistics and SPSS Statistics textbooks. The research methods book surveys qualitative methods and provides alternative means of analysing qualitative data.

■ Level of difficulty

Throughout, the package is designed to remain at a relatively simple level even when complex statistics are being explained. The material is aimed at the vast majority of students who, although having some mathematical skills, nevertheless do not relish complex formulae and abstract explanations of obscure mathematical procedures. Our interest is in the development of students beyond their degrees and into their careers whether in psychology or some other field. The ability to do research and understand empirical data is increasingly a feature of many different professions.

Nevertheless, rigor is not sacrificed to this end. Students following our advice and recommendations carefully will be able to analyse virtually any data effectively and to a competent standard. To this end, we have been scrupulous in ensuring that alternative statistical procedures are mentioned when the limits of applicability of a statistical technique are breached. A good example of this is the inclusion of the Fisher exact probability test when chi-square is not applicable because of small expected frequencies. Students' data sets are often fairly small and must be analysed as they are because the option of collecting more data is not available.

■ Flexibility

The textbook is designed as a menu of statistical techniques, not all of which need be sampled. Chapters 1 to 18 constitute a thorough but compact basic introduction to psychological statistics; they are suitable for use as a basic-level course as they cover descriptive statistics and common inferential statistics. Flexibility was an important feature, planned into the package for the following reasons:

- All instructors teach courses differently. The textbook covers most of the commonly taught techniques and many less common ones too. Instructors may omit some chapters without causing difficulties. The textbook contains pertinent basic and revision information within each chapter wherever possible. In other words, instructors will be able to select their favoured route through the material.

- Some instructors prefer to teach statistics practically through the use of computers. This is made easy by this package which contains both a textbook and a computer manual.

- Many students will have little difficulty in self-study of most chapters. Supervisors of student practical classes and projects may find this particularly appealing as they can direct students to appropriate parts of the textbook.

- However, the flexibility is far greater than this. The package can serve as an introduction to statistics or as a textbook for an intermediate-level course. Not only is this better value for students, it means that the problems of transferring from one textbook to another are bypassed.

There is no right or wrong way of structuring modules in psychological statistics. What is appropriate depends on what students know already, the aims and objectives of the module and, most importantly, the other modules that the students are taking, especially those involving practical research. If statistics is taught as part of practical classes then it may be difficult to include formal lectures on the use of statistics. For these reasons and many others, this text is itself modular in construction. The physical order of the chapters in the text is merely one of several possibilities. Our aim is to give a thorough grounding in descriptive statistics before moving on to the basic principles of significance testing. This is partly because we feel that descriptive statistics is not always handled well by psychology students who too often regard statistical significance as equivalent to statistical analysis, at the expense of understanding and describing their data.

Most lecturers will choose their own route through the material. For example, the chapters on correlation and regression may be omitted or deferred if the lecturer wishes to teach basic experimental design and analysis. For this reason, each chapter lists essential prerequisites in terms of the students' knowledge and also refers to later chapters if these are particularly relevant.

■ Professional relevance

It is increasingly obvious that the statistics taught to students and the statistics contained in journal articles and books are drawing apart. For that reason, the book contains introductions to techniques such as factor analysis, multiple regression, path analysis, power analysis and logistic regression which are common in professional publications and generally easy to do using computer packages. Again, this section of the textbook may form part of an intermediate course.

■ Other features of the package

- Tables of statistical significance have been simplified extensively wherever possible for pedagogic reasons. Students find some books hard and confusing to use because the statistical tables are so obscurely or badly presented. Nevertheless, the book contains among the most extensive selection of tables possible, and some tables not available elsewhere. Although modern computer packages reduce the day to day need to refer to statistical tables, we think that they still have their place and need to be understood by anyone using statistics intelligently.

- Statistical formulae have been kept to a minimum. This is relatively easy since not too many formulae are necessary anyway.

- Every calculation is illustrated with a step-by-step example for students to follow. While we describe the hand calculation of statistical procedures, this is for pedagogic reasons. In the calculation process lies much of the meaning and interpretation of statistics. To understand how to do a statistical calculation is to understand the concepts better. Of course, once understood, there is little to be gained by not using statistical packages routinely for data analysis. There are some statistical analyses which are commonly misinterpreted because the researcher has not got the necessary understanding of just how they work.

- We have preferred to use methods and descriptions that communicate clearly and effectively to students even if they are at times not the most formally rigorous explanations. This introduces a degree of informality that might annoy the most statistically precise thinkers. We think it is for the greater good to avoid too abstract an approach.

- We have tried to provide insight into the ways in which psychologists use statistics.
- Practical advice on the learning and use of statistics in psychology is given at the end of every chapter of the textbook.
- The research methods textbook provides detailed accounts of the theory and practice of research design.
- The package is excellent value for the student as it meets all of their statistical needs for a first degree in psychology, and well beyond into postgraduate research and professional life.

■ Web resources

There is a website (www.pearsoned.co.uk/howitt) associated with this textbook offering multiple-choice testing and other resources. However, it is worthwhile emphasising that there are extensive web resources available to do many of the calculations described in this textbook. If a comprehensive statistical analysis package is not available, these sites are an attractive resource. New ones are constantly becoming available. The quick way of tracking them is simply to enter the name of the statistic into a favourite search engine.

List of figures

List of tables

List of boxes

Acknowledgements

■ **Authors' acknowledgements**

Producing a modern textbook is very much a team effort and so we would like to thank at least some of those who have contributed such a great deal to this fifth edition of *Introduction to Statistics in Psychology*.

Janey Webb was, once again, the most charming of taskmasters and her decision to move the book to full-colour has made a tremendous difference to the text. As ever, she was tirelessly supportive and focused on this fifth edition and her influence pervades every aspect of it. She was magnificently supported by Catherine Morrissey who has now moved on from Pearson Education and we wish her the best in her new job.

In charge of the production of the book have been Beth Wright, Philippa Fiszzon and Christina Venditti. We are well-used to superwomen in this role and the tradition has continued with this edition. They can do things beyond what ought to be possible including organising everything so immaculately.

The contribution of designers can be overlooked but they have a tremendous role to play in terms of the clarity and look of a text like this. Kevin Ancient was responsible for the text design and Nicola Woowat for the cover design. The copy editor for this edition was Ros Woodward and the proofreader was Jonathon Price. Their contribution is enormous and it is so comforting to authors to know that they are in such safe hands. How they remain so polite faced with our numerous errors is beyond comprehension.

The boffins at Pearson Education who design and run the website for the book also risk being unsung heroes – but not in this case. We are grateful to Louise Newman for her hard work on this.

Academic colleagues also contribute an enormous amount to a text like this by reviewing the previous edition and making recommendations and suggestions for the new edition. This is a vital stimulus to us and we would like to thank them for keeping us on our toes but not for keeping us up at night:

William Brown, University of East London
Jane M. Hutchinson, University of Central Lancashire
Dirk Janssen, University of Kent
Richard Rowe, The University of Sheffield
Paul Seager, University of Central Lancashire
Richard Stephens, Keele University
Jane Walsh, National University of Ireland, Galway

Dennis Howitt and Duncan Cramer

◼ Publisher's acknowledgements

We are grateful to the following for permission to reproduce copyright material:

Tables

Table I.1 adapted from Fundamentals of Behavioural Statistics, New York: McGraw Hill (Runyon, R.P. and Haber, A. 1989) Table I The McGraw-Hill Companies; Table I.2 adapted from Fundamentals of Behavioral Statistics, New York: McGraw-Hill (Runyon, R.P. and Haber, A. 1989) Table I The McGraw Hill Companies Inc.; Significance Table 18.3 adapted from Fundamentals of Behavioral Statistics, New York: McGraw-Hill (Runyon, R.P. and Haber A. 1989) Table I McGraw-Hill; Table 31.3 adapted from Relationship of gender, self-esteem, social class and racial identity to depression in blacks, JOURNAL OF BLACK PSYCHOLOGY, 20, pp.157–74 (1994), by Munford M.B. Copyright 1994 by SAGE PUBLICATIONS INC. JOURNALS. Reproduced with permission of SAGE PUBLICATIONS INC. JOURNALS in the format Textbook via Copyright Clearance Center.; Table 32.2 from The relation of formal education to ethnic prejudice: its reliability, validity and explanation, European Journal of Social Psychology, 25, pp.41–56 (Wagner, U. and Zick, A. 1995), John Wiley & Sons.

In some instances we have been unable to trace the owners of copyright material, and we would appreciate any information that would enable us to do so.

The publishers thank all the reviewers for their helpful comments on the book.

CHAPTER 1

Why you need statistics

Types of data

Overview

- Statistics are used to describe our data but also assess what reliance we can place on information based on samples.

- A variable is any concept that we can measure and that varies between individuals or cases.

- Variables should be identified as nominal (also known as category, categorical and qualitative) variables or score (also known as numerical) variables.

- Formal measurement theory holds that there are more types of variable – nominal, ordinal, interval and ratio. These are generally unimportant in the actual practice of doing statistical analyses. It is difficult to distinguish ordinal, interval and ratio measurement in practice in psychology.

- Nominal variables consist of just named categories whereas score variables are measured in the form of a numerical scale which indicates the quantity of the variable.

1.1 Introduction

Imagine a world in which everything is the same; people are identical in all respects. They wear identical clothes; they eat the same meals; they are all the same height from birth; they all go to the same school with identical teachers, identical lessons and identical facilities; they all go on holiday in the same month; they all do the same job; they all live in identical houses; and the sun shines every day. They do not have sex as we know it since there are no sexes so everyone self-reproduces at the age of 30; their gardens have the same plants and the soil is exactly the same no matter whose garden; they all die on their 75th birthdays and are all buried in the same wooden boxes in identical plots of land. They are all equally clever and they all have identical personalities. Their genetic make-up never varies. Mathematically speaking all of these characteristics are constants. If this world seems less than realistic then have we got news for you – you need statistics! Only in a world of standardisation would you not need statistics – in a richly varying world statistics is essential.

If nothing varies, then everything that is to be known about people could be guessed from information obtained from a single person. No problems would arise in generalising since what is true of Sandra Green is true of everyone else – they're all called Sandra Green after all. Fortunately, the world is not like that. Variability is an essential characteristic of life and the social world in which we exist. The sheer quantity of variability has to be tamed when trying to make statements about the real world. Statistics is largely about making sense of variability.

Statistical techniques perform three main functions:

1. They provide ways of summarising the information that we collect from a multitude of sources. Statistics is partly about tabulating your research information or data as clearly and effectively as possible. As such, it merely describes the information collected. This is achieved using tables and diagrams to summarise data, and simple formulae which turn fairly complex data into simple indexes that describe numerically the main features of the data. This branch of statistics is called *descriptive statistics* for very obvious reasons – it describes the information you collect as accurately and succinctly as possible. The first few chapters of this book are largely devoted to descriptive statistics.

2. Another branch of statistics is far less familiar to most of us: *inferential statistics*. This branch of statistics is really about economy of effort in research. There was a time when in order to find out about people, for example, everyone in the country would be contacted in order to collect information. This is done today when the government conducts a *census* of everyone in order to find out about the population of the country at a particular time. This is an enormous and time-consuming operation that cannot be conducted very often. But most of us are familiar with using relatively small *samples* in order to approximate the information that one would get by studying everybody. This is common in public-opinion surveying where the answers of a sample of 1000 or so people may be used, say, to predict the outcome of a national election. Granted that sometimes samples can be misleading, nevertheless it is the principle of sampling that is important. *Inferential statistics* is about the confidence with which we can generalise from a sample to the entire population.

3. The amount of data that a researcher can collect is potentially massive. Some statistical techniques enable the researcher to clarify trends in vast quantities of data using a number of powerful methods. Data simplification, data exploration and data reduction are among the names given to the process. Whatever the name, the objective is the same – to make sense of large amounts of data that otherwise would be

PART 1

Descriptive statistics

PHOTO 1.1	People vary in very obvious ways but they also vary in terms of their psychological characteristics. Just what would a small sample of people such as this tell us about the bigger crowd?

much too confusing. These *data exploration techniques* are mainly dealt with in the later chapters of this book.

1.2 Variables and measurement

The concept of a *variable* is basic but vitally important in statistics. It is also as easy as pie. *A variable is anything that varies and can be measured.* These measurements need *not* correspond very well with everyday notions of measurement such as weight, distance and temperature. So the gender of people is a variable since it can be measured as either male or female – and gender varies between people. Similarly, eye colour is a variable because a set of people will include some with brown eyes, some with blue eyes and some with green eyes. Thus measurement can involve merely categorisation. Clinical psychologists might use different diagnostic categories such as schizophrenia, bipolar disorder and anxiety in research. These diagnostic categories constitute a variable since they are different mental and emotional problems to which people can be allocated. Such categorisation techniques are an important type of measurement in statistics.

Another type of measurement in statistics is more directly akin to everyday concepts of measurement in which numerical values are provided. These *numerical* values are assigned to variables such as weight, length, distance, temperature and the like – for example, 10 kilometres or 30 degrees. These numerical values are called *scores*. In psychological research many variables are measured and *quantified* in much the same way. Good examples are the many tests and scales used to assess intelligence, personality, attitudes and mental abilities. In most of these, people are assigned a number (or score) in order to describe, for example, how neurotic or how extraverted an individual is. Psychologists will speak of a person having an IQ of 112 or 93, for example, or they will say an individual has a low score of 6 on a measure of psychoticism. Usually these numbers are used as if they corresponded exactly to other forms of measurement such as weight or length. For these, we can make statements such as that a person has a weight of 60 kilograms or is 1.3 metres tall.

1.3   Major types of measurement

Traditionally, statistics textbooks for psychologists emphasise different types of measurement – usually using the phrase *scales of measurement*. However, *for virtually all practical purposes there are only two different types of measurement in statistics*. These have already been discussed, but to stress the point:

1. *Score/numerical measurement* This is the assignment of a *numerical* value to a measurement. This includes most physical and psychological measures. In psychological jargon, these numerical measurements are called *scores*. We could record the IQ scores of five people as in Table 1.1. Each of the numerical values in the table indicates the named individual's *score* on the variable IQ. It is a simple point, but note that the numbers contain information that someone with an IQ of 150 has a higher intelligence than someone with an IQ of 80. In other words, the numbers *quantify* the variable.

2. *Nominal/category measurement* This is deciding to which category of a variable a particular case belongs. It is also appropriate to refer to it as a *qualitative measure*. So, if we were measuring a person's job or occupation, we would have to decide whether or not he or she was a lorry driver, a professor of sociology, a debt collector, and so forth. This is called *nominal* measurement since usually the categories are described in words and, especially, given names. Thus the category 'lorry driver' is a name or verbal description of what sort of case should be placed in that category.

   Notice that there are no numbers involved in the process of categorisation as such. A person is either a lorry driver or not. *However, you need to be warned of*

Table 1.1	IQ scores of five named individuals	
Individual		**IQ score**
Stan		80
Mavis		130
Sanjit		150
Sharon		145
Peter		105

Table 1.2	Frequencies of different occupations	
Occupational category		**Number or frequency in set**
Lorry drivers		27
Sociology professors		10
Debt collectors		15
Other occupations		48

a possible confusion that can occur. If you have 100 people whose occupations are known you might wish to count how many are lorry drivers, how many are professors of sociology, and so forth. These counts could be entered into a data table like Table 1.2. Notice that the numbers this time correspond to a count of the *frequency* or number of cases falling into each of the four occupational categories. *They are not scores*, but frequencies. The numbers do not correspond to a single measurement but are the aggregate of many separate (nominal) measurements. There is more about the concept of frequency in Box 1.1.

Make a habit of mentally labelling variables as numerical scores or nominal categories. Doing so is a big step forward in thinking statistically. This is all you really need to know about types of measurement. However, you should be aware that others use more complex systems. Read the following section to learn more about scales of measurement.

Formal measurement theory

Many psychologists speak of four different scales of measurement. Conceptually they are distinct. Nevertheless, for most practical situations in psychologists' use of statistics the nominal category versus numerical scores distinction discussed above is sufficient.

The four 'theoretical' scales of measurement are as follows. The scales numbered 2, 3 and 4 are different types of *numerical* scores.

1. *Nominal categorisation* This is the placing of cases into *named* categories – nominal clearly refers to names. It is exactly the same as our nominal measurement or categorisation process. — Could be 1, 2, 3 ofc

2. *Ordinal (or rank) measurement* The assumption here is that the values of the numerical scores tell us little else other than which is the smallest, the next smallest and so forth up to the largest. In other words, we can place the scores in order (hence ordinal) from the smallest to the largest. It is sometimes called rank measurement since we can assign ranks to the first, second, third, fourth, fifth, etc. in order from the smallest to the largest numerical value. These ranks have the numerical value 1, 2, 3, 4, 5, etc. You will see examples of this later in the book, especially in Chapters 7 and 18. However, few psychologists collect data directly as ranks.

3. *Interval or equal-interval measurement* The basic idea here is that in some cases the intervals between numbers on a numerical scale are equal in size. Thus, if we measure distance on a scale of centimetres then the distance between 0 and 1 centimetre on our scale is exactly the same as the difference between 4 and 5 centimetres or between 11 and 12 centimetres on that scale. This is obvious for some standard physical measurements such as temperature.

> ## Box 1.1   Key concepts
>
> # Frequency
>
> The concept of frequency tends to be taken a little for granted in statistics textbooks although it can cause some confusion in practice. A frequency is simply a count of how often a particular something occurs in your data. So counting the number of people with red hair in your sample gives you the frequency of red-haired people. Quite obviously, therefore, frequency and frequent are not the same – a frequency of 1 cannot usually be described as frequent. In some disciplines, frequency is defined as how often something occurs in a given period of time, such as in the frequency of sound waves. However, in psychology, this usage is not so common and frequency simply means the number of times something occurs in your data. You will find the word count used instead of frequency especially in statistical analysis computer program output.
>
> Frequency is the main statistical procedure which can be used with nominal category data. The analysis of nominal category data is largely in terms of counting the frequency of occurrence of each of the categories of nominal category variables. This is straightforward enough. Things risk getting confused when frequencies are used in relation to score data. So, as we have seen, we can count the frequency of any sort of characteristic in our data such as the frequency of children with dyslexia in a school class. But, equally, we can count the frequency of participants in a research study with an IQ of 140. That is, dyslexia and 140 are both categories (different values) in our data and so their frequencies can be counted. Dyslexia may have a frequency of 15 and the IQ of 140 may have a frequency of 23 or whatever. It is in the idea that the IQ of 140 has the frequency of 23 that the confusion may emerge. Surely 140 and 23 are both numbers just as 15 is a number? Indeed they are all numbers, but 140 is a score on the variable IQ and 23 is its frequency. What this boils down to is as follows:
>
> a) Frequency refer to the number of times that a particular category (or value) of a variable appears in the data. It is irrelevant whether these categories are given a name (e.g. dyslexia) or a number (e.g. 140).
>
> b) Scores refer to the amount or extent or quantity of a variable. So a number can be a frequency or a score. Consequently, it is important to carefully distinguish between the two since both are numbers.
>
> There is another potential confusion in relation to scores. Sometimes, a researcher will count how often a participant does something and use this as a score. So, for example, a researcher might be interested in people's ability to write text messages. A measure of skill at texting might be the number of errors that a person makes while texting for one minute. In this case, each person's frequency of making errors is being used as a score on the variable 'texting errors', for example.

4. *Ratio measurement* This is exactly the same as interval scale measurement with one important proviso. A ratio scale of measurement has an absolute zero point that is measured as 0. Most physical measurements such as distance and weight have zero points that are absolute. Thus zero on a tape measure is the smallest distance one can have – there is no distance between two coincident points. With this sort of scale of measurement, it is possible to work out ratios between measures. So, for example, a town that is 20 kilometres away is twice as far away as a town that is only 10 kilometres away. A building that is 15 metres high is half the height of a building that is 30 metres high. (Not all physical measures have a zero that is absolute zero – this applies particularly to several measures of temperature. Temperatures measured in degrees Celsius or Fahrenheit have points that are labelled as zero. However, these zero points do not correspond to the lowest possible temperature you can have. It is then meaningless to say, for example, that it is twice as hot if the temperature is 20 degrees Celsius than if it were 10 degrees Celsius.)

Nominal Categories

a) Involves putting a variable into a small number of categories
b) The categories do not correspond to numerical values
c) So the categories might be the Australian Team, the British Team, the French Team, and the Canadian Team

Ordinal Measurement or Ranks

a) The scores can be ordered from smallest to largest
b) Only a rank order is implied – e.g. 1st, 2nd, 3rd etc.
c) Rather like 1st, 2nd, 3rd etc. in a race. Knowing that someone came 2nd does not indicate how far or how many seconds they were behind the winner

The Different Scales of Measurement

Interval Measurement

a) The size of the difference between scores is an indication of magnitude
b) So if Bill was 5 seconds behind the winner, Fred was 7 seconds behind the winner etc. then these times are based on an equal interval scale of measurement – that is an interval of 1 second
c) However, unless you have other information, it is not possible to say how long the winner, Bill and Fred took running the race

Ratio Measurement

a) Like Interval Measurement but allows ratios to be calculated between scores meaningfully
b) So if Tom took 50 seconds and Bill took 100 seconds then it can be said that Tom took half the time that Bill did – or that Tom is twice as fast as Bill
c) There has to be a meaningful zero to the measurement

FIGURE 1.1   The different scales of measurement and their main characteristics

These different scales of measurement are illustrated in Figure 1.1 which includes additional examples. Nominal or category measurement is to be found in a distinct, blue box because it is very different from the other three types of measurement. Nominal or category measurement is about categorisation and involves qualities NOT quantification. The types of measurement in the green sections are similar to each other as they involve quantities. In practice, it is hard to separate them in terms of their applicability to psychological data. Thus it is far from easy to apply the last three types of measurement in psychology with certainty. Put another way, it is usually very difficult to distinguish between ordinal, interval and ratio scales of measurement. Most psychological scores do not have any directly observable physical basis which makes it impossible to decide whether they consist of equal intervals or have an absolute zero. It is noteworthy that the most convincing examples of these three different types of measurement come from the physical world such as temperature, length and weight – it is virtually impossible to think of examples from psychology itself.

For many years this problem caused great controversy and confusion among psychologists. For the most part, much current usage of statistics in psychology ignores the distinctions between the three different types of numerical scores. This has the support of many statisticians. On the other hand, some psychologists prefer to emphasise that some data are best regarded as rankable and lack the qualities which are characteristic of interval/ratio data (see Figure 1.2). They are more likely to use the statistical techniques to be found in Chapter 18 and the ranking correlation coefficient (Chapter 7) than others. In other words, for precisely the same data, different psychologists will adopt different statistical techniques. Usually this will make little difference to the outcomes of their statistical analyses – the results. In general, it will cause you few, if any, problems if you ignore the three subdivisions of numerical score measurement in your practical use of statistics. The exceptions to this are discussed in Chapters 7 and 18. Since psychologists rarely if ever collect data in the form of ranks, Chapters 2 to 6 are unaffected by such considerations.

FIGURE 1.2   The two practical types of scales of measurement

Key points

- Always ask yourself what sort of measurement it is you are considering – is it a numerical score on a variable or is it putting individuals into categories?

- Never assume that a number is necessarily a numerical score. Without checking, it could be a *frequency* of observations in a named category.

- Clarity of thinking is a virtue in statistics – you will rarely be expected to demonstrate great creativity in your statistical work. Understanding precisely the meaning of terms is an advantage in statistics.

COMPUTER ANALYSIS

The different types of data discussed in this chapter are extremely important for the simple reason that nominal or category data are dealt with very differently in statistics from data which is in the form of scores (ordinal, interval and ratio data). Computer programs, generally, will not recognise when you have got the two confused. So identifying your data as nominal or category data versus data in the form of scores is down to you. Some computer programs require that you identify the type of data that each variable involves. SPSS Statistics is an example of this (SPSS is an IBM company. SPSS was acquired by IBM in October 2009).

CHAPTER 2

Describing variables

Tables and diagrams

Overview

- Tables and diagrams are important aspects of descriptive statistics (the description of the major features of the data). Examining data in this sort of detail is a vital stage of any statistical analysis and should never be omitted.

- This chapter describes how to create and present tables and diagrams for individual variables.

- Statistical tables and diagrams should effectively communicate information about your data. Beware of complexity. ✔

- The type of data (nominal versus score) largely determines what an appropriate table and diagram will be.

- If the data are nominal, then simple frequency tables, bar charts or pie charts are most appropriate. The frequencies are simply the numbers of cases in each of the separate categories.

- If the data are scores, then frequency tables or histograms are appropriate. However, to keep the presentation uncluttered and to help clarify trends, it is often best to put the data into bands (or ranges) of adjacent scores.

Preparation

Remind yourself what a variable is from Chapter 1. Similarly, if you are still not sure of the nominal (categorisation) form of measurement and the use of numerical scores in measurement then revise these too.

2.1   Introduction

You probably know a lot more about statistics than you think. The mass media regularly feature statistical tables and diagrams; children become familiar with statistical tables and diagrams at school. Skill with these methods is essential because researchers collect large amounts of data from numerous people (see Box 2.1). If we asked 100 people their age, gender, marital status (divorced, married, single, etc.), their number of children and their occupation this would yield 500 separate pieces of information. Although this is small fry compared with much research, it is not very helpful to present these 500 measurements in your research report. Such unprocessed information is called *raw data*. Statistical analysis has to be more than describing the raw ingredients. It requires the data to be structured in ways that *effectively communicate* the major trends. If you fail to structure your data, you may as well just give the reader copies of your questionnaires or observation schedules to interpret themselves.

There are very few rules regulating the production of tables and diagrams in statistics so long as they are clear and concise; they need to communicate quickly the important trends in the data. There is absolutely no point in using tables and diagrams that do not ease the task of communication. Probably the best way of deciding whether your tables and diagrams do their job well is to ask other people to decipher what they mean. Tables which are unclear to other people are generally useless.

Descriptive statistics are, by and large, relatively simple visual and numerical techniques for describing the major features of one's data. Researchers may produce descriptive statistics in order to communicate the major characteristics of the data to others, but in the first instance they are used by researchers themselves in order to understand the distribution of participants' responses in the research. Never regard descriptive statistical analysis as an unnecessary or trivial stage in research. It is probably more informative than any other aspect of data analysis. Box 2.2 explains the crucial role of descriptive statistics in research further.

The distinction between nominal (category) data and numerical scores discussed in the previous chapter is important in terms of the appropriate tables and diagrams to use.

Box 2.1   Focus on

Multiple responses

One of the easiest mistakes to make in research is to allow participants in your research to give more than one answer to a single question. So, for example, if you ask people to name their favourite television programme and allow each person more than one answer, you will find that the data can be very tricky to analyse thoroughly. Take our word for it for now: statistics in general does not handle multiple responses very well. Certainly it is possible to draw up tables and diagrams, but some of the more advanced statistical procedures become difficult to apply. You will sometimes read comments to the effect that the totals in a table exceed the number of participants in the research. This is because the researcher has allowed multiple responses to

a single variable. So only allow the participants in your research to give one piece of data for each variable you are measuring to avoid digging a pit for yourself. If you plan your data analysis in detail before you collect your data, you should be able to anticipate any difficulties.

It is possible to do something about data which allow multiple responses. This is to use dummy coding which is discussed later in Chapter 41 of this book. Essentially what one does is to take every possible response as a separate new variable and code each person's data for the presence or absence of each of these new variables. Of course, if there are a lot of different responses then this involves creating a lot of new variables.

Box 2.2   Key concepts

Descriptive statistics

The basic concept of descriptive statistics is very clear. Descriptive statistics are the various techniques which help us get a picture of what is happening in our data. They include tables which give averages, frequencies and the like and diagrams which represent very much the same things but in a more graphic, pictorial form. Descriptive statistics can involve the examination of one variable on its own or the relationships between two or more variables. Many aspects of descriptive statistics are very familiar to us all even before we study statistics. They are very hard to avoid as newspapers, television and other media are full of them. We were all taught at least some of them at school. One consequence of this is that we tend not to see them as playing the vital part that they should in our research. This is a mistake as descriptive statistical techniques contain what is essential to understanding our data – they provide a window through which we can begin to appreciate what is going on in our data. They are the bedrock on which other statistical techniques are built. To be sure, there are more demanding techniques to learn about in statistics than tables and diagrams. This book and others are full of seemingly complex and, sometimes, difficult new things to learn and so the danger is that we neglect descriptive statistics in favour of these. Indeed, there are some popular statistics textbooks which almost entirely overlook how to construct good tables and diagrams. But it is mainly through the effective use of descriptive

statistics that we can see the trends, patterns, quirks, bumps and irregularities in our data. Keep sight of what descriptive statistics say about your data as this is the key to data analysis. They are an important part of understanding the 'fancier' stuff that comes later.

Qualitative researchers in psychology spend considerable amounts of time and a great deal of effort in familiarising themselves with their data. So why should quantitative researchers not do the same? Try not to think of tables and diagrams as merely something to adorn your practical reports and dissertations. Often, at best these will contain only a fraction of the descriptive statistics that a researcher will have produced during the process of analysing their data. Descriptive statistics are best seen as a tool in the analysis process rather than merely parts of the final product – your research report. Use descriptive techniques to explore your data thoroughly, knowing that you may need to modify your initial attempts in the light of experience. Data analysis is a sort of trial-and-error process of finding out what works for you and for your data. Statistics programs allow you to generate numerous tables and diagrams some of which are useful and illuminating, others verging on the useless. The not-so-good stuff is easily deleted from your computer. Be prepared to devote quite some time to this stage of your analysis. It will pay dividends in the long run and bring you close to the data from your study early on.

2.2   Choosing tables and diagrams

So long as you are able to decide whether your data are either numerical scores or nominal (category) data, there are few other choices to be made since the available tables and diagrams are essentially dependent upon this distinction. Figure 2.1 gives some of the key steps when considering tables and diagrams.

■ Tables and diagrams for nominal (category) data

One of the main characteristics of tables and diagrams for nominal (category) data is that they have to show the *frequencies* of cases in each category used. While there may be as many categories as you wish, it is *not* the function of statistical analysis to communicate all of the data's detail; the task is to identify the major trends. For example, imagine you are researching the public's attitudes towards private health care. If you ask participants in your research their occupations then you might find that they mention

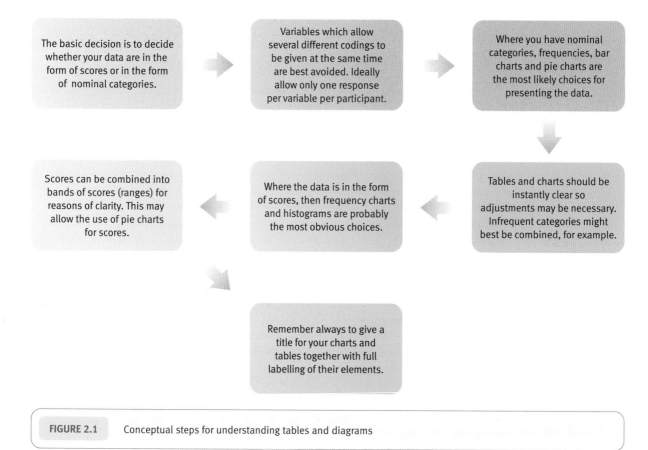

The basic decision is to decide whether your data are in the form of scores or in the form of nominal categories.

Variables which allow several different codings to be given at the same time are best avoided. Ideally allow only one response per variable per participant.

Where you have nominal categories, frequencies, bar charts and pie charts are the most likely choices for presenting the data.

Scores can be combined into bands of scores (ranges) for reasons of clarity. This may allow the use of pie charts for scores.

Where the data is in the form of scores, then frequency charts and histograms are probably the most obvious choices.

Tables and charts should be instantly clear so adjustments may be necessary. Infrequent categories might best be combined, for example.

Remember always to give a title for your charts and tables together with full labelling of their elements.

FIGURE 2.1   Conceptual steps for understanding tables and diagrams

tens if not hundreds of different job titles – newsagents, homemakers, company executives and so forth. Simply counting the frequencies with which different job titles are mentioned results in a vast number of categories. You need to think of relevant and meaningful ways of reducing this vast number into a smaller number of much broader categories that might reveal important trends. For example, since the research is about a health issue you might wish to form a category made up of those involved in health work – some might be dentists, some nurses, some doctors, some paramedics and so forth. Instead of keeping these as different categories, they might be combined into a category 'health worker'. There are no hard-and-fast rules about combining to form broader categories. The following might be useful rules of thumb:

1. Keep your number of categories low, especially when you have only small numbers of participants in your research.

2. Try to make your 'combined' categories meaningful and sensible in the light of the purposes of your research. It would be nonsense, for example, to categorise jobs by the letter of the alphabet with which they start – nurses, nuns, nursery teachers and national footballers. All of these have jobs beginning with the same letter, but it is very difficult to see any other common thread which allows them to be combined meaningfully.

In terms of drawing tables, all we do is to list the categories we have chosen and give the frequency of cases that fall into each of the categories (Table 2.1). The frequencies are presented in two ways in this table – *simple* frequencies and *percentage* frequencies.

Table 2.1	Occupational status of participants in the research expressed as frequencies and percentage frequencies	
Occupation	**Frequency**	**Percentage frequency**
Nuns	17	21.25
Nursery teachers	3	3.75
Television presenters	23	28.75
Students	20	25.00
Other	17	21.25

A percentage frequency is the frequency expressed as a percentage of the total of the frequencies (or total number of cases, usually).

Notice also that one of the categories is called 'other'. This consists of those cases which do not fit into any of the main categories. It is, in other words, a 'rag bag' category or miscellany. Generally, all other things being equal, it is best to have a small number of cases in the 'other' category.

Calculation 2.1

Percentage frequencies

Many readers will not need this, but if you are a little rusty with simple maths, it might be helpful.

The percentage frequency for a particular category, say for students, is the frequency in that category expressed as a percentage of the total frequencies in the data table.

Step 1   What is the category frequency? For students in Table 2.1:

$$\text{category frequency}_{[students]} = 20$$

Step 2   Add up all of the frequencies in Table 2.1:

$$\text{total frequencies} = \text{nuns} + \text{nursery teachers} + \text{TV presenters} + \text{students} + \text{other}$$

$$= 17 + 3 + 23 + 20 + 17$$

$$= 80$$

Step 3

$$\text{percentage frequency}_{[students]} = \frac{\text{category frequency}_{[students]} \times 100}{\text{total frequencies}}$$

$$= \frac{20 \times 100}{80} = \frac{2000}{80} = 25\%$$

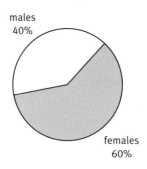

males
40%

females
60%

FIGURE 2.2   A simple pie diagram

One advantage of using computers is that they enable experimentation with different schemes of categorising data in order to decide which is best for your purposes. In this case, you would use initially narrow categories for coding your data. Then you can tell the computer which of these to combine into broader categories.

Sometimes it is preferable to turn frequency tables into diagrams. Good diagrams are quickly understood and add variety to the presentation. The main types of diagram for nominal (category) data are *pie diagrams* and *bar charts*. A pie diagram is a very familiar form of presentation – it simply expresses each category as a slice of a pie which represents all cases (see Figure 2.2).

Notice that the *number* of slices is small – a multitude of slices can be confusing. Each slice is clearly marked with its category name, and the percentage frequency in each category also appears.

Calculation 2.2

Slices for a pie diagram

There is nothing difficult in constructing a pie diagram. Our recommendation is that you turn each of your frequencies into a percentage frequency. Since there are 360 degrees in a circle, if you multiply each percentage frequency by 3.6 you will obtain the angle (in degrees) of the slice of the pie which you need to mark out. In order to create the diagram, you will require a protractor to measure the angles. However, computer graph packages are standard at any university or college and do an impressive job.

In Table 2.1, 25.00% of cases were students. In order to turn this into the correct angle for the slice of the pie, you simply need to multiply 25.00 by 3.6 to give an angle of 90 degrees.

Figure 2.3 shows a *bad* example of a pie diagram for purposes of comparison. There are several problems with this pie diagram:

1. There are too many small slices identified by different shading patterns and the legend takes time to decode.

2. It is not too easily seen what each slice concerns, and the relative sizes of the slices are difficult to judge. We have the size of the slices around the figure and a separate

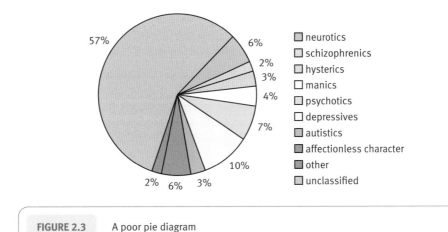

FIGURE 2.3	A poor pie diagram

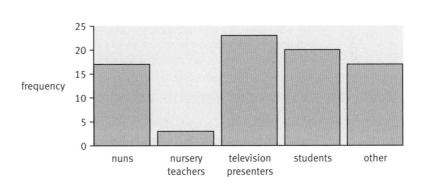

FIGURE 2.4	Bar chart showing occupational categories in Table 2.1

legend or key to identify the components to help cope with the overcrowding problem. In other words, too many categories have resulted in a diagram which is far from easy to read – a cardinal sin in any statistical diagram.

A simple frequency table might be more effective in this case.

Another very familiar form of statistical diagram for nominal (category) data is the *bar chart*. Again these charts are very common in the media. Basically they are diagrams in which bars represent the size of each category. An example is shown in Figure 2.4.

The relative lengths (or heights) of the bars quickly reveal the main trends in the data. With a bar chart, there is very little to remember other than that the bars have a stand-ard space separating them. The spaces indicate that the categories are not in a numerical order; they are frequencies of categories, *not* scores.

It is hard to go wrong with a bar chart (that is not a challenge!) so long as you remember the following:

1. The heights of the bars represent frequencies (number of cases) in a category.

2. Each bar should be clearly labelled as to the category it represents.

3. Too many bars make bar charts hard to follow.

4. Avoid having *many* empty or near-empty categories which represent very few cases. Generally, the information about substantial categories is the most important. (Small categories can be combined together as an 'other' category.)

5. Nevertheless, if *important* categories have very few entries then this needs recording. So, for example, a researcher who is particularly interested in opportunities for women surveys people in top management and finds very few women employed in such jobs. It is important to draw attention to this in the bar chart of males and females in top management. Once again, there are no hard-and-fast rules to guide you – common sense will take you a long way.

6. Make sure that the vertical axis (the heights of the bars) is clearly marked as being frequencies or percentage frequencies.

7. The bars should be of equal width.

In newspapers and on television you are likely to come across a variant of the bar chart called the *pictogram*. In this, the bars of the bar chart are replaced by varying sized drawings of something eye-catching to do with your categories. Thus, pictures of men or women of varying heights, for example, replace the bars. Pictograms are rarely used in professional presentations. The main reason is that pictures of things get wider as well as taller as they increase in size. This can misrepresent the relative sizes of the categories, given that readers forget that it is only the height of the picture that counts.

■ Tables and diagrams for numerical score data

One crucial consideration when deciding what tables and diagrams to use for score data is the number of separate scores recorded for the variable in question. This can vary markedly. So, for example, age in the general population can range from newly born to over 100 years of age. If we merely recorded ages to the nearest whole year then a table or diagram may have entries for 100 different ages. Such a table or diagram would look horrendous. If we recorded age to the nearest month, then we could multiply this number of ages by 12! Such scores can be grouped into bands or ranges of scores to allow effective tabulation (Table 2.2).

Many psychological variables have a much smaller range of numerical values. So, for example, it is fairly common to use questions which pre-specify just a few response alternatives. The so-called Likert-type questionnaire item is a good case in point. Typically this looks something like this:

Statistics is my favourite university subject:
Strongly agree   Agree   Neither agree nor disagree   Disagree   Strongly disagree

Table 2.2	Ages expressed as age bands	
Age range		**Frequency**
0–9 years		19
10–19 years		33
20–29 years		17
30–39 years		22
40–49 years		17
50 years and over		3

Table 2.3	Distribution of students' attitudes towards statistics	
Response category	**Value**	**Frequency**
Strongly agree	1	17
Agree	2	14
Neither agree nor disagree	3	6
Disagree	4	2
Strongly disagree	5	1

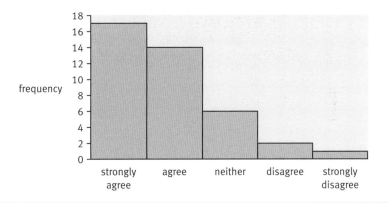

FIGURE 2.5   Histogram of students' attitudes towards statistics

Participants completing this questionnaire circle the response alternative which best fits their personal opinion. It is conventional in this type of research to code these different response alternatives on a five-point scale from one to five. Thus strongly agree might be coded 1, neither agree nor disagree 3, and strongly disagree 5. This scale therefore has only five possible values. Because of this small number of possible answers, a table based on this question will be relatively simple. Indeed, if students are not too keen on statistics, you may well find that they select only the disagree and strongly disagree categories.

Tabulating such data is quite straightforward. Indeed you can simply report the numbers or frequencies of replies for each of the different categories or scores as in Table 2.3.

A *histogram* might be the best form of statistical diagram to represent these data. At first sight, histograms look very much like bar charts but without gaps between the bars. This is because the histogram does not represent distinct unrelated categories but different points on a *numerical* measurement scale. So a histogram of the above data might look like Figure 2.5.

But what if your data have numerous different possible values of the variable in question? One common difficulty for most psychological research is that the number of respondents tends to be small. The large number of possible different scores on the variable is therefore shared between very few respondents. Tables and diagrams should present major features of your data in a simple and easily assimilated form. So, sometimes you will have to use *bands of scores* rather than individual score values, just as you did for Table 2.2. So, if we asked 100 people their ages we could categorise their replies into bands such as 0–9 years, 10–19 years, 30–39 years, 40–49 years and a final category of those 50 years and over. By using bands we reduce the risk of empty parts of the table and allow any trends to become clear (Figure 2.6).

How one chooses the bands to use is an important question. The answer is a bit of luck and judgement, and a lot of trial and error. It is very time-consuming to rejig the ranges of the bands when one is analysing the data by hand. One big advantage of computers is that they will recode your scores into bands repeatedly until you have tables which seem to do the job as well as possible. The criterion is still whether the table communicates information effectively.

The one rule is that the bands ought to be of the same size – that is cover, for example, equal ranges of scores. Generally this is easy except at the upper and lower ends of the distribution. Perhaps you wish to use 'over 70' as your upper range. This, in modern practice, can be done as a bar of the same width as the others, but must be very carefully marked. (Strictly speaking, the width of the band should represent the range of scores involved and the height reduced in the light of this. However, this is rarely done in modern psychological statistics.)

One might redefine the bands of scores and generate another histogram based on identical data but a different set of bands (Figure 2.7).

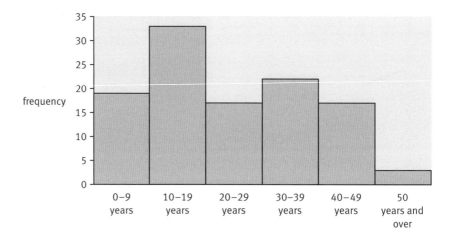

FIGURE 2.6   Use of bands of scores to enable simple presentation

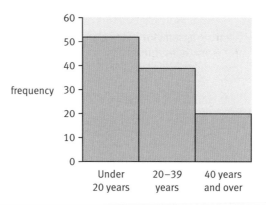

FIGURE 2.7   Histogram showing 'collapsed' categories

It requires some thought to decide which of the diagrams is best for a particular purpose. There are no hard-and-fast rules.

2.3   Errors to avoid

There are a couple of mistakes that you can make in drawing up tables and diagrams:

1. *Do not* forget to head the table or diagram with a succinct description of what it concerns. You will notice that we have done our best throughout this chapter to supply each table and diagram with a clear title.

2. Label everything on the table or diagram as clearly as possible. What this means is that you have to mark your bar charts and histograms in a way that tells the reader what each bar means. Then you must indicate what the height of the bar refers to – probably either frequency or percentage frequency.

Note that this chapter has concentrated on describing a *single* variable as clearly as possible. In Chapter 6, methods of making tables and diagrams showing the relationships between two or more variables are described.

Key points

- Try to make your tables and diagrams useful. It is not usually their purpose to record the data as you collected it in your research. Of course you can list your data in the appendix of projects that you carry out, but this is not useful as a way of illustrating trends. It is part of a researcher's job to make the data accessible to the reader in a structured form that is easily understood by the reader.

- Especially when using computers, it is very easy to generate *useless* tables and diagrams. This is usually because computer analysis encourages you not to examine your raw data in any detail. This implies that you should always regard your first analyses as tentative and merely a step towards something better.

- If a table is not clear to you, it is unlikely to be any clearer to anyone else.

- Check each table and diagram for clear and full labelling of each part. Especially, check that frequencies are clearly marked as such.

- Check that there is a clear, helpful title to each table and diagram.

COMPUTER ANALYSIS

The SPSS Statistics instruction book to this text is Dennis Howitt and Duncan Cramer (2011), *Introduction to SPSS Statistics in Psychology: For version 19 and earlier*, Harlow: Pearson. Chapters 3 (tables) and 4 (diagrams) in that book give detailed step-by-step procedures for the statistics described in this chapter together with advice on how to report the results. Figure 2.8 shows the SPSS Statistics steps to producing tables and diagrams to describe a nominal category variable.

Data	• In Variable View of the Data Editor 'name' the variable, 'label' each of its values and select 'nominal' as the 'measure'. • In Data View of the Data Editor, enter the value of the category for each case.
Analysis	• For a frequency table, select 'Analyze', 'Descriptive Statistics' and 'Frequencies . . .'. • Move variables names to the right hand box for the analysis.
2	• For a graph, select 'Graphs', 'Chart Builder . . . ', 'OK' and move type of graph into box above.
Output	• For frequency tables, the percentage of cases for each category is given for the whole sample first including any missing data and second excluding missing data. If there is no missing data, these percentages will be the same.
2	• Charts may be edited in the Chart Editor.

FIGURE 2.8 SPSS Statistics steps for producing tables and diagrams to describe a nominal category variable

CHAPTER 3

Describing variables numerically

Averages, variation and spread

Overview

- Scores can be described numerically – for example the average of a sample of scores can be given.

- There are several measures of central tendency – the most typical or most likely score.

- The mean score is simply the average score assessed by the total of the scores divided by the number of scores.

- The mode is the numerical value of the most frequently occurring score.

- The median is the score in the middle if the scores are ordered from smallest to largest.

- The spread of scores can be expressed as the range (which is the difference between the largest and the smallest score).

- Variance (an indicator of variability around the average) indicates the spread of scores in the data. Unlike the range, variance takes into account all of the scores. It is a ubiquitous statistical concept.

- Nominal data can only be described in terms of the numbers of cases falling in each category. The mode is the only measure of central tendency that can be applied to nominal (category) data.

- Outliers are unusually large or small values in your data which are very atypical of your data. They can create the impression of trends in your analysis which are not really present. Identifying such outliers and dealing with them effectively can have an important impact on the quality of your research.

Preparation

Revise the meaning of nominal (category) data and numerical score data.

3.1   Introduction

Tables and diagrams take up a lot of space. It can be more efficient to use numerical indexes to describe the distributions of variables. For this reason, you will find relatively few pie charts and the like in published research. One numerical index is familiar to everyone – the numerical average (or arithmetic mean). Large amounts of data can be described adequately using just a few numerical indexes.

What are the major features of data that we might attempt to summarise in this way? Look at the two different sets of scores in Table 3.1. The major differences between these two sets of data are:

1. The sets of scores differ substantially in terms of their typical value – in one case the scores are relatively large (variable B); in the other case the scores are much smaller (variable A).

2. The sets of scores differ in their spread or variability – one set (variable B) seems to have more spread or a greater variability than the other.

3. If we plot these two sets of scores as histograms then we also find that the shapes of the distributions differ markedly. Variable A is much steeper and less spread out than variable B.

Each of these different features of a set of scores can be described using various indexes. They do not generally apply to nominal (category) variables. Figure 3.1 describes some of the key steps you need to consider when describing your data numerically.

FIGURE 3.1   Conceptual steps for understanding how to describe your variables numerically

Table 3.1	Two different sets of scores

Variable A scores	Variable B scores
2	27
2	29
3	35
3	40
3	41
4	42
4	45
4	45
4	49
4	49
5	49
5	
5	

3.2   Typical scores: mean, median and mode

Researchers sometimes speak about the central tendency of a set of scores. By this they are raising the issue of what are the most typical and likely scores in the distribution of measurements. We could speak of the average score, but that can mislead us into thinking that the arithmetic mean is the average score when it is just one of several possibilities. There are three main measures of the typical scores: the arithmetic mean, the mode and the median. These are quite distinct concepts but generally simple enough in themselves.

■ The arithmetic mean

The arithmetic mean is calculated by summing all of the scores in a distribution and dividing by the number of scores. This is the everyday concept of average. In statistical notation we can express this mean as follows:

$$\bar{X}_{\text{mean}} = \frac{\sum X_{\text{[scores]}}}{N_{\text{[number of scores]}}}$$

As this is the first statistical formula we have presented, you should take very careful note of what each symbol means:

X is the statistical symbol for a score

$\sum$ is the summation or sigma sign

$\sum X$ means add up all of the scores X

N is the number of scores

$\bar{X}$ is the statistical symbol for the arithmetic mean of a set of scores

We have added a few comments in small square brackets [just like this]. Although mathematicians may not like them very much, you might find they help you to interpret a formula a little more quickly.

Calculation 3.1

The numerical or arithmetic mean

Although you probably do not need the formula to work out the arithmetic mean, it is useful at this stage to make sure that you understand how to decode the symbols. It is a simple example but contains several of the important elements of statistical formulae. It is good preparation to go through the calculation using the formula.

To illustrate the calculation of the arithmetic mean we can use the following six scores:

$X_1 = 7$ $X_4 = 7$
$X_2 = 5$ $X_5 = 7$
$X_3 = 4$ $X_6 = 5$

The subscripts following the Xs above define a particular score.

$$\bar{X}_{mean} = \frac{\sum X_{[scores]}}{N_{[number\ of\ scores]}}$$

$$= \frac{X_1 + X_2 + X_3 + X_4 + X_5 + X_6}{N}$$

$$= \frac{7 + 5 + 4 + 7 + 7 + 5}{6} = \frac{35}{6} = 5.83$$

■ The median

The median is the middle score of a set if the scores are organised from the smallest to the largest. Thus the scores 7, 5, 4, 7, 7, 5, 3, 4, 6, 8, 5 become 3, 4, 4, 5, 5, 5, 6, 7, 7, 7, 8 when put in order from the smallest to the largest. Since there are 11 scores and the median is the middle score from the smallest to the largest, the median has to be the sixth score, i.e. 5.

With odd numbers of scores all of which are different, the median is easily calculated since there is a single score that corresponds to the middle score in the set of scores. However, if there is an even number of all different scores in the set then the mid-point will not be a single score but two scores. So if you have 12 different scores placed in order from smallest to largest, the median will be somewhere between the sixth and seventh score from smallest. There is no such score, of course, by definition – the 6.5th score just does not exist. What we could do in these circumstances is to take the average of the sixth and seventh scores to give us an estimate of the median.

For the distribution of 40 scores shown in Table 3.2, the middle score from the smallest is somewhere between the 20th and 21st scores. Thus the median is somewhere between score 5 (the 20th score) and score 6 (the 21st score). One could give the average of these two as the median score – that is, the median is 5.5. For most purposes this is good enough.

Table 3.2	Frequency distribution of 40 scores
Score	**Frequency (f)**
1	1
2	2
3	4
4	6
5	7
6	8
7	5
8	3
9	2
10	1
11	0
12	1

You may find that computer programs give different values from this. The computer program is making adjustments since there may be several identical scores near the median, but you need only a fraction of them to reach your mid-point score. So, in the above example the 21st score comes in score category 6 although there are actually eight scores in that category. So in order to get that extra score we need take only one-eighth of score category 6. One-eighth equals 0.125 so the estimated median equals 5.125. To be frank, it is difficult to think of many circumstances in which this level of precision about the value of the median is required in psychological statistics. You ought to regard this feature of computer output as a bonus and adopt the simpler method for your hand calculations.

■ The mode

The mode is the most frequently occurring category of score. It is merely the most common score or most frequent category of scores. In other words, you can apply the mode to any category of data and not just scores. In the above example where the scores were 7, 5, 4, 7, 7, 5 we could represent the scores in terms of their frequencies of occurrence (Table 3.3).

Table 3.3	Frequencies of scores
Score	**Frequency (f)**
4	1
5	2
6	0
7	3

Table 3.4	A bimodel frequency distribution

Score	Frequency (f)
3	1
4	2
5	3
6	1
7	3
8	1

Frequencies are often represented as f in statistics. It is very easy to see in this example that the most frequently occurring score is 7 with a frequency of 3. So the mode of this distribution is 7.

If we take the slightly different set of scores 7, 5, 4, 7, 7, 5, 3, 4, 6, 8, 5, the frequency distribution of these scores is shown in Table 3.4. Here there is no single mode since scores 5 and 7 jointly have the highest frequency of 3. This sort of distribution is called bimodal and the two modes are 5 and 7. The general term multimodal implies that a frequency distribution has several modes.

The mode is the only measure in this chapter that applies to nominal (category) data as well as numerical score data.

Box 3.1	Key concepts

Outliers and identifying them statistically

Outliers, potentially, put your analysis at risk of erroneous conclusions. This is because they are scores which are so atypical of your data in general that they distort any trend in the data because they are unusually large or small. In other words, outliers are a few cases which are out of step with the rest of the data and can mislead the researcher. Outliers may be the result of a wide range of different factors. One does not have to identify what is causing such big or small values, but it is important to eliminate them because they can be so misleading. Routinely, good researchers examine their data for possible outliers simply by inspecting tables of frequencies or scatterplots, for example. This is normally sufficient but does involve an element of judgement which you may not be comfortable with. There are more objective ways of identifying outliers which reduce this subjective element. Essentially, what is done is to define precise limits beyond which a score is suspected of being an outlier. One simple way of doing this is based on the interquartile range which is not affected by outliers since it is based on the middle 50% of scores put in order of their size (p.26).

To calculate the interquartile range, essentially the scores on a variable are arranged from smallest to largest and the 25% of smallest scores and the 25% of largest scores ignored. This leaves the 50% of scores in the middle of the original distribution. The difference between the largest and the smallest score in this middle 50% is the interquartile range. Outliers, which by definition are unusually large or small scores, cannot affect the interquartile range since they will be in the top or bottom 25% of scores and thus eliminated in calculating the interquartile range.

Imagine that we had the following scores for the IQs (Intelligence Quotients) from a sample of 12 individuals:

120, 115, 65, 140, 122, 142, 125, 135, 122, 136, 144, 118

Common sense would suggest that the score of 65 is uncharacteristic of the sample's IQs in general so we would probably identify it as a potential outlier anyway.

To calculate the interquartile range we would first rearrange the scores from smallest to largest (or get a computer to do all of the work for us). This gives us:

65, 115, 118, 120, 122, 122, 125, 135, 136, 140, 142, 144

Since there are 12 scores, to calculate the interquartile range we delete the three (i.e. 25%) lowest scores and also delete the three (i.e. 25%) highest scores. The three lowest scores are 65, 115 and 118 and the three highest scores are 140, 142 and 144. With the extreme quarters deleted, we have the following six scores which are the middle 50% of scores:

120, 122, 122, 125, 135, 136

The interquartile range is the largest of these scores minus the smallest. Thus the interquartile range is 136 − 120 = 16 in this case.

This interquartile range is multiplied by 1.5 which gives us $1.5 \times 16 = 24$. Outliers among the low scores are defined as any score which is smaller than the smallest score in the interquartile range − 24 = 120 − 24 = 96. Outliers among the high scores are defined as any score which is bigger than the largest score in the interquartile range + 24 = 136 + 24 = 160. In other words, scores which are not between 96 and 160 are outliers in this example. The IQ of 65 is thus regarded as an outlier. On the assumption that the scores are normally distributed, then less than 1% of scores would be defined as outliers. This method identifies the moderate outliers.

Extreme outliers are identified in much the same way, but the interquartile range is multiplied by 3 (rather than 1.5). This gives us $3 \times 16 = 48$. Extreme outliers among the low scores are scores which are smaller than 120 − 48 = 72. Extreme outliers among the high scores are scores larger than 136 + 48 = 184. Thus the participant who has an IQ of 65 would be identified as an extreme outlier. In normally distributed scores, extreme outliers will occur only about once in half a million scores.

It would be usual practice to delete outliers from your data. You might also wish to compare the outcome of the analysis with the complete data and with outliers excluded. However, it is important to mention what you have done in any report about your research.

3.3 Comparison of mean, median and mode

Usually the mean, median and mode will give different values of the central tendency when applied to the same set of scores. It is only when a distribution is perfectly symmetrical and the distribution peaks in the middle that they coincide completely. Regard big differences between the mean, median and mode as a sign that your distribution of scores is rather asymmetrical or lopsided.

Distributions of scores do not have to be perfectly symmetrical for statistical analysis, but symmetry tends to make some calculations a little more accurate. It is difficult to say how much lack of symmetry there can be without it becoming a serious problem. There is more about this later, especially in Chapter 18 and Appendix A which make some suggestions about how to test for asymmetry. This is done relatively rarely in our experience.

3.4 The spread of scores: variability

The concept of variability is essential in statistics. Variability is a non-technical term and is related to (but is not identical with) the statistical term variance. Variance is nothing more or less than a mathematical formula that serves as a useful indicator of variability. But it is not the only way of assessing variability.

The following set of ages of 12 university students can be used to illustrate some different ways of measuring variability in our data:

18 years   21 years   23 years   18 years   19 years   19 years
19 years   33 years   18 years   19 years   19 years   20 years

These 12 students vary in age from 18 to 33 years. In other words, the range covers a 15-year period. The interval from youngest to oldest (or tallest to shortest, or fattest to thinnest) is called the range – a useful statistical concept. As a statistical concept, range is always expressed as a single number such as 20 centimetres and seldom as an interval, say, from 15 to 25 centimetres.

One trouble with range is that it can be heavily influenced by extreme cases. Thus the 33-year-old student in the above set of ages is having a big influence on the range of ages of the students. This is because he or she is much older than most of the students. For this reason, the interquartile range has advantages. To calculate the interquartile range, we split the age distribution into quarters and take the range of the middle two quarters (or middle 50%), ignoring the extreme quarters. Since we have 12 students, we delete the three youngest (the three 18-year-olds) and the three oldest (aged 33, 23 and 21). This leaves us with the middle two quarters (the middle 50%) which includes five 19-year-olds and one 20-year-old. The range of this middle two quarters, or the interquartile range, is one year (from 19 years to 20 years). The interquartile range is sometimes a better indicator of the variability of, say, age than the full range because extreme ages are excluded.

Useful as the range is, a lot of information is ignored. It does not take into account all of the scores in the set, merely the extreme ones. For this reason, measures of spread or variability have been developed which include the extent to which each of the scores in the set differs from the mean score of the set.

One such measure is the mean deviation. To calculate this we have to work out the mean of the set of scores and then how much each score in the set differs from that mean. These deviations are then added up, ignoring the negative signs, to give the total of deviations from the mean. Finally, we can divide by the number of scores to give the average or mean deviation from the mean of the set of scores. If we take the ages of the students listed above, we find that the total of the ages is 18 + 21 + 23 + 18 + 19 + 19 + 19 + 33 + 18 + 19 + 19 + 20 = 246. Divide this total by 12 and we get the average age in the set to be 20.5 years. Now if we subtract 20.5 years from each of the student's ages we get the figures in Table 3.5.

The average amount of deviation from the mean (ignoring the sign) is known as the mean deviation (for the above deviations this would give a value of 2.6 years). Although frequently mentioned in statistical textbooks, it has no practical applications in psychological statistics and is best forgotten. However, there is a very closely related concept, variance, that is much more useful and has widespread and extensive applications. Variance is calculated in an almost identical way to mean deviation but for one thing. When we draw up a table to calculate the variance, we square each deviation from the mean before summing the total of these squared deviations as shown in Table 3.6.

The total of the squared deviations from the mean is 193. If we divide this by the number of scores (12), it gives us the value of the variance, which equals 16.08 in this case. Expressing the concept as a formula:

$$\text{variance} = \frac{\sum (X - \bar{X})^2}{N}$$

Table 3.5	Deviations from the mean

Score − mean	Deviation from mean
18 − 20.5	−2.5
21 − 20.5	0.5
23 − 20.5	2.5
18 − 20.5	−2.5
19 − 20.5	−1.5
19 − 20.5	−1.5
19 − 20.5	−1.5
33 − 20.5	12.5
18 − 20.5	−2.5
19 − 20.5	−1.5
19 − 20.5	−1.5
20 − 20.5	−0.5

Table 3.6	Squared deviations from the mean

Score − mean	Deviation from mean	Square of deviation from mean
18 − 20.5	−2.5	6.25
21 − 20.5	0.5	0.25
23 − 20.5	2.5	6.25
18 − 20.5	−2.5	6.25
19 − 20.5	−1.5	2.25
19 − 20.5	−1.5	2.25
19 − 20.5	−1.5	2.25
33 − 20.5	12.5	156.25
18 − 20.5	−2.5	6.25
19 − 20.5	−1.5	2.25
19 − 20.5	−1.5	2.25
20 − 20.5	−0.5	0.25
	Total = 0	Total = 193

This formula defines what variance is – it is the defining formula. This is the most precise definition of variance there is although the problem is that it does not correspond precisely to more everyday or common sense ideas. The calculation of variance above corresponds to this formula. However, in statistics there are often quicker ways of doing calculations. These quicker methods involve computational formulae. The computational formula for variance is important and worth memorising as it occurs in many contexts.

Box 3.2   Focus on

Using negative (–) values

Although psychologists rarely collect data that involve negative signs, some statistical techniques can generate them. Negative values occur in statistical analyses because working out differences between scores is common. The mean is often taken away from scores, for example, or one score is subtracted from another. Generally speaking, negative values are not a problem since either the computer or the calculator will do them for you. A positive value is one which is bigger than zero. Often the + sign is omitted as it is taken for granted.

A negative value (or minus value or – value) is a number which is smaller than (less than) zero. The negative sign is never omitted. A value of –20 is a smaller number than –3 (whereas a value of +20 is a bigger number than +3).

Negative values should cause few problems in terms of calculations – the calculator or computer has no difficulties with them. With a calculator you will need to enter that a number is a negative. A key labelled +/– is often used to do this. On a computer, the number must be entered with a – sign.

Probably, the following are the only things you need to know to be able to understand negative numbers in statistics:

- If a negative number is multiplied by another negative number the outcome is a positive number. So -2×-3 = +6. This is also the case when a number is squared. Thus $-3^2 = +9$. You need this information to understand how the standard deviation and variance formulae work, for example.

- Psychologists often speak of negative correlations and negative regression weights. This needs care because the negative in this case indicates that there is a *reverse* relationship between two sets of scores. That is, for example, the more intelligent a person is, the less time will they take to complete a crossword puzzle.

- If you have got negative values for your scores, it is usually advantageous to add a number of sufficient size to make all of the scores positive. This normally makes absolutely no difference to the outcome of your statistical analysis. For example, the variance and standard deviation of –2, –5 and –6 are exactly the same if we add 6 to each of them. That is, calculate the variance and standard deviation of +4, +1 and 0 and you will find them to be identical to those for –2, –5 and –6. It is important that the same number is added to all of your scores. Doing this is helpful since many of us experience anxiety about negative values and prefer it if they are not there.

Standard deviation (see Chapter 5) is a concept which computationally is very closely related to variance. Indeed, many textbooks deal with them at the same time. Unfortunately, this tends in our view to confuse two very distinct concepts and adds nothing to clarity.

Calculation 3.2

Variance using the computational formula

The computational formula for variance speeds the calculation since it saves having to calculate the mean of the set of scores and subtract this mean from each of the scores. The formula is:

$$\text{variance}_{\text{[computational formula]}} = \frac{\sum X^2 - \dfrac{\left(\sum X^2\right)}{N}}{N}$$

→

Take care with elements of this formula:

X = the general symbol for each member of a set of scores
Σ = sigma or the summation sign, i.e. add up all the things which follow
ΣX^2 = the sum of the square of each of the scores
$(\Sigma X)^2$ = sum all the scores and square that total
N = the number of scores

Step 1 Applying this formula to our set of scores, it is useful to draw up a table (Table 3.7) consisting of our scores and some of the steps in the computation. N (number of scores) equals 12.

Table 3.7 A set of scores and their squares for use in the computing formula for variance

Score X	Squared score X^2
18	324
21	441
23	529
18	324
19	361
19	361
19	361
33	1089
18	324
19	361
19	361
20	400
$\Sigma X = 246$	$\Sigma X^2 = 5236$
$(\Sigma X)^2 = 246^2 = 60\ 516$	

Step 2 Substituting these values in the computational formula:

$$\text{variance}_{[\text{computational formula}]} = \frac{\Sigma X^2 - \dfrac{(\Sigma X^2)}{N}}{N} = \frac{5236 - \dfrac{60\ 516}{12}}{12} = \frac{5236 - 5043}{12} = \frac{193}{12} = 16.08$$

Interpreting the results Variance is difficult to interpret in isolation from other information about the data since it is dependent on the measurement in question. Measures which are based on a wide numerical scale for the scores will tend to have higher variance than measures based on a narrow scale. Thus if the range of scores is only 10 then the variance is likely to be less than if the range of scores is 100. Frequently variance is treated comparatively – that is, variances of different groups of people are compared (see Chapter 19).

Reporting the results Usually variance is routinely reported in tables which summarise a variable or a number of variables along with other statistics such as the mean and range. This is shown in Table 3.8.

Table 3.8 Illustrating the table for descriptive statistics

Variable	N	Mean	Variance	Range
Age	12	20.50 years	16.08	15 years

Box 3.3   Key concepts

Variance estimate

There is a concept called the *variance estimate* (or estimated variance) which is closely related to variance. The difference is that the variance estimate is your best guess as to the variance of a population of scores *if* you only have the data from a small set of scores from that population on which to base your estimate. The variance estimate is described in Chapter 11. It involves a slight amendment to the variance formula in that instead of dividing by N one divides by $N - 1$.

The formula for the estimated variance is:

$$\text{estimated variance} = \frac{\sum X^2 - \dfrac{\left(\sum X\right)^2}{N}}{N - 1}$$

Some psychologists prefer to use this formula in all practical circumstances. Similarly, some textbooks and some computer programs give you calculations based on this formula rather than the one we used in Calculation 3.2. Since virtually all statistical analyses in psychology are based on samples and we normally wish to generalise from these samples to all cases, then the estimated variance is likely to be used in practice. Hence it is reasonable to use the estimated variance as the general formula for variance. The drawback to this is that if we are merely describing the data, this practice is theoretically imprecise.

Key points

- Because they are routine ways of summarising the typical score and the spread of a set of scores, it is important always to report the following information for each of your variables:

  - mean, median and mode

  - range and variance

  - number of scores in the set of scores.

- *The above does not apply to nominal categories.* For these, the frequency of cases in each category exhausts the main possibilities.

- It is worth trying to memorise the definitional and computational formulae for variance. You will be surprised how often these formulae appear in statistics.

- When using a computer, look carefully for variables that have zero variance. They can cause problems and generally ought to be omitted from your analyses (see Chapter 7). Normally the computer will not compute the calculations you ask for in these circumstances. The difficulty is that if all the scores of a variable are the same, it is impossible to calculate many statistical formulae. If you are calculating by hand, variables with all the scores the same are easier to spot.

COMPUTER ANALYSIS

The SPSS Statistics instruction book to this text is Dennis Howitt and Duncan Cramer (2011), *Introduction to SPSS Statistics in Psychology: For version 19 and earlier*, Harlow: Pearson. Chapter 5 in that book gives detailed step-by-step procedures for the statistics described in this chapter together with advice on how to report the results. Figure 3.2 gives the SPSS Statistics steps for producing descriptive statistics.

Data	• Name the variables in Variable View of the Data Editor. • Enter the data under the appropriate variable names in Data View of the Data Editor.
Analysis	• Select 'Analyze'. 'Descriptive Statistics' and 'Frequencies . . .'. • Move the variables to be analysed to the right hand box.
2	• Select 'Statistics . . .', 'Mean', 'Median', 'Mode', 'Variance' and 'Range'.
Output	• These statistics are presented in a single table.

FIGURE 3.2 SPSS Statistics steps for descriptive statistics

CHAPTER 4

Shapes of distributions of scores

Overview

- The shape of the distribution of scores is a major consideration in statistical analysis. It simply refers to the characteristics of the frequency distribution (i.e. histogram) of the scores.

- The normal distribution is an ideal because it is the theoretical basis of many statistical techniques. It is best remembered as a bell-shaped frequency diagram.

- The normal distribution is a symmetrical distribution. That is, it can be folded perfectly on itself at the mean. Symmetry is another ideal in many statistical analyses. Distributions which are not symmetrical are known as skewed distributions.

- Kurtosis indicates how steep or flat a curve is compared with the normal (bell-shaped) curve.

- Cumulative frequencies are ones which include all of the lower values on an accumulating basis. So the highest score will always have a cumulative frequency of 100% since it includes all of the smaller scores.

- Percentiles are the numerical values of the score that cut off the lowest 10%, 30%, 95% or what have you of the distribution of scores.

Preparation

Be clear about numerical scores and how they can be classified into ranges of scores (Chapter 2).

4.1   Introduction

The final important characteristic of sets of scores is the particular shape of their distribution. It is useful for a researcher to be able to describe this shape succinctly. Obviously it is possible to find virtually any shape of distribution amongst the multitude of variables that could be measured. So, intuitively, it seems unrealistic to seek to describe just a few different shapes. But there are some advantages in doing so, as we shall see. The key steps when planning to discuss the shapes of data distributions are given in Figure 4.1.

4.2   Histograms and frequency curves

Most of us have very little difficulty in understanding histograms; we know that they are plots of the frequency of scores (the vertical dimension) against a numerical scale (the horizontal dimension). Figure 4.2 is an example of a histogram based on a relatively small set of scores. This histogram has quite severe steps from bar to bar. In other words, it is quite angular and not a smooth shape at all. Part of the reason for this is that the horizontal numerical scale moves along in discrete steps, so resulting in this pattern. Things would be different if we measured on a *continuous scale* on which every possible score could be represented to the smallest fraction. For example, we might decide to measure people's heights in centimetres to the nearest whole centimetre. But we know that heights do not really conform to this set of discrete steps or points; people who

FIGURE 4.1   Conceptual steps for understanding shapes of distributions

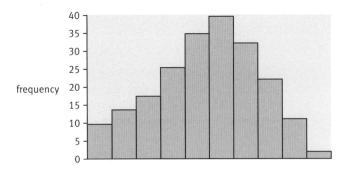

FIGURE 4.2   Histogram showing steep steps

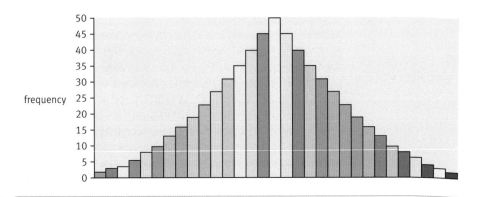

FIGURE 4.3   A smooth curve based on small blocks

measure 120 centimetres actually differ in height by up to a centimetre from each other. Height can be measured in fractions of centimetres, not just whole centimetres. In other words height is a continuous measurement with infinitesimally small steps between measures so long as we have sufficiently precise measuring instruments.

So a histogram of heights measured in centimetre units is at best an approximation to reality. Within each of the blocks of the histogram is a possible multitude of smaller steps. For this reason, it is conventional when drawing frequency curves for theoretical purposes to smooth out the blocks to a continuous curve. In essence, this is like taking much finer and more precise measurements and redrawing the histogram. Instead of doing this literally we approximate it by drawing a smooth curve through imaginary sets of extremely small steps. When this is done our histogram is 'miraculously' turned into a continuous unstepped curve (Figure 4.3).

A frequency curve can, of course, be of virtually any shape but one shape in particular is of concern in psychological statistics – the normal curve.

4.3   The normal curve

The normal curve describes a particular shape of the frequency curve. Although this shape is defined by a formula and can be described mathematically, for most purposes it is sufficient to regard it as a symmetrical bell shape (Figure 4.4).

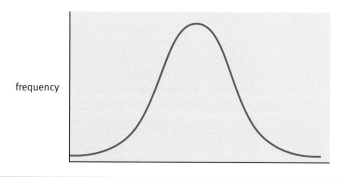

frequency

| **FIGURE 4.4** | A normal (bell-shaped) frequency curve |

It is called the 'normal' curve because it was once believed that distributions in the natural world corresponded to this shape. Even though it turns out that the normal curve is not universal, it is important because many distributions are more or less this shape – at least sufficiently so for most practical purposes. The crucial reason for its use in statistics is that theoreticians developed many statistical techniques on the assumption that the distributions of scores were bell shaped, or normal. It so happens that these assumptions which are useful in the development of statistical techniques have little bearing on their day-to-day application. The techniques may generally be applied to data which are only very roughly bell shaped without too much inaccuracy. In run-of-the-mill psychological statistics, the question of whether a distribution is normal or bell shaped is relatively unimportant. Exceptions to this will be mentioned as appropriate in later chapters.

Don't forget that for the perfectly symmetrical, bell-shaped (normal) curve the values of the mean, median and mode are identical. Disparities between the three are indications that you have an asymmetrical curve.

| Box 4.1 | Focus on |

How normal are my curves?

One thing which may trouble you is the question of how precisely your data need fit this normal or bell-shaped ideal. Is it possible to depart much from the ideal without causing problems? The short answer is that usually a lot of deviation is possible without affecting things too much. So, in the present context, you should not worry too much if the mean, median and mode do differ somewhat; for practical purposes, you can disregard deviations from the ideal distribution, especially when dealing with about 30 or more scores. Unfortunately, all of this involves a degree of subjective judgement since there are no useful ways of assessing what is an acceptable amount of deviation from the ideal when faced with the small amounts of data that student projects often involve. If you wish you can use statistics which do not involve the normal curve (Chapter 18).

| 4.4 | Distorted curves |

The main concepts which deal with distortions in the normal curve are *skewness* and *kurtosis*.

■ Skewness

It is always worth examining the shape of your frequency distributions. Gross skewness is the exception to our rule of thumb that non-normality of data has little influence on statistical analyses. By skewness we mean the extent to which your frequency curve is lopsided rather than symmetrical. A mid-point of a frequency curve may be skewed either to the left or to the right of the range of scores (Figures 4.5 and 4.6).

There are special terms for left-handed and right-handed skew:

- *Negative skew:*
  - more scores are to the left of the mode than to the right
  - the mean and median are smaller than the mode.

- *Positive skew:*
  - more scores are to the right of the mode than to the left
  - the mean and median are bigger than the mode.

There is also an index of the amount of skew shown in your set of scores. With hand-calculated data analyses, the best approach is usually to look at your frequency curve. With computer analyses the ease of obtaining the index of skewness makes using complex formulae methods unnecessary. The index of skewness is positive for a positive skew and negative for a negative skew. Appendix A explains how to test for skewness in your data.

■ Kurtosis (or steepness/shallowness)

Some symmetrical curves may look rather like the normal bell-shaped curve except that they are excessively steep or excessively flat compared to the mathematically defined normal bell-shaped curve (Figures 4.7 and 4.8).

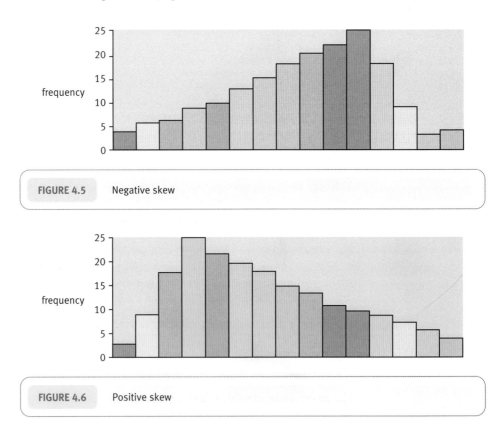

| FIGURE 4.5 | Negative skew |

| FIGURE 4.6 | Positive skew |

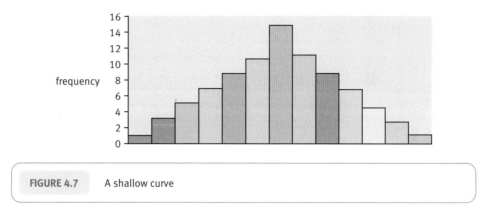

FIGURE 4.7   A shallow curve

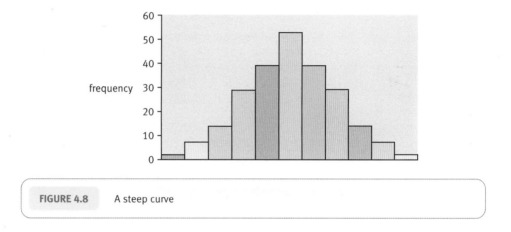

FIGURE 4.8   A steep curve

Kurtosis is the term used to identify the degree of steepness or shallowness of a distribution. There are technical words for different types of curve:

● a steep curve is called *leptokurtic*

● a normal curve is called *mesokurtic*

● a flat curve is called *platykurtic*.

Although they are terms beloved of statistics book writers, since the terms mean nothing more than steep, middling and flat there seems to be good reason to drop the Greek words in favour of everyday English.

It is possible to obtain indexes of the amount of shallowness or steepness of your distribution compared with the mathematically defined normal distribution. These are probably most useful as part of a computer analysis. For most purposes, an inspection of the frequency curve of your data is sufficient in hand analyses. Knowing what the index means should help you cope with computer output; quite simply:

● a positive value of kurtosis means that the curve is steep

● a zero value of kurtosis means that the curve is middling

● a negative value of kurtosis means that the curve is flat.

Steepness and shallowness have little or no bearing on the statistical techniques you use to analyse your data, quite unlike skewness.

4.5   Other frequency curves

■ Bimodal and multimodal frequency distributions

Of course, there is no rule that says that frequency curves have to peak in the middle and tail off to the left and right. As we have already explained, it is perfectly possible to have a frequency distribution with twin peaks (or even multiple peaks). Such twin-peaked distributions are called *bimodal* since they have two modes – most frequently occurring scores. Such a frequency curve might look like Figure 4.9.

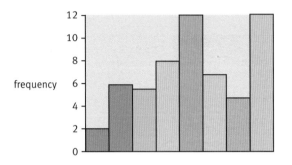

FIGURE 4.9   A bimodal frequency histogram

■ Cumulative frequency curves

There are any number of different ways of presenting a single set of data. Take, for example, the 50 scores in Table 4.1 for a measure of extraversion obtained from airline pilots.

One way of tabulating these extraversion scores is simply to count the number of pilots scoring at each value of extraversion from 1 to 5. This could be presented in several forms, for example Tables 4.2 and 4.3, and Figure 4.10.

Exactly the same distribution of scores could be represented using a *cumulative* frequency distribution. A simple frequency distribution merely indicates the number of people who achieved any particular score. A cumulative frequency distribution gives the number scoring, say, one, two or less, three or less, four or less, and five or less. In other words, the frequencies accumulate. Examples of cumulative frequency distributions are given in Tables 4.4 and 4.5, and Figure 4.11. Cumulative frequencies can be given also as cumulative percentage frequencies in which the frequencies are expressed as percentages and these percentages accumulated. This is shown in Table 4.4.

Table 4.1	Extraversion scores of 50 airline pilots								
3	5	5	4	4	5	5	3	5	2
1	2	5	3	2	1	2	3	3	3
4	2	5	5	4	2	4	5	1	5
5	3	3	4	1	4	2	5	1	2
3	2	5	4	2	1	2	3	4	1

Table 4.2	Frequency table based on data in Table 4.1
Number scoring 1	7
Number scoring 2	11
Number scoring 3	10
Number scoring 4	9
Number scoring 5	13

Table 4.3	Alternative layout for data in Table 4.1

Number of pilots scoring				
1	2	3	4	5
7	11	10	9	13

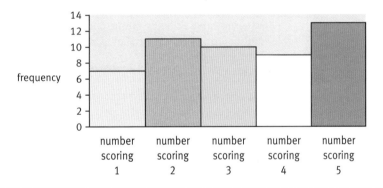

FIGURE 4.10	Histogram of Table 4.1

Table 4.4	Cumulative frequency distribution of pilots' extraversion scores from Table 4.1

Score range	Cumulative frequency	Cumulative percentage frequency
1	7	14%
2 or less	18	36%
3 or less	28	56%
4 or less	37	74%
5 or less	50	100%

Table 4.5	Alternative style of cumulative frequency distribution of pilots' extraversion scores from Table 4.1			
Number of pilots scoring				
1	2 or less	3 or less	4 or less	5 or less
7	18	28	37	50

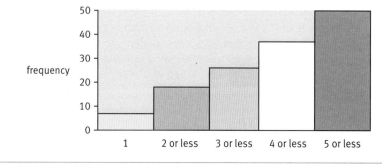

FIGURE 4.11	Cumulative histogram of the frequencies of pilots' extraversion scores from Table 4.1

There is nothing difficult about cumulative frequencies – but you must label such tables and diagrams clearly or they can be very misleading.

■ Percentiles

Percentiles are merely a form of cumulative frequency distribution, but instead of being expressed in terms of accumulating scores from lowest to highest, the categorisation is in terms of whole numbers of percentages of people. In other words, the percentile is the score which a given percentage of scores equals or is less than. You do not necessarily have to report every percentage point and units of 10 might suffice for some purposes. Such a distribution would look something like Table 4.6. The table shows that 10% of

Table 4.6	Example of percentiles

Percentile	Score
10th	7
20th	9
30th	14
40th	20
50th	39
60th	45
70th	50
80th	61
90th	70
100th	78

scores are equal to 7 or less and 80% of scores are equal to 61 or less. Note that the 50th percentile corresponds to the median score.

Percentiles are commonly used in standardisation tables of psychological tests and measures. For these it is often very useful to be able to describe a person's standing compared with the set of individuals on which the test or measure was initially researched. Thus if a particular person's neuroticism score is described as being at the 90th percentile it means that they are more neurotic than about 90% of people. In other words, percentiles are a quick method of expressing a person's score relative to those of others.

In order to calculate the percentiles for any data, it is first necessary to produce a table of cumulative percentage frequencies. This table is then examined to find the score which cuts off, for example, the bottom 10%, the bottom 20%, the bottom 30%, etc. of scores. It should be obvious that calculating percentiles in this way is actually easier if there are a large number of scores so that the cut-off points can be found precisely. Generally speaking, percentiles are used in psychological tests and measures that have been standardised on large numbers of people.

Key points

- The most important concept in this chapter is that of the normal curve or normal distribution. It is worth extra effort to memorise the idea that the normal curve is a bell-shaped symmetrical curve.

- Be a little wary if you find that your scores on a variable are very *skewed* since this can lose precision in certain statistical analyses.

COMPUTER ANALYSIS

The SPSS Statistics instruction book to this text is Dennis Howitt and Duncan Cramer (2011), *Introduction to SPSS Statistics in Psychology: For version 19 and earlier*, Harlow: Pearson. Chapter 6 in that book gives detailed step-by-step procedures for the statistics described in this chapter together with advice on how to report the results. Figure 4.12 gives the SPSS Statistics steps for producing frequency tables and histograms.

Data	• Name the variable in Variable View of the Data Editor. • Enter the data under the appropriate variable names in Data View of the Data Editor.
Analysis	• For frequency tables, select 'Analyze', 'Descriptive Statistics' and 'Frequencies . . .'. • Move variables to be analysed to right hand side box.
2	• For histograms, select 'Graphs', 'Chart Builder . . .', 'OK' and 'Histogram' to box above.
Output	• The frequency table shows the frequency as well as the percentage of the frequency for each value. • If needed, use the Chart Editor to edit the histogram.

FIGURE 4.12 SPSS Statistics steps for frequency tables and histograms

CHAPTER 5

Standard deviation and z-scores

The standard unit of measurement in statistics

Overview

- Standard deviation computationally is the square root of variance (Chapter 3).

- Conceptually standard deviation is distance along a frequency distribution of scores.

- Because the normal (bell-shaped) curve is a standard shape, it is possible to give the distribution as percentages of cases which lie between any two points on the frequency distribution. Tables are available to do this relatively simply.

- It is common to express scores as z-scores. A z-score for a particular score is simply the number of standard deviations that the score lies from the mean of the distribution. (A negative sign is used to indicate that the score lies below the mean.) Z-scores are also referred to as standardised scores.

Preparation

Make sure you know the meaning of variables, scores, Σ and scales of measurement – especially nominal, interval and ratio (Chapter 1).

5.1   Introduction

Measurement ideally uses standard or universal units. It would be really stupid if, when we ask people how far it is to the nearest railway station, one person says 347 cow's lengths, another says 150 poodle jumps, and a third person says three times the distance between my doctor's house and my dentist's home. If you ask us how hot it was on midsummer's day you would be pretty annoyed if one of us said 27 degrees Howitt and the other said 530 degrees Cramer. We measure in standard units such as centimetres, degrees Celsius, kilograms and so forth. The advantages of doing so are obvious: standard units of measurement allow us to communicate easily, precisely and effectively with other people.

It is much the same in statistics – the trouble is the perplexing variety of types of units possible because of the universality of statistics in many research disciplines. Some variables are measured in physical ways such as metres and kilograms. Others use more abstract units of measurement such as scores on an intelligence test or a personality inventory. Although it would be nice if statisticians had a standard unit of measurement, it is not intuitively obvious what this should be.

5.2   Theoretical background

Imagine a 30 centimetre rule – it will be marked in 1 centimetre units from 0 centimetres to 30 centimetres (Figure 5.1). The standard unit of measurement here is the centimetre. But you could have a different sort of rule in which instead of the scale being from 0 to 30 centimetres, the mid-point of the scale is 0 and the scale is marked as –15, –14, –13, . . . , –1, 0, +1, . . . , +13, +14, +15 centimetres. This rule is in essence marked in deviation units (Figure 5.2).

The two rules use the same unit of measurement (the centimetre) but the deviation rule is marked with 0 in the middle, not at the left-hand side. In other words, the mid-point of the scale is marked as 0 deviation (from the mid-point). The standard deviation is similar to this rule in so far as it is based on *distances or deviations* from the average or mid-point.

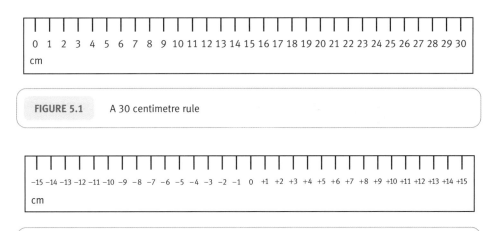

0 1 2 3 4 5 6 7 8 9 10 11 12 13 14 15 16 17 18 19 20 21 22 23 24 25 26 27 28 29 30
cm

FIGURE 5.1   A 30 centimetre rule

–15 –14 –13 –12 –11 –10 –9 –8 –7 –6 –5 –4 –3 –2 –1 0 +1 +2 +3 +4 +5 +6 +7 +8 +9 +10 +11 +12 +13 +14 +15
cm

FIGURE 5.2   A 30 centimetre rule using deviation units

As it is the standard unit of measurement in statistics, it is a pity that statisticians chose to call it standard deviation rather than 'standard statistical unit'. The latter phrase would better describe what it is. In contrast to a lot of measurements such as metres and kilograms, the standard deviation corresponds to no single standard of measurement that can be defined in *absolute terms* against a physical entity locked in a vault somewhere.

The standard deviation of a set of scores is measured *relative* to all of the scores in that set. Put as simply as possible, *the standard deviation is the 'average' amount by which scores differ from the mean or average score*. Now this is an odd idea – basing your standard measure on a set of scores rather than on an absolute standard. Nevertheless, it is an important concept to grasp. Don't jump ahead at this stage – there are a couple of twists in the logic yet. Perhaps you are imagining that if the scores were 4, 6, 3 and 7 then the mean is 20 divided by 4 (the number of scores), or 5. Each of the four scores deviates from the average by a certain amount – for example, 7 deviates from the mean of 5 by just 2. The sum of the deviations of our four scores from the mean of 5 is 1 + 1 + 2 + 2 which equals 6. Surely, then, the standard deviation is 6 divided by 4, which equals 1.5?

But this is *not* how statisticians work out the average deviation for their standard unit. Such an approach might seem logical, but it turns out to be not very useful in practice. Instead *standard deviation uses a different type of average which most mortals would not even recognise as an average.*

The big difference is that standard deviation is calculated as the average *squared* deviation. What this implies is that instead of taking our four deviation scores (1 + 1 + 2 + 2) we square each of them ($1^2 + 1^2 + 2^2 + 2^2$) which gives 1 + 1 + 4 + 4 = 10. If we divide this total deviation of 10 by the number of scores (4), this gives a value of 2.5. However, this is still not quite the end of the story since *we then have to calculate the square root of this peculiar average deviation from the mean*. Thus we take the 2.5 and work out its square root – that is, 1.58. In words, *the standard deviation is the square root of the average squared deviation from the mean.*

And that really is it – honest. It is a pity that one of the most important concepts in statistics is less than intuitively obvious, but there we are. To summarise:

1. The standard deviation is the standard unit of measurement in statistics.

2. The standard deviation is simply the 'average' amount that the scores on a variable deviate (or differ) from the mean of the set of scores. In essence, the standard deviation is the average deviation from the mean. Think of it like this since most of us will have little difficulty grasping it in these terms. Its peculiarities can be safely ignored for most purposes.

3. Although the standard deviation is an average, it is not the sort of average which most of us are used to. However, it is of greater use in statistical applications than any other way of calculating the average deviation from the mean.

The standard deviation gives greater numerical emphasis to scores which depart by larger amounts from the mean. The reason is that it involves *squared* deviations from the mean which give disproportionately more emphasis to larger deviations.

It should be stressed that the *standard deviation is not a unit-free measure*. If we measured a set of people's heights in centimetres, the standard deviation of their heights would also be a certain number of *centimetres*. If we measured 50 people's intelligences using an intelligence test, the standard deviation would be a certain number of IQ points. It might help you to remember this, although most people would say or write things like 'the standard deviation of height was 4.5' without mentioning the units of measurement. Figure 5.3 gives the key steps in relation to using standard deviation.

Standard deviation is simply the average amount by which the scores deviate from the mean score.

However, it is calculated in a somewhat 'unusual' way in which these deviations are squared, summed and then their square root taken.

So every score can be described in terms of how many of these standard deviations it is from the mean.

These are known as *z*-scores and are very important in statistics.

A score at the mean is 0 standard deviations from the mean.

Tables tell one how many scores are (say) bigger than a certain number of standard deviations below the mean.

These tables apply IF your data is normally distributed.

The estimated standard deviation is for the population but is based on a sample of scores taken from that population.

Standard deviation is often used interchangeably with variance and standard error to indicate spread.

FIGURE 5.3   Conceptual steps for understanding standard deviation

Calculation 5.1

Standard deviation

The defining formula for standard deviation is as follows:

$$\text{standard deviation} = \sqrt{\frac{\sum (X - \bar{X})^2}{N}}$$

or the computationally quicker formula is:

$$\text{standard deviation} = \sqrt{\frac{\sum X^2 - \frac{(\sum X)^2}{N}}{N}}$$

Table 5.1 lists the ages of nine students (N = number of scores = 9) and shows steps in calculating the standard deviation. Substituting these values in the standard deviation formula:

$$\text{standard deviation} = \sqrt{\frac{\sum X^2 - \frac{(\sum X)^2}{N}}{N}} = \sqrt{\frac{5115 - \frac{(207)^2}{9}}{9}}$$

$$= \sqrt{\frac{5115 - 4761}{9}}$$

$$= \sqrt{\frac{354}{9}} = \sqrt{39.333} = 6.27 \text{ years}$$

(You may have spotted that the standard deviation is simply the square root of the variance.)

Table 5.1	Steps in the calculation of the standard deviation	
Scores (X) (age in years)		**Scores squared (X^2)**
20		400
25		625
19		361
35		1225
19		361
17		289
15		225
30		900
27		729
$\sum X = 207$		$\sum X^2 = 5115$

Interpreting the results Like variance, standard deviation is difficult to interpret without other information about the data. Standard deviation is just a sort of average deviation from the mean. Its size will depend on the scale of the measurement in question. The bigger the units of the scale, the bigger the standard deviation is likely to be.

Reporting the results Usually standard deviation is routinely reported in tables which summarise a variable or a number of variables along with other statistics such as the mean and range. This is shown in Table 5.2.

Table 5.2	Illustrating the table for descriptive statistics			
Variable	**N**	**Mean**	**Range**	**Standard deviation**
Age	9	23.00 years	20.00 years	6.27 years

The standard deviation is important in statistics for many reasons. The most important is that the *size* of the standard deviation is an indicator of how much variability there is in the scores for a particular variable. The bigger the standard deviation the more spread there is in the scores. However, this is merely to use standard deviation as a substitute for its close relative variance.

Box 5.1	Key concepts

Estimated standard deviation

In this chapter the standard deviation is discussed as a descriptive statistic; that is, it is used like the mean and median, for example, to characterise important features of a set of scores. Be careful to distinguish this from the *estimated* standard deviation which is discussed in Chapter 11. Estimated standard deviation is your best guess as to the standard deviation of a population of scores based on information known about only a small subset or sample of scores from that population. Estimated standard deviation involves a modification to the standard deviation formula so that the estimate is better – the formula is modified to read $N - 1$ instead of just N.

The formula for the estimated standard deviation is:

$$\text{estimated standard deviation} = \sqrt{\frac{\sum X^2 - \frac{(\sum X)^2}{N}}{N - 1}}$$

If you wish, this formula could be used in all of your calculations of standard deviation. Some textbooks and some computer programs give you calculations based on the above formula in all circumstances. Since virtually all statistical analyses in psychology are based on samples and we normally wish to generalise from these samples to all cases then there is good justification for this practice. The downside is that if we are describing the data rather than generalising from them then the formula is theoretically a little imprecise.

5.3 Measuring the number of standard deviations – the *z*-score

Given that one of the aims of statisticians is to make life as simple as possible for themselves, they try to use the minimum number of concepts possible. Expressing standard statistical units in terms of standard deviations is just one step towards trying to express many measures in a consistent way. Another way of achieving consistency is to express all scores in terms of a *number* of standard deviations. That is, we can abandon the original units of measurements almost entirely if all scores are re-expressed as a number of standard deviations.

It is a bit like calculating all weights in terms of kilograms or all distances in terms of metres. So, for example, since there are 2.2 pounds in a kilogram, something that weighs 10 pounds converts to 4.5 kilograms. We simply divide the number of pounds weight by the number of pounds in a kilogram in order to express our weight in pounds in terms of our standard unit of weight, the kilogram.

It is very much like this in statistics. If we know that the size of the standard deviation is, say, 7, we know that a score which is 21 above the mean score is 21/7 or three standard deviations above the mean. A score which is 14 below the mean is 14/7 or two standard deviations below the mean. So, once the size of the standard deviation is known, all scores can be re-expressed in terms of the *number of standard deviations they are from the mean*. One big advantage of this is that, unlike other standard units of measurement such as distance and weight, the *number* of standard deviations will apply no matter what the variable being measured is. Thus it is equally applicable if we are measuring time, anxiety, depression, height or any other variable. So *the number of standard deviations is a universal scale* of measurement. But note the stress on the *number* of standard deviations.

Despite sounding a bit space-age and ultra-modern, the *z-score* is nothing other than the *number* of standard deviations a particular score lies above or below the mean of the set of scores – precisely the concept just discussed. So in order to work out the z-score for a particular score (X) on a variable we also need to know the mean of the set of scores on that variable and the value of the standard deviation of that set of scores. Sometimes it is referred to as the *standard score* since it allows all scores to be expressed in a standard form.

Calculation 5.2

Converting a score into a z-score

To convert the age of a 32-year-old to a z-score, given that the mean of the set of ages is 40 years and the standard deviation of age is 6 years, just apply the following formula:

$$z\text{-score} = \frac{X - \bar{X}}{SD}$$

where X stands for a particular score, $\bar{X}$ is the mean of the set of scores and SD stands for standard deviation.

The z-score of any age (e.g. 32) can be obtained as follows:

$$z\text{-score}_{[\text{of a 32-year-old}]} = \frac{32 - 40}{6} = \frac{-8}{6} = -1.33$$

The value of −1.33 means that:

1. A 32-year-old is 1.33 standard deviations from the mean age of 40 for this set of age scores.

2. The minus sign simply means that the 32-year-old is younger (lower) than the mean age for the set of age scores. A plus sign (or no sign) would mean that the person is older (higher) than the mean age of 40 years.

Interpreting the results There is little to be added about interpreting the z-score since it is defined by the formula as the number of standard deviations a score is from the mean score. Generally speaking, the larger the z-score (either positive or negative) the more atypical a score is of the typical score in the data. A z-score of about 2 or more is fairly rare.

Reporting the results As z-scores are scores they can be presented as you would any other score using tables or diagrams. Usually there is no point in reporting the mean of a set of z-scores since this will be 0.00 if calculated for all of the cases.

5.4 A use of z-scores

z-scores, at first sight, deter a lot of students. They are an odd, abstract idea which needs a little time to master. In addition, they seem to achieve very little for students who do their statistics using computer programs. There is some truth in this, but it overlooks the fact that standardised scores (very like z-scores) appear in many of the more advanced statistical techniques to be found later in this book. So if you master z-scores now, this will make your learning at later stages much easier.

So z-scores are merely scores expressed in terms of the *number* of standard statistical units of measurement (standard deviations) they are from the mean of the set of scores. One big advantage of using these standard units of measurement is that variables measured in terms of many different units of measurement can be compared with each other and even combined.

A good example of this comes from a student project (Szostak, 1995). The researcher was interested in the amount of anxiety that child tennis players exhibited and its effect on their performance (serving faults) in competitive situations as compared with practice. One consideration was the amount of commitment that parents demonstrated to their children's tennis. Rather than base this simply on the extent to which parents claimed to be involved, she asked parents the amount of money they spent on their child's tennis, the amount of time they spent on their child's tennis and so forth:

1. How much money do you spend *per week* on your child's *tennis coaching*?

2. How much money do you spend *per year* on your child's *tennis equipment*?

3. How much money do you spend *per year* on your child's *tennis clothing*?

4. How many *miles per week* on average do you spend travelling to *tennis events*?

5. How many *hours per week* on average do you spend watching your child *play tennis*?

6. How many *LTA tournaments* does your child participate in *per year*?

This is quite straightforward information to collect, but it causes difficulties in analysing the data. The student wanted to combine these six different measures of commitment to give an overall commitment score for each parent. However, the six items are based on radically different units of measurement – time, money and so forth. Her solution was simply to turn each parent's score on each of the questionnaire items into a *z*-score. This involves only the labour of working out the mean and standard deviation of the answers to each questionnaire and then turning each score into a *z*-score. These six *z*-scores are then added (including the + or − signs) to give a total score on the amount of commitment by each parent, which could be a positive or negative value since *z*-scores can be + or −.

This was an excellent strategy since this measure of parental commitment was the best predictor of a child performing poorly in competitive situations; the more parental commitment the worse the child does in real matches compared with practice.

There are plenty of other uses of the standard deviation in statistics, as we shall see.

5.5   The standard normal distribution

There is a remaining important use of standard deviation. Although it should now be obvious that there are some advantages in converting scores into standard units of measurement, you might get the impression that, in the end, the scores themselves on a variable contain information which the *z*-score does not fully capture. In particular, if one looks at a distribution of the original scores, it is possible to have a good idea of how a particular individual scores relative to other people. So, for example, if you know the distribution of weights in a set of people, it should be possible to say something about the weight of a particular person relative to other people. A histogram giving the weights of 38 children in a school class allows us to compare a child with a weight of, say, 42 kilograms with the rest of the class (Figure 5.4).

We can see that a child of 42 kilograms is in the top four of the distribution – that is, in about the top 10% of the weight distribution. Counting the frequencies in the histogram tells us the percentage of the part of the distribution the child falls in. We can also work out that 34 out of 38 (about 90%) of the class are lighter than this particular child.

Surely this cannot be done if we work with standard deviations? In fact it is relatively straightforward to do so since there are ready-made tables to tell us precisely how

FIGURE 5.4 Distribution of weights in a set of children

a particular score (expressed as a *z*-score or number of standard deviations from the mean) compares with other scores. This is achieved by using a commonly available table which gives the frequency curve of *z*-scores assuming that this distribution is bell shaped or normal. This table is known as either the standard normal distribution or the *z*-distribution. To be frank, some versions of the table are rather complicated, but we have opted for the simplest and most generally useful possible. Many statistical tables are known as *tables of significance* for reasons which will become more apparent later on.

Significance Table 5.1 gives the percentage number of scores which will be higher than a score with a given *z*-score. Basically this means that the table gives the proportion of the frequency distribution of *z*-scores which lie in the shaded portions in the example shown in Figure 5.5. The table assumes that the distribution of scores is normal or bell shaped. The table usually works sufficiently well even if the distribution departs somewhat from the normal shape. Of course, since the area of the entire curve is 100% then it is quite easy to work out other characteristics of the curve. So if you know, for example, that 15.87% of scores will be above 1 standard deviation above the mean, it is a quick calculation to say that 100% − 15.87% = 84.13% will be below 1 standard deviation above the mean.

Calculation 5.3

Using the table of the standard normal distribution

Significance Table 5.1 is easy to use. Imagine that you have the IQs of a set of 250 people. The mean ($\bar{X}$) of these IQs is 100 and you calculate that the standard deviation (SD) is 15. You could use this information to calculate the *z*-score of Darren Jones who scored 90 on the test:

$$z\text{-score} = \frac{X - \bar{X}}{SD} = \frac{90 - 100}{15}$$

$$= \frac{-10}{15} = -0.67 = -0.7 \text{ (to 1 decimal place)}$$

Taking a *z*-score of −0.7, Significance Table 5.1 tells us that 75.80% of people in the set would have IQs equal to or greater than Darren's. In other words, he is not particularly intelligent. If the *z*-score of Natalie Smith is +2.0 then this would mean that only 2.28% of scores are equal to or higher than Natalie's – she's very bright.

Of course, you could use the table to calculate the proportion of people with *lower* IQs than Darren and Natalie. Since the total amount of scores is 100%, we can calculate that there are 100% − 75.80% = 24.20% of people with IQs equal to or smaller than his. For Natalie, there are 100% − 2.28% = 97.72% of scores equal to or lower than hers.

| Significance Table 5.1 | The standard normal *z*-distribution: this gives the percentage of *z*-scores which are higher than the tabled values | | |

z-score	Percentage of scores higher than this particular *z*-score	*z*-score	Percentage of scores higher than this particular *z*-score
−4.00	99.997%	0.00	50.00%
−3.00	99.87%	+0.10	46.02%
−2.90	99.81%	+0.20	42.07%
−2.80	99.74%	+0.30	38.21%
−2.70	99.65%	+0.40	34.46%
−2.60	99.53%	+0.50	30.85%
−2.50	99.38%	+0.60	27.43%
−2.40	99.18%	+0.70	24.20%
−2.30	98.93%	+0.80	21.19%
−2.20	98.61%	+0.90	18.41%
−2.10	98.21%	+1.00	15.87%
−2.00	97.72%	+1.10	13.57%
−1.96	97.50%	+1.20	11.51%
z-scores above this point are in the		+1.30	9.68%
extreme 5% of scores in either direction		+1.40	8.08%
from the mean (i.e. the extreme 2.5%		+1.50	6.68%
below the mean)		+1.60	5.48%
−1.90	97.13%	*z-scores below this point are in the extreme*	
−1.80	96.41%	*5% above the mean*	
−1.70	95.54%	+1.64	5.00%
−1.64	95.00%	+1.70	4.46%
z-scores above this point		+1.80	3.59%
are in the extreme 5% below the mean		+1.90	2.87%
−1.60	94.52%	*z-scores below this point are in the*	
−1.50	93.32%	*extreme 5% of scores in either direction*	
−1.40	91.92%	*from the mean (i.e. the extreme 2.5%*	
−1.30	90.32%	*above the mean)*	
−1.20	88.49%	+1.96	2.50%
−1.10	86.43%	+2.00	2.28%
−1.00	84.13%	+2.10	1.79%
−0.90	81.59%	+2.20	1.39%
−0.80	78.81%	+2.30	1.07%
−0.70	75.80%	+2.40	0.82%
−0.60	72.57%	+2.50	0.62%
−0.50	69.15%	+2.60	0.47%
−0.40	65.54%	+2.70	0.35%
−0.30	61.79%	+2.80	0.26%
−0.20	57.93%	+2.90	0.19%
−0.10	53.98%	+3.00	0.13%
0.00	50.00%	+4.00	0.0003%

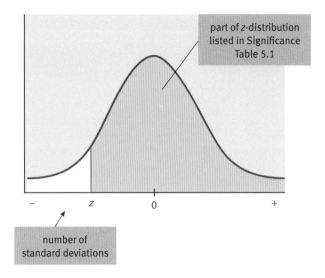

FIGURE 5.5   The part of the *z*-distribution which is listed in Significance Table 5.1

■ More about Significance Table 5.1

Significance Table 5.1 is just about as simple as we could make it. It is not quite the same as similar tables in other books:

1. We have given negative as well as positive values of *z*-scores.

2. We have only given *z*-scores in intervals of 0.1 with a few exceptions.

3. We have given percentages – many other versions of the table give *proportions* out of 1. In order to convert the values in Significance Table 5.1 into proportions, simply divide the percentage by 100 and delete the % sign.

4. We have introduced a number of 'cut-off points' or zones into the table. These basic-ally isolate extreme parts of the distribution of *z*-scores and identify those *z*-scores which come into the extreme 5% of the distribution. If you like, these are the excep-tionally high and exceptionally low *z*-scores. The importance of this might not be obvious right now but will be clearer later on. The extreme zones are described as 'significant'. We have indicated the extreme 5% in either direction (that is, the extreme 2.5% above and below the mean) as well as the extreme 5% in a particular direction.

Box 5.2   Focus on

Negative signs

One thing which can cause confusion is when psychologists talk about plus two standard deviations or minus one standard deviation. The first thing to say is that a standard deviation can never itself have a negative value – a standard deviation is positive. The reason why psychologists talk about minus standard deviations is because they are saying how many standard deviations a score is BELOW the mean. Thus a plus indicates that a score is so many standard deviations above the mean and a minus means that the score is so many standard deviations below the mean. Really, what they should be saying is that a score has a *z*-score of +2 or a *z*-score of −1 since this is where the pluses and minuses come from and nobody would get confused.

5.6   An important feature of *z*-scores

By using *z*-scores the researcher is able to say an enormous amount about a distribution of scores extremely succinctly. If we present the following information:

- the mean of a distribution
- the standard deviation of the distribution
- that the distribution is roughly bell shaped or normal

then we can use this information to make very clear statements about the relative position of any score on the variable in question. In other words, rather than present an entire frequency distribution, these three pieces of information are virtually all that is required. Indeed, the third assumption is rarely mentioned since in most applications it makes very little difference.

Key points

- Do not despair if you have problems in understanding standard deviation; it is one of the most abstract ideas in statistics, but so fundamental that it cannot be avoided. It can take some time to absorb completely.

- Remember that the standard deviation is a sort of average deviation from the mean and you will not go far wrong.

- Remember that using *z*-scores is simply a way of putting variables on a standard unit of measurement irrespective of special characteristics of that variable. Standardised values are common in the more advanced statistical techniques so it is good to master them at an early stage.

- Remember that virtually any numerical score variable can be summarised using the standard deviation and that virtually any measurement can be expressed as a *z*-score. The main exception to its use is measurements which are in *nominal* categories like occupation or eye colour. Certainly if a score is *interval or ratio* in nature, standard deviation and *z*-scores are appropriate.

COMPUTER ANALYSIS

You may find a disparity between computer calculations of standard deviations and the calculations in this chapter. This is because computer programs such as SPSS Statistics calculate the estimated standard deviation rather than the standard deviation as in this chapter. The difference between the two is not important in the long run since the estimated standard deviation is most commonly used in practice because your analyses will usually be estimating population characteristics from sample characteristics. The same is true for the *z*-scores in this chapter and those found on computer output.

The SPSS Statistics instruction book to accompany this text is Dennis Howitt and Duncan Cramer (2011), *Introduction to SPSS Statistics in Psychology: For version 19 and earlier*, Harlow: Pearson. Chapter 7 in that book gives detailed step-by-step procedures for the statistics described in this chapter together with advice on how to report the results. Figure 5.6 shows the SPSS Statistics steps for calculating the standard deviation and *z*-scores. However, you will find that standard deviations are automatically produced for the output for a number of different statistical procedures so you may not have to do the calculation separately.

Data
- Name the variables in Variable View of the Data Editor.
- Enter the data under the appropriate variable names in Data View of the Data Editor.

Analysis
- Select 'Analyze', 'Descriptive Statistics' and 'Descriptives . . .'.
- Move the variables to be analysed to the right hand box.

2
- Select 'Save standardised values as variables'.

Output
- The standardised values are presented in the next free column of Data View in the Data Editor with the name of the original variable following the letter g with a Z.

FIGURE 5.6 SPSS Statistics steps for standard deviation and *z*-scores

CHAPTER 6

Relationships between two or more variables

Diagrams and tables

Overview

- Most research in psychology involves the relationships between two or more variables.

- Relationships between two score variables may be represented pictorially as a scattergram (or scatterplot). Alternatively, a crosstabulation table with the scores broken down into ranges (or bands) is sometimes effective.

- If both variables are nominal (category) then compound bar charts of various sorts may be used or, alternatively, crosstabulation tables.

- If there is one score variable and one nominal (category) variable then often tables of means of the score variable tabulated against the nominal (category) variable will be adequate. It is possible, alternatively, to employ a compound histogram.

Preparation

You should be aware of the meaning of variables, scores and the different scales of measurement, especially the difference between nominal (category) measurement and numerical scores.

6.1   Introduction

Although it is fundamental and important to be able to describe the characteristics of each variable in your research both diagrammatically and numerically, *interrelationships* between variables are more characteristic of research in most areas of psychology and the social sciences. Public opinion polling is the most common use of single-variable statistics that most of us come across. Opinion pollsters ask a whole series of questions about political leaders and voting intentions which are generally reported separately. However, researchers often report relationships between two variables. So, for example, if one asks whether the voting intentions of men and women differ it is really to enquire whether there is a relationship between the variable 'gender' and the variable 'voting intention'. Similarly, if one asks whether the popularity of the President of the USA changed over time, this really implies that there may be a relationship between the variable 'time' and the variable 'popularity of the President'. Many of these questions seem so familiar to us that we regard them almost as common sense. Given this, we should not have any great difficulty in understanding the concept of interrelationships among variables.

Interrelationships between variables form the bedrock of virtually all psychological research. It is rare in psychology to have research questions which require data from only one variable at a time. Much of psychology concerns explanations of why things happen – what causes what – which clearly is about relationships between variables. This chapter describes some of the main graphical and tabular methods for presenting interrelationships between variables. Diagrams and tables often overlap in function as will become apparent in the following discussion. We should emphasise that graphs and tables are not simply ways of smartening up a report or dissertation. Their function in statistical analysis is much deeper than this and they are at the heart of the analytic work of the researcher. Graphs and tables should be the mainstay of a good statistical analysis not the end product. Their role is crucial from the start of the analysis as part of the familiarisation process with one's data which leads to understanding of what is going on in the data. So looking at charts which first of all give the distributions of each of the variables in your study is the initial stage. This can lead you to identify problems such as very skewed distributions for a variable or bunching and clustering around particular data points. Then you can move onto the graphs and tables which allow you to understand the relationships between two variables. This may well be your first indication that your expectations are being confirmed by your data. But it may show that the relationships that you are expecting are more complex than you imagined or that there is a possibility that there are outliers which spuriously appear to create a relationship between your variables but there is no relationship for the bulk of the data. One has to enter this phase with an open mind since it involves getting to understand your data and becoming familiar with its characteristics. This is why you do research. They may seem like very basic procedures compared with the riches of more advanced statistics but they are basic because they are the base from which your analysis is built. Figure 6.1 gives the key steps to consider when describing relationships between two variables in diagram and table form.

6.2   The principles of diagrammatic and tabular presentation

Choosing appropriate techniques to show relationships between two variables requires an understanding of the difference between nominal category data and numerical score

Table 6.1	Types of relationships based on nominal categories and numerical scores	
	Variable *X* = numerical scores	Variable *X* = nominal categories
Variable *Y* = numerical scores	type A	type C
Variable *Y* = nominal categories	type C	type B

FIGURE 6.1   Conceptual steps for showing relationships between two variables

data. If we are considering the interrelationships between *two* variables (*X* and *Y*) then the types of variable involved are as shown in Table 6.1.

Once you have decided to which category your pair of variables belongs, it is easy to suggest appropriate descriptive statistics. We have classified different situations as type A, type B and type C. Thus type B has both variables measured on the nominal category scale of measurement.

6.3   Type A: both variables numerical scores

Where both variables take the form of numerical scores, generally the best form of graphical presentation is the *scattergram* or scatterplot. This is a sort of graph in which the values on one variable are plotted against the values on the other variable. The most familiar form of graph is one that plots a variable against time. These are very familiar from newspapers, especially the financial sections (see Figure 6.2).

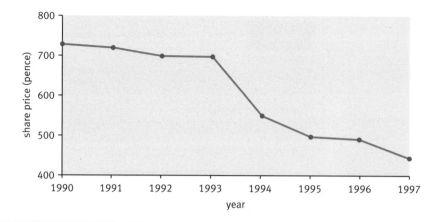

FIGURE 6.2   The dramatic fall in share price in the Timeshare Office Company

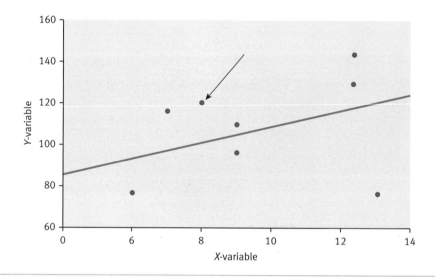

FIGURE 6.3   A scattergram showing the relationship between two variables

Time is no different, statistically speaking, from a wide range of other numerical scores. Figure 6.3 is an example of a scattergram from a psychological study. You will see that the essential features remain the same. In Figure 6.3, the point marked with an arrow represents a case whose score on the X-variable is 8 and whose score on the Y-variable is 120. It is sometimes possible to see that the points of a scattergram fall more or less on a straight line. This line through the points of a scattergram is called the *regression line*. Figure 6.3 includes the regression line for the points of the scattergram.

One complication you sometimes come across is where several points on the scattergram overlap completely. In these circumstances you may well see a number next to a point which corresponds to the number of overlapping points at that position on the scattergram.

In line with general mathematical notation, the horizontal axis or horizontal dimension is described as the X-axis and the vertical axis or vertical dimension is called the Y-axis. It is helpful if you remember to label one set of scores the X scores since these belong on the horizontal axis, and the other set of scores the Y scores because these belong on the vertical axis (Figure 6.4).

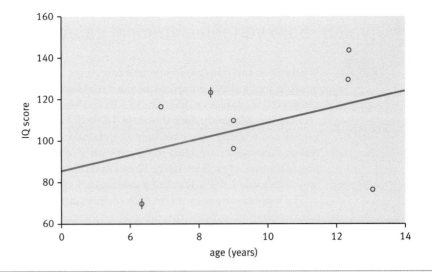

| | FIGURE 6.4 | A scattergram with the *X*- and *Y*-axes labelled and overlapping points illustrated |

Table 6.2	Use of bands of scores to tabulate the relationship between two numerical score variables				
Variable X	**Variable Y**				
	1–5	**6–10**	**11–15**	**16–20**	**21–25**
0–9	15	7	6	3	4
10–19	7	12	3	5	4
20–29	4	9	19	8	4
30–39	1	3	2	22	3
40–49	3	2	3	19	25

In Figure 6.4, overlapping points are marked not with a number but with lines around the point on the scattergram. These are called 'sunflowers' – the number of 'petals' is the number of cases overlapping at the same point. So if there are two 'petals' then there are *two* people with the same pattern of scores on the two variables. If there are three 'petals' then *three* people have exactly the same pattern of scores on the two variables. Another way of indicating overlaps is simply to put the *number* of overlaps next to the scattergraph point.

Apart from cumbersomely listing all of your pairs of scores, it is often difficult to think of a succinct way of presenting data from pairs of numerical scores in tabular form. The main possibility is to categorise each of your score variables into 'bands' of scores and express the data in terms of *frequencies* of occurrence in these bands; a table like Table 6.2 might be appropriate.

Such tables are known as 'crosstabulation' or 'contingency' tables. In Table 6.2 there does seem to be a relationship between variable *X* and variable *Y*. People with low scores on variable *X* also tend to get low scores on variable *Y*. High scorers on variable *X* also tend to score highly on variable *Y*. However, the trend in the table is less easily discerned than in the equivalent scattergram.

6.4 Type B: both variables nominal categories

Where both variables are in nominal categories, it is necessary to report the frequencies in all of the possible groupings of the variables. If you have more than a few nominal categories, the tables or diagrams can be too big.

Take the imaginary data shown in Table 6.3 on the relationship between a person's gender and whether they have been hospitalised at any time in their life for a psychiatric reason. These data are ideal for certain sorts of tables and diagrams because *there are few categories of each variable*. Thus a suitable table for summarising these data might look like Table 6.4 – it is called a contingency or crosstabulation table.

The numbers (frequencies) in each category are instantly obvious from this table. You might prefer to express the table in percentages rather than frequencies, but some thought needs to go into the choice of percentages. For example, you could express the frequencies as percentages of the total of males and females (Table 6.5).

Table 6.3	Gender and whether previously hospitalised for a set of 89 people	
Person	**Gender**	**Previously hospitalised**
1	male	yes
2	male	no
3	male	no
4	male	yes
5	male	no
. . .	. . .	. . .
85	female	yes
86	female	yes
87	female	no
88	female	no
89	female	yes

Table 6.4	Crosstabulation table of gender against hospitalisation	
	Male	**Female**
Previously hospitalised	$f = 20$	$f = 25$
Not previously hospitalised	$f = 30$	$f = 14$

Table 6.5	Crosstabulation table with all frequencies expressed as a percentage of the total number of frequencies	
	Male	**Female**
Previously hospitalised	22.5%	28.1%
Not previously hospitalised	33.7%	15.7%

You probably think that Table 6.5 is not much of an improvement in clarity. An alternative is to express the frequencies as percentages of males *and* percentages of females (Table 6.6). By presenting the percentages based on males and females separately, it is easier to see the trend for females to have had a previous psychiatric history relatively more frequently than males.

The same data can be expressed as a *compound bar chart*. In a compound bar chart information is given about the subcategories based on a pair of variables. Figure 6.5 shows one example in which the proportions are expressed as percentages of the males and females separately.

The golden rule for such data is to ensure that the number of categories is manageable. In particular, avoid having too many empty or near-empty categories. The compound bar chart shown in Figure 6.6 is a particularly bad example and is *not to be copied*. This chart fails any reasonable clarity test and is too complex to decipher quickly.

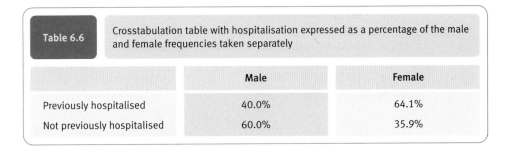

Table 6.6	Crosstabulation table with hospitalisation expressed as a percentage of the male and female frequencies taken separately	
	Male	**Female**
Previously hospitalised	40.0%	64.1%
Not previously hospitalised	60.0%	35.9%

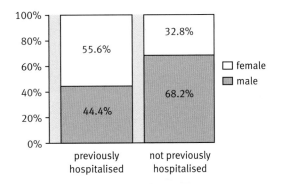

FIGURE 6.5	Compound percentage bar chart showing gender trends in previous hospitalisation

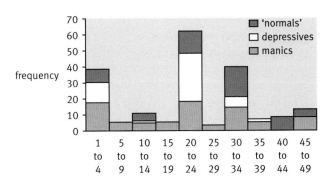

FIGURE 6.6	How *not* to do a compound bar chart

6.5 Type C: one variable nominal categories, the other numerical scores

This final type of situation offers a wide variety of ways of presenting the relationships between variables. We have examined the compound bar chart so it is not surprising to find that there is also a *compound histogram*. To be effective, a compound histogram needs to consist of:

● a small number of categories for the nominal category variable

● a few *ranges* for the numerical scores.

So, for example, if we wish to plot the relationship between managers' anxiety scores and whether they are managers in a high-tech or a low-tech industry, we might create a compound histogram like Figure 6.7 in which there are only two values of the nominal variable (high-tech and low-tech) and four bands of anxiety score (low anxiety, medium anxiety, high anxiety and very high anxiety).

An alternative way of presenting such data is to use a crosstabulation table as in Table 6.7. Instead, however, it is almost as easy to draw up a table (Table 6.8)

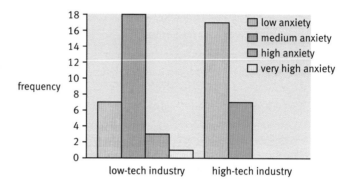

FIGURE 6.7   A compound histogram

Table 6.7	Crosstabulation table of anxiety against type of industry			
	Frequency of anxiety score			
	0–3	**4–7**	**8–11**	**12–15**
Low-tech industry	7	18	3	1
High-tech industry	17	7	0	0

Table 6.8	Comparison of the statistical characteristics of anxiety in two different types of industry				
	Mean	**Median**	**Mode**	**Interquartile range**	**Variance**
High-tech industry	3.5	3.9	3	2.3–4.2	2.2
Low-tech industry	5.3	4.7	6	3.9–6.3	3.2

which gives the mean, median, mode, etc. for the anxiety scores of the two different groups.

Key points

- Never assume that your tables and diagrams are good enough at the first attempt. They could probably be improved with a little care and adjustment.

- Do not forget that tables and diagrams are there to present clearly the major trends in your data (or lack of them). There is not much point in having tables and diagrams that do not clarify your data.

- Your tables and diagrams are not means of tabulating your unprocessed data. If you need to present your data in full then most of the methods to be found in this chapter will not help you much.

- Labelling tables and diagrams clearly and succinctly is an important part of the task – without clear titling and labelling you are probably wasting your time.

COMPUTER ANALYSIS

The SPSS Statistics instruction book to this text is Dennis Howitt and Duncan Cramer (2011), *Introduction to SPSS Statistics in Psychology: For version 19 and earlier*, Harlow: Pearson. Chapters 8 (tables) and 9 (diagrams) in that book give detailed step-by-step procedures for the statistics described in this chapter together with advice on how to report the results. Figure 6.8 gives the SPSS Statistics steps for producing contingency tables, compound charts and histograms.

Data	• Name the variables in Variable View of the Data Editor. • Enter the data under the appropriate variable names in Data View of the Data Editor.
Analysis	• For a contingency table, select 'Analyze', 'Table' and 'Custom Tables . . .'.
2	• Select 'OK' and move the appropriate variables to the column and row boxes.
3	• For compound bar charts or histograms, select 'Graphs', 'Chart Builder . . .', 'OK' and appropriate graph.
4	• Move graph to box above and select appropriate variables and statistics.
Output	• Check charts are correct. They can be edited in the Chart Editor if required.

FIGURE 6.8 SPSS Statistics steps for contingency tables, compound charts and histograms

CHAPTER 7

Correlation coefficients

Pearson correlation and Spearman's rho

Overview

- Correlation coefficients are numerical indexes of the relationship between two variables. They are the bedrock of much statistical analysis.

- The correlation coefficient may be positive or negative depending on whether both sets of scores increase together (positive correlation) or whether one set increases as the other decreases (negative correlation).

- The numerical size of the correlation coefficient ranges from 0 (no relationship) to 1 (a perfect relationship). Intermediary values indicate different amounts of spread around the best-fitting straight line through the points (i.e. the spread around the regression line).

- The Pearson correlation is used for score variables (though it can be used where a variable is a nominal variable with just two categories).

- Spearman's correlation is used when the scores are ranked from smallest to largest.

- Great care should be taken to inspect the scattergram between the two variables in question in order to make sure that the best-fitting line is a straight line rather than a curve. Also, small numbers of very extreme scores can substantially mask the true trend in the data – these are called outliers. The chapter explains what to do about them.

- The statistical significance of correlation coefficients is dealt with in Chapter 10.

Preparation

Revise variance (Chapter 3) and the use of the scattergram to show the relationship between two variables (Chapter 6).

7.1 Introduction

Although the scattergram is an important statistical tool for showing relationships between two variables, it is space consuming. For many purposes, it is more convenient to have the main features of the scattergram expressed as a single numerical index – the *correlation coefficient*. This is merely a numerical index which summarises some, but not all, of the key features of a scattergram. The commonest correlation coefficient is the *Pearson correlation*, also known more grandly and obscurely as the Pearson product-moment correlation coefficient. It includes two major pieces of information:

1. The closeness of the fit of the points of a scattergram to the best-fitting straight line through those points.

2. Information about whether the slope of the scattergram is positive or negative.

It therefore omits other information such as the scales of measurement of the two variables and specific information about individuals.

The correlation coefficient thus neatly summarises a great deal of information about a scattergram. It is especially useful when you have several variables which would involve drawing numerous scattergrams, one for each pair of variables. It most certainly does not replace the scattergram entirely but merely helps you to present your findings rather more concisely than other methods. Indeed, we recommend that you draw a scattergram for every correlation coefficient you calculate even if that scattergram is not intended for inclusion in your report.

Although the correlation coefficient is a basic descriptive statistic, it is elaborated in a number of sophisticated forms such as partial correlation, multiple correlation and factor analysis. It is of paramount importance in many forms of research, especially survey, questionnaire and similar kinds of research. Figure 7.1 overleaf gives the key steps to consider when using the correlation coefficient.

7.2 Principles of the correlation coefficient

The correlation coefficient basically takes the following form:

$$r_{[\text{correlation coefficient}]} = +1.00$$
$$\text{or} \quad 0.00$$
$$\text{or} \quad -1.00$$
$$\text{or} \quad 0.30$$
$$\text{or} \quad -0.72, \text{ etc.}$$

So a correlation coefficient consists of two parts:

1. A positive or negative sign (although for positive values the sign is frequently omitted).

2. Any numerical value in the range of 0.00 to 1.00.

The + or – sign tells us something important about the slope of the correlation line (i.e. the best-fitting straight line through the points on the scattergram). A positive value means that the slope is *from the bottom left to the top right* of the scattergram (Figure 7.2). On

The correlation coeffient is a numerical index of the direction and extent of the relationship between two variables.

A correlation merely shows an association, it does not in itself establish a causal relation.

If your data are in the form of scores then the Pearson product moment correlation coefficient is the most appropriate, usually.

The larger the numerical value then the closer the relationship between the two variables is.

The values of the correlation are from +1 to 0 if there is a positive correlation, –1 to 0 for negative correlations.

If the assumptions of the Pearson correlation coefficient are not met then you may prefer to use the Spearman rank correlation coefficient.

A value of 0 indicates that there is no relationship between the two variables.

Covariance is a measure of how much scores on one variable increase with scores on the other variable.

The Pearson correlation coefficient is simply the covariance divided by the maximum that the covariance could be.

These correlations only deal with straight-line relationships, eta deals with curvilinear ones.

The coefficient of determination is the square of the correlation coeffient – it indicates the amount of shared variance.

Always draw a scattergram as this is a visual way of checking for problems which can make the correlation coefficient misleading.

FIGURE 7.1 Conceptual steps for understanding the correlation coefficient

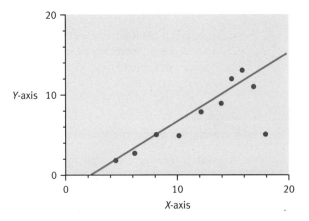

FIGURE 7.2 Positive correlation between two variables

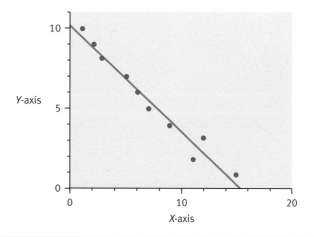

FIGURE 7.3   Negative correlation between two variables

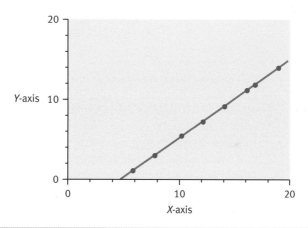

FIGURE 7.4   Perfect correlation between two variables

the other hand, if the sign is negative (−) then the slope of the straight line goes *from upper left to lower right* on the scattergram (Figure 7.3).

The numerical value of the correlation coefficient (0.50, 0.42, etc.) is an index of how close the points on the scattergram fit the best-fitting straight line. A value of 1.00 means that the points of the scattergram all lie exactly on the best-fitting straight line (Figure 7.4), unless that line is perfectly vertical or perfectly horizontal, in which case it means that there is no variation in the scores on one of the variables and so no correlation can be calculated.

A value of 0.00 means that the points of the scattergram are randomly scattered around the straight line. It is purely a matter of luck if any of them actually touch the straight line (Figure 7.5). In this case, the best-fitting straight line for the scattergram could be virtually any line you arbitrarily decide to draw through the points. Conventionally it is drawn as a horizontal line, but any other angle of slope would do just as well since there is no discernible trend in the relationship between the two variables on the scattergram.

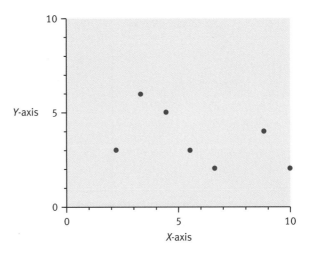

FIGURE 7.5   Near-zero correlation between two variables

A value of 0.50 would mean that although the points on the scattergram are generally close to the best-fitting straight line, there is considerable spread of these points around that straight line.

The correlation coefficient is merely an index of the amount of variance of the scattergram points from the straight line. However, it is calculated in such a way that the *maximum* variance around that straight line results in a correlation of zero. In other words, the closer the relationship between the two variables, the higher is the correlation coefficient, up to a maximum value of 1.00.

To summarise, the components of the correlation coefficient are the sign (+ or −), which indicates the direction of the slope, and a numerical value which indicates how much variation there is around the best-fitting straight line through the points (i.e. the higher the numerical value the closer the fit).

■ Covariance

The actual computation of the correlation coefficient involves little more than an elaboration of the formula for variance:

$$\text{variance} = \frac{\sum (X - \bar{X})^2}{N}$$

If you wished (you will see why in a moment), the formula for variance could be re-expressed as:

$$\text{variance} = \frac{\sum (X - \bar{X})(X - \bar{X})}{N}$$

All we have done is to expand the formula so as not to use the square sign. (A square is simply a number multiplied by itself.)

In the formula for the correlation coefficient we use something called the *covariance*. This is almost exactly the same as the formula for variance, but instead of multiplying scores by themselves we multiply the score on one variable (X) by the score on the second variable (Y):

$$\text{covariance}_{\text{[of variable X with variable Y]}} = \frac{\sum(X - \bar{X})(Y - \bar{Y})}{N}$$

where

X = scores on variable X

$\bar{X}$ = mean score on variable X

Y = scores on variable Y

$\bar{Y}$ = mean score on variable Y

N = number of pairs of scores

We get a large positive value of covariance if there is a strong positive relationship between the two variables, and a big negative value if there is a strong negative relationship between the two variables. If there is no relationship between the variables then the covariance is zero. Notice that, unlike variance, the covariance can take positive or negative values.

However, the size of the covariance is affected by the size of the variances of the two separate variables involved. The larger the variances, the larger is the covariance, potentially. Obviously this would make comparisons difficult. So the covariance is adjusted by dividing by the square root of the product of the variances of the two separate variables. (Because N, the number of pairs of scores, in the variance and covariance formulae can be cancelled out in the correlation formula, the usual formula includes no division by the number of scores.) Once this adjustment is made to the covariance formula, we have the formula for the correlation coefficient:

$$r_{\text{[correlation coefficient]}} = \frac{\sum(X - \bar{X})(Y - \bar{Y})}{\sqrt{\sum(X - \bar{X})^2}\sqrt{\sum(Y - \bar{Y})^2}}$$

The lower part of the formula actually gives the largest possible value of the covariance of the two variables – that is, the theoretical covariance if the two variables lay perfectly on the straight line through the scattergram. Dividing the covariance by the maximum value it could take (if there were no spread of points away from the straight line through the scattergram) ensures that the correlation coefficient can never be greater than 1.00. The covariance formula also contains the necessary sign to indicate the slope of the relationship.

A slightly quicker computational formula which does not involve the calculation of the mean scores directly is as follows:

$$r_{\text{[correlation coefficient]}} = \frac{\sum XY - \dfrac{\sum X \sum Y}{N}}{\sqrt{\left(\sum X^2 - \dfrac{(\sum X^2)}{N}\right)\left(\sum Y^2\right) - \dfrac{\sum Y^2}{N}}}$$

The resemblance of parts of this formula to the computational formula for variance should be fairly obvious. This is not surprising as the correlation coefficient is a measure of the *lack* of variation around a straight line through the scattergram.

Box 7.1 Key concepts

Covariance

Many of the basic concepts taught in introductory statistics are relevant even at the advanced level. The concept of covariance is one of these. As we have seen, covariance is basically the average of the deviation from the mean for the variable X multiplied by the deviation of the variable Y. In other words, it is the top part of the Pearson correlation formula. The correlation coefficient is simply the ratio of the covariance over the largest value that the covariance could take for a particular pair of variables. In other words, it is a standardised measure of covariance. But the term covariance crops up throughout this book in a number of different contexts. It is involved in ANOVA (especially the Analysis of Covariance) and regression, for example – lots of places, some of them unexpected.

One phrase that might cause some consternation is that of the 'variance-covariance' matrix for a number of variables. This is simply a table (matrix) which includes the variances of each variable in the diagonal and their covariances off of the diagonal. This is illustrated for variables X, Y and Z in Table 7.1. The diagonal contains the variances but the other numbers are the covariances – each of

Table 7.1	Variance-covariance matrix for three variables		
	Variable X	**Variable Y**	**Variable Z**
Variable X	2.400	1.533	1.244
Variable Y	1.533	4.933	3.733
Variable Z	1.244	3.733	5.156

The variances are in the green diagonal boxes.
The covariances are in the yellow boxes.

these is presented twice because the covariance of X with Z is the same as the covariance of Z with Z.

Similar matrices are produced for correlation coefficients. However, in this case the diagonal consist of 1.00s (the correlation of a variable with itself is always 1) and the off-diagonals have the correlation coefficients of each variable with the other different variables.

Calculation 7.1

The Pearson correlation coefficient

Our data for this calculation come from scores on the relationship between mathematical ability and musical ability for a group of 10 children (Table 7.2).

It is always sound practice to draw the scattergram for any correlation coefficient you are calculating. For these data, the scattergram will be like Figure 7.6. Notice that the slope of the scattergram is negative, as one could have deduced from the tendency for those who score highly on mathematical ability to have low scores on musical ability. You can also see not only that a straight line is a pretty good way of describing the trends in the points on the scattergram but that the points fit the straight line reasonably well. Thus we should expect a fairly high negative correlation from the correlation coefficient.

Step 1 Set the scores out in a table (Table 7.3) and follow the calculations as shown. Here N is the number of *pairs* of scores, i.e. 10.

Step 2 Substitute the values from Table 7.3 in the formula:

→

Table 7.2	Scores on musical and mathematical ability for 10 children	
Individual	**Music score**	**Mathematics score**
Angela	2	8
Arthur	6	3
Peter	4	9
Mike	5	7
Barbara	7	2
Jane	7	3
Jean	2	9
Ruth	3	8
Alan	5	6
Theresa	4	7

FIGURE 7.6	Scattergram for Calculation 7.1

$$r_{[\text{correlation coefficient}]} = \frac{\sum XY - \dfrac{\sum X \sum Y}{N}}{\sqrt{\left(\sum X^2 - \dfrac{\left(\sum X^2\right)}{N}\right)\left(\sum Y^2\right) - \dfrac{\sum Y^2}{N}}}$$

$$= \frac{240 - \dfrac{45 \times 62}{10}}{\sqrt{\left(233 - \dfrac{45^2}{10}\right)\left(446 - \dfrac{62^2}{10}\right)}}$$

$$= \frac{240 - \dfrac{2790}{10}}{\sqrt{\left(233 - \dfrac{2025}{10}\right)\left(446 - \dfrac{3844}{10}\right)}}$$

→

Table 7.3	Essential steps in the calculation of the correlation coefficient			
X score (music)	Y score (maths)	X^2	Y^2	$X \times Y$
2	8	4	64	16
6	3	36	9	18
4	9	16	81	36
5	7	25	49	35
7	2	49	4	14
7	3	49	9	21
2	9	4	81	18
3	8	9	64	24
5	6	25	36	30
4	7	16	49	28
$\Sigma X = 45$	$\Sigma Y = 62$	$\Sigma X^2 = 233$	$\Sigma Y^2 = 446$	$\Sigma XY = 240$

$$= \frac{240 - 279}{\sqrt{(233 - 202.5)(446 - 384.4)}}$$

$$= \frac{-39}{\sqrt{30.5 \times 61.6}}$$

$$= \frac{-39}{43.35}$$

$$= -0.90$$

Interpreting the results So the value obtained for the correlation coefficient equals −0.90. This value is in line with what we suggested about the scattergram which serves as a rough check on our calculation. There is a very substantial negative relationship between mathematical and musical ability. In other words, the good mathematicians tended to be the poor musicians and vice versa. It is not claimed that they are good at music *because* they are poor at mathematics but merely that there is an inverse association between the two.

Reporting the results When reporting a correlation coefficient it is usual to report its statistical significance. The meaning of statistical significance is explained in Chapters 9 and 10 and especially Calculation 10.1. You could ignore Chapter 8 and proceed directly to these chapters. However, the important point for now is to remember that statistical significance is invariably reported with the value of the correlation coefficient.

We would write something like: 'It was found that musical ability was inversely related to mathematical ability. The Pearson correlation coefficient was −0.90 which is statistically significant at the 5% level with a sample size of 10.' The information in the final sentence will not be informative to you until you have studied Chapters 9 and 10.

If we were to heed the advice of the 2010 Publication Manual of the American Psychological Association (APA) we could write: 'Musical ability was significantly inversely related to mathematical ability, $r(8) = -.90$, $p < .05$'. The number in brackets after r is the sample size minus 2. This number is called the degrees of freedom and is explained in Chapter 20, Section 20.4. Statistical significance is usually reported as a proportion rather than a percentage. Computer packages like SPSS Statistics give the exact significance level. We should report this as a figure as it is more informative.

7.3   Some rules to check out

1. You should make sure that a straight line is the best fit to the scattergram points. If the best-fitting line is a *curve* such as in Figure 7.7 then you should not use the Pearson correlation coefficient. The reason for this is that the Pearson correlation assumes a straight line which is a gross distortion if you have a curved (curvilinear) relationship.

2. Make sure that your scattergram does not contain a few extreme cases which are unduly influencing the correlation coefficient (Figure 7.8). In this diagram you can see that the points at the top left of the scattergram are responsible for the apparent negative correlation between the two variables. Your eyes probably suggest that for virtually all the points on the scattergram there is no relationship at all. You could in these circumstances eliminate the 'outliers' (i.e. extreme, highly influential points) and recalculate the correlation coefficient based on the remaining, more

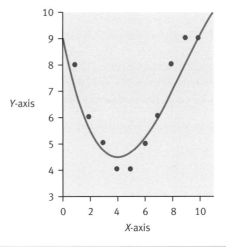

FIGURE 7.7   A curved relationship between two variables

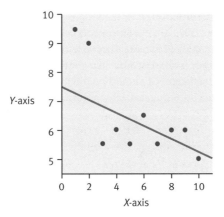

FIGURE 7.8   Influence of outliers on a correlation

typical group of scores. If the correlation remains significant with the same sign as before then your interpretation of your data is likely to remain broadly unchanged. However, there needs to be good reason for deleting the 'outliers'; this should not be done simply because the data as they stand do not support your ideas. It may be that something unusual had happened – perhaps an outlier arose from the responses of a slightly deaf person who could not hear the researcher's instructions, for example.

Box 7.2   Key concepts

Correlation and causality

It is typically argued that a correlation does not prove causality. Because two variables are related to each other is not reason to say anything other than that they are related. Statistical analysis is basically incapable of showing that one variable influenced the other variable directly one way or the other. Questions such as whether one variable affected the other are addressed primarily through the nature of your research design and not through the statistical analysis as such. Conventionally psychologists have turned to laboratory experiments in which variables could be systematically manipulated by the researcher in order to be able to enhance their confidence in making causal interpretations about relationships between variables.

Be careful when you read phrases such as 'the effect of Variable A on Variable B' in psychological writings. This can be misleading as it does not always mean causal effect. Instead, sometimes it merely means that there is a relationship, causal or otherwise.

7.4   Coefficient of determination

The correlation coefficient is an index of how much variance two variables have in common. However, you need to square the correlation coefficient in order to know precisely how much variance is shared. The squared correlation coefficient is also known as the *coefficient of determination*.

The proportion of variance shared by two variables whose correlation coefficient is 0.5 equals 0.5^2 or 0.25. This is a proportion out of 1 so as a percentage it is $0.25 \times 100\%$ = 25%. A correlation coefficient of 0.8 means that $0.8^2 \times 100\%$ or 64% of the variance is shared. A correlation coefficient of 1.00 means that $1.00^2 \times 100\%$ = 100% of the variance is shared. Since the coefficient of determination is based on *squaring* the correlation coefficient, it should be obvious that the amount of variance shared by the two variables declines increasingly rapidly as the correlation coefficient gets smaller (Table 7.4).

7.5   Significance testing

Some readers who have previously studied statistics a little will be familiar with the notion of significance testing and might be wondering why this has not been dealt with for the correlation coefficient. The answer is that we will be dealing with it, but not until Chapter 10. In the present chapter we are presenting the correlation coefficient as a

Table 7.4	Variance shared by two variables	
Correlation coefficient		**Variance the two variables share**
1.00		100%
0.90		81%
0.80		64%
0.70		49%
0.60		36%
0.50		25%
0.40		16%
0.30		9%
0.20		4%
0.10		1%
0.00		0%

descriptive statistic which numerically summarises a scattergram between two variables. For those who wish to understand significance testing for the correlation coefficient, simply skip Chapter 8 on regression for now and proceed to Chapters 9 and 10.

7.6 Spearman's rho – another correlation coefficient

Spearman's rho is often written as r_s. We have not used this symbol in the following discussion although it is common in textbooks.

The Pearson correlation coefficient is the dominant correlation index in psychological statistics. There is another called *Spearman's rho* which is not very different – practically identical, in truth. Instead of taking the scores directly from your data, the scores on a variable are ranked from smallest to largest. That is, the smallest score on variable *X* is given rank 1, the second smallest score on variable *X* is given rank 2, and so forth. The smallest score on variable *Y* is given rank 1, the second smallest score on variable *Y* is given rank 2, etc. Then Spearman's rho is calculated like the Pearson correlation coefficient between the two sets of ranks as if the ranks were scores. A special procedure is used to deal with *tied ranks*.

Sometimes certain scores on a variable are identical. There might be two or three people who scored 7 on variable *X*, for example. This situation is described as *tied scores* or *tied ranks*. The question is what to do about them. The conventional answer in psychological statistics is to pretend first of all that the tied scores can be separated by fractional amounts. Then we allocate the appropriate ranks to these 'separated' scores but give each of the tied scores the average rank that they would have received if they could have been separated (Table 7.5)

The two scores of 5 are each given the rank 2.5 because if they were slightly different they would have been given ranks 2 and 3, respectively. But they cannot be separated and so we average the ranks as follows:

Table 7.5	Ranking of a set of scores when tied (equal) scores are involved								
Scores	4	5	5	6	7	8	9	9	9	10
Ranks	1	2.5	2.5	4	5	6	8	8	8	10

$$\frac{2 + 3}{2} = 2.5$$

This average of the two ranks corresponds to what was entered into Table 7.5.

There are three scores of 9 which would have been allocated the ranks 7, 8 and 9 if the scores had been slightly different from each other. These three ranks are averaged to give an average rank of 8 which is entered as the rank for each of the three tied scores in Table 7.5.

There is a special computational formula (see Calculation 7.3 later in this chapter) which can be used which is quicker than applying the conventional Pearson correlation formula to data in the form of ranks. It is nothing other than a special case of the Pearson correlation formula. Most statistics textbooks provide this formula for routine use. Unfortunately this formula is only accurate when you have absolutely no tied ranks at all – otherwise it gives a slightly wrong answer. As tied ranks are common in psychological research it is dubious whether there is anything to be gained in using the special Spearman's rho computational formula as opposed to the Pearson correlation coefficient applied to the ranks.

You may wonder why we have bothered to turn the scores into ranks before calculating the correlation coefficient. The reason is that ranks are commonly used in psychological statistics when the distributions of scores on a variable are markedly unsymmetrical and do not approximate (even poorly) a normal distribution. In the past it was quite fashionable to use rankings of scores instead of the scores themselves, but we would suggest that you avoid ranking if possible. Use ranks only when your data seem extremely distorted from a normal distribution. We realise that others may argue differently. The reasons for this are explained in Chapter 18.

Calculation 7.2

Spearman's rho with or without tied ranks

We could apply the Spearman rho correlation to the data on the relationship between mathematical ability and musical ability for a group of 10 children which we used previously. But we must rank the two sets of scores before applying the normal Pearson correlation formula since there are tied ranks (see Table 7.6). In our calculation, N is the number of *pairs* of ranks, i.e. 10. For this calculation we have called the maths score the X score and the music score the Y score (the reverse of Calculation 7.1). This makes no difference to the calculation of the correlation coefficient.

Table 7.6		Steps in the calculation of Spearman's rho correlation coefficient					
Person	Maths score	Music score	Maths rank	Maths rank squared	Music rank	Music rank squared	Maths rank × music rank
	X score	Y score	X_r	X_r^2	Y_r	Y_r^2	$X_r \times Y_r$
1	8	2	7.5	56.25	1.5	2.25	11.25
2	3	6	2.5	6.25	8	64.00	20.00
3	9	4	9.5	90.25	4.5	20.25	42.75
4	7	5	5.5	30.25	6.5	42.25	35.75
5	2	7	1	1.00	9.5	90.25	9.50
6	3	7	2.5	6.25	9.5	90.25	23.75
7	9	2	9.5	90.25	1.5	2.25	14.25
8	8	3	7.5	56.25	3	9.00	22.50
9	6	5	4	16.00	6.5	42.25	26.00
10	7	4	5.5	30.25	4.5	20.25	24.75
			$\sum X_r = 55$	$\sum X_r^2 = 383$	$\sum Y_r = 55$	$\sum Y_r^2 = 383$	$\sum X_r Y_r = 230.50$

We then substitute the totals in the computational formula for the Pearson correlation coefficient, although now we call it Spearman's rho:

$$r_{\text{[correlation coefficient]}} = \frac{\sum X_r Y_r - \dfrac{\sum X_r \sum Y_r}{N}}{\sqrt{\left(\sum X_r^2 - \dfrac{\left(\sum X_r\right)^2}{N}\right)\left(\sum Y_r^2 - \dfrac{\left(\sum Y_r\right)^2}{N}\right)}}$$

$$= \frac{230.5 - \left(\dfrac{55 \times 55}{10}\right)}{\sqrt{\left(383 - \dfrac{55^2}{10}\right)\left(383 - \dfrac{55^2}{10}\right)}}$$

$$= \frac{230.5 - 302.5}{\sqrt{(383 - 302.5)(383 - 302.5)}}$$

$$= \frac{-72.00}{\sqrt{(80.5)(80.5)}}$$

$$= \frac{-72.00}{80.5}$$

$$= -0.89$$

Interpreting the results So, Spearman's rho gives a substantial negative correlation just as we would expect from these data. You can interpret the Spearman correlation coefficient more or less in the same way as the Pearson correlation coefficient so long as you remember that it is calculated using ranks.

It so happens in this case that the Spearman coefficient gives virtually the same numerical value as Pearson's applied to the same data. *This is fortuitous. Usually there is a discrepancy between the two.*

Reporting the results Just as with the Pearson correlation (Calculation 7.1), when reporting the Spearman's rho correlation coefficient it is normal to report the statistical significance of the coefficient. The meaning of statistical significance is explained in Chapters 9 and 10 and especially Calculation 10.2. Proceed to these chapters for a discussion of statistical significance. The most important thing for the time being is to remember that statistical significance is almost invariably reported with the value of the correlation coefficient.

We would write up the results something like: 'It was found that musical ability was inversely related to mathematical ability. The value of Spearman's rho correlation coefficient was −0.89 which is statistically significant at the 5% level with a sample size of 10.' The last sentence will not mean much until Chapters 9 and 10 have been studied.

Alternatively, following the recommendations of the APA (2010) Publication Manual we could write it as 'Musical ability was significantly inversely related to mathematical ability, $r_s(8) = −.89, p < .05$'.

We referred earlier to a special computational formula which could be used to calculate Spearman's rho when there are no ties. There seems little point in learning this formula, since a lack of tied ranks is not characteristic of psychological data. You may as well simply use the method of Calculation 7.2 irrespective of whether there are ties or not. For those who want to save a little time when there are no tied ranks, the procedure of Calculation 7.3 may be used.

Calculation 7.3

Spearman's rho where there are no tied ranks

The formula used in this computation applies only when there are no tied scores. If there are any, the formula becomes increasingly inaccurate and the procedure of Calculation 7.2 should be applied. However, some psychologists use the formula whether or not there are tied ranks, despite the inaccuracy problem.

For illustrative purposes we will use the same data on maths ability and musical ability despite there being ties, as listed in Table 7.7. Once again, $N = 10$.

$$r_{[\text{Spearman's rho}]} = 1 - \frac{6\sum D^2}{N(N^2 - 1)}$$

$$= 1 - \frac{6 \times 305}{10(10^2 - 1)}$$

$$= 1 - \frac{1830}{10 \times (100 - 1)}$$

$$= 1 - \frac{1830}{10 \times 99}$$

$$= 1 - \frac{1830}{990}$$

$$= 1 - 1.848$$

$$= -0.848$$

$$= -0.85 \text{ to 2 decimal places}$$

→

Table 7.7	Steps in the calculation of Spearman's rho correlation coefficient using the speedy formula					
Person	Maths score X score	Music score Y score	Maths rank X_r	Music rank Y_r	Maths rank − music rank D (difference)	Square of previous column D^2
1	8	2	7.5	1.5	6.0	36.00
2	3	6	2.5	8	−5.5	30.25
3	9	4	9.5	4.5	5	25.00
4	7	5	5.5	6.5	−1.0	1.00
5	2	7	1	9.5	−8.5	72.25
6	3	7	2.5	9.5	−7.0	49.00
7	9	2	9.5	1.5	8.0	64.00
8	8	3	7.5	3	4.5	20.25
9	6	5	4	6.5	−2.5	6.25
10	7	4	5.5	4.5	1.0	1.00
						$\sum D^2 = 305$

Interpreting the results It should be noted that this value of Spearman's rho is a little different from its correct value (−0.89) as we calculated it in Calculation 7.2. The reason for this difference is the inaccuracy of the speedy formula when there are tied scores. Although the difference is not major, you are strongly recommended not to incorporate this error. Otherwise the interpretation of the negative correlation is the same as we have previously discussed.

Reporting the results As with the Pearson correlation (Calculation 7.1), when reporting the Spearman's rho correlation coefficient we would report the statistical significance of the coefficient. The meaning of statistical significance is explained in Chapters 9 and 10 and especially Calculation 10.2. Ignore Chapter 8 and proceed directly to these chapters for an explanation. However, the important point for now is to remember that statistical significance is invariably reported with the value of the correlation coefficient.

We would write up the results something along the lines of the following: 'It was found that musical ability was inversely related to mathematical ability. The value of Spearman's rho correlation coefficient was −0.85 which is statistically significant at the 5% level with a sample size of 10.' The last sentence will not mean much until Chapters 9 and 10 have been studied.

7.7   An example from the literature

Pearson correlation coefficients are extremely common in published research. They can be found in a variety of contexts so choosing a typical example is virtually meaningless. The correlation coefficient is sometimes used as an indicator of the validity of a psychological test. So it might be used to indicate the relationship between a test of intelligence and children's performance in school. The test is a valid predictor of school performance if there is a substantial correlation between the test score and school performance.

The correlation coefficient is also very useful as an indicator of the reliability of a psychological test. This might mean the extent to which people's scores on the test are consistent over time. You can use the correlation coefficient to indicate whether those who perform well now on the test also performed well a year ago. For example, Gillis (1980) in the manual accompanying the Child Anxiety Scale indicates that he retested 127 US schoolchildren in the first to third grades immediately after the initial testing. The reliability coefficients (test–retest reliability) or the correlation coefficients between the two testings were:

Grade 1 = 0.82
Grade 2 = 0.85
Grade 3 = 0.92

A sample of children retested after a week had a retest reliability coefficient of 0.81. It is clear from this that the reliability of the measure is good. This means that the children scoring the most highly one week also tend to get the highest scores the next week. It does not mean that the scores are identical from week to week – only that the relative scores are the same.

Practically all reliability and validity coefficients used in psychological testing are variants on much the same theme and are rarely much more complex than the correlation coefficient itself.

Key points

Most of the major points have been covered already. But they bear repetition:

- Check the scattergram for your correlation coefficient for signs of a nonlinear relationship – if you find one you should not be using the Pearson correlation coefficient. In these circumstances you should use coefficient eta (η) which is designed for curvilinear relationships. However, eta is a relatively obscure statistic. It is mentioned again in Chapter 34.

- Check the scattergram for outliers which may spuriously be producing a correlation when over-whelmingly the scattergram says that there is a poor relationship.

- Examine the scattergram to see whether there is a positive or negative slope to the scatter and form a general impression of whether the correlation is good (the points fit the straight line well) or poor (the points are very widely scattered around the straight line). Obviously you will become more skilled at this with experience, but it is useful as a rough computational check among other things.

- Before concluding your analysis, check out Chapter 10 to decide whether or not to generalise from your set of data.

COMPUTER ANALYSIS

The SPSS Statistics instruction book to this text is Dennis Howitt and Duncan Cramer (2011), *Introduction to SPSS Statistics in Psychology: For version 19 and earlier*, Harlow: Pearson. Chapter 10 in that book gives detailed step-by-step procedures for the statistics described in this chapter together with advice on how to report the results. Figure 7.9 shows the SPSS Statistics steps for Pearson's correlation and Figure 7.10 for a scattergram.

Data
- The data are entered as different variables in different columns – each row equals a person.
- Name each variable.

Analysis
- Select 'Analyze'.
- Select 'Correlate' then Select 'Bivariate'.

2
- Move variables to correlate to right hand side box.
- Select 'Pearson' or 'Spearman' according to what is appropriate.

Output
- The output is a correlation matrix even with just two variables so take care.
- The matrix includes the correlation of each variable with itself and does not provide a significance level.

FIGURE 7.9 SPSS Statistics steps for correlation coefficient

Data
- Data have already been entered for the correlation coefficient.

Analysis
- Select 'Graphs', 'Chart Builder', 'OK' and move 'Simple Scatter' to the box above.

2
- Move appropriate variables names to the vertical and horizontal axes.

Output
- A regression line can be fitted by double clicking anywhere on the scattergram to bring up the Chart Editor.
- Select 'Elements' and 'Fit Line at Total'.

FIGURE 7.10 SPSS Statistics steps for scattergrams

CHAPTER 8

Regression

Prediction with precision

Overview

- Regression basically identifies the regression line (that is best-fitting straight line) for a scatterplot between two variables. (By this token, the correlation coefficient can be seen as an index of the spread of the data points around this regression line.)

- It uses a variable X (which is the horizontal axis of the scatterplot) and a variable Y (which is the vertical axis of the scatterplot).

- Sometimes (somewhat misleadingly) the X variable is known as the independent variable and the Y variable is known as the dependent variable. Alternatively, the X variable may be called the predictor variable and the Y variable is known as the criterion variable.

- To describe the regression line, one needs the slope of the line and the point at which it touches the vertical axis (the intercept).

- Using this information, it is possible to estimate the most likely score on the variable Y for any given score on variable X. Sometimes this is referred to as making predictions.

- Standard error is a term used to describe the variability of any statistical estimate including those of the regression calculation. So there is a standard error of the slope, a standard error of the intercept and so forth. Standard error is analogous to standard deviation and indicates the likely spread of any of the estimates.

- Regression is the foundation of many of the more advanced techniques described later in this book. So the better you understand the concept at this stage, the easier will be your later work.

Preparation

You should have a working knowledge of the scattergram, of the relationship between two variables (Chapter 6) and understand the correlation coefficient (Chapter 7).

8.1 | Introduction

Regression, like the correlation coefficient, numerically describes important features of a scattergram relating two variables. However, it does it in a different way from the correlation coefficient. Among its important uses is that it allows the researcher to make predictions (for example, when choosing the best applicant for a job on the basis of an aptitude or ability test).

Assume that research has shown that a simple test of manual dexterity is capable of distinguishing between the better and not-so-good assembly workers in a precision components factory. Manual dexterity is a *predictor* variable and job performance the *criterion* variable. So it should be possible to predict which applicants are likely to be the more productive employees from scores on this easily administered test of manual dexterity. Using the test might be a lot cheaper than employing people who do not make the grade. Imaginary data for such a study are shown in Table 8.1.

The scattergram (Figure 8.1) shows imaginary data on the relationship between scores on the manual dexterity test and the number of units per hour the employee produces in the components factory. Notice that we have made scores on the manual dexterity test the horizontal dimension (*X*-axis) and the number of units produced per hour the vertical dimension (*Y*-axis).

In regression in order to keep the number of formulae to the minimum, the horizontal dimension (*X*-axis) should always be used to represent the variable from which the prediction is being made, and the vertical dimension (*Y*-axis) should always represent what is being predicted.

It is clear from the scattergram that the number of units produced by workers is fairly closely related to scores on the manual dexterity test. If we draw a straight line as best we can through the points on the scattergram, this line could be used as a basis for making predictions about the most likely score on work productivity from the aptitude test score of manual dexterity. This line through the points on a scattergram is called the *regression line*. In order to predict the likeliest number of units per hour corresponding to a score of 70 on the manual dexterity test, we simply draw a right angle from the score 70 on the horizontal axis (manual dexterity test score) to the regression line, and then a right angle from the vertical axis to meet this point. In this way we can find the productivity

Table 8.1	Manual dexterity and number of units produced per hour
Manual dexterity score	**Number of units produced per hour**
56	17
19	6
78	23
92	22
16	9
23	10
29	13
60	20
50	16
35	19

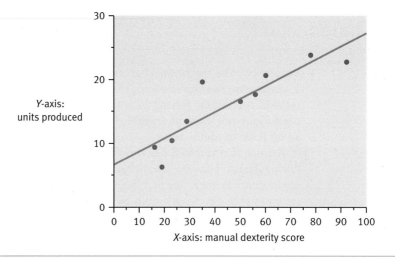

FIGURE 8.1   Scattergram of the relationship between manual dexterity and productivity

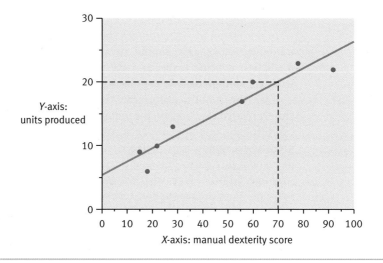

FIGURE 8.2   Using a regression line to make approximate predictions

score which best corresponds to a particular manual dexterity score (Figure 8.2). Estimating from this scattergram and regression line, it appears that the best prediction from a manual dexterity score of 70 is a productivity rate of about 19 or 20.

There is only one major problem with this procedure – the prediction depends on the particular line drawn through the points on the scattergram. You might draw a somewhat different line from the one we did. Subjective factors such as these are not desirable and it would be better to have a method which was not affected in this way. So mathematical ways of determining the regression line have been developed. Fortunately, the computations are generally straightforward.

Regression is a component of many of the more advanced statistical techniques which we describe later in this book and a good understanding of the basics will make your more advanced work easier. See Box 8.1 for a discussion of the General Linear Model which underlies a great deal of the statistical analyses used by psychologists. Figure 8.3 describes the key steps when using regression.

Regression is a numerical way of describing the best-fitting straight line through a scatterplot. So the data must be scores.

The best-fitting straight line is the one for which the sum of the (squared) deviations of the data points from the line is minimised.

The cut-point (constant or intercept) is the point at which the best-fitting straight line cuts the vertical axis of the scatterplot.

It is possible to make the best prediction, by multiplying a score on the X variable by the regression weight (*b*) and then adding the cut-point (or constant).

Regression coefficients indicate the slope of the regression line and may be sometimes expressed in a standardised way (i.e. beta coefficients).

It is crucial to have the predictor (independent) variable as the X-axis and the criterion (dependent) variable as the Y-axis.

FIGURE 8.3   Conceptual steps for understanding regression

Box 8.1   Key concepts

The General Linear Model

GLM, the General Linear Model, is the basis of many of the statistical techniques discussed in this book. It is quite simple – it simply refers to the assumption that the effects of variables on other variables are additive. In other words, an increase of 1 unit on variable *A* leads to an increase of *x* on variable *B*. This is basically assumed to be the case irrespective of where the increase of 1 unit is on variable *A* (i.e. at the top, middle or bottom of the distribution, etc.). The basis of the General Linear Model is the formula that you can see in Calculation 8.1 which is used to predict values on one variable from values on another. The formula only needs slight modification to give the relationship between one set of data *Y* and another set of data *X*:

$$Y_{data\ set} = a_{constant} + (b_{regression\ weight} \times X_{scores}) + \cancel{e_{error}}$$

All that we have done is to add in *e* for error. That is, there is not a perfect relationship between the *Y* data and the *X* data. The imperfection is the result of error in the measurements.

The General Linear Model is actually more general than this basic formula implies. The reason is that there may be several *Y* variables (as in multivariate ANOVA – Chapter 26), several *X* variables (as in multiple regression – Chapter 31), several intercept values for each *X* variable and several regression coefficients also for each *X* variable. But the basic regression equation is the simplest version of the General Linear Model.

8.2   Theoretical background and regression equations

The line through a set of points on a scattergram is called the regression line. In order to establish an objective criterion, the regression line is chosen which gives the closest fit to the points on the scattergram. In other words, the procedure ensures that there is a minimum sum of distances of the regression line to the points in the scattergram. So, in theory, one could keep trying different possible regression lines until one is found which has the minimum deviation of the points from it.

The sum of the deviations ($\sum d$) of the scattergram points from the regression line should be minimal. Actually, the precise criterion is the sum of the *squared* deviations.

This is known as the *least squares solution*. But it would be really tedious work drawing different regression lines then calculating the sum of the squared deviations for each of these in order to decide which regression line has the smallest sum of squared deviations. Fortunately things are not done like that and trial and error is not involved at all. The formulae for regression do all of that work for you.

In order to specify the regression line for any scattergram, you quantify two things:

1. The point at which the regression line cuts the vertical axis at $X = 0$ – this is a number of units of measurement from the zero point of the vertical axis. It can take a positive or negative value, denoting whether the vertical axis is cut above or below its zero point. It is normally denoted in regression as point a or the *intercept*.

2. The *slope* of the regression line or, in other words, the gradient of the best-fitting line through the points on the scattergram. Just as with the correlation coefficient, this slope may be positive in the sense that it goes up from bottom left to top right or it can be negative in that it goes downwards from top left to bottom right. The slope is normally denoted by the letter b.

The intercept and slope are both shown in Figure 8.4. To work out the slope, we have drawn a horizontal dashed line from $X = 30$ to $X = 50$ (length 20) and a vertical dashed line up to the regression line (length about 4 up the Y-axis). The slope b is the increase (+) or decrease (−) of the units produced (in this case +4) divided by the increase in the manual dexterity score (in this case 20), i.e. +0.2.

The slope is simply the number of units that the regression line moves up the vertical axis for each unit it moves along the horizontal axis. In other words, you mark a single step along the horizontal axis and work out how much increase this represents on the vertical axis. So, for example, if you read that the slope of a scattergram is 2.00, this means that for every increase of 1.00 on the horizontal axis (X-axis) there is an increase of 2.00 on the vertical axis (Y-axis). If there is a slope of −0.5 then this means that for every increase of 1 on the horizontal axis (X-axis) there is a decrease of 0.5 on the vertical axis (Y-axis).

In our example, for every increase of 1 in the manual dexterity score, there is an increase of 0.2 (more accurately, 0.21) in the job performance measure (units produced per hour). We have estimated this value from the scattergram – it may not be exactly the answer that we would have obtained had we used mathematically more precise

FIGURE 8.4   Slope *b* and intercept *a* of a regression line

methods. This increase defines the slope. (Note that you do not work with angles, merely distances on the vertical and horizontal axes.)

Fortunately, the application of two relatively simple formulae (see Calculation 8.1) provides all the information we need to calculate the slope and the intercept. A third formula is used to make our predictions from the horizontal axis to the vertical axis.

The major differences between correlation and regression are:

1. Regression retains the original units of measurement so direct comparisons between regression analyses based on different variables are difficult. Correlation coefficients can readily be compared as they are essentially on a standardised measurement scale and free of the original units of measurement.

2. The correlation coefficient does *not* specify the slope of a scattergram. Correlation indicates the amount of spread or variability of the points around the regression line in the scattergram.

In other words, correlation and regression have somewhat different functions despite their close similarities.

Box 8.2 Focus on

Regression lines

One of the things which can cause difficulty when using regression is the question of what variable should go on the horizontal axis and what variable should go on the vertical axis. Get them the wrong way around and your calculation will be incorrect. There are, in reality, always two regression lines between two variables: that from which variable A is predicted from variable B, and that from which variable B is predicted from variable A. They almost always have different slopes. But you probably will never come across these two different formulae. The reason is that life is made simpler if we always have the predictor on the horizontal axis and the criterion to be predicted on the vertical axis. You need to be careful what you are trying to predict and from what and make sure that you put your predictor on the horizontal axis. If you are using regression weights to calculate actual scores on the dependent variable then it is sensible to produce a scattergram for your data. From this you should be able to estimate what the correct answer should be. If this is very different from what your calculation says, then one possibility is that you have got the axes the wrong way round.

Calculation 8.1

Regression equations

To facilitate comparison, we will take the data used in the computation of the correlation coefficient (Chapter 7). The data concern the relationship between mathematical and musical ability for a group of 10 individuals. The 10 scores need to be set out in a table like Table 8.2 and the various intermediate calculations carried out. However, it is important with regression to make the X scores the predictor variable; the Y scores are the criterion variable. N is the number of *pairs* of scores, i.e. 10. (Strictly speaking the Y^2 and $\sum Y^2$ calculations are not necessary for regression but are included here because they highlight the similarities between the correlation and regression calculations.)

Table 8.2	Important steps in calculating the regression equation				
Person	Maths score X score	Music score Y score	X^2	Y^2	XY
1	8	2	64	4	16
2	3	6	9	36	18
3	9	4	81	16	36
4	7	5	49	25	35
5	2	7	4	49	14
6	3	7	9	49	21
7	9	2	81	4	18
8	8	3	64	9	24
9	6	5	36	25	30
10	7	4	49	16	28
	$\sum X = 62$	$\sum Y = 45$	$\sum X^2 = 446$	$\sum Y^2 = 233$	$\sum XY = 240$

The slope b of the regression line is given by the following formula:

$$b = \frac{\sum XY - \left(\dfrac{\sum X \sum Y}{N}\right)}{\sum X^2 - \dfrac{\left(\sum X\right)^2}{N}}$$

Thus, substituting the values from the table in the above formula:

$$b_{[slope]} = \frac{240 - \left(\dfrac{62 \times 45}{10}\right)}{446 - \dfrac{(62)^2}{10}} = \frac{240 - \dfrac{2790}{10}}{446 - \dfrac{3844}{10}}$$

$$= \frac{240 - 279}{446 - 384.4} = \frac{-39}{61.6} = -0.63$$

This tells us that the slope of the regression line is negative – it moves downwards from top left to bottom right. Furthermore, for every unit one moves along the horizontal axis, the regression line moves 0.63 units *down* the vertical axis since in this case it is a *negative* slope.

We can now substitute in the following formula to get the cut-off point or intercept a of the regression line on the vertical axis:

$$a_{[\text{intercept on vertical axis}]} = \frac{\sum Y - b \sum X}{N} = \frac{45 - (-0.63 \times 62)}{10}$$

$$= \frac{45 - (-39.06)}{10}$$

$$= \frac{84.06}{10} = 8.41$$

This value for *a* is the point on the vertical axis (musical ability) cut by the regression line.

If one wishes to predict the most likely score on the vertical axis from a particular score on the horizontal axis, one simply substitutes the appropriate values in the following formula:

$$Y_{[\text{predicted score}]} = a_{[\text{intercept}]} + (b_{[\text{slope}]} \times X_{[\text{known score}]})$$

Thus if we wished to predict musical ability for a score of 8 on mathematical ability, given that we know the slope *b* is −0.63 and the intercept is 8.41, we simply substitute these values in the formula:

$$\begin{aligned} Y_{[\text{predicted score}]} &= a_{[\text{intercept}]} + (b_{[\text{slope}]} \times X_{[\text{known score}]}) \\ &= 8.41 + (-0.63 \times 8] \\ &= 8.41 + (-5.04) \\ &= 3.37 \end{aligned}$$

This is the *best* prediction – it does not mean that people with a score of 8 on mathematical ability inevitably get a score of 3.37 on musical ability. It is just our most intelligent estimate.

Interpreting the results The proper interpretation of the regression equations depends on the scattergram between the two variables showing a more or less linear (i.e. straight line) trend. If it does not show this, then the interpretation of the regression calculations for the slope and intercept will be misleading since the method assumes a straight line. Curvilinear relationships (see Chapter 7) are difficult to handle mathematically.

If the scattergram reveals a linear relationship, then the interpretation of the regression equations is simple as the formulae merely describe the scattergram mathematically.

Reporting the results This regression analysis could be reported as follows: 'Because of the negative correlation between mathematical and musical abilities, it was possible to carry out a regression analysis to predict musical ability from mathematical ability. The slope of the regression of mathematical ability on musical ability *b* is −0.63 and the intercept *a* is 8.41.'

Box 8.3   Focus on

Problems interpreting regression

The use of regression in prediction is a fraught issue not because of the statistical methods but because of the characteristics of the data used. In particular, note that our predictions about job performance are based on data from the people already in the job. So, for example, those with the best manual dexterity might have developed these skills on the job rather than having them when they were interviewed. Thus it may not be that manual dexterity determines job performance but that they are both influenced by other (unknown) factors. Similarly, if we found that age was a negative predictor of how quickly people get promoted in a banking corporation, this may simply reflect a bias against older people in the profession rather than greater ability of younger people.

<table>
<tr><td>8.3</td><td>

Standard error: how accurate are the predicted score and the regression equations?

</td></tr>
</table>

You may prefer to leave studying the following material until you have had the opportunity to study Chapter 11.

The accuracy of the predicted score on the criterion is dependent on the closeness of the scattergram points to the regression line; if there is a strong correlation between the variables there is little error in the prediction. Examining the scattergram between two variables will give you an idea of the variability around the regression line and hence the precision of the estimated or predicted scores.

Statisticians prefer to calculate what they call the standard error to indicate how certain one can be about aspects of regression such as the prediction of the intercept or cut-off points, and the slope. A standard error is much the same as the standard deviation except it applies to the means of samples rather than individual scores. So the standard error of something is the average deviation of sample means from the mean of the sample means. Don't worry too much if you don't quite understand the concept yet, since we come back to it in Chapters 11 and 12. *Just regard standard error of an estimate as the average amount by which an estimate is likely to be wrong.* As you might expect, since this is statistics, the average is calculated in an unexpected way, as it was for the standard deviation, which is little different.

Box 8.4	Key concepts

Standard error

Standard error is discussed again in later chapters. Superficially, it may appear to be quite different from the ideas in this chapter. However, remember that whenever we use any characteristic of a sample as the basis for estimating the characteristic of a population, we are likely to be wrong to some extent. The standard error is merely the average amount by which the characteristics of *samples* from the population differ from the characteristic of the *whole* population. In other words, the standard error is the standard deviation but applied to sample means and not to scores.

Although the formulae for calculating the standard errors of the various aspects of the regression line are readily available, they add considerably to the computational labour involved in regression, so we recommend that you use a computer to relieve you of this computational chore.

The main standard errors involved in regression are:

1. The one for your predicted (or estimated) value on the criterion (this is known as the standard error of the estimate of *y*).

2. The one for the slope of the regression line *b*.

3. The one for the intercept on the vertical axis *a*.

Don't forget that the formulae for calculating these standard errors merely give you the average amount by which your estimate is wrong.

It might be more useful to estimate the likely range within which the true value of the prediction, slope or intercept is likely to fall. In other words, to be able to say that, for example, the predicted score on the criterion variable is likely to be between 2.7 and 3.3. In statistics, this likely range of the true value is known as the *confidence interval*. Actually there are several confidence intervals depending on how confident you wish to be that you have included the true value – the interval is obviously going to be wider if you wish to be *very* confident rather than just confident. In statistics one would routinely use the 95% confidence interval. This 95% confidence interval indicates the range of values within which the true value will fall 95% of the time. That is, we are likely to be wrong only 5% of the time.

The following is a rule of thumb which is accurate enough for your purposes for now. Multiply the standard error by two. This gives you the amount which you need to *add and subtract* from the estimated value to cut off the middle 95% of the possible values – that is the 95% confidence interval. In other words, if the estimated value of the criterion (Y-variable) is 6.00 and the standard error of this estimate is 0.26, then the 95% confidence interval is 6.00 ± (2 × 0.26) which is 6.00 ± 0.52. This gives us a 95% confidence interval of 5.48 to 6.52. Thus it is almost certain that the person's score will actually fall in the range of 5.48 to 6.52 although the most likely value is 6.00.

Exactly the same applies to the other aspects of regression. If the slope is 2.00 with a standard error of 0.10, then the 95% confidence interval is 2.00 ± (2 × 0.10), which gives a confidence interval of 1.80 to 2.20.

The use of confidence intervals is not as common as it ought to be despite the fact that it gives us a realistic assessment of the precision of our estimates.

The above calculations of confidence intervals are approximate if you have fewer than about 30 pairs of scores. If you have between 16 and 29 pairs of scores the calculation will be more accurate if you multiply by 2.1 rather than 2.0. If you have between 12 and 15 pairs of scores then multiplying by 2.2 would improve the accuracy of the calculation. With fewer than 12 pairs the method gets a little more inaccurate. When you have become more knowledgeable about statistics, you could obtain precise confidence intervals by multiplying your standard error by the appropriate value of t from Significance Table 12.1 (Chapter 12). The appropriate value is in the row headed 'Degrees of freedom', corresponding to your number of pairs of scores minus 2 under the column for the 5% significance level (i.e. if you have 10 pairs of scores then you would multiply by 2.31).

Key points

- Drawing the scattergram will invariably illuminate the trends in your data and strongly hint at the broad features of the regression calculations. It will also provide a visual check on your computations.

- These regression procedures assume that the best-fitting regression line is a straight line. If it looks as if the regression line ought to be curved or curvilinear, do not apply these numerical methods. Of course, even if a relationship is curvilinear you could use the curved-line scattergram to make graphically based predictions.

- It may be that you have more than one predictor variable that you wish to use – if so, look at Chapter 31 on multiple regression.

COMPUTER ANALYSIS

The SPSS Statistics instruction book to this text is Dennis Howitt and Duncan Cramer (2011), *Introduction to SPSS Statistics in Psychology: For version 19 and earlier*, Harlow: Pearson. Chapter 11 in that book gives detailed step-by-step procedures for the statistics described in this chapter together with advice on how to report the results. Figure 8.5 shows the SPSS Statistics steps for doing simple regression.

Data	• Like for the correlation coefficient, the data are entered as different variables in different columns – each row equals a person. • Name each variable.
Analysis	• Select 'Analyze'. • Select 'Regression' then select 'Linear'.
2	• Select the dependent variable and move to 'Dependent' box. • Select the independent variable and move to the 'Independent(s)' box. Only use one independent variable.
3	• Select 'Statistics' and then 'Confidence Intervals' or any other option you wish. • Select 'Continue' and then select 'OK'.
Output	• The output gives the regression weight as well as its significance. • The confidence intervals are presented as a range – take care as it is also given for the constant.
Extras	• If you want the scattergram, follow the instructions as found in Chapter 7 for the correlation coefficient.

FIGURE 8.5 SPSS Statistics steps for performing simple regression

PART 2

Significance testing

CHAPTER 9

Samples and populations

Generalising and inferring

Overview

- Samples are characteristic of all research. Their use requires inferential statistical techniques in the analysis of data.

- A population in statistics is all of the scores on a particular variable and a sample is a smaller set of these scores.

- Random samples are systematically drawn samples in which each score in the population has an equal likelihood of being selected.

- Random samples tend to be like the population from which they are drawn in terms of characteristics such as the mean and variability of scores.

- Standard error is a measure of the variation in the means of samples drawn from a population. It is essentially the standard deviation of the sample means.

Preparation

This chapter introduces some important new ideas. They can be understood by anyone with a general familiarity with Chapters 1–8.

9.1   Introduction

Most research in psychology relies on just a small sample of data from which general statements are made. The terms *sample* and *population* are familiar to most of us, although the fine detail may be a little obscure. So far we have mainly discussed *sets* of data. This was deliberate since *everything that we have discussed in previous chapters is applicable to either samples or populations*. The next stage is to understand how we can use a sample of scores to make general statements or draw general conclusions that apply well beyond that sample. This is a branch of statistics called *inferential* statistics because it is about drawing inferences about all scores in the population from just a sample of those scores.

9.2   Theoretical considerations

We need to be careful when defining our terms. A *sample* is fairly obvious – it is just a small number of scores selected from the entirety of scores. A *population* is the entire set of scores. In other words, a sample is a small set, or a subset, taken from the full set or population of scores.

You need to notice some special features of the terminology we have used. We have mentioned a population of *scores* and a sample of *scores*. In other words, population and sample refer to scores on a variable. We do not deal with a population of people or even a sample of people. So, in statistical terms, all of the people living in Scotland do not constitute a population. Similarly, all of the people working in clothing factories in France or all of the goats on the Isle of Capri are not *statistical* populations. They may be populations for geographers or for everyday purposes, but they are not statistical populations. A statistical population is merely *all* of the scores on a particular variable.

This notion can take a little getting used to. However, there is another feature of statistical populations that can cause confusion. In some cases, all of the scores are potentially obtainable, for example the ages of students entering psychology degree courses in a particular year. However, often the population of scores is infinite and otherwise impossible to specify. An example of this might be the amount of time people take to react to an auditory signal in a laboratory. The number of possible measures of reaction time in these circumstances is bounded only by time and resources. No one could actually find out the population of scores other than by taking measurement after measurement – and then there is always another measurement to be taken. The notion of population in statistics is much more of a conceptual tool than something objective. Normally a psychologist will only have a few scores (his or her sample) and no direct knowledge of what all the scores or the population of scores are.

Thus the sample is usually known about in detail in research whereas the population generally is unknown. But the real question is what can we possibly say about the population based on our knowledge of this limited entity, the sample? Quite a lot. The use of sampling in public-opinion polls, for example, is so familiar that we should need little convincing of the value of samples. Samples may only approximate the characteristics of the population but generally we accept that they are sufficient to base decisions on.

If we know nothing about the population other than the characteristics of a sample drawn from that population of scores, our best guess or inference about the characteristics of the population is the characteristics of the sample from that population. It does not necessarily have to be particularly precise since an informed guess has to be better than nothing. So, in general, if we know nothing else, our best guess as to the mean of the population is the mean of the sample, our best guess as to the mode of the population is the mode of the sample, and our best guess as to the variance of the population is the variance of the sample. It is a case of beggars not being able to be choosers.

In statistical inference, it is generally assumed that samples are drawn *at random* from the population. Such samples are called *random samples* from the population. The concept of randomness is sometimes misunderstood. Randomness is not the same as arbitrariness, informality, haphazardness or any other term that suggests a casual approach to drawing samples. A random sample of scores from a population entails selecting scores in such a way that each score in the population has an equal chance of being selected. In other words, a random sample favours the selection of no particular scores in the population. Although it is not difficult to draw a random sample, it does require a systematic approach. Any old sample you choose because you like the look of it is not a random sample.

There are a number of ways of drawing a random sample. Here are just a couple:

1. Put the information about each member of the population on a slip of paper, put all of the slips into a hat, close your eyes, give the slips a long stir with your hand and finally bring one slip out of the hat. This slip is the first member of the sample; repeat the process to get the second, third and subsequent members of the sample. *Technically the slip of paper should be returned to the container after being selected so it may be selected again. However, this is not done, largely because with a large population it would make little difference to the outcome.*

2. Number each member of the population. Then press the appropriate randomisation button on your scientific calculator to generate a random number. If it is not one of the numbers in your population, ignore it and press the button again. The member of the population corresponding to this number becomes a member of the sample. Computer programs are also available for generating random numbers.

Low-tech researchers might use the random number tables found in many statistics textbooks. Essentially what you do is choose a random starting point in the table (a pin is recommended) and then choose numbers using a predetermined formula. For example, you could take the first three numbers after the pin, then a gap of seven numbers and then the three numbers following this, then a gap of seven numbers and then the three numbers following this, etc. Do not laugh at these procedures – they are all valid and convenient ways of choosing random samples. However, they are a little labour intensive given that there are available computer programs and applets on the Internet which will generate a random sequence of numbers for you. These are clearly preferable but less intuitive than the above approaches. Figure 9.1 gives the key steps in significance testing.

9.3 The characteristics of random samples

In Table 9.1 there is a population of 100 scores – the mode is 2, the median is 6.00 and the mean is 5.52. Have a go at drawing random samples of, say, five scores from this population. Repeat the process until you have a lot of sets (or samples) of scores. For each sample calculate any of the statistics just mentioned – the mean is a particularly useful statistic.

Random means that everything has an equal chance of being selected.

That is, random sampling is not systematically biased.

Most randomly drawn samples from a population have a mean very close to the population mean – a few samples, though, are markedly different.

The confidence interval is the range of sample means most likely to occur 95% or 99% of the time if we randomly sample from the population.

The standard deviation of the sample means drawn from a population is known as the standard error.

FIGURE 9.1   Conceptual steps for understanding significance testing

Table 9.1	A population of 100 scores								
7	5	11	3	4	3	5	8	9	1
9	4	0	2	2	2	9	11	7	12
4	8	2	9	7	0	8	0	8	10
10	7	4	6	6	2	2	1	12	2
2	5	6	7	10	6	6	2	1	9
3	4	2	4	9	7	5	1	6	4
5	7	12	2	8	8	3	4	6	5
9	2	6	0	7	7	5	9	10	8
6	1	7	12	3	5	2	7	2	7
2	2	8	11	4	5	8	6	4	6

Table 9.2	Means of 40 samples each of five scores taken at random from the population in Table 9.1						
2.20	5.60	4.80	5.00	8.40	6.80	4.60	6.60
4.00	3.00	5.00	5.60	8.80	5.60	4.60	6.80
3.00	8.20	8.20	3.80	5.40	6.00	4.80	5.20
3.20	5.20	3.00	5.00	5.40	4.80	6.00	7.40
5.00	2.00	3.60	4.60	5.60	4.60	4.40	6.00

We have drawn 40 samples from this population at random using a random sampling procedure from a computer program. The means of each of the 40 samples are shown in Table 9.2. It is noticeable that these means vary quite considerably. However, if we plot them graphically we find that sample means that are close to the population mean of 5.52 are relatively common. The average of the sample means is 5.20 which is close to the population mean. The minimum sample mean is 2.00 and the maximum is 8.80; these contrast with minimum and maximum values of 0 and 12 in the population. Sample means that are very different from this population mean become relatively uncommon the further away they go from the population mean.

We could calculate the standard deviation of these 40 sample means by entering each mean into the standard deviation formula:

$$\text{standard deviation} = \sqrt{\dfrac{\sum X^2 - \dfrac{(\sum X^2)}{N}}{N}}$$

This gives us a standard deviation of sample means of 1.60. The standard deviation of sample means has a technical name, although the basic concept differs only in that it deals with means of samples and not scores. The special term is *standard error*.

So, in general, it would seem that sample means are a pretty good estimate of population means although not absolutely necessarily so.

All of this was based on samples of size 5. Table 9.3 shows the results of exactly the same exercise with samples of size 20.

Table 9.3	Means of 40 samples each of size 20 taken at random from the population in Table 9.1						
4.50	5.70	5.90	5.15	4.25	5.25	5.60	5.00
5.35	5.90	6.85	5.55	5.30	5.60	5.70	4.55
6.35	6.30	4.40	5.25	4.65	5.30	4.80	5.65
4.85	5.35	5.70	4.35	5.25	5.10	6.45	5.05
5.50	6.15	5.65	5.05	5.15	5.10	4.65	4.95

Much the same trends appear with these larger samples but for the following:

1. The spread of the sample means is reduced somewhat and they appear to cluster closer to the population mean. The minimum value is 4.25 and the maximum value is 6.85. The overall mean of these samples is 5.33, close to the population mean of 5.52.

2. The standard deviation of these means (i.e. the standard error) of larger samples is smaller. For Table 9.3 the standard deviation is 0.60.

3. The distribution of sample means is a steeper curve than for the smaller samples.

The conclusion of all this is that the larger sample size produces better estimates of the mean of the population. For statistics, this verges on common sense.

Great emphasis is placed on the extreme samples in a distribution. We have seen that samples from the above population differ from the population mean by varying amounts, that the majority of samples are close to that mean, and that the bigger the sample the closer to the population mean it is likely to be. There is a neat trick in statistics by which we try to define which sample means are very unlikely to occur through random sampling. It is true that in theory just about any sample mean is possible in random sampling, but those very different from the population mean are relatively rare. In statistics, the extreme 5% of these samples are of special interest. Statisticians identify the extreme 2.5% of means on each side of the population mean for special consideration. Two 2.5s make 5%. These extreme samples come in the zone of relative rarity and are termed *significant*. Significance in statistics really means that we have a sample with characteristics very different from those of the population from which it was drawn. Significance at the 5% level of confidence means falling into the 5% of samples which are most different from the population. These extremes are, as we have seen, dependent on the size of sample being used.

9.4 Confidence intervals

There is another idea that is fundamental to some branches of statistics – *confidence interval of the mean*. In public opinion surveys you often read of the margin of error being a certain percentage. The margin of error is simply the amount for, say, voting intention which defines the middle 95% most likely sample means. This is expressed relative to the obtained sample mean. So when public opinion pollsters say that the margin of error is a certain percentage they are telling us the cut-off points from the obtained percentage which would include the middle 95% of sample means. The confidence interval in more general statistics is the range of means that cuts off the extreme 5% of sample means. So the 95% confidence interval merely gives the range of sample means which occupies the middle 95% of the distribution of sample means. The confidence interval will be larger for smaller samples, all other things being equal.

Finally, a little more jargon. The correct term for characteristics of samples such as their means, standard deviations, ranges and so forth is *statistics*. The same characteristics of populations are called *parameters*. In other words, you use the statistics from samples to estimate or infer the parameters of the population from which the sample came.

Key points

- The material in this chapter is not immediately applicable to research. Regard it as a conceptual basis for the understanding of inferential statistics.

- You need to be a little patient since the implications of this chapter will not be appreciated until later.

COMPUTER ANALYSIS

There are a number of applets on the web which allow you to generate a sequence of random numbers. These are quicker to use for this purpose than SPSS Statistics. SPSS Statistics allows you to take a random sample of the cases that you have. The instructions for doing this are to be found in Figure 9.2.

The SPSS Statistics instruction book to this text is Dennis Howitt and Duncan Cramer (2011), *Introduction to SPSS Statistics in Psychology: For version 19 and earlier*, Harlow: Pearson. Chapter 47 in that book gives detailed step-by-step procedures for the statistics described in this chapter together with advice on how to report the results.

Data
- If you have the data you wish to use on file then select that file – otherwise enter the data and name your variable.

Analysis
- Select 'Data'.
- Select 'Cases'.

2
- Select 'Random sample of cases'.
- Select 'Sample'.

3
- Enter 10 next to 'Approximately' to obtain about 10% of cases for instance.
- Alternatively, select 'Exactly' and give number of cases required out of whatever number of cases you enter in the next box.

Output
- The cases not selected for inclusion in your sample are struck out in the very first column of the data spreadsheet and a 'filter_$' column is added to indicate inclusion (1) or exclusion (0).

Extras
- You may carry out any procedure you wish using 'Analyze', etc.

FIGURE 9.2 SPSS Statistics steps for selecting a random sample of cases

CHAPTER 10

Statistical significance for the correlation coefficient

A practical introduction to statistical inference

Overview

- It is generally essential to report the statistical significance of the correlation coefficient and many other statistical techniques.

- Statistical significance is little other than an indication that your statistical findings are unlikely to be the result of chance factors.

- It can be shown that samples drawn randomly from a population generally tend to have similar characteristics to those of the population. However, there are some samples which tend to be unlike the population.

- The null hypothesis always states that there is no relation between two variables. Significance testing always seeks to assess the validity of the null hypothesis.

- If our data sample is in the middle 95% of samples if the null hypothesis is true, we say that our sample is not statistically significant at the 5% level and prefer the null hypothesis.

- However, if our data sample is in the extreme 5% of samples if the null hypothesis is true, our sample does not seem to support the null hypothesis. In this case, we tend to prefer the alternative hypothesis and reject the null hypothesis. We also say that our findings are statistically significant.

Preparation

You must be familiar with correlation coefficients (Chapter 7) and populations and samples (Chapter 9).

10.1 Introduction

Researchers have correlated two variables for a sample of 20 people. They obtained a correlation coefficient of 0.56. The problem is that they wish to generalise beyond this sample and make statements about the trends in the data which apply more widely. However, their analyses are based on just a small sample which might not be characteristic of the trends in the population.

10.2 Theoretical considerations

We can all sympathise with these researchers. The reason why they are concerned is straightforward. Imagine that Table 10.1 contains the *population* of pairs of scores. Overall, the correlation between the two variables in this population is 0.00. That is, there is absolutely no relationship between variable X and variable Y in the population.

| Table 10.1 | An imaginary population of 60 pairs of scores with zero correlation between the pairs | | | | | | | |

Pair	Variable		Pair	Variable		Pair	Variable	
	X	Y		X	Y		X	Y
01	14	12	02	5	11	03	12	5
04	3	13	05	14	9	06	10	14
07	5	12	08	17	17	09	4	8
10	15	5	11	3	3	12	19	12
13	16	7	14	14	9	15	12	13
16	13	8	17	15	11	18	15	7
19	12	17	20	11	14	21	5	13
22	12	11	23	11	9	24	15	14
25	5	12	26	15	9	27	12	13
28	6	13	29	14	7	30	18	13
31	12	1	32	19	12	33	12	19
34	11	14	35	12	17	36	13	9
37	14	12	38	15	5	39	18	13
40	17	11	41	3	12	42	16	9
43	16	12	44	11	9	45	18	2
46	12	14	47	12	14	48	15	11
49	16	12	50	12	14	51	8	14
52	5	11	53	7	8	54	16	8
55	13	13	56	12	15	57	18	2
58	3	1	59	7	8	60	11	6

What happens, though, if we draw many samples of, say, eight pairs of scores at random from this population and calculate the correlation coefficients for *each* sample? Some of the correlation coefficients are indeed more-or-less zero, but a few are substantially different from zero as we can see from Table 10.2. Plotted on a histogram, the distribution of these correlation coefficients looks like Figure 10.1. It is more or less a normal distribution with a mean correlation of zero and most of the correlations being

Table 10.2	Two hundred correlation coefficients obtained by repeatedly random sampling eight pairs of scores from Table 10.1								
−0.56	−0.30	0.36	0.54	−0.27	0.05	−0.33	−0.19	0.54	0.18
−0.54	0.11	0.25	−0.15	−0.57	−0.31	−0.24	0.17	−0.69	−0.19
−0.53	0.68	−0.22	−0.22	−0.26	−0.42	0.08	−0.30	−0.41	0.29
−0.45	−0.09	−0.06	−0.30	−0.72	−0.53	0.04	−0.66	0.65	−0.53
−0.39	−0.21	0.07	−0.80	−0.68	0.08	0.13	0.76	−0.04	0.18
−0.36	−0.19	0.29	0.24	0.38	−0.55	−0.40	0.50	−0.09	−0.30
−0.30	−0.56	0.68	−0.14	0.35	−0.28	0.56	−0.38	−0.16	0.15
−0.29	−0.23	−0.42	−0.27	0.01	0.43	0.01	−0.33	−0.20	0.49
−0.26	−0.41	−0.09	0.00	0.54	0.17	0.34	0.52	−0.11	0.67
−0.26	−0.16	−0.70	0.00	−0.17	0.40	0.03	−0.02	0.35	−0.01
−0.23	0.03	0.30	−0.52	−0.05	−0.26	−0.32	−0.37	−0.51	0.18
−0.20	−0.17	−0.43	−0.39	0.37	0.23	−0.10	0.32	0.02	0.52
−0.18	0.38	0.45	−0.50	−0.58	0.28	−0.34	−0.28	0.24	0.53
−0.17	−0.02	−0.34	−0.23	−0.54	0.25	−0.71	0.72	0.03	−0.13
−0.08	−0.30	−0.06	−0.10	−0.65	0.27	−0.04	0.32	−0.52	−0.42
−0.04	0.59	−0.29	−0.31	0.48	−0.48	0.02	−0.30	0.81	−0.23
0.10	−0.12	−0.51	−0.19	0.08	0.18	−0.27	−0.67	−0.69	0.50
0.15	−0.54	−0.15	0.05	0.01	0.52	0.19	0.19	0.07	0.27
0.34	−0.44	−0.11	−0.21	−0.02	−0.07	0.17	−0.30	−0.06	−0.49
0.57	−0.10	−0.23	0.01	−0.09	−0.27	0.22	−0.28	0.43	−0.34

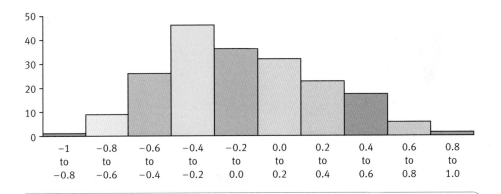

FIGURE 10.1   Distribution of correlation coefficients presented in Table 10.2

close to that zero point. However, some of the correlation coefficients are substantially different from 0.00. This shows that even where there is zero relationship between the two variables in the population, random samples can appear to have correlations which depart from 0.00.

Just about anything is possible in samples although only certain things are likely. Consequently, we try to stipulate which are the *likely* correlations in samples of a given size and which are the *unlikely* ones (if the population correlation is zero). Actually all we say is that correlations in the *middle* 95% of the distribution of samples are likely if the population correlation is zero. Correlations in the extreme 5% (usually the extreme 2.5% in each direction) are unlikely in these circumstances. These are arbitrary cut-off points, but they are conventional in statistics and have long antecedents. It is also not an unreasonable cut-off for most purposes to suggest that if a sample has only a 1 in 20 chance of occurring then it is unlikely to represent the population value.

If a correlation is in the extreme 5% of the distribution of samples from a *population* where the correlation is zero, it is deemed *statistically significant*. We should be sitting up and taking notice if this happens. In other words, statistical significance merely signals the statistically unusual or unlikely. In the above example, by examining Table 10.2 we find that the correlations 0.81, 0.76, 0.72, 0.68 and 0.68 and −0.80, −0.72, −0.71, −0.70 and −0.69 are in the extreme 5% of correlations away from zero. This extreme 5% is made up of the extreme 2.5% positive correlations and the extreme 2.5% negative correlations. Therefore, a correlation of between 0.68 and 1.00 or −0.69 and −1.00 is in the extreme 5% of correlations. This is the range which we describe as statistically significant. Statistical significance simply means that our sample falls in the relatively extreme part of the distribution of samples obtained if the null hypothesis (see the next section) of no relationship between the two variables is true.

These ranges of significant correlations mentioned above only apply to samples of size eight. A different size of sample from the same population results in a different spread of correlations obtained from repeated sampling. The spread is bigger if the samples are smaller and less if the samples are larger. In other words, there is more variation in the distribution of samples with small sample sizes than with larger ones.

On the face of things, all of this is merely a theoretical meandering of little value. We have assumed that the population correlation is zero. A major difficulty is that we are normally unaware of the population correlation since our information is based solely on a sample which may or may not represent the population very well. However, it is not quite the futile exercise it appears. Some information provided by a sample can be used to infer or estimate the characteristics of the population. For one thing, information about the variability or variance of the scores in the sample is used *to estimate the variability of scores in the population*.

10.3 Back to the real world: the null hypothesis

There is another vitally important concept in statistics – the hypothesis. Hypotheses in psychological statistics are usually presented as antithetical pairs – the *null hypothesis* and its corresponding *alternative hypothesis*:

1. The *null hypothesis* is in essence a statement that there is no relationship between two variables. The following are all examples of null hypotheses:

   (a) There is no relationship between brain size and intelligence.

   (b) There is no relationship between gender and income.

(c) There is no relationship between baldness and virility.

(d) There is no relationship between children's self-esteem and that of their parent of the same sex.

(e) There is no relationship between ageing and memory loss.

(f) There is no relationship between the amount of carrots eaten and ability to see in the dark.

2. The *alternative hypothesis* simply states that there is a relationship between two variables. In its simplest forms the alternative hypothesis says only this:

(a) There is a relationship between the number of years of education people have and their income.

(b) There is a relationship between people's gender and how much they talk about their emotional problems.

(c) There is a relationship between people's mental instability and their artistic creativity.

(d) There is a relationship between abuse in childhood and later psychological problems.

(e) There is a relationship between birth order and social dominance.

(f) There is a relationship between the degree of similarity of couples and their sexual attraction for each other.

So the difference between null and alternative hypotheses is merely the word 'no'. Of course, sometimes psychologists dress their hypotheses up in fancier language than this but the basic principle is unchanged. (Actually there is a complication – directional hypotheses – but these are dealt with in Chapter 17.)

The statistical reason for using the null hypothesis and alternative hypothesis is that they *clarify* the populations in statistical analyses. *In statistics, inferences are based on the characteristics of the population as defined by the null hypothesis.* Invariably the populations defined by the null hypothesis are ones in which there is no relation between a pair of variables. Thus, the population defined by the null hypothesis is one where the correlation between the two variables under consideration is 0.00. The characteristics of a sample can be used to assess whether it is likely that the correlation for the sample comes from a population in which the correlation is zero.

So the basic trick is to use certain of the characteristics of a sample together with the notion of the null hypothesis to define the characteristics of a population. Other characteristics of the sample are then used to estimate the likelihood that this sample comes from this particular population. To repeat and summarise:

1. The null hypothesis is used to define a population in which there is no relationship between two variables.

2. Other characteristics, especially the variability of this population, are estimated or inferred from the known sample.

It is then possible to decide whether or not it is likely that the sample comes from this population defined by the null hypothesis. If it is *unlikely* that the sample comes from the null hypothesis-based population, the possibility that the null hypothesis is true is rejected. Instead the view that the alternative hypothesis is true is accepted. That is, the alternative hypothesis that there really is a relationship is preferred. This is the same thing as saying that we can safely generalise from our sample.

Box 10.1   Focus on

Do correlations differ?

Notice that throughout this chapter we are comparing a particular correlation coefficient obtained from our data with the correlation coefficient that we would expect to obtain if there were no relationship between the two variables at all. In other words, we are calculating the likelihood of obtaining the correlation coefficient based on our sample of data if, in fact, the correlation between these two variables in the population from which the sample was taken is actually 0.00. However, there are circumstances in which the researcher might wish to assess whether two correlations obtained in their research are significantly different from each other. Imagine, for example, that the researcher is investigating the relationship between satisfaction with one's marriage and the length of time that individuals have been married. The researcher notes that the correlation between satisfaction and length

of marriage is 0.25 for male participants but 0.53 for female participants. There is clearly a difference here, but is it a statistically significant one? So essentially the researcher needs to know whether a correlation of 0.53 is significantly different from a correlation of 0.25 (the researcher has probably already tested the significance of each of these correlations separately using the sorts of methods described in this chapter but, of course, this does not answer the question of whether the two correlation coefficients differ from each other). It is a relatively simple matter to do this calculation. It has to be done by hand, unfortunately. The procedure for doing this is described in Chapter 35, Section 35.7 *Comparing a study with a previous study*. In this section you will read about how to assess whether two correlation coefficients are significantly different from each other.

10.4   Pearson's correlation coefficient again

The null hypothesis for research involving the correlation coefficient is that there is *no* relationship between the two variables. In other words, the null hypothesis implies that the correlation coefficient between two variables is 0.00 in the population (defined by the null hypothesis). So what if, in a sample of 10 pairs of scores, the correlation is 0.94 as for the data in Table 10.3?

Is it likely that such a correlation would occur in a sample if it actually came from a population where the true correlation is zero? We are back to our basic problem of how

Table 10.3	A sample of 10 pairs of scores	
Pair number	***X* score**	***Y* score**
1	5	4
2	2	1
3	7	8
4	5	6
5	0	2
6	1	0
7	4	3
8	2	2
9	8	9
10	6	7

likely it is that a correlation of 0.94 would occur if there really is no correlation in the population. We need to plot the distribution of correlations in random samples of 10 pairs drawn from this population. Unfortunately we do not have the population of scores, only a sample of scores. However, statisticians can use the variability of this sample of scores to estimate the variability in the population. Then the likely distribution of correlations in repeated samples of a given size drawn from the population with this amount of variability can be calculated. Mere mortals like us use tables provided by statisticians.

Tables are available which, for any given size of sample, tell you the minimum size of a correlation coefficient which cuts the middle 95% of correlations from the extreme 5% of correlations (assuming the null hypothesis is true in the population). These cut-off points are usually called *critical values*:

1. If the sample's correlation is in the middle 95% of correlations then we accept the null hypothesis that there is no relationship between the two variables. By accept, we mean that in the absence of any other information or considerations, the null hypothesis is a more plausible explanation of the data than the hypothesis.

2. However, if the correlation in the sample is in the extreme 5% of correlations then the alternative hypothesis is accepted (that there is a relationship between the two variables).

Significance Table 10.1	5% significance values of the Pearson correlation coefficient (two-tailed test). An extended and conventional version of this table is given in Appendix C						
Sample size	**Significant at 5% level Accept hypothesis**						
5	−0.88	to	−1.00	or	+0.88	to	+1.00
6	−0.81	to	−1.00	or	+0.81	to	+1.00
7	−0.75	to	−1.00	or	+0.75	to	+1.00
8	−0.71	to	−1.00	or	+0.71	to	+1.00
9	−0.67	to	−1.00	or	+0.67	to	+1.00
10	−0.63	to	−1.00	or	+0.63	to	+1.00
11	−0.60	to	−1.00	or	+0.60	to	+1.00
12	−0.58	to	−1.00	or	+0.58	to	+1.00
13	−0.55	to	−1.00	or	+0.55	to	+1.00
14	−0.53	to	−1.00	or	+0.53	to	+1.00
15	−0.51	to	−1.00	or	+0.51	to	+1.00
16	−0.50	to	−1.00	or	+0.50	to	+1.00
17	−0.48	to	−1.00	or	+0.48	to	+1.00
18	−0.47	to	−1.00	or	+0.47	to	+1.00
19	−0.46	to	−1.00	or	+0.46	to	+1.00
20	−0.44	to	−1.00	or	+0.44	to	+1.00
25	−0.40	to	−1.00	or	+0.40	to	+1.00
30	−0.36	to	−1.00	or	+0.36	to	+1.00
40	−0.31	to	−1.00	or	+0.31	to	+1.00
50	−0.28	to	−1.00	or	+0.28	to	+1.00
60	−0.25	to	−1.00	or	+0.25	to	+1.00
100	−0.20	to	−1.00	or	+0.20	to	+1.00

Your value must be in the listed ranges for your sample size to be significant at the 5% level (i.e. to accept the hypothesis).

If your required sample size is not listed, then take the nearest *smaller* sample size. Alternatively, extrapolate from listed values.

Significance Table 10.1 reveals that for a sample size of 10, a correlation has to be between −0.63 and −1.00 *or* between 0.63 and 1.00 to be sufficiently large as to be in the extreme 5% of correlations which support the alternative hypothesis. Correlations closer to 0.00 than these come in the middle 95% which are held to support the null hypothesis. Figure 10.2 gives the key steps in testing statistical significance.

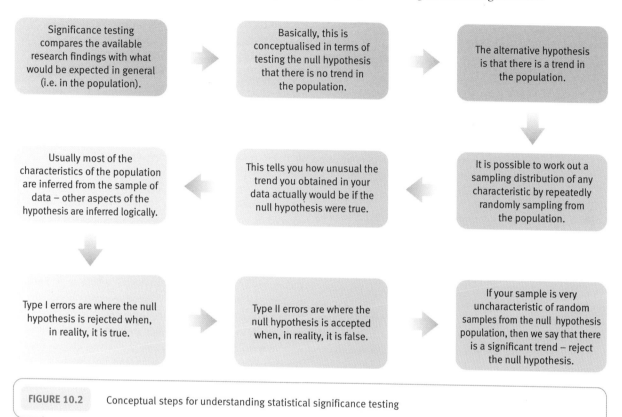

FIGURE 10.2   Conceptual steps for understanding statistical significance testing

Calculation 10.1

Statistical significance of a Pearson correlation coefficient

Having calculated your value of the Pearson correlation coefficient, make a note of the sample size and consult Significance Table 10.1. In the example in Chapter 7 (Calculation 7.1), the correlation between mathematical scores and musical scores was found to be −0.90 with a sample size of 10. If this correlation is in the range of correlations listed as being in the extreme 5% of correlations for this sample size, the correlation is described as being statistically significant at the 5% level of significance.

Interpreting the results In this case, since our obtained value of the correlation coefficient is in the significant range of the correlation coefficient (−0.63 to −1.00 and 0.63 to 1.00), we reject the null hypothesis in favour of the alternative hypothesis that there is a relationship between mathematical and musical scores.

Reporting the results In our report of the study we would conclude by writing something to the following effect: 'There is a negative correlation of −0.90 between mathematical and musical scores which is statistically significant at the 5% level with a sample size of 10.' Alternatively, following the recommendations of the APA (2010) Publication Manual we could say something like 'Mathematical scores were significantly negatively correlated with musical scores, $r(8) = -.90, p < .05$.'

Box 10.2   Key concepts

Type I and II errors

- The terms *Type I error* and *Type II error* frequently appear in statistics textbooks although they are relatively uncommon in reports and other publications. They refer to the risk that no matter what decision you make in research based on your statistical analysis there is always a chance that you have made the wrong decision. There are two types of wrong decision – one involves deciding that there is a trend when there is in reality no trend; the other involves deciding that there is not a trend when in reality there is.

- A Type I error is deciding that the null hypothesis is false when it is actually true.

- A Type II error is deciding that the null hypothesis is true when it is actually false. Powerful statistical tests are those in which there is less chance of a Type II error.

Figure 10.3 shows the process by which correct decisions are made and the processes by which Type I errors and Type II errors are made. Of course, these are not errors which it is easy to do anything about since the researcher simply does not know what is truly the case in general (i.e. in the population) since they only have information from the sample of data that they have collected. So these are rather abstract concepts rather than concrete situations. You may have also noticed that if the researcher does something to minimise the risk of a Type I error then the risk of a Type II error increases. So to avoid a Type I error then the researcher could set a more stringent level of significance than the 5% level – say the 1% level – but this would reduce the risk of a Type I error at the cost of increasing the risk of a Type II error. The main issue in succeeding chapters is significance testing and the Type I error. However, Chapter 39 discusses statistical power which is greatly related to the matter of the Type II error.

Unfortunately, the terms are not particularly useful in the everyday application of statistics where it is hard enough making a decision let alone worrying about the chance that you have made the wrong decision. Given that statistics deals with probabilities and not certainties, it is important to remember that there is always a chance that any decision you make is wrong in statistical analysis.

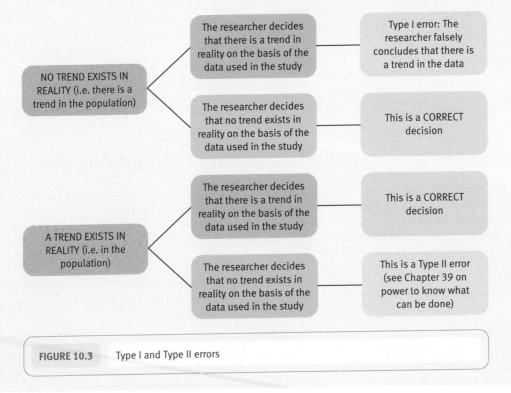

FIGURE 10.3   Type I and Type II errors

10.5 The Spearman's rho correlation coefficient

If you followed our advice in Chapter 7 to use the standard Pearson correlation coefficient formula on the ranked scores instead of using the Spearman rho formula (Calculation 7.3) then the significance of your calculation should be assessed using Significance Table 10.1. This is the approach used by standard computer packages such as SPSS Statistics. However, assuming that you used the Spearman rho formula in Calculation 7.2, especially if there are tied scores, then Significance Table 10.2 should be used.

Significance Table 10.2	5% significance values of the Spearman correlation coefficient (two-tailed test). An extended and conventional version of this table is given in Appendix D						
Sample size	**Significant at 5% level** **Accept hypothesis**						
5			−1.00	or	+1.00		
6	−0.89	to	−1.00	or	+0.89	to	+1.00
7	−0.79	to	−1.00	or	+0.79	to	+1.00
8	−0.74	to	−1.00	or	+0.74	to	+1.00
9	−0.68	to	−1.00	or	+0.68	to	+1.00
10	−0.65	to	−1.00	or	+0.65	to	+1.00
11	−0.62	to	−1.00	or	+0.62	to	+1.00
12	−0.59	to	−1.00	or	+0.59	to	+1.00
13	−0.57	to	−1.00	or	+0.57	to	+1.00
14	−0.55	to	−1.00	or	+0.55	to	+1.00
15	−0.52	to	−1.00	or	+0.52	to	+1.00
16	−0.51	to	−1.00	or	+0.51	to	+1.00
17	−0.49	to	−1.00	or	+0.49	to	+1.00
18	−0.48	to	−1.00	or	+0.48	to	+1.00
19	−0.46	to	−1.00	or	+0.46	to	+1.00
20	−0.45	to	−1.00	or	+0.45	to	+1.00
25	−0.40	to	−1.00	or	+0.40	to	+1.00
30	−0.36	to	−1.00	or	+0.36	to	+1.00
40	−0.31	to	−1.00	or	+0.31	to	+1.00
50	−0.28	to	−1.00	or	+0.28	to	+1.00
60	−0.26	to	−1.00	or	+0.26	to	+1.00
100	−0.20	to	−1.00	or	+0.20	to	+1.00

Your value must be in the listed ranges for your sample size to be significant at the 5% level (i.e. to accept the hypothesis).

If your required sample size is not listed, then take the nearest *smaller* sample size. Alternatively, extrapolate from listed values.

Calculation 10.2

Statistical significance of Spearman's rho correlation coefficient

In Chapter 7 (Calculation 7.2) we calculated Spearman's rho correlation coefficient between mathematical score and musical score. The correlation was found to be −0.89 with a sample size of 10. Significance Table 10.2 reveals that in order to be significant at the 5% level with a sample size of 10, correlations have to be in the range 0.65 to 1.00 *or* −0.65 to −1.00.

Interpreting the results Since our obtained value of the Spearman's rho correlation coefficient is in the range of significant correlations we accept the alternative hypothesis that mathematical and musical scores are (inversely) related and reject the null hypothesis.

Reporting the results We can report a significant correlation: 'There is a negative correlation of −0.89 between mathematical and musical scores which is statistically significant at the 5% level with a sample size of 10.'

Alternatively, following the APA (2010) Publication Manual recommendations we could write something like 'Mathematical scores were significantly negatively correlated with musical scores, $r_s(8) = -.89$, $p < .05$'.

Key points

- There is nothing complex in the calculation of statistical significance for the correlation coefficients. However, statistical tables normally do not include every sample size. When a particular sample size is missing you can simply use the nearest (lower) tabulated value. Alternatively you could extrapolate from the nearest tabulated value above and the nearest tabulated value below your actual sample size.

- It is a bad mistake to report a correlation without indicating whether it is statistically significant.

- Chapter 16 explains how to report your significance levels in a more succinct form. Try to employ this sort of style as it eases the writing of research reports and looks professional.

- Beware that some statistical textbooks provide significance tables which are distributed by degrees of freedom rather than sample size. For any given sample size, the degrees of freedom are *two* less. Thus, for a sample size of 10, the degrees of freedom are 10 − 2, or 8.

COMPUTER ANALYSIS

The new step in this chapter is the calculation of significance levels for the correlation coefficient. SPSS Statistics automatically produces this in the correlation coefficient output so follow the steps in Figure 10.4 to calculate both the size of the correlation coefficient and its significance.

The SPSS Statistics instruction book to this text is Dennis Howitt and Duncan Cramer (2011), *Introduction to SPSS Statistics in Psychology: For version 19 and earlier*, Harlow: Pearson. Chapter 10 in that book gives detailed step-by-step procedures for the statistics described in this chapter together with advice on how to report the results.

Data
- The data are entered as different variables in different columns – each row equals a person.
- Name each variable.

Analysis
- Select 'Analyze'.
- Select 'Correlate' then select 'Bivariate'.

2
- Move variables to be correlated to right hand side box.
- Select 'Pearson' or 'Spearman' according to what is appropriate.

Output
- Significance levels are given for correlations between different variables but not for the correlation of a variable with itself. The matrix includes the correlation of each variable with itself and does not provide a significance level.

FIGURE 10.4 SPSS Statistics steps for the significance of the correlation coefficient

CHAPTER 11

Standard error

The standard deviation of the means of samples

Overview

- Standard error is the term for the standard deviation of a number of sample means. It is important theoretically.

- We never calculate the standard error directly but estimate its value from the characteristics of our sample of data.

- The standard error is simply estimated by dividing the standard deviation of scores in the population by the square root of the sample size for which we need to calculate the standard error.

- We estimate the standard deviation of the population of scores from the standard deviation of our sample of scores. There is a slight adjustment when calculating this estimated standard error – that is, the standard deviation formula involves division by $N - 1$ (i.e. the sample size minus one) rather than simply by N.

Preparation

Review z-scores and standard deviation (Chapter 5) and sampling from populations (Chapter 9).

11.1 Introduction

Most psychological research involves the use of samples drawn from a particular population. Just what are the characteristics of samples drawn from a population? In theory, it is possible to draw samples with virtually any mean score if we randomly sample from a population of scores. So is it possible to make any generalisations about the characteristics of randomly drawn samples from a population?

Standard error is one way of summarising the diversity of sample means drawn from a population. This chapter explains the concept of standard error. However, the practical use of standard error in psychological research will not become obvious until the next two chapters which deal with the *t*-tests. Nevertheless, it is essential to understand standard error before moving on to its practical applications. Figure 11.1 illustrates the key steps in understanding standard error.

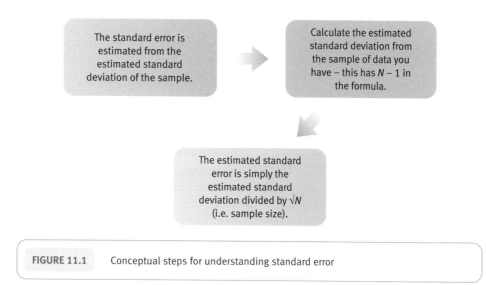

FIGURE 11.1   Conceptual steps for understanding standard error

11.2 Theoretical considerations

Table 11.1 contains a population of 25 scores with a mean of 4.20. We have selected, at random, samples of four scores until we have 20 samples. These are arbitrary decisions

Table 11.1	A population of 25 scores			
5	7	9	4	6
2	6	3	2	7
1	7	5	4	3
3	6	1	2	4
2	5	3	3	4

Table 11.2	Means of 20 samples each of four scores taken at random from the population of 25 scores in Table 11.1		
3.75	6.00	4.00	4.25
3.00	3.75	4.50	3.50
4.50	3.00	4.25	2.50
3.50	5.00	3.00	4.25
4.00	3.00	4.50	5.75

for illustrative purposes. For each of these 20 samples the mean has been calculated, giving 20 separate sample means. They are shown in Table 11.2.

The distribution of the sample means is called a *sampling distribution*. Clearly, in Table 11.2 the 20 sample means differ to varying degrees from each other and from the population mean of 4.20. In fact, the average of the sample means is 4.00. The standard deviation of these 20 sample means is 0.89. This was calculated using the normal formula for the standard deviation (see Calculation 5.1). There is a special name for the standard deviation formula when it is applied to a set of sample means – the *standard error*. Therefore the standard error is 0.89. The implication of this is that the standard error is directly comparable to the standard deviation. Consequently, the standard error is simply the average deviation of sample means from the mean of the sample means. Although this is clumsy to write down or say, it captures the essence of standard error effectively. (The average of sample means, if you have a lot of samples, will be more or less identical to the mean of the population. Thus, it is more usual to refer to the population mean rather than the average of sample means.)

If we sampled from the population of scores in Table 11.1 but using a different sample size, say samples of 12, we would get a rather different sampling distribution. In general, all other things being equal, the standard error of the means of bigger samples is less than that of smaller sized samples. This is just a slightly convoluted way of supporting the common-sense belief that larger samples are more precise estimates of the characteristics of populations than are smaller samples. In other words, we tend to be more convinced by large samples than small samples.

A frequency curve of the means of samples drawn from a population will tend to get taller and narrower as the sample size involved increases. It also tends to be normal in shape, i.e. bell shaped. The more normal (bell shaped) the population of scores on which the sampling is done, the more normal (bell shaped) the frequency curve of the sample means.

11.3 Estimated standard deviation and standard error

The difficulty with the concept of standard error is that we rarely have information about anything other than a sample taken from the population. This might suggest that the standard error is unknowable. After all, if we only have a single sample mean, how on earth can we calculate the standard error? There is only one sample mean which obviously cannot vary from itself. Fortunately we can estimate the standard error from the characteristics of a sample of scores. The first stage in doing this involves estimating the *population* standard deviation from the standard deviation of a *sample* taken from that population. There is a relatively easy way of using the standard deviation of a sample of scores in order to estimate the standard deviation of the population.

The formula is:

$$\text{estimated standard deviation} = \sqrt{\frac{\sum X^2 - \dfrac{\left(\sum X^2\right)}{N}}{N-1}}$$

The above formula is exactly the same as the standard deviation computational formula given in Chapter 5 with one difference. You will see in the lower half of the formula the term $N-1$. In our previous version of the formula, N occurred rather than $N-1$. So if we know the scores in a sample, we can use them to estimate the standard deviation of the scores in the population.

You may be wondering about the $N-1$ in the above formula. The reason is that if we try to extrapolate the standard deviation of the whole population directly from the standard deviation of a sample from this population, we get things somewhat wrong. However, this is easily corrected by adjusting the standard deviation by dividing by $N-1$ instead of N. The adjusted standard deviation formula gives the *estimated* standard deviation. We can also estimate the variance of the population from the characteristics of the sample:

$$\text{estimated variance} = \frac{\sum X^2 - \dfrac{\left(\sum X^2\right)}{N}}{N-1}$$

These formulae for estimated standard deviation and estimated variance apply when you are using a sample to estimate the characteristics of a population. However, some researchers also use these estimating formulae (in which you divide by N – 1) in place of the variance and standard deviation formulae (in which you divide by N) when dealing with populations. Generally this makes little difference in practice since psychologists are usually working with samples and trying to estimate the characteristics of the population.

The term $N-1$ is called the *degrees of freedom*.

There is a second step in estimating the standard error from the characteristics of a sample. The standard error involves sample *means*, not the *scores* involved in the standard deviation and estimated standard deviation. How does one move from scores to sample means? Fortunately a very simple relationship exists between the standard deviation of a population of scores and the standard error of samples of scores taken from that population. The standard error is obtained by dividing the population standard deviation by the *square root* of the sample size involved. This implies that the standard deviation of large samples taken from the population of scores is smaller than the standard deviation of small samples taken from the population. The formula is basically the same whether we are using the standard deviation of a known population or the estimated standard deviation of a population based on the standard deviation of a sample.

$$\text{(estimated) standard error} = \frac{\text{(estimated) standard deviation of population}}{\sqrt{N}}$$

Obviously it is possible to combine the (estimated) standard deviation and the (estimated) standard error formulae:

$$\text{(estimated) standard error} = \frac{\sqrt{\dfrac{\sum X^2 - \dfrac{\left(\sum X^2\right)}{N}}{N-1}}}{\sqrt{N}}$$

Calculation 11.1

Estimated standard error of sample means from scores for a single sample from the population

Table 11.3 is a sample of six scores taken at random from the population: 5, 7, 3, 6, 4, 5.

Table 11.3	Steps in calculating the standard error	
	X (scores)	**X² (squared scores)**
	5	25
	7	49
	3	9
	6	36
	4	16
	5	25
	$\sum X = 30$	$\sum X^2 = 160$

Step 1 Using this information we can estimate the standard error of samples of size 6 taken from the same population. Taking our six scores (X), we need to produce Table 11.3, where $N = 6$.

Step 2 Substitute these values in the standard error formula:

$$\text{(estimated) standard error} = \frac{\sqrt{\dfrac{\sum X^2 - \dfrac{\left(\sum X^2\right)}{N}}{N-1}}}{\sqrt{N}}$$

$$= \frac{\sqrt{\dfrac{160 - \dfrac{30^2}{6}}{6-1}}}{\sqrt{6}}$$

$$= \frac{\sqrt{\dfrac{160 - \dfrac{900}{6}}{5}}}{2.449}$$

$$= \frac{\sqrt{\dfrac{160 - 150}{5}}}{2.449}$$

$$= \frac{\sqrt{\dfrac{10}{5}}}{2.449}$$

→

$$= \frac{\sqrt{2}}{2.449}$$

$$= \frac{1.414}{2.449}$$

$$= 0.58$$

Interpreting the results Roughly speaking, this suggests that on average sample means differ from the population mean by 0.58.

Reporting the results Standard error is not routinely reported although sometimes it is seen. It is no more informative than the standard deviation which is more likely to be included in reports. Many psychologists report the variance or standard deviation instead since this is just as informative descriptive statistics as the standard error.

The term standard *error* is used because it is the standard or average amount by which you would be wrong if you tried to estimate the mean of the population from the mean of a sample from that population.

Key points

- The standard error is often reported in computer output and in research publications. Very much like standard deviation, it can be used as an indicator of the variability in one's data. Variables with different standard errors essentially have different variances so long as the number of scores is the same for the two variables.

- Standard error is almost always really *estimated* standard error in psychological statistics. However, usually this estimate is referred to simply as the standard error. This is a pity since it loses sight of the true nature of standard error.

COMPUTER ANALYSIS

Standard error calculation is a routine feature of statistical analysis computer programs so you will rarely have to calculate it separately from the rest of your calculations. Figure 11.2 gives instructions about how to obtain standard error on SPSS Statistics.

The SPSS Statistics instruction book to this text is Dennis Howitt and Duncan Cramer (2011), *Introduction to SPSS Statistics in Psychology: For version 19 and earlier*, Harlow: Pearson. Chapter 12 in that book gives detailed step-by-step procedures for the statistics described in this chapter together with advice on how to report the results.

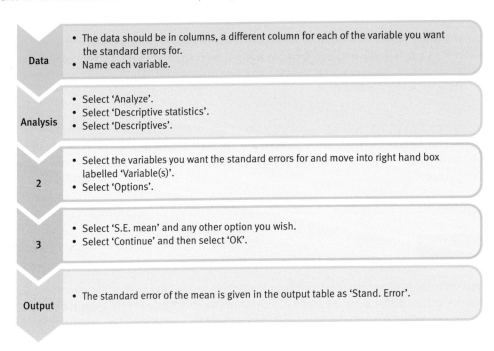

Data
- The data should be in columns, a different column for each of the variable you want the standard errors for.
- Name each variable.

Analysis
- Select 'Analyze'.
- Select 'Descriptive statistics'.
- Select 'Descriptives'.

2
- Select the variables you want the standard errors for and move into right hand box labelled 'Variable(s)'.
- Select 'Options'.

3
- Select 'S.E. mean' and any other option you wish.
- Select 'Continue' and then select 'OK'.

Output
- The standard error of the mean is given in the output table as 'Stand. Error'.

FIGURE 11.2 SPSS Statistics steps for standard error

CHAPTER 12

The *t*-test

Comparing two samples of correlated/related/paired scores

Overview

- The related *t*-test is mainly used when we have data in the form of scores collected at two separate times from a single sample of participants. So it is useful when assessing change over time.

- It is also used when the two sets of scores are correlated with each other as when matching is used.

- It assesses whether the mean of one set of scores is different from the mean of another set of scores.

- The *t*-test is simply the number of standard errors by which the sample means differ from each other.

- There are tables of the *t*-distribution which can be used to assess statistical significance. Generally computer programs calculate significance automatically.

Preparation

Review z-scores and standard deviation (Chapter 5) and standard error (Chapter 11).

12. 1   Introduction

Many research projects involve comparisons between two groups of scores. Each group of scores is a sample from a population of scores. There is a test called the related (correlated) *t*-test which compares the means of two *related* samples of scores to see whether the means differ significantly. The meaning of related samples can be illustrated by the following examples:

1. People's scores on a psychological test of creativity are measured at two different points in time in order to see if any improvement has taken place (see Table 12.1). Notice that we have mentioned individuals by name to stress that they are being measured twice – they are *not* different individuals in the two conditions. Also, some of the data have been omitted.

2. A group of students' memory test scores are measured in the morning and in the afternoon in order to see whether memory is affected by time of day (Table 12.2).

3. A group of participants in an experiment are assessed in terms of their reaction time to a coloured light when they have taken the anti-depressant drug 'Nogloom' and when they have taken an inert control tablet (placebo) (see Table 12.3).

In each of the above studies, the researcher wishes to know whether the means of the two conditions differ from each other. The question is whether the mean scores in the two conditions are sufficiently different from each other that they fall in the extreme 5% of cases. If they do, this allows us to generalise from the research findings. In other words, are the two means significantly different from each other?

Table 12.1	Creativity scores measured at two different times	
	1 March	**6 months later**
Sam	17	19
Jack	14	17
. . .	. . .	. . .
Karl	12	19
Shahida	19	25
Mandy	10	13
Mean	$\bar{X}_1 = 15.09$	$\bar{X}_2 = 18.36$

Table 12.2	Time of day and memory performance scores	
	Morning	**Afternoon**
Rebecca	9	15
Sharon	16	23
. . .	. . .	. . .
Neil	18	24
Mean	$\bar{X}_1 = 17.3$	$\bar{X}_2 = 22.1$

Table 12.3	Reaction time in seconds for drug and no-drug conditions	
	'Nogloom'	**Placebo**
Jenny	0.27	0.25
David	0.15	0.18
. . .	. . .	. . .
Mean	$\bar{X}_1 = 0.22$	$\bar{X}_2 = 0.16$

The key characteristics of all of the previous studies is that a group of participants is measured twice on a single variable in slightly different conditions or circumstances. So in the previous studies, creativity has been measured twice, memory has been measured twice and reaction time has been measured twice. In other words, they are *repeated measures designs* for the obvious reason that participants have been measured more than once on the same variable. Repeated measures designs are also called *related measures designs* and *correlated scores designs*.

Box 12.1   Key concepts

Counterbalancing

Repeated measures designs of the sort described in this chapter can be problematic. For example, since the participants in the research are measured under both the experimental and control conditions, it could be that their experiences in the experimental condition affect the way they behave in the control condition. Many of the problems can be overcome by *counterbalancing* conditions. By this we mean that a random selection of half of the participants in the research are put through the experimental condition first; the other half are put through the control condition first.

In our opening paragraph we mentioned the related (correlated) *t*-test. There are in fact two versions of the *t*-test – a correlated/related and an uncorrelated/unrelated samples version. The latter is more likely to be of use to you simply because unrelated designs are more common in psychological statistics. However, the correlated/related *t*-test is substantially simpler to understand and is useful as a learning aid prior to tackling the more difficult unrelated *t*-test, which is described in Chapter 13.

Box 12.2   Key concepts

Matching

It is also possible to have a related design if you take pairs of subjects *matched* to be as similar as possible on factors which might be related to their scores on the dependent variable. So pairs of participants might be matched on gender and age so that each member of the pair in question is of the same gender and age group (or

Table 12.4	A matched pairs design testing memory score	
Matched pairs	**Morning score**	**Afternoon score**
Both male and under 20	16	17
Both female and under 20	21	25
Both male and over 20	14	20
Both female and over 20	10	14

as close as possible). One member of the pair would be assigned at *random* to one experimental condition, the other member to the other experimental condition. Using the effect of time of day on the memory research question (Table 12.2), the arrangement for a matched pairs or matched subjects design might be as in Table 12.4. Of course, this is only the basic design – the full design would repeat Table 12.4 several times to get a large enough sample size overall.

The purpose of matching, like using the same person twice, is to reduce the influence of unwanted variables on the comparisons.

12.2 Dependent and independent variables

The scores in Tables 12.1–12.3 are scores on the *dependent variable*. They include the variables creativity, memory and reaction time in the experiments.

However, there is another variable – the *independent variable*. This refers to the various conditions in which the measurements are being taken. In Table 12.1 measurements are being taken at two different points in time – on 1 March and six months later. The alternative hypothesis is that there *is* a relationship between the independent variable 'time of measurement' and the dependent variable 'creativity score'. Obviously, it is being assumed that creativity scores are *dependent* on the variable time.

12.3 Some basic revision

A *z*-score is simply the number of standard deviations a score is away from the mean of the set of scores. The formula is:

$$z\text{-score} = \frac{X - \bar{X}}{SD}$$

where X is a particular score, $\bar{X}$ is the mean of the set of scores and SD is the standard deviation of the set of scores.

Remember, once you have obtained the *z*-score, it is possible to use the table of the standard normal distribution (*z*-distribution) (Significance Table 12.1) to identify the relative position of the particular score compared to the rest of the set.

Significance Table 12.1	5% significance values of related *t* (two-tailed test). Appendix E gives a fuller and conventional version of this table

Degrees of freedom (always $N - 1$ for related *t*-test)	Significant at 5% level Accept hypothesis
3	±3.18 or more extreme
4	±2.78 or more extreme
5	±2.57 or more extreme
6	±2.45 or more extreme
7	±2.37 or more extreme
8	±2.31 or more extreme
9	±2.26 or more extreme
10	±2.23 or more extreme
11	±2.20 or more extreme
12	±2.18 or more extreme
13	±2.16 or more extreme
14	±2.15 or more extreme
15	±2.13 or more extreme
18	±2.10 or more extreme
20	±2.09 or more extreme
25	±2.06 or more extreme
30	±2.04 or more extreme
40	±2.02 or more extreme
60	±2.00 or more extreme
100	±1.98 or more extreme
∞	±1.96 or more extreme

Your value must be in the listed ranges for your degrees of freedom to be significant at the 5% level (i.e. to accept the hypothesis).

If your required degrees of freedom are not listed, then take the nearest *smaller* listed values. Refer to Appendix E if you need a more precise value of *t*.

'More extreme' means that, for example, values in the ranges of +3.18 to infinity or −3.18 to (minus) infinity are statistically significant with 3 degrees of freedom.

12.4 Theoretical considerations

As we have seen, the most important theoretical concept with any inferential statistical test is the null hypothesis. This states that there is *no* relationship between the two variables in the research. In the previous example the independent variable is time of day and the dependent variable is memory. The null hypothesis is that there is no relation between the independent variable time and the dependent variable memory. This implies, by definition, that the two samples, according to the null hypothesis, come from the same population. In other words, in the final analysis the overall trend is for pairs of samples drawn from this population to have identical means. However, that is the trend over many pairs of samples. The means of some pairs of samples will differ somewhat from each other simply because samples from even the same population tend to vary. Little differences will be more common than big differences.

Another important concept is that of the *t*-distribution. This is a theoretical statistical distribution which is similar to the *z*-distribution discussed in Chapter 5. There is also a *t*-score which is similar to the *z*-score. The *t*-score is based on analogous logic to the *z*-score. The major difference is that the *t*-score involves *standard error* and not standard deviation. As we saw in the previous chapter, the standard error is nothing other than the standard deviation of a set of sample means. Using the *z*-distribution, it is possible to work out the standing of any score relative to the rest of the set of scores. Exactly the same applies where one has the standard error of a set of sample means. One can calculate the relative extent to which a particular sample mean differs from the average sample mean. (The average sample mean with many samples will be the same as the mean of the population, so normally the population mean is referred to rather than the average of sample means.) The key formulae are as follows:

$$z = \frac{\text{particular score} - \text{sample mean of scores}}{\text{standard deviation of scores}}$$

$$t = \frac{\text{particular sample mean} - \text{average of sample means}}{\text{standard error of sample means}}$$

or

$$t = \frac{\text{particular sample mean} - \text{population mean}}{\text{standard error of sample means}}$$

As you can see, the form of each of these formulae is identical.

Both *z* and *t* refer to standard distributions which are symmetrical and bell shaped. The *z*-distribution is a normal distribution – the standard normal distribution. Similarly, the *t*-distribution is also a normal distribution when large sample sizes are involved. In fact *z* and *t* are identical in these circumstances. As the sample size gets smaller, however, the *t*-distribution becomes a decidedly flatter distribution. Significance Table 12.1 is a table of the *t*-distribution which reports the value of the *t*-score needed to put a sample mean outside the middle 95% of sample means and into the extreme 5% of sample means that are held to be unlikely or *statistically significant* sample means. Notice that the table of the *t*-distribution is structured according to the *degrees of freedom*. Usually this is the sample size minus one if a single sample is used to *estimate* the standard error, otherwise it may be different.

The *t*-test can be applied to the data on the above population. Assume that for a given population, the population mean is 1.0. We have estimated the standard error by taking a known sample of 10 scores, calculating its estimated standard deviation and dividing by the square root of the sample size. All of these stages are combined in the following formula, which was discussed in Chapter 11:

$$(\text{estimated) standard error} = \frac{\sqrt{\sum X^2 \frac{\left(\sum X\right)^2}{N}}}{\frac{N-1}{\sqrt{N}}}$$

This gives the (estimated) standard error to be 2.5. We can calculate if a sample with a mean of 8.0 ($N = 10$) is statistically unusual. We simply apply the *t*-test formula to the information we have:

$$t = \frac{\text{particular sample mean} - \text{population mean}}{\text{standard error of sample means}}$$

$$= \frac{8.0 - 1.0}{2.5}$$

$$= \frac{7.0}{2.5}$$

$$= 2.8$$

In other words, our sample mean is actually 2.8 standard errors *above* the average sample mean (i.e. population mean) of 1.0.

We can now use Significance Table 12.1. This table is distributed according to the number of degrees of freedom involved in the estimation of the population standard deviation. Since the sample size on which this estimate was based is 10, the degrees of freedom are 1 less than 10, i.e. $N - 1 = 9$ degrees of freedom. Significance Table 12.1 tells us that we need a *t*-score of 2.26 or more to place our particular sample mean in the extreme 5% of sample means drawn from the population. Our obtained *t*-score was 2.8. This means that our sample mean is within the extreme 5% of sample means, i.e. that it is statistically significantly different from the average of sample means drawn from this particular population.

Wonderful! But what has this got to do with our research problem which we set out at the beginning of this chapter? The above is simply about a single sample compared with a multitude of samples. What we need to know is whether or not *two* sample means are sufficiently different from each other that we can say that the difference is statistically significant. There is just one remaining statistical trick that statisticians employ in these circumstances. That is, *the two samples of scores are turned into a single sample by subtracting one set of scores from the other*. We calculate the difference between a person's score in one sample and their score in the other sample. This leaves us with a sample of difference scores *D* which constitutes the single sample we need.

The stylised data in Table 12.5 show just what is done. The difference scores in the final column are the single sample of scores which we use in our standard error formula. For this particular sample of difference scores the mean is 4.0. According to the null hypothesis, the general trend should be zero difference between the two samples – that is, the mean of the difference scores would be zero if the sample reflected precisely the null hypothesis. Once again we are reliant on the null hypothesis to tell us what the population characteristics are. Since the null hypothesis has it that there is no difference between the *samples*, there should be zero difference in the population, that is, the average difference score should be 0. (Since the difference between sample means – under the

Table 12.5	Basic rearrangement of data for the related samples *t*-test		
Person	**Sample 1** (X_1)	**Sample 2** (X_2)	**Difference** $X_1 - X_2 = D$
A	9	5	4
B	7	2	5
C	7	3	4
D	11	6	5
E	7	5	2

FIGURE 12.1   Conceptual steps for understanding the related/correlated *t*-test

null hypothesis that the two samples do not differ – is zero by definition, the population mean should be zero. In other words, we can delete the population mean from the formula for *t*-scores.) We would of course expect some samples of difference scores to be above or below zero by varying amounts. The question is whether a mean difference of 4.0 is sufficiently different from zero to be statistically significant. If it comes in the middle 95% of the distribution of sample means then we accept the null hypothesis. If it comes in the extreme 5% then we describe it as significant and reject the null hypothesis in favour of the alternative hypothesis. We achieve this by using the *t*-test formula applied to the sample of difference scores. We then test the significance of *t* by comparing it to the values in Significance Table 12.1. For a sample of 4, since the degrees of freedom are *N* – 1 which equals 3, the table tells us that we need a *t*-score of 3.18 at the minimum to put our sample mean in the significant extreme 5% of the distribution of sample means. Figure 12.1 gives the key steps in carrying out a related/correlated samples *t*-test.

Calculation 12.1

The related/correlated/paired samples *t*-test

The data are taken from an imaginary study which looked at the relationship between the age of an infant and the amount of eye contact it makes with its mother. The infants were six months old and nine months old at the time of testing – age is the independent variable. The dependent variable is the number of one-minute segments during which the infant made any eye contact with its mother over a ten-minute session. The null hypothesis is that there is no relation between age and eye contact. The data are given in Table 12.6, which includes the difference between the six-month and nine-month scores as well as the square of this difference. The number of cases, *N*, is the number of difference scores, i.e. 8.

We can clearly see from Table 12.6 that the nine-month-old babies are spending more periods in eye contact with their mothers, on average, than they did when they were six months old. The average difference in eye contact is 1.5. The question remains, however, whether this difference is statistically significant.

Table 12.6	Steps in calculating the related/correlated samples *t*-test (number of one-minute segments with eye contact)			
Subject	**6 months** X_1	**9 months** X_2	**Difference** $D = X_1 - X_2$	**Difference²** D^2
Baby Clara	3	7	−4	16
Baby Martin	5	6	−1	1
Baby Sally	5	3	2	4
Baby Angie	4	8	−4	16
Baby Trevor	3	5	−2	4
Baby Sam	7	9	−2	4
Baby Bobby	8	7	1	1
Baby Sid	7	9	−2	4
Sums of columns	$\sum X_1 = 42$	$\sum X_2 = 54$	$\sum D = -12$	$\sum D^2 = 50$
Means of columns	$\bar{X}_1 = 5.25$	$\bar{X}_2 = 6.75$	$\bar{D} = 1.5$	

Step 1   The formula for the standard error of the difference (*D*) scores is as follows. It is exactly as for Calculation 11.1 except that we have substituted *D* for *X*.

$$\text{standard error} = \frac{\sqrt{\dfrac{\sum D^2 - \dfrac{\left(\sum D\right)^2}{N}}{N-1}}}{\sqrt{N}}$$

Substituting the values from Table 12.6

$$= \frac{\sqrt{\dfrac{50 - \dfrac{(-12)^2}{8}}{8-1}}}{\sqrt{8}} = \frac{\sqrt{\dfrac{50 - \dfrac{144}{8}}{7}}}{2.828}$$

$$= \frac{\sqrt{\dfrac{50 - 18}{7}}}{2.828} = \frac{\sqrt{\dfrac{32}{7}}}{2.828} = \frac{\sqrt{4.571}}{2.828} = \frac{2.138}{2.828} = 0.756$$

Step 2   We can now enter our previously calculated values in the following formula:

$$t\text{-score} = \frac{\bar{D}}{SE}$$

where $\bar{D}$ is the average difference score and *SE* is the standard error

$$t\text{-score} = \frac{-1.5}{0.756} = -1.98$$

➡

Step 3 If we look up this *t*-score in Significance Table 12.1 for $N - 1 = 7$ degrees of freedom, we find that we need a *t*-value of 2.37 or more (or −2.37 or less) to put our sample mean in the extreme 5% of sample means. In other words, our sample mean of −1.5 is in the middle 95% of sample means which are held to be statistically not significant. In these circumstances we prefer to believe that the null hypothesis is true. In other words, there is no significant difference between the babies' scores at six and nine months.

Interpreting the results Check the mean scores for the two conditions in order to understand which age group has the highest levels of eye contact. Although eye contact was greater at nine months, the *t*-test is not significant which indicates that the difference between the two ages was not sufficient to allow us to conclude that the two groups truly differ from each other.

Reporting the results We would write something along the lines of the following in our report: 'Eye contact was slightly higher at nine months ($\bar{X} = 6.75$) than at six months ($\bar{X} = 5.25$). However, the difference did not support the hypothesis that eye contact differs in six-month and nine-month-old babies since the obtained value of a *t* of −1.98 is not statistically significant at the 5% level.'

Alternatively, following the recommendations of the APA (2010) Publication Manual we could write: 'Eye contact was slightly higher at nine months ($M = 6.75$) than at six months ($M = 5.25$). However, the difference did not support the hypothesis that the amount of eye contact differs significantly at six months and nine months, $t(7) = -1.98$, $p > 0.05$.'

The material in the last part of the second sentence simply gives the statistic used (the *t*-test), the degrees of freedom (7), its value (−1.98), and the level of significance which is more than that required for the 5% level ($p > 0.05$). Chapter 16 explains this in greater detail.

> *Warning* *The distribution of the difference scores should not be markedly skewed if the t-test is to be used. Appendix A explains how to test for significant skewness. If the distribution of difference scores is markedly skewed, you might wish to consider the use of the Wilcoxon matched pairs test (Chapter 18, Calculation 18.2).*

12.5 Cautionary note

Many psychologists act as if they believe that it is the design of the research which determines whether you should use a related test. Related designs are those, after all, in which people serve in both research conditions. It is assumed that there is a correlation between subjects' scores in the two conditions. What if there is no correlation between the two samples of scores? The standard error becomes relatively large compared to the number of degrees of freedom so your research is less likely to be statistically significant (especially if the samples are small). So while trying to control for unwanted sources of error, if there is no correlation between the scores in the two conditions of the study, the researcher may simply reduce the likelihood of achieving statistical significance. The reason is that the researcher may have obtained non-significant findings simply because (*a*) they have reduced the error degrees of freedom, which therefore (*b*) increases the error estimate, thereby (*c*) reducing the significance level perhaps to non-significance. Some computer programs print out the correlation between the two variables as part of the correlated *t*-test output. If this correlation is not significant then you might be wise to think again about your test of significance. This situation is particularly likely to occur where you are using a matching procedure (as opposed to having the same people in both conditions). Unless your matching variables actually do correlate with the dependent variable, the matching can have no effect on reducing the error variance.

In the previous calculation, we found no significant change in eye contact in older babies compared with younger ones. It is worth examining the correlation between the two sets of scores to see if the assumption of correlation is fulfilled. The correlation is 0.42 but we need a correlation of 0.71 or greater to be statistically significant. In other words, the correlated scores do not really correlate – certainly not significantly. Even applying the uncorrelated version of the *t*-test described in the next chapter makes no difference. It still leaves the difference between the two age samples non-significant. We are not suggesting that if a related *t*-test fails to achieve significance you should replace it by an unrelated *t*-test, merely that you risk ignoring trends in your data which may be important. The most practical implication is that matching variables should relate to the dependent variable, otherwise there is no point in matching in the first place.

Key points

- The related or correlated *t*-test is merely a special case of the one-way analysis of variance for related samples (Chapter 21). Although it is frequently used in psychological research it tells us nothing more than the equivalent analysis of variance would do. Since the analysis of variance is generally a more flexible statistic, allowing any number of groups of scores to be compared, it might be your preferred statistic. However, the common occurrence of the *t*-test in psychological research means that you need to have some idea about what it is.

- The related *t*-test assumes that the distribution of the difference scores is not markedly skewed. If it is then the test may be unacceptably inaccurate. Appendix A explains how to test for skewness.

- If you compare many pairs of samples with each other in the same study using the *t*-test, you should consult Chapter 23 to find out about appropriate significance levels. There are better ways of making multiple comparisons, as they are called, but with appropriate adjustment to the critical values for significance, multiple *t*-tests can be justified.

- If you find that your related *t*-test is not significant, it could be that your two samples of scores are not correlated, thus not meeting the assumptions of the related *t*-test.

- Significance Table 12.1 applies whenever we have estimated the standard error from the characteristics of a sample. However, if we had actually known the population standard deviation and consequently the standard error was the actual standard error and not an estimate, we should not use the *t*-distribution table. In these rare (virtually unknown) circumstances, the distribution of the *t*-score formula is that for the *z*-scores.

- Although the correlated *t*-test can be used to compare any pairs of scores, it does not always make sense to do so. For example, you could use the correlated *t*-test to compare the weights and heights of people to see if the weight mean and the height mean differ. Unfortunately, it is a rather stupid thing to do since the numerical values involved relate to radically different things which are not comparable with each other. It is the comparison which is nonsensical in this case. The statistical test is not to blame. On the other hand, one could compare a sample of people's weights at different points in time quite meaningfully.

COMPUTER ANALYSIS

The calculation of the related/correlated *t*-test using SPSS Statistics is given in Figure 12.2.

The SPSS Statistics instruction book to this text is Dennis Howitt and Duncan Cramer (2011), *Introduction to SPSS Statistics in Psychology: For version 19 and earlier*, Harlow: Pearson. Chapter 13 in that book gives detailed step-by-step procedures for the statistics described in this chapter together with advice on how to report the results.

Data	• The two related variables are entered into the spreadsheet as separate variables with the data for each participant in the same row. • Label the variables clearly.
Analysis	• Select 'Analyze'. • Select 'Compare Means'. • Select 'Paired-Samples *T* test'.
2	• Select and move the two variables into the 'Paired Variables' box. • Select 'OK'.
Output	• Includes means, Ns and standard deviations of both variables. • Check that there is a correlation between the two variables – the related/correlated *t* test assumes that there is.
2	• The value of *t*, the degrees of freedom and the exact significance level is given. These are normally given when reporting the outcome of the analysis.

FIGURE 12.2 SPSS Statistics steps for calculating the related/correlated *t* test

CHAPTER 13

The *t*-test

Comparing two samples of unrelated/uncorrelated scores

Overview

- The unrelated *t*-test is used to compare the mean scores of two different samples on a single variable. So it is used with score data.

- It tells you whether the two means are statistically significant or not: that is, whether to accept the alternative hypothesis or the null hypothesis that there is, or is not, a difference between the two means.

- The unrelated *t*-test combines the variation in the two sets of scores to estimate standard error. This leads to a rather clumsy calculation which superficially is very daunting.

- The *t*-value is simply the number of standard errors that the two means are apart by.

- The statistical significance of this *t*-value may be obtained from tables though many prefer to use computer output which usually gives statistical significance levels.

Preparation

This chapter will be easier if you have mastered the related *t*-test of Chapter 12. Revise dependent and independent variables from that chapter.

13.1   Introduction

The *t*-test described in this chapter has various names. The unrelated *t*-test, the uncorrelated scores *t*-test and the independent samples *t*-test are the most common variants. It is also known as the Student *t*-test after its inventor who used the pen-name Student.

Often researchers compare two groups of scores from two separate groups of individuals to assess whether the average score of one group is higher than that of the other group. The possible research topics involved in such comparisons are limitless:

1. One might wish to compare an experimental group with a control group. For example, do volunteer women who are randomly assigned to a sexually abstinent condition have more erotic dreams than those in the sexually active control group? The independent variable is sexual activity (which has two levels – sexually abstinent and sexually active) and the dependent variable is the number of erotic dreams in a month (see Table 13.1). The independent variable differentiates the two groups being compared. In the present example, this is the amount of sexual activity (sexually abstinent versus sexually active). The dependent variable is the variable which might be influenced by the independent variable. These variables correspond to the scores given in the main body of the table (i.e. number of erotic dreams).

2. A group of experienced managers may be compared with a group of inexperienced managers in terms of the amount of time which they take to make complex decisions. The independent variable is experience in management (which has two levels – experienced versus inexperienced) and the dependent variable is decision-making time (Table 13.2).

3. A researcher might compare the amount of bullying in two schools, one with a strict and punitive policy and the other with a policy of counselling on discipline infringements. A sample of children from each school is interviewed and the number of times they have been bullied in the previous school year obtained. The independent

Table 13.1	Number of erotic dreams per month in experimental and control groups
Experimental group **Sexually abstinent**	**Control group** **Sexually active**
17	10
14	12
16	7

Table 13.2	Decision time (seconds) in experienced and inexperienced managers
Experienced managers	**Inexperienced managers**
24	167
32	133
27	74

Table 13.3	Number of times bullied in a year in schools with different discipline policies	
	Strict policy	**Counselling**
	8	12
	5	1
	2	3

variable is policy on discipline (which has two levels – strict versus counselling); and the dependent variable is the number of times a child has been bullied in the previous school year (see Table 13.3).

The basic requirements for the unrelated/uncorrelated scores *t*-test are straightforward enough – two groups of scores coming from two distinct groups of people. The scores should be roughly similar in terms of the shapes of their distributions. Ideally both distributions should be bell shaped and symmetrical. However, there can be marked deviance from this ideal and the test will remain sufficiently accurate.

The *t*-test is the name of a statistical technique which examines whether the two groups of scores have significantly *different* means – in other words, how likely is it that there could be a difference between the two groups as big as the one obtained if there is no difference in reality in the population?

13.2   Theoretical considerations

The basic theoretical assumption underlying the use of the *t*-test involves the characteristics of the null hypothesis. We explained null hypotheses in Chapter 10. The following explanation uses the same format for null hypotheses as we used in that chapter. Figure 13.1 gives the steps in carrying out a *t*-test.

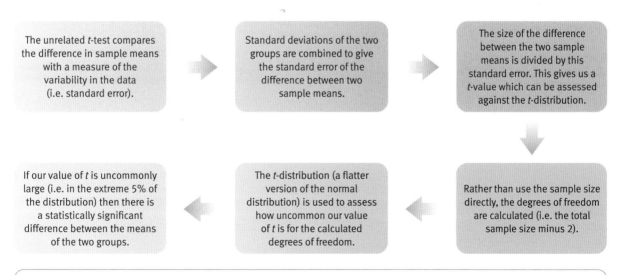

| FIGURE 13.1 | Conceptual steps for understanding the *t*-test |

Null hypotheses are statements that there is no relationship between two variables. The two variables in question at the moment are the independent and dependent variables. *This is another way of saying that there is no difference between the means of the two groups (i.e. columns) of scores.* The simplest null hypotheses for the above three studies are:

- There is no relationship between sexual activity and the number of erotic dreams that women have.

- Managerial experience is not related to speed of complex decision-making.

- The disciplinary style of a school is not related to the amount of bullying.

The alternative hypotheses to these null hypotheses can be obtained by simply deleting *no* or *not* from each of the above. Notice that the above way of writing the null hypothesis is relatively streamlined compared with what you often read in books and journals. So do not be surprised if you come across null hypotheses expressed in much more clumsy language such as:

- Women who abstain from sex will have the same number of erotic dreams as women who are sexually active.

- Erotic dreams do not occur at different frequencies in sexually active and sexually inactive women.

These two statements tend to obscure the fact that null hypotheses are fundamentally similar irrespective of the type of research under consideration.

The erotic dreams experiment will be used to illustrate the theoretical issues. There are two different samples of scores defined by the independent variable – one for the sexually abstinent group and the other for the sexually active group. The scores in Table 13.4 are the numbers of sexual dreams that each woman in the study has in a seven-day period. We can see that, on average, the sexually active women have fewer erotic dreams. Does this reflect a generalisable (significant) difference? The data might be as in Table 13.4. Apart from suggesting that Wendy's fantasy life is wonderful, the table indicates that sexual abstinence leads to an increase in erotic dreams.

The *null hypothesis* suggests that the scores in the two samples come from the same population since it claims that there is no relationship between the independent and dependent variables. That is, for all intents and purposes, the two samples can be

Table 13.4	Possible data from the sexual activity and erotic dreams experiment (dreams per seven days)		
Participant	**Sexually abstinent**	**Participant**	**Sexually active**
Lindsay	6	Janice	2
Claudine	7	Jennifer	5
Sharon	7	Joanne	4
Natalie	8	Anne-Marie	5
Sarah	9	Helen	6
Wendy	10	Amanda	6
Ruth	8	Sophie	5
Angela	9		

Table 13.5	Imaginary population of scores for erotic dreams study			
Experimental group Sexually abstinent			**Control group Sexually active**	
8	3		6	6
7	6		8	4
6	7		7	7
7	7		4	9
5	9		6	8
5	8		9	7
2	7		10	5
4	6		2	7
6	7		3	5
10	8		6	5
9	6		7	7
7	4		8	6
5			7	

construed as coming from a single population of scores; there is no difference between them due to the independent variable. Any differences between samples drawn from this null-hypothesis-defined population are due to chance factors rather than a true relationship between the independent and dependent variables. Table 13.5 is an imaginary population of scores from this null-hypothesis-defined population on the dependent variable 'number of erotic dreams'. The table also indicates whether the score is that of a sexually abstinent woman or a sexually active one. If the two columns of scores are examined carefully, there are no differences between the two sets of scores. In other words, they have the same average scores. Statistically, all of the scores in Table 13.5 can be regarded as coming from the same population. There is no relationship between sexual activity and the number of erotic dreams.

Given that the two samples (sexually abstinent and sexually active) come from the same population of scores on erotic dreams, in general we would expect no difference between pairs of samples drawn at random from this single population. Of course, sampling always introduces a chance element so some pairs of samples would be different, but mostly the differences will cluster around zero. Overall, numerous pairs of samples will yield an *average* difference of zero. We are assuming that we consistently subtract the sexually active mean from the sexually abstinent mean (or vice versa – it does not matter so long as we always do the same thing) so that positive and negative differences cancel each other out.

Since in this case we know the population of scores under the null hypothesis, we could pick out samples of 10 scores at random from the population to represent the sexually abstinent sample and, say, nine scores from the population to represent the sexually active sample. (Obviously the sample sizes will vary and they do not have to be equal.) Any convenient randomisation procedure could be used to select the samples (e.g. computer generated, random number tables or numbers drawn from a hat). The two samples selected at random, together with their respective means, are listed in Table 13.6.

Table 13.6	Random samples of scores from population in Table 13.5 to represent experimental and control conditions	
Experimental group **Sexually abstinent**		**Control group** **Sexually active**
4		5
5		5
10		10
7		9
7		7
5		7
7		8
9		6
9		2
		8
$\bar{X}_1 = 7$		$\bar{X}_2 = 6.7$

Examining Table 13.6, we can clearly see that there is a difference between the two sample means. This difference is 7.100 − 6.556 = 0.544. This difference between the two sample means has been obtained despite the fact that we know that there is no relationship between the independent variable and the dependent variable in the null-hypothesis-defined population. This is the nature of the random sampling process.

We can repeat this experiment by drawing more pairs of samples of these sizes from the null-hypothesis-defined population. This is shown for 40 new pairs of variables in Table 13.7.

Many of the differences between the pairs of means in Table 13.7 are very close to zero. This is just as we would expect since the independent and dependent variables are not related. Nevertheless, the means of some pairs of samples are somewhat different. In Table 13.7, 95% of the differences between the two means come in the range 0.922 to −1.400. (Given the small number of samples we have used, it is not surprising that this range is not symmetrical. If we had taken large numbers of samples, we would have expected more symmetry. Furthermore, had we used normally distributed scores, the symmetry may have been better.) The middle 95% of the distribution of differences between pairs of sample means are held clearly to support the null hypothesis. The extreme 5% beyond this middle range are held more likely to support the alternative hypothesis.

The standard deviation of the 40 'difference' scores gives the standard error of the differences. Don't forget we are dealing with *sample* means so the term standard error is the correct one. The value of the standard error is 0.63. This is the 'average' amount by which the differences between sample means is likely to deviate from the population mean difference of zero.

Table 13.7	Forty pairs of random samples from the population in Table 13.5	

Experimental group Sexually abstinent $N = 10$	Control group Sexually active $N = 9$	Difference (column 1 − column 2)
6.100	6.444	−0.344
6.300	5.444	0.856
6.000	6.556	−0.556
6.400	6.778	−0.378
6.600	6.111	0.489
5.700	6.111	−0.411
6.700	6.111	0.589
6.300	5.667	0.633
6.400	6.667	−0.267
5.900	5.778	0.122
6.400	6.556	−0.156
6.360	6.444	−0.084
6.400	6.778	−0.378
6.200	6.222	−0.022
5.600	5.889	−0.289
6.100	6.222	−0.122
6.800	6.667	0.133
6.100	6.222	−0.122
6.900	6.000	0.900
7.200	5.889	1.311
5.800	7.333	−1.533
6.700	6.889	−0.189
6.200	6.000	0.200
6.500	6.444	0.056
5.900	6.444	−0.544
6.000	6.333	−0.333
6.300	6.778	−0.478
6.100	5.778	0.322
6.000	6.000	0.000
6.000	6.667	−0.667
6.556	6.778	−0.222
6.700	5.778	0.922
5.600	7.000	−1.400
6.600	6.222	0.378
5.600	6.667	−1.067
5.900	7.222	−1.322
6.000	6.667	−0.667
7.000	6.556	0.444
6.400	6.556	−0.156
6.900	6.222	0.678

13.3　Standard deviation and standard error

The trouble with all of the above is that it is abstract theory. Normally, we know nothing for certain about the populations from which our samples come. Fortunately, quite a lot can be inferred about the population given the null hypothesis and information from the samples:

1. Since the null hypothesis states that there is no relationship between the independent and dependent variables in the population, it follows that there should be no systematic difference between the scores in the pair of samples. That is, the average difference between the two means should be zero over many pairs of samples.

2. We can use the scores in a sample to estimate the standard deviation of the scores in the population. However, if we use our usual standard deviation formula the estimate tends to be somewhat too low. Consequently we have to modify our standard deviation formula (Chapter 5) when estimating the standard deviation of the population. The change is minimal – the N in the bottom half of the formula is changed to $N - 1$:

$$\text{estimated standard deviation} = \sqrt{\frac{\sum X^2 - \frac{\left(\sum X\right)^2}{N}}{N - 1}}$$

The net effect of this adjustment is to increase the estimated standard deviation in the population – the amount of adjustment is greatest if we are working with small sample sizes for which subtracting 1 is a big adjustment.

But this only gives us the estimated standard deviation of the *scores* in the population. We really need to know about the standard deviation (i.e. standard error) of sample means taken from that population. Remember, there is a simple formula which converts the estimated standard deviation of the population to the estimated standard error of sample means drawn from that population: we simply divide the estimated standard deviation by the square root of the sample size. It so happens that the computationally most useful way of working out the standard error is as follows:

$$\text{standard error} = \frac{\sqrt{\frac{\sum X^2 - \frac{\left(\sum X\right)^2}{N}}{N - 1}}}{\sqrt{N}}$$

Still we have not finished because this is the estimated standard error of *sample means*; we want the estimated standard error of *differences between pairs of sample means*. It makes intuitive sense that the standard error of differences between pairs of sample means is likely to be the sum of the standard errors of the two samples. After all, the standard error is merely the average amount by which a sample mean differs from the population mean of zero. So the standard error of the differences between pairs of sample means drawn from a population should be the two separate standard errors combined.

Well, that is virtually the procedure. However, the two different standard errors (SE) are added together in a funny sort of way:

$$SE_{\text{[of differences between sample means]}} = \sqrt{(SE_1^2 + SE_2^2)}$$

Finally, because the sample sizes used to estimate the two individual standard errors are not always the same, it is necessary to adjust the equation to account for this, otherwise you end up with the wrong answer. The computational formula for the estimated standard error of differences between pairs of sample means is as follows:

Standard error of differences between pairs of sample means

$$= \sqrt{\left(\frac{\left(\sum X_1^2 - \dfrac{\left(\sum X_1\right)^2}{N_1}\right) + \left(\sum X_2^2 - \dfrac{\left(\sum X_2\right)^2}{N_2}\right)}{N_1 + N_2 - 2}\right)\left(\frac{1}{N_1} + \frac{1}{N_2}\right)}$$

Although this looks appallingly complicated, the basic idea is fairly simple. It looks complex because of the adjustment for different sample sizes.

Now we simply use the *t*-test formula. The average difference between the pairs of sample means is zero assuming the null hypothesis to be true. The *t* formula is:

$$t = \frac{\text{sample 1 mean} - \text{sample 2 mean} - 0}{\text{standard error of differences between sample means}}$$

or

$$t = \frac{\text{differences between the two sample means} - 0}{\text{standard error of differences between sample means}}$$

Since in the above formula the population mean of difference between pairs of sample means is always zero, we can omit it:

$$t = \frac{\text{sample 1 mean} - \text{sample 2 mean}}{\text{standard error of differences between sample means}}$$

The formula expressed in full looks very complicated:

$$t = \frac{\bar{X}_1 - \bar{X}_2}{\sqrt{\left(\dfrac{\left(\sum X_1^2 - \dfrac{\left(\sum X_1\right)^2}{N_1}\right) + \left(\sum X_2^2 - \dfrac{\left(\sum X_2\right)^2}{N_2}\right)}{N_1 + N_2 - 2}\right)\left(\dfrac{1}{N_1} + \dfrac{1}{N_2}\right)}}$$

So *t* is the number of standard errors by which the difference between our two sample means differs from the population mean of zero. The distribution of *t* is rather like the distribution of *z* if you have a large sample – thus it approximates very closely the normal distribution. However, with smaller sample sizes the curve of *t* becomes increasingly flat and more spread out than the normal curve. Consequently we need different *t*-distributions for different sample sizes.

Significance Table 13.1 gives values for the *t*-distributions. Notice that the distribution is dependent on the degrees of freedom which for this *t*-test is the total number of scores in the two samples combined minus 2.

Significance Table 13.1	5% significance values of unrelated t (two-tailed test). Appendix E gives a fuller and conventional version of this table

Degrees of freedom (always $N - 2$ for unrelated t-test)	Significant at 5% level Accept hypothesis
3	±3.18 or more extreme
4	±2.78 or more extreme
5	±2.57 or more extreme
6	±2.45 or more extreme
7	±2.37 or more extreme
8	±2.31 or more extreme
9	±2.26 or more extreme
10	±2.23 or more extreme
11	±2.20 or more extreme
12	±2.18 or more extreme
13	±2.16 or more extreme
14	±2.15 or more extreme
15	±2.13 or more extreme
18	±2.10 or more extreme
20	±2.09 or more extreme
25	±2.06 or more extreme
30	±2.04 or more extreme
40	±2.02 or more extreme
60	±2.00 or more extreme
100	±1.98 or more extreme
∞	±1.96 or more extreme

Your value must be in the listed ranges for your degrees of freedom to be significant at the 5% level (i.e. to accept the hypothesis).

If your required degrees of freedom are not listed, then take the nearest *smaller* listed values. Refer to Appendix E if you need a precise value of t.

'More extreme' means that, for example, values in the ranges of +3.18 to infinity or −3.18 to (minus) infinity are statistically significant with 3 degrees of freedom.

Calculation 13.1

The unrelated (uncorrelated) t-test

The calculation of the unrelated t-test uses the following formula:

$$t = \frac{\bar{X}_1 - \bar{X}_2}{\sqrt{\left(\frac{\left(\sum X_1^2 - \frac{(\sum X_1)^2}{N_1}\right) + \left(\sum X_2^2 - \frac{(\sum X_2)^2}{N_2}\right)}{N_1 + N_2 - 2}\right)\left(\frac{1}{N_1} + \frac{1}{N_2}\right)}}$$

→

Table 13.8	Emotionality scores in two-parent and lone-parent families
Two-parent family X_1	**Lone-parent family X_2**
12	6
18	9
14	4
10	13
19	14
8	9
15	8
11	12
10	11
13	9
15	
16	

Horrific, isn't it? Probably the worst formula that you are likely to use in psychological statistics. However, it contains little new. It is probably best to break the formula down into its component calculations and take things step by step. However, if you prefer to try to work directly with the above formula do not let us stand in your way.

The data are from an imaginary study involving the emotionality of children from lone-parent and two-parent families. The independent variable is family type which has two levels – the lone-parent type and the two-parent type. The dependent variable is emotionality on a standard psychological measure – the higher the score on this test, the more emotional is the child. The data are listed in Table 13.8.

A key thing to note is that we have called the scores for the two-parent family condition X_1 and those for the lone-parent family condition X_2.

Step 1   Extend the data table by adding columns of squared scores and column totals as in Table 13.9. The sample size for $X_1 = N_1 = 12$; the sample size for $X_2 = N_2 = 10$.

$\sum X_1$ = sum of scores for two-parent family sample

$\sum X_1^2$ = sum of squared scores for two-parent family sample

$\sum X_2$ = sum of scores for lone-parent family sample

$\sum X_2^2$ = sum of squared scores for lone-parent family sample

Step 2   Do each of the following calculations.

Calculation of A:

$$A = \bar{X}_1 - \bar{X}_2$$

$$= \frac{\sum X_1}{N_1} - \frac{\sum X_2}{N_2}$$

$$= \frac{161}{12} - \frac{95}{10}$$

$$= 13.417 - 9.500 = 3.917$$

➜

Table 13.9	Table 13.8 extended to include steps in the calculation		
Two-parent family X_1	Square previous column X_1^2	Lone-parent family X_2	Square previous column X_2^2
12	144	6	36
18	324	9	81
14	196	4	16
10	100	13	169
19	361	14	196
8	64	9	81
15	225	8	64
11	121	12	144
10	100	11	121
13	169	9	81
15	225		
16	256		
$\sum X_1 = 161$	$\sum X_1^2 = 2285$	$\sum X_2 = 95$	$\sum X_2^2 = 989$

Calculation of B:

$$B = \sum X_1^2 \frac{\left(\sum X_1\right)^2}{N_1}$$

$$= 2285 - \frac{161^2}{12} = 2285 - \frac{25\,921}{12}$$

$$= 2285 - 2160.0833$$

$$= 124.9167$$

Calculation of C:

$$C = \sum X_2^2 \frac{\left(\sum X_2\right)^2}{N_2}$$

$$= 989 - \frac{95^2}{10} = 989 - \frac{9025}{10}$$

$$= 989 - 902.5$$

$$= 86.5$$

Calculation of D:

$$D = N_1 + N_2 - 2$$

$$= 12 + 10 - 2$$

$$= 20$$

→

Calculation of E:

$$E = \frac{1}{N_1} + \frac{1}{N_2} = \frac{1}{12} + \frac{1}{10}$$

$$= 0.0833 + 0.1000 = 0.1833$$

Calculation of F:

$$F = \left(\frac{B+C}{D}\right) \times E$$

$$= \left(\frac{124.9167 + 86.5000}{20}\right) \times 0.1833$$

$$= \left(\frac{211.4167}{20}\right) \times 0.1833$$

$$= 10.57083 \times 0.1833 = 1.938$$

Calculation of G:

$$G = \sqrt{F} = \sqrt{1.938} = 1.392$$

Calculation of t:

$$t = \frac{A}{G} = \frac{3.917}{1.392} = 2.81$$

Step 3 t is the t-score or the number of standard errors our sample data are away from the population mean of zero. We use Significance Table 13.1 to check the statistical significance of our value of 2.81 by checking against the row for degrees of freedom (i.e. $N_1 + N_2 - 2 = 20$ degrees of freedom). This table tells us that our value of t is in the extreme 5% of the distribution because it is larger than 2.09; so we reject the null hypothesis that family structure is unrelated to emotionality. Our study showed that emotionality is significantly greater in the two-parent family structure as opposed to the lone-parent family structure.

Interpreting the results Remember to check carefully the mean scores for both groups in order to know which of the two groups has the higher scores on the dependent variable. In our example, this shows that the greater emotionality was found in the children from the two-parent families. The significant value of the t-test means that we are reasonably safe to conclude that the two groups do differ in terms of their emotionality.

Reporting the results The statistical analysis could be reported in the following style: 'It was found that emotionality was significantly higher ($t = 2.81$, $df = 20$, $p < 0.05$) in the two-parent families ($\bar{X} = 13.42$) than in the lone-parent families ($\bar{X} = 9.50$).'

The material in the final brackets simply reports the significance test used (the t-test), its value (2.81), the degrees of freedom ($df = 20$) and that the value of t is statistically significant ($p < 0.05$). Chapter 16 explains the approach in greater detail.

Alternatively, following the recommendations of the APA (2010) Publication Manual, we could write the results as follows: 'It was found that emotionality was significantly higher, $t(20) = 2.81$, $p < 0.05$, in the two-parent families ($M = 13.42$) than in the lone-parent families ($M = 9.50$).'

Box 13.1   Focus on

Avoiding rounding errors

When calculating by hand, you need to use rather more decimal places than when reporting your findings. If this is not done then *rounding errors* will result in your getting a different answer from that calculated by a computer. Generally speaking, you need to work to at least three decimal places on your calculator though the actual calculated figures given by the calculator are best and easiest to use. Because of limitations of space and for clarity, the calculations reported in this book have been given to a small number of decimal places – usually three decimal places. When you report the results of the calculation, however, round the figure to no more than two decimal places. Remember to be consistent in the number of decimal places you present in your results.

13.4   Cautionary note

You should not use the *t*-test if your samples are markedly skewed, especially if they are skewed in opposite directions. Appendix A explains how to test for skewness. You might consider using the Mann–Whitney *U*-test in these circumstances (Chapter 18, Calculation 18.3).

Key points

- The *t*-test is commonly used in psychological research, so it is important that you have an idea of what it does. However, it is only a special case of the analysis of variance (Chapter 20) which is a much more flexible statistic. Given the analysis of variance's ability to handle any number of samples, you might prefer to use it instead of the *t*-test in most circumstances. To complicate matters, some use the *t*-test in the analysis of variance.

- The *t*-test assumes that the variances of the two samples are similar so that they can be combined to yield an overall estimate. However, if the variances of the two samples are significantly different from each other, you should not use this version of the *t*-test. The way to see if two variances are dissimilar is to use the variance ratio test described in Chapter 19.

- If you wish to use the *t*-test but find that you fall foul of this *F*-ratio requirement, there is a version of the *t*-test which does not assume equal variances. The best way of doing such *t*-tests is to use a computer package which applies both tests to the same data. Unfortunately, the calculation for the degrees of freedom is a little complex (you can have decimals involved in the values) and it goes a little beyond reasonable hand calculations. The calculation details are provided in Blalock (1972).

COMPUTER ANALYSIS

SPSS Statistics provides one of the better ways of calculating the *t*-test since an alternative calculation is provided for where the variances of the two groups differ significantly. The steps for the unrelated *t*-test are shown in Figure 13.2. It is important to remember that data entry is a little different for the unrelated *t*-test since all of the scores on the dependent variable are put in one column as a single variable, but the group to which a score belongs is identified in a second column using, for example, 1 to indicate one group and 2 to indicate the other group.

The SPSS Statistics instruction book to this text is Dennis Howitt and Duncan Cramer (2011), *Introduction to SPSS Statistics in Psychology: For version 19 and earlier*, Harlow: Pearson. Chapter 14 in that book gives detailed step-by-step procedures for the statistics described in this chapter together with advice on how to report the results.

Data
- The data are entered as two columns – 1. the scores on the dependent variable and 2. a code number to indicate the group that the score comes from, e.g. code 1 for Group 1, code 2 for Group 2.

Analysis
- Select 'Analyze'.
- Select 'Compare Means'.
- Select 'Independent Samples T Test . . .'.

2
- Select the dependent variable and move to the box 'Test Variable(s):'.
- Select the variable containing the group codes and move it into the box 'Grouping Variable:'.

3
- Select 'Define Groups' to identify the two groups for the *t*-test.
- Enter 1 to identify scores from the first group, enter 2 to define scores from the second group.

4
- Select 'Continue'.
- Select 'OK'.

Output
- 'Group Statistics' gives means, standard deviations and standard errors.

2
- In Independent Samples Test use the first row (Equal variances assumed) unless Levene's Test is significant then use the second row values of *t* etc.

FIGURE 13.2 SPSS Statistics steps for the unrelated *t*-test

CHAPTER 14

Chi-square

Differences between samples of frequency data

- Chi-square is used with nominal (category) data in the form of frequency counts. A minimum of two categories is involved.

- It tests whether the frequency counts in the various nominal categories could be expected by chance or whether there is a relationship.

- One-sample chi-square compares the frequencies obtained in each category with a known expected frequency distribution. It is relatively uncommon in psychological research because psychological research usually uses score rather than category measures.

- Two-sample chi-square uses a crosstabulation or frequency table for two variables. This gives the frequencies in the various possible combinations of categories of these two variables.

- The disparity between the actual frequencies in the data and what the frequencies would be if the null hypothesis were true is at the heart of the calculation. The bigger the disparity, the bigger the value of chi-square and the more one's findings are statistically significant.

- When the chi-square table has more than four cells (i.e. combinations of categories), interpretation becomes difficult. It is possible to subdivide a big table into a number of smaller chi-squares in order to facilitate interpretation. This is known as partitioning.

- Sometimes data may violate the mathematical foundations of chi-square too much. In these circumstances, the data may have to be modified to meet the mathematical requirements, or an alternative measure such as the Fisher exact test may be employed.

Preparation

You should be familiar with crosstabulation and contingency tables (Chapter 6) and samples and populations (Chapter 9).

14.1 Introduction

Often, chi-square is written as χ^2. However, we have avoided Greek letters as far as possible.

If a researcher has several samples of data which involve *frequencies* rather than scores, a statistical test designed for frequency data must be used. The following are some examples of research of this sort:

1. Male and female schoolchildren are compared in terms of wanting to be psychologists when they leave school (Table 14.1).

2. The sexual orientations of a sample of religious men are compared with those of a non-religious sample (Table 14.2).

3. Choosing to play with either a black or a white doll in black and white children (Table 14.3).

In each of these examples, both variables consist of a relatively small number of categories. In other words, schematically each study approximates to the form shown in Table 14.4 in which the independent variable is the sample and the dependent variable consists of one of several categories.

The precise number of samples may vary from study to study and the number of categories of the dependent variable can be two or more. As a rule of thumb, *it is better to have just a few samples and a few categories*, since large tables can be difficult to interpret and generally require large numbers of participants or cases to be workable.

Table 14.1	Relationship between gender and wanting to be a psychologist	
Intention	**Male**	**Female**
Wants to be a psychologist	$f = 17$	$f = 98$
Does not want to be a psychologist	$f = 67$	$f = 35$

Table 14.2	Relationship between sexual orientation and religion	
Orientation	**Religious**	**Non-religious**
Heterosexual	57	105
Gay	13	27
Bisexual	8	17

Table 14.3	Relationship between doll choice and ethnicity		
Choice	**Black child**	**White child**	**Mixed-parentage**
Black doll	19	17	5
White doll	16	18	9

Table 14.4	Stylised table for chi-square		
Category	**Sample 1**	**Sample 2**	**Sample 3**
Category 1	27	21	5
Category 2	19	20	19
Category 3	9	17	65

The 'cells' of Table 14.4 (called a *crosstabulation* or *contingency* table) contain the frequencies of individuals in that particular sample and that particular category. So the 'cell' that corresponds to sample 2 and category 3 contains the frequency 17. This means that in your data there are 17 cases in sample 2 which also fit category 3. In other words, a cell is the intersection of a row and a column.

The statistical question is whether the distribution of frequencies in the different samples is so varied that it is unlikely that these all come from the same population. As ever, this population is the one defined by the null hypothesis (which suggests that there is no relationship between the independent and dependent variables).

14.2 Theoretical issues

Imagine a research study in which children are asked to choose between two television programmes, one violent and the other non-violent. Some of the children have been in trouble at school for fighting and the others have not been in trouble. The researcher wants to know if there is a relationship between the violence of the preferred television programme and having been in trouble for fighting at school. The data might look something like Table 14.5.

We can see from Table 14.5 that the fighters (sample 1) are more likely to prefer the violent programme and the non-fighters (sample 2) are more likely to prefer the non-violent programme. The frequencies obtained in the research are known as the *observed* frequencies. This merely refers to the fact that we obtain them from our empirical *observations* (that is, the data).

Assume that both of the samples come from the same population of data in which there is no relationship between the dependent and independent variables. This implies that any differences between the samples are merely due to the chance fluctuations of sampling. A useful index of how much the samples differ from each other is based on how different each sample is from the population distribution defined by the null hypothesis. As ever, since we do not know the population directly in most research, we have to estimate its characteristics from the characteristics of samples.

Table 14.5	Relationship between preferred TV programme and fighting	
Preference	**Sample 1 Fighters**	**Sample 2 Non-fighters**
Violent TV preferred	40	15
Non-violent TV preferred	30	70

Table 14.6	Relationship between preferred TV programme and fighting including the marginal frequencies (column and row frequencies)		
Preference	Sample 1 Fighters	Sample 2 Non-fighters	Row frequencies
Violent TV preferred	40	15	55
Non-violent TV preferred	30	70	100
Column frequencies	70	85	Overall frequency = 155

With the chi-square test, we simply *add* together the frequencies for whatever number of samples we have. These sums are then used as an estimate of the distribution of the different categories in the population. Since differences between the samples under the null hypothesis are solely due to chance factors, by combining samples the best possible estimate of the characteristics of the population is obtained. In other words, we simply add together the characteristics of two or more samples to give us an estimate of the population distribution of the categories. The first stage of doing this is illustrated in Table 14.6.

So in the null-hypothesis-defined population, we would expect 55 out of every 155 to prefer the violent programme and 100 out of 155 to prefer the non-violent programme. But we obtained 40 out of 70 preferring the violent programme in sample 1, and 15 out of 85 preferring the violent programme in sample 2. How do these figures match the expectations from the population defined by the null hypothesis? We need to calculate the expected frequencies of the cells in Table 14.6. This calculation is based on the assumption that the null hypothesis population frequencies are our best information as to the relative proportions preferring the violent and non-violent programmes if there truly was no difference between the samples.

Sample 1 contains 70 children; if the null hypothesis is true then we would expect 55 out of every 155 of these to prefer the violent programme. Thus our expected frequency of those preferring the violent programme in sample 1 is:

$$70 \times \frac{55}{155} = 70 \times 0.355 = 24.84$$

Remember that these figures have been rounded for presentation and give a slightly different answer from that generated by a calculator.

Similarly, since we expect under the null hypothesis 100 out of every 155 to prefer the non-violent programme, then our expected frequency of those preferring the non-violent programme in sample 1, out of the 70 children in that sample, is:

$$70 \times \frac{100}{155} = 70 \times 0.645 = 45.16$$

Notice that the sum of the expected frequencies for sample 1 is the same as the number of children in that sample (24.84 + 45.16 = 70).

We can apply the same logic to sample 2 which contains 85 children. We expect that 55 out of every 155 will prefer the violent programme and 100 out of every 155 will prefer the non-violent programme. The expected frequency preferring the violent programme in sample 2 is:

$$85 \times \frac{55}{155} = 85 \times 0.355 = 30.18$$

Table 14.7	Contingency table including both observed and expected frequencies		
Preference	Sample 1 Fighters	Sample 2 Non-fighters	Row frequencies
Violent TV preferred	*observed frequency = 4* *expected frequency = 24.84*	*observed frequency = 15* *expected frequency = 30.16*	55
Non-violent TV preferred	*observed frequency = 30* *expected frequency = 45.16*	*observed frequency = 70* *expected frequency = 54.84*	100
Column frequencies (i.e. sum of observed frequencies in column)	70	85	Overall frequencies = 155

The expected frequency preferring the non-violent programme in sample 2 is:

$$85 \times \frac{100}{155} = 85 \times 0.645 = 54.83$$

We can enter these expected frequencies (population frequencies under the null hypothesis) into our table of frequencies (Table 14.7).

The chi-square statistic is based on the differences between the observed and the expected frequencies. It should be fairly obvious that the greater the disparity between the observed frequencies and the population frequencies under the null hypothesis, the less likely is the null hypothesis to be true. Thus if the samples are very different from each other, the differences between the observed and expected frequencies will be large. Chi-square involves calculating the overall disparity between the observed and expected frequencies over all the cells in the table. To be precise, the chi-square formula involves the squared deviations over the expected frequencies, but this is merely a slight diversion to make our formula fit a convenient statistical distribution which is called chi-square. The calculated value of chi-square is then compared with a table of critical values of chi-square (Significance Table 14.1) in order to estimate the probability of obtaining our pattern of frequencies by chance (if the null hypothesis of no differences between the samples was true). This table is organised according to degrees of freedom, which is always (number of columns of data − 1) × (number of rows of data − 1). This would be (2 − 1) × (2 − 1) or 1 for Table 14.7. Figure 14.1 gives the key steps when carrying out a chi-square test.

Box 14.1 Focus on

Yates's correction

Yates's correction is a slightly outmoded statistical procedure when the expected frequencies in chi-square are small. This is intended to make such data fit the theoretical chi-square distribution a little better. In essence, all you do is subtract 0.5 from each (observed frequency − expected frequency) in the chi-square formula prior to squaring that difference. With large expected frequencies, this has virtually no effect. With small tables, it obviously reduces the size of chi-square and therefore its statistical significance. We have opted for not using it in our calculations. Really it is a matter of personal choice as far as convention goes.

Significance Table 14.1	5% and 1% significance values of chi-square (two-tailed test). Appendix F gives a fuller and conventional version of this table	
Degrees of freedom	**Significant at 5% level Accept hypothesis**	**Significant at 1% level Accept hypothesis**
1	3.8 or more	6.7 or more
2	6.0 or more	9.2 or more
3	7.8 or more	11.3 or more
4	9.5 or more	13.3 or more
5	11.1 or more	15.1 or more
6	12.6 or more	16.8 or more
7	14.1 or more	18.5 or more
8	15.5 or more	20.1 or more
9	16.9 or more	21.7 or more
0	18.3 or more	23.2 or more
11	19.7 or more	24.7 or more
12	21.0 or more	26.2 or more

Your value must be in the listed ranges for your degrees of freedom to be significant at the 5% level (column 2) or the 1% level (column 3) (i.e. to accept the hypothesis).

Should you require more precise values than those listed below, these are to be found in the table in Appendix F.

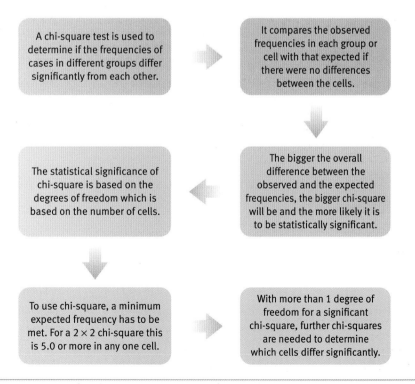

A chi-square test is used to determine if the frequencies of cases in different groups differ significantly from each other.

It compares the observed frequencies in each group or cell with that expected if there were no differences between the cells.

The bigger the overall difference between the observed and the expected frequencies, the bigger chi-square will be and the more likely it is to be statistically significant.

The statistical significance of chi-square is based on the degrees of freedom which is based on the number of cells.

To use chi-square, a minimum expected frequency has to be met. For a 2 × 2 chi-square this is 5.0 or more in any one cell.

With more than 1 degree of freedom for a significant chi-square, further chi-squares are needed to determine which cells differ significantly.

FIGURE 14.1   Conceptual steps for understanding the chi-square test

Calculation 14.1

Chi-square

The calculation of chi-square involves several relatively simple but repetitive calculations. For each cell in the chi-square table you calculate the following:

$$\frac{(\text{observed frequency} - \text{expected frequency})^2}{\text{expected frequency}}$$

The only complication is that this small calculation is repeated for each of the cells in your crosstabulation or contingency table. The formula in full becomes:

$$\text{chi-square} = \sum \frac{(O - E)^2}{E}$$

where O = observed frequency and E = expected frequency.

The following is an imaginary piece of research in which teenage boys and girls were asked to name their favourite type of television programme from a list of three: (1) soap operas, (2) crime dramas and (3) neither of these. The researcher suspects that gender may be related to programme preference (Table 14.8).

We next need to calculate the expected frequencies for each of the cells in Table 14.8. One easy way of doing this is to multiply the row total and the column total for each particular cell and divide by the total number of observations (i.e. total frequencies). This is shown in Table 14.9.

Table 14.8	Relationship between favourite type of TV programme and gender of respondent			
Respondents	**Soap opera**	**Crime drama**	**Neither**	**Totals**
Males	observed = 27	observed = 14	observed = 19	row 1 = 60
Females	observed = 17	observed = 33	observed = 9	row 2 = 59
Total	**Column 1 = 44**	**Column 2 = 47**	**Column 3 = 28**	**Total = 119**

Table 14.9	Calculation of expected frequencies by multiplying appropriate row and column totals and then dividing by overall total			
Respondents	**Soap opera**	**Crime drama**	**Neither**	**Total**
Males	*observed = 27*	*observed = 14*	*observed = 19*	row 1 = 60
	expected = 60 × 44/119 = 22.185	*expected = 60 × 47/119 = 23.697*	*expected = 60 × 28/119 = 14.118*	
Females	*observed = 17*	*observed = 33*	*Observed = 9*	row 2 = 59
	expected = 59 × 44/119 = 21.815	*expected = 59 × 47/119 = 23.303*	*expected = 59 × 28/119 = 13.882*	
Total	**Column 1 = 44**	**Column 2 = 47**	**Column 3 = 28**	**Total = 119**

→

We then simply substitute the above values in the chi-square formula:

$$\text{chi-square} = \sum \frac{(O - E)^2}{E}$$

$$= \frac{(27 - 22.185)^2}{22.185} + \frac{(14 - 23.697)^2}{23.697} + \frac{(19 - 14.118)^2}{14.118}$$

$$+ \frac{(17 - 21.185)^2}{21.185} + \frac{(33 - 23.303)^2}{23.303} + \frac{(9 - 13.882)^2}{13.882}$$

$$= \frac{4.815^2}{22.185} + \frac{(-9.697)^2}{23.697} + \frac{4.882^2}{14.118} + \frac{(-4.185)^2}{21.185} + \frac{9.697^2}{23.303} + \frac{(-4.882)^2}{13.882}$$

$$= \frac{23.184}{22.185} + \frac{94.032}{23.697} + \frac{23.834}{14.118} + \frac{23.184}{21.815} + \frac{94.032}{23.303} + \frac{23.834}{13.882}$$

$$= 1.045 + 3.968 + 1.688 + 1.063 + 4.035 + 1.717$$

$$= 13.52$$

The degrees of freedom are (the number of columns − 1) × (the number of rows − 1) = (3 − 1) × (2 − 1) = 2 degrees of freedom.

We then check the table of the critical values of chi-square (Significance Table 14.1) in order to assess whether or not our samples differ amongst each other so much that they are unlikely to be produced by the population defined by the null hypothesis. The value must equal or exceed the tabulated value to be significant at the listed level of significance. Some tables will give you more degrees of freedom, but you will be hard pressed to do a sensible chi-square that exceeds 12 degrees of freedom.

Interpreting the results Our value of chi-square is well in excess of the minimum value of 6.0 needed to be significant at the 5% level for 2 degrees of freedom, so we reject the hypothesis that the samples came from the population defined by the null hypothesis. Thus we accept the hypothesis that there is a relationship between television programme preferences and gender.

Only if you have a 2 × 2 chi-square is it possible to interpret the significance level of the chi-square directly in terms of the trends revealed in the data table. As we will see in Section 14.3, if we have a bigger chi-square than this (say 3 × 2 or 3 × 3) then a significant value of chi-square merely indicates that the samples are dissimilar to each other overall without stipulating which samples are different from each other.

Because the sample sizes generally differ in contingency tables, it is helpful to convert the frequencies in each cell to percentages of the relevant sample size at this stage. It is important, though, never to actually calculate chi-square itself on these percentages as you will obtain the wrong significance level if you do. It seems from Table 14.10 that males prefer soap operas more often than females do, females have a preference for crime drama, and males are more likely than females to say that they prefer another type of programme. Unfortunately, as things stand we are not able to say which of these trends are statistically significant unless we partition the chi-square as described in Section 14.3.

Table 14.10	Observed percentages in each sample based on the observed frequencies in Table 14.8		
Respondents	**Soap opera**	**Crime drama**	**Neither**
Males	45.0%	23.3%	31.7%
Females	28.8%	55.9%	15.3%

Reporting the results The results could be written up as follows: 'The value of chi-square was 13.52 which was significant at the 5% level with 2 degrees of freedom. Thus there is a gender difference in favourite type of TV programme. Compared with females, males were more likely to choose soap operas and less likely to choose crime dramas as their favourite programmes and more likely to prefer neither of these.'

However, as this table is bigger than a 2 × 2 table, it is advisable to partition the chi-square as discussed in Section 14.3 in order to say which of these trends are statistically significant.

Alternatively, following the recommendations of the APA (2010) Publication Manual we could write: 'There was a significant gender difference in favourite type of TV programme, $\chi^2(2, N = 119) = 13.52$, $p < 0.05$. Compared with females, males were more likely to choose soap operas and less likely to choose crime dramas as their favourite programmes and more likely to prefer neither of these.' Chapter 16 explains how to report statistical significance in the shorter, professional way used in this version.

14.3   Partitioning chi-square

There is no problem when the chi-square contingency table is just two columns and two rows. The chi-square in these circumstances tells you that your two samples are different from each other. But if you have, say, a 2 × 3 chi-square (e.g. you have two samples and three categories) then there is some uncertainty as to what a significant chi-square means – does it mean that all three samples are different from each other, that sample 1 and sample 2 are different, that sample 1 and sample 3 are different, or that sample 2 and sample 3 are different? In the television programmes example, although we obtained a significant overall chi-square, there is some doubt as to why we obtained this. The major differences between the genders are between the soap opera and crime drama conditions rather than between the soap opera and the 'other' conditions.

It is a perfectly respectable statistical procedure to break your large chi-square into a number of 2 × 2 chi-square tests to assess precisely where the significant differences lie. Thus in the TV programmes study you could generate *three* separate chi-squares from the 2 × 3 contingency table. These are illustrated in Table 14.11.

These three separate chi-squares each have just one degree of freedom (because they are 2 × 2 tables). If you calculate chi-square for each of these tables you hopefully should be able to decide precisely where the differences are between samples and conditions.

The only difficulty is the significance levels you use. Because you are doing three separate chi-squares, the normal significance level of 5% still operates, but it is *divided between the three chi-squares* you have carried out. In other words, we share the 5% between three to give us the 1.667% level for each – any of the three chi-squares would have to be significant at this level to be reported as being significant at the 5% level. Significance Table 14.2 gives the adjusted values of chi-square required to be significant

Significance Table 14.2	Chi-square 5% two-tailed significance values for 1–10 unplanned comparisons									
Degree of freedom	**Number of comparisons being made**									
	1	**2**	**3**	**4**	**5**	**6**	**7**	**8**	**9**	**10**
1	3.84	5.02	5.73	6.24	6.64	6.96	7.24	7.48	7.69	7.88

To use this table, simply look under the column for the number of separate comparisons you are making using chi-square. Your values of chi-square must equal or exceed the listed value to be significant at the 5% level with a two-tailed test.

Table 14.11	Three partitioned sub-tables from the 2 × 3 contingency table (Table 14.8)

Soap opera versus crime drama

Respondents	Soap opera	Crime drama	Totals
Males	27	14	row 1 = 41
Females	17	33	row 2 = 50
Totals	Column 1 = 44	Column 2 = 47	Total = 91

Soap opera versus neither

Respondents	Soap opera	Neither	Totals
Males	27	19	row 1 = 46
Females	17	9	row 2 = 26
Totals	Column 1 = 44	Column 3 = 28	Total = 72

Crime drama versus neither

Respondents	Crime drama	Neither	Totals
Males	14	19	row 1 = 33
Females	33	9	row 2 = 42
Totals	Column 2 = 47	Column 3 = 28	Total = 75

at the 5% level (two-tailed test). Thus if you have three comparisons to make, the minimum value of chi-square that is significant is 5.73. The degrees of freedom for these comparisons will always be 1 as they are always based on 2 × 2 contingency tables.

14.4 Important warnings

Chi-square is rather less user friendly than is warranted by its popularity among psychologists. The following are warning signs not to use chi-square or to take very great care:

1. If the expected frequencies in any cell fall lower than 5 then chi-square becomes rather inaccurate. Some authors suggest that no more than one-fifth of values should be below 5, but this is a more generous criterion. Some computers automatically print an alternative to chi-square if this assumption is breached.

2. Never do chi-square on percentages or anything other than frequencies.

3. Always check that your total of frequencies is equal to the number of participants in your research. Chi-square should not be applied where participants in the research are contributing more than one frequency each to the total of frequencies.

14.5 Alternatives to chi-square

The situation is only salvageable if your chi-square violates the expected cell frequencies rule – none should fall below 5. Even then you cannot always save the day. The alternatives are as follows:

Table 14.12	A 3 × 3 contingency table		
Sample	**Category 1**	**Category 2**	**Category 3**
Sample 1	10	6	14
Sample 2	3	12	4
Sample 3	4	2	5

1. If you have a 2 × 2 or a 2 × 3 chi-square table then you can use the Fisher exact probability test which is not sensitive to small expected frequencies (see Calculation 14.2 below).

2. Apart from omitting very small samples or categories, sometimes you can save the day by combining samples and/or categories in order to avoid the small expected frequencies problem; by combining in this way, you should increase the expected frequencies somewhat. So, for example, take the data set out in Table 14.12. It should be apparent that by combining two samples and/or two categories you are likely to increase the expected frequencies in the resulting chi-square table.

But you cannot simply combine categories or samples at a whim – the samples or categories have to be combined meaningfully. So, if the research was on the relationship between the type of degree that students take and their hobbies, you might have the following categories and samples:

category 1 – socialising

category 2 – dancing

category 3 – stamp collecting

sample 1 – English literature students

sample 2 – media studies students

sample 3 – physics students

Looking at these, it would seem reasonable to combine categories 1 and 2 and samples 1 and 2 since they seem to reflect rather similar things. No other combinations would seem appropriate. For example, it is hard to justify combining dancing and stamp collecting.

Calculation 14.2

The Fisher exact probability test

The Fisher exact probability test is not usually presented in introductory statistics books. We will only give the calculation of a 2 × 2 Fisher exact probability test although there is a version for 2 × 3 tables. The reason for its inclusion is that much student work for practicals and projects has very small sample sizes. As a consequence, the assumptions of the chi-square test are frequently broken. The Fisher exact probability test is not subject to the same limitations as the chi-square and can be used when chi-square cannot. It is different from chi-square in that it calculates the exact probability rather than a critical value. Apart from that, a significant result is interpreted much as the equivalent chi-square would be, so we will not explain it further.

A number followed by ! is called a factorial. So 5! = 5 × 4 × 3 × 2 × 1 = 120. And 9! = 9 × 8 × 7 × 6 × 5 × 4 × 3 × 2 × 1 = 362 880. Easy enough but it can lead to rather big numbers which make the calculation awkward to handle. Table 14.13 lists factorials up to 15.

The Fisher exact probability test is applied to a 2×2 contingency table by extending the table to include the marginal row and column totals of frequencies as well as the overall total (see Table 14.14).

The formula for the exact probability is as follows:

$$\text{exact probability} = \frac{W!X!Y!Z!}{N!a!b!c!d!}$$

Table 14.13	Factorials of numbers from 0 to 15
Number	**Factorial**
0	1
1	1
2	2
3	6
4	24
5	120
6	720
7	5 040
8	40 320
9	362 880
10	3 628 800
11	39 916 800
12	479 001 600
13	6 227 020 800
14	87 178 291 200
15	1 307 674 368 000

Table 14.14	Symbols for the Fisher exact probability		
	Column 1	**Column 2**	**Row totals**
Row 1	a	b	$W (= a + b)$
Row 2	c	d	$X (= c + d)$
Column totals	$Y (= a + c)$	$Z (= b + d)$	Overall total $= N$

Table 14.15	Steps in calculating the Fisher exact probability			
Respondents	**Photographic memory**	**No photographic memory**	**Row totals**	
Males	$a = 2$	$b = 7$	$W (= a + b) = 9$	
Females	$c = 4$	$d = 1$	$X (= c + d) = 5$	
Column totals	$Y (= a + c) = 6$	$Z (= b + d) = 8$	Overall total = 14	

Imagine you have collected data on a small group of exceptionally gifted children. You find that some have 'photographic' memories and others do not. You wish to know if there is a relationship between gender of subject and having a photographic memory (Table 14.15).

Substituting in the formula gives:

$$\text{exact probability} = \frac{9!5!6!8!}{14!2!7!4!1!}$$

The values of each of these factorials can be obtained from Table 14.13:

$$\text{exact probability} = \frac{362\ 880 \times 120 \times 720 \times 40\ 320}{87\ 178\ 291\ 200 \times 2 \times 5040 \times 24 \times 1}$$

Unfortunately you will need a scientific calculator to do this calculation.

The alternative is to cancel wherever possible numbers in the upper part of the formula with those in the lower part:

exact probability

$$= \frac{9 \times 8 \times 7 \times 6 \times 5 \times 4 \times 3 \times 2 \times 1 \times 5 \times 4 \times 3 \times 2 \times 1 \times 6 \times 5 \times 4 \times 3 \times 2 \times 1 \times 8 \times 7 \times 6 \times 5 \times 4 \times 3 \times 2 \times 1}{14 \times 13 \times 12 \times 11 \times 10 \times 9 \times 8 \times 7 \times 6 \times 5 \times 4 \times 3 \times 2 \times 1 \times 2 \times 1 \times 7 \times 6 \times 5 \times 4 \times 3 \times 2 \times 1 \times 4 \times 3 \times 2 \times 1 \times 1}$$

$$= \frac{5 \times 4 \times 3 \times 6 \times 5 \times 8}{14 \times 13 \times 12 \times 11 \times 10 \times 1} = \frac{14\ 440}{240\ 240} = 0.060$$

The value of 0.06 is the probability of getting exactly two males in the photographic memory condition. This then is not the end of the calculation. The calculation also ought to take into account the more extreme outcomes which are relevant to the hypothesis. Basically the Fisher exact probability calculation works out (for any pattern of column and row totals) the probability of getting the obtained data or data more extreme than our obtained data. Table 14.16 gives all of the possible versions of the table if the marginal totals in Table 14.15 are retained along with the probability of each pattern calculated using the above formula.

Notice that some patterns are not possible with our marginal totals. For example, one with 0 in the top left-hand cell. If 0 goes in that cell then we could only make the figures fit the marginal totals by using negative values. And that would be meaningless as one cannot have a negative case in a contingency table.

The calculation of significance levels is as follows:

1. One-tailed significance is simply the sum of the probability of the actual outcome (0.060) plus the probability of any possible outcome which has a more extreme outcome in the predicted direction. That is, in the present example, $0.060 + 0.003 = 0.063$. The precise number of values to be added will depend on a number of factors and will sometimes vary from our example according to circumstances.

Table 14.16	All of the possible patterns of data keeping the marginal row and column totals unchanged from Table 14.15

1	8
5	0

$p = 0.003*$

2	7
4	1

$p = 0.060*$
* The sum of the probabilities of these two tables is the one-tailed significance level.

3	6
3	1

$p = 0.280$

4	5
2	3

$p = 0.420$

5	4
1	4

$p = 0.210$

6	3
0	5

$p = 0.028**$
** The two-tailed probability level is the one-tailed probability calculated above plus the probability of this table. That is, the two-tailed probability is $0.063 + 0.028 = 0.091$.

2. Two-tailed significance is not accurately estimated by doubling the one-tailed probability for the simple reason that the distribution is not symmetrical. Instead, two-tailed significance is calculated by adding to the one-tailed probability (0.063) any probabilities at the other end of the distribution from the obtained distribution which are smaller than the probability of the obtained distribution. In our example, the probability of the distribution of data in Table 14.15 is 0.060. At the other end of the distribution, only one probability is equal or less than 0.060 – the final table has a probability of 0.028. We therefore add this 0.028 to the one-tailed probability of 0.063 to give a two-tailed probability of 0.091.

Our two-tailed probability value of 0.091 is *not* statistically significant at the conventional 5% level (neither would the one-tailed test if that were appropriate).

Interpreting the results The two-tailed significance level is 0.09 which is not statistically significant at the 0.05 (or 5%) level. Thus we cannot reject the null hypothesis that the incidence of photographic memory is related to gender. It would be useful to convert the frequencies in Table 14.15 into percentages of the relevant sample size when interpreting these data as we have different numbers of males and females. Such a table would show that 80% of the females had photographic memories but only 22% of the males. Despite this, with such a small amount of data, the trend is not statistically significant.

Reporting the results The following would be an appropriate description: 'Although photographic memory was nearly four times more common in females than in males, this proved not to be statistically significant using the Fisher exact probability test. The exact probability was 0.09 which is not significant at the 0.05 level. Thus we must reject the hypothesis that photographic memory is related to gender.'

Alternatively, following the recommendations of the APA (2010) Publication Manual we could write something like: 'Photographic memory was nearly four times more common in females than in males. However, the difference was not statistically significant, Fisher, $p = 0.091$. Thus we must reject the hypothesis that photographic memory is related to gender.' This style of presenting statistical significance is explained in detail in Chapter 16.

Table 14.17	Stages in the calculation of a 2 × 3 Fisher exact probability test			
	Column 1	**Column 2**	**Column 3**	**Row totals**
Row 1	a	b	c	$W (= a + b + c)$
Row 2	d	e	f	$X (= d + e + f)$
Column totals	$K (= a + d)$	$L (= b + e)$	$M (= c + f)$	Overall total = N

■ Fisher exact probability test for 2 × 3 tables

This is calculated in a very similar way as for the Fisher 2 × 2 test, the difference being simply the increased numbers of cells (Table 14.17). The formula for the 2 × 3 exact probability of the obtained outcome is as follows:

$$\text{exact probability} = \frac{W!X!K!L!M!}{N!a!b!c!d!e!f!}$$

The calculation needs to be extended to cover all of the more extreme outcomes just as with the 2 × 2 version. Nevertheless, this is a very cumbersome calculation and best avoided by hand if possible.

14.6 Chi-square and known populations

Sometimes, but rarely, in research we know the distribution in the population. If the population distribution of frequencies is known then it is possible to employ the single-sample chi-square. Usually the population frequencies are known as relative frequencies or percentages. So, for example, if you wished to know the likelihood of getting a sample of 40 university psychology students in which there are 30 female and 10 male students *if* you know that the population of psychology students is 90% female and 10% male, you simply use the latter proportions to calculate the expected frequencies of females and males in a sample of 40. If the sample were to reflect the population then 90% of the 40 should be female and 10% male. So the expected frequencies are 40 × 90/100 for females and 40 × 10/100 for males = 36 females and 4 males. These are then entered into the chi-square formula, but note that there are only two cells. The degrees of freedom for the one-sample chi-square is the number of cells minus 1 (i.e. 2 − 1 = 1).

Calculation 14.3

The one-sample chi-square

The research question is whether a sample of 80 babies of a certain age in foster care show the same level of smiling to their carer as a population of babies of the same age assessed on a developmental test. On this developmental test, 50% of babies at this age show clear evidence of the smiling response, 40% clearly show no evidence, and for 10% it is impossible to make a judgement. This is the population from which the foster babies are considered to be a sample. It is found that 35 clearly showed evidence of smiling, 40 showed no clear evidence of smiling and the remaining 5 were impossible to classify (Table 14.18).

We can use the population distribution to work out the expected frequency in the sample of 80 if this sample precisely matched the population. Thus 50% of the 80 (= 40) should be clear smilers, 40% of the 80 (= 32) should be clear non-smilers, and 10% of the 80 (= 8) should be impossible to classify. Table 14.18 gives the expected frequencies (i.e. population based) and observed frequencies (i.e. sample based).

These observed and expected frequencies are entered into the usual chi-square formula. The only difference is that the degrees of freedom are not quite the same – they are the number of conditions minus 1 (i.e. $3 - 1 = 2$ in the above example):

$$\text{chi-square} = \sum \frac{(O - E)^2}{E}$$

$$= \frac{(35 - 40)^2}{40} + \frac{(40 - 32)^2}{32} + \frac{(5 - 8)^2}{8}$$

$$= \frac{(-5)^2}{40} + \frac{8^2}{32} + \frac{(-3)^2}{8}$$

$$= \frac{25}{40} + \frac{64}{32} + \frac{9}{8}$$

$$= 0.625 + 2.000 + 1.125 = 3.75$$

But from Significance Table 14.1 we can see that this value of chi-square is far below the critical value of 6.0 required to be significant at the 5% level. Thus the sample of foster babies is not significantly different from the population of babies in terms of their smiling response.

Interpreting the results A significant value of the one-sample chi-square means that the distribution over the various categories departs markedly from that of the known population. That is, the sample is significantly different from the population and is unlikely to come from that population. In our example, however, the sample does not differ significantly from the population. This shows that smiling behaviour in our sample of babies is no different from that

Table 14.18	Data for a one-sample chi-square		
	Clear smilers	**Clear non-smilers**	**Impossible to classify**
Observed frequency	35	40	5
Expected frequency	40	32	8

→

of the population of babies. For the one-sample chi-square, it is sufficient to compare the observed frequencies with the expected frequencies (which are the population values). In our example, there seems to be little difference between the sample and the population values.

Reporting the results The following would summarise the findings of this study effectively: 'It was possible to compare smiling behaviour in babies in foster care with population values of known smiling behaviour on a standard developmental test. A one-sample chi-square test yielded a chi-square value of 3.75 which was not statistically significant with two degrees of freedom. Thus it can be concluded that the fostered babies were no different in terms of smiling behaviour from the general population of babies of this age.'

Alternatively, following the recommendations of the APA (2010) Publication Manual we could write: 'It was found that smiling behaviour in babies in foster care was not different from population figures obtained from a standard developmental test, $\chi^2(2, N = 80) = 3.75$, *p ns*. Thus it can be concluded that the fostered babies were no different in terms of smiling behaviour from the general population of babies of this age.' This style of reporting statistical significance is discussed in greater detail in Chapter 16.

14.7 Chi-square for related samples – the McNemar test

It is possible to use chi-square to compare *related* samples of frequencies. Essentially, this involves arranging the data in such a way that the chi-square contingency table only includes two categories: those that change from the first to the second occasion. For example, data are collected on whether or not teenage students wish to go to university; following a careers talk favouring university education the same informants are asked again whether they wish to go to university. The data can be tabulated as in Table 14.19.

We can see from this table that although some students did not change their minds as a consequence of the talk (30 wanted to go to university before the talk and did not change their minds, 32 did not want to go to university before the talk and did not change their minds), some students did change. Fifty changed their minds and wanted to go to university following the talk and 10 changed their minds and did not want to go to university after the talk.

The McNemar test simply uses the data on those who changed; non-changers are ignored. The logic of the test is that if the talk did not actually affect the teenagers, just as many would change their minds in one direction after the talk as change their minds in the other direction. That is, 50% should change towards wanting to go to university and 50% should change against wanting to go to university, *if the talk had no effect*. We simply create a new table (Table 14.20) which only includes changers and calculate chi-square on the basis that the null hypothesis of no effect would suggest that 50% of the changers should change in each direction.

The calculation is now exactly like that for the one-sample chi-square. This gives us a chi-square value of 25.35 with one degree of freedom (since there are two conditions).

Table 14.19	Illustrative data for the McNemar test	
	Before talk 'yes'	Before talk 'no'
After talk 'yes'	30	50
After talk 'no'	10	32

Table 14.20	Table of those who changed in a positive or negative direction based on Table 14.19	
	Positive changers	**Negative changers**
Observed frequency	50	10
Expected frequency	30	30

Table 14.21	Relationship between ethnicity and selection	
	Selected	**Not selected**
Ethnic minority	1	3
Ethnic majority	17	45
	Chi-square = 0.43; p = ns	

This is very significant when checked against the critical values in Significance Table 14.1. Thus there appears to be more change towards wanting to go to university following the careers talk than change towards not wanting to go to university.

14.8   Example from the literature

In a study of the selection of prison officers, Crighton and Towl (1994) found the relationship shown in Table 14.21 between the ethnicity of the candidate and whether or not they were selected during the recruitment process.

The interpretation of this table is that there is no significant relationship (p = ns) between selection and ethnicity. In other words, the table does not provide evidence of a selection bias in favour of white applicants, for example. While this is not an unreasonable conclusion based on the data if we ignore the small numbers of ethnic minority applicants, the statistical analysis itself is not appropriate. In particular, if you calculate the expected frequencies for the four cells you will find that 50% of the expected frequencies are less than 5, thus a rule has been violated. The Fisher exact probability test would be better for these data.

Key points

● Avoid as far as possible designing research with a multiplicity of categories and samples for chi-square. Large chi-squares with many cells are often difficult to interpret without numerous sub-analyses.

● Always make sure that your chi-square is carried out on frequencies and that each participant contributes only one to the total frequencies.

● Check for expected frequencies under 5; if you have any then take one of the escape routes described if possible.

COMPUTER ANALYSIS

The SPSS Statistics instruction book to this text is Dennis Howitt and Duncan Cramer (2011), *Introduction to SPSS Statistics in Psychology: For version 19 and earlier*, Harlow: Pearson. Chapters 16 (chi-square) and 17 (McNemar) in that book give detailed step-by-step procedures for the statistics described in this chapter together with advice on how to report the results. Figure 14.2 shows the SPSS Statistics steps for producing a chi-square.

Data
- Name the variables in Variable View of the Data Editor.
- Enter the data under the appropriate variable names in Data View of the Data Editor.

Analysis
- For a one-sample chi-square, select 'Analyze', 'Nonparametric Tests' and 'Chi-Square Test . . .'.

2
- Move category variable to right hand box and enter 'Expected Values' of frequencies for the categories of that variable.

3
- For a more than one-sample chi-square, select 'Analyze', 'Descriptive Statistics' and 'Crosstabs . . .'.

4
- Move appropriate variables to 'Row' and 'Column' box.

5
- Select 'Statistics . . .' and 'Chi-square'.
- Select 'Cells . . .' and 'Expected' and 'Unstandardized'.

6
- For a McNemar test, select 'Analyze', 'Nonparametric Tests' and '2-Related Samples . . .'.

7
- Move appropriate pair of variables to box to right and select 'McNemar'.

Output
- Check that the minimum expected frequencies have been met.
- Check that the test is statistically significant with $p = .05$ or less.

2
- Determine direction of significant difference.

FIGURE 14.2 SPSS Statistics steps for chi-square test

Recommended further reading

Maxwell, A.E. (1961), *Analysing Qualitative Data*, London: Methuen.

CHAPTER 15

Probability

Overview

- Although probability theory is at the heart of statistics, in practice the researcher needs to know relatively little of this.

- The addition rule basically suggests that the probability of, say, any of three categories occurring is the sum of the three individual probabilities for those categories.

- The multiplication rule suggests that the probability of different events occurring in a particular sequence is the product of the individual probabilities.

Preparation

General familiarity with previous chapters.

15.1 Introduction

From time to time, researchers need to be able to calculate the probabilities associated with certain patterns of events. One of us remembers being a student in a class that carried out an experiment based on newspaper reports of a Russian study in which people appeared to be able to recognise colours through their finger tips. So we designed an experiment in which a blind-folded person felt different colours in random order. Most of us did not do very well but some in the class seemed excellent. The media somehow heard about the study and a particularly good identifier in our experiment quickly took part in a live TV demonstration of her skills. She was appallingly bad at the task this time.

The reason why she was bad on television was that she had no special skills in the first place. It had been merely a matter of chance that she had done well in the laboratory. On the television programme, chance was not on her side and she turned out to be as bad as the rest of us. Actually, this reflects a commonly referred to phenomenon called *regression to the mean*. Choose a person (or group) because of their especially high (or, alternatively, especially low) scores and they will tend to score closer to the mean on the next administration of the test or measurement. This is because the test or measure is to a degree unreliable and by choosing exceptional scores you have to an extent capitalised on chance factors. With a completely unreliable test or measure, the reversion towards the mean will be dramatic. In our colour experiment the student did badly on TV because she had been selected totally on the basis of a criterion that was fundamentally unreliable – that is, completely at random.

Similar problems occur in any investigation of individual paranormal or psychic powers. For example, a spiritual medium who addresses a crowd of 500 people is doing nothing spectacular if in Britain she claims to be speaking to a dead relative of someone and that relative is Mary or Martha or Margaret. The chances of someone in the 500 having such a relative are very high.

15.2 The principles of probability

When any of us use a test of significance we are utilising probability theory. This is because most statistical tests are based on it. Our working knowledge of probability in most branches of psychology does not have to be very great for us to function well. We have been using probability in previous chapters on significance testing when we talked about the 5% level of significance, the 1% level of significance and the 95% confidence intervals. Basically what we meant by a 5% level of significance is that a particular event (or outcome) would occur on five occasions out of 100. Although we have adopted the percentage system of reporting probabilities in this book, statisticians would normally not write of a 5% probability. Instead they would express it as being out of a *single* event rather than 100 events. Thus:

- 0.05 (or just .05) is an alternative way of writing 5%

- 0.10 (or .10) is an alternative way of writing 10%

- 1.00 is an alternative way of writing 100%.

The difficulty for some of us with this alternative, more formal, way of writing probability is that it leaves everything in decimals, which does not appeal to the less mathematically skilled. However, you should be aware of the alternative notation since it appears in many research reports. Furthermore, much computer output can give probabilities to several decimal places which can be confusing. For example, what does a probability of 0.000 01 mean? The answer is one chance in 100 000 or a 0.001% probability $\left(\dfrac{1}{100\,000} \times 100 = 0.001\% \right)$.

There are two rules of probability with which psychologists ought to be familiar. They are the *addition rule* and the *multiplication rule*.

1. The *addition rule* is quite straightforward. It merely states that for a number of mutually exclusive outcomes the sum of their probabilities adds up to 1.00. So if you have a set of 150 people of whom 100 are women and 50 are men, the probability of picking a woman at random is 100/150 or 0.667. The probability of picking a man at random is 50/150 or 0.333. However, the probability of picking either a man or a woman at random is 0.667 + 0.333 or 1.00. In other words, it is certain that you will pick either a man or a woman. The assumption is that the categories or outcomes are mutually exclusive, meaning that a person cannot be in both the man and woman categories. Being a man excludes that person from also being a woman. In statistical probability theory, one of the two possible outcomes is usually denoted p and the other is denoted q, so $p + q = 1.00$. Outcomes that are not mutually exclusive include, for example, the categories man and young since a person could be a man and young.

2. The *multiplication rule* is about a set of events. It can be illustrated by our set of 150 men and women in which 100 are women and 50 are men. Again the assumption is that the categories or outcomes are mutually exclusive. We could ask how likely it is that the first five people that we pick at random will all be women, given that the probability of choosing a woman on a single occasion is 0.667. The answer is that we multiply the probability associated with the first person being a woman by the probability that the second person will be a woman by the probability that the third person will be a woman by the probability that the fourth person will be a woman by the probability that the fifth person will be a woman:

$$\text{Probability of all five being women} = p \times p \times p \times p \times p$$

$$= 0.667 \times 0.667 \times 0.667 \times 0.667 \times 0.667$$

$$= 0.13$$

Therefore there is a 13% probability (0.13) that we will choose a sample of five women at random. That is not a particularly rare outcome. However, picking a sample of all men from our set of men and women is much rarer:

$$\text{Probability of all five being men} = p \times p \times p \times p \times p$$

$$= 0.333 \times 0.333 \times 0.333 \times 0.333 \times 0.333$$

$$= 0.004$$

Therefore there is a 0.4% probability (0.004) of choosing all men.

The multiplication rule as stated here assumes that once a person is selected for inclusion in the sample, he or she is replaced in the population and possibly selected again. This is called random sampling with replacement. However, normally we do not do this in psychological research, though if the population is big then not replacing the individual back into the population has negligible influence on the outcome. Virtually all statistical analyses assume replacement, but it does not matter that people are usually not selected more than once for a study in psychological research.

15.3   Implications

Such theoretical considerations concerning probability theory have a number of implications for research. They ought to be carefully noted.

1. *Repeated significance testing within the same study* It is tempting to carry out several statistical tests on data. Usually we find that a portion of these tests are statistically significant at the 5% level whereas a number are not. Indeed, even if there were absolutely no trends in the population, we would expect, by chance, 5% of our comparisons to be significant at the 5% level. This is the meaning of statistical significance, after all. The more statistical comparisons we make on our data the more significant findings we would expect. If we did 20 comparisons we would expect one significant finding even if there are no trends in the population. In order to cope with this, the correct procedure is to make the statistical significance more stringent the more tests of significance we do. So, if we did two tests then our significance level per test should be 5%/2 or 2.5%; if we did four comparisons our significance level would be 5%/4 or 1.25% significance per test. In other words, we simply divide the 5% significance level by the number of tests we are doing. Although this is the proper thing to do, few psychological reports actually do it. However, the consequence of not doing this is to find more significant findings than you should.

2. *Significance testing across different studies* An application of the multiplication rule in assessing the value of replicating research shows the dramatic increase in significance that this can achieve. Replication means the essential repeating of a study at a later date and possibly in radically different circumstances such as other locations. Imagine that the significance level achieved in the original study is 5% ($p = 0.05$). If one finds the same significance level in the replication, the probability of two studies producing this level of significance by chance is $p \times p$ or $0.05 \times 0.05 = 0.0025$ or 0.25%. This considerably enhances our confidence that the findings of the research are not the result of chance factors but reflect significant trends.

Calculation 15.1

The addition rule

A psychologist wishes to calculate the chance expectations of marks on a multiple choice test of general knowledge. Since a person could get some answers correct simply by sticking a pin into the answer paper, there has to be a minimum score below which the individual is doing no better than chance. If each question has four response alternatives then one would expect that by chance a person could get one in four or one-quarter of the answers correct. That is intuitively obvious. But what if some questions have three alternative answers and others have four alternative answers? This is not quite so obvious, but we simply apply the law of addition and add together the probabilities of being correct for all of the questions on the paper. This entails adding together probabilities of 0.33 and 0.25 since there are three or four alternative answers. So if there are 10 questions with three alternative answers and five questions with four alternative answers, the number of answers correct by chance is $(10 \times 0.33) + (5 \times 0.25) = 3.3 + 1.25 = 4.55$.

Calculation 15.2

The multiplication rule

A psychologist studies a pair of male twins who have been brought up separately and who have never met. The psychologist is surprised to find that the twins are alike on seven out of ten different characteristics, as presented below. The probability of their characteristics occurring in the general population is given in brackets:

1. They both marry women younger than themselves (0.9).

2. They both marry brunettes (0.7).

3. They both drive (0.7).

4. They both swim (0.6).

5. They have both spent time in hospital (0.8).

6. They both take foreign holidays (0.5).

7. They both part their hair on the left (0.9).

However, they are different in the following ways:

8. One attends church (0.4) and the other does not.

9. One has a doctorate (0.03) and the other does not.

10. One smokes (0.3) and the other does not.

The similarities between the two men are impressive if it is exceptional for two randomly selected men to be similar on each of the items. The probabilities of each of the outcomes are presented in brackets above. These probabilities are the proportions of men in the general population demonstrating these characteristics. For many of the characteristics it seems quite likely that they will be similar. So two men taken at random from the general population are most likely to marry a younger woman. Since the probability of marrying a younger woman is 0.9, the probability of any two men marrying younger women is $0.9 \times 0.9 = 0.81$. The probability of two men taken at random both being drivers is $0.7 \times 0.7 = 0.49$. In fact the ten characteristics listed above are shared by randomly selected pairs of men with the following probabilities:

1. $0.9 \times 0.9 = 0.81$

2. $0.7 \times 0.7 = 0.49$

3. $0.7 \times 0.7 = 0.49$

4. $0.6 \times 0.6 = 0.36$

5. $0.8 \times 0.8 = 0.64$

6. $0.5 \times 0.5 = 0.25$

7. $0.9 \times 0.9 = 0.81$

8. $0.4 \times 0.4 = 0.16$

9. $0.03 \times 0.03 = 0.0009$

10. $0.3 \times 0.3 = 0.09$

The sum of these probabilities is 4.10. Clearly the pair of twins are more alike than we might expect on the basis of chance. However, it might be that we would get a different answer if instead of taking the general population of men, we took men of the same age as the twins.

Key points

- Although probability theory is of crucial importance for mathematical statisticians, psychologists generally rely on an intuitive approach to the topic. This may be laziness on their part, but we have kept the coverage of probability to a minimum given the scope of this book. It can also be very deterring to anyone not too mathematically inclined. If you need to know more, especially if you need to estimate precisely the likelihood of a particular pattern or sequence of events occurring, we suggest that you consult books such as Kerlinger (1986) for more complete accounts of mathematical probability theory.

- However, it is important to avoid basic mistakes such as repeated significance testing on the same data without adjusting your significance levels to allow for the multitude of tests. This is not necessary for tests designed for multiple testing such as those for the analysis of variance, some of which we discuss later (Chapter 23), as the adjustment is built in.

CHAPTER 16

Reporting significance levels succinctly

Overview

- A glance at reports in psychology journals suggests that relatively little space is devoted to reporting the outcomes of statistical analysis.

- Usually, authors report their findings using very succinct methods which occupy very little space.

- Normally the test statistic, the sample size (or degrees of freedom), significance level and if it is a one-tailed test are reported.

- It is recommended that students adopt this succinct style of reporting for their research as it will result in a more professional-looking product.

Preparation

You need to know about testing significance, from Chapter 11 onwards.

16.1   Introduction

So far, the reporting of statistical significance in this book has been a relatively clumsy and long-winded affair. In contrast, a glance at any psychology journal will suggest that precious little space is devoted to reporting significance. Detailed expositions of the statistical significance of your analyses have no place in professional reports. Researchers can make life much simpler for themselves by adopting the standard style of reporting statistical significance. Clarity is one great benefit; another is the loss of wordiness.

Although the standard approach to reporting statistical significance does vary slightly, there is little difficulty with this. At a minimum, the following should be mentioned when reporting statistical significance:

1. The statistical distribution used (e.g. F, chi-square, r, z, t, etc.).

2. The degrees of freedom (df). Alternatively, for some statistical techniques you may report the sample size (N).

3. The value of the calculation (e.g. the value of your z-score or your chi-square).

4. The probability or significance level. Sometimes 'not significant', 'not sig.' or 'ns' is used.

5. If you have a one-tailed hypothesis then this should be also mentioned. Otherwise a two-tailed hypothesis is assumed. You can also state that you are using a two-tailed test. This is most useful when you have several analyses and some are one-tailed and others are two-tailed.

16.2   Shortened forms

In research reports, comments such as the following are to be found:

- The hypothesis that drunks slur their words was supported ($t = 2.88$, degrees of freedom = 97, $p < 0.01$).

- There was a trend for drunks to slur their words more than sober people ($t = 2.88$, df = 97, significance = 1%).

- The null hypothesis that drunks do not slur their words more than sober people was rejected ($t = 2.88$, degrees of freedom = 97, $p = 0.01$).

- The analysis supported the hypothesis since drunks tended to slur their words the most often (t (97) = 2.88, $p = 0.01$, two-tailed test).

- The hypothesis that drunks slur their words was accepted (t (97) = 2.88, $p = 0.005$, 1-tail).

All of the above say more or less the same thing. The symbol t indicates that the t-test was used. The symbol < indicates that your probability level is smaller than the given value. Thus $p < 0.01$ could mean that the probability is, say, 0.008 or 0.005. That is, the test is statistically significant at better than the reported level of 0.01. Sometimes, the degrees of freedom are put in brackets after the symbol for the statistical test used, as in t (97) = 2.88. In all of the above examples, the hypothesis was supported and the null hypothesis rejected.

The following are examples of what might be written if the hypothesis was not supported by your data:

- The hypothesis that drunks slur their words was rejected ($t = 0.56$, degrees of freedom = 97, $p > 0.05$).

- Drunks and sober people did not differ in their average rates of slurring their speech ($t = 0.56$, df = 97, not significant).

- The hypothesis that drunks slur their words was rejected in favour of the null hypothesis ($t = 0.56$, df = 97, $p > 0.05$, not significant).

The last three statements mean much the same. The symbol > means that your probability is greater than the listed value. It is used to indicate that your calculation is not statistically significant at the stated level.

Notice throughout this chapter that the reported significance levels are not standardised on the 5% level of significance. It is possible, especially with computers, to obtain much more exact values of probability than the critical values used in tables of significance. While there is nothing at all technically wrong with using the more precise values if you have them to hand, there is one objection. Statistical significance can become a holy grail in statistics, supporting the view 'the smaller the probability the better'. Although significance is important, the size of the trends in your data is even more crucial. A significant result with a strong trend is the ideal which is not obtained simply by exploring the minutiae of probability.

One thing causes a lot of confusion in the significance levels given by computers. Sometimes values like $p < 0.0000$ are listed. All that this means is that the probability level for the statistical test is less than 0.0001. In other words, the significance level might be, say, 0.000 03 or 0.000 000 4. These are very significant findings, statistically speaking. We would recommend that you report them slightly differently in your writings. Values such as 0.0001 or 0.001 are clearer to some readers. So change your final 0 in the string of zeros to 1.

16.3 Examples from the published literature

■ Example 1

> . . . a post hoc comparison was carried out between means of the adult molesters' and adult control groups' ratings using Student's t-test. A significant (t (49) = 2.96, $p < 0.001$) difference was found between the two groups.
>
> (Johnston and Johnston, 1986, p. 643)

The above excerpt is fairly typical of the ways in which psychologists summarise the results of their research. To the practised eye, it is not too difficult to decipher. However, some difficulties can be caused to the novice statistician. A little patience at first will help a lot. The extract contains the following major pieces of information:

1. The statistical test used was the t-test. The authors mention it by name, but it is also identified by the t mentioned in the brackets. However, the phrase 'Student's t-test' might be confusing. Student was the pen-name of a researcher at the Guinness Brewery who invented the t-test. It is quite redundant nowadays – the name Student, not Guinness!

2. The degrees of freedom are the (49) contained in the brackets. If you check the original paper you will find that the combined sample size is 51. It should be obvious, then, that this is an unrelated or uncorrelated t-test since the degrees of freedom are clearly $N - 2$ in this case.

3. The value of the *t*-test is 2.96.

4. The difference between the two groups is statistically significant at the 0.001 or 0.1% level of probability. This is shown by $p < 0.001$ in the above excerpt.

5. *Post hoc* merely means that the researchers decided to do the test after the data had been collected. They had not planned it prior to collecting the data.

6. No mention is made of whether this is a one-tailed or a two-tailed test so we would assume that it is a two-tailed significance level.

Obviously, there are a variety of ways of writing up the findings of any analysis. The following is a different way of saying much the same thing:

. . . a post hoc comparison between the means of the adult molesters' and adult control groups' ratings was significant ($t = 2.96$, df = 49, $p < 0.001$).

■ Example 2

The relationship of gender of perpetrators and victims was examined. Perpetrators of female victims were more often male (13 900 of 24 947, 55.8%) while perpetrators of males were more often female (10 977 of 21 373, 51.4%, χ^2 (1) = 235.18, $p < 0.001$).

(Rosenthal, 1988, p. 267)

The interpretation of this is as follows:

1. The chi-square test was used. χ is the Greek symbol for chi, so chi-square can be written as χ^2.

2. The value of chi-square is 235.18.

3. It is statistically very significant as the probability level is less than 0.001 or less than 0.1%.

4. Chi-square is usually regarded as a directionless test. That is, the significance level reported is for a two-tailed test unless stated otherwise.

5. Although the significance level in this study seems impressive, just look at the sample sizes involved – over 46 000 children in total. The actual trends are relatively small – 55.8% versus 51.4%. This is a good example of when not to get excited about statistically significant findings.

An alternative way of saying much the same thing is:

Female victims were offended against by males in 55.8% of cases ($N = 24$ 947). For male victims, 51.4% of offenders were female ($N = 21$ 373). Thus victims were more likely to be offended against by a member of the opposite sex (chi-square = 235.18, degrees of freedom = 1, $p < 0.1\%$).

■ Example 3

A 2×2 analysis of variance (ANOVA) with anger and sex of target as factors was conducted on the BP2 (after anger manipulation) scores. This analysis yielded a significant effect for anger, F (1, 116) = 43.76, $p < 0.004$, with angered subjects revealing a larger increase in arousal ($M = 6.01$) than the nonangered subjects ($M = 0.01$).

(Donnerstein, 1980, p. 273)

This should be readily deciphered as:

1. A two-way analysis of variance with two different levels of each independent variable. One of the independent variables is anger (angered and non-angered conditions are the categories). The other independent variable is the gender of the target of aggression. Something called BP2 (whatever that may be – it turns out to be blood pressure) is the dependent variable. (We cover two-way analysis of variance in Chapter 22.)

2. The mean BP2 score for the angered condition was 6.01 and the mean for the non-angered condition was 0.01. The author is using M as the symbol of the sample mean.

3. The test of significance is the F-ratio test. We know this because this is an analysis of variance but also because the statistic is stated to be F.

4. The value of F, the variance ratio, equals 43.76.

5. There are 1 and 116 degrees of freedom for the F-ratio for the main effect of the variable anger. The 1 degree of freedom is because there are two different levels of the variable anger (df $= c - 1$ or the number of groups of data minus one). The 116 degrees of freedom means that there must have been 120 participants in the experiment. The degrees of freedom for a main effect is N – number of cells $= 120 - (2 \times 2) = 120 - 4 = 116$. All of this is clarified in Chapter 22.

6. The difference between the angered and non-angered conditions is statistically significant at the 0.4% level.

A slightly different style of describing these findings is:

Blood pressure following the anger manipulation was included as the dependent variable on a 2×2 analysis of variance. The two independent variables were gender of the target of aggression and anger. There was a significant main effect for anger ($F = 43.76$, df $= 1, 116$, $p < 0.4\%$). The greater mean increase in blood pressure was for the angered group (6.01) compared to the non-angered group (0.01).

Box 16.1   Focus on

APA (2010) Publication Manual recommended practice of reporting statistical significance

The American Psychological Association produces a Publication Manual which sets out the ways in which manuscripts should be typed to be considered for publication in the journals that they publish. The latest publication manual is the sixth edition and was published in 2010. The recommendations of this guide are also used by the British Psychological Society for manuscripts to be submitted to the journals that they publish. The recommendations for reporting statistics seem to be relatively straightforward. Some of the main ones are listed below.

- Decimals should generally be reported to no more two decimal places.

- One exception to this are probability values which may be reported to three decimal places.

→

- Probability values of less than .001 should be reported as < .001.

- Leading zeroes (i.e. zeroes before the decimal point) should not be used for numbers which cannot be more than 1.00 such as correlation coefficients. For example, correlations should not be reported with a leading zero such as 0.67.

- It is preferable to report the exact significance level to three decimal places as given by statistics software such as SPSS Statistics. For example, it is more informative to report $p = .343$ than $p > .05$ or p *ns*.

- Means (M), standard deviations (SD) and confidence intervals (95% CI) when reported within sentences should be appropriately abbreviated and reported within round brackets. The value of the lower limit should be followed by a comma and the value of the upper limit. Both values should be placed within square brackets. For example, we could write 'Post-test

depression was lower in the treated ($M = 3.52$, $SD = 1.09$, 95% CI [3.42, 3.62]) than in the untreated group ($M = 5.39$, $SD = 2.13$, 95% CI [5.20, 5.68]).' Confidence intervals are discussed in Chapter 37.

- Details of the results of the inferential test are placed after a comma and are not bracketed. Bracketing is reserved for the degrees of freedom. The appropriate letter of the statistical test is given first (e.g. t, χ^2) followed by the degrees of freedom in brackets, an = sign, the value of the statistical test to two decimal places, a comma, p, an = sign and the probability level to three decimal places or a < sign and .001.

- Effect sizes should be reported if these are readily available and you are familiar with them. They are discussed in Chapter 35.

When reporting your results in this style, it is worth checking out a recent paper published by the APA on this topic.

Key points

- Remember that the important pieces of information to report are:

  - the symbol for the statistic (t, T, r, etc.)

  - the value of the statistic for your analysis – two decimal places are enough

  - an indication of the degrees of freedom or the sample size involved (df = . . . , N = . . .)

  - the probability or significance level

  - whether a one-tailed test was used.

- Sometimes you will see symbols for statistical techniques that you have never heard of. Do not panic since it is usually possible to work out the sense of what is going on. Certainly if you have details of the sort described in this chapter, you know that a test of significance is involved.

- Using the approaches described in this chapter creates a good impression and ensures that you include pertinent information. However, standardise on one of the variants in your report. Eventually if you submit papers to a journal for consideration, you should check out that journal's method of reporting significance.

- Some statistical tests are regarded as being directionless. That is, their use always implies a two-tailed test. This is true of chi-square and the analysis of variance. These tests can only be one-tailed if the degrees of freedom equal one. Otherwise, the test is two-tailed. Even when the degrees of freedom equal one, only use a one-tailed test if you are satisfied that you have reached the basic requirements of one-tailed testing (see Chapter 17).

COMPUTER ANALYSIS

Modern statistical packages almost invariably provide precise significance levels in their output. However, traditionally the 0.05 (5%) and 0.01 (1%) levels of significance were the main ones reported. There are advantages in just the two levels as these provide a relatively simple choice. Exact levels of significance can cause some confusion when they are given as, say, the 0.000 level of significance. This is correct and is a significance level of less than 0.0005 rounded to three decimal places. The exact levels of significance can have their uses when trying to calculate the correct levels of significance of multiple statistical tests (e.g. Chapter 23).

The SPSS Statistics instruction book to this text is Dennis Howitt and Duncan Cramer (2011), *Introduction to SPSS Statistics in Psychology: For version 19 and earlier*, Harlow: Pearson. This book gives detailed step-by-step procedures for the statistics described in this chapter including significance levels. It also provides examples on how to report the results.

CHAPTER 17

One-tailed versus two-tailed significance testing

Overview

- Hypotheses which do not or cannot stipulate the direction of the relationship between variables are called *non-directional*. So far we have only dealt with non-directional tests of hypotheses. These are also known as two-tailed tests.

- Some hypotheses stipulate the direction of the relationship between the variables – either a positive relation or a negative relation. These are known as directional hypotheses. They are also known as one-tailed tests.

- Directional tests for any given data result in more significant findings than non-directional tests when applied to the same data.

- However, there are considerable restrictions on when directional tests are allowable. Without very carefully planning, it is wise to deal with one's data as if it were non-directional. Most student research is likely to fail to meet the requirements of one-tail testing.

Preparation

Revise the null hypothesis and alternative hypothesis (Chapter 10) and significance testing.

17.1   Introduction

Sometimes researchers are so confident about the likely outcome of their research that they make pretty strong predictions about the relationship between their independent and dependent variables. So, for example, rather than say that the *independent variable* age is correlated with verbal ability, the researcher predicts that the *independent variable* age is *positively* correlated with the *dependent variable* verbal ability. In other words, it is predicted that the older participants in the research will have better verbal skills. Equally the researcher might predict a *negative* relationship between the independent and dependent variables.

It is conventional in psychological statistics to treat such *directional* predictions differently from *non-directional* predictions. Normally psychologists speak of a directional prediction being one-tailed whereas a non-directional prediction is two-tailed. The crucial point is that if you have a directional prediction (one-tailed test) the critical values of the significance test become slightly different.

In order to carry out a one-tailed test you need to be satisfied that you have met the criteria for one-tailed testing. These, as we will see, are rather stringent. In our experience, many one-tailed hypotheses put forward by students are little more than hunches and certainly not based on the required strong past research or strong theory. In these circumstances it is unwise and wrong to carry out one-tailed testing. It would be best to regard the alternative hypothesis as non-directional and choose two-tailed significance testing exactly as we have done so far in this book. One-tailed testing is a contentious issue and you may be confronted with different points of view; some authorities reject it although it is fairly commonplace in psychological research.

17.2   Theoretical considerations

If we take a directional alternative hypothesis (such as that intelligence correlates positively with level of education) then it is necessary to revise our understanding of the null hypothesis somewhat. (The same is true if the directional alternative hypothesis suggests a negative relationship between the two variables.) In the case of the positively worded alternative hypothesis, the null hypothesis is:

Intelligence does not correlate *positively* with level of education.

Our previous style of null hypothesis would have left out the word *positively*. There are two different circumstances which support the null hypothesis that intelligence does not correlate *positively* with level of education:

If intelligence *does not correlate* at all with level of education, *or*

If intelligence correlates *negatively* with level of education.

That is, it is only research which shows a *positive* correlation between intelligence and education which supports the directional hypothesis – if we found an extreme negative correlation between intelligence and education this would lead to the rejection of the alternative hypothesis just as would zero or near-zero relationships. Because, in a sense, the dice is loaded against the directional alternative hypothesis, it is conventional to argue that we should not use the extremes of the sampling distribution in both directions

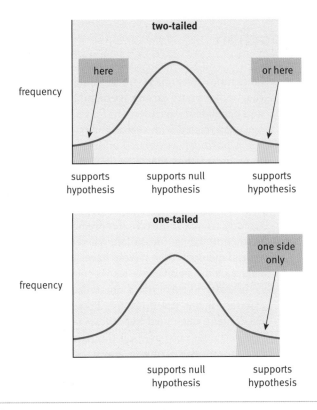

FIGURE 17.1   Areas of statistical significance for two-tailed and one-tailed tests

for our test of significance for the directional hypothesis. Instead we should take the extreme samples in the positive direction (if it is positively worded) or the extreme samples in the negative direction (if it is negatively worded). In other words, our extreme 5% of samples which we define as significant should all be from one side of the sampling distribution, not 2.5% on each side as we would have done previously (see Figure 17.1).

Because the 5% of extreme samples, which are defined as significant, are all on the same side of the distribution, you need a smaller value of your significance test to be in that extreme 5%. Part of the attraction of directional or one-tailed significance tests of this sort is that basically you can get the same level of significance with a smaller sample or smaller trend than would be required for a two-tailed test. Essentially the probability level can be halved – what would be significant at the 5% level with a two-tailed test is significant at the 2.5% level with a one-tailed test.

There is a big proviso to this. If you predicted a positive relationship but found what would normally be a significant negative relationship, with a one-tailed test you ought to ignore that negative relationship – it merely supports the null hypothesis. The temptation is, however, to ignore your original directional alternative hypothesis and pretend that you had not predicted the direction. Given that significant results are at a premium in psychology and are much more likely to get published, it is not surprising that psychologists seeking to publish their research might be tempted to 'adjust' their hypotheses slightly.

It is noteworthy that the research literature contains very few tests of significance of directional hypotheses which are rejected when the trend in the data is strongly (and significantly with a two-tailed test) in the opposite direction to that predicted. The only example we know of was written by one of us. Figure 17.2 gives the key steps to consider in understanding one- and two-tailed significance testing.

Two-tailed significance testing is the failsafe option for most research. A difference or trend in either direction is tested in this case.

One-tailed testing is employed if there are STRONG theoretical and empirical reasons (based on previous research) for expecting the trend to be in a particular direction.

The problem is that these strong reasons rarely apply. Strong theoretical justifications are hard to find and the research literature tends to demonstrate inconsistent findings.

Unfortunately, if the findings go in the opposite direction then the researcher should reject the hypothesis and is not justified in proceeding to a two-tail test instead.

One-tail testing allows the researcher to obtain significant results with smaller sample sizes.

It is insufficient to simply offer a directional hypothesis since this, for example, could be based on guesswork rather than a convincing and rational argument.

Two-tailed testing is the conservative approach and is recommended for all student research.

It is wrong to inspect the data before deciding whether to carry out a one- or two-tailed significance test.

Quite simply, the requirements for one-tail significance testing are very difficult to meet routinely in student research, in particular.

FIGURE 17.2   Conceptual steps for understanding one-tailed and two-tailed significance testing

17.3   Further requirements

There are a number of other rules which are supposed to be followed if one is to use a directional hypothesis. These include:

1. The prediction is based on strong and well-researched theory and not on a whim or intuition.

2. The prediction is based on previous similar research demonstrating consistent trends in the predicted direction.

3. One should make the above predictions in advance of any information about the trends in the data about which the prediction is to be made. That is, for example, you do not look at your scattergrams and then predict the direction of the correlation between your variables. That would be manifestly cheating but a 'good' way otherwise of getting significant results with a one-tailed test when they would not quite reach significance with a two-tailed test.

There is another practical problem in the use of directional hypotheses. That is, if you have *more than two groups* of scores it is often very difficult to decide what the predicting trends between the groups would be. For this reason, many statistical techniques are commonly regarded as directionless when you have more than two groups of scores or subjects. This applies to techniques such as chi-square, the analysis of variance and other related tests.

Although this is clearly a controversial area, you will probably find that as a student you rarely if ever have sufficient justification for employing a one-tailed test. As you might have gathered, most of these criteria for selecting a one-tailed test are to a degree subjective which makes the use of one-tailed tests less objective than might be expected. We would recommend that you choose a two-tailed or directionless test unless there is a pressing and convincing reason to do otherwise. Otherwise the danger of loading things in favour of significant results is too great.

In addition to two-tailed critical values, the significance tables in the appendices give the one-tailed values where these are appropriate.

Key points

- Routinely make your alternative hypotheses two-tailed or directionless. This is especially the case when the implications of your research are of practical or policy significance. However, this may not be ideal if you are testing theoretical predictions when the direction of the hypothesis might be important. Nevertheless, it is a moot point whether you should take advantage of the 'less stringent' significance requirements of a one-tailed test.

- If you believe that the well-established theoretical or empirical basis for predicting the direction of the outcomes is strong enough, then still be a little cautious about employing one-tailed tests. In particular, do not formulate your hypothesis *after* collecting or viewing your data.

- You cannot be faulted for using two-tailed tests since they are less likely to show significant relationships. Thus they are described as being statistically more conservative. Student research often does not arise out of previous research or theory. Often the research is initiated before earlier research and theory have been reviewed. In these circumstances one-tailed tests are not warranted.

CHAPTER 18

Ranking tests

Nonparametric statistics

Overview

- There are many statistical techniques which are not based on the notion of the normal curve.

- Some data violate the assumption of normality which underlies many of the statistical tests in this book. However, violations rarely have much impact on the outcome of a statistical analysis.

- Nonparametric and distribution-free statistics are often helpful where one's data violate the assumptions of other tests too much.

- For each of the tests discussed in the earlier chapters of this book, a nonparametric or distribution-free alternative is appropriate.

- Unfortunately, in many cases there is no satisfactory alternative to the parametric tests.

Preparation

Be aware of the *t*-tests for related and unrelated samples. Revise ranking (Chapter 7).

18.1   Introduction

From time to time, any researcher will be faced with the distinction between parametric and nonparametric significance tests. The difference is quite straightforward. Many statistical techniques require that the details are known or estimates can be made of the characteristics of the population. These are known as *parametric* tests (a parameter is a characteristic of a population). Almost invariably, as we have seen, the population is the population defined by the null hypothesis. Generally speaking, the numerical scores we used had to roughly approximate to the normal (bell-shaped) distribution in order for our decisions to be precise. The reason for this is that the statistician's theoretical assumptions, when developing the test, included the normal distribution of the data. It is widely accepted that the assumption of a bell-shaped or normal distribution of scores is a very broad criterion and that the distribution of scores on a variable would have to be very lopsided (skewed) in order for the outcomes to be seriously out of line. Appendix A explains how to test for such skewness.

But what if assumptions such as that of symmetry are so badly violated that the use of the test seems somewhat unacceptable? One traditional alternative approach is called *nonparametric* testing because it makes few or no assumptions about the distribution in the population. Many nonparametric tests of significance are based on rankings given to the original numerical scores – it is unusual for researchers to collect their data in the form of ranks in the first place.

Conventionally these tests for ranks are regarded as relatively easy computations for students – this is part of their appeal. Up to a point this can be true, but the difficulties are as follows:

1. They become disproportionately cumbersome with increasing amounts of data.

2. They also suffer from the difficulty that many psychological data are gathered using rather restricted ranges of scores. This often results in the same values appearing several times in a set of data. The tests based on ranks also become cumbersome with increased tied scores and, consequently, somewhat inaccurate.

3. Worst of all, the variety and flexibility of these nonparametric statistical techniques are nowhere as great as for parametric statistics. For this reason it is generally best to err towards using parametric statistics in our opinion. Certainly current research practice seems to increasingly disfavour nonparametric statistics.

Figure 18.1 gives some of the key steps in deciding to use non-parametric statistics.

18.2   Theoretical considerations

Ranking merely involves the ordering of a set of scores from the smallest to the largest. The smallest score is given the rank 1, the second smallest score is given the rank 2, the 50th smallest score is given the rank 50 and so on.

Since many nonparametric statistical techniques use ranks, the question is raised why this is so. The answer is very much the same as the reason for using the normal distribution as the basis for parametric statistics – it provides a standard distribution of scores with standard characteristics. It is much the same for the tests based on ranks. Although there are incalculable varieties in samples of data, for any given number of scores the ranks are always the same. So the ranks of 10 scores which represent the IQs of the 10 greatest

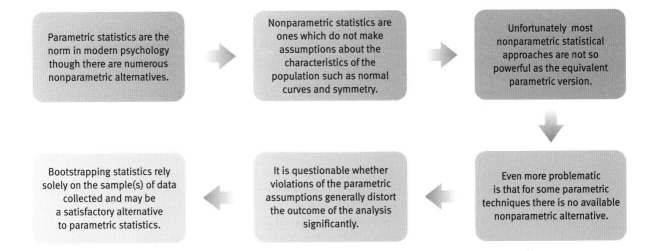

FIGURE 18.1   Conceptual steps for understanding nonparametric statistics

geniuses of all time are exactly the same as the ranks for the scores on introversion of the 10 members of the local stamp collectors' club: 1, 2, 3, 4, 5, 6, 7, 8, 9 and 10.

Since all sets of 10 scores use exactly the same set of ranks, this considerably eases the statistician's calculations of the distribution of the ranks under the null hypothesis that there is no relationship between pairs of variables. Instead of an infinite variety of 10 scores, there is just this one set of 10 ranks on which to do one's calculations. Only sample size makes a difference to the ranks, not the precise numerical values of the scores themselves.

The other advantage, of course, is that it uses ideas which can be seen as fairly common-sensical and more intuitive.

Box 18.1   Key concepts

Bootstrapping

Probably the history of statistics in psychology would have been somewhat different if computers had been available earlier. Many of the statistical techniques which modern psychologists routinely compute using powerful computer programs are actually quite elderly and, in some ways, creak a little when used in this digital age. In particular, the various standard statistical distributions such as the t-distribution and the F-distribution which are used in statistics were particularly important because they enabled calculations to be carried out relatively easily, even before electronic calculators had been invented. But could things have been different if computers had been available to the early statisticians?

Bootstrapping refers to a number of techniques which do not assume a particular shape or distribution to the population, as does the t-test for example which basically assumes that the data are normally distributed. Instead it simply assumes that a sample or samples of scores represents what is going on in the population. In other words, the population simply has the characteristics of the sample(s). So if the distribution of scores in a sample is 6, 8, 9, 9, 11, 12, 13 then it is assumed that the population is exactly the same. Wait a minute, you might be saying, just how does this help? We cannot work out a sampling distribution of samples of seven scores if we only have seven scores. There is only one sample of seven possible from seven scores. This is quite right. The 'trick' in bootstrapping is to take these seven scores and reproduce them, say, a thousand times, so that instead of seven scores we have 7,000 scores. There is nothing in this bootstrapped 'population' that was not in the sample – everything is just reproduced many times.

Now it is possible to work out a sampling distribution of samples of seven taken from this bootstrapped population. Actually, literally hundreds if not thousands of samples are drawn and the distribution, say, of their means can be plotted. So it is possible to work out the likelihood of getting a particular sample mean given this bootstrapped sampling distribution. This is number crunching with a vengeance but the sort of work that computers are excellent at doing. The good news is that it is no longer necessary to do the bootstrapping calculations yourself since SPSS Statistics does bootstrapping as part of some of the statistical routines that it carries out – for example, the *t*-test. Where it is available, bootstrapping only requires the minimum effort of selecting the bootstrapping option.

Bootstrapping is capable of calculating things which are not easily calculated by traditional means – for example, it can work out the standard deviation of the median and any number of other statistics. From the point of view of the present chapter on nonparametric statistics, bootstrapping does not make assumptions about the data of the sort that parametric statistical tests do. Consequently, it can be seen as a powerful alternative to parametric testing but based on the same routines as the parametric test.

18.3 Nonparametric statistical tests

There is an extensive battery of nonparametric tests, although many are interchangeable with each other or rather obscure with very limited applications. In this chapter we will consider only a small number of tests which you may come across during your university courses or general reading. We have discussed chi-square (for frequencies) and Spearman's rho (for correlations) elsewhere in this book. The nonparametric tests discussed in this chapter are usually applicable in very much the same experimental designs as the parametric tests we have discussed elsewhere (see Table 18.1).

■ Tests for related samples

Two nonparametric tests are common in the literature – the sign test (which is not based on ranks) and the Wilcoxon matched pairs test (which is based on ranks). Because they would apply to data for the related *t*-test, we will use the data for the worked example in Chapter 12 to illustrate the application of both of these tests.

Table 18.1	Similar parametric and nonparametric tests	
Parametric test		**Nonparametric equivalent**
Related *t*-test		Wilcoxon matched pairs test
		Sign test
Unrelated *t*-test		Mann–Whitney *U*-test
One-way ANOVA		Kruskal-Wallis Test (Appendix B2)
Related ANOVA		Friedman Test (Appendix B2)

Calculation 18.1

The sign test

The sign test is like the related *t*-test in that it takes the differences between the two related samples of scores. However, instead of considering the *size* of the difference, the sign test merely uses the *sign* of the difference. In other words, it loses a lot of the information inherent in the size of the difference.

Step 1 Delete from the analysis any case which has identical scores for both variables. They are ignored in the sign test. Take the second group of scores away from the first group (Table 18.2). Remember to include the sign of the difference (+ or −).

Table 18.2	Steps in the calculation of the sign test		
Subject	**Six months** X_1	**Nine months** X_2	**Difference** $D = X_1 - X_2$
Baby Clara	3	7	−4
Baby Martin	5	6	−1
Baby Sally	5	3	+2
Baby Angie	4	8	−4
Baby Trevor	3	5	−2
Baby Sam	7	9	−2
Baby Bobby	8	7	+1
Baby Sid	7	9	−2

Step 2 Count the *number* of scores which are positively signed and then count the *number* of scores which are negatively signed. (Don't forget that zero differences are ignored in the sign test.)

Step 3 Take whichever is the smaller number – the number of positive signs or the number of negative signs.

Step 4 Look up the significance of this smaller number in Significance Table 18.1. You need to find the row which contains the *sum* of the positive and negative signs (i.e. ignoring zero differences). Your value has to be in the tabulated range to be statistically significant.

In our example, there are 6 negative and 2 positive signs; 2 is the smaller number. The sum of positive and negative signs is 8. Significance Table 18.1 gives the significant values of the smaller number of signs as 0 only. Therefore our value is not statistically unusual and we accept the null hypothesis.

It would be a good approximation to use the one-sample chi-square formula (Calculation 14.3), given that you would expect equal numbers of positive and negative differences under the null hypothesis that 'the two samples do not differ'. That is, the distributions of the sign test and the McNemar test (Section 14.7) for the significance of changes are the same.

Significance Table 18.1	5% significance values for the sign test giving values of T (the smaller of the sums of signs) (two-tailed test). An extended table is given in Appendix G

Number of pairs of scores (ignoring any tied pairs)	Significant at 5% level Accept hypothesis
6–8	0 only
9–11	0 to 1
12–14	0 to 2
15–16	0 to 3
17–19	0 to 4
20–22	0 to 5
23–24	0 to 6
25	0 to 7
26–28	0 to 8
29–30	0 to 9
31–33	0 to 10
34–35	0 to 11
36–38	0 to 12
39–40	0 to 13
41–42	0 to 14
43–45	0 to 15
46–47	0 to 16
48–49	0 to 17
50	0 to 18

Your value must be in the listed ranges for your sample size to be significant at the 5% level (i.e. to accept the hypothesis).

Interpreting the results The mean scores for eye contact at six months and nine months need to be checked in order to know what the trend is in the data. Although eye contact was greater at nine months, the sign test is not significant which means that we should accept the null hypothesis of no differences in eye contact at the two ages.

Reporting the results The following could be written: 'Eye contact was higher at nine months ($\bar{X} = 6.75$) than at six months ($\bar{X} = 5.25$). However, this difference was insufficient to cause us to reject the null hypothesis that the amount of eye contact is the same at six months and nine months of age (sign test, $n = 8$, p *ns*).'

Alternatively, following the APA (2010) Publication Manual recommendations, we could rewrite these results as follows: 'Eye contact was higher at nine months ($M = 6.75$) than at six months ($M = 5.25$). However, this difference was insufficient to cause us to reject the null hypothesis that the amount of eye contact is the same at six months and nine months of age, sign test ($n = 8$), p *ns*).'

The calculation steps for the Wilcoxon matched pairs (or signed ranks) test are similar. However, this test retains a little more information from the original scores by ranking the differences.

Calculation 18.2

The Wilcoxon matched pairs test

The test is also known as the Wilcoxon signed ranks test. It is similar to the sign test except that when we have obtained the difference score we rank-order the differences ignoring the sign of the difference.

Step 1 The difference scores are calculated and then ranked ignoring the sign of the difference (Table 18.3). Notice that where there are tied values of the differences, we have allocated the average of the ranks which would be given if it were possible to separate the scores. Thus the two difference scores which equal 1 are both given the rank 1.5 since if the scores did differ minutely one would be given the rank 1 and the other the rank 2. Take care: zero differences are ignored and are *not* ranked.

Table 18.3	Steps in the calculation of the Wilcoxon matched pairs test			
Subject	**Six months** X_1	**Nine months** X_2	**Difference** $D = X_1 - X_2$	**Rank of difference ignoring sign during ranking**
Baby Clara	3	7	−4	7.5−
Baby Martin	5	6	−1	1.5−
Baby Sally	5	3	2	4.5+
Baby Angie	4	8	−4	7.5−
Baby Trevor	3	5	−2	4.5−
Baby Sam	7	9	−2	4.5−
Baby Bobby	8	7	1	1.5+
Baby Sid	7	9	−2	4.5−

Step 2 The ranks of the differences can now have the sign of the difference reattached.

Step 3 The sum of the positive ranks is calculated = 4.5 + 1.5 = 6. The sum of the negative ranks is calculated = 7.5 + 1.5 + 7.5 + 4.5 + 4.5 + 4.5 = 30.

Step 4 We then decide which is the smaller of the two sums of ranks – in this case it is 6. This is normally designated *T*.

Step 5 We then find the significance values of *T* (the smaller of the two sums of ranks) from Significance Table 18.2. This is structured in terms of the number of pairs of scores used in the calculation, which is 8 in the present case. The critical value for a two-tailed test at the 5% level is 4 or less. Our value is 6 which is not statistically significant.

If your sample size is larger than Significance Table 18.2 deals with, Appendix B1 explains how to test for significance.

Interpreting the results As always, it is important to examine the means of the two sets of scores in order to know what the trend in the data is. Although the amount of eye contact at nine months was greater

Significance Table 18.2	5% significance values for the Wilcoxon matched pairs test (two-tailed test). An extended and conventional significance table is given in Appendix H

Number of pairs of scores (ignoring any tied pairs)	Significant at 5% level Accept hypothesis
6	0 only
7	0 to 2
8	0 to 4
9	0 to 6
10	0 to 8
11	0 to 11
12	0 to 14
13	0 to 17
14	0 to 21
15	0 to 25
16	0 to 30
17	0 to 35
18	0 to 40
19	0 to 46
20	0 to 52
21	0 to 59
22	0 to 66
23	0 to 74
24	0 to 81
25	0 to 90

Your value must be in the listed ranges for your sample size to be significant at the 5% level (i.e. to accept the hypothesis).

than at six months, the Wilcoxon matched pairs test failed to reach statistical significance so it is not possible to reject the null hypothesis of no differences in eye contact at the two ages.

Reporting the results The following gives a reasonably concise account of our findings: 'Eye contact was slightly higher at nine months ($\bar{X} = 6.75$) than at six months ($\bar{X} = 5.25$). However, this difference did not reach statistical significance so it was not possible to reject the null hypothesis that eye contact does not change between these ages ($T = 6$, $n = 8$, $p > 0.05$, ns).'

Alternatively, following the APA (2010) Publication Manual recommendations we could rewrite the results as follows: 'Eye contact was slightly higher at nine months ($M = 6.75$) than at six months ($M = 5.25$). However, this difference did not reach statistical significance so it was not possible to reject the null hypothesis that eye contact does not change between these ages, $T(n = 8) = 6$, $p > .05$.'

Generally speaking, it is difficult to suggest circumstances in which the sign test is to be preferred over the Wilcoxon matched pairs test. The latter uses more of the information contained within the data and so is more likely to detect significant differences where they exist.

The sign test can be applied in virtually any circumstance in which the expected population distribution under the null hypothesis is 50% of one outcome and 50% of another. In other words, the table of significance of the sign test can be used to check for departures from this 50/50 expectation.

■ Tests for unrelated samples

The major nonparametric test for differences between two groups of unrelated or uncorrelated scores is the Mann–Whitney U-test.

Calculation 18.3

The Mann–Whitney U-test

The most common nonparametric statistic for unrelated samples of scores is the Mann–Whitney U-test. This is used for similar research designs as the unrelated or uncorrelated scores t-test (Chapter 13). In other words, it can be used whenever you have two groups of scores which are independent of each other (i.e. they are usually based on different samples of people). We will use the identical data upon which we demonstrated the calculation of the unrelated/uncorrelated scores t-test (Chapter 13).

Step 1 Rank all of the scores from the smallest to the largest (Table 18.4). Scores which are equal are allocated the average of ranks that they would be given if there were tiny differences between the scores.

Table 18.4	Steps in the calculation of the Mann–Whitney U-test

Two-parent families (X_1)	Rankings	Lone-parent families (X_2)	Rankings
(This column is for the larger group)		*(This column is for the smaller group)*	
12	12.5	6	2
18	21	9	6
14	16.5	4	1
10	8.5	13	14.5
19	22	14	16.5
8	3.5	9	6
15	18.5	8	3.5
11	10.5	12	12.5
10	8.5	11	10.5
13	14.5	9	6
15	18.5		
16	20		
	$\Sigma R_1 = 174.5$		
	(Note that this is the sum of ranks for the larger group)		

→

Be careful! All of your scores are ranked irrespective of the group they are in. To avoid confusion, *use the first column for the larger group* of scores. If both groups are equal in size then either can be entered in the first column. Group size $N_1 = 12$ for the two-parent families and $N_2 = 10$ for the lone-parent families.

Step 2   Sum the ranks for the *larger* group of scores. This is R_1. (If the groups are equal in size then either can be selected.)

Step 3   The sum of ranks (R_1) of Group 1 (174.5) (the larger group) and its sample size N_1 ($N_1 = 12$) together with the sample size N_2 of Group 2 ($N_2 = 10$) are entered into the following formula which gives you the value of the statistic U:

$$U = (N_1 \times N_2) + \frac{N_1 \times (N_1 \times 1)}{2} - R_1$$

$$= (12 \times 10) + \frac{12 \times (12 + 1)}{2} - 174.5$$

$$= 120 + \frac{12 \times 13}{2} - 174.5$$

$$= 120 + \frac{156}{2} - 174.5$$

$$= 120 + 78 - 174.5$$

$$= 198 - 174.5$$

$$= 23.5$$

Step 4   Check the significance of your value of U by consulting Significance Table 18.3. In order to use this table, you need to find your value of N_1 in the column headings and your value of N_2 in the row headings. (However, since the table is symmetrical it does not matter if you use the rows instead of the columns and vice versa.) The table gives the *two* ranges of values of U which are significant. Your value must be in *either* of these two ranges to be statistically significant. (Appendix B1 explains what to do if your sample size exceeds the largest value in the table.)

The table tells us that for sample sizes of 12 and 10, the ranges are 0 to 29 or 91 to 120. Our value of 23.5 therefore is significant at the 5% level. In other words, we reject the null hypothesis that the independent variable is unrelated to the dependent variable in favour of the view that family structure has an influence on scores of the dependent variable.

Interpreting the results The means of the two groups of scores must be examined to know which of the two groups has the higher scores on the dependent variable. In our example, greater emotionality was found in the children from the two-parent families. The significant value of the Mann–Whitney U-test suggests that we are reasonably safe to conclude that the two groups do differ in terms of their emotionality.

Reporting the results The statistical analysis could be reported in the following APA (2010) Publication Manual style: 'It was found that emotionality was significantly higher, $U(n = 22) = 23.5$, $p < .05$, in the two-parent families ($M = 13.42$) than in the lone-parent families ($M = 9.50$).'

Significance Table 18.3

5% significance values for the Mann–Whitney U-test (two-tailed test)

Sample size for smaller group	Sample size for larger group											
	5	6	7	8	9	10	11	12	13	14	15	20
5	0–2	0–3	0–5	0–6	0–7	0–8	0–9	0–11	0–12	0–13	0–14	0–20
	23–25	27–30	30–35	34–40	38–45	42–50	46–55	49–60	53–65	57–70	61–75	80–100
6	0–3	0–5	0–6	0–8	0–10	0–11	0–13	0–14	0–16	0–17	0–19	0–27
	27–30	31–36	36–42	40–48	44–54	49–60	53–66	58–72	62–78	67–84	71–90	93–120
7	0–5	0–6	0–8	0–10	0–12	0–14	0–16	0–18	0–20	0–22	0–24	0–34
	30–35	36–42	41–49	46–56	51–63	56–71	61–77	66–84	71–91	76–98	81–105	106–140
8	0–6	0–8	0–10	0–13	0–15	0–17	0–19	0–22	0–24	0–26	0–29	0–41
	34–40	40–48	46–56	51–64	57–72	63–80	69–88	74–96	80–104	86–112	91–120	119–160
9	0–7	0–10	0–12	0–15	0–17	0–20	0–23	0–26	0–28	0–31	0–34	0–48
	38–45	44–54	51–63	57–72	64–81	70–90	76–99	82–108	89–117	95–126	101–135	130–180
10	0–8	0–11	0–14	0–17	0–20	0–23	0–26	0–29	0–33	0–36	0–39	0–55
	42–50	49–60	56–70	63–80	70–90	77–100	84–110	91–120	97–130	104–140	111–150	145–200
11	0–9	0–13	0–16	0–19	0–23	0–26	0–30	0–33	0–37	0–40	0–44	0–62
	46–55	53–66	61–77	69–88	76–99	84–110	91–121	99–132	106–143	114–154	121–165	158–220
12	0–11	0–14	0–18	0–22	0–26	0–29	0–33	0–37	0–41	0–45	0–49	0–69
	49–60	58–72	66–84	74–96	82–108	91–120	99–132	107–144	115–156	123–168	131–180	171–240
13	0–12	0–16	0–20	0–24	0–28	0–33	0–37	0–41	0–45	0–50	0–54	0–76
	53–65	62–78	71–91	80–104	89–117	97–130	106–143	115–156	124–169	132–182	141–195	184–260
14	0–13	0–17	0–22	0–26	0–31	0–36	0–40	0–45	0–50	0–55	0–59	0–83
	57–70	67–84	76–98	86–112	95–126	104–140	114–154	123–168	132–182	141–196	151–210	197–280
15	0–14	0–19	0–24	0–29	0–34	0–39	0–44	0–49	0–54	0–59	0–64	0–90
	61–75	71–90	81–105	91–120	101–135	111–150	121–165	131–180	141–195	151–210	161–225	210–300
20	0–20	0–27	0–34	0–41	0–48	0–55	0–62	0–69	0–76	0–83	0–90	0–127
	80–100	93–120	106–140	119–160	130–180	145–200	158–220	171–240	184–260	197–280	210–300	273–400

Source: Adapted and extended from Table I of R.P. Runyon and A. Haber (1989). *Fundamentals of Behavioral Statistics*. New York: McGraw-Hill. With the kind permission of the publisher. Your value must be in the listed ranges for your sample sizes to be significant at the 5% level (i.e. to accept the hypothesis).

18.4   Three or more groups of scores

The Kruskal–Wallis test and the Friedman test are essentially extensions of the Mann–Whitney U-test and the Wilcoxon matched pairs test, respectively. Appendix B2 gives information on how to calculate these nonparametric statistics.

Key points

- Often you will not require nonparametric tests of significance of the sort described in this chapter. The t-test will usually fit the task better.

- Only when you have marked symmetry problems in your data will you require the nonparametric tests. But even then remember that a version of the unrelated t-test is available to cope with some aspects of the problem (Chapter 13).

- The computations for the nonparametric tests may appear simpler. A big disadvantage is that when the sample sizes get large the problems in ranking escalate disproportionately.

- Some professional psychologists tend to advocate nonparametric techniques for entirely outmoded reasons.

- There is no guarantee that the nonparametric test will always do the job better when the assumptions of parametric tests are violated.

- There are large sample formulae for the nonparametric tests reported here for when your sample sizes are too big for the printed tables of significance. However, by the time this point is reached the computation is getting clumsy and can be better handled by a computer; also the advantages of the nonparametric tests are very reduced.

COMPUTER ANALYSIS

The SPSS Statistics instruction book to this text is Dennis Howitt and Duncan Cramer (2011), *Introduction to SPSS Statistics in Psychology: For version 19 and earlier*, Harlow: Pearson. Chapter 18 in that book gives detailed step-by-step procedures for the statistics described in this chapter together with advice on how to report the results. Figure 18.2 shows the SPSS Statistics steps for the sign, Wilcoxon and Mann–Whitney nonparametric tests.

Data	• Name the variables in Variable View of the Data Editor. • Enter the data under the appropriate variable names in Data View of the Data Editor.
Analysis	• For the 2 related data tests, select 'Analyze', 'Nonparametric Tests' and '2-Related Samples . . .'.
2	• Move the appropriate pair of variables to the box to the right and select 'Sign'. Wilcoxon is already selected.
3	• For the Mann–Whitney test, select 'Analyze', 'Nonparametric Tests' and '2 Independent Samples . . .'.
4	• Move the appropriate test (dependent) and grouping (independent) variable to the two boxes to the right.
Output	• Check to see if the *p* value is significant at .05 or less. • If it is determine the direction of the difference.

FIGURE 18.2 SPSS Statistics steps for the sign, Wilcoxon and Mann–Whitney nonparametric tests

Recommended further reading

Mariscuilo, L.A. and McSweeney, M. (1977), *Nonparametric and Distribution-free Methods for the Social Sciences*, Monterey, CA: Brooks/Cole.

Siegel, S. and Castellan, N.J. (1988), *Nonparametric Statistics for the Behavioral Sciences*, New York: McGraw-Hill.

PART 3

Introduction to analysis of variance

CHAPTER 19

The variance ratio test

The *F*-ratio to compare two variances

Overview

- The variance ratio test (the *F*-ratio test) assesses whether the variances of two different samples are significantly different from each other.

- That is, it tests whether the spread of scores for the two samples is significantly different. This is not dependent on the value of the means of each sample.

- However, it is more commonly used as part of other statistical techniques such as the analysis of variance.

- It is also used to test the assumptions of the *t*-test since the common version of this assumes that the variances of the two sets of scores are more or less equal (i.e. not significantly different).

Preparation

Make sure that you understand variance and the variance estimate (Chapters 3 and 11). Familiarity with the *t*-test will help with some applications (Chapters 12 and 13).

19.1 Introduction

In a number of circumstances in research it is important to compare the variances of two samples of scores. The conventions of psychological research stress comparing the sample *means* with each other. However, it is perfectly possible to find that despite the means of two groups being identical, their variances are radically different. Take the following simple experiment in which men and women are shown advertisements for tights, set out in Table 19.1. The dependent variable is the readers' degree of liking for the product rated on a scale from 1 to 7 (on which 1 means that they strongly disliked the advertisement and 7 means that they strongly liked the advertisement).

Table 19.1	Data comparing men and women on ratings of tights
Men	**Women**
5	1
4	6
4	7
3	2
5	6
4	7
3	5
6	7
5	2
5	6
	1
	2

The big difference between the two groups is not in terms of their means – the men's mean is 4.4 whereas the women's mean is 4.3. This is a small and unimportant difference. What is more noticeable is that the women seem to be split into two camps. The women's scores tend to be large or small with little in the centre. There is more variance in the women's scores. Just how does one test to see whether the differences in variances are significant?

There are other circumstances in which we compare variances:

1. For the unrelated *t*-test, it is conventional to make sure that the two samples do not differ significantly in terms of their variances – if they do then it is better to opt for an 'unpooled' *t*-test (see Chapter 13). This is in addition to testing for the significance of the difference between the sample means.

2. Another major application is the analysis of variance in which variance estimates are compared (see Chapter 20).

The statistical test to use in all these circumstances is called the *F*-ratio test or the variance ratio test.

19.2   Theoretical issues and an application

The variance ratio simply compares two variances in order to test whether they come from the same population. In other words, are the differences between the variances simply the result of chance sampling fluctuations? Of course, since we are comparing samples from a population we need the variance estimate formula. In the simpler applications of the variance ratio test (F-ratio), the variance estimate involves using the sample size minus one (N – 1) as the denominator (lower part) of the variance estimate formula. (This does not apply in quite the same way in the more advanced case of the analysis of variance, as we will see in Chapter 20 onwards.)

The variance ratio formula is as follows:

$$F = \frac{\text{larger variance estimate}}{\text{smaller variance estimate}}$$

There is a table of the F-distribution (Significance Table 19.1) which is organised according to the degrees of freedom of the two variance estimates. Unlike the t-test, the F-ratio is a one-tailed test. It determines whether the numerator, the top part of the formula, is larger than the denominator, the lower part. The variance ratio cannot be smaller than one. The 5% or .05 applies to the upper or right-hand tail of the distribution. The larger the F-ratio is, the more likely it is that the larger variance estimate is significantly larger than the lower variance estimate.

Figure 19.1 shows the key steps in the variance test.

Significance Table 19.1	5% significance values of the F-distribution for testing differences in variance estimates between two samples (one-tailed test). Additional values are given in Significance Table 20.1					
Degrees of freedom for smaller variance estimate (denominator)	**Degrees of freedom for larger variance estimate (numerator)**					
	5	**7**	**10**	**20**	**50**	**∞**
5	5.1 or more	4.9	4.7	4.6	4.4	4.4
6	4.4	4.1	4.1	3.9	3.8	3.7
7	4.0	3.8	3.6	3.4	3.3	3.2
8	3.7	3.5	3.3	3.2	3.0	2.9
10	3.3	3.1	3.0	2.8	2.6	2.5
12	3.1	2.9	2.8	2.5	2.4	2.3
15	2.9	2.7	2.6	2.3	2.2	2.1
20	2.7	2.5	2.4	2.1	2.0	1.8
30	2.5	2.3	2.2	1.9	1.8	1.6
50	2.4	2.2	2.0	1.8	1.6	1.4
100	2.3	2.1	1.9	1.7	1.5	1.3
∞	2.2	2.0	1.8	1.6	1.4	1.0

Your value has to equal or be larger than the tabulated value to be significant at the 5% level.

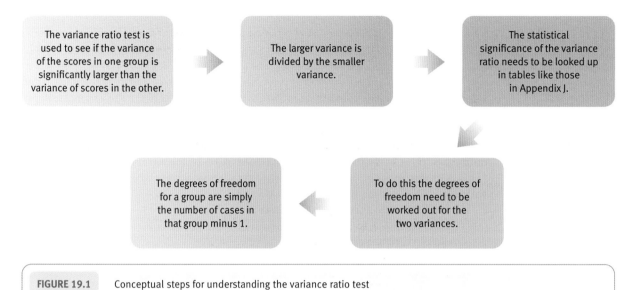

The variance ratio test is used to see if the variance of the scores in one group is significantly larger than the variance of scores in the other.

The larger variance is divided by the smaller variance.

The statistical significance of the variance ratio needs to be looked up in tables like those in Appendix J.

The degrees of freedom for a group are simply the number of cases in that group minus 1.

To do this the degrees of freedom need to be worked out for the two variances.

FIGURE 19.1   Conceptual steps for understanding the variance ratio test

Calculation 19.1

The variance ratio (*F*-ratio)

Imagine a very simple piece of clinical research which involves the administration of electroconvulsive therapy (ECT). There are two experimental conditions: in one case the electric current is passed through the left hemisphere of the brain and in the other case it is passed through the right hemisphere of the brain. The dependent variable is scores on a test of emotional stability following treatment. Patients were assigned to one or other group at random. The scores following treatment were as listed in Table 19.2.

Table 19.2	Emotional stability scores from a study of ECT to different hemispheres of the brain

Left hemisphere	Right hemisphere
20	36
14	28
18	4
22	18
13	2
15	22
9	1
Mean = 15.9	Mean = 15.9

Quite clearly there is no difference in terms of the mean scores on emotional stability. Looking at the data, though, it looks as if ECT to the right hemisphere tends to push people to the extremes whereas ECT to the left hemisphere leaves a more compact distribution.

To calculate the variance ratio, the variance *estimates* of the two separate samples (left and right hemispheres) have to be calculated using the usual variance estimate formula. The following is the computational formula version of this:

$$\text{estimated variance} = \frac{\sum X^2 - \frac{(\sum X)^2}{N}}{N - 1}$$

Step 1   Calculate the variance of the first group of scores (i.e. the left hemisphere group), as in Table 19.3. The sample size (number of scores) is $N_1 = 7$.

Substituting in the formula:

$$\text{variance estimate}_{[\text{group 1}]} = \frac{\sum X_1^2 - \frac{(\sum X_1)^2}{N_1}}{N_1 - 1} = \frac{1879 - \frac{111^2}{7}}{7 - 1} = \frac{1879 - \frac{12\,321}{7}}{6}$$

$$= \frac{1879 - 1760.143}{6} = \frac{118.857}{6}$$

$$= 19.81 \text{ (degrees of freedom} = N_1 - 1 = 6)$$

Table 19.3	Step 1 in the calculation of the variance estimate	
X_1 = left hemisphere	**X_1^2**
20	400
14	196
18	324
22	484
13	169
15	225
9	81
$\sum X_1 = 111$	**$\sum X_1^2 = 1879$**

Step 2   The variance estimate of the right hemisphere group is calculated using the standard computational formula as in Table 19.4. The sample size $N_2 = 7$.

Substituting in the formula:

$$\text{variance estimate}_{[\text{group 2}]} = \frac{\sum X_2^2 - \frac{(\sum X_2)^2}{N_2}}{N_2 - 1} = \frac{2909 - \frac{111^2}{7}}{7 - 1} = \frac{2909 - \frac{12\,321}{7}}{6}$$

$$= \frac{2909 - 1760.143}{6} = \frac{1148.857}{6}$$

$$= 191.48 \text{ (degrees of freedom} = N_2 - 1 = 6)$$

→

Table 19.4	Step 2 in the calculation of the variance estimate	
X_1 = right hemisphere		X_1^2
36		1296
28		784
4		16
18		324
2		4
22		484
1		1
$\sum X_2 = 111$		$\sum X_2^2 = 2909$

Step 3

The larger variance estimate is divided by the smaller:

$$F = \frac{\text{larger variance estimate}}{\text{smaller variance estimate}}$$

$$= \frac{191.48}{19.81}$$

$$= 9.67 \text{ (df larger variance estimate = 6, df smaller variance estimate = 6)}$$

Step 4

We need to check whether or not a difference between the two variance estimates as large as this ratio implies would be likely if the samples came from the same population of scores. Significance Table 19.1 contains the critical values for the F-ratio. To use the table you find the intersection of the column for the degrees of freedom for the larger variance estimate and the degrees of freedom for the smaller variance estimate. Notice that the degrees of freedom we want are not listed for the numerator, so we take the next smaller listed value. Thus the table tells us we need a value of 4.4 at a minimum to be significant at the 5% level with a one-tailed test. Our calculated value of F is substantially in excess of the critical value. Thus we conclude that it is very unlikely that the two samples come from the same population of scores. We accept the hypothesis that the two sample variances are significantly different from each other.

Interpreting the results The interpretation of the F-ratio test is simply a matter of examining the two variance estimates to see which is the largest value. If the F-ratio is statistically significant then the larger of the variance estimates is significantly larger than the smaller one.

Reporting the results The results could be written up according to the APA (2010) Publication Manual recommendations as follows: 'Despite there being no difference between the mean scores on emotionality following ECT to left and right brain hemispheres, the variance of emotionality was significantly higher for ECT to the right hemisphere, $F(6, 6) = 9.67$, $p < 0.05$. This suggests that ECT to the right hemisphere increases emotionality in some people but decreases it in others.'

Key points

- Psychologists often fail to explore for differences in variances. It is good practice to routinely examine your data for them.

- The F-ratio is a necessary adjunct to applying the unrelated t-test correctly. Make sure that you check that the variances are indeed similar before using the t-test.

- Be very careful when you use the F-ratio in the analysis of variance (Chapter 20 onwards). The F-ratio in the analysis of variance is not quite the same. In this you do not always divide the larger variance estimate by the smaller variance estimate.

COMPUTER ANALYSIS

The SPSS Statistics instruction book to this text is Dennis Howitt and Duncan Cramer (2011), *Introduction to SPSS Statistics in Psychology: For version 19 and earlier*, Harlow: Pearson. Chapter 20 in that book gives detailed step-by-step procedures for the statistics described in this chapter together with advice on how to report the results. SPSS Statistics does not give the results of this test. However, it does give the variances which can then be used to calculate the F ratio as shown in Figure 19.2.

Data	• Name the variables in Variable View of the Data Editor. • Enter the data under the appropriate variable names in Data View of the Data Editor.
Analysis	• Select 'Analyze', 'Compare Means' and 'Means . . .'. • Move the appropriate variable names to the 'Dependent:' and 'Independent:' boxes to the right.
2	• Select 'Options . . .' and move 'Variance' from the 'Statistics' to the 'Cell Statistics:' box.
Output	• Divide the larger variance by the smaller variance and look up in the tables in Appendix J under the appropriate degrees of freedom whether the ratio is statistically significant.

FIGURE 19.2 SPSS Statistics steps for computing variance

CHAPTER 20

Analysis of variance (ANOVA)

Introduction to the one-way unrelated or uncorrelated ANOVA

Overview

- The one-way analysis of variance compares the means of a minimum of two groups but is most commonly used when there are three or more mean scores to compare.

- This chapter concentrates on the case where the samples of scores are unrelated – that is, there is no relation between the samples.

- The scores are the dependent variable, the groups are the independent variable.

- In essence, the ANOVA estimates the variance in the population due to the cell means (between variance) and the variance in the population due to random (or error) processes (within variance). These are compared using the F-ratio test.

- Error is variation which is not under the researcher's control.

- A significant finding for the analysis of variance means that overall some of the means differ from each other.

Preparation

It is pointless to start this chapter without a clear understanding of how to calculate the basic variance estimate formula and the computational formula for variance estimate (Chapter 3). A working knowledge of the variance ratio test (F-ratio test) is also essential (Chapter 19).

20.1 Introduction

Up to this point we have discussed research designs comparing the means of just *two* groups of scores. The analysis of variance (ANOVA) can do this but in addition can extend the comparison to three or more groups of scores. Analysis of variance takes many forms but is primarily used to analyse the results of experiments. Nevertheless, the simpler forms of ANOVA are routinely used in surveys and similar types of research. This chapter describes the one-way analysis of variance. This can be used whenever we wish to compare two or more groups in terms of their mean scores on a dependent variable. The scores must be independent (uncorrelated or unrelated). In other words, each respondent contributes just one score to the statistical analysis. Stylistically, Table 20.1 is the sort of research design for which the (uncorrelated or unrelated) one-way analysis of variance is appropriate.

Table 20.1	Stylised table of data for unrelated analysis of variance		
Group 1	**Group 2**	**Group 3**	**Group 4**
9	3	1	27
14	1	4	24
11	5	2	25
12	5	31	

The scores are those on the dependent variable. The groups are the independent variable. There are very few limitations on the research designs to which this is applicable:

1. It is possible to have any number of groups with the minimum being two.

2. The groups consist of independent samples of scores. For example the groups could be:

    (a) men versus women

    (b) an experimental versus one control group

    (c) four experimental groups and one control group

    (d) three different occupational types – managers, office personnel and production workers.

3. The scores (the dependent variable) can be for virtually any variable. The main thing is that they are numerical scores suitable for calculating the mean and variance.

4. It is *not* necessary to have equal numbers of scores in each group. With other forms of analysis of variance, not having equal numbers can cause complications.

20.2 Some revision and some new material

You should be familiar with most of the following. Remember the formula for *variance*:

$$\text{variance}_{[\text{definitional formula}]} = \frac{\sum(X - \bar{X})^2}{N}$$

If you wish to estimate the variance of a population from the variation in a sample from that population, you use the *variance estimate* formula which is:

$$\text{variance estimate}_{\text{[definitional formula]}} = \frac{\sum(X - \bar{X})^2}{N - 1}$$

(By dividing by $N - 1$ we get an unbiased estimate of the population variance from the sample data.)

It is useful if you memorise the fact that the top part of the formula, i.e.

$$\sum(X - \bar{X})^2$$

is called the *sum of squares*. It is the sum of the squared deviations from the mean. The phrase 'sum of squares' occurs repeatedly in all forms of the analysis of variance so cannot be avoided.

The bottom part of the variance formula (N) or variance estimate formula ($N - 1$) is called in the analysis of variance the *degrees of freedom*. It is a little complex in that its calculation can vary. Nevertheless, memorising that the phrase 'degrees of freedom' refers to the bottom part of the variance formulae is a useful start.

We can rewrite this formula as a *computational formula*:

$$\text{variance estimate}_{\text{[computational formula]}} = \frac{\sum X^2 - \frac{\left(\sum X\right)^2}{N}}{N - 1}$$

20.3   Theoretical considerations

The analysis of variance involves very few new ideas. However, some basic concepts are used in a relatively novel way. Unfortunately, most textbooks confuse readers by presenting the analysis of variance rather obscurely. In particular, they use a variant of the computational formula for the calculation of the variance estimate which makes it very difficult to follow the logic of what is happening. This is a pity since the analysis of variance is relatively simple in many respects. The main problem is the number of steps which have to be coped with.

All measurement assumes that a score is made up of two components:

● the 'true' value of the measurement

● an 'error' component.

Most psychological measurements tend to have a large error component compared to the true component. Error results from all sorts of factors – tiredness, distraction, unclear instructions and so forth. Normally we cannot say precisely to what extent these factors influence our scores. It is further assumed that the 'true' and 'error' components add together to give the obtained scores (i.e. the data). So, for example, an obtained score of 15 might be made up of:

$$15_{\text{[obtained score]}} = 12_{\text{[true]}} + 3_{\text{[error]}}$$

or an obtained score of 20 might be made up as follows:

$$20 = 24 + (-4)$$

The error score may take a positive or negative value.

We have no certain knowledge about anything other than the obtained scores. *The true and error scores cannot be known directly. However, in some circumstances we can infer them through intelligent guesswork.*

In the analysis of variance, each score is separated into the two components – true scores and error scores. This is easier than it sounds. Look at the data of some fictitious research in Table 20.2. It is a study of the effects of two different hormones and an inert (placebo) control on depression scores in men.

Tables 20.3 and 20.4 give the best estimates possible of the 'true' scores and 'error' scores in Table 20.2. Try to work out the simple 'tricks' we have employed. All we did to produce these two new tables was the following:

Table 20.2	Stylised table of data for unrelated analysis of variance with means		
Group 1 Hormone 1	**Group 2 Hormone 2**	**Group 3 Placebo control**
9	4	3
12	2	6
8	5	3
Mean = 9.667	Mean = 3.667	Mean = 4.000
		Overall mean = 5.778

Table 20.3	'True' scores based on the data in Table 20.2		
Group 1 Hormone 1	**Group 2 Hormone 2**	**Group 3 Placebo control**
9.667	3.667	4.000
9.667	3.667	4.000
9.667	3.667	4.000
Mean = 9.667	Mean = 3.667	Mean = 4.000
		Overall mean = 5.778

Table 20.4	'Error' scores based on the data in Table 20.2		
Group 1 Hormone 1	**Group 2 Hormone 2**	**Group 3 Placebo control**
−0.667	0.333	−1.000
2.333	−1.667	2.000
−1.667	1.333	−1.000
Mean = 0.000	Mean = 0.000	Mean = 0.000
		Overall mean = 0.000

1. In order to obtain a table of 'true' scores we have simply substituted the column mean for each group for the individual scores, the assumption being that the obtained scores deviate from the 'true' score because of the influence of varying amounts of error in the measurement. In statistical theory, error is assumed to be randomly distributed. Thus we have replaced all of the scores for Group 1 by the mean of 9.667. The column mean is simply the best estimate of what the 'true' score would be for the group if *we could get rid of the 'error' component*. As all of the scores are the same, there is absolutely no error component in any of the conditions of Table 20.3. The assumption in this is that the variability within a column is due to error so the average score in a column is our best estimate of the 'true' score for that column. Notice that the column means are unchanged by this.

2. We have obtained the table of 'error' scores (Table 20.4) simply by subtracting the scores in the 'true' scores table (Table 20.3) away from the corresponding score in the original scores table (Table 20.2). What is not a 'true' score is an 'error' score by definition. Notice that the error scores show a mixture of positive and negative values, *and* that the sum of the error scores in each column (and the entire table for that matter) is zero. This is always the case with error scores and so constitutes an important check on your calculations. An alternative way of obtaining the error scores is to take the column (or group) mean away from each score in the original data table.

So what do we do now that we have the 'true' scores and 'error' scores? The two derived sets of scores – the 'true' and the 'error' scores – are used separately to estimate the variance of the population of scores from which they are samples. (That is, the calculated variance estimate for the 'true' scores is an estimate of the 'true' variation in the population, and the calculated variance estimate of the 'error' scores is an estimate of the 'error' variation in the population.) Remember, the null hypothesis for this research would suggest that differences between the three groups are due to error rather than real differences related to the influence of the independent variable. The null hypothesis suggests that both the 'true' and 'error' variance estimates are similar since they are both the result of error. *If the null hypothesis is correct*, the variance estimate derived from the 'true' scores should be no different from the variance estimate derived from the 'error' scores. After all, under the null hypothesis the variation in the 'true' scores is due to error anyway. *If the alternative hypothesis is correct*, then there should be rather more variation in the 'true' scores than is typical in the 'error' scores.

We calculate the variance estimate of the 'true' scores and then calculate the variance estimate for the 'error' scores. Next the two variance estimates are examined to see whether they are significantly different using the *F*-ratio test (the variance ratio test). This involves the following calculation:

$$F = \frac{\text{variance estimate}_{[\text{of true scores}]}}{\text{variance estimate}_{[\text{of error scores}]}}$$

(The error variance is always at the bottom in the analysis of variance. This is different from the *F*-ratio test described in the previous chapter. This is because we want to know if the variance estimate of the true scores is *bigger* than the variance estimate of the 'error' scores. We are not simply comparing the variance of two conditions.)

It is then a fairly straightforward matter to use Significance Table 20.1 for the *F*-distribution to decide whether or not these two variance estimates are significantly different from each other. We just need to be careful to use the appropriate numbers of degrees of freedom. The *F*-ratio calculation was demonstrated in Chapter 19. If the variance estimates are similar then the variance in 'true' scores is little different from the

| Significance Table 20.1 | 5% significance values of the *F*-ratio for unrelated ANOVA. Additional values are given in Significance Table 19.1 | | | | | |

Degrees of freedom for error or within cells mean square (or variance estimate)	Degrees of freedom for true or between-treatment mean square (or variance estimate)					
	1	2	3	4	5	∞
1	161 or more	200	216	225	230	254
2	18.5	19.0	19.2	19.3	19.3	19.5
3	10.1	9.6	9.3	9.1	9.0	8.5
4	7.7	6.9	6.6	6.4	6.3	5.6
5	6.6	5.8	5.4	5.2	5.1	4.4
6	6.0	5.1	4.8	4.5	4.4	3.7
7	5.6	4.7	4.4	4.1	4.0	3.2
8	5.3	4.5	4.1	3.8	3.7	2.9
9	5.1	4.3	3.9	3.6	3.5	2.7
10	5.0	4.1	3.7	3.5	3.3	2.5
13	4.7	3.8	3.4	3.2	3.0	2.2
15	4.5	3.7	3.3	3.1	2.9	2.1
20	4.4	3.5	3.1	2.9	2.7	1.8
30	4.2	3.3	2.9	2.7	2.5	1.6
60	4.0	3.2	2.8	2.5	2.4	1.4
∞	3.8	3.0	2.6	2.4	2.2	1.0

Your value has to equal or be larger than the tabulated value for an effect to be significant at the 5% level.

variance in the 'error' scores; since the estimated 'true' variance is much the same as the 'error' variance in this case, both can be regarded as 'error'. On the other hand, if the *F*-ratio is significant it means that the variation due to the 'true' scores is much greater than that due to 'error'; the 'true' scores represent reliable differences between groups rather than chance factors.

As mentioned in Chapter 19, the *F*-ratio, unlike the *t*-test, is a one-tailed test. It simply determines whether the true variance estimate is bigger than the error variance estimate. The *F*-ratio cannot be smaller than zero. In other words, it is always positive. The 5% or .05 probability only applies to the upper or right-hand tail of the distribution. The larger the *F*-ratio is, the more likely it is to be statistically significant.

And that is just about it for the one-way analysis of variance. There is just one remaining issue: the *degrees of freedom*. If one were to work out the variance estimate of the original data in our study we would use the formula as given above:

$$\text{variance estimate}_{[\text{original data}]} = \frac{\sum X^2 - \dfrac{\left(\sum X\right)^2}{N}}{N - 1}$$

where $N - 1$ is the number of degrees of freedom.

However, the calculation of the number of degrees of freedom varies in the analysis of variance (it is not always $N - 1$). With the 'true' and 'error' scores the degrees of freedom

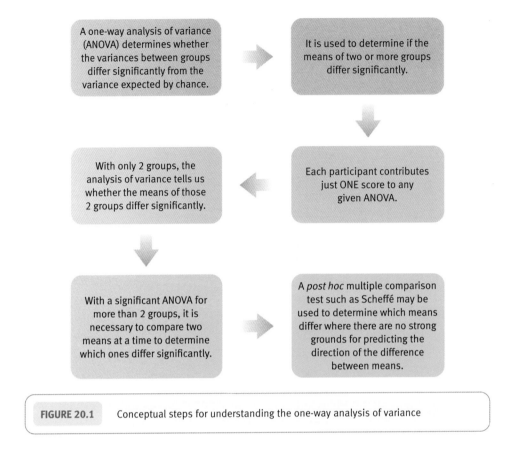

FIGURE 20.1   Conceptual steps for understanding the one-way analysis of variance

are a little more complex although easily calculated using formulae. But the idea of degrees of freedom can be understood at a more fundamental level with a little work. Figure 20.1 gives the key steps for an unrelated analysis of variance.

20.4 Degrees of freedom

This section gives a detailed explanation of degrees of freedom. You may find it easier to return to this section when you are a little more familiar with ANOVA.

Degrees of freedom refer to the distinct items of information contained in your data. By information we mean something which is new and not already known. For example, if we asked you what is the combined age of your two best friends and then asked you the age of the younger of the two, you would be crazy to accept a bet that we could tell you the age of your older best friend, the reason being that if you told us that the combined ages of your best friends was 37 years and that the younger was 16 years, any fool could work out that the older best friend must be 21 years. The age of your older best friend is contained within the first two pieces of information. The age of your older friend is redundant because you already know it from your previous information.

It is much the same sort of idea with degrees of freedom – which might be better termed the quantity of distinct information.

Table 20.5 repeats the table of the 'true' scores that we calculated earlier as Table 20.3. The question is how many items of truly new information the table contains. You have

Table 20.5	'True' scores based on the data in Table 20.2	
Group 1 **Hormone 1**	**Group 2** **Hormone 2**	**Group 3** **Placebo control**
9.667	3.667	4.000
9.667	3.667	4.000
9.667	3.667	4.000
Mean = 9.667	**Mean = 3.667**	**Mean = 4.000**
		Overall mean = 5.778

Table 20.6	Insertion of arbitrary values in the first column	
Group 1	**Group 2**	**Group 3**
10.000	–	–
10.000	–	–
10.000	–	–
Mean = 10.000		
		Overall mean = 5.778

to bear in mind that what we are looking at is the variance estimate of the scores which is basically their variation around the overall mean of 5.778. Don't forget that the overall mean of 5.778 is our best estimate of the population mean under the null hypothesis that the groups do not differ.

Just how many of the scores in this table are we able to alter and still obtain this same overall mean of 5.778? For this table, we simply start rubbing out the scores one by one and putting in any value we like. So *if we start with the first person in group 1* we can arbitrarily set their score to 10.000 (or any other score you can think of). But, once we have done so, each score in group 1 has to be changed to 10.000 because the columns of the 'true' score table have to have identical entries. Thus the first column has to look like the column in Table 20.6 (the dashes represent parts of the table we have not dealt with yet). The scores in italics are ones which are not free to vary.

We have been free to vary just one score so far. We can now move on to the group 2 column. Here we can arbitrarily put in a score of 3.000 to replace the first entry. Once we do this then the remaining two scores in the column have to be the same because this is the nature of 'true' tables – all the scores in a column have to be identical (Table 20.7).

Thus so far we have managed to vary only two scores independently. We can now move on to group 3. We could start by entering, say, 5.000 to replace the first score, but there is a problem. The overall mean has to end up as 5.778 and the number 5.000 will not allow this to happen given that all of the scores in group 3 would have to be 5.000. There is only one number which can be put in the group 3 column which will give an overall mean of 5.778, that is 4.333 (Table 20.8).

We have not increased the number of scores we were free to vary by changing group 3 – we have changed the scores but we had no freedom other than to put one particular score in their place.

Table 20.7	Insertion of arbitrary values in the second column		
Group 1	**Group 2**	**Group 3**
10.000	3.000	–
10.000	3.000	–
10.000	3.000	–
Mean = 10.000	Mean = 3.000	
		Overall mean = 5.778

Table 20.8	Forced insertion of a particular value in the third column because of the requirement that the overall mean is 5.778		
Group 1	**Group 2**	**Group 3**
10.000	3.000	4.333
10.000	3.000	4.333
10.000	3.000	4.333
Mean = 10.000	Mean = 3.000	Mean = 4.333
		Overall mean = 5.778

Table 20.9	'Error' scores based on the data in Table 20.2		
Group 1	**Group 2**	**Group 3**
−0.667	0.333	−1.000
2.333	−1.667	2.000
−1.667	1.333	−1.000
Mean = 0.000	Mean = 0.000	Mean = 0.000
		Overall mean = 0.000

Thus we have varied only *two* scores in the 'true' scores table – notice that this is one less than the number of groups we have. We speak of *the 'true' scores having two degrees of freedom.*

It is a similar process with the error table. The requirements this time are (a) that the column averages equal zero and (b) that the overall average equals zero. This is because they are error scores which must produce these characteristics – if they do not they cannot be error scores. Just how many of the scores can we vary this time and keep within these limitations? (We have 'adjusted' the column means to ignore a tiny amount of rounding error.)

The answer is six scores (Table 20.9). The first *two* scores in each group can be varied to any values you like. However, having done this the value of the third score has to be fixed in order that the column mean equals zero. Since there are three equal-size groups then there are *six degrees of freedom for the error table* in this case.

Just in case you are wondering, for the *original data* table the degrees of freedom correspond to the number of scores minus one. This is because there are no individual column constraints – the only constraint is that the overall mean has to be 5.778. The lack of column constraints means that the first eight scores could be given any value you like and only the final score is fixed by the requirement that the overall mean is 5.778. In other words, the variance estimate for the original data table uses $N - 1$ as the denominator – thus the formula is the usual variance estimate formula for a sample of scores.

Also note that the degrees of freedom for the 'error' and 'true' scores tables add up to $N - 1$.

◼ Quick formulae for degrees of freedom

Anyone who has difficulty with the above explanation of degrees of freedom should take heart. Few of us would bother to work out the degrees of freedom from first principles. It is much easier to use simple formulae. For the one-way analysis of variance using unrelated samples, the degrees of freedom are as follows:

N = number of scores in the table
degrees of freedom$_{[original\ data]}$ = $N - 1$
degrees of freedom$_{['true'\ scores]}$ = number of columns $- 1$
degrees of freedom$_{['error'\ scores]}$ = $N -$ number of columns

This is not cheating – most textbooks ignore the meaning of degrees of freedom and merely give the formulae anyway.

Calculation 20.1

Unrelated/uncorrelated one-way analysis of variance

Step-by-step, the following is the calculation of the analysis of variance.

Step 1 Draw up your data table using the format shown in Table 20.10. The degrees of freedom for this table are the number of scores minus one = $9 - 1 = 8$.

Table 20.10 Data table for an unrelated analysis of variance

Group 1 Hormone 1	Group 2 Hormone 2	Group 3 Placebo control
9	4	3
12	2	6
8	5	3
Mean = 9.667	Mean = 3.667	Mean = 4.000
		Overall mean = 5.778

→

Although this is not absolutely necessary you can calculate the variance estimate of your data table as a computational check – the sum of squares for the data table should equal the total of the sums of squares for the separate components. Thus, adding together the true and error sums of squares should give the total sum of squares for the data table. Similarly, the data degrees of freedom should equal the total of the true and error degrees of freedom. We will use the computational formula:

$$\text{variance estimate}_{\text{[original data]}} = \frac{\sum X^2 - \frac{\left(\sum X\right)^2}{N}}{df}$$

$\sum X^2$ means square each of the scores and then sum these individual calculations:

$$\sum X^2 = 9^2 + 4^2 + 3^2 + 12^2 + 2^2 + 6^2 + 8^2 + 5^2 + 3^2$$
$$= 81 + 16 + 9 + 144 + 4 + 36 + 64 + 25 + 9$$
$$= 388$$

$(\sum X)^2$ means add up all of the scores and then square the total:

$$\left(\sum X\right)^2 = (9 + 4 + 3 + 12 + 2 + 6 + 8 + 5 + 3)^2 = (52)^2 = 2704$$

The number of scores N equals 9. The degrees of freedom (df) equal $N - 1 = 9 - 1 = 8$. Substituting in the formula:

$$\text{variance estimate}_{\text{[original data]}} = \frac{\sum X^2 - \frac{\left(\sum X\right)^2}{N}}{df} = \frac{388 - \frac{2704}{9}}{8}$$
$$= \frac{388 - 300.444}{8} = \frac{87.556}{8} = 10.944$$

Step 2   Draw up Table 20.11 of 'true' scores by replacing the scores in each column by the column mean.

$$\sum X^2 = 9.667^2 + 3.667^2 + 4.000^2 + 9.667^2 + 3.667^2 + 4.000^2 + 9.667^2 + 3.667^2 + 4.000^2$$
$$= 93.451 + 13.447 + 16.000 + 93.451 + 13.447 + 16.000 + 93.451 + 13.447 + 16.000$$
$$= 368.694$$

$$\left(\sum X\right)^2 = (9.667 + 3.667 + 4.000 + 9.667 + 3.667 + 4.000 + 9.667 + 3.667 + 4.000)^2$$
$$= (52.000)^2 = 2704$$

Table 20.11	'True' scores based on the data in Table 20.10	
Group 1	**Group 2**	**Group 3**
9.667	3.667	4.000
9.667	3.667	4.000
9.667	3.667	4.000
Mean = 9.667	Mean = 3.667	Mean = 4.000
		Overall mean = 5.778

The number of scores N equals 9. The degrees of freedom (df) are given by:

degrees of freedom$_{[true\ scores]}$ = number of columns − 1 = 3 − 1 = 2

We can now substitute in the formula:

$$\text{variance estimate}_{[true\ scores]} = \frac{\sum X^2 - \dfrac{\left(\sum X\right)^2}{N}}{df}$$

$$= \frac{368.694 - \dfrac{2704}{9}}{2}$$

$$= \frac{368.694 - 300.444}{2} = \frac{68.250}{2} = 34.125$$

Step 3   Draw up the table of the 'error' scores (Table 20.12) by subtracting the 'true' scores table from the original data table (Table 20.10). Remember all you have to do is to take the corresponding scores in the two tables when doing this subtraction. The alternative is to take the appropriate column mean away from each score in your data table.

$$\text{variance estimate}_{[error]} = \frac{\sum X^2 - \dfrac{\left(\sum X\right)^2}{N}}{df}$$

$$\sum X^2 = (-0.667)^2 + 0.333^2 + (-1.000)^2 + 2.333^2 + (-1.667)^2 + 2.000^2 + (-1.667)^2 + 1.333^2 + (-1.000)^2$$

$$= 0.445 + 0.111 + 1.000 + 5.443 + 2.779 + 4.000 + 2.779 + 1.777 + 1.000$$

$$= 19.334$$

$$\left(\sum X\right)^2 = [(-0.667) + 0.333 + (-1.000) + 2.333 + (-1.667) + 2.000 + (-1.667) + 1.333 + (-1.000)]^2$$

$$= 0$$

The number of scores N equals 9. The degrees of freedom (df) equal N minus the number of columns, i.e. 9 − 3 = 6. We can now substitute in the above formula:

$$\text{variance estimate}_{[error]} = \frac{\sum X^2 - \dfrac{\left(\sum X\right)^2}{N}}{df} = \frac{19.334 - \dfrac{0}{9}}{6} = 3.222$$

Table 20.12	'Error' scores based on the data in Table 20.10	
Group 1	**Group 2**	**Group 3**
−0.667	0.333	−1.000
2.333	−1.667	2.000
−1.667	1.333	−1.000
Mean = 0.000	**Mean = 0.000**	**Mean = 0.000**
		Overall mean = 0.000

Step 4   We can now work out the *F*-ratio by dividing the variance estimate$_{[\text{true scores}]}$ by the variance estimate$_{[\text{error scores}]}$:

$$F\text{-ratio} = \frac{\text{variance estimate}_{[\text{true scores}]}}{\text{variance estimate}_{[\text{error scores}]}}$$

$$= \frac{34.125}{3.222}$$

$$= 10.6 \text{ (degrees of freedom} = 2 \text{ for true and } 6 \text{ for error)}$$

From Significance Table 20.1, we need a value of *F* of 5.1 or more to be significant at the 5% level of significance. Since our value of 10.6 is substantially larger than this, we can reject the null hypothesis and accept the hypothesis that the groups are significantly different from each other at the 5% level of significance.

20.5   The analysis of variance summary table

The analysis of variance calculation can get very complicated with complex experimental designs. In preparation for this, it is useful to get into the habit of recording your analysis in an analysis of variance summary table. This systematically records major aspects of the calculation. Table 20.13 is appropriate for this. Notice that the sums of squares for 'true' and 'error' added together are the same as the sum of squares of the original data (allowing for rounding errors). Don't forget that the sum of squares is simply the upper part of the variance estimate formula. Similarly the degrees of freedom of 'true' and 'error' scores added together give the degrees of freedom for the original data. The degrees of freedom are the lower part of the variance estimate formula.

In Table 20.13, we have used the terminology from our explanation. This is not quite standard in discussions regarding the analysis of variance. It is more usual to see the analysis of variance summary table in the form of Table 20.14 which uses slightly different terms.

Tables 20.13 and 20.14 are equivalent except for the terminology and the style of reporting significance levels:

1. 'Mean square' is analysis of variance terminology for variance estimate. Unfortunately the name 'mean square' loses track of the fact that it is an estimate and suggests that it is something new.

2. 'Between' is another way of describing the variation due to the 'true' scores. The idea is that the variation of the 'true' scores is essentially the differences between the groups or experimental conditions. Sometimes these are called the 'treatments'.

Table 20.13	Analysis of variance summary table for unrelated ANOVAs				
Source of variation	Sum of squares	Degrees of freedom	Variance estimate	*F*-ratio	Significance
'True' scores	68.222	2	34.111	10.6	5%
'Error' scores	19.334	6	3.222		
Original data	87.556	8	10.944		

Table 20.14	Analysis of variance summary table for unrelated ANOVAs using alternative terminology			
Source of variation	Sum of squares	Degrees of freedom	Mean square	F-ratio
Between groups	68.222	2	34.111	10.6*
Within groups	19.334	6	3.222	
Total	87.556	8	10.944	

*Significant at 5% level.

3. 'Within' is just another way of describing the 'error' variation. It is called 'within' since the calculation of 'error' is based on the variation *within* a group or experimental condition.

4. Total is virtually self-explanatory – it is the variation of the original scores which combine 'true' and 'error' components.

20.6 Quick calculation methods for ANOVA

The following step-by-step procedure describes the quick way for calculating the unrelated/uncorrelated one-way ANOVA by hand. This is less error prone than the conceptually clearer method described in Calculation 20.1 which often suffers from accumulated rounding errors. Statistics textbooks usually describe the quick formula method. It is based on the computational formula for the variance estimate (p. 121).

Calculation 20.2

One-way unrelated analysis of variance: quick method

The following calculation involves three different conditions (levels) of the independent variable. The method is easily adapted to any other number of conditions from a minimum of two.

Step 1 Draw up a data table using the format shown in Table 20.15. Calculate the totals for each column separately (i.e. T_1, T_2, T_3). (Notice that you are calculating totals rather than means with this method.) Remember that this table gives us the data on the influence of the independent variable (drug treatment, which has three levels – hormone 1, hormone 2 and placebo control) on the dependent variable (depression).

1. Calculate the overall (or grand) total of the scores: $G = 9 + 12 + 8 + 4 + 2 + 5 + 3 + 6 + 3 = 52$, or simply add the column totals to obtain this value.

2. Calculate the number of scores: $N = 9$.

Table 20.15	Stylised data table for an unrelated analysis of variance

Group 1 Hormone 1	Group 2 Hormone 2	Group 3 Placebo control
9	4	3
12	2	6
8	5	3
$N_1 = 3$	$N_2 = 3$	$N_3 = 3$
Total $= T_1 = 9 + 12 + 8 = 29$	Total $= T_2 = 4 + 2 + 5 = 11$	Total $= T_3 = 3 + 6 + 3 = 12$

3. Insert the number of scores for each group (N_1, N_2 and N_3). In our example these are all 3 as the group sizes are equal, but this does not have to be so with the unrelated one-way analysis of variance.

4. Total degrees of freedom for the data table is: number of scores $- 1 = 9 - 1 = 8$.

Step 2   Square each of the scores (X) and then sum all of these squared scores (i.e. to give the sum of squared scores or $\sum X^2$):

$$\sum X^2 = 9^2 + 12^2 + 8^2 + 4^2 + 2^2 + 5^2 + 3^2 + 6^2 + 3^2$$

$$= 81 + 144 + 64 + 16 + 4 + 25 + 9 + 36 + 9$$

$$= 388.000$$

Step 3   Calculate the 'correction factor' (G^2/N) by substituting the values of G and N previously obtained in steps 1 and 2. (The correction factor is merely part of the computational formula for the variance estimate (p. 121) expressed as (G^2/N) rather than ($\sum X)^2/N$.)

$$\text{correction factor} = \frac{G^2}{N} = \frac{52^2}{9} = \frac{2704}{9}$$

$$= 300.444$$

Step 4   The outcome of step 2 minus the outcome of step 3 gives the total sum of squares ($SS_{[total]}$) for the data table. It is equivalent to part of the computational formula for the calculation of the variance estimate (p. 121). Substituting the previously calculated values:

$$SS_{[total]} = \sum X^2 - \frac{G^2}{N}$$

$$= 388.000 - 300.444 = 87.556$$

Enter this value of the total sum of squares into an analysis of variance summary table such as Table 20.16. Enter the degrees of freedom for the total sum of squares. This is always $N - 1$ or the number of scores $- 1 = 9 - 1 = 8$.

Step 5   The sum of squares between groups ($SS_{[between]}$) can be calculated as follows using the correction factor (from step 3) and the column totals (T_1, etc.) and cell sizes (N_1, etc.) from Table 20.15.

Table 20.16	Analysis of variance summary table			
Source of variation	Sum of squares	Degrees of freedom	Mean square (variance estimate)	F-ratio
Between groups	68.222	2	34.111	$\dfrac{34.111}{3.222} = 10.59$[a]
Error (within groups)	19.334	6	3.222	
Total	87.556	8		

[a] Significant at the 5% level.

$$SS_{[between]} = \frac{T_1^2}{N_1} + \frac{T_2^2}{N_2} + \frac{T_3^2}{N_3} - \frac{G^2}{N} = \frac{29^2}{3} + \frac{11^2}{3} + \frac{12^2}{3} - 300.444$$

$$= \frac{841}{3} + \frac{121}{3} + \frac{144}{3} - 300.444$$

$$= 280.333 + 40.333 + 48.000 - 300.444$$

$$= 368.666 - 300.444$$

$$= 68.222$$

The degrees of freedom between subjects is columns $- 1 = c - 1 = 3 - 1 = 2$.

The mean square between groups is $SS_{[between]}$/degrees of freedom$_{[between]}$ = 68.222/2 = 34.111. These values are entered in Table 20.16.

Step 6   Calculate the error (i.e. error or within) sum of squares ($SS_{[error]}$) by subtracting the between sum of squares from the total sum of squares:

$$SS_{[error]} = SS_{[total]} - SS_{[between]} = 87.566 - 68.222 = 19.344$$

The degrees of freedom for error are the number of scores minus the number of columns: $N - c = 9 - 3 = 6$. The mean square for error is $SS_{[error]}$/degrees of freedom$_{[error]}$ = 19.334/6 = 3.222. These values are entered in Table 20.16.

Step 7   The F-ratio is the between-groups mean square divided by the error mean square. This is 34.111/3.222 = 10.6. This value can be checked against Significance Table 20.1. We need a value of F of 5.1 or more to be significant at the 5% level of significance with two degrees of freedom for the between-groups mean square and six degrees of freedom for the error mean square. Thus our obtained F-ratio of 10.6 is statistically significant at the 5% level.

Interpreting the results   The most important step in interpreting your data is simple. You need a table of the means for each of the conditions such as Table 20.17. It is obvious from this table that two of the cell means are fairly similar whereas the mean of Group 1 is relatively high. This would suggest to an experienced researcher that *if* the one-way analysis of variance is statistically significant, then a multiple comparisons test (Chapter 23) is needed in order to test for significant differences between pairs of group means.

→

Table 20.17	Table of cell means	
Group 1 Hormone 1	Group 2 Hormone 2	Group 3 Placebo control
Mean = M_1 = 9.67	Mean = M_2 = 3.67	Mean = M_3 = 4.00

Reporting the results The results of this analysis could be written up following the APA (2010) Publication Manual recommendations as: 'The data were analysed using an unrelated one-way analysis of variance. It was found that there was a significant effect of the independent variable drug treatment on the dependent variable depression, $F(2, 6) = 10.59$, $p < 0.05$. The mean for the hormone 1 group ($M = 9.67$) appears to indicate greater depression scores than for the hormone 2 group ($M = 3.67$) and the placebo control ($M = 4.00$).'

Of course, you can use Appendix J to test for significance at other levels.

In order to test whether the mean for group 1 is significantly greater than for the other two groups, it is necessary to apply a multiple comparisons test such as the Scheffé test (Chapter 23) if the differences had not been predicted. The outcome of this should also be reported.

We have given intermediary calculations for the F-ratio; these are not usually reported but may be helpful for calculation purposes.

Key points

- The *t*-test is simply a special case of one-way ANOVA, so these tests can be used interchangeably when you have two groups of scores. They give identical significance levels. The square of the two-tailed *t* value equals the one-tailed F value (e.g. $1.96^2 = 3.8416$) and the square root of the one-tailed F value equals the two-tailed *t* value (e.g. $\sqrt{3.8416} = 1.96$).

- Do not be too deterred by some of the strange terminology used in the analysis of variance. Words like treatments and levels of treatment merely reveal the agricultural origins of these statistical procedures; be warned that it gets worse. Levels of treatment simply refers to the number of different conditions for each independent variable. Thus if the independent variable has three different values it is said to have three different levels of the treatment.

- The analysis of variance with just two conditions or sets of scores is relatively easy to interpret. You merely have to examine the difference between the means of the two conditions. It is not so easy where you have three or more groups. Your analysis may not be complete until you have employed a multiple comparisons procedure as in Chapter 23. Which multiple comparisons test you use may be limited by whether your ANOVA is significant or not.

- We have used computational procedures which are not identical to those in most textbooks. We have tried to explain the analysis of variance by referring to the basic notion of variance estimate. Virtually every textbook we have seen merely gives computational procedures alone. More typical calculation methods are also included in this book.

● When the *F*-ratio is statistically significant for a one-way analysis of variance with more than two groups, you need to determine which groups differ significantly from each other. If you had good grounds for predicting which groups differed, you could use an unrelated *t*-test to see if the difference was significant (see Chapter 13). If you did not have a sound basis for predicting which groups differed, you would use a multiple comparison test such as the Scheffé test (Chapter 23).

COMPUTER ANALYSIS

The SPSS Statistics instruction book to this text is Dennis Howitt and Duncan Cramer (2011), *Introduction to SPSS Statistics in Psychology: For version 19 and earlier*, Harlow: Pearson. Chapter 21 in that book gives detailed step-by-step procedures for the statistics described in this chapter together with advice on how to report the results. Figure 20.2 gives the SPSS Statistics steps for a one-way analysis of variance.

Data
- Name the variables in Variable View of the Data Editor.
- Enter the data under the appropriate variable names in Data View of the Data Editor.

Analysis
- Select 'Analyze', 'Compare Means' and 'One-Way ANOVA . . .'.
- Move the dependent and independent (Factor) variable names to the appropriate boxes to the right.

2
- Select 'Post Hoc . . .', the post hoc test you want and 'Continue'.

3
- Select 'Options', 'Descriptive', 'Homogeneity of variance test' and 'Continue'.

Output
- Check if the Sig(nificance) of the *F* ratio is significant at .05 or less.
- If so, check that the Sig(nificance) of the homogeneity of variances is not significant at more than .05.

2
- Check which means differ significantly with the *post hoc* test or further unrelated *t*-tests.

FIGURE 20.2 SPSS Statistics steps for one-way analysis of variance

CHAPTER 21

Analysis of variance for correlated scores or repeated measures

Overview

- The related analysis of variance is used to compare two or more related samples of means. For example, when the same group of participants is assessed three times on a measure. That is, measurement takes place under a number of conditions.

- The scores are the dependent variable, the different occasions the measure is taken constitute the independent variable.

- Because individuals are measured more than once, it is possible to estimate the impact of the characteristics of the individual on the scores. This allows a separate assessment of the variation in the data due to these individual differences. Effectively this variation can be removed from the data.

- The amount of error variance is lower in related designs since the variation due to individual differences is removed. What remains of the error is known as the 'residual'. The value of the residual is compared to the variation due to the condition using the *F*-ratio.

- A significant value of the *F*-ratio shows that the means in the conditions differ from each other overall.

Preparation

You need a good understanding of the unrelated/uncorrelated analysis of variance (Chapter 20). In addition, the difference between correlated/related samples and unrelated/uncorrelated samples (or repeated measures) should be revised.

21.1   Introduction

The analysis of variance covered in this chapter is also called the related, related scores, related samples, repeated measures and matched analysis of variance.

Correlated or related research designs are held to be efficient forms of planning research. Generally these designs involve the same group of participants being assessed in two or more research conditions. The assumption is that by doing so many of the differences between people are 'allowed for' by having each person 'serve as their own control' – that is, appear in all of the research conditions.

The different sets of scores in the related or correlated analysis of variance are essentially different treatment conditions. We can describe them as either different levels of the treatment or different experimental conditions (Table 21.1).

The numerical scores are scores on the *dependent variable*. They can be any measures for which it is possible to calculate their means and variances meaningfully, in other words basically numerical scores. The treatments are the levels of the independent variable. There are very few limitations to the use of this research design:

1. It is possible to have any number of treatments with two being the minimum.

2. The groups consist of related or correlated sets of scores, for example:

    (a) children's IQs assessed at the age of 5 years, then again at 8 years and finally at 10 years (Table 21.2)

    (b) two experimental conditions versus two control conditions so long as the same subjects are in each of the conditions. The research is a study of reaction time to recognising words. The two experimental conditions are very emotive words (four-letter words) and moderately emotive words (mild swear words). The two control conditions are using neutral words and using nonsense syllables; the dependent variable is reaction time (Table 21.3)

Table 21.1	Stylised research design for the analysis of variance			
Case	**Treatment 1**	**Treatment 2**	**Treatment 3**	**Treatment 4**
Case 1 (John)	9	14	6	18
Case 2 (Heather)	7	12	9	15
Case 3 (Jane)	5	11	6	17
Case 4 (Tracy)	10	17	12	24
Case 5 (Paul)	8	15	7	19

Table 21.2	Research design of IQ assessed sequentially over time		
Child	**Age 5 years**	**Age 8 years**	**Age 10 years**
John	120	125	130
Paula	93	90	100
Sharon etc.	130	140	110

Table 21.3	Reaction time in seconds comparing two experimental conditions with two control conditions			
Subject	Four-letter words	Mild swear words	Neutral words	Nonsense syllables
Darren	0.3	0.5	0.2	0.2
Lisa etc.	0.4	0.3	0.3	0.4

Table 21.4	Weight in pounds before and after dieting	
Dieter	Before diet	After diet
Ben	130	120
Claudine etc.	153	141

Table 21.5	Stylised ANOVA design using matched samples			
Matched set	Treatment 1	Treatment 2	Treatment 3	Treatment 4
Matched set 1	9	14	6	18
Matched set 2	7	12	9	15
Matched set 3	5	11	6	17
Matched set 4	10	17	12	24
Matched set 5	8	15	7	19

    (c) a group of weight watchers' weights before and after dieting. The dependent variable is their weight in pounds (Table 21.4).

3. It is necessary to have equal numbers of scores in each group since this is a related subjects or repeated measures design. Obviously in the above examples we have used small numbers of cases.

The related/correlated analysis of variance can also be applied when you have *matched sets* of people (Table 21.5). By this we mean that although there are different people in each of the treatment conditions, they are actually very similar. Each set is as alike as possible on specified variables such as age or intelligence. One member of each matched set is assigned at random to each of the treatment conditions. The variables forming the basis of the matching are believed or known to be correlated with the dependent variable. There is no point in matching if they are not. The purpose of matching is to reduce the amount of 'error' variation.

One advantage of using matched sets of people in experiments rather than the same person in several different treatment conditions is their lack of awareness of the other treatment conditions. That is, they only respond in one version of the experimental design and so cannot be affected by their experience of the other conditions. Matching can be done on any variables you wish but it can get cumbersome if there are too many variables on which to match. So, for example, if you believed that age and sex were related to the dependent variable, you could control for these variables by using matched sets which contained people of the same sex and a very similar age. In this way variation due to sex and age is equally spread between the different treatments or conditions. Thus, matched set 1 might consist of four people matched in that they are all females in the age range 21–25 years. Each one of each of these is randomly assigned to one of the four treatment conditions. Matched set 2 might consist of four males in the age range 16 to 20 years. Once again, one of each of these four people is randomly assigned to one of the four treatment conditions.

21.2   Theoretical considerations

It is a very small step from the uncorrelated to the correlated analysis of variance. All that is different in the correlated ANOVA is that the *error* scores are reduced (or adjusted) by removing from them the contribution made by *individual differences*. By an individual difference we mean the tendency of a particular person to score generally high or generally low irrespective of the research treatment or condition they are being tested in. So, for example, bright people will tend to score higher on tests involving intellectual skills no matter what the test is. Less bright people may tend to score relatively poorly no matter what the intellectual test is. In *uncorrelated* research designs there is no way of knowing the contribution of individual differences. In effect, the individual differences have to be lumped together with the rest of the variance which we have called error. But *repeated/related/correlated* designs allow us to subdivide the error variance into two sorts: (a) that which is explained (as individual differences) and (b) that which remains unexplained (or residual error variance). So far we have discussed error variance as if it were purely the result of chance factors, but error variance is to some extent explicable in theory – the problem is that we do not know what causes it. If we can get an estimate of the contribution of an individual's particular characteristics to their scores in our research we should be able to revise the error scores so that they no longer contain any contribution from the individual difference of that participant. (Remember that individual differences are those characteristics of individuals which tend to encourage them to score generally high or generally low on the dependent variable.) Figure 21.1 shows the key steps in related ANOVA.

21.3   Examples

Once we have measured the same participant twice (or more) then it is possible to estimate the individual difference. Take the data from two individuals given in Table 21.6. Looking at these data, we can see the participants' memory ability for both words and numbers. It is clear that Ann Jones tends to do better on these memory tasks irrespective of the precise nature of the task; John Smith generally does worse no matter what the task. Although both of them seem to do better on memory for numbers, this does not alter the tendency for Ann Jones to generally do better. This is not measurement error but a general characteristic of Ann Jones. On average, Ann Jones tends to score six points above John Smith or three points above the overall mean of 15.5 and John Smith tends to score three points below the overall mean of 15.5. In other words, we can give a numerical value to their individual difference relative to the overall mean.

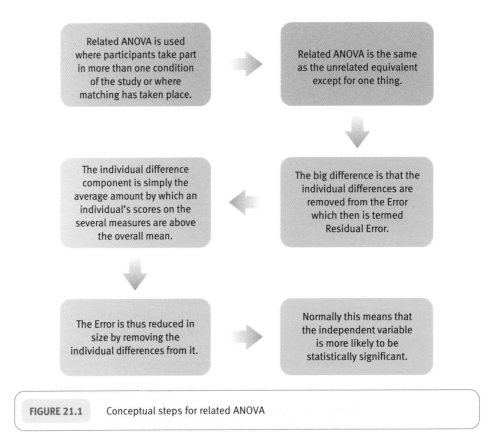

FIGURE 21.1   Conceptual steps for related ANOVA

Table 21.6	Individual differences for two people		
Subject	**Memory for words**	**Memory for numbers**	**Row mean**
Ann Jones	17	20	18.5
John Smith	11	14	12.5
			Overall mean = 15.5

A physiological psychologist is researching the effects of different pain relieving drugs on the amount of relief from pain that people experience in a controlled trial. In one condition people are given aspirin, in another condition they are given the trial drug product X, and in the third condition (the control condition) they are given a tablet which contains no active ingredient (this is known as a placebo). The amount of relief from pain experienced in these conditions is rated by each of the participants. The higher the score, the more pain relief. Just to be absolutely clear, participant 1 (Bob Robertson) gets a relief from pain score of 7 when given one aspirin, 8 when given product X and 6 when given the inactive placebo tablet (Table 21.7). It is obvious that Bob Robertson tends to get the most relief from pain (the row mean for Bob is the highest there is) whereas Bert Entwistle tends to get the least relief from pain (his row mean is the lowest there is).

The related/correlated scores analysis of variance is different in that we make adjustments for these tendencies for individuals to typically score generally high or generally low or generally in the middle. We simply subtract each person's row mean from the table's overall mean of 6.000 to find the amount of adjustment needed to each person's

Table 21.7	Pain relief scores from a drugs experiment			
Participant	Aspirin	Product X	Placebo	Row mean
Bob Robertson	7	8	6	7.000
Mavis Fletcher	5	10	3	6.000
Bob Polansky	6	6	4	5.333
Ann Harrison	9	9	2	6.667
Bert Entwistle	3	7	5	5.000
Column mean	6.000	8.000	4.000	Overall mean = 6.000

Table 21.8	Amount of adjustment of Table 21.7 for individual differences		
Participant	Overall mean	Row mean	Adjustment needed to error scores to allow for individual differences (overall mean − row mean)
Bob Robertson	6.000	7.000	−1.000
Mavis Fletcher	6.000	6.000	0.000
Bob Polansky	6.000	5.333	0.667
Ann Harrison	6.000	6.667	−0.667
Bert Entwistle	6.000	5.000	1.000

score in order to 'eliminate' individual differences from the scores. Thus for Bob Robertson we need to add −1 (i.e. 6.000 − 7.000) to each of his scores in order to overcome the tendency of his scores to be 1.000 higher than the overall mean (i.e. average score in the table). Do not forget that adding −1 is the same as subtracting 1. Table 21.8 shows the amount of adjustment needed to everyone's scores in order to eliminate individual differences.

Apart from the adjustment for individual differences, the rest of the analysis of variance is much as in Chapter 20.

Calculation 21.1

Correlated samples analysis of variance

The end point of our calculations is the analysis of variance summary table (Table 21.9). Hopefully by the time we reach the end of our explanation you will understand all of the entries in this table.

Step 1 To begin, you need to tabulate your data. We will use the fictitious relief from pain experiment described above. This is given in Table 21.10.

Table 21.9	Analysis of variance summary table				
Source of variation	Sum of squares	Degrees of freedom	Mean square (or variance estimate)	F-ratio	Probability (sig.)
Between treatments (i.e. drugs)	40.00	2	20.00	5.10	5%
Between people (i.e. individual differences)	8.67	4	2.17		
Error (i.e. residual)	31.33	8	3.92		
Total	80.00	14			

Table 21.10	Pain relief scores from a drugs experiment			
Participant	Aspirin	Product X	Placebo	Row mean
Bob Robertson	7	8	6	7.000
Mavis Fletcher	5	10	3	6.000
Bob Polansky	6	6	4	5.333
Ann Harrison	9	9	2	6.667
Bert Entwistle	3	7	5	5.000
Column mean	6.000	8.000	4.000	Overall mean = 6.000

If you wish, you may calculate the variance estimate of this table using the standard variance estimate formula. As this is generally only a check on your calculations, it is unnecessary for our present purposes since it contains nothing new. If you do the calculation then you should find that the sum of squares is 80 and the degrees of freedom 14 which would give a variance estimate value of 5.71 (i.e. 80 divided by 14). The first two pieces of information are entered into the analysis of variance summary table.

Step 2 We then produce a table of the 'true' scores. Remember that 'true' scores are usually called the 'between' or 'between groups' scores in analysis of variance. To do this, we simply substitute the column mean for each of the individual scores in that column so leaving no variation within the column – the only variation is between the columns. The results are given in Table 21.11.

Table 21.11	'True' scores (obtained by replacing each score in a column by its column mean)			
Participant	Aspirin	Product X	Placebo	Row mean
Bob Robertson	6.000	8.000	4.000	6.000
Mavis Fletcher	6.000	8.000	4.000	6.000
Bob Polansky	6.000	8.000	4.000	6.000
Ann Harrison	6.000	8.000	4.000	6.000
Bert Entwistle	6.000	8.000	4.000	6.000
Column mean	6.000	8.000	4.000	Overall mean = 6.000

The estimated variance of these data can be calculated using the standard formula:

$$\text{estimated variance}_{\text{[true/between scores]}} = \frac{\sum X^2 - \dfrac{(\sum X)^2}{N}}{df}$$

$$\sum X^2 = 6.000^2 + 8.000^2 + 4.000^2 + 6.000^2 + 8.000^2 + 4.000^2 + 6.000^2 + 8.000^2 + 4.000^2 + 6.000^2 \\ + 8.000^2 + 4.000^2 + 6.000^2 + 8.000^2 + 4.000^2$$

$$= 36.000 + 64.000 + 16.000 + 36.000 + 64.000 + 16.000 + 36.000 + 64.000 + 16.000 \\ + 36.000 + 64.000 + 16.000 + 36.000 + 64.000 + 16.000$$

$$= 580$$

$$(\sum X)^2 = (6.000 + 8.000 + 4.000 + 6.000 + 8.000 + 4.000 + 6.000 + 8.000 + 4.000 + 6.000 \\ + 8.000 + 4.000 + 6.000 + 8.000 + 4.000)^2$$

$$= (90)^2$$

$$= 8100$$

The number of scores N equals 15. The degrees of freedom (df) equals the number of columns of data minus 1 ($3 - 1 = 2$). Substituting in the formula:

$$\text{estimated variance}_{\text{[true/between scores]}} = \frac{\sum X^2 - \dfrac{(\sum X)^2}{N}}{df}$$

$$= \frac{580 - \dfrac{8100}{15}}{2}$$

$$= \frac{580 - 540}{2} = \frac{40}{2}$$

$$= 20.0$$

Step 3   The error table is now calculated as an intermediate stage. As ever, this is done by subtracting the true/between scores from the scores in the original data table (see Table 21.12). Alternatively, we subtract the column mean from each of the scores in the data table.

Table 21.12	'Error' scores (original data table minus true/between scores)			
Participant	**Aspirin**	**Product X**	**Placebo**	**Row mean**
Bob Robertson	1.000	0.000	2.000	1.000
Mavis Fletcher	−1.000	2.000	−1.000	0.000
Bob Polansky	0.000	−2.000	0.000	−0.667
Ann Harrison	3.000	1.000	−2.000	0.667
Bert Entwistle	−3.000	−1.000	1.000	−1.000
Column mean	**0.000**	**0.000**	**0.000**	**Overall mean = 0.000**

This is essentially our table of 'error' scores, but since the row means vary (Bert Entwistle's is −1.000 but Mavis Fletcher's is 0.000) then we still have to remove the effects of the individual differences. This we do simply by taking away the row mean from each of the error scores in the row. That is, we take 1.000 away from Bob Robertson's error scores, 0.000 from Mavis Fletcher's, −0.667 from Bob Polansky's, 0.667 from Ann Harrison's and −1.000 from Bert Entwistle's. (Don't forget that subtracting a negative number is like adding a positive number.) This gives us a revised table of error scores without any individual differences. It is usually called the *residual* scores table in analysis of variance, but it is just a more refined set of error scores (Table 21.13).

Table 21.13	'Residual (error)' scores (obtained by subtracting individual differences or row means from Table 21.12)			
Participant	**Aspirin**	**Product X**	**Placebo**	**Row mean**
Bob Robertson	0.000	−1.000	1.000	0.000
Mavis Fletcher	−1.000	2.000	−1.000	0.000
Bob Polansky	0.667	−1.333	0.667	0.000
Ann Harrison	2.333	0.333	−2.667	0.000
Bert Entwistle	−2.000	0.000	2.000	0.000
Column mean	**0.000**	**0.000**	**0.000**	**Overall mean = 0.000**

Notice that both the column and row means now equal zero. This is because not only have the 'true' or between scores been removed from the table but the individual differences are now gone. We need to check out the degrees of freedom associated with this table. There are more constraints now because the row totals have to equal zero. Thus in the aspirin column we can adjust four scores, but the fifth score is fixed by the requirement that the mean equals zero. In the product X condition we can again vary four scores. However, once we have made these changes, we cannot vary any of the scores in the placebo condition because the row means have to equal zero. In other words, there is a total of eight degrees of freedom in the residual error scores.

The formula for the degrees of freedom is quite straightforward:

$$\text{degrees of freedom}_{[\text{residual error scores}]} = (\text{number of columns of error scores} - 1)$$
$$\times (\text{number of rows of error scores} - 1)$$

The variance estimate of this residual error can be calculated using the standard formula:

$$\text{variance estimate}_{[\text{residual error scores}]} = \frac{\sum X^2 \dfrac{(\sum X)^2}{N}}{df}$$

$$\sum X^2 = 0.000^2 + (-1.000)^2 + 1.000^2 + (-1.000)^2 + 2.000^2 + (-1.000)^2 + 0.667^2 + (-1.333)^2 + 0.667^2$$
$$+ 2.333^2 + 0.333^2 + (-2.667)^2 + (-2.000)^2 + 0.000^2 + 2.000^2$$

$$= 0.000 + 1.000 + 1.000 + 1.000 + 4.000 + 1.000 + 0.445 + 1.777 + 0.445 + 5.443 + 0.111$$
$$+ 7.113 + 4.000 + 0.000 + 4.000$$

$$= 31.334$$

→

$$\left(\sum X\right)^2 = [0.000 + (-1.000) + 1.000 + (-1.000) + 2.000 + (-1.000) + 0.667 + (-1.333)$$
$$+ 0.667 + 2.333 + 0.333 + (-2.667) + (-2.000) + 0.000 + 2.000]^2$$

$$= 0$$

The number of scores N equals 15 as before. The degrees of freedom are given by:

$$\text{degrees of freedom} = (\text{number of columns} - 1) \times (\text{number of rows} - 1)$$

$$= (3 - 1) \times (5 - 1)$$

$$= 2 \times 4 = 8$$

Substituting in the formula:

$$\text{variance estimate}_{[\text{residual error scores}]} = \frac{\sum X^2 - \dfrac{\left(\sum X\right)^2}{N}}{df}$$

$$= \frac{31.334 - \dfrac{0}{15}}{8}$$

$$= \frac{31.334}{8} = 3.92$$

Step 4 This is not absolutely necessary, but the conventional approach to correlated/repeated measures analysis of variance calculates the variance estimate of the individual differences. This is usually described as the between-people variance estimate or 'blocks' variance estimate. (The word 'blocks' originates from the days when the analysis of variance was confined to agricultural research. Different amounts of fertiliser would be put on a single area of land and the fertility of these different 'blocks' assessed. The analysis of variance contains many terms referring to its agricultural origins such as split plots, randomised plots, levels of treatment and so forth.)

If you wish to calculate the between-people (or individual differences) variance estimate, you need to draw up Table 21.14 which consists of the individual differences component in each score (this is obtained by the difference between the row means and the overall mean in the original data). In other

Table 21.14	Between-people (individual difference) scores (obtained by taking the difference between the row means and overall mean in the original data)			

Participant	Aspirin	Product X	Placebo	Row mean
Bob Robertson	1.000	1.000	1.000	1.000
Mavis Fletcher	0.000	0.000	0.000	0.000
Bob Polansky	−0.667	−0.667	−0.667	−0.667
Ann Harrison	0.667	0.667	0.667	0.667
Bert Entwistle	−1.000	−1.000	−1.000	−1.000
Column mean	0.000	0.000	0.000	Overall mean = 0.000

→

words, it is a table of the amount of adjustment required to everyone's scores in order to remove the effect of their individual characteristics.

We calculate the variance estimate of this using the usual variance estimate formula for the analysis of variance. The degrees of freedom are constrained by the fact that the column means have to equal zero and that all the scores in the row are the same. In the end, this means that the degrees of freedom for this table are the number of rows minus one. We have five rows so therefore the number of degrees of freedom is four.

The sum of squares for Table 21.14 is 8.67 and the degrees of freedom are 4, therefore the variance estimate is $8.67/4 = 2.17$. These values can be entered in the analysis of variance summary table. (Strictly speaking, this is another unnecessary stage in the calculation, but it does provide a check on the accuracy of your calculations.)

Step 5 We can enter the calculations into an analysis of variance summary table. It might be more conventional to see an analysis of variance summary table written in the form shown in Table 21.15. Some calculations are unnecessary and we have omitted them.

Table 21.15	Analysis of variance summary table			
Source of variation	**Sum of squares**	**Degrees of freedom**	**Mean square (or variance estimate)**	**F-ratio**
Between treatments (i.e. drugs)	40.00	2	20.00	5.10[a]
Between people (i.e. individual differences)	8.67	4	2.17	–
Error (i.e. residual)	31.33	8	3.92	–
Total	80.00	14	–	–

[a] Significant at 5% level.

Notice that the total sum of squares (80.00) is the same as the sum of the individual components of this total ($40.00 + 8.67 + 31.33$) and this applies also to the degrees of freedom. This can provide a useful check on the accuracy of your calculations.

The most important part of the table is the F-ratio. This is the between-groups variance estimate divided by the error (residual) variance estimate. In other words, it is $20.00/3.92 = 5.10$. The statistical significance of this value has been assessed by the use of Significance Table 21.1. With two degrees of freedom for between treatments and eight for the error, a minimum F-ratio of 4.5 is needed to be statistically significant. Thus the obtained F-ratio of 5.10 is significant at the 5% level.

The significant probability value of 5% tells us that the variance in the between-groups scores is substantially greater than the error (residual) variance. Thus the null hypothesis that the drugs have no effect on the amount of relief from pain is rejected and the hypothesis that the drugs treatments have an effect at the 5% level of significance is accepted.

Significance Table 21.1	5% significance values of the *F*-ratio for related ANOVA (one-tailed test). Additional values are to be found in Significance Table 19.1					
Degrees of freedom for residual or residual error mean square (or variance estimate)	Degrees of freedom for between-treatments mean square (or variance estimate)					
	1	2	3	4	5	∞
1	161 or more	200	216	225	230	254
2	18.5	19.0	19.2	19.3	19.3	19.5
3	10.1	9.6	9.3	9.1	9.0	8.5
4	7.7	6.9	6.6	6.4	6.3	5.6
5	6.6	5.8	5.4	5.2	5.1	4.4
6	6.0	5.1	4.8	4.5	4.4	3.7
7	5.6	4.7	4.4	4.1	4.0	3.2
8	5.3	4.5	4.1	3.8	3.7	2.9
9	5.1	4.3	3.9	3.6	3.5	2.7
10	5.0	4.1	3.7	3.5	3.3	2.5
13	4.7	3.8	3.4	3.2	3.0	2.2
15	4.5	3.7	3.3	3.1	2.9	2.1
20	4.4	3.5	3.1	2.9	2.7	1.8
30	4.2	3.3	2.9	2.7	2.5	1.6
60	4.0	3.2	2.8	2.5	2.4	1.4
∞	3.8	3.0	2.6	2.4	2.2	1.0

Your value has to equal or be larger than the tabulated value for an effect to be significant at the 5% level.

21.4 Quick method for calculating the correlated ANOVA

Calculation 21.1 gives a *conceptual* account of the calculation of the analysis of variance. It suffers from being somewhat laborious and prone to the cumulative effects of rounding which can produce slight errors. The following describes the usual calculation steps involved in the standard quick calculation method. The difficulty is that it gives little insight into what is actually happening with the analysis of variance. However, if you have mastered Calculation 21.1 then you might find it advantageous to try the following approach.

Calculation 21.2

Correlated samples analysis of variance: quick method

Step 1 Tabulate your data. We are using the fictitious relief from pain data given in Table 21.10 so that you may make comparisons with Calculation 21.1 if you wish. These data have been entered into Table 21.16. Certain additional calculations have been included such as the row total for each person in the study (i.e. P_1, etc.) and the column totals (i.e. C_1, etc.). The grand total or G is simply the sum of all of the scores in the table. Thus it could be calculated by adding all of the row totals or all of the column totals.

Table 21.16 The data for the relief from pain study plus additional row and column totals

Participant	Aspirin condition	Product X	Placebo	Row totals
Bob Robertson	7	8	6	$P_1 = 21$
Mavis Fletcher	5	10	3	$P_2 = 18$
Bob Polansky	6	6	4	$P_3 = 16$
Ann Harrison	9	9	2	$P_4 = 20$
Bert Entwistle	3	7	5	$P_5 = 15$
Column totals	$C_1 = 30$	$C_2 = 40$	$C_3 = 20$	Grand total $= G = 90$

Step 2 Calculate the square of each score to obtain the sum of squared scores ($\sum X^2_{[\text{total}]}$):

$$\sum X^2_{[\text{total}]} = 7^2 + 5^2 + 6^2 + 9^2 + 3^2 + 8^2 + 10^2 + 6^2 + 9^2 + 7^2 + 6^2 + 3^2 + 4^2 + 2^2 + 5^2$$

$$= 49 + 25 + 36 + 81 + 9 + 64 + 100 + 36 + 81 + 49 + 36 + 9 + 16 + 4 + 25$$

$$= 620$$

Step 3 Calculate the correction factor G^2/N:

$$\text{correction factor} = \frac{G^2}{N} = \frac{90^2}{15} = \frac{8100}{15} = 540.000$$

G is the grand total or total of all the scores. N is the number of scores. The correction factor is merely the equivalent of $(\sum X)^2/N$ in the calculation formula for the variance estimate (p. 121).

The following calculations should be entered into an analysis of variance summary table such as Table 21.17.

Step 4 Calculate the between people sum of squares. Refer to step 1 and Table 21.16 for the meaning and values of P_1^2 etc.:

$$SS_{[\text{between people}]} = \frac{P_1^2 + P_2^2 + P_3^2 + P_4^2 + P_5^2}{\text{number of columns (i.e. conditions)}} - \frac{G^2}{N}$$

→

Table 21.17	Analysis of variance summary table for quick computation method			
Source of variation	**Sum of squares**	**Degrees of freedom**	**Mean square (or variance estimate)**	**F-ratio**
Between treatments (i.e. drugs)	40.000	2	20.000	$\frac{20.000}{3.917} = 5.11^a$
Between people (i.e. individual differences)	8.667	4	2.167	–
Error (i.e. residual)	31.333	8	3.917	–
Total	80.000	14	–	–

[a] Significant at the 5% level.

The number of columns of data is three. Remember that the final part of the above formula after the minus sign is the correction factor which we calculated to equal 540.000 in step 3.

$$SS_{[between\ people]} = \frac{21^2 + 18^2 + 16^2 + 20^2 + 15}{3} - 540.000$$

$$= \frac{441 + 324 + 256 + 400 + 225}{3} - 540.000$$

$$= \frac{1646}{3} - 540.000$$

$$= 548.667 - 540.000 = 8.667$$

The degrees of freedom for the $SS_{[between\ people]}$ is the number of different people (in this case 5) minus one (i.e. $5 - 1 = 4$).

Step 5 Calculate the between-conditions sum of squares. Refer to step 1 and Table 21.16 for the meaning and values of C_1, etc. Remember that the correction factor has already been calculated to be 540.000 in step 2 so we can simply insert this value.

$$SS_{[between\ conditions]} = \frac{C_1^2 + C_2^2 + C_3^2}{number\ of\ rows\ (i.e.\ different\ people)} - \frac{G^2}{N}$$

$$= \frac{30^2 + 40^2 + 20^2}{5} - 540.000$$

$$= \frac{2900}{5} - 540.000$$

$$= 580.000 - 540.000$$

$$= 40.000$$

The degrees of freedom for the $SS_{[between\ conditions]}$ is the number of columns (i.e. conditions) minus one (i.e. $3 - 1 = 2$).

Step 6

Calculate the sum of squares for the error (i.e. residual error). This is based on the squares of the individual scores as calculated in step 2. All of the separate parts of the formula have already been calculated. Substitute these values from the earlier steps into the following formula:

$$SS_{[\text{residual error}]} = \sum X^2_{\text{total}} - \frac{C_1^2 + C_2^2 + C_3^2}{\underset{\substack{\text{(i.e. different people)}}}{\text{number of rows}}} - \frac{P_1^2 + P_2^2 + P_3^2 + P_4^2 + P_5^2}{\underset{\substack{\text{(i.e. conditions)}}}{\text{number of rows}}} + \frac{G^2}{N}$$

$$= 620.000 - \frac{30^2 + 40^2 + 20^2}{5} - \frac{21^2 + 18^2 + 16^2 + 20^2 + 15^2}{3} + \frac{90^2}{15}$$

$$= 620.000 - 580.000 - 548.667 + 540.000$$

$$= 31.33$$

The degrees of freedom $SS_{[\text{residual error}]}$ = (number of conditions − 1) × (number of rows (or participants) − 1) = (3 − 1) × (5 − 1) = 8.

Step 7

Calculate the means in Table 21.17 by dividing each sum of squares by the relevant degrees of freedom.

Step 8

The essential calculations for the correlated/related one-way analysis of variance are now completed. The F-ratio in Table 21.17 is simply the between-treatments mean square divided by the (residual) error mean square. The interpretation of this table is exactly as for Calculation 21.1 since we have exactly the same ANOVA summary table. (Sometimes the two methods will produce slightly different answers because of the effects of rounding errors.) Use Significance Table 21.1 to check the minimum value to be statistically significant. The between-treatments degrees of freedom indicates the column to choose and the residual error degrees of freedom indicates the row to choose.

Interpreting the results The pattern of condition means (Table 21.18) is crucial for interpreting the data. Tests of significance merely indicate whether the trends can be generalised. The table of means seems to suggest that each of the groups is substantially different from any other.

Table 21.18	Table of condition means		
Aspirin		**Product X**	**Placebo**
M_1 = 6.000		M_2 = 8.000	M_3 = 4.000

Reporting the results The results may be written up following the APA (2010) Publication Manual's recommendations as: 'A related-samples ANOVA was carried out on the data. It was found that there was a significant effect of the independent variable type of drug treatment on the dependent variable relief from pain, $F(2, 8) = 5.10$, $p < 0.05$. Product X produced the greatest relief from pain ($M = 8.00$), aspirin the next highest relief from pain ($M = 6.00$) and the inert placebo tablet the least relief from pain ($M = 4.00$). Thus it is clear that relief from pain was affected by the type of drug given.'

For a complete analysis of the data, also calculate exactly which of the three drug conditions were significantly different from each other – see the panel opposite on multiple comparisons with related designs.

Box 21.1   Key concepts

Multiple comparisons with related designs

Related analyses of variance with three or more groups *may* require that a multiple comparison test is employed in order to assess just where the differences lie (that is, which of the various groups actually differ significantly from each other). This is discussed in Chapter 23 as are some of the tests available for such testing. Unfortunately, this is an area for which it is difficult to present a straightforward satisfactory solution as authorities in the field often seem to differ widely in their advice. In addition, the advice will vary according to how carefully planned the analysis was. If the comparisons have been planned in advance of the analysis (*a priori*) in the light of the requirements of the research hypotheses then we generally do not have a major problem (see p. 279). If, for example, the comparisons are simply made after the data have been collected, perhaps in order to exhaust all of the possibilities for the analysis (that is, *post hoc* analysis), then things become more problematic for the simple reason that the more comparisons one makes then the higher likelihood that one has to find something significant by chance. This needs to be taken into account.

The multiple comparison tests available (see Chapter 23) are designed for unrelated scores. Using them would lose some of the advantage of related designs. If they were used, this would result in a conservative test in that the possibility of obtaining significance is reduced compared to an 'optimum' test. Probably the simplest approach is simply to use the paired *t*-tests adjusted for the multiple comparisons made (see pp. 278–9). Quite simply, the exact significance obtained from SPSS Statistics output, for example, is multiplied by the number of multiple comparisons being made. This would be the Bonferroni adjustment. So if the exact significance of a related *t*-test comparing condition A and condition C is 0.002 and two multiple comparisons are being made in total (i.e. condition B is being compared with condition C also), then the proper significance of the related *t*-test between condition A and condition C is $2 \times 0.002 = 0.004$. Sometimes it is recommended that you carry out multiple comparison testing *only* if the ANOVA itself is statistically significant. However, this advice can be ignored for some multiple comparison tests. The Bonferroni adjustment is probably sufficiently conservative for us not to require the ANOVA to be significant overall prior to the multiple comparisons.

Key points

- Working out this analysis of variance by hand is quite time-consuming and extremely repetitive. Computers will save most people time.

- Do not be too deterred by some of the strange terminology used in the analysis of variance. Words like blocks, split-plots and levels of treatment have their origins in agricultural research, as does ANOVA.

- The analysis of variance in cases in which you have just two conditions or sets of scores is relatively easy to interpret. It is not so easy where you have three or more groups; then your analysis is not complete until you have employed a multiple comparisons procedure as in Chapter 23.

COMPUTER ANALYSIS

The SPSS Statistics instruction book to this text is Dennis Howitt and Duncan Cramer (2011), *Introduction to SPSS Statistics in Psychology: For version 19 and earlier*, Harlow: Pearson. Chapter 22 in that book gives detailed step-by-step procedures for the statistics described in this chapter together with advice on how to report the results. Figure 21.2 shows the SPSS Statistics steps for a repeated measures analysis of variance.

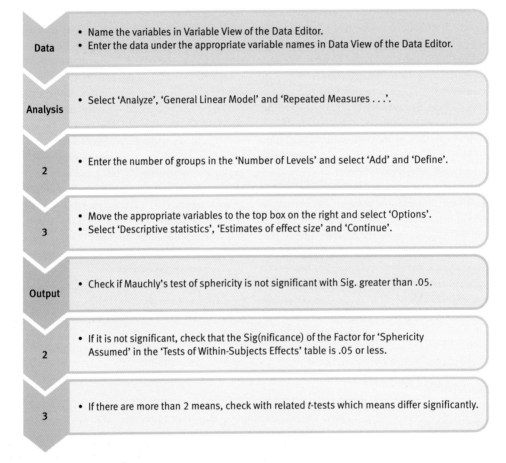

Data
- Name the variables in Variable View of the Data Editor.
- Enter the data under the appropriate variable names in Data View of the Data Editor.

Analysis
- Select 'Analyze', 'General Linear Model' and 'Repeated Measures . . .'.

2
- Enter the number of groups in the 'Number of Levels' and select 'Add' and 'Define'.

3
- Move the appropriate variables to the top box on the right and select 'Options'.
- Select 'Descriptive statistics', 'Estimates of effect size' and 'Continue'.

Output
- Check if Mauchly's test of sphericity is not significant with Sig. greater than .05.

2
- If it is not significant, check that the Sig(nificance) of the Factor for 'Sphericity Assumed' in the 'Tests of Within-Subjects Effects' table is .05 or less.

3
- If there are more than 2 means, check with related *t*-tests which means differ significantly.

FIGURE 21.2 SPSS Statistics steps for a repeated measures analysis of variance

CHAPTER 22

Two-way analysis of variance for unrelated/uncorrelated scores

Two studies for the price of one?

Overview

- The two-way analysis of variance involves two independent variables and a single dependent variable which is the score.

- It then has the potential to indicate the extent to which the two independent variables may combine to influence scores on the dependent variable.

- The main effects are the influence of the independent variables acting separately, the interaction is the influence of the independent variables acting in combination.

- Much of the two-way analysis of variance proceeds like two separate one-way analyses. However, there is the interaction which is really a measure of the multiplicative (rather than additive) influence of the two independent variables acting in combination.

- The two-way analysis of variance can be extended to any number of independent variables though the process rapidly becomes very cumbersome with each additional independent variable.

Preparation

Chapter 20 on the one-way analysis of variance contains material essential to the full understanding of this chapter.

22.1   Introduction

Often researchers wish to assess the influence of more than a single independent variable at a time in experiments. The one-way analysis of variance deals with a single independent variable which can have two or more levels. However, analysis of variance copes with several *independent* variables in a research design. These are known as multifactorial ANOVAs. The number of 'ways' is the number of independent variables. Thus a two-way analysis of variance allows two independent variables to be included, three-way analysis of variance allows three independent variables and five-way analysis of variance means that there are five independent variables. *There is only one dependent variable no matter how many 'ways' in each analysis of variance. If you have two or more *dependent* variables, each of these will entail a separate analysis of variance. Although things can get very complicated conceptually, two-way analysis of variance is relatively straightforward and introduces just one major new concept – interaction.

In this chapter we will be concentrating on examples in which all of the scores are independent (uncorrelated). Each person therefore contributes just one score to the analysis. In other words, it is an *uncorrelated* design.

Generally speaking, the 'multivariate' analysis of variance is best suited to experimental research in which it is possible to allocate participants at random into the various conditions. Although this does not apply to the one-way analysis of variance, there are problems in using two-way and multi-way analyses of variance in survey and other non-experimental research. The difficulty is that calculations become more complex if you do not have equal numbers of scores in each of the cells or conditions. This is difficult to arrange in surveys. (It is possible to work with unequal numbers of scores in the different conditions, or cells, but these procedures tend to be a little cumbersome for hand calculation – see Chapter 24.)

So a typical research design for a two-way analysis of variance is the effect of the *independent variables* alcohol *and* sleep deprivation on the *dependent variable* of people's comprehension of complex video material expressed in terms of the number of mistakes made on a test of understanding of the video material. The research design and data might look like that shown in Table 22.1.

In a sense, one could regard this experiment conceptually as two separate experiments, one studying the effects of sleep deprivation and the other studying the effects of alcohol. The effects of each of the two independent variables are called the *main* effects. Additionally, the analysis normally looks for *interactions* which are basically findings

Table 22.1	Data for typical two-way analysis of variance: number of mistakes on video test		
	Sleep deprivation		
	4 hours	**12 hours**	**24 hours**
Alcohol	16	18	22
	12	16	24
	17	25	32
No alcohol	11	13	12
	9	8	14
	12	11	12

which cannot be explained on the basis of the distinctive effects of alcohol level and sleep deprivation acting separately. For example, it could be that people do especially badly if they have been deprived of a lot of sleep *and* have been given alcohol. They do more badly than the additive effects of alcohol and sleep deprivation would predict. Interactions are about the effects of specific combinations of variables. If we look carefully at Table 22.1, it is possible to see that the scores in the Alcohol–24 hours cell seem to be rather higher on average than the scores in any of the other cells. Similarly, the scores in the No alcohol–4 hours cell seem to be rather smaller, typically, than the other cells. This is an example of what we mean by an interaction – an outcome which does not seem to be the consequence of the two main variables acting separately. We will return to the concept of interaction later.

In the analysis of variance, we sometimes talk of the *levels of a treatment* – this is simply the number of values that any independent variable can take. In the above example, the alcohol variable has two different values – that is, there are two levels of the treatment or variable alcohol. There are three levels of the treatment or variable sleep deprivation. Sometimes, a two-way ANOVA is identified in terms of the numbers of levels of treatment for each of the independent variables. So a 2 × 3 ANOVA has two different levels of the first variable and three for the second variable. This corresponds to the above example.

22.2   Theoretical considerations

Much of the two-way analysis of variance is easy if it is remembered that it largely involves two separate 'one-way' analyses of variance as if there were two separate experiments. Imagine an experiment in which one group of subjects is given iron supplements in their diet to see if iron has any effect on their depression levels. In the belief that women have a greater need for iron than men, the researchers included gender as their other independent variable. The data are given in Table 22.2. Figure 22.1 gives the key steps in a two-way ANOVA.

Table 22.2	Data table for study of dietary supplements		
	Iron supplement	**No iron supplement**	
Males	3	9	
	7	5	
	4	6	
	6	8	
	Cell mean = 5.00	Cell mean = 7.00	Row mean = 6.00
Females	11	19	
	7	16	
	10	18	
	8	15	
	Cell mean = 9.00	Cell mean = 17.00	Row mean = 13.00
	Column mean = 7.00	**Column mean = 12.00**	**Overall mean = 9.50**

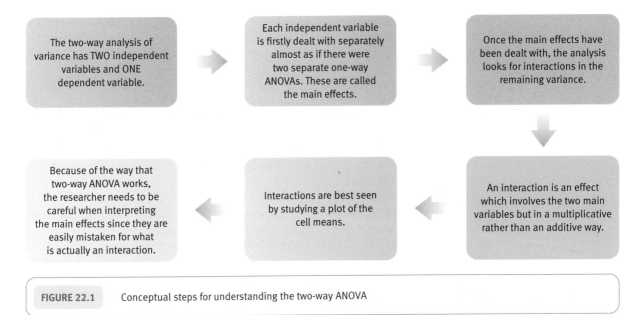

The two-way analysis of variance has TWO independent variables and ONE dependent variable.

Each independent variable is firstly dealt with separately almost as if there were two separate one-way ANOVAs. These are called the main effects.

Once the main effects have been dealt with, the analysis looks for interactions in the remaining variance.

An interaction is an effect which involves the two main variables but in a multiplicative rather than an additive way.

Interactions are best seen by studying a plot of the cell means.

Because of the way that two-way ANOVA works, the researcher needs to be careful when interpreting the main effects since they are easily mistaken for what is actually an interaction.

FIGURE 22.1   Conceptual steps for understanding the two-way ANOVA

Table 22.2 represents a 2 × 2 ANOVA. Comparing the four condition means (cell means), the depression scores for females not receiving the supplement seem rather higher than those of any other groups. In other words, it would appear that the lack of the iron supplement has more effect on women. Certain gender and iron supplement conditions in combination have a great effect on depression scores. This suggests an interaction. That is, particular cells in the analysis have much higher or lower scores than can be explained simply in terms of the gender trends or dietary supplement trends acting separately.

The assumption in the two-way analysis of variance is that the variation in Table 22.2 comes from four sources:

- 'error'
- the main effect of gender
- the main effect of iron supplement
- the interaction of gender and iron supplement.

The first three components above are dealt with exactly as they were in the one-way unrelated analysis of variance. The slight difference is that instead of calculating the variance estimate for one independent variable we now calculate two variance estimates – one for each independent variable. However, the term main effect should not cause any confusion. It is merely the effect of an independent variable acting alone as it would if the two-way design were turned into two separate one-way designs. The only difference is that the error term may be smaller than in a one-way ANOVA as part of the error may now be accounted for by the other independent variable and the interaction of the two independent variables. A smaller error term makes it more likely to obtain significant effects.

The interaction consists of any variation in the scores which is left after we have taken away the 'error' and main effects for the gender and iron supplements sub-experiments. That is, priority is given to finding main effects at the expense of interactions. This is important and can lead to incorrectly interpreted analyses if it is not appreciated.

22.3   Steps in the analysis

■ Step 1

To produce an 'error' table we simply take our original data and subtract the cell mean from every score in the cell. Thus, for instance, we need to subtract 5.00 from each score in the cell for males receiving the iron supplement and 17.00 from each cell for the females not receiving the iron supplement, etc. In the present example the 'error' table is as in Table 22.3.

We calculate the 'error' variance estimate for this in the usual way. The formula, as ever, is:

$$\text{variance estimate}_{[\text{'error'}]} = \frac{\sum X^2 - \frac{(\sum X)^2}{N}}{df}$$

The degrees of freedom (df), analogously to the one-way analysis of variance, is the number of scores minus the number of conditions or cells. This leaves 12 degrees of freedom (16 scores minus 4 conditions or cells).

■ Step 2

To produce a table of the main effects for the iron supplement treatment, simply substitute the column means from the original data for each of the scores in the columns. The iron supplement mean was 7.00 so each iron supplement score is changed to 7.00, thus eliminating any other source of variation. Similarly, the no-iron supplement mean was 12.00 so each score is changed to 12.00 (see Table 22.4).

The variance estimate of the above scores can be calculated using the usual variance estimate formula. The degrees of freedom are calculated in the familiar way – the number of columns minus one (i.e. $df = 1$).

Table 22.3	'Error' scores for study of dietary supplements		
	Iron supplement	**No iron supplement**	
Males	3 − 5 = −2	9 − 7 = 2	
	7 − 5 = 2	5 − 7 = −2	
	4 − 5 = −1	6 − 7 = −1	
	6 − 5 = 1	8 − 7 = 1	
	Cell mean = 0.00	Cell mean = 0.00	Row mean = 0.00
Females	11 − 9 = 2	19 − 17 = 2	
	7 − 9 = −2	16 − 17 = −1	
	10 − 9 = 1	18 − 17 = 1	
	8 − 9 = −1	15 − 17 = −2	
	Cell mean = 0.00	Cell mean = 0.00	Row mean = 0.00
	Column mean = 0.00	**Column mean = 0.00**	**Overall mean = 0.00**

Table 22.4	Diet main effect scores for study of dietary supplements		
Iron supplement	**No iron supplement**		
7.00	12.00	
7.00	12.00	
7.00	12.00	
7.00	12.00	Row mean = 9.50
7.00	12.00	
7.00	12.00	
7.00	12.00	
7.00	12.00	Row mean = 9.50
Column mean = 7.00	Column mean = 12.00	Overall mean = 9.50

■ Step 3

To produce a table of the main effect of gender, remember that the independent variable gender is tabulated as the rows (not the columns). In other words, we substitute the row mean for the males and the row mean for the females for the respective scores (Table 22.5).

The variance estimate of the above scores can be calculated with the usual variance estimate formula. Even the degrees of freedom are calculated in the usual way. However, *as the table is on its side* compared to our usual method, the degrees of freedom are the number of *rows* minus one in this case (2 − 1 or 1 degree of freedom).

The calculation of the main effects (variance estimates) for gender and the iron supplement follows exactly the same procedures as in the one-way analysis of variance.

Table 22.5	Gender main effect scores for study of dietary supplements								
Males	6.00	6.00	6.00	6.00	6.00	6.00	6.00	6.00	Row mean = 6.00
Females	13.00	13.00	13.00	13.00	13.00	13.00	13.00	13.00	Row mean = 13.00

■ Step 4

The remaining stage is to calculate the interaction. This is simply anything which is left over after we have eliminated 'error' and the main effects. So for any score, the interaction score is found by taking the score in your data and subtracting the 'error' score and the gender score and the iron supplement score.

Table 22.6 is our data table less the 'error' variance, in other words a table which replaces each score by its cell mean.

It is obvious that the row means for the males and females are not the same. The row mean for males is 6.00 and the row mean for females is 13.00. To get rid of the gender effect, we can subtract 6.00 from each male score and 13.00 from each female score in the previous table. The results of this simple subtraction are found in Table 22.7.

Table 22.6	Data table with 'error' removed		
	Iron supplement	**No iron supplement**	
Males	5.00	7.00	
	5.00	7.00	
	5.00	7.00	
	5.00	7.00	Row mean = 6.00
Females	9.00	17.00	
	9.00	17.00	
	9.00	17.00	
	9.00	17.00	Row mean = 13.00
	Column mean = 7.00	**Column mean = 12.00**	**Overall mean = 9.50**

Table 22.7	Data table with 'error' and gender removed		
	Iron supplement	**No iron supplement**	
Males	−1.00	1.00	
	−1.00	1.00	
	−1.00	1.00	
	−1.00	1.00	Row mean = 0.00
Females	−4.00	4.00	
	−4.00	4.00	
	−4.00	4.00	
	−4.00	4.00	Row mean = 0.00
	Column mean = −2.50	**Column mean = 2.50**	**Overall mean = 0.00**

You can see that the male and female main effect has been taken into account since now both row means are zero. That is, there remains no variation due to gender. But you can see that there remains variation due to iron treatment. Those getting the supplement now score −2.50 on average and those not getting the iron treatment score +2.50. To remove the variation due to the iron treatment, subtract −2.50 from the iron supplement column and 2.50 from the non-iron supplement column (Table 22.8). Do not forget that *subtracting a negative number is like adding a positive number*.

Looking at Table 22.8, although the column and row means are zero throughout, the scores in the cells are not. This shows that there still remains a certain amount of variation in the scores even after 'error' and the two main effects have been taken away. That is, there is an interaction, which may or may not be significant. We have to check this using the *F*-ratio test.

What the interaction table implies is that women *without* the iron supplement and men *with* the iron supplement are getting the higher scores on the dependent variable.

We can calculate the variance estimate for the interaction by using the usual formula. Degrees of freedom need to be considered. The degrees of freedom for the above table of the interaction are limited by:

Table 22.8	Interaction table, i.e. data table with 'error', gender and iron supplement all removed		
	Iron supplement	**No iron supplement**	
Males	1.5	−1.5	
	1.5	−1.5	
	1.5	−1.5	
	1.5	−1.5	Row mean = 0.00
Females	−1.5	1.5	
	−1.5	1.5	
	−1.5	1.5	
	−1.5	1.5	Row mean = 0.00
	Column mean = 0.00	**Column mean = 0.00**	**Overall mean = 0.00**

- all scores in the cells having to be equal (i.e. no 'error' variance)
- all marginal means (i.e. row and column means) having to equal zero.

In other words, there can be only one degree of freedom in this case.
There is a general formula for the degrees of freedom of the interaction:

$$\text{degrees of freedom}_{[\text{interaction}]} = (\text{number of rows} - 1) \times (\text{number of columns} - 1)$$

Since there are two rows and two columns in this case, the degrees of freedom are:

$$(2 - 1) \times (2 - 1) = 1 \times 1 = 1$$

■ Step 5

All of the stages in the calculation are entered into an analysis of variance summary table (Table 22.9).

Table 22.9	Analysis of variance summary table			
Source of variation	**Sums of squares**	**Degrees of freedom**	**Mean square**	**F-ratio**
Main effects				
Gender	196.00	1	196.00	58.96[a]
Iron supplement	100.00	1	100.00	30.00[a]
Interaction				
Gender with iron supplement	36.00	1	36.00	10.81[a]
'Error'	40.00	12	3.33	–
Total (data)	372.00	15	–	–

[a] Significant at the 5% level.

Notice that there are several *F*-ratios because you need to know whether there is a significant effect of gender, a significant effect of the iron supplement and a significant interaction of the gender and iron supplement variables. In each case, you divide the appropriate mean square by the 'error' mean square. If you wish to check your understanding of the processes involved, see if you can obtain the above table by going through the individual calculations.

The significant interaction indicates that some of the cells or conditions are getting exceptionally high or low scores which cannot be accounted for on the basis of the two main effects acting independently of each other. In this case, it would appear that females getting the iron supplement and males not getting the iron supplement are actually getting higher scores than the gender or supplement acting separately and independently of each other would produce. In order to interpret an interaction, you have to remember that the effects of the independent variables are separately removed from the table (i.e. the main effects are removed first). It is only after this has been done that the interaction is calculated. In other words, ANOVA gives priority to main effects, and sometimes it can confuse interactions for main effects. Table 22.10 presents data from the present experiment in which the cell means have been altered to emphasise the lack of main effects.

In this example, it is absolutely clear that all the variation in the cell means is to do with the female/no-supplement condition. All the other three cell means are identical at 5.00. Quite clearly the males and females in the iron supplement condition have exactly the same average score. Similarly, males in the iron supplement and no-supplement conditions are obtaining identical means. In other words, there seem to be no main effects at all. The females in the no-supplement condition are the only group getting exceptionally high scores.

This would suggest that there is an interaction but no main effects. However, if you do the analysis of variance on these data you will find that there are two main effects and an interaction! The reason for this is that the main effects are estimated before the interaction, so the exceptionally high row mean for females and the exceptionally high column mean for the no-supplement condition will lead to the interaction being mistaken for main effects as your ANOVA summary table might show significant main effects. So you need to examine your data with great care as you carry out your analysis of variance, otherwise you will observe main effects which are an artifact of the method and ignore interactions which are actually there! The analysis of variance may be tricky to execute, but it can be even trickier for the novice to interpret properly – to be frank, many professional psychologists are unaware of the problems.

It is yet another example of the importance of close examination of the data alongside the statistical analysis itself.

Table 22.10	Alternative data table showing different trends		
	Iron supplement	**No iron supplement**	
Males	Cell mean = 5.00	Cell mean = 5.00	Row mean = 5.00
Females	Cell mean = 5.00	Cell mean = 17.00	Row mean = 11.00
	Column mean = 5.00	**Column mean = 11.00**	

Calculation 22.1

Two-way unrelated analysis of variance

Without a safety net we will attempt to analyse the sleep and alcohol experiment mentioned earlier. It is described as a 2 × 3 analysis of variance because one independent variable has two values and the other has three values (Table 22.11).

Table 22.11   Data for sleep deprivation experiment: number of mistakes on video test

	Sleep deprivation		
	4 hours	12 hours	24 hours
Alcohol	16	18	22
	12	16	24
	17	25	32
No alcohol	11	13	12
	9	8	14
	12	11	12

Step 1   *(total variance estimate)* We enter the row and column means as well as the means of each of the six cells (Table 22.12).

Table 22.12   Data for sleep deprivation experiment with the addition of cell, column and row means

	Sleep deprivation			
	4 hours	12 hours	24 hours	
Alcohol	16	18	22	
	12	16	24	
	17	25	32	
	Cell mean = 15.000	Cell mean = 19.667	Cell mean = 26.000	Row mean = 20.222
No alcohol	11	13	12	
	9	8	14	
	12	11	12	
	Cell mean = 10.667	Cell mean = 10.667	Cell mean = 12.667	Row mean = 11.333
	Column mean = 12.833	Column mean = 15.167	Column mean = 19.333	Overall mean = 15.777

$$\text{variance estimate}_{[\text{data}]} = \frac{\sum X^2 - \frac{\left(\sum X\right)^2}{N}}{df}$$

$$\sum X^2 = 16^2 + 18^2 + 22^2 + 12^2 + 16^2 + 24^2 + 17^2 + 25^2 + 32^2 + 11^2 + 13^2 + 12^2 + 9^2$$
$$+ 8^2 + 14^2 + 12^2 + 11^2 + 12^2$$

$$= 256 + 324 + 484 + 144 + 256 + 576 + 289 + 625 + 1024 + 121 + 169$$
$$+ 144 + 81 + 64 + 196 + 144 + 121 + 144$$

$$= 5162$$

$$\left(\sum X\right)^2 = (16 + 18 + 22 + 12 + 16 + 24 + 17 + 25 + 32 + 11 + 13 + 12 + 9 + 8 + 14 + 12 + 11 + 12)^2$$

$$= (284)^2 = 80\,656$$

The number of scores N equals 18. The degrees of freedom (df) equal the number of scores minus one, i.e. 17. Substituting in the formula:

$$\text{variance estimate}_{[\text{data}]} = \frac{\sum X^2 - \frac{\left(\sum X\right)^2}{N}}{df} = \frac{5162 - \frac{80\,656}{18}}{17}$$

$$= \frac{5162 - 4480.889}{17}$$

$$= \frac{681.111}{17} = 40.065$$

The sum of squares here (i.e. 681.111) is called the *total* sum of squares in the ANOVA summary table. (Strictly speaking, this calculation is unnecessary in that its only function is a computational check on your other calculations.)

Step 2 (*'error' variance estimate*) Subtract the cell mean from each of the scores in a cell to obtain the 'error' scores (Table 22.13).

Table 22.13	'Error' scores			
	Sleep deprivation			
	4 hours	**12 hours**	**24 hours**	
Alcohol	1.000	−1.667	−4.000	
	−3.000	−3.667	−2.000	
	2.000	5.333	6.000	Row mean = 0.000
No alcohol	0.333	2.333	−0.667	
	−1.667	−2.667	1.333	
	1.333	0.333	−0.667	Row mean = 0.000
	Column mean = 0.000	**Column mean = 0.000**	**Column mean = 0.000**	**Overall mean = 0.000**

→

Apart from rounding errors, the cell means, the row means, the column means and the overall mean are all zero – just as required of an 'error' table.

We calculate the 'error' variance estimate using the usual variance estimate formula:

$$\text{variance estimate}_{[\text{'error' scores}]} = \frac{\sum X^2 - \dfrac{\left(\sum X\right)^2}{N}}{df}$$

$$\sum X^2 = 1.000^2 + (-1.667)^2 + (-4.000)^2 + (-3.000)^2 + (-3.667)^2 + (-2.000)^2 + 2.000^2$$
$$+ 5.333^2 + 6.000^2 + 0.333^2 + 2.333^2 + (-0.667)^2 + (-1.667)^2 + (-2.667)^2$$
$$+ 1.333^2 + 1.333^2 + 0.333^2 + (-0.667)^2$$

$$= 1.000 + 2.779 + 16.000 + 9.000 + 13.447 + 4.000 + 4.000 + 28.441 + 36.000$$
$$+ 0.111 + 5.443 + 0.445 + 2.779 + 7.113 + 1.777 + 1.777 + 0.111 + 0.445$$

$$= 134.668$$

$$\left(\sum X\right)^2 = [1.000 + (-1.667) + (-4.000) + (-3.000) + (-3.667) + (-2.000) + 2.000$$
$$+ 5.333 + 6.000 + 0.333 + 2.333 + (-0.667) + (-1.667) + (-2.667)$$
$$+ 1.333 + 1.333 + 0.333 + (-0.667)]^2$$

$$= 0$$

(Notice that this latter calculation is unnecessary as it will always equal 0 for 'error' scores.) The number of scores N equals 18. The degrees of freedom (df) equal the number of scores minus the number of cells, i.e. $18 - 6 = 12$. We can now substitute these values in the formula:

$$\text{variance estimate}_{[\text{'error' scores}]} = \frac{\sum X^2 - \dfrac{\left(\sum X\right)^2}{N}}{df} = \frac{134.668 - \dfrac{0}{18}}{12}$$

$$= \frac{134.668}{12}$$

$$= 11.222$$

Step 3 *(sleep deprivation variance estimate)* We now derive our table containing the scores in the three sleep deprivation conditions (combining over alcohol and non-alcohol conditions) simply by replacing each score in the column by the column mean (Table 22.14).

$$\text{variance estimate}_{[\text{'sleep deprivation' scores}]} = \frac{\sum X^2 - \dfrac{\left(\sum X\right)^2}{N}}{df}$$

$$\sum X^2 = 12.833^2 + 15.167^2 + 19.333^2 + 12.833^2 + 15.167^2 + 19.333^2 + 12.833^2$$
$$+ 15.167^2 + 19.333^2 + 12.833^2 + 15.167^2 + 19.333^2 + 12.833^2 + 15.167^2$$
$$+ 19.333^2 + 12.833^2 + 15.167^2 + 19.333^2$$

$$= 164.686 + 230.038 + 373.765 + 164.686 + 230.038 + 373.765 + 164.686$$
$$+ 230.038 + 373.765 + 164.686 + 230.038 + 373.765 + 164.686 + 230.038$$
$$+ 373.765 + 164.686 + 230.038 + 373.765$$

$$= 4610.934$$

$\rightarrow$

Table 22.14	Scores due to sleep deprivation		
	Sleep deprivation		
4 hours	**12 hours**	**24 hours**
12.833	15.167	19.333
12.833	15.167	19.333
12.833	15.167	19.333
12.833	15.167	19.333
12.833	15.167	19.333
12.833	15.167	19.333
Column mean = 12.833	Column mean = 15.167	Column mean = 19.333

$$\left(\sum X\right)^2 = (12.833 + 15.167 + 19.333 + 12.833 + 15.167 + 19.333 + 12.833$$
$$+ 15.167 + 19.333 + 12.833 + 15.167 + 19.333 + 12.833 + 15.167$$
$$+ 19.333 + 12.833 + 15.167 + 19.333)^2$$

$$= 284^2$$

$$= 80\ 656$$

The number of scores N equals 18. The degrees of freedom (df) equal the number of columns minus one, i.e. $3 - 1 = 2$. We can now substitute these values in the formula:

$$\text{variance estimate}_{[\text{'sleep deprivation' scores}]} = \frac{\sum X^2 - \dfrac{\left(\sum X\right)^2}{N}}{df} = \frac{4610.934 - \dfrac{80\ 656}{18}}{2}$$

$$= \frac{4610.934 - 4480.889}{2}$$

$$= \frac{130.045}{2} = 65.023$$

Step 4   *(alcohol variance estimate)* The main effect for alcohol (or the table containing scores for the alcohol and no-alcohol comparison) is obtained by replacing each of the scores in the original data table by the row mean for alcohol or the row mean for no-alcohol as appropriate. In this way the sleep deprivation variable is ignored (Table 22.15).

The variance estimate of these 18 scores gives us the variance estimate for the independent variable alcohol. We calculate:

$$\text{variance estimate}_{[\text{'alcohol' scores}]} = \frac{\sum X^2 - \dfrac{\left(\sum X\right)^2}{N}}{df}$$

→

Table 22.15	Scores due to alcohol effect alone		
Alcohol	20.222	20.222	20.222
	20.222	20.222	20.222
	20.222	20.222	20.222
No alcohol	11.333	11.333	11.333
	11.333	11.333	11.333
	11.333	11.333	11.333

$$\sum X^2 = 20.222^2 + 20.222^2 + 20.222^2 + 20.222^2 + 20.222^2 + 20.222^2 + 20.222^2$$
$$+ 20.222^2 + 20.222^2 + 11.333^2 + 11.333^2 + 11.333^2 + 11.333^2$$
$$+ 11.333^2 + 11.333^2 + 11.333^2 + 11.333^2 + 11.333^2$$

$$= 408.929 + 408.929 + 408.929 + 408.929 + 408.929 + 408.929 + 408.929$$
$$+ 408.929 + 408.929 + 128.437 + 128.437 + 128.437 + 128.437$$
$$+ 128.437 + 128.437 + 128.437 + 128.437 + 128.437$$

$$= 4836.294$$

$$\left(\sum X\right)^2 = (20.222 + 20.222 + 20.222 + 20.222 + 20.222 + 20.222 + 20.222 + 20.222 + 20.222$$
$$+ 11.333 + 11.333 + 11.333 + 11.333 + 11.333 + 11.333 + 11.333 + 11.333 + 11.333)^2$$

$$= (284)^2$$

$$= 80\ 656$$

The number of scores N equals 18. The degrees of freedom (df) equal the number of rows minus one, i.e. $2 - 1 = 1$. We can now substitute these values in the formula:

$$\text{variance estimate}_{[\text{'alcohol' scores}]} = \frac{\sum X^2 - \dfrac{\left(\sum X\right)^2}{N}}{df} = \frac{4836.294 - \dfrac{80\ 656}{18}}{1}$$

$$= \frac{4836.294 - 4480.889}{1}$$

$$= \frac{355.405}{1} = 355.405$$

Step 5

(interaction variance estimate) The final stage is to calculate the interaction. This is obtained by getting rid of 'error', getting rid of the effect of sleep deprivation and then getting rid of the effect of alcohol:

1. Remove 'error' by simply replacing our data scores by the cell mean (Table 22.16).

2. Remove the effect of the alcohol versus no-alcohol treatment. This is done simply by subtracting the row mean (20.222) from each of the alcohol scores and the row mean (11.333) from each of the no-alcohol scores (Table 22.17).

3. Remove the effect of sleep deprivation by subtracting the column mean for each sleep deprivation condition from the scores in the *previous table*. In other words, *subtract* –2.944, –0.611 or 3.556 as appropriate. (Do not forget that subtracting a negative number is like adding the absolute value of that number.) This leaves us with the interaction (Table 22.18).

Table 22.16	Data minus 'error' (each data score replaced by its cell mean)			
	Sleep deprivation			
	4 hours	12 hours	24 hours	
Alcohol	15.000	19.667	26.000	
	15.000	19.667	26.000	
	15.000	19.667	26.000	Row mean = 20.222
No alcohol	10.667	10.667	12.667	
	10.667	10.667	12.667	
	10.667	10.667	12.667	Row mean = 11.333
	Column mean = 12.833	Column mean = 15.167	Column mean = 19.333	Overall mean = 15.777

Table 22.17	Data minus 'error' and alcohol effect (row mean subtracted from each score in Table 22.16)			
	Sleep deprivation			
	4 hours	12 hours	24 hours	
Alcohol	−5.222	−0.555	5.778	
	−5.222	−0.555	5.778	
	−5.222	−0.555	5.778	Row mean = 0.000
No alcohol	−0.666	−0.666	1.334	
	−0.666	−0.666	1.334	
	−0.666	−0.666	1.334	Row mean = 0.000
	Column mean = −2.944	Column mean = −0.611	Column mean = 3.556	Overall mean = 0.000

Table 22.18	Interaction table: data minus 'error', alcohol and sleep deprivation (column mean subtracted from each score in Table 22.17)			
	Sleep deprivation			
	4 hours	12 hours	24 hours	
Alcohol	−2.278	0.056	2.222	
	−2.278	0.056	2.222	
	−2.278	0.056	2.222	Row mean = 0.000
No alcohol	2.278	−0.056	−2.222	
	2.278	−0.056	−2.222	
	2.278	−0.056	−2.222	Row mean = 0.000
	Column mean = 0.000	Column mean = 0.000	Column mean = 0.000	Overall mean = 0.000

→

The variance estimate from the interaction is computed using the usual formula:

$$\text{variance estimate}_{[\text{'interaction' scores}]} = \frac{\sum X^2 - \dfrac{\left(\sum X\right)^2}{N}}{df}$$

$$
\begin{aligned}
\sum X^2 &= (-2.278)^2 + 0.056^2 + 2.222^2 + (-2.278)^2 + 0.056^2 + 2.222^2 + (-2.278)^2 \\
&\quad + 0.056^2 + 2.222^2 + 2.278^2 + (-0.056)^2 + (-2.222)^2 + 2.278^2 + (-0.056)^2 \\
&\quad + (-2.222)^2 + 2.278^2 + (-0.056)^2 + (-2.222)^2
\end{aligned}
$$

$$
\begin{aligned}
&= 5.189 + 0.003 + 4.937 + 5.189 + 0.003 + 4.937 + 5.189 + 0.003 + 4.937 \\
&\quad + 5.189 + 0.003 + 4.937 + 5.189 + 0.003 + 4.937 + 5.189 + 0.003 + 4.937
\end{aligned}
$$

$$= 60.774$$

$$
\begin{aligned}
\left(\sum X\right)^2 &= [(-2.278) + 0.056 + 2.222 + (-2.278) + 0.056 + 2.222 + (-2.278) + 0.056 \\
&\quad + 2.222 + 2.278 + (-0.056) + (-2.222) + 2.278 + (-0.056) + (-2.222) \\
&\quad + 2.278 + (-0.056) + (-2.222)]^2
\end{aligned}
$$

$$= 0$$

(This latter calculation is an unnecessary calculation as it will always equal 0.) The number of scores N equals 18. The degrees of freedom (df) are given by the following formula:

$$df = (\text{number of rows} - 1) \times (\text{number of columns} - 1)$$

$$= (2 - 1) \times (3 - 1)$$

$$= 1 \times 2$$

$$= 2$$

We can now substitute the above values in the formula:

$$\text{variance estimate}_{[\text{'interaction' scores}]} = \frac{\sum X^2 - \dfrac{\left(\sum X\right)^2}{N}}{df} = \frac{60.774 - \dfrac{0}{18}}{2}$$

$$= \frac{60.774 - 0}{2}$$

$$= \frac{60.774}{2} = 30.387$$

Step 6   Table 22.19 is the analysis of variance summary table. The F-ratios are always the mean square of either one of the main effects or the interaction divided by the variance estimate (mean square) due to 'error'. The significance of each F-ratio is checked against Significance Table 22.1. Care must be taken to use the appropriate degrees of freedom. The error in this case is 12, which means that alcohol (with one degree of freedom) must have an F-ratio of 4.8 or more to be significant at the 5% level. Sleep deprivation and the interaction need to have a value of 3.9 or more to be significant at the 5% level. Thus the interaction is not significant, but sleep deprivation is.

The interpretation of the analysis of variance summary table in this case appears to be quite straightforward:

Table 22.19	Analysis of variance summary table			
Source of variation	**Sums of square**	**Degrees of freedom**	**Mean square**	**F-ratio**
Main effects				
Sleep deprivation	130.045	2	65.023	5.79[a]
Alcohol	355.405	1	355.405	31.67[a]
Interaction				
Sleep deprivation with alcohol	60.774	2	30.387	2.71
'Error'	134.668	12	11.222	–
Total (data)	681.111[b]	17	–	–

[a] Significant at 5% level.
[b] This form of calculation has introduced some rounding errors.

Significance Table 22.1	5% significance values of the F-ratio for unrelated ANOVA. Additional values are to be found in Significance Table 19.1					
Degrees of freedom for error or mean square (or variance estimate)	**Degrees of freedom for between-treatments mean square (or variance estimate)**					
	1	**2**	**3**	**4**	**5**	**∞**
1	161 or more	200	216	225	230	254
2	18.5	19.0	19.2	19.3	19.3	19.5
3	10.1	9.6	9.3	9.1	9.0	8.5
4	7.7	6.9	6.6	6.4	6.3	5.6
5	6.6	5.8	5.4	5.2	5.1	4.4
6	6.0	5.1	4.8	4.5	4.4	3.7
7	5.6	4.7	4.4	4.1	4.0	3.2
8	5.3	4.5	4.1	3.8	3.7	2.9
9	5.1	4.3	3.9	3.6	3.5	2.7
10	5.0	4.1	3.7	3.5	3.3	2.5
13	4.7	3.8	3.4	3.2	3.0	2.2
15	4.5	3.7	3.3	3.1	2.9	2.1
20	4.4	3.5	3.1	2.9	2.7	1.8
30	4.2	3.3	2.9	2.7	2.5	1.6
60	4.0	3.2	2.8	2.5	2.4	1.4
∞	3.8	3.0	2.6	2.4	2.2	1.0

Your value has to equal or be larger than the tabulated value for an effect to be significant at the 5% level for a two-tailed test (i.e. to accept the hypothesis).

→

1. Alcohol has a significant influence on the number of mistakes in the understanding of the video.

2. The amount of sleep deprivation has a significant influence on the number of mistakes in the understanding of the video.

3. There is apparently no significant interaction – that is, the differences between the conditions are fully accounted for by alcohol and sleep deprivation acting independently.

But this only tells us that there are significant differences; we have to check the column and row means in order to say precisely which condition produces the greatest number of mistakes. In other words, the analysis of variance summary table has to be interpreted in the light of the original data table with the column, row and cell means all entered.

Carefully checking the data suggests that the above interpretation is rather too simplistic. It seems that sleep deprivation actually has little effect unless the person has been taking alcohol. The high cell means are associated with alcohol and sleep deprivation. In these circumstances, there is some doubt that the main effects explanation is good enough.

We would conclude, in these circumstances, 'Although, in the ANOVA, only the main effects were significant, there is reason to think that the main effects are actually the results of the interaction between the main effects. Careful examination of the cell means suggests that especially high scores are associated with taking alcohol and undergoing higher amounts of sleep deprivation. In contrast, those in the no-alcohol condition were affected only to a much smaller extent by having high amounts of sleep deprivation.'

This is tricky for a student to write up since it requires a rather subtle interpretation of the data which might exceed the statistical skills of the readers of their work.

22.4 More on interactions

A conventional way of illustrating interactions is through the use of graphs such as those in Figures 22.2 and 22.3. These graphs deal with the sleep and alcohol study just analysed. Notice that the means are given for each of the cells of the two-way ANOVA. Thus the vertical axis is a numerical scale commensurate with the scale of the dependent variable; the horizontal axis simply records the different levels of *one* of the independent variables.

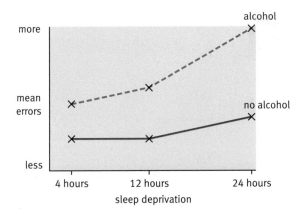

FIGURE 22.2   ANOVA graph illustrating possible interactions

FIGURE 22.3   ANOVA graph illustrating lack of interactions

FIGURE 22.4   ANOVA graph illustrating an alternative form of interaction

In order to indicate the different levels of the second independent variable, the different cell means for each level are joined together by a distinctively different line.

The main point to remember is that main effects are assumed to be effects which can be added directly to the scores in the columns or rows for that level of the main effect and that the effect is assumed to be common and equal in all of the cells involved. This implies that:

1. If there is *no* interaction, then the lines through the points should move more or less parallel to each other.

2. If there *is* an interaction, then the lines through the points will not be parallel; they may touch, move together or move apart.

Figure 22.3 illustrates the sort of pattern we might expect if there is no interaction between the independent variables. Figure 22.4 shows that it is possible for an interaction to involve the crossing of the lines through the points.

Crucially, the pattern illustrated in Figure 22.5 demonstrates the circumstances in which the risk of confusing main effects for the interaction is minimal. This is because, although the two lines are definitely not parallel, the evidence for main effects is not strong but there is evidence of an interaction. Thus there seems to be no sleep deprivation main

FIGURE 22.5   ANOVA graph illustrating interaction when it cannot be mistaken for main effects

effect since the means of the no alcohol and alcohol groups combined vertically are more or less the same. Thus there is no main effect of sleep deprivation in Figure 22.5 because of this similarity. In much the same way, if the three means for the no-alcohol condition are averaged and the three means for the alcohol condition are averaged, these two overall means are very similar. In other words, if the means of the combined conditions are the same, this implies, by definition, there is no interaction. In any of the other circumstances such as in Figures 22.2–22.4, combining the means vertically and combining the means horizontally produces combined means which differ. So be comforted if you obtain the pattern shown in Figure 22.5 in your research; there is no element of judgement involved in its interpretation. In the end, simple statistics usually tell you more about your data than many of the more complex statistics. If, when doing ANOVA, you look at graphs like these then you should be able to work out what is happening in your study. The *F*-ratios and the like simply confirm whether or not what you see is significant.

22.5   Calculation of two-way ANOVA using quick method

Calculation 22.1 gives a *conceptual* account of the two-way analysis of variance calculation. While it has the enormous advantage of showing precisely how your data are being manipulated statistically, it is somewhat laborious and rounding errors can accumulate to give slightly imprecise results. The following calculation uses the computational formula for variance (see p. 151) which saves some effort in the calculation. It gives little or no insight into how the analysis of variance works conceptually. Also remember that this calculation is appropriate only if you have equal numbers of scores in each cell. If not then you are far better off using a computer program which can cope easily with unequal sample sizes and is the preferred approach. If you wish to do a hand calculation, then the simplest procedure is to delete scores *at random* from the larger cells until each is the same size as the smallest cell.

Calculation 22.2

Two-way unrelated analysis of variance: quick method

Step 1 Enter your data into a table such as Table 22.20. These are the data given in Table 22.1 for the study into the effects of sleep deprivation and alcohol on errors on a video test with a few additions. These additions are:

- the totals of scores in each cell (i.e. the cell totals or T_1, etc.)
- the totals of scores in each row (i.e. the row totals or R_1, etc.)
- the totals of scores in each column (i.e. the column totals or C_1, etc.)
- the overall total of all of the scores (i.e. the grand total or G).

These additions are analogous to the calculations in Table 22.12 of the previous computational method. With the quick method we do not calculate the means, merely the totals.

Table 22.20	Data for the two-way analysis of variance with added totals			
	Sleep deprivation			
	4 hours	**12 hours**	**24 hours**	
Alcohol	16	18	22	
	12	16	24	
	17	25	32	
	T_1 = Cell total = 45	T_2 = Cell total = 59	T_3 = Cell total = 78	R_1 = Row total = 182
No alcohol	11	13	12	
	9	8	14	
	12	11	12	
	T_4 = Cell total = 32	T_5 = Cell total = 32	T_6 = Cell total = 38	R_2 = Row total = 102
	$C1$ = Column total = 77	$C2$ = Column total = 91	$C3$ = Column total = 116	G = Grand total = 284

Step 2 Square each of the scores and calculate the total of squared scores ($\sum X^2$):

$$\text{sum of squared scores} = \sum X^2$$

$$= 16^2 + 12^2 + 17^2 + 18^2 + 16^2 + 25^2 + 22^2 + 24^2 + 32^2 + 11^2 + 9^2 + 12^2$$
$$+ 13^2 + 8^2 + 11^2 + 12^2 + 14^2 + 12^2$$

$$= 256 + 144 + 289 + 324 + 256 + 625 + 484 + 576 + 1024 + 121 + 81$$
$$+ 144 + 169 + 64 + 121 + 144 + 196 + 144$$

$$= 5162$$

→

Step 3 Carry out the following essential intermediary calculations to be used in later steps. They are R, C, T and something called the correction factor.

$$C = \frac{C_1^2 + C_2^2 + C_3^2}{\text{number of scores per sleep deprivation condition}}$$

$$= \frac{77^2 + 91^2 + 116^2}{6}$$

$$= \frac{5929 + 8281 + 13\ 456}{6}$$

$$= \frac{27\ 666}{6}$$

$$= 4611.000$$

$$R = \frac{R_1^2 + R_2^2}{\text{number of scores per alcohol condition}} = \frac{182^2 + 102^2}{9}$$

$$= \frac{33\ 124 + 10\ 404}{9}$$

$$= \frac{43\ 528}{9} = 4836.444$$

$$T = \frac{T_1^2 + T_2^2 + T_3^2 + T_4^2 + T_5^2 + T_6^2}{\text{number of scores per cell}}$$

$$= \frac{45^2 + 59^2 + 78^2 + 32^2 + 32^2 + 38^2}{3}$$

$$= \frac{2025 + 3481 + 6084 + 1024 + 1024 + 1444}{3}$$

$$= \frac{15\ 082}{3}$$

$$= 5027.333$$

$$\text{correction factor} = \frac{\text{grand total}^2}{\text{number of scores}} = \frac{G^2}{N} = \frac{284^2}{18} = \frac{80\ 656}{18} = 4480.889$$

Thus

$$C = 4611.000$$

$$R = 4836.444$$

$$T = 5027.333$$

$$\frac{G^2}{N} = 4480.889 \text{ (i.e. correction factor)}$$

→

Table 22.21	Analysis of variance summary table			
Source of variation	Sum of squares	Degrees of freedom	Mean square	F-ratio
Main effects				
Alcohol	355.555	1	355.555	31.67[a]
Sleep deprivation	130.111	2	65.555	5.84[a]
Interaction				
Sleep deprivation with alcohol	60.778	2	30.389	2.71
'Error'	134.667	12	11.222	–
Total	681.111	17	–	–

[a] Significant at the 5% level.

Also $\sum X^2 = 5162$ (from step 2).

Enter the following calculations into the analysis of variance summary table (Table 22.21).

Step 4   Calculate the sum of squares for the independent variable alcohol (i.e. $SS_{[alcohol]}$). (The elements of the calculation have already been calculated in step 3.)

$$SS_{[alcohol]} = R - \frac{G^2}{N}$$

$$= 4836.444 - 4480.889$$

$$= 355.555$$

The degrees of freedom for $SS_{[alcohol]}$ are the number of conditions (or levels) of the alcohol variable minus one (i.e. $2 - 1 = 1$).

Step 5   Calculate the sum of squares for the sleep deprivation variable. (The elements of this calculation have already been calculated in step 3.)

$$SS_{[sleep\ deprivation]} = C - \frac{G^2}{N}$$

$$= 4611.000 - 4480.889$$

$$= 130.111$$

The degrees of freedom are the number of conditions (or levels) of the sleep deprivation variable minus one (i.e. $3 - 1 = 2$).

Step 6   Calculate the interaction sum of squares (i.e. $SS_{[interaction]}$). (All of the elements of this calculation have already been calculated in step 3.) Insert these values:

$$SS_{[interaction]} = T - C - R + \frac{G^2}{N}$$

$$= 5027.333 - 4611.000 - 4836.444 + 4480.889$$

$$= 60.778$$

The degrees of freedom $SS_{[interaction]}$ are (the number of conditions (or levels) of the sleep deprivation variable − 1) × (the number of conditions (or levels) of the alcohol variable − 1) = (3 − 1) × (2 − 1) = 2 × 1 = 2 degrees of freedom.

Step 7 Calculate the error sum of squares. (This is based on the total sum of squares calculated in step 2 and T calculated in step 3.) Enter these values.

$$SS_{[error]} = \sum X^2 - T = 5162 - 5027.333 = 134.667$$

The degrees of freedom for $SS_{[error]}$ are the number of scores − (number of rows) × (number of columns). Thus the degrees of freedom for error are 18 − (2 × 3) = 18 − 6 = 12. This value should be entered in the analysis of variance summary table.

Step 8 The main parts of the computation have now been completed and you should have entered the sums of squares and the degrees of freedom into the analysis of variance summary table. You also need to calculate the three F-ratios in Table 22.21 by dividing the main effect and interaction mean squares by the error mean squares.

Step 9 The statistical significance of each of these F-ratios is obtained by consulting Significance Table 22.1. If your value is larger than the listed value for the appropriate degrees of freedom then the F-ratio is statistically significant at the 5% level of significance. The column entry is the degrees of freedom for the particular main effect or interaction in question, the rows are always the degrees of freedom for error. As you can see, the two main effects in Table 22.21 are statistically significant whereas the interaction is not.

Interpreting the results Remember that the interpretation of any data should be based first of all on an examination of cell means and variances (or standard deviations) as in Table 22.22. The tests of significance merely confirm whether or not your interpretations can be generalised. It would appear from Table 22.22 that the cell means for the no-alcohol condition are relatively unaffected by the amount of sleep deprivation. However, in the alcohol conditions increasing levels of sleep deprivation produce a greater number of mistakes. There also appears to be a tendency for there to be more mistakes when the participants have taken alcohol than when they have not.

Table 22.22	Table of means for the two-way ANOVA			
	Sleep deprivation			
	4 hours	**12 hours**	**24 hours**	
Alcohol	15.000	19.667	26.000	Row mean = 20.222
No alcohol	10.667	10.667	12.667	Row mean = 11.333
	Column mean = 12.833	Column mean = 15.167	Column mean = 19.333	Overall mean = 15.777

→

Reporting the results The results of this analysis may be written up according to the APA (2010) Publication Manual's recommendation as follows: 'A two-way ANOVA was carried out on the data. The two main effects of sleep deprivation, $F(2, 12) = 31.67$, $p < 0.05$, and alcohol, $F(1, 12) = 5.84$, $p < 0.05$, were statistically significant. The number of errors related to the number of hours of sleep deprivation. Four hours of sleep deprivation resulted in an average of 12.83 errors, 12 hours of sleep deprivation resulted in an average of 15.17 errors, and 24 hours of sleep deprivation resulted in 19.33 errors on average. Consuming alcohol before the test resulted on average in 20.22 errors and the no-alcohol condition resulted in substantially fewer errors ($M = 15.78$). The interaction between sleep deprivation was not significant despite the tendency of the scores in the alcohol condition with 24 hours of sleep deprivation to be much higher than those in the other conditions, $F(2, 12) = 2.71$, *p ns*. Inspection of the graph (Figure 22.2) suggests that there is an interaction since the alcohol and no-alcohol lines are not parallel. It would appear that the interaction is being hidden by the main effects in the ANOVA.'

The significant *F*-ratio for the main effect of sleep deprivation needs to be explored further by the use of multiple comparisons tests (Chapter 23). Because there are only two alcohol conditions, this is unnecessary for independent variables having only two levels: there is no doubt where the differences lie in circumstances where there are only two values of an independent variable. Given the implications of the graph for the question of an interaction, it would be sensible to carry out multiple comparisons comparing all of the six cell means of the 2×3 ANOVA with each other (Chapter 23).

22.6 Three or more independent variables

The two-way ANOVA can be extended to include three or more independent variables although you are always restricted to analysing a single dependent variable. Despite this, it should be noted that the complexity of experimental research is constrained by a number of factors including the following:

1. Having a lot of different conditions in an experiment may involve a lot of research and planning time. Preparing complex sets of instructions for participants in the different experimental conditions, randomly assigning individuals to these groups and many other methodological considerations usually limit our level of ambition in research designs. In non-psychological disciplines, the logistics of experiments are different since the units may not be people but, for example, seedlings in pots containing one of several different composts, with different amounts of fertiliser, and one of several different growing temperatures. These are far less time-consuming.

2. Interpreting ANOVA is more skilful than many researchers realise. Care is needed to interpret even a two-way analysis properly because main effects are prioritised in the calculation, which results in main effects being credited with variation which is really due to interaction.

Since theoretically but not practically there is no limit to the number of independent variables possible in the analysis of variance, the potential for complexity is enormous. However, caution is recommended when planning research. The problems of interpretation get somewhat more difficult the more independent variables there are. The complexity is largely the result of the number of possible *interactions*. Although there is just one interaction with a two-way analysis of variance, there are four with a three-way analysis of variance. The numbers accelerate rapidly with greater numbers of independent variables. As far as possible, we would recommend any psychologist to be wary of going far beyond a two-way analysis of variance without very careful planning and without some experience with these less complex designs.

It is possible to disregard the interactions and simply to analyse the different variables in the experiment as if they were several one-way experiments carried out at the same time. The interpretations would be simpler by doing this. However, this is rarely if ever done in psychological research and it is conventional always to consider interactions.

Imagine the following three-way or three-factor analysis of variance. The three independent variables are:

- age – coded as either young or old
- gender – coded as either male or female
- noise – the research takes place in either a noisy or a quiet environment.

So this is a three-way ANOVA with a total of eight different conditions (2 ages × 2 gender × 2 different noise levels). The dependent variable is the number of errors on a numerical memory test in the different conditions. The main features of this research are presented in Table 22.23.

Table 22.23	A stylised three-way analysis of variance study						
		Noisy Conditions			**Quiet Conditions**		
		Young	Old		Young	Old	
Males							
Females							

The sheer number of comparisons possible between sections of the data causes problems. These comparisons are:

1. *The main effect of gender* that is, comparing males and females irrespective of age or noise.

2. *The main effect of age* that is, comparing young and old irrespective of gender or noise.

3. *The main effect of noise* that is, comparing noisy and quiet conditions irrespective of age or gender.

4. *The interaction of age and gender* that is, comparing age and gender groups ignoring the noise conditions. This would look like Table 22.24.

5. *The interaction of age and noise* that is, comparing age and noise groups ignoring gender. This is shown in Table 22.25.

6. *The interaction of noise and gender* that is, comparing the noise and gender groups ignoring age. This is shown in Table 22.26.

7. *There is a fourth interaction* the interaction of noise and gender and age which is represented by Table 22.27. Notice that the cell means of each of the conditions are involved in this.

Although Table 22.27 looks like the format of the original data table (Table 22.23), the scores in the cells will be very different because all of the other sources of variation will have been removed.

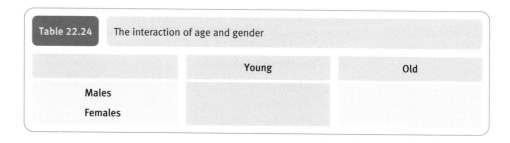

Table 22.24	The interaction of age and gender	
	Young	Old
Males		
Females		

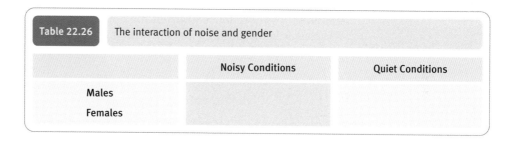

Table 22.25	The interaction of age and noise			
	Noisy Conditions		Quiet Conditions	
	Young	Old	Young	Old

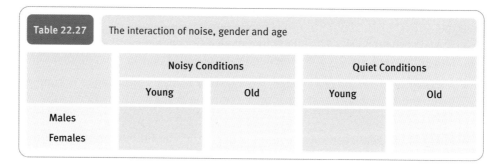

Table 22.26	The interaction of noise and gender	
	Noisy Conditions	Quiet Conditions
Males		
Females		

Table 22.27	The interaction of noise, gender and age			
	Noisy Conditions		Quiet Conditions	
	Young	Old	Young	Old
Males				
Females				

The steps in calculating this three-way analysis of variance follow the pattern demonstrated earlier in this chapter but with extra layers of complexity:

1. The error term is calculated in the usual way by subtracting the cell mean from each score in a particular cell. The variance estimate of this table can then be calculated.

2. The main effect of gender is calculated by substituting the male mean for each of the male scores and the female mean for each of the female scores. The variance estimate of this table can then be calculated.

3. The age main effect is calculated by substituting the mean score of the young people for each of their scores and substituting the mean score of the old people for each of their scores. The variance estimate of this table can then be calculated.

4. The noise main effect is obtained by substituting the mean score in the noisy conditions for each score in the noisy conditions and substituting the mean score in the quiet conditions for each score in the quiet conditions. The variance estimate of this table can then be calculated.

5. The interaction of age and gender is arrived at by taking the table of scores with the error removed and then removing the age and gender difference simply by taking away the column mean and then the row mean. This is the same procedure as we applied to get the interaction in the two-way analysis of variance. The variance estimate of this table can then be calculated.

6. We arrive at the interaction of age and noise by drawing up a similar table and then taking away the appropriate age and noise means in turn. The variance estimate of this table can then be calculated.

7. We arrive at the interaction of noise and gender by drawing up a similar table and then taking away the appropriate noise and gender means in turn. The variance estimate of this table can then be calculated.

8. The three-way interaction (age × noise × gender) is obtained by first of all drawing up our table of the age × noise × gender conditions. We then take away the main effects by subtracting the appropriate age, noise and gender means from this table. But we also have to take away the two-way interactions of age × noise, age × gender and noise × gender by subtracting the appropriate means from the above table. Whatever is left is the three-way interaction. The variance estimate of this final table can then be calculated.

Key points

- Only when you have a 2 × 2 unrelated analysis of variance is the interpretation of the data relatively straightforward. For 2 × 3 or larger analyses of variance, you need to read Chapter 23 as well.

- Although at heart simple enough, the two-way analysis of variance is cumbersome to calculate by hand and is probably best done on a computer if you have anything other than small amounts of data.

- Analysis of variance always requires a degree of careful interpretation of the findings and cannot always be interpreted in a hard-and-fast way. This is a little disconcerting given its apparent mathematical sophistication.

- Before calculating the analysis of variance proper, spend a good deal of effort trying to make sense of the pattern of column, row and cell means in your data table. This should alert you to the major trends in your data. You can use your interpretation in combination with the analysis of variance summary table to obtain as refined an interpretation of your data as possible.

COMPUTER ANALYSIS

The SPSS Statistics instruction book to this text is Dennis Howitt and Duncan Cramer (2011), *Introduction to SPSS Statistics in Psychology*: For version 19 and earlier, Harlow: Pearson. Chapter 23 in that book gives detailed step-by-step procedures for the statistics described in this chapter together with advice on how to report the results. Figure 22.6 shows the SPSS Statistics steps for a two-way analysis of variance.

Data
- Name the variables in Variable View of the Data Editor.
- Enter the data under the appropriate variable names in Data View of the Data Editor.

Analysis
- Select 'Analyze', 'General Linear Model' and 'Univariate . . .'.

2
- Move the dependent variable to the 'Dependent Variable:' box.
- Move the independent variables to the 'Fixed Factor(s):' box.

3
- Select 'Plots . . .'. Move one independent variable (Factor) to the 'Horizontal Axis:' box and the other to the 'Separate Lines:' box. Select 'Add' and 'Continue'.

4
- Select 'Options . . . ', 'Descriptive Statistics', 'Estimates of effect size' and 'Homogeneity tests'.

Output
- Check which *F* ratios are significant by having a Sig(nificance) of .05 or less.

2
- Check that Levene's test shows the variances are homogeneous by having a Sig(nificance) level of more than .05.

3
- If a significant main effect has more than 2 groups, use further tests to determine which means differ.

4
- With a significant interaction use further tests to determine which means differ.

FIGURE 22.6 SPSS Statistics steps for two-way analysis of variance

CHAPTER 23

Multiple comparisons in ANOVA

Just where do the differences lie?

Overview

- Generally speaking, analyses of variance are relatively easy to interpret if the independent variables all have just two different values.

- Interpretation becomes difficult with greater numbers of values of the independent variables.

- This is because the analysis does not stipulate which means are significantly different from each other. If there are only two values of each independent variable, then statistical significance means that those two values are significantly different.

- Multiple comparison tests are available to indicate just where the differences lie.

- These multiple comparison tests have built-in adjustment for the numbers of comparisons being made. Hence they are generally to be preferred over multiple comparisons using the *t*-test.

- It is very difficult to know which multiple comparison tests are the most appropriate for any particular data or purpose. Consequently, it is reasonable advice that several different tests should be used. The only problem that arises is when the different tests yield different conclusions.

- Some multiple comparison tests may be applied whether or not the ANOVA itself is statistically significant.

Preparation

You will need a working knowledge of Chapters 19, 20 and 21 on the analysis of variance. Chapter 14 introduces the problem of multiple comparisons in the context of partitioning chi-square tables.

23.1   Introduction

When in research there are *more than two levels* of an *independent* variable it is not always obvious where the differences between conditions lie. There is no problem when you have only two groups of scores to compare in a one-way or a 2×2 ANOVA. However, if there are three or more different levels of any independent variable the interpretation problems multiply. Take, for example, Table 23.1 of means for a one-way analysis of variance.

Although the analysis of variance for the data which are summarised in this table may well be statistically significant, there remains a very obvious problem. Groups 1 and 2 have virtually identical means and it is group 3 which has the exceptionally large scores. Quite simply we would be tempted to assume that group 1 and group 2 do not differ significantly and that any differences are due to group 3. Our eyes are telling us that only parts of the data are contributing to the significant ANOVA.

Although the above example is very clear, it becomes a little more fraught if the data are less clear-cut than this (Table 23.2). In this case, it may well be that all three groups differ from each other. Just by looking at the means we cannot know for certain since they may just reflect sampling differences.

Table 23.1	Sample means in a one-way ANOVA		
	Group 1	**Group 2**	**Group 3**
Mean	5.6	5.7	12.9

Table 23.2	Sample means in another one-way ANOVA		
	Group 1	**Group 2**	**Group 3**
Mean	5.6	7.3	12.9

Box 23.1   Focus on

Does it matter that the *F*-ratio is not significant?

Traditionally, the advice to users of statistics was that unless the ANOVA itself is statistically significant, no further analyses should be carried out. That is, a significant ANOVA is a prerequisite for multiple comparison testing. Perhaps this was sound advice before the sophisticated modern multiple range tests were developed. However, this is a fairly controversial topic which makes straightforward advice difficult. Some multiple range tests are deemed by some authorities to be permissible in circumstances where ANOVA was not significant. With *post hoc* testing, depending on which multiple comparison test is being contemplated, you do not need a significant ANOVA first. Of course, if the ANOVA is statistically significant then any multiple comparison test is appropriate.

Among a number of multiple comparison tests which can be applied irrespective of overall significance are the Neuman–Keuls test and Duncan's new multiple range test.

If one is operating within the strictures of *a priori* (planned) specific comparisons, then concerns which apply to the *post hoc* test simply do not apply, as explained elsewhere.

Obviously it is essential to test the significance of the differences between the means for all *three* possible *pairs* of sample means from the three groups. These are:

group 1 with group 2

group 1 with group 3

group 2 with group 3

If there had been *four* groups then the pairs of comparisons would be:

group 1 with group 2

group 1 with group 3

group 1 with group 4

group 2 with group 3

group 2 with group 4

group 3 with group 4

This is getting to be a lot of comparisons!

23.2   Methods

There are a number of different procedures which you could employ to deal with this problem. One traditional approach involves comparing each of the pairs of groups using a *t*-test (or you could use one-way analysis of variance for two groups). So for the four-group experiment there would be six separate *t*-tests to calculate (group 1 with group 2, group 1 with group 3, etc.).

The problem with this procedure (which is not so bad really) is the number of separate comparisons being made. The more comparisons you make between pairs of means the more likely is a significant difference merely due to chance (always the risk in inferential statistics). Similar procedures apply to the multifactorial (two-way, etc.) analysis of variance. You can compare different levels of any of the main effect pairs simply by comparing their means using a *t*-test or the equivalent. However, the multiple comparison difficulty remains unless you make an adjustment.

To cope with this problem a relatively simple procedure, the Bonferroni method, is used. It assumes that the significance level should be shared between the *number* of comparisons made. So, if you are making four comparisons (i.e. conducting four separate *t*-tests) then the appropriate significance level for the individual tests is as follows:

$$\text{significance level for each test} = \frac{\text{overall significance level}}{\text{number of comparisons}}$$

$$= \frac{5\%}{4}$$

$$= 1.25\%$$

In other words, a comparison actually needs to be significant at the 1.25% level according to the significance tables before we accept that it is significant at the *equivalent* of the 5% level. This essentially compensates for our generosity in doing many comparisons and reduces the risk of inadvertently capitalising on chance differences. (We adopted this procedure for chi-square in Chapter 14.) Although this is the proper thing to do, we have often seen examples of analyses which fail to make this adjustment. Some researchers tend to stick with the regular 5% level per comparison no matter how many they are doing, although sometimes they point out the dangers of multiple comparisons without making an appropriate adjustment.

So long as you adjust your critical values to allow for the number of comparisons made, there is nothing much wrong with using multiple *t*-tests. Indeed, this procedure, properly applied, is a slightly 'conservative' one in that it errs in favour of the null hypotheses. However, there are better procedures for making multiple comparisons which are especially convenient when using a computer. These include such procedures as the Scheffé test and the Duncan multiple range test. The advantage of these is that they report directly significance levels which are adjusted for the numbers of comparisons being made.

Appendix K contains a table of *t*-values for use when there are a number of comparisons being made (i.e. multiple comparisons). Say you wished to test the statistical significance of the differences between pairs of groups in a three-group one-way analysis of variance. This gives three different comparisons between the pairs. The significant *t*-test values for this are found under the column for three comparisons.

23.3 Planned versus *a posteriori (post hoc)* comparisons

In the fantasy world of statisticians, there is a belief that researchers are meticulous in planning the last detail of their statistical analysis in advance of doing research. As such an ideal researcher, one would have planned in advance precisely what pairs of cells or conditions in the research are to be compared. These choices are based on the hypotheses and other considerations. In other words, they are planned comparisons. More usual, in our experience, is that the details of the statistical analysis are decided upon *after* the data have been collected. Psychological theory is often not so strong that we can predict from it the precise pattern of outcomes we expect. Comparisons decided upon after the data have been collected and tabulated are called *a posteriori* or *post hoc* comparisons.

Since properly planned comparisons are not the norm in psychological research, for simplicity we will just consider the more casual situation in which comparisons are made as the data are inspected. (Basically, if your number of planned comparisons is smaller than your number of experimental conditions, then they can be tested by the multiple *t*-test *without* adjusting the critical values.)

There are a number of tests which deal with the situation in which multiple comparisons are being made. These include Dunnett's test, Duncan's test and others. The Scheffé test will serve as a model of the sorts of things achieved by many of these tests and is probably as good as any other similar test for general application. Some other tests are not quite so stringent in ensuring that the appropriate level of significance is achieved.

23.4 The Scheffé test for one-way ANOVA

Although this can be computed by hand without too much difficulty, the computer output of the Scheffé test is particularly useful as it gives subsets of the groups (or conditions) in your experiment which do not differ significantly from each other. For example, take a look at the following:

Scheffe[a]

Condition	Subset for alpha = .05
	1
3	4.00
1	5.60
2	7.00
Sig.	0.424

[a] Uses Harmonic Mean Sample Size = 3.000.

This indicates that groups 1, 2 and 3 are not significantly different from each other since they all belong in the same group. The right hand column indicates that all three conditions are in the same subset – it also gives the means involved. If you had significant differences between all three groups then you would have three subsets (subset 1, subset 2 and subset 3) each of which contained just one group. If groups 1 and 3 did not differ from each other but they both differed from group 2 then you would obtain something like the following:

Scheffe[a]

Condition	Subset for alpha = .05	
	1	2
3	4.00	
1	5.60	
2		7.00
Sig.	0.975	1.000

[a] Uses Harmonic Mean Sample Size = 3.000.

Calculation 23.1

Multiple comparisons: the Scheffé test

The calculation of the Scheffé test is straightforward once you have carried out an analysis of variance and have the summary table. The test tells you whether two group means in an ANOVA differ significantly from each other. Obviously the calculation has to be repeated for every pair of groups you wish to compare, but no adjustments are necessary for the number of pairs of groups being compared. The following worked example is based on the data in Calculation 20.1. Table 23.3 reminds us about the data and Table 23.4 is the analysis of variance summary table for that calculation.

➔

Table 23.3	Data table for an unrelated analysis of variance

Group 1 Hormone 1	Group 2 Hormone 2	Group 3 Placebo control
9	4	3
12	2	6
8	5	3
Mean = 9.667	Mean = 3.667	Mean = 4.000
$N_1 = 3$	$N_2 = 3$	$N_3 = 3$
		Overall mean = 5.778

Table 23.4	Analysis of variance summary table

Source of variation	Sum of squares	Degrees of freedom	Mean square (variance estimate)	F-ratio
Between groups	68.222	2	34.111	10.59[a]
Error (within-groups)	19.334	6	3.222	
Total	87.556	8		

[a] Significant at the 5% level.

Step 1

The formula used is based on the F-distribution. It involves the two group means in question, the sample sizes in the relevant conditions and the error (within) mean square. All of these are to be found in Tables 23.3 and 23.4.

$$F = \frac{(\text{mean of group}_1 - \text{mean of group}_2)^2}{\text{error mean sqare} \times \dfrac{N_1 + N_2}{N_1 \times N_2}}$$

$$= \frac{(9.667 - 3.667)^2}{3.222 \times \dfrac{3 + 3}{3 \times 3}} = \frac{6.000^2}{3.222 \times \dfrac{6}{9}}$$

$$= \frac{36.000}{3.222 \times 0.667}$$

$$= \frac{36.000}{2.149} = 16.75$$

Step 2

The significance of this F-ratio depends on the degrees of freedom. The degrees of freedom for the columns in Significance Table 22.1 are the number of groups being compared minus one (i.e. $3 - 1 = 2$). The degrees of freedom for the error term (i.e. number of scores − number of groups = $9 - 3 = 6$) corresponds to the rows in Significance Table 22.1. The critical value of the F-ratio for these degrees of freedom needs to be adjusted by number of groups minus one. This critical value is about 5.143 which

→

multiplied by 2 is 10.29. This indicates that the difference between the mean of group 1 and that of group 2 is significant at the 5% level with the Scheffé test since the critical F-value is only 10.29.

Step 3

In essence, step 3 repeats steps 1 and 2 but compares group 1 with group 3 and group 2 with group 3. This gives us:

F when comparing group 1 with group 3 = 14.94 (significant at 5% level)

F when comparing group 2 with group 3 = 0.16 (not significant)

Interpreting the results The use of a multiple comparison test is necessary whenever there are more than two groups to compare in ANOVA. If there are only two groups then any further test is superfluous.

Reporting the results The results of this analysis may be written up according to the APA (2010) Publication Manual's recommendations as follows: 'The main effect was significant, $F(2, 6) = 10.59$, $p < 0.05$. Consequently, the Scheffé test was used to compare pairs of group means in order to assess where the differences lie. Group 1 ($M = 9.67$) was significantly higher than group 2 ($M = 3.67$) and group 3 ($M = 4.00$), $p < .05$, but the means of groups 2 and 3 did not differ from each other. Thus hormone 1 was associated with higher levels of depression than either hormone 2 or the placebo control which did not differ from each other.'

23.5 Multiple comparisons for multifactorial ANOVA

If your experimental design is multifactorial (that is, with two or more independent variables), multiple comparisons are tackled much as for the two-way ANOVA using exactly the same methods (including the adjusted multiple t-test procedure or the Scheffé test). Of course, you would only need such a test if any of the independent variables (factors) have three or more different levels. Otherwise, the significance of the comparisons in the ANOVA is obvious from the ANOVA summary table since there are only two groups of scores to compare with each other (except for interactions).

If you have an independent variable with three or more different levels then multiple comparisons are important to tell you precisely where the significant differences lie. It would be possible to carry out multiple comparisons between every cell mean in the ANOVA, but generally this would not be helpful. All one would do is to produce a table analogous to a one-way ANOVA by making the data in each cell of the multifactorial ANOVA into a column of the one-way ANOVA. The difficulty is that this multiplicity of comparisons would be practically uninterpretable since each cell consists of several sources of variation – the various main effects, for example.

It is much more useful and viable to employ multiple comparisons to compare the means of the several different levels of the independent variable(s). If there are four different levels of the independent variable, then one would essentially set out the table like a one-way ANOVA with four different levels of the independent variable. It is then possible to test the significance of the differences among the four means using, for example, the Scheffé test. Figure 23.1 shows the key steps for multiple comparison tests.

Multiple comparisons testing deals with the problem of where differences lie when the study compares three or more means.

Because one needs to carry out several tests of significance, simply comparing each pair of means carries a risk of finding erroneous significant difference so adjustments need to be made.

However, if the comparisons have been planned in advance of data collection, then it is appropriate simply to use the *t*-test without any adjustment IF the number of comparisons planned does not exceed the number of conditions in the study.

The Bonferroni method is the most direct method of making adjustments, where these are necessary – that is, where the comparisons have not been planned in advance.

However, there is a range of other approaches to make multiple comparisons which are ready available on SPSS Statistics and other programs.

Some methods are more stringent in practice than others. Unfortunately, generally speaking it is not clear which multiple comparison technique is best for a particular purpose.

Consequently, a prudent approach is to employ a selection of different methods. If they all point to identical conclusions then things are simple. If they produce very different outcomes one needs to address the question of which is the most appropriate method.

FIGURE 23.1   Conceptual steps for understanding multiple-comparison testing

---

Key points

- If you have more than two sets of scores in the analysis of variance (or any other test for that matter), it is important to employ one of the procedures for multiple comparisons.

- Even simple procedures such as multiple *t*-tests are better than nothing, especially if the proper adjustment is made for the number of *t*-tests being carried out and you adjust the critical values accordingly.

- Modern computer packages, especially SPSS Statistics, have a range of multiple comparison tests. It is a fine art to know which is the most appropriate for your particular circumstances. Usually it is expedient to compare the results from several tests; often they will give much the same results, especially where the trends in the data are clear.

COMPUTER ANALYSIS

The SPSS Statistics instruction book to this text is Dennis Howitt and Duncan Cramer (2011), *Introduction to SPSS Statistics in Psychology: For version 19 and earlier*, Harlow: Pearson. Chapter 24 in that book gives detailed step-by-step procedures for the statistics described in this chapter together with advice on how to report the results. Figure 23.2 shows the SPSS Statistics steps for carrying out multiple comparison tests.

Data
- Name the variables in Variable View of the Data Editor.
- Enter the data under the appropriate variable names in Data View of the Data Editor.

Analysis
- Select 'Analyze' and appropriate analysis of variance option.

2
- Enter dependent and independent variables in boxes to the right.

3
- Select 'Post Hoc . . .', 'Scheffe' and 'Continue'.

Output
- Check which means differ significantly by seeing if the Sig(nificance) is .05 or less.
- Note the direction of the difference.

FIGURE 23.2 SPSS Statistics steps for multiple-comparison tests

Recommended further reading

Howell, D. (2010), *Statistical Methods for Psychology*, 7th edition, Belmont, CA: Duxbury Press.

CHAPTER 24

Mixed-design ANOVA

Related and unrelated variables together

24.1   Introduction

This chapter deals with a useful variant of the analysis of variance: the mixed design. Although we are moving into quite advanced areas of statistics, the key to most statistical analysis lies more in the interpretation of simple statistics such as cell means. Avoid letting the complex calculations sometimes employed blind you to the major purpose of your analysis – understanding what your data say. The mixed-design analysis of variance is similar to the two-way ANOVA described in Chapter 22. The big difference is that *one* of the independent variables is related and *one* is unrelated – hence the term mixed design. Thus it is used when participants take part in *all* of the conditions of one independent variable but in just *one* condition of the other variable. A good example of this type of design is when a pre-test has been given on the dependent variable before the different experimental treatments and a post-test given afterwards. So all participants are measured on both the pre-test and post-test, making pre-test/post-test a related measure. Of course, the unrelated independent variable involves the important experimental manipulation.

Box 24.1   Focus on

Equal cell sizes?

Before the introduction of computers, it was conventional in many of the variants of the analysis of variance to ensure that *all* conditions or cells had the same number of scores. The reason for this was that the hand calculations are simpler if this is the case. When carrying out laboratory studies, equal cell sizes are relatively easy to achieve even if it involves randomly discarding scores from some cells. However, it is possible to do any analysis of variance with unequal numbers of scores in each condition or cell. The calculations tend to be cumbersome and so it is best to use a computer package such as SPSS Statistics to reduce the computational load.

The exception to this is the one-way analysis of variance described in Chapter 20 which can be calculated with

no adjustments for unequal sample size. Of course, with the related one-way ANOVA it is not possible to have different numbers of participants in different conditions of the experiment since participants have to take part in all conditions.

One issue remains, though, and that is whether it is better to have equal cell sizes no matter whether a computer package is being used or not. The answer to the question is that it is always better to have equal cell sizes for the simple reason that if data are not there then the computer package has to employ estimates. While the bias caused by this is minimal in most cases, anyone employing really complex ANOVA designs would be well advised to try to ensure that equal sample sizes are used.

24.2   Mixed designs and repeated measures

Repeated measures designs have the same subjects (or matched groups of subjects) measured in *all* conditions just as in the repeated measures one-way analysis of variance except that there are two or more independent variables. The repeated measures design is intended to increase the precision of research by measuring the error variance (residual variance) in a way which excludes the individual differences component. The individual difference component is obtained from the general tendency of individual participants to score relatively high or relatively low, say, irrespective of the experimental condition. The trend for each individual can simply be deducted from the error scores to leave (residual) error.

Fully repeated measures designs can be analysed, but they are beyond the scope of this book (see Howell (2010) for calculation methods). Some independent variables do not allow for repeated measures – gender, for example, is not a repeated measure since a person cannot change their gender during the course of an experiment. Only where matching of groups on the basis of gender has been carried out is it possible to have gender as a repeated measure.

Box 24.2   Key concepts

Fixed and random effects

The issue of fixed versus random effects is a typical analysis of variance misnomer. It really means fixed or random choice of the different levels of an independent variable. The implication is that you can select the levels of a treatment (independent variable) either by a systematic decision or by choosing the levels by some random procedure.

Most psychological research assumes a *fixed effects* model, and it is hard to find instances of the use of random effects. A fixed effect is where you as the researcher choose or decide or fix what the different values of the independent variable are going to be. In some cases you have no choice at all – a variable such as gender gives you no discretion since it has just two different values (male and female). Usually we just operate as if we have the choice of the different treatments for each independent variable. We simply decide that the experimental group is going to be deprived of sleep for five hours and the control group not deprived of sleep at all.

But there are many different possible amounts of sleep deprivation – no hours, one hour, two hours, three hours, four hours and so forth. Instead of just selecting the number of hours of sleep deprivation on the basis of a particular whim, practicality or any other similar basis, it is possible to choose the amounts of sleep deprivation at random. We could draw the amount out of a hat containing the possible levels. In circumstances like these we would be using a *random effects* model. Because we have selected the hours of sleep deprivation at random, it could be said that our ability to generalise from our experiment to the effects of sleep deprivation in general is enhanced. We have simply chosen an unbiased way of selecting the amount of sleep deprivation after all.

Since the random effects model rarely corresponds to practice in psychological research it is not dealt with further in this book. Psychologists' research is more likely to be the result of agonising about time, money and other practical constraints on the choices available.

Much more common in psychology are *mixed designs* in which the repeated measure is on just some of the independent variables. Mixed designs are two- or more-way analyses of variance in which participants are measured in more than one experimental condition but not *every* experimental condition. (This means that for at least one of the independent variables in a mixed design, scores on different participants will be found in the different levels of this independent variable.) Usually you will have to check through the experimental design carefully in order to decide whether a researcher has used a mixed design, although many will stipulate the type of design.

One common mixed design is the pre-test/post-test design. Participants are measured on the dependent variable before and after the experimental treatment. This is clearly a related design since the same people are measured twice on the same dependent variable. However, since the experimental and control groups consist of different people, this comparison is unrelated. Hence this form of the pre-test/post-test design is a mixed design. This sort of design is illustrated in Table 24.1. Imagine that the dependent variable is self-esteem measured in children before and after the experimental manipulation. The experimental manipulation involves praising half of the children (the experimental group) for good behaviour but telling the other half (the control group) nothing. Obviously this sort of design allows the researcher to test whether the two groups are similar prior to the experimental manipulation by comparing the experimental and control groups on the pre-test measure. The hypothesis that praise affects self-esteem suggests that the post-test measure should be different for the two groups. (Notice that

Table 24.1	Stylised version of the mixed ANOVA design	
	RELATED VARIABLE	
UNRELATED VARIABLE	Pre-test	Post-test
Experimental Condition		
Control Condition		

the hypothesis predicts an interaction effect in which the related and unrelated independent variables interact to yield rather different scores for the experimental group and the control group on the post-test.)

In virtually all respects, the computation of the mixed design is like that for the two-way (unrelated) ANOVA described in Chapter 22. Both main effects and the interaction are calculated in identical fashion. The error is treated differently though as shown in Tables 24.13 and 24.14 (Calculation 24.1). Although the *total* error is calculated by subtracting the cell mean from each of the data scores to leave the error score (as in Chapter 22), in the mixed design this error is then subdivided into two component parts: (a) the individual differences component and (b) the (residual) error component:

- the error due to individual differences is calculated and then used as the error term for the *unrelated* independent variable (this error term is often called 'subjects within groups')

- the (residual) error term is used as the error term when examining the effects of the related independent variable (this error term is often called 'B × subjects within groups').

Note the slight amendments made to the tables such as Table 24.1 (Calculation 24.1) compared to those given in Chapter 22; columns headed 'subject' and 'subject mean' have been added. If there is variation in the subject mean column it shows that there is still an individual differences component in the scores in the main body of the table. Careful examination of (a) the column means and row means, (b) cell means, (c) subject means and (d) the individual scores in the cells will hint strongly whether there remains any variation due to (a) the main effects, (b) interaction, (c) individual differences and (d) (residual) error. Table 24.2 shows a typical ANOVA summary table for the mixed design. The main effects are A and B and there is an interaction AB. However, there are rows such as that for Subjects within groups and B x subjects within groups. These are used as error terms in the mixed design ANOVA – that is, more than one error term is used. Figure 24.1 shows the key steps in a mixed ANOVA.

Table 24.2	Analysis of variance summary table for the mixed design			
Source of variation	**Sums of squares**	**Degrees of freedom**	**Mean Square**	**F-ratio**
Between subjects				
A (Unrelated variable)				
Subjects within groups				
Within subjects				
B (Related variable)				
AB (Interaction)				
B × subjects within groups				

If you feel confident with the two-way unrelated ANOVA described in Chapter 22, we suggest that you need to concentrate on steps 2 and 7 overleaf as these tell you how to calculate the error terms. The other steps should be familiar.

The mixed ANOVA has at least one related factor and one unrelated factor.

The interaction between the related and unrelated factor is often of the greatest interest.

However, the main effects can indicate both differences between groups and changes over time.

Pre-test-post-test designs are generally concerned with seeing whether experimental conditions show greater changes than control conditions.

Repeated measures designs which control for order of testing need to see whether the order affects the results.

One complexity with mixed ANOVA designs is that there are several different 'error' terms in use for different comparisons.

FIGURE 24.1 Conceptual steps for understanding the mixed ANOVA

Calculation 24.1

Mixed-design two-way unrelated analysis of variance: conceptual method

The variance estimate for the data in Table 24.3 for $N - 1$ degrees of freedom is $76.89/11 = 6.99$. N is the number of scores.

Table 24.3	Example of a mixed ANOVA design			
	Subject	**Pre-test measure**	**Post-test measure**	**Subject mean**
Control	S1	6	5	5.500
	S2	4	6	5.000
	S3	5	7	6.000
		Mean = 5.000	Mean = 6.000	Mean = 5.500
Experimental	S4	7	10	8.500
	S5	5	11	8.000
	S6	5	12	8.500
		Mean = 5.667	Mean = 11.000	Mean = 8.333
		Mean = 5.333	**Mean = 8.500**	**Overall mean = 6.917**

→

Just to remind you, 6.99 is the variance estimate (or mean square) based on the 12 scores in Table 24.3. To avoid repetitious calculations with which you should now be familiar, we have given only the final stages of the calculation of the various variance estimates. This is to allow you to work through our example and check your calculations.

In the mixed-design ANOVA the following steps are then calculated.

Step 1   *(between-subjects scores)* Between-subjects scores are the data but with the pre-test/post-test difference eliminated. In other words, each subject's scores in the pre-test and post-test conditions are replaced by the corresponding subject mean. Thus the column means for the pre-test and post-test have the (residual) error removed since the remaining variation within the cells is due to individual differences. However, there still remains variation within the table due to individual differences as well as the main effects and interaction. (To be absolutely clear, the first entry of 5.500 for both the pre-test and post-test measure is obtained by averaging that first person's scores of 5 and 6 in Table 24.4.)

The variance estimate for the between-subjects scores is 25.40/5 = 5.08 (df = number of subjects − 1, i.e. 6 − 1 = 5).

Step 2   *(subjects within groups scores, i.e. individual difference component)* If we take away the cell mean from the scores in Table 24.4, we are left with the individual difference component for each subject for each score. Thus, S2's scores are on average −0.500 below the row mean. Table 24.5 gives the individual difference component of every score in the original data.

The variance estimate for the subjects within groups scores is 1.32/4 = 0.33 (the df is the number of subjects − number of rows of data, i.e. 6 − 2 = 4).

You will see that these individual difference scores seem rather like error scores – they add to zero for each cell. Indeed they are error scores – the individual differences component of error. The variance estimate of the individual differences is used as the error variance estimate for calculating the significance of the control/experimental comparison (i.e. the *unrelated* independent variable).

Step 3   *(experimental/control scores: main effect)* The best estimate of the effects of the experimental versus the control condition involves simply replacing each score for the control group with the control group mean (5.500) and each score for the experimental group by the experimental group mean (8.333). This is shown in Table 24.6.

The variance estimate for the experimental/control main effect is 24.08/1 = 24.08 (the df is the number of rows of data − 1, i.e. 2 − 1 = 1).

Table 24.4	Table of between-subjects scores, i.e. with (residual) error removed

	Subject	Pre-test	Post-test	Subject mean
Control	S1	5.500	5.500	5.500
	S2	5.000	5.000	5.000
	S3	6.000	6.000	6.000
		Mean = 5.500	Mean = 5.500	Mean = 5.500
Experimental	S4	8.500	8.500	8.500
	S5	8.000	8.000	8.000
	S6	8.500	8.500	8.500
		Mean = 8.333	Mean = 8.333	Mean = 8.333
		Mean = 6.917	**Mean = 6.917**	**Overall mean = 6.917**

Table 24.5	Subjects within groups scores, i.e. error due to individual differences removed			
	Subject	Pre-test	Post-test	Subject mean
Control	S1	5.500 − 5.500 = 0.000	0.000	0.000
	S2	5.000 − 5.500 = −0.500	−0.500	−0.500
	S3	6.000 − 5.500 = 0.500	0.500	0.500
				Mean = 0.000
Experimental	S4	8.500 − 8.333 = 0.167	0.167	0.167
	S5	−0.333	−0.333	−0.333
	S6	0.167	0.167	0.167
				Mean = 0.000
		Mean = 0.000	Mean = 0.000	Overall mean = 0.000

Table 24.6	Main effect (experimental/control comparison)			
	Subject	Pre-test	Post-test	Subject mean
Control	S1	5.500	5.500	5.500
	S2	5.500	5.500	5.500
	S3	5.500	5.500	5.500
				Mean = 5.500
Experimental	S4	8.333	8.333	8.333
	S5	8.333	8.333	8.333
	S6	8.333	8.333	8.333
				Mean = 8.333
		Mean = 6.917	Mean = 6.917	Overall mean = 6.917

The statistical significance of the main effect of the experimental versus control manipulation independent variable involves the variance estimate for the main effects scores in Table 24.6 and the variance estimate for the individual differences error scores in Table 24.5. By dividing the former by the latter variance estimate, we obtain the F-ratio for testing the effects of the experimental versus control conditions. If this is significant then there is an overall difference between the control and experimental group scores.

Step 4 *(within-subjects scores)* Subtract the between-subjects scores (Table 24.4) from the data table (Table 24.3) and you are left the within-subjects scores. In other words, the scores in Table 24.7 are what is left when the effects of the experimental/control comparison and the individual difference component of the scores are removed. Notice that the subject means in Table 24.7 are all zero as are the row means. This indicates that there are no individual differences or differences due to the experimental/control comparison remaining in Table 24.7.

The variance estimate for this table is 51.54/6 = 8.59 (*df* is the number of scores minus the number of subjects = 12 − 6 = 6).

Table 24.7	Within-subjects scores (i.e. the scores with individual differences and control/experimental differences eliminated)			
	Subject	**Pre-test**	**Post-test**	**Subject mean**
Control	S1	0.5	−0.5	0.000
	S2	−1.0	1.0	0.000
	S3	−1.0	1.0	0.000
				Mean = 0.000
Experimental	S4	−1.5	1.5	0.000
	S5	−3.0	3.0	0.000
	S6	−3.5	3.5	0.000
				Mean = 0.000
		Mean = −1.583	Mean = 1.583	Overall mean = 0.000

Table 24.8	The main effects of the pre-test/post-test comparison			
	Subject	**Pre-test**	**Post-test**	**Subject mean**
Control	S1	5.333	8.500	6.917
	S2	5.333	8.500	6.917
	S3	5.333	8.500	6.917
				Mean = 6.917
Experimental	S4	5.333	8.500	6.917
	S5	5.333	8.500	6.917
	S6	5.333	8.500	6.917
				Mean = 6.917
		Mean = 5.333	Mean = 8.500	Overall mean = 6.917

Step 5   *(within-subjects independent variable main effect: pre-test/post-test scores)* This is the main effect of the repeated measure. It is obtained simply by substituting the appropriate column average from the data table (Table 24.3) for each of the scores (Table 24.8).

The variance estimate for the pre-test/post-test main effect is 30.09/1 = 30.09 (the df is the number of columns of data −1, i.e. 2 − 1 = 1).

Step 6   *(the interaction of experimental/control with pre-test/post-test)* The calculation of the interaction is much as for the two-way unrelated ANOVA (Chapter 22):

1. We can eliminate error by making every score in the data table the same as the cell mean (Table 24.9).

2. We can eliminate the effect of the control versus experimental treatment by simply taking the corresponding row means away from all of the scores in Table 24.9 (Table 24.10).

3. Note that Table 24.10 still contains variation between its pre-test and post-test columns. We eliminate this by subtracting the corresponding column mean from each of the scores in the pre-test and post-test columns (Table 24.11).

Table 24.9   Removing (total) error from the data table

	Subject	Pre-test	Post-test	Subject mean
Control	S1	5.000	6.000	5.500
	S2	5.000	6.000	5.500
	S3	5.000	6.000	5.500
				Mean = 5.500
Experimental	S4	5.667	11.000	8.333
	S5	5.667	11.000	8.333
	S6	5.667	11.000	8.333
				Mean = 8.333
		Mean = 5.333	**Mean = 8.500**	**Overall mean = 6.917**

Table 24.10   Removing experimental/control main effect (total error removed in previous step)

	Subject	Pre-test	Post-test	Subject mean
Control	S1	5.000 − 5.500 = −0.500	0.500	0.000
	S2	−0.500	0.500	0.000
	S3	−0.500	0.500	0.000
				Mean = 0.000
Experimental	S4	5.667 − 8.333 = −2.666	2.667	0.000
	S5	−2.666	2.667	0.000
	S6	−2.666	2.667	0.000
				Mean = 0.000
		Mean = −1.583	**Mean = 1.583**	**Overall mean = 0.000**

Table 24.11   Removing pre-test/post-test differences (error and experimental/control main effect already removed in previous two steps)

	Subject	Pre-test	Post-test	Subject mean
Control	S1	−0.500 − (−1.583) = 1.083	−1.083	0.000
	S2	1.083	−1.083	0.000
	S3	1.083	−1.083	0.000
				Mean = 0.000
Experimental	S4	2.666 − (−1.583) = −1.083	1.083	0.000
	S5	−1.083	1.083	0.000
	S6	−1.083	1.083	0.000
				Mean = 0.000
		Mean = 0.00	**Mean = 0.00**	**Overall mean = 0.00**

→

Table 24.11 contains the scores for the interaction. The variance estimate for the interaction is $14.08/1 = 14.08$ (the df is the number of rows of data − 1 × the number of columns of data −1 (i.e. $(2 − 1) × (2 − 1) = 1 × 1 = 1$)).

Step 7   *(pre-test/post-test × subjects within groups) Earlier we explained that pre-test/post-test × subjects within groups is an error term which is in essence the (residual) error that we calculated in Chapter 21. It is actually quite easy to calculate the (residual) error simply by:*

- *drawing up a total error table by subtracting the cell means from each score in the data table (Table 24.8) as we did for the two-way unrelated ANOVA in Chapter 22 and then*

- *taking away from these (total) error scores the corresponding (residual) error in Table 24.10. In other words,*

(Residual) error = (Total) error − Individual difference error

Most statistical textbooks present a rather more abstract computational approach to this which obscures what is really happening. However, to facilitate comparisons with other textbooks, if required, we will present the calculation using essentially the computational method.

The calculation of this error term involves taking the data (Table 24.3) and then (a) subtracting the interaction score (Table 24.11), (b) subtracting the individual differences score (Table 24.4) and (c) adding the between-subjects score (Table 24.8). Notice that the scores in Table 24.12 are just as we would expect of error scores – the cells all add up to zero. It is (residual) error since there is no variation left in the subject mean column.

The variance estimate for the pre-test/post-test × subjects within groups (or residual error) is $7.37/4 = 1.84$ (the df is (number of subjects − number of rows) × (number of columns − 1) = $(6 − 2) × (2 − 1) = 4 × 1 = 4$).

This (residual) error term is used in assessing the significance of the pre-test/post-test comparison as well as the interaction.

The various calculations in steps 1–7 can be made into an analysis of variance summary table. Table 24.13 is a summary table using the basic concepts we have included in this book; Table 24.14 is the same except that it uses the conventional way of presenting mixed designs in statistics textbooks.

You might be wondering about the reasons for the two error terms. The (residual) error is merely that with no individual differences remaining, and in Chapter 21 we examined how removing individual differences helps to control error variation in related designs. Not surprisingly, it is used for the main effect

Table 24.12	The pre-test/post test × subjects within groups scores (i.e. (residual) error)			
	Subject	**Pre-test**	**Post-test**	**Subject mean**
Control	S1	$6 − 5.000 − 5.500 + 5.500 = 1.000$	$5 − 6.000 − 5.500 + 5.500 = −1.000$	0.000
	S2	$4 − 5.000 − 5.000 + 5.500 = −0.500$	$6 − 6.000 − 5.000 + 5.500 = 0.500$	0.000
	S3	$5 − 5.000 − 6.000 + 5.500 = −0.500$	$7 − 6.000 − 6.000 + 5.500 = 0.500$	0.000
				Mean = 0.000
	S4	$7 − 5.667 − 8.500 + 8.333 = 1.167$	$10 − 11.000 − 8.500 + 8.333 = −1.167$	0.000
	S5	$5 − 5.667 − 8.000 + 8.333 = −0.334$	$11 − 11.000 − 8.500 + 8.333 = 0.333$	0.000
	S6	$5 − 5.667 − 8.500 + 8.333 = −0.834$	$12 − 11.000 − 8.500 + 8.333 = 0.833$	0.000
				Mean = 0.000
		Mean = 0.000	**Mean = 0.000**	**Overall mean = 0.000**

Table 24.13	Analysis of variance summary table (using basic concepts)			
Source of variation	**Sums of squares**	**Degrees of freedom**	**Variance estimate**	**F-ratio**
Unrelated				
Main effect (unrelated variable)	24.08	1	24.08	$\frac{24.08}{0.33} = 72.97^a$
Individual differences error	1.32	4	0.33	
Related				
Main effect (related variable)	30.09	1	30.09	$\frac{30.09}{1.84} = 16.35^a$
Interaction (related × unrelated variables)	14.08	1	14.08	$\frac{14.08}{1.84} = 7.65^a$
(Residual) error	7.37	4	1.84	

[a] Significant at the 5% level.

Table 24.14	Analysis of variance summary table (with layout in the conventional form)			
Source of variation	**Sums of squares**	**Degrees of freedom**	**Variance estimate**	**F-ratio**
Between subjects				
A (Praise)	24.08	1	24.08	$\frac{24.08}{0.33} = 72.97^a$
Subjects within groups	1.32	4	0.33	
Within subjects				
B (Time)	30.09	1	30.09	$\frac{30.09}{1.84} = 16.35^a$
AB	14.08	1	14.08	$\frac{14.08}{1.84} = 7.65^a$
B × subjects within groups	7.37	4	1.84	

[a] Significant at the 5% level. The above which is conceptually correct is based on calculations subject to compounded rounding errors. So the figures do not correspond exactly to those in Table 24.16 for example.

and interaction which include related components. However, since the individual differences error contains only that source of variation, it makes a good error term for the unrelated scores comparison. After all, by getting rid of 'true' error variation the design allows a 'refined' error term for the unrelated comparison.

Perhaps we ought to explain why rather unusual names are used conventionally for the error terms in mixed ANOVAs. The reason is that the individual differences component of the scores cannot be estimated totally independently of the interaction between the main variables since they are both dependent on pre-test/post-test differences. Consequently, the estimate of individual differences cannot be totally divorced from the interaction. It follows that both error terms ought to be labelled in ways which indicate this fact. On balance, then, you would be wise to keep to the conventional terminology.

Box 24.3   Focus on

A simpler alternative

The sort of mixed design dealt with in this chapter requires a significant interaction for the experimental hypothesis to be supported. However, it has the drawback that the main effect of the pre-test/post-test comparison may well be affected by this interaction. (Remember that ANOVA takes out main effects first and interactions can be confused for these unless you keep your eye firmly on the descriptive output for the means, etc.) Furthermore, the unrelated comparison can also be affected in the same way. A simpler analysis of these same data, although not so thorough as the mixed design ANOVA, would be a *t*-test comparing the *differences* between the pre-test and post-test scores for the experimental and control groups. In other words, you have two groups of scores based on the change from pre-test scores. So you can compare the amount of change in your experimental group compared to the amount of change in the control group using an unrelated *t*-test.

■ The 'risks' in related subjects designs

The advantage of related designs is that the error component of the data can be reduced by the individual differences component. Similarly, in matched-subject designs the matching variables, if they are carefully selected because they correlate with the dependent variable, reduce the amount of error in the scores. However, there is a trade-off between reducing the error term and the reduction in degrees of freedom involved (Glantz and Slinker, 1990) since the degrees of freedom in an unrelated ANOVA error term are higher than for the related ANOVA error term. If one's matching variables are poorly related to the dependent variable or if the individual differences component of error is very small, there may be no advantage in using the related or matched ANOVA. Indeed, there can be a reduction in the power of the related ANOVA to reject your null hypothesis. This is a complex matter. The most practical advice is:

1. Do not employ matching unless you know that there is a strong relationship between the matching variables and the dependent variable (for example, it is only worthwhile matching subjects by their gender if you know that there is a gender difference in scores on the dependent variable).

2. Do whatever you can to reduce the error variance by standardising your methods and using highly reliable measures of the dependent variable.

Calculation 24.2

Mixed-design two-way analysis of variance: quick method

Calculation 24.1 gives a *conceptual* account of the two-way mixed-design analysis of variance calculation. That method illuminates the calculation of the two-way mixed design analysis of variance, but it is time-consuming and rounding errors can affect it. The following calculation uses the computational formula for variance (p. 151) so it is quicker. Also remember that this calculation is only appropriate if you have equal numbers of scores in each cell. If not, you are far better using a computer program which can cope easily with unequal sample sizes and is the preferred solution. If you wish to do a hand calculation, then the simplest procedure is to delete scores *at random* from the larger cells until they are the same size as the smallest cell.

Step 1 We will analyse the data from Table 24.3. This involves a control group and an experimental group (the unrelated independent variable) together with a pre-test/post-test measure (the related independent variable). Table 24.15 reproduces these data but includes a number of totals instead of the means calculated in the previous method. These totals are:

- the totals of each of the four cells (T_1, T_2, T_3, T_4)

- the column totals (C_1, C_2)

- the row totals (i.e. the control group total R_1, and the experimental group total R_2)

- the subject totals (i.e. the totals for each participant P_1, P_2, etc.)

- the grand total (G) or the total of all of the scores.

Step 2 Square each of the scores and calculate the total of squared scores ($\sum X^2$):

$$\text{Sum of squared scores} = \sum X^2$$

$$= 6^2 + 4^2 + 5^2 + 7^2 + 5^2 + 5^2 + 5^2 + 6^2 + 7^2 + 10^2 + 11^2 + 12^2$$

$$= 36 + 16 + 25 + 49 + 25 + 25 + 25 + 36 + 49 + 100 + 121 + 144$$

$$= 651.000$$

Step 3 Carry out the following essential intermediary calculations to be used in later steps. They are R, C, T, P and the correction factor:

Table 24.15 Data for the mixed-design ANOVA with some totals added

Group	Subject	Pre-test	Post-test	Subject totals	Condition totals
Control	1	6	5	$P_1 = 11$	
	2	4	6	$P_2 = 10$	$R_1 = 33$
	3	5	7	$P_3 = 12$	
		$T_1 = 15$	$T_2 = 18$		
Experimental	4	7	10	$P_4 = 17$	
	5	5	11	$P_5 = 16$	$R_2 = 50$
	6	5	12	$P_6 = 17$	
		$T_3 = 17$	$T_4 = 33$		
		$C_1 = 32$	$C_2 = 51$		$G = 83$

$$C = \frac{C_1^2 + C_2^2}{\text{Number of scores per related variable condition}}$$

$$= \frac{32^2 + 51^2}{6}$$

$$= \frac{1024 + 2601}{6}$$

$$= \frac{3625}{6} = 604.167$$

$$R = \frac{R_1^2 + R_2^2}{\text{Number of scores per column}}$$

$$= \frac{33^2 + 50^2}{6}$$

$$= \frac{1089 + 2500}{6}$$

$$= \frac{3589}{6} = 598.167$$

$$T = \frac{T_1^2 + T_2^2 + T_3^2 + T_4^2}{\text{Number of scores per cell}} = \frac{15^2 + 18^2 + 17^2 + 33^2}{3}$$

$$= \frac{225 + 324 + 289 + 1089}{3}$$

$$= \frac{1927}{3} = 642.333$$

$$P = \frac{P_1^2 + P_2^2 + P_3^2 + P_4^2 + P_5^2 + P_6^2}{\text{Number of scores per subject}}$$

$$= \frac{11^2 + 10^2 + 12^2 + 17^2 + 16^2 + 17^2}{2}$$

$$= \frac{121 + 100 + 144 + 289 + 256 + 289}{2}$$

$$= \frac{1199}{2} = 599.500$$

$$\text{Correction factor} = \frac{\text{Grand total}^2}{\text{Number of scores}} = \frac{G^2}{N} = \frac{83^2}{12} = \frac{6889}{12} = 574.083$$

Thus $C = 604.167$

$\quad\quad R = 598.167$

$\quad\quad T = 642.333$

$\quad\quad P = 599.500$

→

$$\frac{G^2}{N} = 574.083 \text{ (i.e. correction factor)}$$

Also $\sum X^2 = 651.000$ (from step 2).

Step 4 Calculate the sum of squares for the unrelated independent variable experimental/control group (i.e. $SS_{[experimental/control]}$). The elements of the calculation have already been calculated in step 3. We can enter these values.

$$SS_{[experimental/control]} = R - \frac{G^2}{N} = 598.167 - 574.083 = 24.084$$

The degrees of freedom for $SS_{[exp/con]}$ are the number of conditions (or levels) of the experimental/control variable minus one. Thus the degrees of freedom for the main effect of the independent variable experimental/control are $2 - 1 = 1$.

Step 5 Calculate the sum of squares for subjects within groups ($SS_{[subjects \, within \, groups]}$):

$$SS_{[subjects \, within \, groups]} = P - R = 599.500 - 598.167 = 1.333$$

The degrees of freedom for $SS_{[subjects \, within \, groups]}$ are the number of subjects minus the number of rows. There are six subjects and two rows of data, therefore the degrees of freedom = $6 - 2 = 4$.

Step 6 Calculate the sum of squares for the related variable (i.e. the pre-test/post-test comparison.) This is $SS_{[time]}$:

$$SS_{[time]} = C - \frac{G^2}{N} = 604.167 - 574.083 = 30.084$$

The degrees of freedom for $SS_{[time]}$ are the number of conditions (or levels) of the pre-test/post-test variable (i.e. independent variable) minus one. Thus the degrees of freedom for the main effect of the independent variable pre-test/post-test are $2 - 1 = 1$.

Step 7 Calculate the interaction between the related and unrelated variables (i.e. $SS_{[interaction]}$):

$$SS_{[interaction]} = T - R - C + \text{correction factor}$$
$$= 642.333 - 598.167 - 604.167 + 574.083$$
$$= 14.082$$

The degrees of freedom for $SS_{[interaction]}$ are (the number of conditions of the related independent variable $- 1$) $\times$ (the number of conditions of the unrelated independent variable $- 1$) = $(2 - 1) \times (2 - 1) = 1 \times 1 = 1$.

Step 8 Calculate (the sum of squares for the related variable) $\times$ (subjects within groups), that is $SS_{[related \times subjects \, within \, groups]}$:

$$SS_{[related \times subjects \, within \, groups]} = \sum X^2 - T - P + R$$
$$= 651.000 - 642.333 - 599.500 + 598.167$$
$$= 7.334$$

→

The degrees of freedom for $SS_{[related \times subjects within groups]}$ = (number of subjects – number of rows) × (number of columns – 1) = (6 – 2) × (2 – 1) = 4 × 1 = 4.

Once you have entered the above calculations into an analysis of variance summary table (Table 24.16), the appropriate F-ratios need to be calculated as shown in that table and the significance of each F-ratio calculated. Significance Table 22.1 can be used for the 5% levels of significance (or Appendix J if other levels of significance are required). The degrees of freedom for the upper part of each F-ratio are to be found in the columns of this table; the degrees of freedom for the lower part of each F-ratio is the corresponding row of this table. As can be seen from Table 24.16, both the main effects and the interaction are significant.

Interpreting the results The interpretation of the mixed-design two-way ANOVA is virtually identical to the interpretation of any two-way ANOVA design such as the unrelated two-way analysis of variance in Chapter 22. It is the calculation of the error terms which is different and this does not alter the interpretation although obviously may affect the significance level.

Remember that the interpretation of any data should be based first of all on an examination of cell means and variances (or standard deviations) such as those to be found in Table 24.17. It is the pattern that you find in these which tells you just what the data say. The tests of significance merely confirm whether or not your interpretations may be generalised. An examination of Table 24.17 suggests that it is the experimental group at the post-test which has by far the highest mean score. There seems to be little difference between the other cells. This seems to suggest that there is an interaction between the two independent variables. The ANOVA summary table confirms this.

Reporting the results These results may be written up according to the APA (2009) Publication Manual's recommendations as follows: 'A mixed-design analysis of variance with praise as the unrelated independent variable and pre-test versus post-test as the related independent variable was carried out on the dependent variable self-esteem. The independent variable praise had a significant effect on self-esteem, $F(1, 4) = 72.32$, $p < 0.05$. The scores in the control group ($M = 5.50$) were significantly lower than those in the experimental group which was given praise ($M = 8.33$). Similarly, scores at the post-test were significantly higher in the post-test ($M = 8.50$) than in the pre-test ($M = 5.33$), $F(1, 4) = 16.40$, $p < 0.05$.

Table 24.16	Analysis of variance summary table for calculation formula analysis			
Source of variation	**Sums of squares**	**Degrees of freedom**	**Variance estimate (i.e. mean square)**	**F-ratio**
Between subjects				
A (unrelated variable)	24.084	1	24.084	$\dfrac{24.084}{0.333} = 72.32^{a}$
Subjects within groups	1.333	4	0.333	
Within subjects				
B (time)	30.084	1	30.084	$\dfrac{30.084}{1.834} = 16.40^{a}$
AB	14.082	1	14.082	$\dfrac{14.082}{1.834} = 7.68^{a}$
B × subjects within groups	7.334	4	1.834	

[a] Significant at the 5% level.

However, the hypothesis suggests that there is an interaction between the two independent variables such that the post-test measures of the experimental group given praise score more highly on the dependent variable than the other cells. There was a significant interaction, $F(1, 4) = 7.68$, $p < 0.05$. Furthermore, it would seem that it is the experimental groups following the praise manipulation which had the highest self-esteem scores. Table 24.17 shows the cell means for the four conditions of the experiment. It would appear that the variation between the cells is the result of the interaction effect and that the main effects are slight in comparison.'

Table 24.17	Table of means for mixed ANOVA design		
	Pre-test measure	**Post-test measure**	
Control	Cell mean = 5.000	Cell mean = 6.000	Row mean = 5.500
Experimental	Cell mean = 5.667	Cell mean = 11.000	Row mean = 8.333
	Column mean = 5.333	**Column mean = 8.500**	**Overall mean = 6.917**

Key points

- Research designs which require complex statistics such as the above ANOVAs are difficult and cumbersome to implement. Use them only after careful deliberation about what it is you really need from your research.

- Avoid the temptation to include basic demographic variables such as age and gender routinely as independent variables in the analysis of variance. If they are key factors then they should be included, otherwise they can merely lead to complex interactions which may be hard to interpret and not profitable when you have done so.

COMPUTER ANALYSIS

The SPSS Statistics instruction book to this text is Dennis Howitt and Duncan Cramer (2011), *Introduction to SPSS Statistics in Psychology: For version 19 and earlier*, Harlow: Pearson. Chapter 25 in that book gives detailed step-by-step procedures for the statistics described in this chapter together with advice on how to report the results. Figure 24.2 gives the SPSS Statistics steps for a mixed analysis of variance.

Data
- Name the variables in Variable View of the Data Editor.
- Enter the data under the appropriate variable names in Data View of the Data Editor.

Analysis
- Select 'Analyze', 'General Linear Model' and 'Repeated Measures . . .'.
- Enter number of conditions for related independent variable in 'Number of levels:' box. Select 'Add' and 'Define'.

2
- Move the related or repeated measures variables to the 'Within-Subjects Variables:' box.
- Move the unrelated factor to the 'Between-Subjects Variables:' box.

3
- Select 'Plots . . .'. Move related variable to 'Horizontal Axis:' box and unrelated variable to 'Separate Lines:' box. Select 'Add' and 'Continue'.

4
- Select 'Options', 'Descriptive statistics', 'Estimates of effect size', 'Homogeneity tests' and 'Continue'.

Output
- The effect of most interest in a pre-test-post-test design is the interaction between the related and the unrelated variable.

2
- Check whether this interaction is significant in the 'Tests of Within-Subjects Contrasts' table by seeing if the Sig(nificance) is .05 or less.

3
- If it is significant, conduct further tests to determine which means differ significantly.

4
- In a repeated measures design where the order of conditions is controlled, it is important to determine if there is a carryover effect.

FIGURE 24.2 SPSS Statistics steps for a mixed ANOVA

Recommended further reading

Glantz, S.A. and Slinker, B.K. (1990), *Primer of Applied Regression and Analysis of Variance*, New York: McGraw-Hill.

CHAPTER 25

Analysis of covariance (ANCOVA)

Controlling for additional variables

Overview

- The analysis of covariance (ANCOVA) involves procedures by which it is possible to control for additional variables which may be influencing the apparent trends in the data.

- Analysis of covariance designs often include a pre-test measure of the dependent variable. The analysis adjusts for these pre-test differences. Very approximately speaking, it adjusts or controls the data so that the pre-test scores are equal. This is especially useful when participants cannot be randomly allocated to different conditions of the design.

- Remember that in properly randomised experimental designs, extraneous influences are controlled partly by this process of randomly assigning participants to conditions. Of course, this may not always have the desired outcome which is why some researchers will use a pre-test to check that the participants are similar on the dependent variable prior to actually running the experiment. If the pre-test data suggest that the participants are not equated on the dependent variable then ANCOVA may be employed to help correct this.

Preparation

Chapters 20 to 22 are essential as this chapter utilises many of the ideas from different types of ANOVA.

25.1 Introduction

Another useful variant of the analysis of variance is the analysis of covariance. This adds extra complexity but is especially valuable when there is reason to believe that the randomisation process cannot be relied on to have equated participants in the various conditions (cells) prior to the experimental manipulation. Of course, in non-randomised studies using ANOVA this is especially likely to be the case.

The analysis of covariance (ANCOVA) described in this chapter is basically an elaboration of the unrelated analysis of variance (Chapter 22). The crucial difference is that an additional variable known as the covariate is measured in addition to the dependent variable. This covariate is a variable which correlates potentially with the *dependent* variable. That is, the researcher suspects that the covariate is an uncontrolled source of variation which is affecting the outcome of the study. The participants in the various conditions of the experiment may be different in terms of a covariate, for example. Thus not all differences between the experimental conditions are due to the influence of the independent variable (experimental manipulation) on the dependent variable if the covariate is having an influence. In ANCOVA the scores on the dependent variable are adjusted so that they are equated on the covariate. Although the procedures do not actually use the adjusted scores, the cell means for the adjusted scores are obtained as part of an additional stage in the statistical analysis. In experiments random assignment of participants to different conditions of the experiment is used so that any pre-existing differences between participants are randomly distributed – hopefully. However, randomisation does not fully guarantee that participants are similar in all conditions for every study. Randomisation avoids systematic biases, but it cannot ensure that there are no differences between participants in the different conditions prior to the experimental manipulation which affect their scores on the dependent variable. Furthermore, non-experimental studies cannot employ randomisation properly. In one important application of ANCOVA, pre-test measures can be thought of as covariates of the post-test measure and thus handled using the analysis of covariance as an alternative to the mixed design described in the previous chapter. Figure 25.1 shows the key steps in ANCOVA.

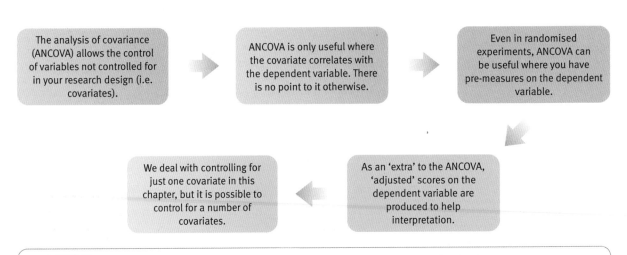

The analysis of covariance (ANCOVA) allows the control of variables not controlled for in your research design (i.e. covariates).

ANCOVA is only useful where the covariate correlates with the dependent variable. There is no point to it otherwise.

Even in randomised experiments, ANCOVA can be useful where you have pre-measures on the dependent variable.

As an 'extra' to the ANCOVA, 'adjusted' scores on the dependent variable are produced to help interpretation.

We deal with controlling for just one covariate in this chapter, but it is possible to control for a number of covariates.

FIGURE 25.1   Conceptual steps for understanding ANCOVA

25.2   Analysis of covariance

The analysis of covariance (ANCOVA) is very much like the analysis of variance. The big difference is that it allows you to take account of any variable(s) which might correlate with the dependent variable (apart, of course, from any independent variables in your analysis of variance design). In other words, it is possible to adjust the analysis of variance for differences between your groups that might affect the outcome. For example, you might find that social class correlates with your dependent variable, and that social class differs for the groups in your ANOVA. Using ANCOVA you can effectively 'adjust' the scores on your dependent variable for these social class differences. This is, in essence, to equate all of the groups so that their mean social class is the same. Although it is possible to calculate ANCOVA by hand, we would recommend the use of a computer package since you are likely to want to equate for several variables, not just one. Furthermore, you should check to see that your covariate does, in fact, correlate with the dependent variable otherwise your analysis becomes less sensitive, not more so.

Table 25.1 gives data that might be suitable for the analysis of covariance. The study is of the effects of different types of treatment on the dependent variable depression. For each participant, a pre-test measure of depression taken prior to therapy is also given. Notice that the pre-test scores of group 3, the no-treatment control group, tend to be larger on this pre-measure. Therefore, it could be that the apparent effects of therapy are to do with pre-existing differences between the three groups. Analysis of covariance could be used to allow for these pre-existing differences.

Table 25.1	Example of analysis of covariance data				
Group 1 Psychotherapy		**Group 2 Anti-depressant**		**Group 3 No-treatment control**	
Independent variable Depression	Covariate Pre-test	Independent variable Depression	Covariate Pre-test	Independent variable Depression	Covariate Pre-test
27	38	30	40	40	60
15	32	27	34	29	52
2	35	24	32	35	57

Calculation 25.1

One-way analysis of covariance

The data are found in Table 25.1. The analysis of covariance involves a number of steps which remove the influence of the covariate on the dependent variable prior to calculating the analysis of variance on these adjusted scores. It is unnecessary to calculate the adjusted scores directly and adjusted sums of squares are used instead. The one-way analysis of covariance involves three major steps:

1. Calculating a one-way ANOVA on the dependent variable (depression) using exactly the same methods as found in Calculation 20.2.

2. Calculating a one-way ANOVA on the covariate (in this case the pre-test scores) again using exactly the same methods as found in Calculation 20.2.

3. Calculating a variation on the one-way ANOVA which involves the regression of the covariate on the dependent variable. In essence this is the covariation which is subtracted from the variation in the scores on the dependent variable to adjust them for the effect of the covariate.

The above steps are then used to calculate the analysis of covariance (ANCOVA).

Finally, in order to judge what the data say after the influence has been removed, we also need a table of the adjusted cell means for the dependent variable, i.e. what is left when the covariate is removed from the dependent variable.

Step 1 *(one-way unrelated ANOVA on the dependent variable)* For clarity we have given the data on the dependent variable in Table 25.2. Consult Calculation 20.2 for fuller details of calculating the one-way ANOVAs.

1. Calculate the sum of the squared scores by squaring each score on the dependent variable and adding to give the total:

$$\sum X^2 = 27^2 + 15^2 + 22^2 + 30^2 + 27^2 + 24^2 + 40^2 + 29^2 + 35^2 = 7309$$

2. Sum the scores to give:

$$G = 27 + 15 + 22 + 30 + 27 + 24 + 40 + 29 + 35 = 249$$

3. Calculate the total number of scores on the dependent variable, $N = 9$.

4. Calculate the correction factor using the following formula:

$$\frac{G^2}{N} = \frac{249^2}{9} = 6889.000$$

5. Obtain the total sum of squares for the dependent variable by taking the sum of the squared scores minus the correction factor. This is $7309 - 6889.000 = 420.000$. This is entered into the ANOVA summary table for the dependent variable (Table 25.3).

6. Enter the degrees of freedom for the total sum of squares for the dependent variable. This is always $N - 1$ or the number of scores $- 1 = 9 - 1 = 8$.

Table 25.2	Scores on the dependent variable		
	Group 1	**Group 2**	**Group 3**
	27	30	40
	15	27	29
	22	24	35

→

Table 25.3	Analysis of variance summary table for scores on the dependent variable			
Source of variation	**Sum of squares**	**Degrees of freedom**	**Mean square (variance estimate)**	**F-ratio**
Between groups[dependent]	268.667	2	134.333	5.33[a]
Error[dependent]	151.333	6	25.222	
Total[dependent]	420.000	8		

[a] Significant at the 5% level.

7. The sum of squares between groups ($SS_{[between]}$) can be calculated as follows using the correction factor calculated above, the totals of each column and the number of scores in each column (e.g. N_1).

$$SS_{[between]} = \frac{T_1^2}{N_1} + \frac{T_2^2}{N_2} + \frac{T_3^2}{N_3} - \frac{G^2}{N}$$

$$= \frac{64^2}{3} + \frac{81^2}{3} + \frac{104^2}{3} - 6889.000$$

$$= 268.667$$

This value of the between-groups sum of squares for the dependent variable is entered into the ANOVA summary table (Table 25.3).

8. Enter the degrees of freedom for the between-groups sum of squares = columns $- 1 = c - 1 = 3 - 1 = 2$.

9. Calculate the error (i.e. error or within) sum of squares ($SS_{[error]}$) by subtracting the between-groups sum of squares from the total sum of squares:

$$SS_{[error]} = SS_{[total]} - SS_{[between]}$$

$$= 420.000 - 268.667$$

$$= 151.333$$

10. The degrees of freedom for error are the number of scores minus the number of columns = $N - c = 9 - 3 = 6$.

Step 2 *(unrelated ANOVA on the covariate)* Again we can create a table of the covariate scores (Table 25.4) and carry out an unrelated ANOVA in exactly the same way as above for the dependent variable.

1. Calculate the sum of the squared scores by squaring each score on the covariate and adding to give the total:

$$\sum X^2 = 38^2 + 32^2 + 35^2 + 40^2 + 34^2 + 32^2 + 60^2 + 52^2 + 57^2 = 17\ 026$$

2. Sum the scores to give:

$$G = 38 + 32 + 35 + 40 + 34 + 32 + 60 + 52 + 57 = 380$$

3. Calculate the total number of scores for the covariate, $N = 9$.

Table 25.4	Scores on the covariate		
	Group 1	**Group 2**	**Group 3**
	38	40	60
	32	34	52
	35	32	57

4. Calculate the correction factor using the following formula:

$$\frac{G^2}{N} = \frac{380^2}{9} = 16\ 044.444$$

5. Obtain the sum of squared scores for the covariate by taking the sum of the squared scores minus the correction factor. This is $17\ 026 - 16\ 044.444 = 981.556$. This is entered into the ANOVA summary table for the covariate (Table 25.5).

6. Enter the degrees of freedom for the total sum of squares for the dependent variable. This is always $N - 1$ or the number of scores $- 1 = 9 - 1 = 8$.

7. The sum of squares between groups ($SS_{[between]}$) can be calculated as follows using the correction factor which has already been calculated, the totals of each column and the number of scores in each column for the covariate (e.g. N_1):

$$SS_{[between]} = \frac{T_1^2}{N_1} + \frac{T_2^2}{N_2} + \frac{T_3^2}{N_3} - \frac{G^2}{N} = \frac{105^2}{3} + \frac{106^2}{3} + \frac{169^2}{3} - 16\ 044.444 = 896.223$$

This value of the between-groups sum of squares for the covariate is entered into the ANOVA summary table (Table 25.5).

8. Also, enter the degrees of freedom for the between-groups sum of squares for the covariate = columns $- 1 = c - 1 = 3 - 1 = 2$.

9. Calculate the error (i.e. error or within) sum of squares ($SS_{[error]}$) by subtracting the between-groups sum of squares from the total sum of squares:

$$SS_{[error]} = SS_{[total]} - SS_{[between]} = 981.556 - 896.223 = 85.333$$

Table 25.5	Analysis of variance summary table for scores on the covariate			
Source of variation	**Sum of squares**	**Degrees of freedom**	**Mean square (variance estimate)**	**F-ratio**
Between groups[covariate]	896.223	2	448.112	31.51[a]
Error[covariate]	85.333	6	14.222	
Total[covariate]	981.556	8		

[a] Significant at the 0.1% level.

The degrees of freedom for error are the number of scores minus the number of columns = $N - c =$ 9 − 3 = 6.

Step 3 *(calculating the covariation summary table)* This is very similar to the calculation of the unrelated ANOVA but is based on the cross-products of the dependent variable and covariate scores (Table 25.6). Basically it involves multiplying each dependent variable score by the equivalent covariate score. In this way it is similar to the calculation of the Pearson correlation coefficient which involves the calculation of the covariance. Table 25.6 can be used to calculate a summary table for the cross-products (Table 25.7). The calculation is analogous to that for ANOVA in steps 1 and 2 above. The only substantial difference is that it involves calculation of the cross-products of $X \times Y$ instead of X^2.

1. Calculate the overall (or grand) total of the X scores:

$$G_X = 27 + 15 + 22 + 30 + 27 + 24 + 40 + 29 + 35 = 249$$

2. Calculate the overall (or grand) total of the Y scores:

$$G_Y = 38 + 32 + 35 + 40 + 34 + 32 + 60 + 52 + 57 = 380$$

3. Calculate the number of scores for the dependent variable, $N = 9$.

Table 25.6   Data and cross-products table

Group 1			Group 2			Group 3		
X Dependent	Y Covariate	$X \times Y$	X Dependent	Y Covariate	$X \times Y$	X Dependent	Y Covariate	$X \times Y$
27	38	1026	30	40	1200	40	60	2400
15	32	480	27	34	918	29	52	1508
22	35	770	24	32	768	35	57	1995
$\Sigma X = 64$	$\Sigma Y = 105$	$\Sigma XY = 2276$	$\Sigma X = 81$	$\Sigma Y = 106$	$\Sigma XY = 2886$	$\Sigma X = 104$	$\Sigma Y = 169$	$\Sigma XY = 5903$

$\Sigma X \Sigma Y = 64 \times 105 = 6720$ $\Sigma X \Sigma Y = 81 \times 106 = 8586$ $\Sigma X \Sigma Y = 104 \times 169 = 17\,576$

$N_1 = 3$ $N_2 = 3$ $N_3 = 3$

Grand total of all X scores $= \Sigma X = G_x = 64 + 81 + 104 = 249$
Grand total of all Y scores $= \Sigma Y = G_y = 105 + 106 + 169 = 380$

Table 25.7   Summary table for the covariation

Source of variation	Sum of squares	Degrees of freedom	Mean square (variance estimate)	F-ratio
Between groups[covariation]	447.334	2		
Error[covariation]	104.333	5		
Total[covariation]	551.667	8		

4. Calculate the correction factor by substituting the already calculated values:

$$\text{Correction factor} = \frac{G_X \times G_Y}{N} = \frac{249 \times 380}{9} = \frac{94\ 620}{9} = 10\ 513.333$$

5. Calculate the number of scores for each group (N_1, N_2, N_3). In our example these are all 3 as the group sizes are equal, but this does not have to be so.

6. Total degrees of freedom for the data table = the number of scores − 1 = 9 − 1 = 8.

7. Multiply each X score by the equivalent Y score to give the cross-products and sum these cross-products to give $\sum XY$ which is the sum of cross-products:

$$\sum XY = (27 \times 38) + (15 \times 32) + (22 \times 35) + (30 \times 40) + (27 \times 34) + (24 \times 32)$$
$$+ (40 \times 60) + (29 \times 52) + (35 \times 57)$$
$$= 1026 + 480 + 770 + 1200 + 918 + 768 + 2400 + 1508 + 1995$$
$$= 11\ 065$$

8. Obtain the total sum of covariation by subtracting the correction factor from the sum of cross-products:

$$\text{Total sum of covariation} = \sum XY - \frac{G_X \times G_Y}{N}$$
$$= 11\ 065 - 10\ 513.333$$
$$= 551.667$$

9. These values of the total sum of covariation (551.667) and the degrees of freedom (8) can be entered into Table 25.7 (the summary table for covariation).

10. Sum the scores on the dependent variable and independent variables separately for each of the groups separately as in Table 25.6. This gives us $\sum X_1$, $\sum X_2$, $\sum X_3$, $\sum Y_1$, $\sum Y_2$, $\sum Y_3$, since we have three groups in our instance.

11. The sum of the covariation between groups is calculated as follows:

$$\text{Sum of covariation between groups} = \frac{\sum X_1 \sum Y_1}{N_1} + \frac{\sum X_2 \sum Y_2}{N_2} + \frac{\sum X_3 \sum Y_3}{N_3} - \frac{G_X G_Y}{N}$$
$$= \frac{64 \times 105}{3} + \frac{81 \times 106}{3} + \frac{104 \times 169}{3} - 10\ 513.333$$
$$= \frac{6720}{3} + \frac{8586}{3} + \frac{17\ 576}{3} - 10\ 513.333$$
$$= 2240.000 + 2862.000 + 5858.667 - 10\ 513.333$$
$$= 447.334$$

12. The degrees of freedom for the covariation between groups is the number of groups − 1 = 3 − 1 = 2.

13. These values of the sum of covariation between groups and degrees of freedom between groups can be entered in Table 25.7.

14. The sum of the covariation of error can be obtained now by subtracting the sum of the between-groups covariation from the total covariation:

➔

Sum of the covariation of error = Total of covariation − Covariation between groups

$$= 551.667 - 447.334$$

$$= 104.333$$

15. This value of the covariation for error can now be entered into Table 25.7.

16. The degrees of freedom for error are calculated in a way which removes one degree of freedom for the covariation. This is simply the total number of scores − the number of groups − 1 = 9 − 3 − 1 = 5. This can be entered in Table 25.7.

The above calculation steps for covariation are only superficially different from those for the analysis of variance in steps 1 and 2. They are actually different only so far as variance and covariance differ (pp. 72–3).

Step 4 *(calculating the ANCOVA summary table, i.e. the dependent table with the covariate partialled out)* This is achieved by taking away the variation in the scores due to the covariate from the variation in the dependent variable. Once we have the three summary tables (dependent variable, covariate and cross-products) then it is a fairly simple matter to calculate the adjusted dependent variable sums of squares and enter them into Table 25.8, the summary table for a one-way ANCOVA.

The formulae are:

$$SSError_{[adjusted]} = SSError_{[dependent]} - \frac{(Error_{[covariation]})^2}{SSError_{[covariate]}}$$

$$SSTotal_{[adjusted]} = SSTotal_{[dependent]} - \frac{(Total_{[covariation]})^2}{SSError_{[covariate]}}$$

Be very careful to distinguish between the covariation and the covariate.

These calculations are as follows:

$$SSError_{[adjusted]} = SSError_{[dependent]} - \frac{(Error_{[covariation]})^2}{SSError_{[covariate]}}$$

$$= 151.333 - \frac{104.333^2}{85.333}$$

$$= 151.333 - \frac{10\,885.375}{85.333}$$

$$= 151.333 - 127.563$$

$$= 23.77$$

Table 25.8	ANCOVA summary table			
Source of variation	**Sum of squares**	**Degrees of freedom**	**Mean square (variance estimate)**	**F-ratio**
Between[adjusted]	86.175	2	43.088	$\frac{43.088}{4.754} = \textbf{9.06}^a$
Error[adjusted]	23.770	5	4.754	
Total[adjusted]	109.945	8		

[a] Significant at the 5% level.

$$SSTotal_{[adjusted]} = SSTotal_{[dependent]} - \frac{(Total_{[covariation]})^2}{SSError_{[covariate]}}$$

$$= 420.000 - \frac{551.667^2}{981.556}$$

$$= 420.000 - \frac{304\,336.479}{981.556}$$

$$= 420.000 - 310.055$$

$$= 109.945$$

Enter these values into the ANCOVA summary table (Table 25.8) and the between sum of squares obtained by subtracting the error sum of squares from the total sum of squares.

Note that the degrees of freedom for the error term in the ANCOVA summary table are listed as 5. This is because we have constrained the degrees of freedom by partialling out the covariate. The formula for the degrees of freedom for the adjusted error is number of scores – number of groups – 1 = 9 – 3 – 1 = 5.

Step 5 The F-ratio in the ANCOVA summary table is calculated in the usual way. It is the between mean square divided by the error mean square. This is 9.06. The significance of this is obtained from Significance Table 22.1 for 2 and 5 degrees of freedom (or Appendix J if other levels of significance are required). We look under the column for 2 degrees of freedom and the row for 5 degrees of freedom. This indicates that our F-ratio is above the minimum value for statistical significance and is therefore statistically significant.

Step 6 *(adjusting group means)* No analysis of variance can be properly interpreted without reference to the means of the data table. This is not simple with ANCOVA as the means in the data are the means un-adjusted for the covariate. Consequently it is necessary to adjust the means to indicate what the mean would be when the effect of the covariate is removed. The formula for this is as follows:

Adjusted group mean = Unadjusted group mean

$$-\frac{(Error_{[covariance]})}{SSError_{[covariate]}} \times (Group\ mean_{[covariate]} - Grand\ mean_{[covariate]})$$

The unadjusted group means are merely the means of the scores on the dependent variable for each of the three groups in our example. These can be calculated from Table 25.2. The three group means are: group 1 = 21.333, group 2 = 27.000 and group 3 = 34.667.

The group means for the covariate can be calculated from Table 25.4. They are group 1 = 35.000, group 2 = 35.333 and group 3 = 56.333.

The grand mean of the covariate is simply the mean of all of the scores on the covariate in Table 25.4 which equals 42.222 for our example.

The sums of squares for error have already been calculated. The sum of squares for error for the cross-products is 104.333 and is found in Table 25.7. The sum of squares for error for the covariate is 85.333 and is found in Table 25.5.

We can now substitute all of these values into the formula and enter these values into Table 25.9.

Group 1: Adjusted mean = 30.27 obtained as follows

$$21.333 - \left(\frac{104.333}{84.333} \times (35.000 - 42.222)\right) = 21.333 - (1.237 \times (-7.222))$$

$$= 21.333 - (-8.934)$$

$$= 30.267$$

Table 25.9	Unadjusted and adjusted means for depression		
Means	**Group 1 Psychotherapy**	**Group 2 Antidepressants**	**Group 3 Control**
Unadjusted	21.33	27.00	34.67
Adjusted	30.27	35.52	17.21

Group 2: Adjusted mean = 35.52 obtained as follows

$$27.000 - \left(\frac{104.333}{84.333} \times (35.333 - 42.222) \right) = 27.000 - (1.237 \times (-6.889))$$

$$= 27.000 - (-8.522)$$

$$= 35.522$$

Group 3: Adjusted mean = 17.21 obtained as follows

$$34.667 - \left(\frac{104.333}{84.333} \times (56.333 - 42.222) \right) = 34.667 - (1.237 \times 14.111)$$

$$= 34.667 - 17.455$$

$$= 17.21$$

Notice how the adjusted means in Table 25.9 show a completely different pattern from the unadjusted means in this case.

Step 7

The simplest way of testing which of the adjusted means are different from the others is to use the Fisher protected LSD (least significant difference) test (Huitema, 1980). It is convenient since the component parts have largely been calculated by now. This test gives us an *F*-ratio with always one degree of freedom for the comparison and N – the number of groups – $1 = 9 - 3 - 1 = 5$ in our example for the error. Because we have three groups, there are three possible comparisons between pairs of groups. We will show the calculation in full for the comparison between groups 1 and 2:

$$F = \frac{(\text{Adjusted group}_1 \text{ mean} - \text{Adjusted group}_2 \text{ mean})^2}{\text{Mean square error adjusted} \times \left[\left(\frac{1}{N_1} + \frac{1}{N_2} \right) + \left(\frac{(\text{Covariate group}_1 \text{ mean} - \text{Covariate group}_2 \text{ mean})^2}{\text{Sum of squares of error for the covariate}} \right) \right]}$$

where:

Adjusted group$_1$ mean is found in Table 25.9.

Adjusted group$_2$ mean is found in Table 25.9.

Mean square error adjusted is found in Table 25.8.

Covariate group$_1$ mean is found by consulting Table 25.4 and dividing the sum of covariate scores for group 1 by the number of scores for group $1 = \Sigma Y/N = 105/3 = 35.000$.

Covariate group$_2$ mean is found in exactly the same way. Consult Table 25.4 and divide the sum of covariate scores for group 2 by the number of scores = 106/3 = 35.333.

Sum of squares of error for the covariate is found in Table 25.5.

$$F = \frac{(30.27 - 35.52)^2}{4.754\left[\left(\dfrac{1}{3} + \dfrac{1}{3}\right) + \dfrac{(35.000 - 35.333)^2}{85.333}\right]}$$

$$= \frac{5.25^2}{4.754\left[(0.333 + 0.333) + \dfrac{(-0.333)^2}{85.333}\right]}$$

$$= \frac{27.563}{4.754\left(0.666 + \dfrac{0.111}{85.333}\right)}$$

$$= \frac{27.563}{4.754(0.666 + 0.001)}$$

$$= \frac{27.563}{4.754(0.667)} = \frac{27.563}{3.11} = 8.692$$

This value of the *F*-ratio with 1 and 5 degrees of freedom is statistically significant at the 5% level. So the adjusted means of group 1 and group 2 are significantly different from each other.

We also carried out the comparisons between group 1 and group 3 (the obtained *F*-ratio of 5.98 was not significant at the 5% level) and group 2 and group 3 (the obtained *F*-ratio 12.09 was statistically significant at the 5% level).

Interpreting the results The analysis of covariance makes it clear that the post-test measures of depression differ overall once the pre-test differences are controlled. However, by considering the means of the adjusted levels of depression it seems clear that the depression scores of the control group were actually lower than those of either of the treatment groups. In other words, once pre-test levels of depression are adjusted for, then the obvious interpretation is that depression is actually being increased by the treatment rather than being reduced relative to the control group. The multiple comparisons test indicates that the significant differences are between the anti-depressant group and the control group and the psychotherapy group and the control group. The two treatment groups did not differ significantly from each other.

Reporting the results This analysis may be written up according to the APA (2010) Publication Manual's recommendations as follows: 'An analysis of covariance (ANCOVA) was applied to the three groups (psychotherapy, anti-depressant and no-treatment control) in order to see whether the different treatments had an effect on post-test levels of depression controlling for pre-test depression. There was found to be a significant effect of the type of treatment, $F(2, 5) = 9.06$, $p < .05$. The unadjusted means indicated that depression was higher in the control group ($M = 34.67$) than with psychotherapy ($M = 21.33$) or with anti-depressant treatment ($M = 35.52$). However, this seems to be the result of the influence of the covariate (pre-therapy levels of depression as measured at the pre-test) since the adjusted means for the groups indicate that the least depression is found in the untreated control group ($M = 17.21$), compared with the psychotherapy group ($M = 30.27$) and the anti-depressant group ($M = 35.52$). Thus, the two treatment conditions increased depression relative to the control group. This was confirmed in a comparison of the adjusted means using the Fisher protected LSD test. The analysis indicated that group 1 (psychotherapy) and group 2 (anti-depressant) differed significantly, $F(1, 5) = 8.69$, $p < .05$. Group 2 (anti-depressant) and group 3 (control condition) differed significantly, $F(1, 5) = 12.09$, $p < .05$. Group 1 (psychotherapy) and group 3 (control) did not differ significantly, $F(1, 5) = 5.98$, p *ns*.'

Key points

- Relying on ANCOVA to deal with the problems due to employing non-randomised allocation to the cells of the ANOVA ignores the basic reason for doing randomised experiments in the first place – that the researcher does not know what unknown factors influence the outcome of the research. Random allocation to conditions is the only practical and sound way of fully controlling for variables not included in the design.

- It is not wise to use ANCOVA to try to correct for the sloppiness of your original design or procedures. Although, especially when using computers, you can include many covariates, it is best to be careful when planning your research to reduce the need for this. In randomised experiments, probably the control of the pre-test measure is the only circumstance requiring ANCOVA. Of course, there are circumstances in which pre-tests are undesirable, especially as they risk sensitising participants as to the purpose of the study or otherwise influencing the post-test measures.

COMPUTER ANALYSIS

The SPSS Statistics instruction book to this text is Dennis Howitt and Duncan Cramer (2011), *Introduction to SPSS Statistics in Psychology: For version 19 and earlier*, Harlow: Pearson. Chapter 26 in that book gives detailed step-by-step procedures for the statistics described in this chapter together with advice on how to report the results. Figure 25.2 gives the SPSS Statistics steps for analysis of covariance.

Data
- Name the variables in Variable View of the Data Editor.
- Enter the data under the appropriate variable names in Data View of the Data Editor.

Analysis
- If the potential covariate is reasonably strongly related to the dependent variable, proceed with ANCOVA.

2
- Select 'Analyze', 'General Linear Model' and 'Univariate . . .'.
- Move dependent variable to 'Dependent Variable:' box, independent variable to 'Fixed Factor:' box and covariate variable to 'Covariate:' box.

3
- To check that the slope of the regression line is similar in each condition, select 'Model' and 'Custom'. Move the independent variable, the covariate and the interaction between the independent variable and covariate box to the box on the right..

4
- If the interaction between the independent variable and the covariate is not significant by having a Sig(nificance) of greater than .05, proceed with the ANCOVA.

5
- Select 'Analyze', 'General Linear Model', 'Univariate . . .', 'Model', 'Full factorial' and 'Continue'. Select 'Options . . .', 'Descriptive statistics' and 'Estimates of effect size'.
- Move the independent variable to the 'Display Means for:' box.

Output
- Check if the independent variable is significant by seeing if its Sig(nificance) is .05 or less.
- If it is and there are more than 2 conditions, conduct further tests to determine which adjusted means differ significantly.

FIGURE 25.2 SPSS Statistics steps for ANCOVA

Recommended further reading

Cramer, D. (2003), *Advanced Quantitative Data Analysis*, Buckingham: Open University Press, Chapter 11.

Glantz, S.A. and Slinker, B.K. (1990), *Primer of Applied Regression and Analysis of Variance*, New York: McGraw-Hill.

Table 26.1	Data table for a study of effects of Therazine on motor skills										
Group (independent variable)											
Therazine condition				**Placebo condition**				**No treatment condition**			
RT*	Sp	Hd	RT	Sp	Hd	W	RT	Sp	Hd	W	
8**	5	7	7	1	3	2	2	4	3	5	4
7	7	6	5	4	5	3	3	1	2	3	6
9	8	5	9	7	2	1	2	3	5	2	6
7	5	8	8	2	5	6	1	1	4	6	2

* RT = reaction time, Sp = clarity of speech, Hd = steadiness of hand and W = writing speed. Scores are from four cases in each column.
** The scores are for the four dependent variables.

- Just one independent variable. This is known as a one-way analysis of variance. The independent variable is that which forms the different groups. (See Table 20.1 for an example.)

- Two or more independent variables. It would be possible to extend our Alzheimer study to include more than one independent variable. A simple example would be to have a second independent variable. We previously referred to this design as a two-way ANOVA design. If we added a third grouping variable (independent variable) then this would be termed a three-way ANOVA design, and so forth. These two-way, three-way and so forth designs are sometimes referred to as factorial designs.

- Any of the above designs with additional covariates controlled for. So, for example, age of participants might be added as a covariate in the above designs. This is known as the analysis of covariance (ANCOVA) (Chapter 25).

MANOVA can deal with all three of the above types of design and more.

Box 26.1	Focus on

Hotelling two sample t^2

You may have a very simple study with just two groups (e.g. experimental and control conditions) yet have several dependent variables which relate to your hypothesis. Such designs are usually analysed using the t-test (Chapter 13). There is a multivariate version of the t-test for research designs in which there are just two groups of participants but where there are several dependent variables. This is known as the Hotelling two sample t^2. (If you want to do this analysis, just remember it is the same as MANOVA which reduces effectively to the Hotelling two sample t^2 if you just have two groups in your study. So simply follow the MANOVA procedures.)

There are two obvious questions to ask about MANOVA at this stage:

1. Just why would one wish to analyse several different dependent variables at the same time rather than do a number of separate ANOVAs?

2. Just how does one combine several dependent variables?

The answers to these questions are not simple:

1. *Why not do several ANOVAs?* The answer to this question partly lies in the common comment in statistics that the more tests of significance one carries out then the more likely that significant findings emerge *by chance*. These do not represent real differences and, consequently, are not meaningful. So the more ANOVAs one does on one's data the more likely that a statistically significant finding will emerge. The consequence of multiple testing of this sort we have dealt with elsewhere under multiple comparisons (Chapter 23). But multiple testing of this sort can create other difficulties which do not at first appear to be statistical in nature. The purpose of research is not primarily to obtain significant findings but to provide an account or narrative or theoretical explanation which links together the findings of the researcher. Thus if the findings are not reliable then one may be trying to explain chance findings as meaningful findings which represent something which is happening in the real world.

    One obvious solution may strike you. Why not apply the Bonferroni adjustment (p. 278) to the significance levels of the ANOVAs carried out on each dependent variable? That is, adjust the probability levels to take into account the number of comparisons made. This is sensible thinking but not entirely satisfactory in this case because multiple significance testing is the biggest problem when the dependent variables correlate with each other poorly (or not at all). Where the dependent variables correlate highly then the risk of a spurious significant ANOVA is not so great. More technically, there is a risk of Type I errors (accepting the hypothesis when it is in fact false) which increases when the dependent variables do not correlate with each other. The use of MANOVA can be thought of as a way of replacing several ANOVAs with one blanket test on a set of dependent variables. It thus protects against Type I errors.

2. *How to combine dependent variables?* At first sight, the answer to this question seems self-evident if the scores are positively correlated – just add up the scores for each participant to give a total score. In this way, one has generated a single dependent variable which can be entered into a regular ANOVA and there would be no reason to bother with MANOVA. There are circumstances in which this would be a good way to proceed. However, the drawback is that by doing something like this you risk losing some of the information contained in your data. If this is not clear then imagine you ask your participants six questions the answers to which are scored on a five-point Likert scale from strongly disagree to strongly agree. Then you give a score from 1 to 5 for each of the different points on the rating scales. Finally you add up each individual's scores to give a total score. Usually, information is lost from the data by doing so. So if someone scores 17 on the scale you simply do not know from that total what answers they gave. There are many possible ways of scoring 17 on the six questions. The total score does represent something, but it has lost some of the detail of the original replies. Hence, ANOVA carried out on the total scores also loses information from the original data.

This is not always a problem. It is a problem when more than one dimension underlies scores on the various dependent variables. If the correlations between our dependent variables show some high correlations but also some low correlations then it is likely that more than one dimension underlies our scores. However, if the variables are highly correlated and constitute a single underlying dimension, totalling the scores and then subjecting the resultant total scores to ANOVA may be extremely effective. It also has the advantage that there is no loss of degrees of freedom in the analysis – loss of degrees of freedom can be a problem in MANOVA, but this is dependent on the total picture of the analysis and there is no simple way of balancing the different advantages and disadvantages of the different approaches.

On a sort of loss–gains analysis, if your dependent variables are highly correlated then more is lost than gained through the use of MANOVA. MANOVA is somewhat more abstract than ANOVA so perhaps best avoided if there is not a clear gain. It would also be legitimate to use just one dependent variable if it is highly intercorrelated with the other dependent variables. However, since psychological measures tend to be unreliable, one cannot generally expect extremely high intercorrelations between variables. Furthermore, there is no advantage of this over the summation approach of adding up the dependent variables to get a total score if the variables correlate highly.

26.2   MANOVA's two stages

Actually MANOVA is a two-stage process. These stages are usually separate in the computer programs most of us do our statistical analyses with nowadays. SPSS Statistics does have a method for doing MANOVA in the GLM procedures, but that only does half the job. In addition, you probably will need to carry out a discriminant function analysis which is a different SPSS Statistics procedure. Let us look at these two stages in turn:

■ Stage 1: MANOVA

In ANOVA the researcher wants to know whether the different groups defined by the independent variable(s) are associated with different mean scores on the dependent variable. This is generally discussed in terms of the sums of squares associated with the different group means compared with the estimated sums of squares associated with error. The ratio between the sums of squares due to the different groups of participants and the sum of squares due to error provides the basis of the statistical significance testing using the F-ratio or something similar. We have illustrated the calculation of this from basics in previous chapters on ANOVA. This is a somewhat tedious and unnecessary process given that the work is better done by computers.

Much the same process is involved in MANOVA except that we have several dependent variables to examine at the same time. So the question is whether the different groups are different in terms of the means that they have on several dependent variables. Once again, these differences in means are turned into sums of squares. But there is a big problem in doing this for a MANOVA design. It is not merely that there are several dependent variables, but also the several dependent variables may well be correlated with each other – that is, they measure, in part, the same thing. The analysis needs to make allowance for the extent to which the dependent variables are correlated. If it did not do so then the analysis would be claiming the same variance several times over. The extent of this depends on the size of the correlation between variables and the number of variables which correlate. Once the sums of squares associated with the different groups in the research design have been calculated, then multivariate tests of significance are computed and a significance level(s) provided. If the analysis is significant, then this shows that the groups of participants differ in terms of their scores over the set of dependent variables combined. It does not tell us which dependent variables are responsible for the differences. That is the job of the second stage.

Things are more complicated than this, of course. Life is never simple towards the end of a statistics textbook. Like all tests of significance, MANOVA was subject to a set of assumptions by the person who developed the procedures. Parts of the computer output for MANOVA simply tell the user whether these assumptions have been met.

■ Stage 2: The relative importance of each dependent variable

From the MANOVA procedure, we know whether the groups in our research are different overall on the several dependent variables combined. That is the basic test of the hypothesis. Of course, if the multivariate test of significance in MANOVA is not significant, this basically is the end of the story. The researcher has drawn a blank in terms of his or her hypothesis and the null hypothesis is preferred over the alternative hypothesis. Even if we get a significant result from the multivariate test of significance, we remain at something of a loss as to what our analysis means since this tells us nothing as such about which groups vary and on what variables. We really need to understand something more about the pattern of variables on which the groups differ – that is, what combinations of variables tend to produce differences in group means?

A less than perfect but intuitively reasonable approach to this is to do a number of ANOVAs – one for each dependent variable. Hold on a minute, you may be thinking, didn't we decide at the start of the chapter that it was not a good idea to do this? The problem was the multitude of tests of significance being employed and this was part of the reason for opting for MANOVA in the first place. But MANOVA gives us protection from Type I errors (accepting the hypothesis when it is in fact false) so we do not need to worry. If the MANOVA is not significant then the analysis is protected from the risk of Type I error simply because no further analyses are carried out on the individual dependent variables.

If the MANOVA is statistically significant, then this supposedly 'protects' the analysis from Type I errors and indicates that it is legitimate to do ANOVAs on each of the various dependent variables. In other words, a significant MANOVA puts a cap on the risk of finding a significant result by chance – that is, committing the Type I error. Unfortunately, this is just not adequate for a number of reasons. The main one is that often there is one variable which is affected by the independent variable and the rest of the dependent variables are not affected. In these circumstances, the significant MANOVA protects the affected dependent variable from Type I errors, but the other variables are not protected. So one of the ANOVAs would be protected but the rest not. Quite what will happen depends on the details of the data and analysis. Some textbooks still recommend doing this second stage analysis but there is an alternative approach so you may choose that instead (unless your local statistical expert advises otherwise in which case it would be politic to follow their advice).

Another problem with it is that even if you test each dependent variable separately, in the end you do not quite know what was affected by the independent variable(s). Although you could name the various significant dependent variables, this does not tell you what it is about the dependent variable which is affected. That is, what do the dependent variables have in common which produces the differences between the groups of participants?

Ideally, the problem of finding which dependent variables are influential on the findings is addressed through the use of discriminant function analysis (see Box 26.2 on p. 326 and Chapter 27). In this chapter, we will simply describe the MANOVA procedure followed up by ANOVAs.

26.3 Doing MANOVA

If you have mastered the basics of ANOVA then you may regard MANOVA, in its essence, as just a small step further. Ignoring discriminant function analysis for now, the major problem in implementing MANOVA lies in seeing the wood for the trees in terms of the computer output. But by this stage, this is probably a familiar difficulty. The reason that MANOVA is essentially easy is that the only new thing that you really need to know is that there are things known as multivariate tests. These are analogous to the *F*-ratios (or Levene's test which is used by SPSS Statistics) which we are familiar with from ANOVA. Actually there are several multivariate tests which, despite being differently calculated, do much the same sort of thing – tell you if your group 'means' are different on the set of dependent variables as a whole. These multivariate tests include Pillai's trace, Wilks' lambda, Hotelling's trace and Roy's largest root. These are the ones that SPSS Statistics calculates for you. You don't have to choose between them – the computer computes them all for you. Figure 26.1 gives the key steps in understanding a MANOVA analysis.

Let's look at the research summarised in Table 26.2. This is basically a one-way MANOVA design in which we have a single independent variable – the group – but several dependent variables. So apart from having several dependent variables, this is much the same as the design in Chapter 20 for one-way ANOVA. The study investigates the efficiency of team-building sessions with a sports psychologist, team-building sessions with a sports coach or no team building. Participants were randomly assigned to these three different conditions. Gender is regarded as a second independent variable. There are equal numbers of male and female participants. If you can, it is best to have equal group sizes for MANOVA as it helps you to avoid problems (see later). Three dependent measures were used: 1) the difference between the liking ratings for the participant's favourite and least favourite team member which is believed to be a measure of team cohesion, 2) the number of voluntary gym sessions the player attends and 3) the number of games each player plays in a season.

The three dependent variables correlate at the levels indicated in Table 26.3. As can be seen, all three measures intercorrelate positively, but there is some considerable variation in the size of the correlations. This suggests that more than one dimension underlies these variables. The variables cannot convincingly be totalled in this case given the wide range in the size of the correlations. So a MANOVA analysis seems appropriate.

The MANOVA analysis of the data produces primarily a MANOVA summary table which is similar to the ANOVA summary table in Chapter 20. There are even values of the *F*-ratio much as in ANOVA. However, this is based on different calculations from ANOVA since it is applied to the multivariate test (e.g. Pillai's trace, Wilks' lambda, Hotelling's trace and Roy's largest root). Pillai's trace is probably the one to rely on

Multivariate analysis of variance (MANOVA) involves multiple dependent variables which are combined in the analysis.		MANOVA basically calculates whether there are significant effects of the independent variables on the 'combined' dependent variable.		Instead of the *F*-ratio, Pillai's trace or another test is used to assess statistical significance.

This still leaves uncertainty about the combination of dependent variables which led to the significance of MANOVA so discriminant function analysis may help.		One approach to 'deconstructing' the findings is separate ANOVAs if the MANOVA is significant. No adjustment to the significance level is necessary.		A significant effect in MANOVA leaves us uncertain as to what aspects of the 'combined' dependent variable are affected by the independent variable.

FIGURE 26.1   Conceptual steps for understanding MANOVA

Table 26.2	Data for the MANOVA analysis								

Group (independent variable)								
Team building with sports psychologist Dependent variables			Team building with sports coach Dependent variables			No team building controls Dependent variables		
Like*	Gym	Game	Like	Gym	Game	Like	Gym	Game
9**	12	14	4	6	15	9	6	10
5	9	14	5	4	12	1	2	5
8	11	12	4	9	15	6	10	12
4	6	5	3	8	8	2	5	6
9	12	3	4	9	9	3	6	7
9	11	14	5	3	8	4	7	8
6	13	14	2	8	12	1	6	13
6	11	18	6	9	11	4	9	12
8	11	22	4	7	15	3	8	15
8	13	22	4	8	28	3	2	14
9	15	18	5	7	10	2	8	11
7	12	18	4	9	9	6	9	10
8	10	13	5	18	18	3	8	13
6	11	22	7	12	24	6	14	22

* Like = difference between ratings of most and least liked team members, Gym = number of gym sessions voluntarily attended and Game = number of games played.
** The scores are the scores on the three dependent variables.

Table 26.3	Correlations between the three dependent variables		

	Difference between ratings of most/least liked team members	Number of gym sessions voluntarily attended	Number of games played
Difference between ratings of most/least liked team members	–	.60	.30
Number of gym sessions voluntarily attended		–	.51
Number of games played			–

because it is more robust and less affected by the data not meeting its requirements. To keep the tables as simple as possible, we have confined our analysis to Pillai's trace only. In MANOVA you do not calculate the sums of squares but the value of Pillai's trace (and possibly the others). The MANOVA summary table (Table 26.4) gives the results of this analysis. Apart from that, you will find much the same statistics as for analysis of variance.

So it should be self-evident from Table 26.4 that we have a significant effect of group (type of team building). Generally speaking, Pillai's trace gives much the same outcome as Wilks' lambda, Hotelling's trace and Roy's largest root. It does not much matter

Table 26.4	Result of multivariate tests				
Effect	**Value**	***F***	**Hypothesis df**	**Error df**	**Sig.**
Intercept Pillai's trace	.94	184.71	3.00	37.00	.00
Groups Pillai's trace	.49	4.11	6.00	76.00	.00

which you choose – and, of course, you can use all four if you so wish though this will clutter your report. If you do not get any significant findings then this is the end of MANOVA – you do not go any further since your hypothesis has been rejected.

Of course, if you have significant findings, then you need to know what they indicate. There are several steps in order to do this:

■ Step 1

The simplest interpretation would be to conclude that there are differences on the composite of the three dependent variables related to the independent variables (groups). This may in any research study be sufficient to confirm the hypothesis. In our particular example, there are differences in the 'means' of the composite of the three dependent variables due to the independent variable group (condition).

■ Step 2

In order to have a better understanding of more precisely what is going on in the data, you need the corresponding univariate ANOVAs to the MANOVA. SPSS Statistics gives you these as part of the basic output from MANOVA. An example is given in Table 26.5. As you can see, there is an ANOVA for each dependent variable. It may look confusing at first, but taking one dependent variable at a time a basic understanding of one-way ANOVA will suffice. What seems clear from Table 26.5 is that two of the three dependent variables show virtually identical significant patterns. That is, the summary table shows that the two main effects for 1) difference between ratings of most and least liked team members and 2) number of gym sessions voluntarily attended are significant. The third dependent variable, number of games played, does not reach significance. This would suggest that the significant MANOVA is largely the result of the first two variables rather than the third variable. But it should be noted that you may obtain a significant MANOVA yet none of the ANOVAs are statistically significant. This means exactly what it says, but you also need to realise that a linear combination of the dependent variables is related to group membership despite the fact that individually the

Table 26.5	Part of a table of the individual ANOVAs for the three dependent variables				
Dependent variable	**Sum of squares**	**Degrees of freedom**	**Mean square**	***F*-ratio**	**Significance**
Number of games played	98.14	2	49.07	1.67	0.20
Difference between ratings of most liked and least liked team members	97.19	2	48.60	15.71	0.00
Number of gym sessions voluntarily attended	122.33	2	61.16	6.86	0.03

dependent variables may fail to be related to group membership. Using these methods, you do not know much about that linear combination of variables. Discriminant function analysis would help you with this (see Chapter 27 and Box 26.2 on this page).

Box 26.2   Focus on

Discriminant function analysis and MANOVA

In the present chapter, we have concentrated on the very basics of MANOVA. A significant MANOVA means that the groups defined by your independent variable are different in terms of the composite of the dependent variables you have used. The next question is just what aspects of the dependent variable are responsible for the significant MANOVA. The approach used in the present chapter is to do a number of ANOVA analyses for the different dependent variables. This tells you if the means for your groups are different for any of the dependent variables. The trouble with this is that one is left somewhat unclear about the nature of the underlying combination variable derived from the several dependent variables.

An improvement in understanding can be achieved using discriminant function analysis (which is covered in detail in Chapter 27). This analysis helps you to understand how your dependent variables were combined to give the significant MANOVA. These combinations of variables are known as *discriminant functions*. In other words, the analysis creates artificial variables which it derives from one or more of the original dependent variables. This is usually done on a computer program such as SPSS Statistics as the calculations are tedious to do by hand – and you would be ill-advised to spend time doing so with the attendant risk of computational errors. There is one centroid (which is a sort of mean score) for each group of participants on each of the discriminant functions. Discriminant functions are obviously abstractions from the original dependent variables and, as such, they cannot be expected to be as clear initially as the variables that you included in the set of dependent variables.

There can be several discriminant functions based on a set of dependent variables as already indicated. If there is just one dependent variable, as in ANOVA, then there is just one discriminant function which is the same as that single dependent variable. With two dependent variables there can be two discriminant functions and so forth. The number of discriminant functions is the smaller number of the number of dependent variables or one less the number of groups. Each discriminant function that emerges in an

analysis is unrelated to the other discriminant functions that emerge. That is, discriminant functions do not correlate with each other.

The term discriminant function seems odd at first, but it means just what it says on the label. It is a mathematical equation (function) which discriminates things. What does it discriminate? Well, it is the mathematical function of the dependent variables which best discriminate between the different groups (i.e. levels of the independent variable). Basically the calculation (computer) works out the pattern of weights to give to each of the dependent variables in order to produce the maximum discrimination between the various groups on the discriminant function. Of course, there are many different possible discriminant functions since it is basically a pattern of weights to apply to the different dependent variables, but only one function will give the greatest degree of discrimination between the different groups. In other words, discriminant function analysis produces a new measure (function) which maximises the difference between the groupings of participants on that measure (function).

As indicated, there may be several discriminant functions. The first discriminant function essentially emerges from the original data whereas the second discriminant function is calculated on the data *after* the first discriminant function has been taken into account. The third discriminant function is calculated from the data after the first and second discriminant functions have been removed.

There is a conceptual problem when we move from MANOVA to discriminant function analysis. In MANOVA we tend to speak of the scores as being the dependent variable and the variable on which the groups differ is the independent variable. Well, discriminant function analysis, like the various forms of regression, works the other way round. In this case, the score variables become the independent variables and the dependent variable is the variable on which the different groups are categorised. Yes, this is confusing, but if you concentrate on the nature of the variable in question (category variable or score) then Chapter 27 should be straightforward.

Table 26.6	Estimated marginal means for groups on each dependent variable		
	Difference between ratings of most and least liked team members	Number of gym sessions voluntarily attended	Number of games played
Teamwork training by sports psychologist	7.29	11.21	14.93
Teamwork training by coach	4.43	8.36	13.86
Control – no teamwork training	3.79	7.14	11.29

■ Step 3

A table of estimated marginal means is helpful at this stage. SPSS Statistics generates separate tables for each of the main effects and each interaction. In the present case, we have reproduced only the estimated marginal means for the significant main effect (the team building variable). This can be seen in Table 26.6. It is clear from this that scores on each of the first two dependent variables are lowest for the control, second highest for team building by a coach, and highest for team building by the psychologist. It is not immediately obvious which of the three dependent variables best discriminates the three conditions.

Remember that this is a down-to-basics account of MANOVA. We do not pretend that it offers the most sophisticated approach. You might wish, especially, to check whether your data actually meet the requirements of MANOVA in terms of the characteristics of the data. One quite important thing is the Box's test of equality of the covariance matrix. We don't need to know too much about this test, but we do need to know what to do if the test is statistically significant. The Box's test is illustrated in Table 26.7. If it yields a significant value (as it does in our case), this means that the covariances are not similar which violates one of the assumptions on which MANOVA was built. This can affect the probability levels obtained in the MANOVA. However, this is crucial only if the MANOVA significance levels just reach the 0.05 level of significance. If your MANOVA findings are very significant then there is not a great problem. You should not worry if the different cells (groupings) of your MANOVA have equal sample sizes as violating the requirements of the MANOVA makes no practical difference to the significance level in this case. If you have very different sample sizes and your findings are close to the boundary between statistical significance and statistical non-significance, then you should worry more – one solution is to equate the sample sizes by randomly

Table 26.7	The Box M test for covariance homogeneity (equality)
Box's M	18.70
F	1.38
df_1	12
df_2	7371
Significance	0.17

dropping cases from cells as necessary. But this could have as much effect on your findings as violating the equal covariances principle anyway. So bear this in mind when designing your MANOVA.

26.4 Reporting your findings

If your MANOVA was not significant, you could write following the APA (2010) Publication Manual's recommendations: 'MANOVA was used to test the hypothesis that team work training had an effect on sporting behaviours, but the null hypothesis was supported, Pillai's $F(6, 76) = 1.08$, p ns.'

However, since the findings were significant, you could write: 'MANOVA showed that teamwork training was effective in improving sporting behaviours, Pillai's $F(6, 76) = 4.12$, $p < .01$. The individual dependent variables were subject to ANOVAs in order to assess whether the three dependent variables showed the same trend. For the measure of the difference between favourite and least favourite team member measure it was found that the psychologist teamwork sessions ($M = 7.29$) were superior to the coach team work sessions ($M = 4.43$) and the control condition ($M = 3.79$), $F(2, 39) = 15.71$, $p < .01$. The mean number of gym sessions attended was higher for the psychologist ($M = 11.21$) than the coach ($M = 8.36$) and control ($M = 7.14$), $F(2, 39) = 6.86$, $p < .05$.'

Key points

- MANOVA basically deals with a very simple problem – the risk of falsely accepting a hypothesis because you have carried out multiple tests of significance.

- Try to avoid an unfocused approach to MANOVA. It is *not* a particularly useful technique for sorting out what to do with numerous dependent variables that you have measured merely because you could.

- MANOVA is not appropriate if all of your dependent variables are highly intercorrelated. It may be better in these circumstances to combine the dependent variables to give a total score which is then analysed using ANOVA, for example.

- A complete MANOVA would preferably involve a discriminant function analysis. This is described in Chapter 27.

COMPUTER ANALYSIS

The SPSS Statistics instruction book to this text is Dennis Howitt and Duncan Cramer (2011), *Introduction to SPSS Statistics in Psychology: For version 19 and earlier*, Harlow: Pearson. Chapter 27 in that book gives detailed step-by-step procedures for the statistics described in this chapter together with advice on how to report the results. Figure 26.2 gives the SPSS Statistics steps for MANOVA.

Data	• Name the variables in Variable View of the Data Editor. • Enter the data under the appropriate variable names in Data View of the Data Editor.
Analysis	• Select 'Analyze', 'General Linear Model' and 'Multivariate . . .'. • Move the dependent variables to the 'Dependent Variables:' box and the independent variable(s) to the 'Independent Variable(s):' box.
2	• Select 'Options . . .' and move the independent variable to the 'Display Means for:' box.
3	• Select the 'Descriptive statistics', 'Estimates of effect size' and 'Continue'.
Output	• Check in the 'Multivariate Tests' table if Pillai's *F* for the independent variable is significant with a Sig(nificance) of .05 or less.
2	• If it is significant, check in the 'Tests of Between-Subjects Effects' table which of the dependent variables the independent variable has a significant effect on with a Sig(nificance) of .05 or less.
3	• If there are more than 2 groups use further tests to determine which means differ significantly from each other.

FIGURE 26.2 SPSS Statistics steps for MANOVA

Recommended further reading

Diekhoff, G. (1992), *Statistics for the Social and Behavioral Sciences*, Dubuque, IL: Wm. C. Brown, Chapter 15.

Hair, J.F., Jr, Anderson, R.E., Tatham, R.L. and Black, W.C. (2009), *Multivariate Data Analysis*, 7th edition, Upper Saddle River, NJ: Pearson Prentice Hall, Chapter 6.

Tabachnick, B.G. and Fidell, L.S. (2007), *Using Multivariate Statistics*, 5th edition, Boston, MA: Allyn & Bacon, Chapter 7.

CHAPTER 27

Discriminant (function) analysis – especially in MANOVA

Overview

- Discriminant function analysis uses a set of score variables to assess the extent to which they are associated with the different groups in a study. In other words, it asks the question of whether it is possible to discriminate between groupings of participants (conditions) on the basis of a set of other variables.

- It is similar to logistic regression (Chapters 41 and 42) in terms of what it does, though it cannot use category variables as predictor variables and is based on more restrictive assumptions.

- The main use of discriminant function analysis is following a significant MANOVA (Chapter 26). It serves as a way of understanding what combinations of a set of variables best differentiate the different groups (conditions) in a study.

- A discriminant function is a variable derived from a set of variables which maximises the differences between the groups on that set of variables. It computes a set of weights which are applied to each variable in the set of score variables. More than one discriminant function may emerge.

- It is important to avoid highly correlated variables since this creates high collinearity which distorts the analysis and puts the meaning of the findings in doubt. If two variables highly correlate then one could be omitted from the analysis (it contains no different information from the other variable with which it correlates highly). To check, the omitted variable could then be used instead of that variable and the analysis repeated and the two outcomes compared.

- Discriminant function analysis can classify participants into groups on the basis of their 'scores' on the discriminant functions. This classification can then be compared with the group that the participants actually belong to.

→

- Discriminant function analysis has concepts which are new – especially those of centroids and canonical correlation. But a centroid is nothing more than the mean of a group on a discriminant function (which is just a special sort of variable) and canonical correlation is just a correlation coefficient but between one *set* of variables and another *set* of variables.

Preparation

Read Chapter 26 on MANOVA, but understanding something about regression (Chapters 8 and 31) and especially logistic regression (Chapters 41 and 42) will be beneficial.

27.1 Introduction

Discriminant function analysis once did the job for which logistic regression is now the preferred technique. For most purposes, logistic regression is better than discriminant function analysis since its underlying basic assumptions are less demanding (restricting). Both techniques tell the researcher whether different groups of participants (categories of the dependent variable) can be accurately classified on the basis of a number of other variables (the independent variables) in combination. For discriminant function analysis, these other variables must be score variables (logistic regression can handle nominal or category variables in addition). The main (perhaps only) reason why discriminant function analysis is included here is its role in relation to MANOVA (see Chapter 26). In many ways, discriminant function analysis and MANOVA are built on the same basic mathematical calculations. Consequently, it is not surprising that when MANOVA cannot answer a particular question, discriminant function analysis is used to fill in the information gap. Apart from that, we would not recommend its use. Its role in relation to MANOVA is to indicate the combination of variables which best discriminate between the different groups of participants. In order to do this, a researcher must examine what the discriminant functions which significantly discriminate between the groups actually represent. This is done by seeing which variables correlate best with the discriminant function. In this regard, it is a little like factor analysis (Chapter 30).

Table 27.1 illustrates a study for which discriminant function analysis is appropriate. It deals with three drug conditions (including one no-treatment control). Much the same data were previously discussed in Chapter 26 on MANOVA, though notice that we have reversed the labelling of the independent variable and the dependent variables. There are four independent variables (reaction time, clarity of speech, steadiness of hand and writing speed). The dependent variable is the drug condition. The research question is basically what pattern or combination of the independent variables best classifies individuals in terms of the group to which they belong. That is, can we predict group membership accurately on the basis of the scores we have on the independent variables?

Some authorities describe discriminant function analysis as the reverse of MANOVA. This is a reasonable description, especially since the independent and dependent variables are reversed between MANOVA and discriminant function analysis. In MANOVA, the categories of the independent variable become the dependent variable in discriminant function analysis. The dependent variables (the score variables) in

Table 27.1	Data table for a study of effects of Therazine on motor skills										
Group (dependent variable)											
Therazine condition Independent variables				**Placebo condition Independent variables**				**No-treatment condition Independent variables**			
RT*	Sp	Hd	W	RT	Sp	Hd	W	RT	Sp	Hd	W
8**	5	7	7	1	3	2	2	4	3	5	4
7	7	6	5	4	5	3	3	1	2	3	6
9	8	5	9	7	2	1	2	3	5	2	6
7	5	8	8	2	5	6	1	1	4	6	2

* RT = Reaction time, Sp = clarity of speech, Hd = steadiness of hand and W = writing speed. Scores are from four cases in each column.
** The scores are for the four independent variables.

MANOVA become the independent variables in discriminant function analysis. There is a strong relationship between ANOVA and multiple regression – indeed many calculations of ANOVA actually use regression techniques. The strongest indication of that is the use of the term intercept (from regression) in some ANOVA analyses. There is also a very strong relationship between MANOVA and discriminant function analysis, as we have indicated.

Of course, what is really confusing is the use of the terms independent and dependent variables, which should not be taken to indicate that one thing causes the other. Predictor and criterion variables are another way of saying the same thing.

No matter, in discriminant function analysis the independent variables are the score variables whereas the dependent variable consists of the different groups of participants. So essentially in discriminant function analysis we are trying to predict which group of participants individuals belong to on the basis of a number of predictor variables. Another way of saying exactly the same thing is to suggest that discriminant function analysis seeks to find whether the different groups of participants are different in terms of their means on the independent variables. This is often expressed in terms of the means of each group on the discriminant functions. These means are called centroids. Though this sounds like a radically new concept, it merely indicates the group mean on a discriminant function.

One thing is vital to understand. A discriminant function is basically a way of totalling or combining the scores on the independent variables. Instead of adding the scores on variables A, B, C and D as follows:

$$A + B + C + D \text{ etc.}$$

in discriminant function analysis, each score variable is given a different weight (w) so that the formula for the discriminant function is:

$$w_1A + w_2B + w_3C + w_4D \text{ etc.}$$

This is little different from the formula for multiple regression (Chapter 31), though we have omitted a constant from the above for the purposes of clarity. Of course, there are any number of different sets of weights that can be applied. However, in discriminant function analysis the discriminant function used is the one which best discriminates (differentiates) the various groups of participants. Only one discriminant function can meet this criterion. One could think of the discriminant function as simply a variable based on a combination of other variables, just as factors in factor analysis are variables (see Chapter 30). Just so long as you remember that this combination variable is one that maximises differences between the groups (conditions) in the study then you cannot go far wrong.

It is a little more complicated than that since there can be several discriminant functions calculated for any set of data. The first discriminant function maximises the differences between the groups of participants (on that discriminant function). In other words, the discriminant function is the weighted combination of the predictor variables that maximises the difference between the groups of participants (i.e. conditions of the study). Thus it is the function (weighted combination of variables) that best discriminates the groups in the study. There may remain important variation in the data after this has been done. So a second discriminant function may sometimes be calculated based on the original data minus variation due to the first discriminant function. The process can continue to produce further discriminant functions depending on the number of groups to differentiate and the number of predictor variables (score variables). The discriminant functions are unrelated to each other – that is to say, they are independent of each other or orthogonal. Basically this means that discriminant functions from an analysis do not correlate.

Actually, discriminant function analysis does not handle more than one dependent variable at a time. This is no great problem as the main effects from the MANOVA can be dealt with one at a time (the main effects of MANOVA are independent of each other).

It is important, so as not to be flustered when you come across new terminology, to know that discriminant function analysis works largely using canonical correlations. These are similar to multiple correlations (see Chapter 31) which are the correlation of several variables with one other variable. Canonical correlation is the correlation of a set of several variables with another set of several variables. In discriminant function analysis there are several independent variables and also several dependent variables since there are usually several different groups. Don't worry. We have read claims that canonical analysis has the dubious distinction of being the hardest multivariate concept to understand. Actually, apart from knowing that there is such a thing as canonical correlations, there is not a great deal more that you need to know about the computer output for discriminant function analysis that you probably don't know already from other parts of this book.

There is a limit to the number of discriminant functions that can be produced for any set of data. The number of groups being discriminated minus 1 is one criterion and the number of (score) variables in the analysis is the other criterion. Whichever is the smaller of the two is the maximum number of discriminant functions.

27.2 Doing the discriminant function analysis

Table 27.2 gives the discriminant function analysis version of the data that we used in Chapter 26 to illustrate the steps in a MANOVA analysis. Chapter 26 left the MANOVA analysis incomplete since it lacked a discriminant function analysis, which adds to our ability to understand what is happening in our data. In the following discussion we concentrate solely on using discriminant function analysis to identify group membership in terms of team-building procedures. We know from MANOVA (Chapter 26) that we have a significant effect of the teamwork condition on the scores on the set of three dependent variables. In the MANOVA chapter, the fact that we had found a significant MANOVA freed us to do several ANOVAs to see which of the dependent variables (score variables) actually were influenced by the particular

Table 27.2	Data for the discriminant function analysis							
Group (dependent variable)								
Team building with sports psychologist Independent variables			**Team building with sports coach Independent variables**			**No team building controls Independent variables**		
Like*	Gym	Game	Like	Gym	Game	Like	Gym	Game
9**	12	14	4	6	15	9	6	10
5	9	14	5	4	12	1	2	5
8	11	12	4	9	15	6	10	12
4	6	5	3	8	8	2	5	6
9	12	3	4	9	9	3	6	7
9	11	14	5	3	8	4	7	8
6	13	14	2	8	12	1	6	13
6	11	18	6	9	11	4	9	12
8	11	22	4	7	15	3	8	15
8	13	22	4	8	28	3	2	14
9	15	18	5	7	10	2	8	11
7	12	18	4	9	9	6	9	10
8	10	13	5	18	18	3	8	13
6	11	22	7	12	24	6	14	22

* Like = difference between ratings of most and least liked team members, Gym = number of gym sessions voluntarily attended and Game = number of games played.
** The scores are the scores on the three independent variables.

group to which participants belonged. We found that teamwork training did not seem to have an influence on the number of games played, but it did have an influence on the other two dependent variables. In other words, we already know quite a bit from the MANOVA. This should be remembered now that we move on to the discriminant function analysis. And don't forget that when we say independent variable in discriminant function analysis we would call it a dependent variable in MANOVA and vice versa. So the group variable is labelled the dependent variable in Table 27.2 and the independent variables are the scores. Figure 27.1 gives the key steps in discriminant function analysis.

■ Step 1

Before we start a discriminant function analysis, there is one important thing to understand. Highly correlated score variables should be avoided. This is because of the problem of collinearity which is discussed in Chapter 31. Basically you need to check the correlations between all of the score variables to make sure that this is not the case. Just compute a correlation matrix between all of your score variables to see whether there are any highly correlated items. In discriminant function analysis, the score variables are the independent or predictor variables. We are thinking of correlations of the order of maybe 0.7 and above. The question, then, is what you can do about this situation. The higher the correlation the more the two variables are assessing more

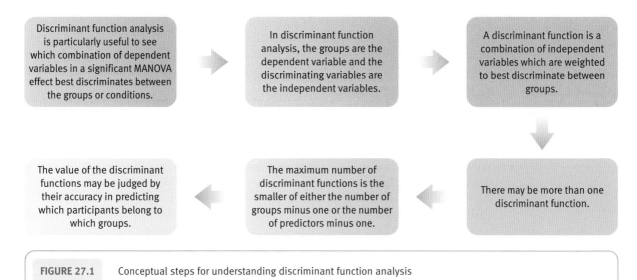

FIGURE 27.1   Conceptual steps for understanding discriminant function analysis

or less the same thing in terms of the variation in scores. So it would be reasonable to do the analysis leaving out one of the two highly correlated variables and any others you find. There is no harm in this since the two variables are virtually the same and so leaving one of them out is no real handicap. Of course, if you wish, you could reinstate those variables and leave out the other variables which you had previously included. Almost certainly, you will find virtually no difference in terms of the two analyses except for the names of the variables involved.

■ Step 2

Having run your data through SPSS Statistics or some other program which does discriminant function analysis, the next thing to do is to look for the eigenvalues in the output. Note that for our example, the maximum number of discriminant functions possible is the number of groups – 1 which is 3 – 1 which is 2 discriminant functions. (The number of variables is the other formula but this is bigger than 2 in this case, so it is ignored.) The first discriminant function is the most discriminating between the groups and the later discriminant functions are the most discriminating *after* the earlier discriminant functions have been removed from the data. Table 27.3 gives the char-acteristic eigenvalue information that is provided. For discriminant function 1, we can see that the eigenvalue is 0.87. This is indicative of the amount of variation in the data which is accounted for by the first discriminant function. Looking at the column for % of variance, this corresponds to 97% of the total variance. This is not the total of the variance in the data but the total of the variance explained by the discriminant functions. It is, in other words, the reliable variance explained and excludes error variance. Thus

Table 27.3	The eigenvalues and variance explained by each discriminant function		
Function	**Eigenvalue**	**% of variance**	**Canonical correlation**
Discriminant function 1	0.87	97	0.68
Discriminant function 2	0.03	3	0.16

in this example the total of the two eigenvalues is 0.87 + 0.03 = 0.90. Thus the proportion of variance explained = 0.87/0.90 which equals 0.97; expressed as a percentage this becomes the figure of 97% of the total variance explained in the penultimate column in Table 27.3. Don't be misled into thinking that the research has identified a weighted set of variables (the discriminant function) which explains 97% of the variation in the data. That would be phenomenal. What it means is that the researcher has found a discriminant function which explains the reliable variance (i.e. with error variance ignored) which is much less impressive.

Also notice that a cumulative % of variance explained figure is given. Since there is a maximum of two discriminant functions possible where one has three groups, then it is hardly surprising that those two discriminant functions account for all of the variation that could be accounted for by the discriminant functions. It is all the reliable variance that can be explained.

The final column in Table 27.3 gives the canonical correlation for the first discriminant function as being 0.68. If you interpret this much as you would do any correlation, it is clear that it is quite a substantial correlation and indicative of a strong relationship between the predictor (score) variables and the groups of participants. In contrast, the second discriminant function not only explains very little of the variance but the canonical correlation is fairly low at 0.16. Again, if this were an ordinary correlation coefficient we would regard the value as fairly low. This is exactly the same for the canonical correlation. So we are left with the impression that there is one substantial discriminant function and a rather unsubstantial second discriminant function for these data.

■ Step 3

A crucial part of the analysis is the information on Wilks' lambda (Table 27.4). The table can be a little confusing at first. What the analysis basically does is to indicate whether or not your discriminant function analysis is statistically significant. It does so by first of all giving the significance of all of your discriminant functions together. So where you see in the first column 1 through 2 this includes all of the discriminant functions in the analysis. For our example, the maximum is two so that row reads 1 through 2. If we had four groupings then this would read 1 through 3 because 3 is the maximum number of discriminant functions with four groupings (see above). The next row in our example reads just 2. This is the test for the second discriminant function *alone*. So, as we can see, discriminant functions 1 and 2 together are very significant at 0.00, but discriminant function 2 on its own is not significant. Of course, this means that the discriminant functions do not individually have to be statistically significant in order that you have a significant discriminant function analysis overall. The table for Wilks' lambda becomes more complex with increasing numbers of discriminant functions. But, despite this, the key is the first row in the table since if that is not significant then you need proceed no further in examining the output. (You probably would not have done the discriminant function analysis anyway since the MANOVA that you probably have computed previously would have indicated a lack of significance in your data already.)

Table 27.4	The values of Wilks' lambda			
Test of function(s)	**Wilks' lambda**	**Chi-square**	**df**	**Sig.**
Discriminant functions 1 through 2	0.52	24.69	6	0.00
Discriminant function 2	0.97	1.01	2	0.61

If the Wilks' lambda is statistically significant then this indicates that the means (centroids) of the different groups on the discriminant function(s) are statistically different. The value of lambda can range from 0 to 1. It is the amount of variation in the discriminant function which cannot be accounted for by the different groups (conditions). The value of lambda will increase as you go down the column for lambda since the discriminant functions lower down the list have more variance than cannot be explained by differences between the groups in the analysis. We know that already, since they are the discriminant functions which are poorest at differentiating the groups in the analysis.

■ Step 4

The main point of doing the discriminant function analysis following MANOVA (and we would not recommend it for any other purpose) is to understand which of your predictor (independent) variables are associated with the discriminant functions that have been calculated. In other words, just what weights are given to the predictor variables in calculating each of the discriminant functions. Just knowing the weights as such is not very helpful at all since the weights depend on the exact scale and range of scores on each variable. These may be different for each of your predictor variables, so it is better to have a standardised version of the weights (coefficients) as this then allows meaningful comparison. These standardised weights can be seen in Table 27.5. The big weights given to the first discriminant function are for 'difference between ratings of most and least liked team members' (0.85). The number of gym sessions voluntarily attended has a smaller *relative* weight (0.30). It is also notable that 'number of games played' has a near zero weight (−0.04). Thus, the first discriminant function is most clearly identified with the variable concerning the most and least favourite team member, though there is also a component of the discriminant function which is associated with the voluntary attendance at gym session.

The second discriminant function, which we already have seen is in itself not statistically significant, has its major weighting solely for number of games played.

Alternatively, we could look at the correlations between the predictor variables and the standardised discriminant functions (the structure matrix). Although the value of the correlations in Table 27.6 naturally differ from the weights shown in Table 27.5, the direction of the results is similar. The variable that is most highly correlated with the first standardised discriminant function in Table 27.6 is the difference between the most and least liked team members (0.97). This variable also has the largest weight (0.85) on the first standardised discriminant function in Table 27.5. The variable that is most highly correlated with the second discriminant function in Table 27.6 is the number of games played (0.96). This variable also has the greatest weight (1.00) on the second discriminant function in Table 27.5.

Table 27.5	Standardised coefficients for the different discriminant functions	
Group (condition)	**Function**	
	Discriminant function 1	**Discriminant function 2**
Difference between ratings of most and least liked team members	0.85	−0.31
Number of gym sessions voluntarily attended	0.30	0.05
Number of games played	−0.04	1.00

Table 27.6	The structure matrix of the correlation of the predictors and the standardised discriminant functions	
Group (condition)	**Discriminant function 1**	**Discriminant function 2**
Difference between ratings of most and least liked team members	0.97	−0.09
Number of gym sessions voluntarily attended	0.64	0.38
Number of games played	0.27	0.96

So the picture seems to be that the first discriminant function consists largely of 'difference between ratings of most and least liked team members' with a smaller contribution from 'number of gym sessions voluntarily attended'. The second discriminant function is the 'number of games played', though it is fairly clear by now that this function is unimportant relative to the first discriminant function and non-significant statistically.

While this interpretation makes sense and fits the statistical analysis, it has to be said that the discriminant function analysis does not shed a great deal of light on the combination of predictor variables which best discriminate between the groups. It is not like, say, exploratory factor analysis (Chapter 30) which can unveil patterns which are meaningful and informative. This is partly because that is not really the job of discriminant function analysis. More light may be shed if you have more variables than in this case. However, if you have many variables (such as where you have administered a lengthy questionnaire) then it would be wise to subject this questionnaire to factor analysis initially rather than throw all of the variables into a discriminant function analysis.

■ Step 5

Since the discriminant scores are variables of a special sort, it is useful to examine the mean 'scores' for each discriminant function for each group of participants. These are shown in Table 27.7. Remember that discriminant functions are just variables so each participant can be scored on each discriminant function. So it is possible to find the average score for each group on the discriminant functions. This basically tells us which groups are high and low on each discriminant function. So in terms of the first discriminant function, the teamwork talk by the sports psychologist generates the highest mean (remember that the discriminant function is largely about the 'difference between the most and least favourite team member'). The other two groups are more similar to each other on this discriminant function. The second discriminant function (number of games

Table 27.7	Means (centroids) for the groups (conditions) on each discriminant function	
Group	**Discriminant function 1**	**Discriminant function 2**
Team psychologist	1.24	−0.04
Team coach	−0.42	0.21
Control	−0.83	−0.17

Table 27.8	Accuracy of the classification based on the discriminant functions		
Actual group membership	**Predicted group membership**		
	Psychologist teamwork	**Coach teamwork**	**Controls**
Psychologist teamwork	11 (78.6%)	2 (14.3%)	1 (7.1%)
Coach teamwork	3 (21.4%)	4 (28.6%)	7 (50.0%)
Controls	4 (28.6%)	2 (14.3%)	8 (57.1%)

played was the most associated variable) seems to suggest that the teamwork talk by the team coach produced higher scores. However, this second discriminant function is to be discounted because of its lack of significance.

■ Step 6

Finally, we need to ask to what extent the discriminant functions can be used to accurately classify participants in terms of the group that they were in. This is done by comparing the predicted group based on the discriminant functions with the actual group membership. Examining Table 27.8, it can be seen that the accuracy of the prediction depends on which group one is considering. The discriminant functions accurately classified 78.6% of the 14 participants who underwent the team-building sessions with the psychologist, but only 28.6% of the 14 participants who had team-building sessions with the coach were correctly classified. For the control group, accuracy was 57.1% since 8 out of the 14 members of the control group were accurately classified by the discriminant functions. Fifty per cent of those allocated to the coach teamwork condition were actually misclassified as being in the control condition.

■ Step 7

There is an alternative way of doing the discriminant function analysis – using a stepwise process. Stepwise processes are discussed in Chapter 31. In SPSS Statistics, this involves pressing a single extra button. Stepwise would have advantages in terms of simplicity of the output. This is because it chooses the biggest discriminant functions and does not include any discriminant function which is not statistically significant. Thus in the above tables, only one discriminant would be mentioned because only the first discriminant function is significant. This is a considerable saving of effort, of course. Unfortunately, and this may be sufficient reason for you not to use stepwise, this is not the same model as the original MANOVA employed. In that MANOVA, essentially all discriminant functions were used as the basis of the calculation (though it would not be apparent that this was what was happening) – that is, the significant MANOVA is based on all of the discriminant functions. So there is no reason why this should change for the discriminant function analysis. But by using stepwise you are probably violating the MANOVA model. Some textbooks, nevertheless, advise the use of stepwise discriminant function analysis. In truth, it probably makes very little difference to the way you understand your analysis.

27.3   Reporting your findings

One way of summarising the results of this analysis according to the APA (2010) Publication Manual's recommendations is as follows. 'A direct discriminant analysis was carried out using the three predictors of the difference between the most and least liked team member, the number of gym sessions voluntarily attended and the number of games played to determine which of these variables best discriminate between teams built with a sports psychologist, teams built with a coach and teams built with neither of these (the control condition). Two discriminant functions were calculated, explaining about 97 per cent and 3 per cent of the variance, respectively. Wilks' lambda was significant for the combined functions, $X^2(6, N = 42) = 24.69$, $p < .001$ but was not significant when the first function was removed, $X^2(2, N = 42) = 1.01$, $p = .605$. The first discriminant function maximally differentiated the psychologist's teamwork training from the other two groups and correlated most highly with the difference between the most and least liked members (.96) and the number of gym sessions attended (.64). The second discriminant function maximally distinguished the coach's team from the other two groups and loaded most strongly with the number of games played (.96). About 80 per cent of the cases were correctly classified compared with 33 per cent expected by chance. About 79 per cent of the psychologist's team members were correctly identified with 14 per cent misclassified as the coach's team members. Fifty-seven per cent of the control team members were correctly identified with 29 per cent misclassified as the psychologist's team members. Twenty-nine per cent of the coach's team members were correctly identified with 50 per cent misclassified as the control team members.'

Key points

- Although discriminant function analysis is a general technique to assess the accuracy with which different groups can be classified on the basis of a set of score variables, it is not the best technique for doing so. It is important in relation to MANOVA since discriminant function analysis and MANOVA are based on very similar assumptions and mathematics.

- Check out logistic regression (Chapters 41 and 42) if you simply want to know which variables accurately classify groups of participants. Discriminant function analysis has drawbacks compared to logistic regression.

- Only where you have a significant MANOVA do you need to consider using discriminant function analysis.

COMPUTER ANALYSIS

The SPSS instruction book to this text is Dennis Howitt and Duncan Cramer (2011), *Introduction to SPSS Statistics in Psychology: For version 19 and earlier*, Harlow: Pearson. Chapter 28 in that book gives detailed step-by-step procedures for the statistics described in this chapter together with advice on how to report the results. Figure 27.2 gives the SPSS Statistics steps for a discriminant function analysis.

→

Data
- Name the variables in Variable View of the Data Editor.
- Enter the data under the appropriate variable names in Data View of the Data Editor.

Analysis
- Select 'Analyze', 'Classify' and 'Discriminant . . .'.
- Move grouping variable to 'Grouping Variable:' box.

2
- Select 'Define Range'. Put the lowest group number code in the 'Minimum:' box and the highest in the 'Maximum:' box. Select 'Continue'.

3
- Move predictor variables to the 'Independents:' box and select 'Statistics'.

4
- Select 'Means', 'Box's M' and 'Continue'.
- Select 'Classify', 'Compute from group size', 'Summary table' and 'Continue'.

Output
- Check whether any of the Wilks' lambda for the discriminant functions are significant with a Sig(nificance) of .05 or less.

2
- If so check in the 'Structure Matrix' table which predictors are most highly correlated as these best discriminate the groups.

3
- Determine the percentage of correct classification for the groups.

FIGURE 27.2 SPSS Statistics steps for a discriminant function analysis

Recommended further reading

Cramer, D. (2003), *Advanced Quantitative Data Analysis*, Buckingham: Open University Press, Chapter 13.

Diekhoff, G. (1992), *Statistics for the Social and Behavioral Sciences*, Dubuque, IL: Wm. C. Brown, Chapter 14.

Hair, J.F., Jr, Anderson, R.E., Tatham, R.L. and Black, W.C. (2009), *Multivariate Data Analysis*, 7th edition, Upper Saddle River, NJ: Pearson Prentice Hall, Chapter 5.

Tabachnick, B.G. and Fidell, L.S. (2007), *Using Multivariate Statistics*, 5th edition, Boston, MA: Allyn & Bacon, Chapter 9.

CHAPTER 28

Statistics and the analysis of experiments

Overview

- There is a temptation to regard statistical analyses as something to be left until the last minute. This is far from ideal.

- It is a good discipline to sketch out the statistical analysis of your data as part of the planning of the research. This may help you find solutions to methodological problems when something can be done about them.

- Choosing an appropriate statistical analysis depends on a clear statement of the hypotheses (i.e. relationships) to be tested, clearly identifying what variables are nominal (category) variables and what are score variables, and whether you are looking for correlations or for differences in mean scores.

- It is essential to feel free to manipulate the data to create new variables or develop composite measures based on several items.

Preparation

Make sure that you understand hypotheses (Chapter 10) and nominal category data versus numerical score data (Chapter 1).

28.1   Introduction

Feeling jaded and listless? Don't know what stats to use to analyse your experiment? Make money from home. Try Professor Warburton's Patent Stats Pack. All the professional tricks revealed. Guaranteed not to fail. Gives hope where there is no hope. Professor Warburton's Stats Pack troubleshoots the troubleshooters.

Since the death of Professor Warburton in 1975, through thrombosis of the wallet, his Patent Stats Pack had been feared lost. Libraries on three continents were searched. Miraculously it was discovered after many years in Australia in a trunk under the bed of a dingo farmer. Auctioned recently at Sotheby's to an unknown buyer – reputedly a German antiquarian – it broke all records. Controversy broke out when scholars claimed that Professor Warburton was a fraud and never held an academic appointment in his life. To date, it has not been possible to refute this claim.

These are vile slurs against Professor Warburton whom many regard as the founder of the post-modernist statistics movement and the first person to deconstruct statistics. Judge for yourself.

28.2   The Patent Stats Pack

Principle 1

Practically nothing needs to be known about statistical calculations and theory to choose appropriate procedures to analyse your data. The characteristics of your research are the main considerations – not knowledge of statistics books.

Principle 2

Ideally you should not undertake research without being able to sketch out the likely features of your tables and diagrams.

Principle 3

You *can* make a silk purse out of a sow's ear. First catch your silk pig. . . . A common mistake is thinking that the data as they are collected are the data as they will be analysed. Sometimes, especially when the statistical analysis has not been planned prior to collecting data, you may have to make your data fit the available statistical techniques. Always remember that you may need to alter the format of your data in some way in order to make them suitable for statistical analysis. These changes include:

- adding scores from several variables to get a single overall or composite variable

- separating a variable into several different components (especially where you have collected data as frequencies in nominal categories and have allowed multiple answers).

Box 28.1   Focus on

Where to get advice

One should be wary about from where to get statistical advice. A little knowledge can be a dangerous thing and this applies to statistical advice as much as anything. Sometimes a sort of blind panic sets in whereby a student, for example, feels that they cannot cope with the demands of a quantitative analysis of their data and so becomes reliant on anyone who will listen and appears to know a little more than they do. It is easy to impress by bandying about statistical terminology and alluding to the inherent problems of various statistical techniques. None of this is particularly helpful to the person with a pressing need to get on with analysing their data. What we are trying to say, hopefully subtly, is that in our experience students' difficulties with statistical analysis are made worse by being given wrong or impracticable advice given the circumstances. Worse still, sometimes this third party advice is communicated with such conviction that the hapless student is torn between this advice and what they know about statistics in general. Consequently, because they lack confidence in their statistical ability, this contradictory advice pushes them into a tail-spin from which it is difficult to recover.

28.3   Checklist

Years of experience providing statistical advice suggests that rarely is the statistical analysis the basic problem – far more important is the inadequate conceptualisation which underlies the research design. Statistics is of some help – but limited – even where a research design was inadequate. It is far better to get your research design clear before you start. Profound knowledge of statistical techniques is probably not the most important skill of the researcher. Instead, apparently simple skills such as being able to understand how one's research aims can be met using your chosen research questions are more important. Just what is there in the research design which allows one to answer the research question? If you can't answer this question satisfactorily then there is likely to be some sort of conceptual muddle which is hindering your process. If you knew virtually nothing about statistics, how could you use your data to answer your research question? For example, you might answer this question by saying draw a scattergram between this variable and that variable or the average score in one group should be higher than the average score in another group. That is, just what would you look for in your data to answer your research question?

Of course, prevention is better than cure in statistical analysis. Sometimes it is easy to see the root cause of the conceptual muddle which has resulted in someone seeking statistical advice. It is hard to be clear about concepts, and the more concepts involved in a study then the greater the capacity for muddle. It is important to be able to write your ideas down, but it is equally or even more important to be able to talk about your ideas to other people. By talking about your plans to your research supervisor, colleagues and friends then you are actively engaging with the all important building blocks of your study. It may be embarrassing to do so, sometimes, but this might encourage a re-think if it proves problematic to communicate your ideas clearly to others.

So what can be done where the statistical analysis does not seem to flow from your research design? The following are some of the major considerations which will help you choose an appropriate statistical analysis for your data.

1. Write down your hypothesis. Probably the best way of doing this is to simply fill in the blanks in the following:

'My hypothesis is that there is a relationship between variable 1 ___ and variable 2 ___'

Do not write in the names of more than two variables. There is nothing to stop you having several hypotheses. Write down as many hypotheses as seems appropriate – but only *two* variable names per hypothesis. Treat each hypothesis as a separate statistical analysis at least for now.

If you cannot name the two variables you see as correlated then it is possible that you wish only to compare a single sample with a population. In this case check out the single-sample chi-square (Chapter 14) or the single-sample t-test (Chapter 12).

2. If you cannot meet the requirements of 1 above then you are possibly confused about the purpose of the research. *Go no further until you have sorted this out* – do not blame statistics for your conceptual muddle. Writing out your hypotheses until they are clear may sound like a chore, but it is an important part of statistical analysis.

3. Classify each of the variables in your hypothesis into either of the following categories:

   (a) numerical score variables

   (b) nominal (category) variables – and count the number of categories.

4. Based on 3, decide which of the following statements is true of your hypothesis:

   (a) I have *two* numerical score variables. (Yes/No)
       (if yes then go to 5)

   (b) I have *two* nominal category variables. (Yes/No)
       (if yes then go to 6)

   (c) I have *one* nominal category variable and *one* numerical score variable. (Yes/No)
       (if yes then go to 7)

5. If you answered yes to 4(a) above (i.e. you have two numerical score variables) then your statistical analysis involves the correlation coefficient. This might include Pearson correlation, Spearman correlation or regression. Turn to Chapter 33 on the analysis of questionnaire research for ideas of what is possible.

6. If you answered yes to 4(b), implying that you have two nominal category variables, then your statistical analysis has to be based on contingency tables using chi-square or closely related tests. The range available to you is as follows:

   (a) chi-square

   (b) Fisher exact probability test for 2 × 2 or 2 × 3 contingency tables, especially if the samples are small or expected frequencies low

   (c) The McNemar test if you are studying *change* in the same sample of people.

The only problem you are likely to experience with such tests is if you have allowed the participants in your research to give more than one answer to a question. If you have, then the solution is to turn each category into a separate variable and code each individual according to whether or not they are in that category. This is referred to as dummy coding and is covered in detail later in this book (Chapter 41). So, for example, in a frequency table such as Table 28.1 it is pretty obvious that multiple responses have been allowed since the total of the frequencies is in excess of the sample size of 50. This table could be turned into four new tables:

- Table 1: The number of vegetarians (19) versus the number of non-vegetarians (31)

- Table 2: The number of fast food preferrers (28) versus the non-fast food preferrers (22)

Table 28.1	Food preferences of a sample of 50 teenagers	
Food type		**Frequency**
Vegetarian		19
Fast food		28
Italian		9
Curry		8

- Table 3: Italian preferrers (9) versus Italian non-preferrers (41)

- Table 4: Curry preferrers (8) versus non-curry preferrers (42).

7. If you answered yes to 4(c) then the nominal (category) variable is called the *independent* variable and the numerical score variable is called the *dependent* variable. The number of categories for the independent variable partly determines the statistical tests you can apply:

   (a) If you have two categories for the independent (nominal category) variable then:

      (i) the *t*-test is a suitable statistic (Chapters 12 and 13)

      (ii) the one-way analysis of variance is suitable (Chapters 20 and 21).

   The choice between the two is purely arbitrary as they give equivalent results. Remember to check whether your two sets of scores are independent or correlated/related. If your scores on the dependent variable are correlated then it is appropriate to use the related or correlated versions of the *t*-test (Chapter 12) and the analysis of variance (Chapter 21).

   (b) If you have *three or more* categories for the independent (nominal category) variable then your choice is limited to the one-way analysis of variance. Again, if your dependent variable features correlated or related scores, then the related or correlated one-way analysis of variance can be used (Chapters 19 and 20).

Box 28.2	Focus on

Problematic data

If it becomes clear that the basic assumptions of parametric tests are violated by your data (which for all practical purposes means that the distribution of scores is *very* skewed), then you might wish to employ a nonparametric equivalent (Chapter 18 and Appendix B2). However, you may wish to look at bootstrapping procedures (see Box 18.1) which are not as reliant on symmetrical and normally distributed data as conventionally many of the parametric tests are. Bootstrapping makes no more assumptions about the nature of the data than can be seen from your data. The big advantage of bootstrapping procedures is that they can be applied to many conventional parametric techniques. Bootstrapping is a welcome recent feature in SPSS Statistics. The use of a computer package is essential for bootstrapping procedures which involve vast numbers of samples drawn randomly from your data set (which is multiplied numerous times in order to get a large sample).

Sometimes you may decide that you have *two or more independent* variables for each dependent variable. Here you are getting into the complexities of the analysis of variance and you need to consult Chapters 22 and 24 for advice.

28.4 Special cases

■ Multiple items to measure the same variable

Sometimes instead of measuring a variable with a single question or with a single technique, that variable is measured in several ways. Most likely is that a questionnaire has been used which contains several questions pertaining to the same thing. In these circumstances, you will probably want to combine these questions to give a single numerical score on that variable. The techniques used to do this include the use of standard scores and factor analysis (which are described in Chapters 5 and 30). Generally by combining these different indicators of a major variable together to give a single score you improve the reliability and validity of your research. The combined scores can be used as a single variable and analysed with *t*-tests or analyses of variance, for example.

■ Assessing change over time

The simplest way of studying change over time is to calculate the difference between the first testing and the second testing. This is precisely what a repeated measures *t*-test, for example, does. However, these difference scores can themselves be used in whatever way you wish. In particular, it would be possible to compare difference scores from two or more different samples in order to assess if the amount of change over time depended on gender or any other independent variable. In other words, it is unnecessary to have a complex analysis of variance design which includes time as one independent variable and gender as the other.

Key points

- Nobody ever learned to play a musical instrument simply by reading a book and never practising. It takes time to become confident in choosing appropriate statistical analyses.

- Simple statistical analyses are not automatically inferior to complex ones.

- Table 28.2 should help you choose an appropriate statistical procedure for your experimental data. It is designed to deal only with studies in which you are comparing the *means* of two or more groups of scores. It is not intended to deal with correlations between variables.

Table 28.2	An aid to selecting appropriate statistical analyses for different experimental designs					
Type of data	One sample compared with known population	Two independent samples	Two related samples	Two or more independent samples	Two or more related samples	Two or more independent variables
Nominal (category) data	one-sample chi-square	chi square	McNemar test	chi-square	not in this book[a]	chi-square
Numerical score data	one-sample t-test	unrelated t test, unrelated one way ANOVA	related t-test, related one-way ANOVA	unrelated ANOVA	related ANOVA	two-way, etc. ANOVA
Numerical score data which violate assumptions of parametric tests	not in this book[a]	Mann–Whitney U test	Wilcoxon matched pairs test	Kruskal–Wallis (Appendix B2)	Friedman (Appendix B2)	not in this book[a]

[a] These are fairly specific nonparametric tests which are rarely used.

COMPUTER ANALYSIS

The SPSS instruction book to this text is Dennis Howitt and Duncan Cramer (2011), *Introduction to SPSS Statistics in Psychology: For version 19 and earlier*, Harlow: Pearson. This guide gives detailed step-by-step procedures for the statistics described in this chapter together with advice on how to report the results.

PART 4

More advanced correlational statistics

CHAPTER 29

Partial correlation

Spurious correlation, third or confounding variables, suppressor variables

Overview

- Partial correlation is used to statistically adjust a correlation to take into account the possible influence of a third (or confounding) variable or variables. These are sometimes known as control variables.

- That is, partial correlation deals with the third-variable problem in which additional variables may be the cause of spurious correlations or hide (suppress) the relationship between two variables.

- If one control variable is used then we have a first-order partial correlation. If two control variables are used then the result is a second-order partial correlation.

- Partial correlation may be helpful in trying to assess the possibility that a relationship is a causal relationship.

Preparation

Revise the Pearson correlation coefficient (Chapter 7) if necessary. Make sure you know what is meant by a causal relationship.

29.1 Introduction

The partial correlation coefficient is particularly useful when trying to make causal statements from field research. It is not useful in experimental research where different methods are used to establish causal relationships. Look at the following research outlines taking as critical a viewpoint as possible:

Project 1

Researchers examine the published suicide rates in different geographical locations in the country. They find that there is a significant relationship between unemployment rates in these areas and suicide rates. They conclude that unemployment causes suicide.

Project 2

Researchers examine the relationship between shoe size and liking football matches. They find a relationship between the two but claim that it would be nonsense to suggest that liking football makes your feet grow bigger.

Although both of these pieces of research are superficially similar, the researchers draw rather different conclusions. In the first case it is suggested that unemployment *causes* suicide whereas in the second case the researchers are reluctant to claim that liking football makes your feet grow bigger. The researchers in both cases may be correct in their interpretation of the correlations, but should we take their interpretations at face value? The short answer is no, since correlations do not demonstrate causality in themselves.

In both cases, it is possible that the relationships obtained are spurious (or artificial) ones which occur because of the influence of other variables which the researcher has not considered. So, for example, the relationship between shoe size and liking football might be due to gender – men tend to have bigger feet than women and tend to like football more than women do. So the relationship between shoe size and liking football is merely a consequence of gender differences. The relationship between unemployment and suicide, similarly, could be due to the influence of a third variable. In this case, the variable might be social class. If we found, for example, that being from a lower social class was associated with a greater likelihood of unemployment *and* with being more prone to suicide, this would suggest that the relationship between unemployment and suicide was due to social class differences, not because unemployment leads directly to suicide.

Partial correlation is a statistically precise way of calculating what the relationship between two variables would be if one could take away the influence of one (or more) additional variables. Sometimes this is referred to as controlling for a third variable or partialling out a third variable. In essence it revises the value of your correlation coefficient to take into account third variables.

Causality

This is intended as a timely reminder of things discussed in depth earlier in this book. Partial correlation can never confirm that causal relationships exist between two variables. The reason is that partialling out a third, fourth or fifth variable does not rule out the possibility that there is an additional variable which has not been considered which is the cause of the correlation. However, partial correlation may be useful in examining the validity of claims about specified variables which might be causing the relationship. Considerations of causality are a minor aspect of partial correlation.

29.2   Theoretical considerations

Partial correlation can be applied to your own data if you have the necessary correlations available. However, partial correlation can also be applied to published research without necessarily obtaining the original data itself – so long as the appropriate correlation coefficients are available. All it requires is that the values of the correlations between your two main variables and the possible third variable are known. It is not uncommon to have the necessary tables of correlations published in books and journal articles, although the raw data (original scores) are rarely included in published research.

A table of correlations between several variables is known as a correlation matrix. Table 29.1 is an example featuring the following three variables: numerical intelligence test score (which we have labelled X in the table), verbal intelligence test score (which we have labelled Y in the table) and age (which we have labelled C in the table) in a sample of 30 teenagers.

Notice that the diagonal from top left to bottom right consists of 1.00 repeated three times. This is because the correlation of numerical score with itself, verbal score with itself and age with itself will always be a perfect relationship ($r = 1.00$) – it has to be since you are correlating exactly the same numbers together. Also notice that the matrix is symmetrical around the diagonal. This is fairly obvious since the correlation of the numerical score with the verbal score has to be exactly the same as the correlation of the verbal score with the numerical score. More often than not a researcher would report just half of Table 29.1, so the correlations would look like a triangle. It doesn't matter which triangle you choose although it is usual to display the lower left triangle as we read from left to right.

Table 29.1	A correlation matrix involving three variables		
	Variable X Numerical score	**Variable Y Verbal score**	**Variable C Age in years**
Variable X Numerical score	1.00	0.97	0.80
Variable Y Verbal score	0.97	1.00	0.85
Variable C Age in years	0.80	0.85	1.00

Remember that we have used the letters X, Y and C for the different columns and rows of the matrix. The C column and C row are the column and row, respectively, for the *control* variable (age in this case).

Not only is partial correlation an important statistical tool in its own right, it also forms the basis of other techniques such as multiple regression (Chapter 31).

Box 29.2   Key concepts

Mediator and moderator variables

There is a crucial conceptual distinction in research which has a bearing on our discussion of partialling or controlling for third variables. This is the difference between moderator and mediator variables. This is not a statistical issue, as such, but a key issue in relation to research design and methodology. A knowledge of statistics, however, is helpful in understanding the distinction and putting it into effect. Put crudely, a *mediator* variable is a variable which explains the relationship between two other variables (usually best expressed as the independent and dependent variable). For example, imagine that there is a correlation between annual income (independent variable) and happiness (dependent variable) such that richer people are happier. Although this relationship would be interesting, it is somewhat unsatisfactory from a psychological and theoretical point of view since we do not know the psychological processes which create the relationship. So we might imagine another variable, extensiveness of social network, which might be influenced by annual income and might lead to greater happiness. We know from previous research that a supportive social network contributes to happiness. Now the reason why income may be associated with happiness may be because having more money allows one to socialise more and that the more one socialises the more likely it is that one forms an extensive social network. The variable, extensiveness of social network, can be described as a mediator variable since it mediates the relationship between income and happiness. The way that we have described this implies a causal relationship. That is, basically, higher income (independent variable) influences social networking (the mediator variable) which then influences happiness (the dependent variable). This is only established in randomised studies as is any causal relationship. That is, in order to really establish a causal relationship the researcher would have to randomly allo-

cate participants to the richer and poorer conditions and study the effects of this on both the mediator variable (social networking) and the dependent variable (happiness). Without randomisation, the causal interpretation is much more tentative. For instance, it is perfectly possible that people with extensive social networks have higher incomes as a consequence of their ability to network rather than vice versa.

A moderator variable is something quite different. It is a variable which reveals that the relationship between the independent and dependent variable is not consistent throughout the data. Imagine that, once again, the researcher is investigating the relationship between income (independent variable) and happiness (the dependent variable). However, this time the researcher is interested in whether the genders differ in terms of the size of the relationship. Imagine that for men the correlation between income and happiness is 0.6 but that for women the correlation is only 0.0. This implies quite different conclusions for men and for women. In one case there is quite a substantial correlation and in the other case no correlation. In other words, gender moderates the relationship between income and happiness. Quite clearly, how we understand the relationship between income and happiness would be different for men and women. A moderator variable does not explain the relationship, of course. We would have to consider further the explanation of why the relationship is different in women and men. It could be, for example, that women's social networks are more influenced by having children and so mixing with other women with children than men's social networks. Perhaps men's social networks are more affected by having the money to go to the pub, the golf club or the yacht club, for instance. This, of course, is to begin to ask why gender moderates the relationship between income and happiness – notice that we are hinting at possible mediating variables. Moderator variables, in themselves, are not directly about establishing causal relationships so randomisation is not an issue for the research design. Chapter 38 covers moderator variables in detail.

Quite clearly, the techniques that we have described in this chapter are ways of studying moderator and mediator variables. But there are other techniques described in this book which can also contribute. For example, interactions in ANOVA (Chapter 22) can be regarded as evidence of moderator effects as explained in Chapter 38 on moderator variables. The same is true for significant log-linear interactions (Chapter 40). The appropriate statistics really depend on whether you have score or category variables or both. However, it is the research design which influences whether or not a variable is conceived as a moderator or mediator variable. For example, if a variable cannot be influenced by the independent variable, then it can only be conceived as a moderator variable. For example, income (independent variable) cannot affect a person's gender so gender cannot be a mediator variable between income and happiness. It can, however, be a moderator variable in the relationship between income and happiness.

29.3   The calculation

The calculation of the partial correlation coefficient is fairly speedy so long as you have a correlation matrix ready made. Assuming this, the calculation should cause no problems. Computer programs for the partial correlation will normally be capable of calculating the correlation matrix for you, if necessary. Calculation 29.1 works out the relationship between verbal and numerical scores in the Table 29.1 controlling for age ($r_{XY.C}$).

Calculation 29.1

Partial correlation coefficient

The calculation is based on the correlations found in Table 29.1. The formula is as follows:

$$r_{XY.C} = \frac{r_{XY} - (r_{XC} \times r_{YC})}{\sqrt{1 - r_{XC}^2}\sqrt{1 - r_{YC}^2}}$$

where

$r_{XY.C}$ = correlation of verbal and numerical scores with age controlled as denoted by C

r_{XY} = correlation of numerical and verbal scores (= 0.97)

r_{XC} = correlation of numerical scores and age (the control variable) (= 0.80)

r_{YC} = correlation of verbal scores and age (the control variable) (= 0.85).

→

Using the values taken from the correlation matrix in Table 29.1 we find that

$$r_{XY.C} = \frac{0.97 - (0.80 \times 0.85)}{\sqrt{1 - 0.80^2}\sqrt{1 - 0.85^2}}$$

$$= \frac{0.97 - (0.68)}{\sqrt{1 - 0.64}\sqrt{1 - 0.72}}$$

$$= \frac{0.29}{\sqrt{0.36}\sqrt{0.28}} = \frac{0.29}{0.6 \times 0.53} = \frac{0.29}{0.32} = 0.91$$

Thus controlling for age has hardly changed the correlation coefficient – it decreases only very slightly from 0.97 to 0.91.

Interpreting the results   A section on interpretation follows. However, when interpreting a partial correlation you need to consider what the unpartialled correlation is. This is the baseline against which the partial correlation is understood. Although usually we would look to see if partialling reduces the size of the correlation, it can increase it.

Reporting the results   The following is one way of reporting this analysis: 'Since age was a correlate of both verbal and numerical ability, it was decided to investigate the effect of controlling for age on the correlation. After partialling, the correlation of .97 declined slightly to .91. However, this change is very small and the correlation remains very significant so age had little or no effect on the correlation between verbal and numerical abilities.'

29.4   Interpretation

What does the result of Calculation 29.1 mean? The original correlation between numerical and verbal scores of 0.97 is reduced to 0.91 when we control for age. This is a very small amount of change and we can say that controlling for age has no real influence on the original correlation coefficient.

The following is the original pattern of relationships between the three variables: the partial correlation essentially removes all the variation between verbal scores and age and also between numerical scores and age. This is rather like making these correlations zero. But, in this case, when we make these correlations zero we still find that there is a very substantial correlation between verbal and numerical scores:

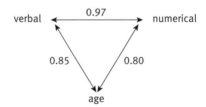

This is an important lesson since it suggests that controlling for a third variable does not always affect the correlation, despite the fact that in this case the control variable age had quite substantial relationships with both verbal and numerical ability scores. *This should be a warning that simply showing that two variables are both correlated with a third variable does not in itself establish that the third variable is responsible for the main correlation.*

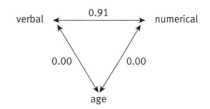

Despite this, often the partial correlation coefficient substantially changes the size of the correlation coefficient. Of course, it is important to know that a third variable does not change the correlation value. In contrast, the example in Section 29.7 and Calculation 29.3 shows a major change following partialling.

Calculation 29.2

Statistical significance of the partial correlation

The calculation of statistical significance for the partial correlation can be carried out simply using tables of the significance of the Pearson correlation coefficient such as Significance Table 10.1 or the table in Appendix C. However, in order to do this you will need to adjust the sample size by subtracting three. Thus if the sample size is 10 for the Pearson correlation, it is 10 − 3 = 7 for the partial correlation coefficient with one variable controlled. So in our example in Table 29.1, which was based on a sample of 30 teenagers, we obtain the 5% significant level from the table in Appendix C by finding the 5% value for a sample size of 30 − 3 = 27. The minimum value for statistical significance at the 5% level is 0.367 (two-tailed).

Interpreting the results The statistical significance of the partial correlation coefficient is much the same as for the Pearson correlation coefficient on which it is based. A statistically significant finding means that the partial correlation coefficient is unlikely to have been drawn from a population in which the partial correlation is zero.

Reporting the results The statistical significance of the partial correlation may be reported in exactly the same way as for any correlation coefficient. The degrees of freedom are different since they have to be adjusted for the number of control variables. If the sample size for the correlation is 10, then subtract three to give seven degrees of freedom if just one variable is being controlled for. In other words, subtract the total number of variables including the two original variables plus all of the control variables. So if there were 4 control variables in this example, the degrees of freedom become 10 − 2 − 4 = 4.

29.5 Multiple control variables

It may have struck you that there might be several variables that a researcher might wish to control for at the same time. For example, a researcher might wish to control for age and social class at the same time, or even age, social class and gender. This can be done relatively easily on a computer but is rather cumbersome to do by hand.

There are a number of terms that are used which are relatively simple if you know what they mean:

1. *Zero-order correlation* The correlation between your main variables (e.g. r_{XY}).

2. *First-order partial correlation* The correlation between your main variables controlling for just *one* variable (e.g. $r_{XY.C}$).

3. *Second-order partial correlation* The correlation between your main variables controlling for *two* variables at the same time (the symbol for this might be $r_{XY.CD}$).

Not surprisingly, we can extend this quite considerably; for example, a *fifth*-order partial correlation involves *five* control variables at the same time (e.g. $r_{XY.CDEFG}$). The principles remain the same no matter what order of partial correlation you are examining.

29.6 Suppressor variables

Sometimes you might find that you actually obtain a low correlation between two variables which you had expected to correlate quite substantially. In some instances this is because a third variable actually has the effect of reducing or suppressing the correlation between the two main variables. Partial correlation is useful in removing the inhibitory effect of this third variable. In other words, it can sometimes happen that controlling the influence of a third variable results in a *larger* correlation. Indeed, it is possible to find that an initially negative correlation becomes a positive correlation when the influence of a third variable is controlled. Figure 29.1 outlines the key steps in partial correlation.

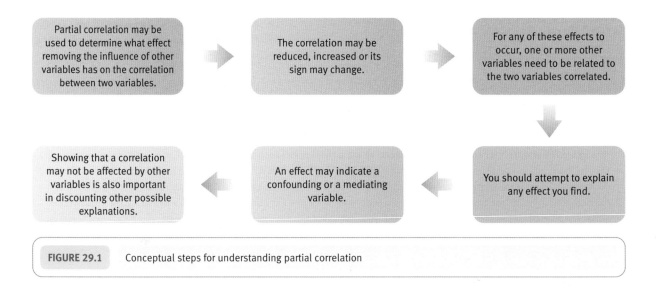

FIGURE 29.1 Conceptual steps for understanding partial correlation

29.7 An example from the research literature

Baron and Straus (1989) took the officially reported crime rates for rapes from most US states and compared these with the circulation figures for soft-core pornography in these areas. The correlation between rape rates and the amounts of pornography over these states was 0.53. (If this confuses you, the correlations are calculated 'pretending' that each state is like a person in calculating the correlation coefficient.) The temptation

Table 29.2	Correlation between rape, pornography and divorce		
	Variable *X* Rape rates	Variable *Y* Pornography circulation	Variable *C* Proportion of divorced men
Variable *X*: Rape rates	1.00	0.53	0.67
Variable *Y*: Pornography circulation		1.00	0.59
Variable *C*: Proportion of divorced men			1.00

is to interpret this correlation as suggesting that pornography leads to rape. Several authors have done so.

However, Howitt and Cumberbatch (1990) took issue with this. They pointed out that the proportions of divorced men in these areas also correlated substantially with both pornography circulation rates and rape rates. The data are listed in Table 29.2.

It might be the case that rather than pornography causing rape, the apparent relationship between these two variables is merely due to the fact that divorced men are more likely to engage in these 'alternative sexual activities'. It is a simple matter to control for this third variable, as set out in Calculation 29.3.

Calculation 29.3

Partial correlation coefficient for rape and pornography controlling for proportion of divorced men

The formula is

$$r_{XY.C} = \frac{r_{XY} - (r_{XC} \times r_{YC})}{\sqrt{1 - r_{XC}^2} \sqrt{1 - r_{YC}^2}}$$

where

$r_{XY.C}$ = correlation of rape rates with pornography controlling for proportion of divorced men

r_{XY} = correlation of rape and pornography (= 0.53)

r_{XC} = correlation of rape and proportion of divorced men (= 0.67)

r_{YC} = correlation of pornography and proportion of divorced men (= 0.59).

Using the values taken from the correlation matrix in Table 29.2 we find that:

$$r_{XY.C} = \frac{0.53 - (0.67 \times 0.59)}{\sqrt{1 - 0.67^2} \sqrt{1 - 0.59}} = 0.22$$

→

In this case, the correlation when the third variable is taken into account has changed substantially to become much nearer zero. It would be reasonable to suggest that the partial correlation coefficient indicates that there is *no* causal relationship between pornography and rape – quite a dramatic change in interpretation from the claim that pornography causes rape. The argument is not necessarily that the proportion of divorced men directly causes rape and the purchase of pornography. However, since it is an unlikely hypothesis that rape and pornography *cause* divorce then the fact that partialling out divorce reduces greatly the correlation between rape and pornography means that our faith in the original 'causal' link is reduced.

29.8 An example from a student's work

It is becoming increasingly common to teach children with special educational needs in classrooms along with other children rather than in special schools. Butler (1995a) measured the number of characteristics a sample of 14 teachers possessed which have been held to be of special importance in the effective teaching of special needs children. These qualities would include 'empathy towards special needs children', 'attitude towards integrating special needs children' and about ten others.

In order to assess the quality of the learning experience, the student researcher time-sampled children's task-centred behaviour. By this is meant the number of time periods during which the child was concentrating on the task in hand rather than, say, just wandering around the classroom causing a nuisance. The researcher rated one special needs child and one 'normal' child from each teacher's class. She found that there was a very high correlation of 0.96 between the number of qualities that a teacher possessed and the amount of time that the special needs children spent 'on task' ($df = 12$, $p < 0.01$). Interestingly, the correlation of the measure of teacher qualities with the behaviour of normal children in the class was only 0.23. The student used partial correlation to remove the task-oriented behaviour of the 'normal' children in order to control for the extent to which teacher qualities had a beneficial effect on ordinary teaching. This made absolutely no difference to the correlation between the number of qualities the teacher possessed and the amount of time special needs children spent on educational tasks. In other words, the student could be confident that she had identified qualities of teachers which were especially beneficial to special needs children.

In terms of the research design there might be some worries, as the student was well aware. In particular, in an ideal research design there would be a second observer rating the behaviour of the children in order to check the consistency of the ratings between different observers.

Key points

- If you are doing a *field* rather than a laboratory project, check your research hypotheses. If they appear to suggest that one variable *causes* another then consider using partial correlation. It can potentially enhance one's confidence about making causal interpretations if a significant correlation remains after partialling. However, caution should still be applied since there always remains a risk that an additional variable suppresses the relationship between your two main variables.

- Do not forget that even after partialling out third variables, any causal interpretation of the correlation coefficient remaining has to be tentative. No correlation coefficient (including partial correlation coefficients) can establish causality in itself. You establish causality largely through your research design, not the statistics you apply.

- Do not overlook the possibility that you may need to control more than one variable.

- Do not assume that partial correlation has no role except in seeking causal relationships. Sometimes, for example, the researcher might wish to control for male–female influences on a correlation without wishing to establish causality. Partial correlation will reveal the strength of a non-causal relationship having controlled for a third variable. Causality is something the researcher considers; it is not something built into a correlation coefficient as such.

- Do not forget to test the statistical significance of the partial correlation – as shown above, it is very easy.

COMPUTER ANALYSIS

The SPSS Statistics instruction book to this text is Dennis Howitt and Duncan Cramer (2011), *Introduction to SPSS Statistics in Psychology: For version 19 and earlier*, Harlow: Pearson. Chapter 29 in that book gives detailed step-by-step procedures for the statistics described in this chapter together with advice on how to report the results. Figure 29.2 shows the SPSS Statistics steps for a partial correlation.

Data
- Name the variables in Variable View of the Data Editor.
- Enter the data under the appropriate variable names in Data View of the Data Editor.

Analysis
- Select 'Analyze', 'Correlate' and 'Partial . . .'.

2
- Move the two variables to be correlated to the 'Variables:' box and move the variables to be controlled to the 'Controlled for:' box.

3
- Select 'Options . . .' if 'Means and standard deviations', 'Zero-order correlations' or 'Exclude cases pairwise' is needed.

Output
- Check for any difference in size and sign between the zero-order correlation and the partial correlation.
- Note whether the partial correlation is significant with a Significance of .05 or less.

FIGURE 29.2 SPSS Statistics steps for partial correlation

CHAPTER 30

Factor analysis

Simplifying complex data

Overview

- Factor analysis is used largely when the researcher has substantial numbers of variables seemingly measuring similar things. It has proven particularly useful with questionnaires.
- It examines the pattern of correlations between the variables and calculates new variables (factors) which account for the correlations. In other words, it reduces data involving a number of variables down to a smaller number of factors which encompass the original variables.
- Factors are simply variables. The correlations of factors with the original variables are known as factor loadings, although they are merely correlation coefficients. Hence they range from −1.0 through 0.0 to +1.0. It is usual to identify the nature of each factor by examining the original variables which correlate highly with it. Normally each factor is identified by a meaningful name.
- Because the process is one of reducing the original variables down to the smallest number of factors, it is important not to have too many factors. The scree plot may be used to identify those factors which are likely to be significantly different from a chance factor.
- Factors are mathematically defined to have the maximum sum of squared factor loadings at every stage. They may be more easily interpreted if they are rotated. This maximises the numbers of large factor loadings and small factor loadings while minimising the number of moderate factor loadings, making interpretation easier.
- Factor scores provide a way of treating factors like any other variable. They are similar to standard or z-scores in that they have symmetrical numbers of positive and negative values and their mean is 0.00. They can be used to compare groups in terms of their mean factor scores.

Preparation

Review variance (Chapter 5), correlation coefficient (Chapter 7) and correlation matrix (Chapter 29).

<h2>30.1   Introduction</h2>

Researchers frequently collect large amounts of data. Sometimes, speculatively, they add extra questions to a survey without any pressing reason. With data on so many variables, it becomes difficult to make sense of the complexity of the data. With questionnaires, one naturally seeks patterns in the correlations between questions. However, the sheer number of interrelationships makes this hard. Take the following brief questionnaire:

Item 1: It is possible to bend spoons by rubbing them.

Agree strongly   Agree   Neither   Disagree   Disagree strongly

Item 2: I have had 'out of body' experiences.

Agree strongly   Agree   Neither   Disagree   Disagree strongly

Item 3: Satanism is a true religion.

Agree strongly   Agree   Neither   Disagree   Disagree strongly

Item 4: Tarot cards reveal coming events.

Agree strongly   Agree   Neither   Disagree   Disagree strongly

Item 5: Speaking in tongues is a peak religious experience.

Agree strongly   Agree   Neither   Disagree   Disagree strongly

Item 6: The world was saved by visiting space beings.

Agree strongly   Agree   Neither   Disagree   Disagree strongly

Item 7: Most people are reincarnated.

Agree strongly   Agree   Neither   Disagree   Disagree strongly

Item 8: Astrology is a science, not an art.

Agree strongly   Agree   Neither   Disagree   Disagree strongly

Item 9: Animals have souls.

Agree strongly   Agree   Neither   Disagree   Disagree strongly

Item 10: Talking to plants helps them to grow.

Agree strongly   Agree   Neither   Disagree   Disagree strongly

Agree strongly could be scored as 1, agree scored as 2, neither as 3, disagree as 4 and disagree strongly as 5. This turns the words into numerical scores. Correlating the answers to each of these 10 questions with each of the others for 300 respondents generates a large correlation matrix (a table of all possible correlations between all of the possible pairs of questions). Ten questions will produce 10^2 or 100 correlations. Although the correlation matrix is symmetrical about the diagonal from top left to bottom right, there remain 45 *different* correlations to examine. Such a matrix might be much like the one in Table 30.1.

Table 30.1	Correlation matrix of 10 items									
	Item 1	Item 2	Item 3	Item 4	Item 5	Item 6	Item 7	Item 8	Item 9	Item 10
Item 1	1.00	0.50	0.72	0.30	0.32	0.20	0.70	0.30	0.30	0.10
Item 2	0.50	1.00	0.40	0.51	0.60	0.14	0.17	0.55	0.23	0.55
Item 3	0.72	0.40	1.00	0.55	0.64	0.23	0.12	0.17	0.22	0.67
Item 4	0.30	0.51	0.55	1.00	0.84	0.69	0.47	0.44	0.56	0.35
Item 5	0.32	0.60	0.64	0.84	1.00	0.14	0.77	0.65	0.48	0.34
Item 6	0.20	0.14	0.23	0.69	0.14	1.00	0.58	0.72	0.33	0.17
Item 7	0.70	0.17	0.12	0.47	0.77	0.58	1.00	0.64	0.43	0.76
Item 8	0.30	0.55	0.17	0.44	0.65	0.72	0.64	1.00	0.27	0.43
Item 9	0.30	0.23	0.22	0.56	0.48	0.33	0.43	0.27	1.00	0.12
Item 10	0.10	0.55	0.67	0.35	0.34	0.17	0.76	0.43	0.12	1.00

It is not easy to make complete sense of this; the quantity of information makes over-all interpretation difficult. Quite simply, large matrices are too much for our brains to comprehend. This is where factor analysis can be beneficial. It is a technique which helps you overcome the complexity of correlation matrices. In essence, it takes a matrix of correlations and generates a much smaller set of 'supervariables' which characterise the main trends in the correlation matrix. These supervariables or factors are generally much easier to understand than the original matrix.

30.2   A bit of history

Factor analysis is not a new technique – it dates back to shortly after the First World War. It is an invention largely of psychologists, originally to serve a very specific purpose in the field of mental testing. There are numerous psychological tests of different sorts of intellectual ability. The purpose of factor analysis was to detect which sorts of mental skills tend to go together and which are distinct abilities. It has proven more generally useful and is used in the development of psychological tests and questionnaires. Personality, attitude, intelligence and aptitude tests are often based on it since it helps select which items from the tests and measures to retain. By using factors, it is possible to obtain 'purer' measures of psychological variables. Not surprisingly, then, some theorists have used it extensively. The personality theories of researchers Raymond Cattell and Hans Eysenck (Cramer, 1992) are heavily dependent on factor analysis. The development of high-speed electronic computers has made the technique relatively routine since no longer does it require months of hand calculations.

Box 30.1	Focus on

Data issues in factor analysis

One crucial question is what sample size is appropriate for a factor analysis. There is no simple answer to this. Well, that is not quite true – often it is suggested that for every variable in the analysis there should be many more participants. You will read suggestions such as have ten times as many participants as variables in a factor analysis to get reliable outcomes. As the advice we have seen ranges from just two participants per variable in the analysis to 20 participants per variable, you have quite a lot of discretion! The alternative has tended to be to stipulate a minimum number of participants, though, once again, as these recommendations vary from 100 to 1000 participants you might well feel a little confused. Furthermore, students rarely have the opportunity to collect data from this sort of number of participants. Does this mean that they should never carry out a factor analysis?

It is not just a difficult issue for students. Professional researchers may have problems in getting samples of this sort of size. This is not merely a matter of sloth on their part. It can be notoriously difficult to obtain particular sorts of sample. For example, how much effort would be involved in getting a sample of 100 serial killers in the United Kingdom? Again, should researchers ignore factor analysis as an analytic technique in these circumstances? There are no alternatives to factor analysis which could be effectively used to do much the same job as factor analysis.

The advice we would offer is simple – but there is a more complex version that you should consider. The simple advice is to have as big a sample size as possible – the more variables, the bigger the sample size should be. Your work is almost certain to be acceptable to most researchers if it is based on 300 or more participants. The smaller your sample size is below this, the more your work is likely to be criticised by someone.

So what should one do in circumstances where this conventional criterion cannot be met? One thing to remember is that none of the sample size criteria has a real empirical justification and little in psychology is ever accepted simply on the basis of a single study. So there are circumstances in which one might be justified carrying out a factor analysis on a smaller sample size – for example, the more exploratory your study is the more you are likely to be simply trying to find interesting aspects of your data for future further exploration. Of course, one should acknowledge the limitations of your factor analysis

because of the small sample size. But we would also suggest that you consider the following:

1. It is bad practice to simply throw a bunch of variables into a factor analysis. The axiom 'junk in, junk out' applies here. Be selective about which variables you put into a factor analysis. Probably you could do a factor analysis on most of your data in the sense that a computer will perform a calculation. But what is the point of this? It is better to confine yourself to variables which you feel are likely to measure a particular concept which you think important as well. As soon as you begin to be selective, the smaller the number of variables you put into the factor analysis and the less will small sample size be a problem.

2. If you have a small sample size, then be especially vigilant when you carry out your basic examination of your data using descriptive statistics. For example, variables that have little variability; variables that produce the same response from the vast majority of participants because, for example, they are rarely agreed with; variables for which many of your participants fail to give an answer; and variables that participants have difficulty understanding may be omitted from the factor analysis. In other words, get rid of variables which are in some way problematic as they contribute junk (error) to your data. You would be well advised to do this anyway for any data.

3. The bigger the typical correlation there is between your variables, the more likely is it that your factor analysis will be reliable (stable across studies) so the more acceptable would be a smaller sample size. Similarly, the bigger the communality estimates, the smaller the sample size can be.

4. The more variables you have for each factor you extract, the more stable your analysis is likely to be. In other words, if you have only one or two factors rather than 10 factors then the more reliable your factor analysis will be.

The minimum sample size issue tends to be most strongly expressed in relation to factor analysis. Other statistical techniques tend not to be subject to the same stringency. It is important to bear in mind the sample size issue since you need to be able to estimate roughly the confidence you can place in your analysis.

Concepts in factor analysis

In order to understand factor analysis, it is useful to start with a simple and highly stylised correlation matrix such as the one in Table 30.2.

You can probably detect that there are *two* distinct clusters of variables. Variables *A*, *C* and *E* all tend to correlate with each other pretty well. Similarly, variables *B*, *D* and *F* all tend to correlate with each other. Notice that the members of the first cluster (*A*, *C*, *E*) do not correlate well with members of the second cluster (*B*, *D*, *F*) – they would not be very distinct clusters if they did. In order to make the clusters more meaningful, we need to decide what variables contributing to the first cluster (*A*, *C*, *E*) have in common; next we need to explore the similarities of the variables in the second cluster (*B*, *D*, *F*). Calling the variables by arbitrary letters does not help us very much. But what if we add a little detail by identifying the variables more clearly and relabelling the matrix of correlations as in Table 30.3?

Interpretation of the clusters is now possible. Drawing the clusters from the table we find:

1st Cluster
variable *A* = skill at batting
variable *C* = skill at throwing darts
variable *E* = skill at juggling

Table 30.2	Stylised correlation matrix between variables *A* to *F*					
	Variable A	**Variable B**	**Variable C**	**Variable D**	**Variable E**	**Variable F**
Variable *A*	1.00	0.00	0.91	−0.05	0.96	0.10
Variable *B*	0.00	1.00	0.08	0.88	0.02	0.80
Variable *C*	0.91	0.08	1.00	−0.01	0.90	0.29
Variable *D*	−0.05	0.88	−0.01	1.00	−0.08	0.79
Variable *E*	0.96	0.02	0.90	−0.08	1.00	0.11
Variable *F*	0.10	0.80	0.29	0.79	0.11	1.00

Table 30.3	Stylised correlation matrix with variable names added					
	Batting	**Crosswords**	**Darts**	**Scrabble**	**Juggling**	**Spelling**
Batting	1.00	0.00	0.91	−0.05	0.96	0.10
Crosswords	0.00	1.00	0.08	0.88	0.02	0.80
Darts	0.91	0.08	1.00	−0.01	0.90	0.29
Scrabble	−0.05	0.88	−0.01	1.00	−0.08	0.79
Juggling	0.96	0.02	0.90	−0.08	1.00	0.11
Spelling	0.10	0.80	0.29	0.79	0.11	1.00

2nd Cluster
variable *B* = skill at doing crosswords
variable *D* = skill at doing the word game Scrabble
variable *F* = skill at spelling

Once this 'fleshing out of the bones' has been done, the meaning of each cluster is somewhat more apparent. The first cluster seems to involve a general skill at hand–eye coordination; the second cluster seems to involve verbal skill.

This sort of interpretation is easy enough in clear-cut cases like this and with small correlation matrices. Life and statistics, however, are rarely that simple. Remember that in Chapter 29 on partial correlation we found that a zero correlation between two variables may become a large positive or negative correlation when we take away the influence of a third variable or a suppressor variable which is hiding the true relationship between two main variables. Similar sorts of things can happen in factor analysis. Factor analysis enables us to handle such complexities which would be next to impossible by just inspecting a correlation matrix.

Factor analysis is a mathematical procedure which reduces a correlation matrix containing many variables into a much smaller number of factors or supervariables. A supervariable cannot be measured directly and its nature has to be inferred from the relationships of the original variables with the abstract supervariable. However, in identifying the clusters above we have begun to grasp the idea of supervariables. The abilities which made up cluster 2 were made meaningful by suggesting that they had verbal skill in common.

The *output* from a factor analysis based on the correlation matrix presented above might look rather like the one in Table 30.4.

What does this table mean? There are two things to understand:

1. Factor 1 and factor 2 are like the clusters of variables we have seen above. They are really variables, but we are calling them supervariables because they take a large number of other variables into account. Ideally there should only be a small number of factors to consider.

2. The numbers under the columns for factor 1 and factor 2 are called *factor loadings*. Really they are nothing other than correlation coefficients recycled with a different name. So the variable 'skill at batting' correlates 0.98 with the supervariable which is factor 1. 'Skill at batting' does not correlate at all well with the supervariable which is factor 2 (the correlation is nearly zero at −0.01). Factor loadings follow all of the rules for correlation coefficients so they vary from −1.00 through 0.00 to +1.00.

Table 30.4	Factor loading matrix	
Variable	**Factor 1**	**Factor 2**
Skill at batting	0.98	−0.01
Skill at crosswords	0.01	0.93
Skill at darts	0.94	0.10
Skill at Scrabble	−0.07	0.94
Skill at juggling	0.97	−0.01
Skill at spelling	0.15	0.86

We interpret the meaning of factor 1 in much the same way as we interpreted the clusters above. We find the variables which correlate best with the supervariable or factor in question by looking at the factor loadings for each of the factors in turn. Usually you will hear phrases like 'batting, darts and juggling load highly on factor 1'. All this means is that they correlate highly with the supervariable, factor 1. Since we find that batting, darts and juggling all correlate well with factor 1, they must define the factor. We try to see what batting, darts and juggling have in common – once again we would suggest that hand–eye coordination is the common element. We might call the factor hand–eye coordination. Obviously there is a subjective element in this since not everyone would interpret the factors identically.

In order to interpret the meaning of a factor we need to decide which items are the most useful in identifying what the factor is about. While every variable may have something to contribute, those with the highest loadings on a factor probably have the most to contribute to its interpretation. So where does one draw the line between useful factor loadings and not so useful? Generally speaking, you will not go far wrong if you take factor loadings with an absolute value of 0.50 and above as being important in assessing the meaning of the factor. Now this is a rule of thumb and with a very big sample size then smaller factor loadings may be taken into account. With a very small sample size, then the critical size of the loading might be increased to 0.60. Generally speaking, this is not a vital issue.

When you have identified the highly loading items on the factor, write them out as a group on a piece of paper. Then peruse these items over and over again until you are able to suggest what these items seem to have in common or what it is they represent. There are no rules for doing this and, of course, different researchers may well come up with different interpretations of exactly the same list of items. This is not a problem any more than it is whenever we try to label any sort of concept.

30.4   Decisions, decisions, decisions

This entire section can be ignored by the faint-hearted who are not about to carry out a factor analysis.

Now that you have an idea of how to interpret a factor loading matrix derived from a factor analysis, it is time to add a few extra complexities. As already mentioned, factor analysis is more subjective and judgmental than most statistical techniques you have studied so far. This is not solely because of the subjectivity of interpreting the meaning of factors. There are many variants of factor analysis. By and large these are easily coped with as computers do most of the hard work. However, there are five issues that should be raised as they underlie the choices to be made.

■ Rotated or unrotated factors?

The most basic sort of factor analysis is the principal components method. It is a mathematically based technique which has the following characteristics:

1. The factors are extracted in order of magnitude from the largest to smallest in terms of the amount of variance explained by the factor. Since factors are variables they will have a certain amount of variance associated with them.

2. Each of the factors explains the *maximum amount* of variance that it possibly can.

The amount of variance 'explained' by a factor is related to something called the *eigenvalue*. This is easy to calculate since it is merely the *sum* of the *squared* factor loadings of a particular factor. Thus the eigenvalue of a factor for which the factor loadings are 0.86, 0.00, 0.93, 0.00, 0.91 and 0.00 is $0.86^2 + 0.00^2 + 0.93^2 + 0.00^2 + 0.91^2 + 0.00^2$ which equals 2.4.

But maximising each successive eigenvalue or amount of variance is a purely mathematical choice which may not offer the best factors for the purposes of understanding the conceptual underlying structure of a correlation matrix. For this reason, a number of different criteria have been suggested to determine the 'best' factors. Usually these involve maximising the number of high factor loadings on a factor and minimising the number of low loadings (much as in our stylised example). This is not a simple process because a factor analysis generates several factors – adjustments to one factor can adversely affect the satisfactoriness of the other factors. This process is called *rotation* because in pre-computer days it involved rotating (or twisting) the axes on a series of scattergrams until a satisfactory or 'simple' (i.e. easily interpreted) factor structure was obtained. Nowadays we do not use graphs to obtain this simple structure but procedures such as varimax do this for us. Principal components are the unadjusted factors which explain the greatest amounts of variance but are not always particularly easy to interpret.

These are quite abstract ideas and you may still feel a little confused as to which to use. Experimentation by statisticians suggests that the rotated factors tend to reveal underlying structures a little better than unrotated ones. We would recommend that you use rotated factors until you find a good reason not to.

Orthogonal or oblique rotation?

Routinely researchers will use *orthogonal rotations* rather than *oblique rotations*. The difference is not too difficult to grasp if you remember that factors are in essence variables, albeit supervariables:

1. Orthogonal rotation simply means that none of the factors or supervariables are actually allowed to correlate with each other. This mathematical requirement is built into the computational procedures.

2. Oblique rotation means that the factors or supervariables are allowed to correlate with each other (although they can end up uncorrelated) if this helps to simplify the interpretation of the factors. Computer procedures such as promax and oblimin produce correlated or oblique factors.

There is something known as *second-order factor analysis* which can be done if you have correlated factors. Since the oblique factors are supervariables which correlate with each other, it is possible to produce a correlation matrix of the correlations between factors. This matrix can then be factor analysed to produce new factors. Since second-order factors are 'factors of factors' they are very general indeed. You cannot get second-order factors from uncorrelated factors since the correlation matrix would contain only zeros. Some of the controversy among factor analysts is related to the use of such second-order factors.

How many factors?

We may have misled you into thinking that factor analysis reduces the number of variables that you have to consider. It can, but not automatically so, because in fact without some intervention on your part you could have as many factors as variables you started off with. This would not be very useful as it means that your factor matrix is as complex as your correlation matrix. Furthermore, it is difficult to interpret all of the factors since the later ones tend to be junk and consist of nothing other than error variance.

You need to limit the number of factors to those which are 'statistically significant'. There are no commonly available and universally accepted tests of the significance of a factor. However, one commonly accepted procedure is to ignore any factor for which the eigenvalue is less than 1.00. The reason for this is that a factor with an eigenvalue of less than 1.00 is not receiving its 'fair share' of variance by chance. What this means is that a factor with an eigenvalue under 1.00 cannot possibly be statistically significant – although this does not mean that those with an eigenvalue greater than 1.00 are actually statistically significant. For most purposes it is a good enough criterion although skilled statisticians might have other views.

Another procedure is the scree test. This is simply a graph of the amount of variance explained by successive factors in the factor analysis. The point at which the curve flattens out indicates the start of the non-significant factors.

Getting the number of factors right matters most of all when one is going to rotate the factors to a simpler structure. If you have too many factors the variance tends to be shared very thinly.

■ Communality

Although up to this point we have said that the diagonal of a correlation matrix from top left to bottom right will consists of ones, an exception is usually made in factor analysis. The reason for this is quite simple if you compare the two correlation matrices in Tables 30.5 and 30.6.

You will notice that matrix 1 contains substantially higher correlation coefficients than matrix 2. Consequently the ones in the diagonal of matrix 2 contribute a disproportionately large amount of variance to the matrix compared to the equivalent ones in matrix 1 (where the rest of the correlations are quite large anyway). The factors obtained from matrix 2 would largely be devoted to variance coming from the diagonal. In other words, the factors would have to correspond more or less to variables *A*, *B* and *C*. Hardly a satisfactory simplification of the correlation matrix. Since most psychological data tend to produce low correlations, we need to do something about the problem. The difficulty is obviously greatest when the intercorrelations between the variables tend to be small than where the intercorrelations tend to be large. This is simply because the value in the diagonal is disproportionately larger than the correlations.

Table 30.5	Correlation matrix 1		
	Variable *A*	**Variable *B***	**Variable *C***
Variable *A*	1.00	0.50	0.40
Variable *B*	0.50	1.00	0.70
Variable *C*	0.40	0.70	1.00

Table 30.6	Correlation matrix 2		
	Variable *A*	**Variable *B***	**Variable *C***
Variable *A*	1.00	0.12	0.20
Variable *B*	0.12	1.00	0.30
Variable *C*	0.20	0.30	1.00

The solution usually adopted is to substitute different values in the diagonal of the correlation matrix in place of the ones seen above. These replacement values are called the *communalities*. Theoretically, a variable can be thought of as being made of three different types of variance:

1. *Specific variance* Variance which can only be measured by that variable and is specific to that variable.

2. *Common variance* Variance which a particular variable has in common with other variables.

3. *Error variance* Just completely random variance which is not systematically related to any other source of variance.

A correlation of any variable with itself is exceptional in that it consists of all of these types of variance (that is why the correlation of a variable with itself is 1.00), whereas a correlation between two different variables consists only of variance that is common to the two variables (common variance).

Communality is in essence the correlation that a variable would have with itself based solely on common variance. Of course, this is a curious abstract concept. Obviously it is not possible to know the value of this correlation directly since variables do not come ready broken down into the three different types of variance. All that we can do is estimate the communality as best we can. The highest correlation that a variable has with any other variable in a correlation matrix is used as the communality. This is shown in Table 30.7.

So if we want to know the communality of variable *A* we look to see what its highest correlation with anything else is (in this case it is the 0.50 correlation with variable *B*). Similarly we estimate the communality of variable *B* as 0.70 since this is its highest correlation with any other variable in the matrix. Likewise the communality of variable *C* is also 0.70 since this is its highest correlation in the matrix with another variable. We then substitute these communalities in the diagonal of the matrix as shown in Table 30.8.

Table 30.7	Correlation matrix 1 (communality italicised in each column)		
	Variable *A*	Variable *B*	Variable *C*
Variable *A*	1.00	0.50	0.40
Variable *B*	*0.50*	1.00	*0.70*
Variable *C*	0.40	*0.70*	1.00

Table 30.8	Correlation matrix 1 but using communality estimates in the diagonal		
	Variable *A*	Variable *B*	Variable *C*
Variable *A*	0.50	0.50	0.40
Variable *B*	0.50	0.70	0.70
Variable *C*	0.40	0.70	0.70

Table 30.9	Part of a factor loading matrix		
		Factor 1	Factor 2
Variable A		0.50	0.70
Variable B		0.40	0.30

These first estimates can be a little rough and ready. Normally in factor analysis, following an initial stab using methods like this, better approximations are made by using the 'significant' factor loading matrix in order to 'reconstruct' the correlation matrix. For any pair of variables, the computer multiplies their two loadings on each factor, then sums the total. Thus if part of the factor loading matrix was as shown in Table 30.9, the correlation between variables A and B is $(0.50 \times 0.40) + (0.70 \times 0.30) = 0.20 + 0.21 = 0.41$. This is not normally the correlation between variables A and B found in the original data but one based on the previously estimated communality and the significant factors. However, following such a procedure for the entire correlation matrix does provide a slightly different value for each communality compared with our original estimate. These new communality estimates can be used as part of the factor analysis. The whole process can be repeated over and over again until the best possible estimate is achieved. This is usually referred to as a process of *iteration* – successive approximations to give the best estimate.

Actually, as a beginner to factor analysis you should not worry too much about most of these things for the simple reason that you could adopt an off-the-peg package for factor analysis which, while not satisfying every researcher, will do the job pretty well until you get a little experience and greater sophistication.

Factor scores

We often carry out a factor analysis to determine whether we can group a larger number of variables such as questionnaire items into a smaller set of 'supervariables' or factors. For example, we may have made up 10 questions to measure the way in which people express anxiety and a further 10 questions to assess how they exhibit depression. Suppose that the results of our factor analysis show that all or almost all of the 10 questions on anxiety load most highly on one of these factors and all or almost all of the 10 questions on depression load most highly on the other factor. This result would suggest that rather than analyse each of the 20 questions separately we could combine the answers to the 10 questions on anxiety to form one measure of anxiety and combine the answers to the 10 questions on depression to form a measure of depression. In other words, rather than have 20 different measures to analyse, we now have two measures. This greatly simplifies our analysis.

The most common way of combining variables which are measured on the same scale is to simply add together the numbers which represent that scale. This is sometimes referred to as a summative scale. For example, if respondents only had to answer 'Yes' or 'No' to each of our 20 questions, then we could assign an answer which indicated the presence of either anxiety or depression a higher number than an answer which reflected the absence of either anxiety or depression. We could assign the number 2 to show the presence of either anxiety or depression and the number 1 to show the absence of either anxiety or depression. Alternatively, we could assign the number 1 to indicate the presence of either anxiety or depression and the number 0 to the absence of either. We would then add together the numbers for the anxiety items to form a total or overall anxiety score and do the same for the depression items. If we had assigned the number 2 to indicate the presence of either anxiety or depression, then the total score for these two variables would vary between a minimum score of 10 and a maximum score of 20. Alternatively, if we had assigned the number 1 to reflect the presence of either anxiety or depression, then the total score for these two variables would vary between a minimum score of 0 and a maximum score of 10.

Another way of assigning numbers to each of the variables or items that go to make up a factor is to use the factor score for each factor. There are various ways of producing factor scores and this is generally done with the computer program which carries out the factor analysis. A factor score may be based on all the items in the factor analysis. The items which load or correlate most highly on a factor are generally weighted the most heavily. So, for example, anxiety items which load or correlate most highly with the anxiety factor will make a larger contribution to the factor score for that factor. Factor scores may be positive or negative but will have a mean of zero. The main advantage of factor scores is that they are more closely related to the results of the factor analysis. In other words, scores represent these factors more accurately. Their disadvantage is that the results of a factor analysis of the same variables are likely to vary according to the method used and from sample to sample so that the way that the factor scores are derived is likely to vary. Unless we have access to the data, we will not know how the factor scores were calculated.

One key thing to remember about factor scores is that they allow you to use the factors as if they were like any other variable. So they can be correlated with other variables, for example, or they might be used as the dependent variable in ANOVA.

30.5   Exploratory and confirmatory factor analysis

So far, we have presented factor analysis as a means of simplifying complex data matrices. In other words, factor analysis is being used to explore the structure (and, as a consequence, the meaning) of the data. This is clearly a very useful analytical tool. Of course, the danger is that the structure obtained through these essentially mathematical procedures is assumed to be the basis for a definitive interpretation of the data. This is problematic because of the inherent variability of most psychological measurements which suggest that the factors obtained in exploratory factor analysis may themselves be subject to variability.

As a consequence, it has become increasingly common to question the extent to which exploratory factor analysis can be relied upon. One development from this is the notion of confirmatory factor analysis. Put as simply as possible, confirmatory factor analysis is a means of confirming that the factor structure obtained in exploratory factor analysis is robust and not merely the consequence of the whims of random variability in one's data. Obviously it would be silly to take the data and re-do the factor analysis. That could only serve to check for computational errors. However, one could obtain a new set of data using more or less the same measures as in the original study. Then it is possible to factor analyse these data to test the extent to which the characteristics of the original factor analysis are reproduced in the fresh factor analysis of fresh data. In this way, it may be possible to confirm the original analysis. Box 30.2 contains more information about confirmatory factor analysis. Figure 30.1 gives the key steps in exploratory factor analysis.

Exploratory factor analysis is useful for seeing whether a number of variables such as questionnaire items can be grouped together to form a single index or factor.

Factor analysis produces as many factors as there are variables.

The factors are produced in terms of the amount of variance they account for with the first factor explaining the most variance and the last factor the least variance.

Factors are rotated to make their meaning clearer by maximising the higher correlations of variables with a factor and minimising the lower correlations.

The meaning of a factor needs to be interpreted in terms of the meaning of the variables that correlate most highly with it.

The variables that correlate most highly together may be combined to form a single score or index.

FIGURE 30.1 Conceptual steps for exploratory factor analysis

Box 30.2 Key concepts

Confirmatory versus exploratory factor analysis

Most of this chapter discusses factor analysis as a means of exploring data. Probably this process is best regarded as a way of throwing up hypotheses about the nature of relationships between variables than definitive evidence that the underlying structure of the data is that indicated by the factors. There are a number of reasons why one should be careful about exploratory factor analyses such as the ones described in this chapter. One reason is that sometimes we have to interpret the factors on the basis of very limited information. Another reason is that the results of a factor analysis are somewhat dependent on the choice of method of factor analysis adopted. So when some authorities write of factor analysis as being a good hypothesis generating tool rather than a good hypothesis confirming tool, the reasons for caution become obvious as well as the reasons for the great popularity of factor analysis. It is probably going too far to describe exploratory factor analysis as 'shotgun empiricism' or 'empiricism gone mad'. Anyone who has carried out an exploratory factor analysis will realise that identifying the nature of a factor is a somewhat creative act – and often based on relatively little information.

So why confirmatory factor analysis? The reasons are not to do with the inadequacies of the factor analysis methods described in this chapter. Factor analysis is generally regarded as a very powerful analytic technique. The problem lies more with the way in which it is employed rather than its computational procedures. Ideally, in research, knowledge and understanding should be built on previous research. Out of this previous research, 'models' or sets of variables are built up which effectively account for observed data. Frequently factor analysis is used simply to explore the data and to suggest the underlying nature of the relationships between variables. As a consequence, there is no model or hypothesis to test. It is at the stage at which there is a clear model or hypothesis that analyses can be used to properly test that model or hypothesis. So the reason why factor analysis cannot be used for model and hypothesis testing is that there is nothing to be tested. If there was a model or hypothesis available, then factor analysis could be used to test that model or hypothesis. This is a traditional approach which uses principal axes factor analysis. The researcher would include 'indicator variables' in the data to be factor analysed. These indicator variables would have predicted relationships with the factors. For example, if a factor is proposed to be 'feminist attitudes' an appropriate indicator variable for this might be gender as it might be a reasonable supposition that females would be more inclined towards feminist views. Gender would load heavily on the factor if the factor and its relationship with the indicator variable was as expected by the researcher.

The modern approach is to use some sort of structural equation modelling procedure such as employed by the computer software *LISREL*, though there are others. The researcher must begin with a hypothesis about the relationships between variables and factors as well as which (if any) factors are interrelated with each other. The hypothesis is based on a reserve of theoretical and empirical resources which have been built up from previous investigations in that research field. Typically the researcher will have an idea of how many different factors are required to account for the data which ultimately consist of a correlation matrix of relationships between variables. The researcher will have hypotheses about what variables will correlate with which factors or which factors will correlate with each other. Of course, a number of different models will always be potentially viable for any given set of data. Hence the researcher will have more than a single model to compare.

Models are specified by the research by fixing (or freeing) certain specific characteristics of the model. This could be the number of factors or the size of the correlation between factors or any other aspect deemed appropriate. These various models are compared for their adequacy by assessing how well the different models may fit the data. The best fitting model is, of course, the preferred model – though if there is any competition then the simplest (most parsimonious) model will be selected. Of course, there may be a better model that the researcher has not formulated or tested. The fit of the models to the data is assessed by a number of statistics including the chi-square/degrees of freedom or a number of alternative statistics.

30.6 An example of factor analysis from the literature

Butler (1995b) points out that children at school spend a lot of time looking at the work of their classmates. Although the evidence for this is clear, the reasons for their doing so are not researched. She decided to explore children's motives for looking at the work of other children and proposed a four component model of the reasons they gave. Some children could be concerned mainly about learning to do the task and developing their skills and mastery of a particular type of task; other children might be more concerned with the quality of the product of their work. Furthermore, a child's motivation might be to evaluate themselves (self-evaluation); on the other hand, their primary motivation might be in terms of evaluating the product of their work on the task. In other words, Butler proposed two dichotomies which might lead to a fourfold categorisation of motivations for looking at other children's work (Table 30.10).

Based on this sort of reasoning, the researcher developed a questionnaire consisting of 32 items, 'Why I looked at other children's work'. Raters allocated a number of items to each of the above categories and the best eight items in each category were chosen for this questionnaire.

Table 30.10	Butler's model of reasons to look at the work of others	
	Product improvement	**Self-improvement**
Performance oriented	Doing better than others with little effort	Comparing task skills with those of others
Mastery oriented	Wanting to learn and improve	Checking whether own work needs improving

An example of a question from this questionnaire is:

I wanted to see if my work is better or worse than others.

The children's answers had been coded from 1 to 5 according to their extent of agreement with the statements.

Each child was given a page of empty circles on which they drew many pictures using these circles as far as possible. When this had been completed, they answered the 'Why I looked at other children's work' questionnaire. The researcher's task was then to establish whether her questionnaire actually consisted of the four independent 'reasons' for looking at the work of other children during the activity.

An obvious approach to this questionnaire is to correlate the scores of the sample of children on the various items on the questionnaire. This produced a 32 × 32 correlation matrix which could be factor analysed to see whether the four categories of motives for looking at other children's work actually emerged:

> 'Principal-components analysis[1] with oblique rotation[2] yielded five factors with eigenvalues greater than 1.0[3] which accounted for 62% of the variance[4] . . . Three factors corresponded to the mastery-oriented product improvement (MPI), performance-oriented product improvement (PPI), and performance-oriented self-evaluation (PSE) categories, but some items loaded high on more than one factor[5]. Items expected a priori to load on a mastery-oriented self-evaluation (MSE) category formed two factors. One (MSE) conformed to the original conceptualization, and the other (checking procedure [CP]) reflected concern with clarifying task demands and instructions.'

(Butler, 1995b, p. 350, superscripts added)

The meaning of the superscripted passages is as follows:

1. Principal components analysis was the type of factor analysis employed – it means that communalities were *not* used. Otherwise the term 'principal axes' is used where communalities have been estimated.

2. Oblique rotation means that the factors may well correlate with each other. That is, if one correlates the factor loadings on each factor with the factor loadings on each of the other factors, a correlation matrix would be produced in which the correlations may differ from zero. Orthogonal rotation would have produced a correlation matrix of the factors in which the correlation coefficients are all zero.

3. This means that there are five factors which are potentially statistically significant – the minimum value of a potentially significant eigenvalue is 1.0 although this is only a *minimum* value and no guarantee of statistical significance.

4. These five factors explain 62% of the variance, apparently. That is, the sum of the squared factor loadings on these five factors is 62% of the squared correlation coefficients in the 32 × 32 correlation matrix. Doing this is problematic for oblique rotation as the factors are correlated which means that the variance of a factor is not specific to that factor.

5. In factor analysis, some items may load on more than one factor – this implies that they are measuring aspects of more than one factor.

Table 30.11 gives an adapted version of the factor analysis table in which some items have been omitted for simplicity's sake in the presentation.

You will notice from Table 30.11 that many factor loadings are missing. This is because the researcher has chosen not to report low factor loadings on each factor. This

Table 30.11	Butler's factor loading matrix				
Item: I wanted to see . . .	Performance-oriented self-evaluation	Mastery-oriented product improvement	Checking procedures	Performance-oriented product improvement	Mastery-oriented self-evaluation
Who had the most ideas	0.61	–	–	−0.37	–
Whose work was best	0.74	–	–	–	–
If others had better ideas than me	0.68	–	–	–	–
Whether there were ideas I hadn't thought of	–	0.68	–	–	0.34
Ideas which would help me develop my own ideas	–	0.68	–	–	–
If I'd understood what to do	–	–	0.85	–	–
Whether my drawings were appropriate	–	–	0.86	–	–
If I was working at the appropriate speed	–	–	–	–	0.63
How I was progressing on this new task	–	–	–	–	0.70
I didn't want to hand in poor work	–	–	–	0.67	–
I didn't want my page to be emptier than others'	–	–	–	0.74	–

Factor loadings with absolute values less than 0.30 are not reported.
Source: Table adapted from Butler (1995b).

has the advantage of simplifying the factor loading matrix by emphasising the stronger relationships. The disadvantage is that the reporting of the analysis is incomplete and it is impossible for readers of the report to explore the data further. (If the original 32×32 correlation matrix had been included then it would be possible to reproduce the factor analysis and carry out variants on the original analysis.)

The researcher has inserted titles for the factors in the matrix. Do not forget that these titles are arbitrary and the researcher's interpretation. Consequently, you may wish to consider the extent to which her titles are adequate. The way to do this is to examine the set of questions which load highly on each of the factors to see whether a radically different interpretation is possible. Having done this you may feel that Butler's interpretations are reasonable. Butler's difficulty is that she has five factors when her model would predict only four. While this means that she is to a degree wrong, her model is substantially correct because the four factors she predicted appear to be present in the factor analysis. The problem is that some of the questionnaire items do not appear to measure what she suggested they should measure.

Some researchers might be tempted to re-do the factor analysis with just four factors. The reason for this is that the proper number of factors to extract in factor analysis is not clear-cut. Because Butler used a minimal cut-off point for significant factors (eigenvalues of 1.0 and above), she may have included more factors than she needed to. It would strengthen Butler's argument if such a re-analysis found that four factors reproduced Butler's model better. However, we should stress that factor analysis does not lead to hard-and-fast solutions and that Butler would be better confirming her claims by the analysis of a fresh study using the questionnaire.

30.7 Reporting the results

There is no standard way of reporting the results of a factor analysis which will suffice irrespective of circumstances. However, it is essential to report the type of factor analysis, the type of rotation, how the number of factors was determined, and the relative importance of the factors in terms of variance explained or eigenvalues. Although the original author's description is given above, the following is another way of writing much the same. More examples are to be found in the companion computer guide to this book (see the end of the chapter).

'A principal components factor analysis was conducted on the correlation matrix of the 36 items on the "Why I looked at other children's work" questionnaire. Five factors were extracted which accounted for 62% of the variance overall. Three of these factors corresponded to components of the proposed model. Oblique rotation of the factors was employed which yielded the factor structure given in Table 30.11. One factor was identified as *mastery-oriented product improvement (MPI)*, another was *performance-oriented product improvement (PPI)* and a third was *performance-oriented self-evaluation (PSE)*. These are as the model predicted. The fourth category predicted by the model (*mastery-oriented self-evaluation (MSE)*) was also identified but some of the items expected to load on this actually formed the fifth factor *checking procedures*.'

Notice that some aspects of this description would be fairly general to any factor analysis, but there are other aspects which are idiosyncratic in nature and due to the distinctive characteristics and purposes of this particular study. Ideally, you should study reports of factor analyses which are similar to yours (coming from the same area of research) for more precise examples of how your work could be reported.

Key points

- Do not be afraid to try out factor analysis on your data. It is not difficult to do if you are familiar with using simpler techniques on a computer.

- Do not panic when faced with output from a factor analysis. It can be very lengthy and confusing because it contains things that mere mortals simply do not want to know. Usually the crucial aspects of the factor analysis are to be found towards the end of the output. If in doubt, do not hesitate to contact your local expert – computer output is not always user friendly.

- Take the factor analysis slowly – it takes a while to build your skills sufficiently to be totally confident.

- Do not forget that interpreting the factors can be fairly subjective – you might not always see things as other people do and it might not be you who is wrong.

- Factor analysis can be applied only to correlations calculated using the Pearson correlation formula.

COMPUTER ANALYSIS

The SPSS Statistics instruction book to this text is Dennis Howitt and Duncan Cramer (2011), *Introduction to SPSS Statistics in Psychology: For version 19 and earlier*, Harlow: Pearson. Chapter 30 in that book gives detailed step-by-step procedures for the statistics described in this chapter together with advice on how to report the results. Chapter 51 does this for confirmatory factor analysis using LISREL. Figure 30.2 shows the SPSS Statistics steps for exploratory factor analysis.

Data
- Name the variables in Variable View of the Data Editor.
- Enter the data under the appropriate variable names in Data View of the Data Editor.

Analysis
- Select 'Analyze', 'Dimension on Reduction' and 'Factor . . .'.
- Move the variables to be analysed to the 'Variables:' box.

2
- Select 'Descriptives . . .', 'Univariate descriptives' and 'Continue'.
- Select 'Extraction . . .', 'Method' of extraction if different from principal components, 'Scree test' and 'Continue'.

3
- Select 'Rotation . . .', method of rotation and 'Continue'.
- Select 'Options . . .', 'Sorted by size' and 'Continue'.

Output
- The analysis may not complete if any variable has no variance and if the number of iterations needed is greater than the default of 25. Adjust analysis accordingly.
- Check the sample size in the 'Descriptive Statistics' table.

2
- Check the meaning of the variables correlating most highly on the rotated factors to determine the meaning of the factors.

3
- You may need to redo the analysis on the basis of your judgement of how many factors should be extracted. This judgement is dependent on the outcome of the Scree test.

FIGURE 30.2 SPSS Statistics steps for exploratory factor analysis

Recommended further reading

Bryman, A. and Cramer, D. (2007), *Quantitative Data Analysis with SPSS 14 and 15: A Guide for Social Scientists*, London: Routledge, Chapter 11.

Child, D. (1970), *The Essentials of Factor Analysis*, London: Holt, Rinehart & Winston.

Kline, P. (1994), *An Easy Guide to Factor Analysis*, London: Routledge.

Tabachnick, B.G. and Fidell, L.S. (2007), *Using Multivariate Statistics*, 5th edition, New York: Allyn and Bacon, Chapter 13.

CHAPTER 31

Multiple regression and multiple correlation

Overview

- So far we have studied regression and correlation in which just two variables are used – variable X and variable Y. We can consider variable X the independent or predictor variable and variable Y the dependent or criterion variable.

- The terms independent and dependent variable do not imply a causal relationship between the two variables.

- Multiple regression and correlation are extensions of the two variable regressions to include several different X variables (X_1, X_2, X_3, . . .). Only one Y variable is involved. If we wish to relate how well a student does in an examination, we may wish to correlate examination performance with intelligence. This would be simple or bivariate correlation (or regression). If we considered an additional variable – amount of preparation – to intelligence then we might expect higher correlations with examination performance.

- Multiple regression and correlation basically indicate the best predictor of the Y variable, then the next best predictor (correlate) and so forth. They indicate how much weight to give to each predictor to yield the best prediction or correlation.

- There are many versions of multiple regression which are appropriate in different circumstances.

- Usually there are two versions of multiple regression. One works with the original scores and yields unstandardised regression or b-weights. Another version works with the scores turned into z-scores. This yields standardised regression or beta (β) weights which are essentially correlation coefficients. The advantage of beta weights is that they are standardised values and so independent of the variance of the original variables. This means that they can be compared directly.

→

31.1   Introduction

Traditionally, psychologists have assumed that the primary purpose of research is to isolate the influence of one variable on another. So researchers might examine whether paternal absence from the family during childhood leads to poor mathematical skills in children. The fundamental difficulty with this is that other variables which might influence a child's mathematical skills are ignored. In real life, away from the psychology laboratory, variables do not act independently of each other. An alternative approach is to explore the complex pattern of variables which may relate to mathematical skills. Numerous factors may be involved in mathematical ability including maternal educational level, the quality of mathematical teaching at school, the child's general level of intelligence or IQ, whether or not the child went to nursery school, the gender of the child and so forth. We rarely know all the factors which might be related to important variables such as mathematical skills before we begin research; so we will tend to include some variables which turn out to be poor predictors of the criterion. Multiple regression quite simply helps us choose empirically the most effective set of predictors for any criterion.

Multiple regression can be carried out with scores or standardised scores (z-scores). Standardised multiple regression has the advantage of making the regression values directly analogous to correlation coefficients. The consequence of this is that it is easy to make direct comparisons between the influence of different variables. In unstandardised multiple regression the variables are left in their original form. Standardised and unstandardised multiple regression are usually done simultaneously by computer programs.

31.2   Theoretical considerations

The techniques described in this chapter concern linear multiple regression which assumes that the relationships between variables fall approximately on a straight line.

Multiple regression is an extension of simple (or bivariate) regression (Chapter 8). In simple regression, a single dependent variable (or criterion variable) is related to a single independent variable (or predictor variable). For example, marital satisfaction may be regressed against the degree to which the partners have similar personalities. In other words, can marital satisfaction be predicted from the degree of personality similarity between partners? In multiple regression, on the other hand, the criterion is regressed against several potential predictors. For example, to what extent is marital satisfaction related to various factors such as socio-economic status of both partners, similarity in socio-economic status, religious affiliation, similarity in religious affiliation, duration of courtship, age of partners at marriage and so on? Of course, personality similarity might be included in the list of predictors studied.

Multiple regression serves two main functions:

1. To determine the minimum number of predictors needed to predict a criterion. Some of the predictors which are significantly related to the criterion may also be correlated with each other and so may not all be necessary to predict the criterion. Say, for example, that the two predictors of attraction to one's spouse and commitment to one's marriage both correlate highly with each other and that both these variables were positively related to the criterion of marital satisfaction (although marital commitment is more strongly related to marital satisfaction than is attraction to the spouse). If most of the variation between marital satisfaction and attraction to the spouse was also shared with marital commitment, then marital commitment alone may be sufficient to predict marital satisfaction. Another example of this would be the industrial psychologist who wished to use psychological tests to select the best applicants for a job. Obviously a lot of time and money could be saved if redundant or very overlapping tests could be weeded out, leaving just a minimum number of tests which predict worker quality.

2. To explore whether certain predictors remain significantly related to the criterion when other variables are controlled or held constant. For example, marital commitment might be partly a function of religious belief so that those who are more religious may be more satisfied with their marriage. We may be interested in determining whether marital commitment is still significantly related to marital satisfaction when strength of religious belief is controlled.

To explain multiple regression, it is useful to remember the main features of simple regression. These are listed below as a quick summary of what you need to know already so that you can study this chapter effectively. Generally speaking, multiple regression as dealt with in this chapter is a relatively straightforward extension of simple regression:

1. Simple regression can be represented by the scatterplot in Figure 31.1 in which values of the criterion are arranged along the vertical axis and values of the predictor are arranged along the horizontal axis. For example, marital satisfaction may be the criterion and personality similarity the predictor. Each point on the scatterplot indicates the position of the criterion and predictor scores for a particular individual in the sample. The relationship between the criterion and the predictor is shown by the slope of the straight line through the points on the scattergram. This best-fitting straight line is the one which minimises the sum of the (squared) distances between the points and their position on the line. This slope is known as the regression coefficient.

2. The intercept constant is the point at which the regression line intersects or cuts the vertical axis, in other words, the value on the vertical axis when the value on the horizontal axis is zero. Confusingly, in multiple regression this is sometimes referred to as the coefficient of the intercept. It is a constant and so is not variable.

3. To determine the predicted score of the criterion from a particular score of the predictor, we draw a line parallel to the vertical axis from the score on the horizontal axis to the regression line. From here we draw a second line parallel to the horizontal axis to the vertical axis, which gives us the predicted score of the criterion. More precisely, we can use the regression weights to make our prediction. In this, we simply multiply the regression weight by the score that we are interested in on the independent variable and add the regression weight (i.e. cut point) for the intercept. This gives us our predicted score.

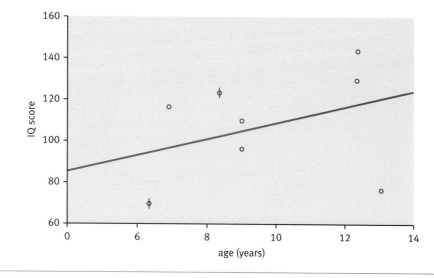

FIGURE 31.1 A simple scatterplot

4. Unless there is a perfect relationship between the predictor and the criterion, the predicted score of the criterion will usually differ from the actual score for a particular case.

5. Unlike the correlation coefficient, regression is dependent on the variability of the units of measurement involved. This makes regressions on different samples and different variables very difficult to compare. However, we can standardise the scores on the predictor and the criterion variables. By expressing them as standard scores (i.e. z-scores), each variable will have a mean of 0 and a standard deviation of 1. Furthermore, the intercept or intercept constant will always be 0 in these circumstances.

■ Regression equations

Simple regression is usually expressed in terms of the following regression equation as we have already mentioned in the brief notes on simple regression:

$$\underset{\substack{\text{predicted score on} \\ \text{criterion variable}}}{Y} = \underset{\text{intercept constant}}{a} + \underset{\substack{\text{regression coefficient} \\ \times \text{predictor score}}}{bX}$$

In other words, to predict a particular criterion score, we multiply the particular score of the predictor by the regression coefficient and add to it the intercept constant. Note that the values of the intercept constant and the regression coefficient remain the same for the equation, so the equation can be seen as describing the relationship between the criterion and the predictor.

When the scores of the criterion and the predictor are standardised to z-scores, the regression coefficient is the same as Pearson's correlation coefficient and ranges from +1.00 through 0.00 to −1.00. Regression weights standardised in this way are known as beta weights.

In multiple regression, the regression equation is the same except that there are several predictors and each predictor has its own (partial) regression coefficient:

$$Y = a + b_1X_1 + b_2X_2 + b_3X_3 + \ldots$$

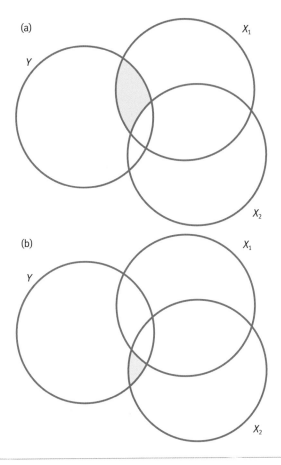

FIGURE 31.2   Venn diagrams illustrating partial regression coefficients

A partial regression coefficient expresses the relationship between a particular predictor and the criterion controlling for, or partialling out, the relationship between that predictor and all the other predictors in the equation. This ensures that each predictor variable provides an independent contribution to the prediction.

The relationship between the criterion and the predictors is often described in terms of the percentage of variance of the criterion that is *explained* or *accounted for* by the predictors. (This is much like the coefficient of determination for the correlation coefficient.) One way of illustrating what the partial regression coefficient means is through a Venn diagram (Figure 31.2) involving the criterion Y and the two predictors X_1 and X_2. Each of the circles signifies the amount of variance of one of the three variables. The area shaded in Figure 31.2a is common only to X_1 and Y, and represents the variance of Y that it shares with variable X_1. The shaded area in Figure 31.2b is shared only by X_2 and Y, and signifies the amount of variance of Y that it shares with variable X_2. Often a phrase such as 'the amount of variance explained by variable X' is used instead of 'the amount of variance shared by variable X'. Both terms signify the amount of overlapping variance.

> ## Box 31.1 Focus on

Standardised or unstandardised regression weights

Regression can involve the raw scores or standard scores. Computers will usually print out both sorts.

1. Regression involving 'standard scores' gives regression coefficients (weights) which can more readily be compared in terms of their size since they range between +1.0 and −1.0 like simple correlation coefficients (i.e. Pearson correlation). In other words, the predictor variables are comparable irrespective of the units of measurement on which they were originally based. This is just like any other standard scores (Chapter 5). The regression weights for this are usually called beta (β).

2. Regression involving 'non-standardised scores' or raw scores is about the 'nuts and bolts' of prediction. The unstandardised regression coefficient (weight) can take, theoretically, any positive or negative value. Like our account of simple regression, it provides predicted numerical values for the criterion variable based on an individual's scores on the various predictor variables. However, the size of the regression coefficient (weight) is no indication of the importance of the unstandardised predictor since the size is dependent on the units of measurement involved. The unstandardised regression weight is usually given the symbol b.

■ Selection

Since multiple regression is particularly useful with a large number of predictors, such an analysis potentially would involve many regression equations. That is to say, one might stipulate a wide variety of different 'models' to examine in the multiple regression. Obviously the complexity of the analysis could be awesome. In practice, however, a researcher does not need to consider every possible regression equation when carrying out multiple regression. This involves deciding the broad analysis strategy for the multiple regression and stipulating this as part of the analysis and when running multiple regression on a computer package. A number of different approaches have been suggested for selecting and testing predictors. These approaches include *hierarchical* (or *blockwise*) *selection* and *stepwise selection*. Hierarchical selection enters predictors into the regression equation on some practical or theoretical consideration. Stepwise selection employs statistical criteria to choose the smallest set of predictors which best predict the variation in the criterion. In contrast to these methods, entering all predictors into the regression equation is known as *standard* or *simultaneous* multiple regression. Finally, *setwise* regression compares all possible sets of predictors such as all predictors singly, in pairs, in trios and so on until the best set of predictors is identified.

1. *Hierarchical selection* Predictors are entered singly or in blocks according to some practical or theoretical rationale. For example, potentially confounding variables such as socio-demographic factors may be statistically controlled by entering them first into the regression equation. Alternatively, similar variables may be grouped (or 'blocked') together and entered as a block, such as a block of personality variables, a block of attitude variables and so on. The computer tells us the net influence of each block in turn.

2. *Stepwise selection* The predictor with the highest zero-order correlation is entered first into the regression equation if it explains a significant proportion of the variance of the criterion. The second predictor to be considered for entry is that which has the highest partial correlation with the criterion. If it explains a significant proportion of the variance of the criterion, it is entered into the equation. At this point, the

Multiple regression is often used to determine which predictors are significantly associated with a criterion taking into account that the predictors may be significantly related to each other.

It is also used to determine the amount of variance in the criterion that is explained by predictors or groups of predictors.

The relative importance of predictors may be compared by examining the size of the standardised (partial) regression or beta coefficients between the criterion and the predictors.

The sign of the coefficient indicates the direction of the relation between the criterion and a predictor.

Bigger coefficients indicate a stronger relation between the criterion and a predictor than smaller coefficients.

It may also be judged by the amount of variance in the criterion that is explained just by that predictor taking other predictors into account.

FIGURE 31.3 Conceptual steps for a multiple regression

predictor which was entered first is examined to see if it still explains a significant proportion of the variance of the criterion. If it no longer does so, it is dropped from the equation. The analysis continues with the predictor which has the next highest partial correlation with the criterion. The process stops when no more predictors are entered into or removed from the equation.

Box 31.2 gives an overview of some of the possibilities for multiple regression analyses. Figure 31.3 shows the key steps in a multiple regression.

Box 31.2   Focus on

Different approaches to multiple regression

Among the choices of methods for multiple regression are:

- Single-stage entry of all predictors and all predictors are employed whether or not they are likely to be good predictors (i.e. irrespective of their potential predictive power).

- Blocks: There are circumstances in which the researcher does not wish to enter all of the variables at the same time. Instead, it is possible to enter the predictors in sets, one set at a time. These are sets specified by the researcher and are usually called blocks. There can be any number of variables in a block from a minimum of one. There are a number of advantages to this. Putting variables into blocks allows the variables in the block to be analysed together, either before or after

other variables. One might put variables into blocks because they are similar in some way. For instance, they may be a particular type of variable (e.g. health variables, education variables, social class variables could all form separate blocks). Another use is to 'control' for certain variables first – that is, age and social class may be entered as the first block. This is often done as a way of controlling for the influence of demographic variables. If the first block included demographic variables such as gender, age and social class, this is the equivalent of partialling them out of the analysis (see Chapter 29). Once this is done, one can compare the outcome of this block with what happens when other predictors are introduced. This is known as hierarchical multiple regression.

- Finding best predictors: The analysis may proceed on a stepwise basis by finding the best predictors in a set of predictors and eliminating the poor predictors. This is particularly appropriate where the main objective of the researcher is to predict with the highest possible accuracy – rather than to find explanatory models of influences on the dependent variable.

- Reverse (backwards) elimination of predictors: In this the first model is initially employed. That is, the model in our earlier example is calculated. All of the predictor variables are included. Having done that, the worst predictor is dropped. Usually this is the least significant predictor. Essentially the model is recalculated on the basis of the remaining predictors. Then the remaining worst predictor is dropped and again the model re-calculated. The researcher is looking to see whether dropping a variable or variables actually substantially worsens the model. This is not simply a matter of the goodness-of-fit of the model to the data; some models may be better at predicting one value of the dependent variable rather than the other. If one is trying to avoid letting men out of prison early if they are likely to re-offend, the model which maximises the number of recidivists (re-offenders) correctly identified may be preferred over the model which misclassifies recidivists

as likely to be non-recidivists. This is obviously a complex judgement based on a wide variety of considerations.

- There are models which mix blocks and stepwise approaches.

- In this chapter, we largely deal with individual predictors acting alone or their combined effects on the dependent variable. Following the General Linear Model (see Box 8.1), this essentially means that the analysis adds a standard amount to the prediction of the dependent variable for each increment in each of the predictor (independent) variables. In other words, the effects of the independent variables are additive. It is, however, possible to deal with interactions between predictors in multiple regression just as we do in analysis of variance (ANOVA). This is discussed in detail in Chapter 38 which deals with moderator variables.

Except for the simple case where the maximum possible accuracy of prediction is required and all variables may be entered en masse, the choice of approach is a matter of judgement that partly comes with experience and practice. It does no harm to try out a variety of approaches on one's data, especially if one is inexperienced with the techniques. Though, of course, one has to be able to justify the final choice of model.

31.3 Stepwise multiple regression example

Since we will need to use standard multiple regression to carry out path analysis in the next chapter, we will illustrate stepwise multiple regression in the present chapter. Our example asks whether a person's educational achievement (the criterion variable) can be predicted from their intellectual ability, their motivation to do well in school and their parents' interest in their education (the predictor variables). The minimum information we need to carry out a multiple regression is the number of people in the sample and the correlations between all the variables, though you would normally work with the actual scores when carrying out a multiple regression. It has been suggested that with stepwise regression it is desirable to have 40 times more cases than predictors. Since we have three predictors, we will say that we have a sample of 120 cases. (However, much reported research fails to follow this rule of thumb.) In order to interpret the results of multiple regression it is usually necessary to have more information than this, but for our purposes the fictitious correlation matrix presented in Table 31.1 should be sufficient. The full analysis along with the data can be found in the companion computer analysis book – see the end of the chapter.

The calculation of multiple regression with more than two predictors is complicated and so will not be shown. However, the basic results of a stepwise multiple regression analysis are given in Table 31.2. What this simple example shows is that only two of the three 'predictors' actually explain a significant percentage of variance in educational

Table 31.1	Correlation matrix for a criterion (educational achievement) and three predictors		
	Educational achievement	Intellectual ability	School motivation
Intellectual ability	0.70		
School motivation	0.37	0.32	
Parental interest	0.13	0.11	0.34

Table 31.2	Some regression results – significant predictors only				
Predictor variables	r	b	Beta β	t	Significance
Intellectual ability	0.70	0.83	0.65	9.56	0.001
School motivation	0.37	0.17	0.16	2.42	0.02
Constant = -0.17, $R^2 = 0.52$, Adjusted $R^2 = 0.51$, $R = 0.72$					

achievement. That they are significant is assessed using a t-test. The values of t are given in Table 31.2 along with their two-tailed significance levels. A significance level of 0.05 or less is regarded as statistically significant.

The two significant predictor variables are intellectual ability and school motivation. The first variable to be considered for entry into the regression equation is the one with the highest zero-order correlation with educational achievement. This variable is intellectual ability. The *proportion* of variance in educational achievement explained or predicted by intellectual ability is the square of its correlation with educational achievement which is 0.49 ($0.7^2 = 0.49$). The next predictor to be considered for entry into the regression equation is the variable which has the highest partial correlation with the criterion (after the variance due to the first predictor variable has been removed). These partial correlations have not been presented; however, school motivation is the predictor variable with the highest partial correlation with the criterion variable educational achievement.

The two predictors together explain 0.52 of the variance of educational achievement. The figure of the total proportion of variance explained is arrived at by squaring the overall R (the multiple correlation) which is 0.72^2 or 0.52. The multiple correlation is likely to be bigger the smaller the sample and for more predictors. Consequently, this figure is usually adjusted for the size of the sample and the number of predictors, which reduces it in size somewhat. Finally, the partial regression or beta coefficients for the regression equation containing the two predictors are also shown in Table 31.2 and are 0.65 for intellectual ability and 0.16 for school motivation. There is also a constant (usually denoted as a) which is -0.17 in this instance. The constant is the equivalent to the cut-point described in Chapter 8. We can write this regression equation as follows:

Educational achievement = a + (0.83 × intellectual ability) + (0.17 × school motivation)

According to our fictitious example, intellectual ability is more important than school motivation in predicting educational achievement.

Box 31.3   Key concepts

Multicollinearity

There is a concept, *multicollinearity*, which needs consideration when planning a multiple regression analysis. This merely refers to a situation in which several of the predictor variables correlate with each other very highly. This results in difficulties because small sampling fluctuations may result in a particular variable appearing to be a powerful predictor while other variables may appear to be relatively weak predictors. So variables *A* and *B*, both of which predict the criterion, may correlate with each other at, say, 0.9. However, because variable *A*, say, has a *minutely* better correlation with the criterion it is selected first by the computer. Variable *B* then appears to be a far less good predictor. When the intercorrelations of your predictor variables are very high, perhaps above 0.8 or so, then the dangers of multicollinearity are also high. In terms of research design, it is a well-known phenomenon that if you measure several different variables using the same type of method then there is a tendency for the variables to intercorrelate simply because of that fact. So, if all of your measures are based on self-completion questionnaires or on ratings by observers then you may find strong intercorrelations simply because of this. Quite clearly, care should be exercised to ensure that your predictor measures do not intercorrelate highly. If multicollinearity is apparent then be very careful about claiming that one of the predictors is far better than another.

Box 31.4   Focus on

Prediction in multiple regression

Prediction in regression is often not prediction at all. This can cause some confusion. In everyday language, prediction is indicating what will happen in the future on the basis of some sign in the present. Researchers, however, often use regression analysis with no intention of predicting future events. Instead, they collect data on the relation between a set of variables (let's call them X_1, X_2 and X_3) and another variable (called *Y*). They think that the *X* variables may be correlated with *Y*. The data on all of these variables are available to the researcher. The analysis proceeds essentially by calculating the overall correlation of the several *X* variables with the *Y* variable. The overall correlation of a set of variables with another single variable is called multiple correlation. If there is a multiple correlation between the variables then this means that we can use the value of this correlation together with other information to estimate the value of the *Y* variable from a pattern of *X* variables. Since the multiple correlation is rarely a perfect correlation, then our estimate of *Y* is bound to be a little inaccurate. Explained this way, we have not used the concept of prediction. If we know the multiple correlation between variables based on a particular sample of participants, we can use the size of the correlation to estimate the value of *Y* for other individuals based on knowing their pattern of scores on the *X* variables. That is the task of multiple regression. Prediction in multiple regression, then, is really estimating the unknown value of *Y* for an individual who was not part of the original research sample from that individual's known pattern of scores on the *X* variables.

31.4   Reporting the results

Multiple regression can be performed in a variety of ways for a variety of purposes. Consequently, there is no standard way of presenting results from a multiple regression analysis. However, there are some things which are best routinely mentioned. In particular, the reader needs to know the variables on which the analysis was conducted, the particular form of the multiple regression used, regression weights and the main pattern of predictors. Other information may be added as appropriate. By all means consult journal articles in your field of study for other indications as to style. We would say the following when reporting the simple example in Section 31.3 (though this contains additional information from the companion computer analysis book – see the end of the chapter): 'A stepwise multiple regression was carried out in order to investigate the best pattern of variables for predicting educational achievement. Intellectual ability was selected for entry into the analysis first and explained 49% of the variance in educational achievement. School motivation was entered second and together with intellectual ability explained 52% of the variance in educational achievement. Greater educational attainment was associated with greater intellectual ability and school motivation. A third variable, parental interest, was not included in the analysis as it was not a significant, independent predictor of educational achievement.'

31.5 An example from the published literature

Munford (1994) examined the predictors of depression in African–Americans. The research involved her administering the following measures:

1. The Beck Depression Inventory

2. The Rosenberg self-esteem scale

3. The Hollingshead two-factor index of social position – this is a measure of the occupational social class and educational standards (i.e. a measure of social class)

4. The gender (self-reported sex) of the individual

5. The Racial identity attitude scale which measures several different stages in the development of racial identity:

   (a) Pre-encounter: the stage before black people become exposed to racism. It is the stage at which they accept the definitions of themselves imposed by the white racist community

   (b) Encounter: the stage where identity is challenged by direct experiences of racism

   (c) Immersion: the individual is learning to value his or her own race and culture

   (d) Internalisation: the individual has achieved a mature and secure sense of his or her own race and identity.

As one might expect, Munford was interested in the relationship between depression as measured by the Beck Depression Inventory (the criterion variable) and the remaining variables (the predictor variables). She computed a correlation matrix between all of the variables, but as this involved 28 different correlation coefficients it is obvious that she needed a means of simplifying its complexity. She subjected her correlation matrix to a stepwise regression which yielded the outcome shown in Table 31.3.

As you can see, many of the predictors are not included in the table, indicating that they were not significant independent predictors of depression (thus social class and internalisation, for example, are excluded). Self-esteem is the best predictor of depression – those with the higher self-esteem tended to have lower depression scores. One cannot

Table 31.3	Summary of stepwise multiple regression: self-esteem, gender, social class and racial identity attitudes as predictors of depression		
Predictor	**R^2 increments**	**R^2 (adjusted) total**	**Beta F**
Self-esteem	0.37	0.37	134.10
Pre-encounter	0.02	0.39	8.97
Encounter	0.01	0.41	4.71
Gender	0.01	0.42	4.77

Source: Adapted from Munford, 1994

tell this directly from the table as it presents squared values which would have lost any negative signs. *We have to assess the direction of the relationship from the sign of the regression coefficient.* This sign is negative.

Although pre-encounter, encounter and gender all contribute something to the prediction, the increment in the amount of variation explained is quite small for each of them. Thus R^2 for pre-encounter is only 0.02 which means (expressed as a percentage) that the increase in variation explained is only 2% (i.e. $0.02 \times 100\%$).

Beta F in essence reports F-ratios (Chapter 20) for each of the predictor variables. All of those presented are statistically significant since otherwise the variable in question would not correlate significantly with depression.

Key points

- Multiple regression is only practicable in most cases using a computer since the computations are numerous.

- Normally one does not have to compute the correlation matrix independently between variables. The computer program usually does this on the raw scores. There may be a facility for entering correlation matrices which might be useful once in a while when you are reanalysing someone else's correlation matrix.

- Choose hierarchical selection for your multiple regression if you are trying to test out theoretical predictions or if you have some other rationale. One advantage of this is that you can first of all control for any social or demographic variables (gender, social class, etc.) which might influence your results. Then you can choose your remaining predictors in any order which you think best meets your needs.

- Choose stepwise selection methods in circumstances in which you simply wish to choose the best and smallest set of predictors. This would be ideal in circumstances in which you wish to dispense with time-consuming (and expensive) psychological tests, say in an industrial setting involving personnel selection. The main considerations here are entirely practical.

- Avoid construing the results of multiple regression in cause and effect terms.

COMPUTER ANALYSIS

The SPSS Statistics instruction book to this text is Dennis Howitt and Duncan Cramer (2011), *Introduction to SPSS Statistics in Psychology: For version 19 and earlier*, Harlow: Pearson. Chapters 32 and 48 in that book give detailed step-by-step procedures for the statistics described in this chapter together with advice on how to report the results. Figure 31.4 gives the SPSS Statistics steps for a stepwise multiple regression.

Data
- Name the variables in Variable View of the Data Editor.
- Enter the data under the appropriate variable names in Data View of the Data Editor.

Analysis
- Select 'Analyze', 'Regression' and 'Linear . . .'.

2
- Move the criterion or dependent variable to the 'Dependent:' box and the predictors or independent variables to the 'Independent(s):' box.

3
- In the 'Method:' box select 'Stepwise'.
- Select 'Statistics . . .' and then '*R* squared change', 'Descriptives', 'Part and partial correlations', 'Collinearity diagnostics' and 'Continue'.

Output
- Check the sample size in the 'Descriptive Statistics' table.
- In the 'Model Summary' table note the predictor and *R* Square Change in each step.
- In the 'Coefficients' table check that the Tolerance level is above 0.1.

FIGURE 31.4 SPSS Statistics steps for stepwise multiple regression

Recommended further reading

Cramer, D. (2003), *Advanced Quantitative Data Analysis*, Buckingham: Open University Press, Chapters 5 and 6.

Glantz, S.A. and Slinker, B.K. (1990), *Primer of Applied Regression and Analysis of Variance*, New York: McGraw-Hill.

Pedhazur, E.J. (1982), *Multiple Regression in Behavioral Research: Explanation and Prediction*, 2nd edition, New York: Holt, Rinehart & Winston, Chapter 6.

Tabachnick, B.G. and Fidell, L.S. (2007), *Using Multivariate Statistics*, 5th edition, Boston, MA: Allyn & Bacon, Chapter 5.

CHAPTER 32

Path analysis

Overview

- Path analysis is based on multiple regression, but its conceptualisation of the predictors (independent variables) is more complex.

- The primary objective of path analysis is to indicate likely relationships between the independent variables as predictors of the dependent variable.

- There are numerous possible relationships among the predictor variables. Variable X_1 may affect variable X_2, or variable X_2 may affect variable X_1, or they may both affect each other (a bidirectional relationship).

- The relationships between variables in path analysis are present as path coefficients. These are essentially correlation coefficients based on the beta weights (standardised regression coefficients) calculated in multiple regression.

- Path analysis is about trying to establish a causal model of how predictor variables are combined to affect the level of the dependent variable.

Preparation

Path analysis requires that you understand the basic principles of multiple regression (Chapter 31).

32.1 Introduction

As modern psychology has increasingly drawn from real issues and non-laboratory research methods, the problems of establishing what variables affect what other variables have changed. The methodological sophistication of laboratory experiments in which causal linkages are determined by random assignment of individuals to an experimental and control group has been supplemented by a strong wish to understand people better in their natural environment. Causal modelling is merely a generic name for attempts to explore the patterns of interrelationships between variables in order to suggest how some variables might be causally influencing others. Of course, some suggestions might be rather better than others; some theoretical links might not fare well against actual empirical data. In path analysis, it is possible to estimate how well a particular suggested pattern of influences fits the known data. The better the model or causal pattern is supported by the actual data then the more likely we are to believe that the model is a useful theoretical development.

There is no suggestion intended that path analysis will always provide indisputable evidence strongly favouring one particular causal model over a number of other possibilities. It is not a question of showing that one model is the best model. Path analysis simply seeks to describe a particular path which explains the relationships among the variables well and precisely; the researcher may have overlooked other variables when planning the study or analysing it and it is feasible that these variables, if they had been included, would radically change our understanding of what is happening in the data. Thought is part of the process just as much as statistics. For example, we can exclude some causal pathways on logical grounds such as changes in a causal influence need to precede changes in the variable that we are trying to explain. Thus, childhood experiences might possibly influence our adult behaviour and so it is reasonable to include childhood experiences as influences on adult behaviour. However, the reverse pattern is not viable. Our childhood experiences cannot possibly be caused by things that happen to us in our adult years; the temporal sequence is wrong. In other words, some causal models are not convincing simply because they are not logically so feasible as other models.

32.2 Theoretical considerations

Path analysis involves specifying the assumed causal relationships among several variables. Take, for example, the variables:

- marital satisfaction,

- the love between a couple and

- remaining married.

A reasonable assumption which might lead to a causal model is that couples who love one another are more likely to be satisfied with their marriage and consequently are more likely to stay together. Such a pattern of influences (or causal model) can be drawn as a path diagram such as the one in Figure 32.1. This is little more than a flow diagram indicating the direction of influence of one variable on another. In this particular model (and it clearly is just one of several possibilities), variables to the left (marital love) are thought to influence variables towards the right (marital satisfaction and remaining married). Right-facing arrows between variables indicate the causal direction. So the

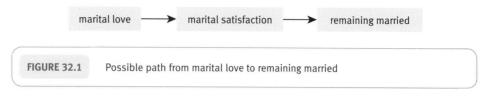

> **FIGURE 32.1**   Possible path from marital love to remaining married

model is quite simply that marital love causes marital satisfaction which in turn is responsible for remaining married.

Of course, the temptation is simply to correlate together scores on the three variables in this model. Suppose that we find that they all intercorrelate – then what? Well this might appear to be evidence in support of the suggested model, but it would also support many other models based on these three variables. The main point is that relationships between variables do not, in themselves, establish that marital love really causes marital satisfaction. Just taking two variables at a time results in four possible causal relationships:

● As suggested by our model, marital love may increase marital satisfaction.

● The opposite effect may occur with marital satisfaction heightening marital love.

● Both variables may affect each other, marital love bringing about marital satisfaction and marital satisfaction enhancing marital love. This kind of relationship is variously known as a *two-way*, *bidirectional*, *bilateral*, *reciprocal* or *non-recursive* relationship.

● The relationship may not really exist but may appear to exist because both variables are affected by some further confounding factor(s). For example, both marital love and marital satisfaction may be weaker in emotionally unstable people and stronger in emotionally stable people. This creates the impression that marital love and marital satisfaction are related when they are not, because emotionally unstable people are lower in both marital love and marital satisfaction while emotionally stable people are higher in both. This fourth sort of relationship is known as a *spurious relationship*.

In path analysis, a distinction is often made between *exogenous* and *endogenous* variables:

1. An exogenous variable is one whose assumed causes have not been measured or tested as part of the model. In other words, it refers to those variables which do not have arrows pointing to them in a path diagram.

2. An endogenous variable is one for which one or more possible causes have been measured and have been posited in the causal model. In other words, endogenous variable have arrows pointing to them in the path diagram.

So, in the above model, marital love is an exogenous variable while marital satisfaction and remaining married are endogenous variables.

There will be some variation in endogenous variables which is unaccounted for or unexplained by causal variables in the model. This unexplained variance in an endogenous variable is indicated by vertical arrows pointing towards that variable as shown in the path diagram in Figure 32.2. For example, the variance in marital satisfaction *not* explained by marital love is represented by the vertical arrow from e_2. Similarly, the variance in remaining married unaccounted for by marital satisfaction is depicted by the vertical arrow from e_3. The *e* stands for *error* – the term used to describe unexplained variance. The word *residual* is sometimes used instead to refer to the variance that remains to be explained and the phrase *disturbance term* is also applied, in path analysis, to exactly the same concept. It is important to realise that *e* refers to the influence of unknown factors rather than random error. In other words, the variance *e* may eventually be explained by a more complex model.

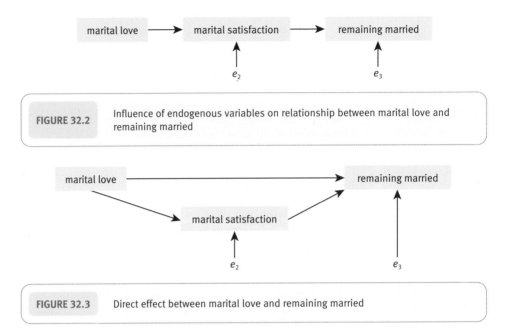

FIGURE 32.2 Influence of endogenous variables on relationship between marital love and remaining married

FIGURE 32.3 Direct effect between marital love and remaining married

In this model, marital love is assumed to have an *indirect* effect on remaining married through its effect on marital satisfaction. However, marital love may also have a *direct* effect on remaining married as shown in the path diagram of Figure 32.3.

■ Path coefficients

The values of the direct effects are expressed as *path coefficients*. They are usually the standardised beta coefficients taken from the sort of multiple regression analysis which was introduced in the previous chapter (see Chapter 31). In other words, they can essentially be understood as analogous to correlation coefficients. The values of the paths reflecting error (or residual) variance are known as error or residual path coefficients.

We will use the following symbols:

- p_1 for the path coefficient for the direct effect of marital love on marital satisfaction

- p_2 for the direct effect of marital love on remaining married

- p_3 for the direct effect of marital satisfaction on remaining married

- p_4 for the path reflecting the error variance of marital satisfaction

- p_5 for the path reflecting error variance for remaining married.

These are illustrated in Figure 32.4.

FIGURE 32.4 Path coefficients

To calculate these path coefficients we need to calculate the following two regression equations which are essentially the same as for the multiple regression discussed in the previous chapter:

marital satisfaction = $a + p_1$ marital love

remaining married = $b + p_2$ marital love + p_3 marital satisfaction

(In these equations a and b are intercept coefficients for the regression equations. Intercept coefficients are the points at which the regression lines cut the vertical axis. They are identified with different symbols in our example simply because they refer to different things. However, they will always take a value of 0.00 if we are using standardised multiple regression as we do in path analysis. We can, therefore, ignore them for present purposes.)

Suppose that the correlation between marital love and marital satisfaction is 0.50, between marital love and remaining married 0.40 and between marital satisfaction and remaining married 0.70 for a sample of 100 couples. These are correlations which have been made up for the purposes of this example. We have carried out our multiple regression using this correlation matrix. This is possible, for example, with SPSS Statistics though one has to use syntax commands. Normally this is not necessary as the researcher will have the raw data. So the path coefficients about to be discussed are based on this analysis. The path coefficients are the standardised beta coefficients for these two equations which are:

marital satisfaction = $a + 0.50$ marital love

remaining married = $b + 0.07$ marital love + 0.67 marital satisfaction

In other words, the path coefficient for p_1 is 0.50, for p_2, 0.07 and for p_3, 0.67 as shown in Figure 32.5.

Since there is only one predictor variable in the first regression, the standardised beta coefficient of 0.50 is the same as the zero-order correlation of 0.50 between marital love (the predictor variable) and marital satisfaction (the criterion variable). (If there are several predictors then partial regression coefficients would be involved.) Note that the path coefficient between marital love and remaining married is virtually zero (0.07) and statistically not significant. This means that marital love does not directly affect remaining married. The path coefficient (0.67) between marital satisfaction and remaining married differs little from the correlation (0.70) between them. This indicates that the relationship between marital satisfaction and remaining married is not due to the spurious effect of marital love.

To determine an indirect effect (such as that between marital love and remaining married which is mediated by marital satisfaction), the path coefficient between marital love and marital satisfaction (0.50) is multiplied by the path coefficient between marital satisfaction and remaining married (0.67). This gives an indirect effect of 0.335 (0.50 × 0.67 = 0.335). To calculate the total effect of marital love on remaining married, we add

FIGURE 32.5   Actual values of path coefficients inserted

the direct effect of marital love on remaining married (0.07) to its indirect effect (0.335) which gives a sum of 0.405. The total effect of one variable on another should be, within rounding error, the same as the zero-order correlation between the two variables. As we can see, the total effect of marital love on remaining married is 0.405, which is very close to the value of the zero-order correlation of 0.40. In other words, path analysis breaks down or decomposes the correlations between the endogenous and exogenous variables into their component parts, making it easier to see what might be happening. So, for example, the correlation between marital love and remaining married is decomposed into (a) the indirect effect of marital love on remaining married and (b) the direct effects of marital love on marital satisfaction and of marital satisfaction on remaining married. Doing this enables us to see that although the correlation between marital love and remaining married is moderately strong (0.40), this relationship is largely mediated indirectly through marital satisfaction.

The correlation between marital satisfaction and remaining married can also be decomposed into the direct effect we have already calculated (0.67) and a spurious component due to the effect of marital love on both marital satisfaction and remaining married. This spurious component is the product of the direct effect of marital love on marital satisfaction (0.50) and of marital love on remaining married (0.07) which gives 0.035 (0.50 × 0.07 = 0.035). This is clearly a small value. We can reconstitute the correlation between marital satisfaction and remaining married by summing the direct effect (0.67) and the spurious component (0.035) which gives a total of 0.67 + 0.035 = 0.705. This value is very similar to the original correlation of 0.70.

To calculate the proportion of variance not explained in an endogenous variable we subtract the adjusted multiple R squared value for that variable from 1. The adjusted multiple R squared value is 0.24 for marital satisfaction and 0.48 for remaining married. So 0.76 (1 − 0.24 = 0.76) or 76% of the variance in marital satisfaction is not explained, and 0.52 (1 − 0.48) or 52% of the variance in remaining married is not explained. In path analysis, it is assumed that the variables representing error are unrelated to any other variables in the model (otherwise it would not be error). Consequently, the error path coefficient is the correlation between the error and the endogenous variable which can be obtained by taking the square root of the proportion of unexplained variance in the endogenous variable. In other words, the residual path coefficient is 0.87 ($\sqrt{0.76} = 0.87$) for marital satisfaction and 0.72 ($\sqrt{0.52} = 0.72$) for remaining married (Figure 32.6).

Where there is a relationship between two variables whose nature is not known or specified, this relationship is depicted in a path diagram by a curved double-headed arrow. Suppose, for example, the two exogenous variables of similarity in personality and similarity in physical attractiveness, which were assumed to influence marital satisfaction, were known to be related, but this relationship was thought not to be causal. This relationship would be shown in a path diagram as in Figure 32.7.

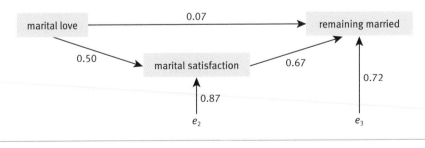

FIGURE 32.6   Residual path coefficients

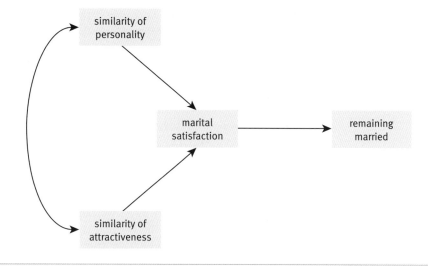

The correlation between these two exogenous variables is not used in calculating the effect of these two variables on marital satisfaction and remaining married. Figure 32.8 shows the key steps in a path analysis.

■ Generalisation

To determine whether our path analysis is generalisable from the sample to the population, we calculate how well our model reflects the original correlation matrix between the variables in that model using the large sample chi-square test. This will not be described here other than to make these two points:

- If this chi-square test is statistically significant, then this means that the model does not fit the data.

- Other things being equal, the larger the sample, the more likely it is that the chi-square test is statistically significant and the model is to be rejected.

A variable which is explained by other variables is the dependent or criterion variable in the multiple regression while the other variables are the independent or predictor variables.	→	Multiple regression for path analysis can only be used where there is only one final endogenous variable or criterion in the model.	→	Variables which are thought to affect other variables should be placed to the right of those variables and connected with a single rightward facing arrow.
The path coefficients between variables are the standardised or beta regression coefficients so their relative size can be compared.	←	Remember that if there is not a significant correlation between two variables then it is unlikely there will be significant path coefficient.	←	Ideally the model should be relatively simple without excessive pathways included.

FIGURE 32.8   Conceptual steps for understanding a path analysis

Table 32.1	Original and recomposed correlations	
Pairs of variables	**Original correlations**	**Recomposed correlations**
Marital love and marital satisfaction	0.50	0.500
Marital love and remaining married	0.40	0.405
Marital satisfaction and remaining married	0.70	0.705

In terms of our model in Figure 32.6, we can see that the recomposed correlations for the model are very similar to the original correlations between the three variables as shown in Table 32.1. This is not always true as explained in Box 32.1.

Box 32.1   Key concepts

Identification

Although in Table 32.1 we give an example where the correlations between the variables and the recomposed correlations based on path analysis are very similar, not all models which emerge in path analysis demonstrate this feature. It is always true when the model is just-identified. Identification is an important concept in path analysis. There are three types of identification:

- *Just-identified* This means that all the variables in the path analysis model put forward by the researcher are connected by unidirectional paths (single-headed arrows). Actually, even with the arrows entirely reversed in direction this would still be the case. Since the standardised beta coefficients are essentially correlation coefficients, this entirely reversed model would fit our data just as well as our preferred model. In other words, the recomposed correlations for this reversed just-identified model are just the same as for the forward model. *The reconstituted correlations for any just-identified model are similar to the original correlations. Consequently it is not possible to use the match between the model and the data as support for the validity of the model.*

- *Under-identified* In this, there are assumed to be one or more bidirectional pathways (double-headed arrows between variables) in the model. For example, the relationship between marital love and marital satisfaction

may be thought of as being reciprocal, both variables having an influence on each other. Since it is impossible to provide an estimate of the influence of marital love on marital satisfaction which is entirely independent of the influence of marital satisfaction on marital love, it is not possible to say what the unique estimate for these pathways would be. Consequently, we would need to modify our model to avoid this. That is, we need to respecify it as a just-identified or an over-identified model in order to deal with this problem.

- *Over-identified* In an over-identified model, it is assumed that some pairs of variables do not relate. Using our example, an over-identified model assumes that there is no relationship between two pairs of variables. For instance, take the following model which postulates that marital love does not lead directly to remaining married:

  marital love → marital satisfaction → remaining married

This is over-identified because a third possible pathway between marital love and remaining married has not been suggested (that is, the direct pathway from marital love to remaining married). Thus there are more variables (three) than pathways (two).

32.3   An example from published research

Path analysis can be as simple or as complex as the researchers' theories about the inter-relationships between variables in their research. Increasing the numbers of variables under consideration rapidly accelerates the complexity in the path diagram. Not only does the analysis look more daunting if many variables are involved, but the path diagram becomes harder to draw. In this section we will discuss a path analysis by Wagner and Zick (1995) of the causes of blatant ethnic prejudice as a typical example of path analysis in psychology. It is fairly well known and established that there is a relationship between people's level of formal education and their expressions of prejudice: the more prejudiced tend to have the least formal education. This suggests that there is something about education which leads to less prejudice, but what is the mechanism involved? Does education act directly to reduce prejudice or does it do so indirectly through some mediating variable (Figure 32.9)?

Thus there are two possible paths: (1) the *direct* path from formal education to blatant prejudice and (2) the *indirect* path which involves a mediating variable(s).

As we have indicated, the apparent complexity of this path diagram can be increased if several mediating variables are used rather than just one. Furthermore, if several direct variables are used instead of formal education alone, the diagram will become increasingly complex. Wagner and Zick (1995) collected information in a number of European countries on several potential mediating variables linking formal education and blatant prejudice:

1. *Individual (relative) deprivation* The feeling of an individual that he or she is economically deprived compared with other people.

2. *Group (relative) deprivation* The feeling that one's social group (e.g. ethnic group) has fared badly economically compared with the rest of society.

3. *Perceived incongruency* The incompatibility between an ethnic group's values and those dominant in society.

4. *Political conservatism* The individual's position on the political left-wing to right-wing dimension.

5. *National pride* Pride in being a member of the national group (e.g. French or German).

6. *Contact with foreign people* The numbers of foreign people living in one's neighbourhood.

Although this list of mediating variables far from exhausts the possibilities, it does identify a number of variables which are related to blatant ethnic prejudice according to a number of empirical studies.

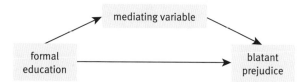

FIGURE 32.9   Path diagram of the direct and indirect influence of formal education on blatant prejudice

In addition, the researchers had other measures which they could have included in the path diagram (e.g. gender and age) but omitted because the researchers did not consider them relevant to their immediate task. However, they were used by the researchers as control variables, as we shall see. There was another variable, *social strata*, which was a measure of social class. This was included in the path diagram by the researchers as social class was actually affected by a person's level of education.

There is no mystery about the path diagram; it is merely one of several path diagrams which the researchers could have studied. Most of the possibilities were ignored and the researchers concentrated on why those with the most formal education tend to express the least blatant prejudice. Drawing the diagram is a paper-and-pencil task based on elaborating the simple path diagram in Figure 32.9. Wagner and Zick's path diagram is shown in Figure 32.10. It includes both direct and indirect (mediated) relationships. Arrows pointing more or less towards the right are the only ones included as these indicate possible causal directions. Having drawn the elaborated diagram, the researchers inserted the values of the relationships between the variables (i.e. path coefficients which are in essence correlation coefficients) next to the appropriate arrows. These path coefficients were obtained, of course, using multiple regression. The researchers omitted arrows (pathways) when the path coefficient did not reach statistical significance. However, because the sample was big ($N = 3788$), very small values were significant at the 5% level. A correlation of 0.04 is statistically significant, but its coefficient of determination or amount of variation shared by the two variables is 0.04^2 or 0.0016 or 0.16%. The square of $e = 0.83$ in Figure 32.10 indicates how much variation in blatant prejudice is *unexplained* by the path diagram.

The path coefficients themselves are to be found in Table 32.2. As you can see, this contains a lot of information. The following are the main considerations that you need to bear in mind when considering this table:

1. A zero-order correlation is merely the Pearson correlation coefficient as described in Chapter 7. First-order, second-order, etc. correlations are partial correlations as described in Chapter 29.

2. The upper triangle of the matrix in the table is merely a correlation matrix involving the range of measures in the path diagram with age and gender added.

3. Correlation coefficients are not used in the path analysis but are used in a multiple regression to obtain the beta weights.

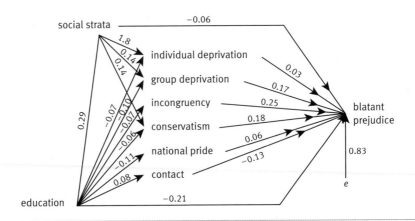

FIGURE 32.10   Significant path on blatant prejudice (adapted from Wagner and Zick, 1995)

Table 32.2 Zero-order correlations between variables (upper part) and results of a path analysis (lower part)

	Age	Gender	Education	Social strata	Individual deprivation	Group deprivation	Incongruency	Conservatism	National pride	Contact	Blatant prejudice
Age		-0.02	-0.28*	-0.01	0.07*	0.03*	0.06*	0.13*	0.18*	-0.24*	0.23*
Gender	-0.02		-0.07*	-0.02	0.04†	0.02	-0.02	0.02	-0.01	-0.14*	0.04*
Education	-0.28*[a]	-0.08*[a]		0.27*	-0.13*	-0.14*	-0.08*	-0.05*	-0.15*	0.17*	-0.34*
Social strata	0.07*[a]	0.01[a]	0.29*[a]		-0.20*	-0.17*	-0.02	0.13*	-0.02	0.34*	-0.14*
Individual deprivation	0.05*[a]	0.03[a]	-0.07*[a]	-0.18*[a]		0.30*	0.01	-0.09*	-0.07*	-0.08*	0.12*
Group deprivation	0.01[a]	0.01[a]	-0.10*[a]	-0.14*[a]	0.28*[b]		0.12*	0.01	0.03†	0.01	0.25*
Incongruency	0.04*[a]	-0.02[a]	-0.07*[a]	0.00[a]	-0.02[b]	0.11*[b]		0.09*	0.04†	-0.01	0.32*
Conservatism	0.12*[a]	0.02[a]	-0.06*[a]	0.14*[a]	-0.07*[b]	-0.03[b]	0.08*[b]		0.23*	-0.10*	0.24*
National pride	0.15*[a]	-0.01[a]	-0.11*[a]	0.01[a]	-0.09*[b]	0.04[b]	0.01[b]	0.20*[b]		-0.09*	0.18*
Contact	-0.22*[a]	-0.13*[a]	0.09*[a]	0.01[a]	-0.08*[b]	0.06[b]	0.01[b]	-0.07*[b]	-0.03[b]		-0.21
Blatant prejudice	0.08*[a]	0.00[a]	-0.21*[a]	-0.06*[a]	0.03*[a]	0.17*[a]	0.25*[a]	0.18*[b]	0.06*[a]	-0.13*[a]	

[a] beta-coefficient from a simultaneous regression (i.e. the enter method on SPSS Statistics).

[b] partial correlation with the effects of age, gender, education and social strata partialled out unless otherwise indicated: Pearson correlation coefficient.

* $p \leq 0.01$; † $p \leq 0.05$.

Source: Table reproduced from Wagner and Zick (1995) © John Wiley and Sons Limited. Reproduced with permission.

4. Wagner and Zick (1995) carried out a simultaneous multiple regression on the correlation matrix in order to predict blatant prejudice from age, gender, formal education, social strata and the mediating variables (individual deprivation, group deprivation, etc.). Standard or simultaneous multiple regression is called the enter method on SPSS Statistics. It simply means that all of the predictor variables are included in the analysis at the same time rather than being entered in stepwise order, for example, such as where the variable explaining the most variance is dealt with as a priority.

5. The beta weights from this multiple regression are indicated by a letter *b* in the lower half of the matrix in Table 32.2.

6. The coefficients marked *c* in the lower half of the matrix in Table 32.2 are partial correlations which take away the effects of age, gender, education and social strata from the relationships between the pairs of variables. That is, one needs to insert in the *indirect* pathways the correlations having removed the influence of age, gender, education and social strata. In other words, the coefficients marked *c* are the partial correlation coefficients controlling for age, gender, education and social strata simultaneously, they are fourth-order correlation coefficients. Although this procedure is perfectly adequate, it is more conventional to use hierarchical multiple regression to achieve much the same end. This would involve having the four control variables as the first block in a hierarchical multiple regression. This essentially controls for these variables in the later blocks of the analysis.

32.4 Reporting the results

Path analysis is a difficult procedure to apply and few students would carry out such analysis at undergraduate level. Even at the postgraduate level, novices to path analysis would probably be wise to seek some experienced support. Part of the difficulty in writing a simple way of reporting the results of a path analysis is that the reasons for this particular analysis can be complex and dependent on elaboration of previous theory. Nevertheless, readers may find it helpful to read Wagner and Zick's description of the results of their path analysis:

> 'The path analysis shows that the predictors of ethnic prejudice mentioned above are determined by formal education, even though some of the direct paths from education are relatively weak. However, for individual and group relative deprivation, and for political conservatism, social strata mediates part of the determination by formal education. The influence of mediating variables means that the covariation of formal education and ethnic prejudice can be partially explained especially by variations in social strata, group deprivation, incongruency, conservatism and acceptance of contact with foreigners. In addition to this, the path analysis indicates a strong direct path from education to blatant prejudice which cannot be explained by the mediation variables measured. A chi-square analysis shows that a restricted model without the assumption of a direct path from education to prejudice is significantly worse than the full model presented (chi-square = 84.02, df = 1). Thus, the path analysis demonstrates that part of the educational differences in ethnic outgroup rejection can be accounted for by the mediating psychological variables, even though a substantial proportion of the covariance of respondents' education and outgroup rejection remained unexplained.'

(Wagner and Zick, 1995, pp. 53–4)

Major points which might clarify the Wagner and Zick quotation include:

1. Education influences variables which influence blatant prejudice. Often the influences are very weak. Most studies would use far smaller sample sizes so the tiny coefficients sometimes obtained in the study would be dismissed as not significant.

2. The chi-square tests whether the indirect paths model is significantly improved by adding in the direct path from formal education to blatant prejudice. The results of the analysis suggest that the direct plus indirect effects model is superior to the indirect effects alone model.

Key points

- Path analysis requires a degree of mastery of statistical concepts which many students will not achieve during their degree course. Anyone who is convinced that it is appropriate for their research will need to consult supplementary sources and any local expert who might be available.

- The complexity of path analysis should not be allowed to interfere with one's critical faculties. A path analysis cannot be any better than the quality of the data which go into it.

- Path analysis involves exploring data in ways which seem alien to those who feel that statistics should be a hard-and-fast discipline in which there is only one right way of doing things. It is an example of a statistical technique which is an exploratory tool rather than a fixed solution to a fixed problem.

COMPUTER ANALYSIS

The SPSS Statistics instruction book to this text is Dennis Howitt and Duncan Cramer (2011), *Introduction to SPSS Statistics in Psychology: For version 19 and earlier*, Harlow: Pearson. Chapters 33 to 35 in that book give detailed steps for the Enter procedure for a hierarchical multiple regression together with advice on how to report the results. This procedure with all relevant variables entered in a single step is the procedure to use in a path analysis. Chapters 52 to 54 give the steps for a simple path analysis using LISREL. Figure 32.11 shows the SPSS Statistics for the Enter regression procedure.

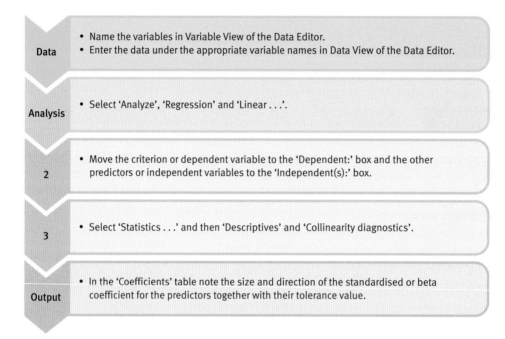

Data
- Name the variables in Variable View of the Data Editor.
- Enter the data under the appropriate variable names in Data View of the Data Editor.

Analysis
- Select 'Analyze', 'Regression' and 'Linear . . .'.

2
- Move the criterion or dependent variable to the 'Dependent:' box and the other predictors or independent variables to the 'Independent(s):' box.

3
- Select 'Statistics . . .' and then 'Descriptives' and 'Collinearity diagnostics'.

Output
- In the 'Coefficients' table note the size and direction of the standardised or beta coefficient for the predictors together with their tolerance value.

FIGURE 32.11 SPSS Statistics steps for the enter regression procedure

Recommended further reading

Bryman, A. and Cramer, D. (2007), *Quantitative Data Analysis with SPSS 14 and 15: A Guide for Social Scientists*, London: Routledge, Chapter 10.

Cramer, D. (2003), *Advanced Quantitative Data Analysis*, Buckingham: Open University Press, Chapter 7.

Pedhazur, E.J. (1982), *Multiple Regression in Behavioral Research: Explanation and Prediction*, 2nd edition, New York: Holt, Rinehart & Winston, Chapter 15.

CHAPTER 33

The analysis of a questionnaire/ survey project

Overview

- One of the hardest things facing newcomers to research is the transition between the contents of statistics textbooks and collecting and analysing data. This chapter attempts to clarify how to develop an appropriate statistical analysis in circumstances in which planning has been less than perfect. Although it is ideal that the data analysis is planned in advance at the same time as the data collection is planned, this is probably beyond the skills of student researchers.

- A researcher needs clear understanding of what they are trying to achieve in the research. Hence it is important to clarify the broad research question and any hypotheses that derive from this. Hypotheses are merely statements of relationships that one wishes to explore.

- The data need to be mapped to identify the characteristics of variables. Identifying what is a score variable and what is a nominal (category) variable is important. Nominal (category) variables with just two categories can be treated as scores by giving the values 1 and 2 to the two alternative values.

- Data may need recoding to make the analysis acceptable.

- Ineffective variables are removed through a process of data cleaning.

- Data analysis consists of presenting descriptive statistics on the major variables and finding the extent of relationships among variables. This may be more or less complex.

Preparation

Review correlation (Chapter 7) and regression (Chapter 8).

33.1 Introduction

This chapter examines the analysis of questionnaire and/or survey projects. A lot of research planned by students adopts this style. The key feature is the number of variables involved; this type of research tempts researchers to write lengthy questionnaires with numerous items. It takes little effort to write a question, even less to write a poor question. Still less time is required to answer the questions if they are in a closed-ended format in which just one alternative is circled. An exploratory or pilot study will not always identify faulty questions and, more often than not, the pressures on students' time are such that pilot studies are rudimentary and based on very few individuals. So inadequacies are often built in from the very beginning.

Some students, wanting to get closer to the experiences of the participants in their research, choose to ask the questions themselves rather than have a self-completion questionnaire. This form of open questioning can have many advantages in terms of the quality of data collected in some studies. However, the basic problem remains very much the same – too much data. The difference is that with the open-ended interview approach the data have to be coded in a form suitable for statistical analysis. The coding process has its own problems – largely what coding categories to use and whether the categories used are easily used by the coders. Profound disagreements between the coders suggest either that the categories are inadequate or that they have been very poorly defined.

Of course, there are student projects which utilise ready-made questionnaires purchased from a supplier of psychological tests and measures, downloaded from the Web, or found in books and journal articles. Although there are numerous questions involved, these are reduced to a single 'score' or measurement (or sometimes a small number of sub-scores). The groundwork of turning the questionnaire into a small number of 'scores' has already been done by its writers and will not be elaborated upon here.

33.2 The research project

Sarah Freeman is a bright young psychology student who has partied for most of her time at university. So when it is time to plan a research project she has little background knowledge of psychological research and theory. Stuck for a final-year project, she designs a piece of research based on her main interest in life – thinking about sex. Her project explores the hypothesis that a religious upbringing leads to sexual inhibitions. Naturally, her supervisor is reluctant to let Sarah loose on the public at large and so insists that the research is carried out on a consenting sample of fellow students. Pressured by deadlines for coursework essays, she hastily prepares a questionnaire which she pushes under bedroom doors in the Elisha Briggs Hall of Residence. Participants in the research are to return the completed questionnaires to her via the student mail system.

Her questionnaire is a simple enough affair. Sarah's questions – with spelling corrected – are as follows.

1. My gender is

   Male   Female

2. My degree course is ___

3. I am ___ years of age

4. My religion is ___

5. I would rate my religious faith as:

   Very strong   Strong   Neither   Weak   Very weak

6. I attend a place of worship per year

7. My faith in God is important to me

   Strongly agree   Agree   Neither   Disagree   Strongly disagree

8. I am a virgin

   Agree   Disagree

9. I am sexually promiscuous

   Strongly agree   Agree   Neither   Disagree   Strongly disagree

10. I fantasise about sex with several partners at the same time

    Strongly agree   Agree   Neither   Disagree   Strongly disagree

11. I feel guilty after sex with more than three people at the same time

    Strongly agree   Agree   Neither   Disagree   Strongly disagree

12. Oral sex is an abomination

    Strongly agree   Agree   Neither   Disagree   Strongly disagree

13. Sadomasochism is appealing to me

    Strongly agree   Agree   Neither   Disagree   Strongly disagree

14. I like sex

    Once a week   Twice a week   Every day   Every morning and evening   All the time

15. Pornography

    Is disgusting   Is a stimulant   Is best home-made

Suddenly Sarah sees the light of day – just a few months before she finishes at university and is launched onto the job market. Despite being due for submission, the project is in a diabolical mess. No more partying for her – she has become a serious-minded student (well, sort of) and she is determined to resurrect her flagging and ailing attempts at research. No longer does she burn the candle at one end – she now burns it at both ends trying to make sense of statistics and research methods books. Pretty dry stuff it all is. If only she had spent some time on statistics in her misspent youth she would not have been in this hole. Can she get out of the mess?

The short answer is no. The longer answer is that she could improve things considerably with a well-thought-out analysis of her data. Research has to be carefully planned to be at its most effective. She needed to consider her hypotheses, methods and statistical analysis in advance of even collecting the data. Sarah is paying for the error of her ways. One positive aspect of all this is that Sarah can at least show that she is aware of the major issues and problems with her sort of research.

33.3   The research hypothesis

Although statistics is not particularly concerned about the details of the hypotheses underlying research, a clear statement of the purposes of the research often transforms the analysis of haphazardly planned research. Of course, it is by far the best to plan meticulously before doing your research. However, this does not always happen in research – even in research by professionals.

Simply stated, Sarah's research aims to discover whether there is a relationship between religious upbringing and sexual inhibitions. The trouble with this is that it is unclear quite what is meant by a religious upbringing – does it matter which sort of religion or how intensely it is part of family life? Furthermore, it is unclear what she means by sexual inhibitions – for example, not carrying out certain activities might be the result of inhibitions, but it may also be that the person does not find them arousing.

Given the limited range of questions which Sarah included in her questionnaire, we might suggest to her that she has several measures of religiousness:

1. The first is what religion they claim to be. The range is wide and includes Roman Catholic, Protestant, Muslim and a variety of other religions. Is it possible for Sarah to make suggestions as to which religions are most likely to encourage sexual repression – perhaps she thinks that Roman Catholicism and Islam are the religions most likely to inculcate sexual inhibitions? If so, she could formulate a hypothesis which relates aspects of the religion to sexual inhibition.

2. There is a question about actual attendance at church. It could be that involvement in the religious community is a key variable in the influence of religion on sexual inhibitions. This might be specified as a hypothesis.

3. There are two questions which involve the importance of religious beliefs in the lives of the respondents. Again, a hypothesis might specify religious beliefs as the important element in the possible relationship.

In terms of her measures of sexual activity, there are some very obvious things to point out. The first is that it is very difficult to relate any of the sex questions to sexual inhibition as such. Some of the questions deal with frequency of sexual activities, some deal with sexual fantasy and others deal with somewhat 'unusual' sexual practices. Probably Sarah is stuck with a fatal flaw in her research – that is, she failed to *operationalise* her concept properly; she may not have turned her *idea* of sexual inhibitions into a *measure* of that thing. It may or may not be that her measures do reflect sexual inhibitions. This is really a matter of the validity of her measures for her purposes. At the level of the superficial validity of the questions we may have our doubts. Clearly Sarah might have done better to include some questions which ask about sexual inhibitions. In the circumstances, it might be appropriate for Sarah to reformulate her hypothesis to suggest that religious upbringing influences sexual behaviours and sexual fantasy. At least this might make more sense in terms of her questionnaire. Unfortunately there is a downside to this – sexual inhibition seemed to be a psychologically interesting concept.

33.4 Initial variable classification

It is useful for novice researchers to classify the variables that they have collected into category variables and numerical scores:

1. You should remember that psychologists frequently turn answers on a verbal scale into numerical scores. So questions 5, 7 and 9–14 of Sarah's questionnaire all have fixed answer alternatives. Although they do not involve numbers, it is conventional in psychological research to impose a numerical scale of 1 to 5 onto these answer categories. The reason for this is that the categories have verbal labels which imply increasing quantities of something. Scaling from 1 to 5 is arbitrary but has been shown to work pretty well in practice.

2. Some variables which appear at first to be just nominal categories can be turned into numerical scores simply and easily. The classic example of this in research is the variable gender which consists of just two categories: male and female. Innumerable research reports code the gender variable numerically as 1 = male and 2 = female. The logic is obvious, the numerical codings implying different quantities of the variable femaleness (or maleness). However, such variables can legitimately be treated in either way.

So, with these points in mind, we can classify each of our variables as 'category' or 'numerical score' or 'other' – meaning anything we are uncertain about (as in Table 33.1).

This is quite promising in terms of statistical analysis as 12 out of the 15 variables can be classified as numerical scores. This allows some of the more powerful correlational statistical techniques to be used if required. This still leaves three variables classified as categories. These are the degree course the student is taking, their religion and their

Table 33.1	Sarah's 15 questions classified as category or score variables	
Nominal or category variables	**Numerical score variables**	**Other**
Question 1: Gender[a]	Question 1: Gender[a]	
Question 2: Degree course		
	Question 3: Age	
Question 4: Religion		
	Question 5: Faith	
	Question 6: Attend	
	Question 7: God	
	Question 8: Virgin	
	Question 9: Promiscuous	
	Question 10: Fantasise	
	Question 11: Guilty	
	Question 12: Oral	
	Question 13: Sadomasochism	
	Question 14: Like sex	
Question 15: Pornography		

[a] Means that the variable may be placed in more than one column.

views on pornography. These are probably quite varied in terms of their answers any-way. So, Sarah may find that there may be 20 or more different degree courses included in the list of replies with only a few students in each of these 20 or more categories. Similarly, the religion question could generate a multiplicity of different replies. *As they stand, these three variables are of little use in statistical analysis – they need to be recoded in some way.*

33.5   Further coding of data

It is difficult to know why Sarah included the degree course question – it does not seem to have much to do with the issues at hand – so one approach is to discreetly ignore it. Probably a better approach is to recode the answers in a simple but appropriate way. One thing which could be done is to recode them as science or arts degree courses. In other words, the degree course could be coded as 1 if it is science and 2 if it is arts. If this is done then the variable could be classified as a numerical score much as the gender variable could be.

The religion question is more of a problem. Given that the answers will include Catholics, Mormons, Baptists and many more, the temptation might be to classify the variable simply as *religion given* versus *no religion given*. However, this may not serve Sarah's purposes too well since it may be that the key thing is whether the religion is sexually controlling or not. One approach that Sarah could take is to obtain the services of people who are knowledgeable about various religions. They could be asked to rate the religions in terms of their degree of sexual control over their members. This could be done on a short scale such as:

| Very sexually controlling | Sexually controlling | Not sexually controlling |

This would transform the religion variable into a numerical scale if ratings were applied from 0 to 2, for example. Those not mentioning a religion might be deemed to be in the 'not sexually controlling' category. Obviously Sarah should report the degree of agree-ment between the raters of the religion (i.e. the interrater reliability).

Of course, Sarah might decide to categorise the religions in a category form:

1. None

2. Catholic

3. Protestant

4. Muslim

5. Other.

Unfortunately, this classification retains the nominal category characteristics of the original data although reducing the numbers of categories quite substantially.

The question about pornography seems to be a natural nominal category variable given the response alternatives. Perhaps it is best to treat it as such although it could be recoded in such a way that the 'is a stimulant' and 'is best home-made' answers are classified together as being pro-pornography while the 'is disgusting' answer is given a different score. There are no hard-and-fast rules about these decisions and at some stage you have to come to terms with the fact that some choices seem almost arbitrary. That does not mean that you should not try to base your decisions on rational arguments as far as possible.

33.6   Data cleaning

There is little point in retaining variables in your research which contain little or no variance. It is particularly important with analyses of questionnaire-type materials to systematically exclude useless variables since they can create misleading impressions at a later stage.

The important steps are as follows:

1. Draw up or print out frequency counts of the values of each variable you have. This can be done as frequency tables or histograms/bar charts. It should become obvious to you if virtually every participant in the research gives much the same answer to a question. Consider deleting such non-discriminating questions.

2. In the case of variables which have a multiplicity of different values, you might consider recoding these variables into a small number of ranges. This might apply in the case of the age question in Sarah's research.

3. Where you find empty or virtually empty response categories then consider combining categories. Some categories may contain just a few cases. These are probably useless for your overall analysis.

33.7   Data analysis

■ A relatively simple approach

If Sarah follows our advice, all or virtually all of the variables will be coded as numerical scores. Any variables not coded in this way will have to be analysed by statistics suitable for category data – this might be the chi-square but more likely they will be treated as different values of the independent variable for the analysis of variance or a similar test. We would recommend, as far as possible within the requirements of your hypotheses, that all variables are transformed into numerical scores.

Accepting this, it would be a relatively simple matter to calculate the correlations between all of the variables in Sarah's list and each other. The trouble with this is that it results in a rather large correlation matrix of 15×15 correlation coefficients – in other words a table of 225 coefficients. Although the table will be symmetrical around the diagonal of the matrix, this still leaves over 100 different correlations. It is not the purpose of statistical analysis to pour complexity on your research; statistics are there to simplify as far as is possible.

In Sarah's research, the sex questions are quite numerous. She has eight different questions about sexual matters. Obviously it would be satisfactory if there were some way of combining these different answers in order that a single measure of 'sexual inhibition' could be developed. One simple thing that might be done is simply to add the scores on the questions together. This would require the following:

1. That the different questions are scored in the same direction. Looking at Sarah's questionnaire we see that, for example, the question 'I like sex' if scored numerically from left to right would give a bigger score to those who liked sex most often. However, the answers to the question on sadomasochism if scored numerically from left to right would give a lower score to those who liked sadomasochistic sex. It is necessary to recode her answers in such a way that they are consistent. In this case,

all the answers which are more sexual could be rescored as necessary to make the high scores pro-sex.

2. That the standard deviations of scores on questions to be added together are similar, otherwise the questions with the biggest standard deviations will swamp the others. If they differ radically, then it is best to convert each score on a variable to a standard score and then add up answers to several questions (Chapter 5).

A similar sort of thing could be done with the three religious questions, although it might be equally appropriate, given their relatively small number, to treat them as three separate variables.

In order to test her hypotheses, Sarah could correlate the sex and religion variables together. A significant relationship in the predicted direction would support Sarah's hypotheses. (It would be equally appropriate to apply *t*-tests or analyses of variance with religion as the independent variable and sex questions as the dependent variables.)

The advantage of using correlations is that it is then possible to control for (or partial out) obvious background variables which might influence the relationships found. In this study gender and age are of particular interest since both of them might relate to our main variables of interest. Partial correlation could be used to remove the influence of gender and age from the correlation between religion and sexual inhibition.

■ A more complex approach

Given the number of questions Sarah has included on her questionnaire, it is arguable that she ought to consider using factor analysis on the sex questions to explore the pattern of interrelations between the variables. She may well find that the answers to the sex questions tend to cluster together to form small groups of questions which tend to measure separate aspects of sex. For example, questions which deal with unusual sexual practices might be grouped together.

Factor analysis would identify the important clusters or factors. In addition, factor analysis will usually give factor scores which are weighted scores for each individual on each factor separately. These are expressed on the same scale and so are comparable. In other words, they have already been expressed in terms of standard scores.

It is then possible to relate scores on the religion variable(s) with scores on each of the factors just as before. Partialling out gender and age might also be appropriate.

■ An alternative complex approach

One could also employ multiple regression (Chapter 31). Probably the best approach is to use religion as the dependent (criterion) variable(s) and the separate sex variables as the independent (predictor) variables. In this way, it is possible to find out which of the sex variables contribute to the prediction of the religious experiences of the participants in childhood. Sarah may find that only certain of the questions are particularly and independently related to religion. Actually, Sarah could control for age and gender by forcing them into the regression early in the analysis.

Key points

- Although statistics can help structure poor data, it is impossible to remedy all faults through statistics. Research design and planning are always vital.

- Statistics is useful in simplifying complex data into a small number of variables. Unfortunately, for most practical purposes it is impossible to do this without resorting to computer analysis. This is because of the sheer number of variables to be analysed.

- Do not let your partying outstrip your studying.

COMPUTER ANALYSIS

To help her with her analysis, Sarah may want to refer to our SPSS Statistics instruction book to this text which is Dennis Howitt and Duncan Cramer (2011), *Introduction to SPSS Statistics in Psychology: For version 19 and earlier*, Harlow: Pearson. This book gives detailed step-by-step procedures for what she could do together with advice on how to report the results.

PART 5

Assorted advanced techniques

CHAPTER 34

The size of effects in statistical analysis

Do my findings matter?

Overview

- Statistical significance is not the key attribute of a successful statistical analysis. Significance is merely a matter of whether the trend in the sample is likely if there is not a trend in the population.

- More important is the size of the relationship or difference obtained. This is not always easily assessed on the basis of tests of significance.

- One standardised way of indicating the strength of a relationship is simply to turn the statistic into a correlation coefficient. This is easily done for chi-square, the t-test, nonparametric tests and the analysis of variance using the simple formulae presented in this chapter. There are other ways of doing this including Cohen's d which is discussed in later chapters.

Preparation

Significance testing (Chapter 10) and the correlation coefficient (Chapter 7) are the basic ideas. Since this chapter contrasts with much of current practice in the use of statistics by academic psychologists, a degree course at the University of Real Life might help.

34.1 Introduction

One of the most neglected questions in statistical analysis is that of whether or not the researcher's findings are of any real substance. Obviously part of the answer depends very much on the particular research question being asked. One needs to address issues such as:

- Is this a theoretically important issue?
- Is this an issue of social relevance? and
- Will this research actually help people?

None of these are statistical matters. Statistics can help quantify the strength of the relationships established in the research. Very few research publications seriously discuss this issue with respect to the research they describe.

34.2 Statistical significance

Students sometimes get confused as to the meaning of significance in statistics. Perhaps it is a pity that the word significance was ever used in this context since all that it actually means is that it is reasonable to generalise from your sample data to the population. That is to say, significance merely tells you the extent to which you can be confident that your findings are not simply artefacts of your particular sample or samples. It has absolutely nothing to do with whether or not there are really substantial trends in your data. Researchers tend to keep a little quiet about the substance of their findings, preferring merely to report the statistical significance. It is common – but bad – practice to dwell on statistical significance, but this is encouraged by the fact that publication of one's research in psychology depends to some extent on obtaining statistical significance.

The size of the samples being used has a profound effect on the statistical significance of one's research. A correlation of 0.81 is needed to be statistically significant at the 5% level with a sample size of 6. However, with a much larger sample size (say, 100), a much smaller correlation of 0.20 is statistically significant at the 5% level. In other words, with a large enough sample size quite small relationships can be statistically significant. This is discussed extensively in Chapter 39 on statistical power analysis.

We have already seen that the *squared* correlation coefficient basically gives us the proportion of the total variance shared by two variables. Sometimes r^2 is referred to as the *coefficient of determination*. With a correlation of $r = 1.00$ the value of r^2 is still 1.00 (i.e. the total amount of variance). That means that all of the variation in one of the variables is predictable from the other variable. In other words, 100% of the variation on one variable is determinable from the variation in the other variable. Expressed graphically, it would mean that all of the points on a scattergram would fit perfectly on a straight line. If, however, the correlation between two variables is 0.2 then this means that r^2 equals 0.04. That is to say, the two variables have only 4% of their variance in common. This is not very much at all despite the fact that such a small correlation may well be statistically significant given a large enough sample size. The scatterplot of such a small correlation has points which tend to scatter quite a lot from the best-fitting straight line between the points – in other words, there is a lot of error variance compared to the strength of the relationship between the two variables.

34.3 Method and statistical efficiency

Before going any further, we should emphasise that the quality of your research methods is an important factor determining the strength of the relationships found in your research. Sloppy research methods or poor measurements are to be avoided at all costs. Anything which introduces measurement error into your research design will reduce the apparent trends in the research. So, for example, a laboratory experimenter must take scrupulous care in standardising her or his procedures as far as possible.

This is clearly demonstrated if we consider a researcher trying to assess the relationship between children's ages and their heights in a sample of pre-school children. An excellent method for doing this would be to obtain each child's birth certificate to obtain his or her age and to take the child down to the local clinic to have the child's height precisely measured by the clinic nurse who is experienced at doing this. In these circumstances, there is probably very little we can do further to maximise our chances of assessing the true relationship between age and height in children.

A much sloppier way of doing this research on the relation between children's ages and heights might be as follows. The researcher asks the child's nursery teacher to estimate the child's height and tells them to guess if they complain that they do not know. The children's ages are measured by asking the children themselves. It is pretty obvious that these measures of age and height are a little rough and ready. Using these approximate measures we would expect rather poor correlations between age and height – especially compared with the previous, very precise method. In other words, the precision of our measurement procedures has an important influence on the relationships we obtain.

The difference between the two studies is that the second researcher is using very unreliable measures of height and age compared with the very reliable measures of the first researcher. There are a number of ways of measuring reliability in psychology including interrater reliability which is essentially the correlation between a set of measurements taken by person A with those taken by person B. So, for example, we would expect that the birth certificate method of measuring age would produce high correlations between the calculations of two different people, and that asking the children themselves would not produce very reliable measures compared with the answer we would get from the same children even the next day.

If you can calculate the reliability of your measurements, it is possible to adjust the correlation between two measures for the unreliability of each of the measures. This essentially inflates the reliability coefficients upwards towards 1.00. In other words, you get the correlation between age and height assuming that the measures were totally reliable. The formula for doing this is:

$$r_{x_\infty y_\infty} = \frac{r_{xy}}{\sqrt{r_{xx}r_{yy}}}$$

The symbol $r_{x_\infty y_\infty}$ is the coefficient of attenuation. It is merely the correlation between variables x and y if these variables were perfectly reliable. The symbols r_{xx} and r_{yy} are the separate reliability coefficients of the variables x and y.

Often in research we do not have estimates of the reliability of our measures so the procedure is not universally applicable.

Although it is relatively easy to see the size of the relationships in correlation research, it is not quite so obvious in relation to experiments which have been analysed using *t*-tests, chi-square or a nonparametric test such as the Wilcoxon matched pairs. One of the approaches to this is to find ways of turning each of these statistics into a correlation coefficient. Generally this is computationally easy. The resulting correlation coefficient makes it very easy to assess the size of your relationships as it can be interpreted like any other correlation coefficient.

■ Chi-square

It is easy to turn a 2×2 chi-square into a sort of correlation coefficient by substituting the appropriate values in the following formula:

$$r_{\text{phi}} = \sqrt{\frac{\text{chi-square}}{N}}$$

r_{phi} is simply a Pearson correlation coefficient for frequency scores. In fact, it is merely a special name for the Pearson correlation coefficient formula used in these circumstances. Interpret it more or less like any other correlation coefficient. It is always positive because chi-square itself can only have positive values. Remember that N in the above formula refers to the number of subjects and *not* to the degrees of freedom.

If your chi-square is bigger than a 2×2 table, you can calculate the *contingency coefficient* instead. The formula for this is:

$$\text{contingency coefficient} = \sqrt{\frac{\text{chi-square}}{\text{chi-square} + N}}$$

As above, N in this case is the sample size, *not* the number of degrees of freedom.

It is possible to interpret the contingency coefficient *very approximately* as if it were a Pearson correlation coefficient. But avoid making precise parallels between the two.

■ The *t*-test

Essentially what is done here is to turn the *independent variable* into numerical values. That is to say, if the research design has, say, an experimental and a control group we code one group with the value 1 and the other group with the value 2. Take the research design in Table 34.1, for example, which compares men and women in terms of level of job ambition (the dependent variable).

Of course, normally we would analyse the difference between the means in terms of the *t*-test or something similar. However, we can correlate the scores on the dependent variable (job ambition) if we code the independent variable as 1 for a man and 2 for a woman (Table 34.2). The two sets of scores can then be correlated using a Pearson correlation. This should be a simple calculation for you. However, if you have already worked out your *t*-values for the *t*-test you can use the following formula to enable you to calculate the correlation quicker:

$$r_{\text{bis}} = \sqrt{\frac{t^2}{t^2 + df}}$$

Table 34.1	Scores of men and women on a dependent variable

Men	Women
5	2
4	1
9	3
6	2
4	1
7	6
5	2
1	2
4	

Table 34.2	Arranging the data in Table 34.1 so that gender can be correlated with the dependent variable

Score on dependent variable (job ambition)	Score on independent variable gender (men coded as 1, women coded as 2)
5	1
4	1
9	1
6	1
4	1
7	1
5	1
1	1
4	1
2	2
1	2
3	2
2	2
1	2
6	2
2	2
2	2

where t is the value of the t-statistic and df equals the degrees of freedom for the t-test.

Do not worry too much about r_{bis} since it is merely the Pearson correlation coefficient when one variable (e.g. gender) has just one of two values.

34.5   An approximation for nonparametric tests

We have to approximate to obtain a correlation coefficient for nonparametric tests such as the Mann–Whitney U-test. One possible procedure is to work out the statistic (e.g. Mann–Whitney U-test), check its probability value (significance level) and then look up what the value of the t-test would be for that same significance level and sample size. For example, if we get a value of the Mann–Whitney U of 211 which we find to be significant at the 5% level (two-tailed test) on a sample of 16 subjects, we could look up in the t-table the value of t which would be significant at the 5% level (two-tailed test) on a sample of 16 subjects (i.e. the degrees of freedom = 14). This value of t is 2.15 which could be substituted in the formula:

$$r_{\text{bis}} = \sqrt{\frac{t^2}{t^2 + df}}$$

34.6   Analysis of variance (ANOVA)

It is possible to compute from analysis of variance data a correlation measure called *eta*. This is analogous to a correlation coefficient but describes a curvilinear rather than the linear relationship which the Pearson correlation coefficient does. It is of particular use in the analysis of variance since it is sometimes difficult to know which of the independent variables explains the most variance. The probability value of an F-ratio in itself does not enable us to judge which of the independent variables accounts for the largest amount of the variance of the dependent variable. Table 34.3 is a summary table from an analysis of variance considering the influence of intelligence and social class on a dependent variable. It is difficult to know from the table whether intelligence or social class explains more of the variance as the degrees of freedom differ.

In order to calculate the value of eta for any of the variables all we need to do is substitute in the following formula:

$$\text{eta} = \sqrt{\frac{\text{treatment } df \times F - \text{ratio}}{(\text{treatment } df \times F - \text{ratio}) + \text{within } df}}$$

So, for example, if we take intelligence then we substitute the values from Table 34.3 in the formula:

Table 34.3	Analysis of variance summary table				
Source of variance	**Sum of squares**	**Degrees of freedom**	**Mean square**	**F-ratio**	**Significance**
Intelligence	1600	2	800	8.9	1%
Social class	2400	3	800	8.9	1%
Interaction	720	6	120	1.3	ns
Within (error)	9720	108	90		

Table 34.4	Analysis of variance summary table with values of eta added					
Source of variance	Sum of squares	Degrees of freedom	Mean square	F-ratio	Significance	Eta
Intelligence	1600	2	800	8.9	1%	0.38
Social class	2400	3	800	8.9	1%	0.44
Interaction	720	6	120	1.3	ns	0.26
Within (error)	9720	108	90			

$$\text{eta} = \sqrt{\frac{2 \times 8.9}{(2 \times 8.9) + 108}} = \sqrt{\frac{17.8}{17.8 + 108}}$$

$$= \sqrt{\frac{17.8}{125.8}} = \sqrt{0.1415} = 0.38$$

If we do a similar calculation for the two other sources of variation, we can extend our summary table to include eta (Table 34.4). What this extra information tells us is that social class accounts for more variation in the dependent variable than does either intelligence or the interaction. Eta is calculated by some statistics packages such as SPSS Statistics.

Key points

- *Do not* expect the things in this chapter to feature regularly in other researchers' reports. They tend to get ignored despite their importance.

- *Do* be aware of the need to assess the degree of explanatory power obtained in your research as part of your interpretation of the value of your findings. All too frequently psychologists seek statistical significance and forget that their findings may be trivial in terms of the amount of variance explained.

- Do try to design your research in such a way that the error and unreliability are minimised as far as possible.

COMPUTER ANALYSIS

The SPSS Statistics instruction book to this text is Dennis Howitt and Duncan Cramer (2011), *Introduction to SPSS Statistics in Psychology: For version 19 and earlier*, Harlow: Pearson. Chapter 23 in that book gives detailed step-by-step procedures for obtaining eta together with advice on how to report this result.

CHAPTER 35

Meta-analysis

Combining and exploring statistical findings from previous research

Overview

- A review of the findings of previous research is a typical component of any research report. However, this is a very difficult thing to do adequately given the availability of many research studies in some areas.

- Meta-analysis provides a way of handling the complexity of the multiple research studies available on many topics.

- It consists of methods of assessing the size of relationships between variables or differences between sample means. The finding of each study is converted into a standard measure of effect such as a Pearson correlation coefficient or Cohen's d. We concentrate on the correlation coefficient.

- Effect sizes from several studies may be combined to give an overall effect size.

- Furthermore, studies may be coded in a number of ways such as the type of study, the number of participants and even the geographic location of the study. The relationship between these variables and effect size can be calculated. The findings may suggest that, for example, laboratory studies reveal greater effects than field studies.

Preparation

Review effect size (Chapter 34). In particular, make sure that you understand the difference between statistical significance and effect size.

35.1   Introduction

Meta-analysis is a general term to describe statistical techniques which allow a researcher to analyse the pattern of findings from a variety of published and unpublished studies into a particular research question. Most statistical analyses investigate the data from a single research study. However, when we review the research literature we frequently find a number of studies researching similar hypotheses and similar variables. Such studies can vary enormously in terms of the method they employ (for example, field studies versus laboratory studies) or the populations they sample (for example, students versus the general population). Sometimes a number of studies may find positive evidence in favour of the hypothesis whereas others support the reverse trend. The main objectives of meta-analysis are as follows:

1. To assess the strength of relationships over a range of studies and, if possible, to combine these into a single overall indicator of the relationship.

2. To assess the influence of various characteristics of pertinent studies (the type of sample, the type of method, etc.) on the strength of the relationships found in the studies.

Meta-analysis involves some new concepts. Although relatively rare in student work, a meta-analysis is a feasible proposition where time and resources are available for a thorough literature search.

A crucial feature of any research study is the process of reviewing the available empirical literature on a particular topic. To date, meta-analysis has not routinely been applied to these reviews. Usually a meta-analysis is carried out as an independent exercise because of a number of difficulties in its use:

1. Because meta-analysis is a study of studies, it is necessary to obtain copies of relevant reports and publications dealing with the statistical analysis of the relationship in question. Sometimes these may have to be obtained, say, from other libraries (or from the researchers themselves if the study has been recently published). Sometimes publications will be untraceable. The process of obtaining research reports costs time and there may be financial charges involved. Since there may be a bias towards the publishing of significant research findings, ideally a meta-analysis should also include unpublished research findings. These can be even more difficult to identify and obtain.

2. The meta-analyst needs to be familiar with computerised database searches. Unless a variety of databases are searched using a variety of keywords, important research studies may be overlooked. Published articles and books may be sources of additional studies which have not been found using the databases.

3. There is inconsistency in the reporting of research findings. Sometimes important pieces of information are missing. A meta-analysis can be done with very minimal information – sample size and significance level. If effect size were routinely reported for every research study there would be no problem. Increasingly, journals are requiring this information. Nevertheless, meta-analysts may have to use a range of formulae to transpose published findings into measures of effect size.

4. There is a good deal of non-computer work involved in meta-analysis. Meta-analysis is not available on any of the standard statistical packages. However, much of the work is computationally easy with just a hand calculator. Computers can be useful in later stages of the analysis, but they are far from essential.

5. Meta-analysis involves defining the variables and types of study of interest with some precision. This requires some understanding of the field of study which is difficult to achieve within the timescale of student projects.

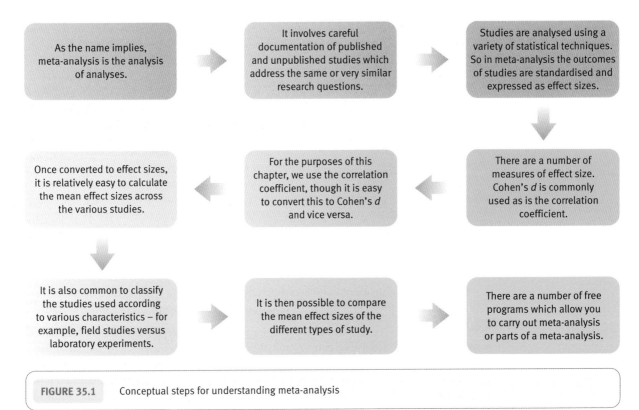

As the name implies, meta-analysis is the analysis of analyses.

It involves careful documentation of published and unpublished studies which address the same or very similar research questions.

Studies are analysed using a variety of statistical techniques. So in meta-analysis the outcomes of studies are standardised and expressed as effect sizes.

There are a number of measures of effect size. Cohen's *d* is commonly used as is the correlation coefficient.

For the purposes of this chapter, we use the correlation coefficient, though it is easy to convert this to Cohen's *d* and vice versa.

Once converted to effect sizes, it is relatively easy to calculate the mean effect sizes across the various studies.

It is also common to classify the studies used according to various characteristics – for example, field studies versus laboratory experiments.

It is then possible to compare the mean effect sizes of the different types of study.

There are a number of free programs which allow you to carry out meta-analysis or parts of a meta-analysis.

FIGURE 35.1   Conceptual steps for understanding meta-analysis

It is to be hoped that readers will not be too deterred by the above comments. After all, they imply diligence, planning, hard work and understanding of the chosen field of research. These are reasonable targets for any researcher whether or not using meta-analysis.

Criticisms of meta-analysis usually apply equally to conventional reviews of the empirical studies. So, for example, problems of retrieval of studies, biases in selection of statistically significant findings in research publications, glossing over details in particular studies and similar issues are common to both meta-analytic and other attempts to synthesise the literature.

This chapter provides a practical introduction to meta-analysis which should be sufficient to guide students through the major stages involved. It does not pretend to be an exhaustive coverage. Figure 35.1 gives the key steps to consider in understanding meta-analysis.

35.2   The Pearson correlation coefficient as the effect size

Effect size is the central concept in meta-analysis. It means exactly what it says – the size of the effect of one variable on a second. In other words, the effect size indicates the amount of relationship between one variable and another variable in a standardised way. This should not be confused with a causal effect, though in controlled experiments it may actually mean causal effect. Ultimately, and largely for practical reasons, the most convenient measure of effect size is the Pearson correlation coefficient between the two variables (say the independent variable and the dependent variable). In Chapter 34, the correlation coefficient was used as a measure of effect size (i.e. the strength of the relationship between the two variables). Effect size is not the same as statistical significance, which is about generalising from a sample to a population. The larger the correlation coefficient between two variables, the larger the effect of one variable on the other.

Chapter 34 also showed just how easy it is to convert a number of different statistical tests such as the *t*-test and chi-square into a Pearson correlation coefficient. It is the ease of such conversions that ensures the Pearson correlation coefficient's practical utility as a measure of effect size. Irrespective of the nature of the statistical analysis reported by the researcher in the primary report, it is highly likely that a correlation coefficient can be obtained from this information. The minimum information required is significance level and sample size.

Do not assume that effect size is useful only when comparing independent variables and dependent variables in experimental studies. Meta-analysis can be used in virtually any type of study. Also, remember that the techniques can be useful when combining the results of just two studies.

35.3   Other measures of effect size

Cohen's *d* is the other common measure of effect size. Its major disadvantage is that it can be more difficult to calculate from the statistical analyses usually presented in reports of psychological research. Cohen's *d* is the difference between the mean of one group of participants and the mean of the other group adjusted by dividing by the standard deviation of the scores. In other words, it is the difference between the two groups standardised by dividing by the standard deviation. Just as we can turn any score into a *z*-score by dividing the score by the standard deviation, we can generate a standardised effect score by dividing the unstandardised effect size (for example, the difference between the experimental and control group) by the size of the standard deviation of the scores. Expressed as a formula, Cohen's *d* is usually given as:

$$\text{Cohen's } d = \frac{\text{mean of Group A} - \text{mean of Group B}}{\text{standard deviations of both groups of scores pooled together}}$$

The standard deviation is obtained by subtracting the experimental group scores from the experimental group's mean and subtracting the control group scores from the control group's mean. These difference scores are then pooled (combined) as a first step in computing their standard deviation. Actually, this is not Cohen's formulation since he simply recommended using the standard deviation of one of the populations on the assumption that both populations should have the same standard deviation. It is possible to find on the Web a number of programs and applets which will calculate Cohen's *d* for you. G*Power, which is discussed in Chapter 39, can do this as part of power analysis. See the Computer analysis section at the end of the present chapter. Although there is a similarity, it is not true to say that Cohen's *d* is the same as the *t*-test despite overlaps in their calculation. In the *t*-test, the division is by the standard error of the difference between the sample means; in Cohen's *d*, the division is by the standard deviation of the pooled groups of scores. (In essence the two standard deviations are combined arithmetically.)

Although Cohen's *d* is commonly used in meta-analysis, it is not quite as flexible in use as the Pearson correlation coefficient. Most important is the fact that it is much easier to estimate the Pearson correlation coefficient from the minimal information that researchers sometimes supply. We saw in Chapter 34 how we can calculate a correlation coefficient from a range of tests of significance. This is not so easy with Cohen's *d*.

35.4 Effects of different characteristics of studies

Modern meta-analyses are not simply about determining the effect size over a range of studies. They also try to estimate what characteristics of studies may be responsible for large effect sizes and what characteristics of studies may be responsible for smaller effect sizes. It is usual to select a range of possible study variables which may be related to effect size. These may include:

- the gender of the participants
- the size of the study
- the quality of the study as rated by a panel of psychologists or from the prestige of the journal in which the study was published
- whether the study involved behavioural rather than attitudinal measures
- the sex of the researcher
- whether the study was a laboratory experiment or field study
- any other variable that the meta-analyst judges to be pertinent and which can be assessed from the primary published reports of studies or by other means such as ratings by experts.

This list is not the ideal or complete list. The study variables you choose may be very different from the above list which should not simply be routinely applied without further consideration.

The selection of study variables is a subjective matter in the sense that it depends on knowledge, skill and a degree of insight. These are much the same characteristics that are required by any researcher. Note that the information the meta-analyst wants may not be given in the available research reports – for example, the researcher may not have analysed data for males and females separately.

The basic procedures for investigating the influence of study variables on effect size are very simple. So if a meta-analyst wished to study effect size in studies involving female participants compared with those involving male participants, the following effect sizes could be calculated:

1. The overall (combined) effect size for relevant studies irrespective of the gender of the participants.

2. The overall (combined) effect size for female participant studies.

3. The overall (combined) effect size for male participant studies.

Table 35.1	Meta-analysis table for different age and gender combinations	
	Young	**Older**
Males	$r = 0.32$	$r = 0.13$
	$r = 0.45$	$r = -0.03$
	$r = 0.35$	
Females	$r = 0.22$	$r = -0.04$
	$r = 0.12$	$r = 0.05$
	$r = 0.15$	$r = 0.15$
		$r = 0.11$

It may well be that the overall effect size is more or less the same for both males and females. However, the male and female effect sizes could be very different. Such a simple analysis may be insufficient for the analyst's particular purposes. For example, the analysis would be a little more complicated if the analyst wished to compare the effect sizes for young males, young females, older males and older females. This would involve the calculation of effect sizes for the four different age/gender combinations (see Table 35.1).

Not all meta-analyses investigate the influence of study characteristics. Carry out such an analysis only if it is relevant to your purposes.

35.5   First steps in meta-analysis

■ Step 1: Define the variables of interest to you

Decide precisely which two variables you are investigating in your meta-analysis. (Other pairs of variables can also be considered and treated in the same way in parallel.) This is in essence deciding the nature of the research hypothesis to be tested.

■ Step 2: Plan your database search

Plan your search for relevant studies involving your chosen variables. This search should involve a computer search of the relevant databases. Perusing studies referred to in relevant research publications may generate additions to your list of relevant studies. Of course, you may wish to omit certain types of study because they are not relevant or do not meet other criteria. It is important to do this using stipulated criteria rather than on whims. If possible, seek out unpublished studies.

■ Step 3: Obtain research reports

Obtain copies of research reports containing the statistical analyses of the relevant studies. These may be available in your local university or college library, but sometimes they have to be ordered from other libraries. The authors of recently published studies may be contacted by mail or e-mail to obtain copies of reports. Databases usually contain an adequate address for the senior author. Remember that at the very minimum, you need a significance level and sample size to calculate an effect size.

Sometimes a previous meta-analytic study may supply you with details of otherwise unobtainable studies. It may be possible to use the effect sizes reported in this earlier meta-analysis. Cohen's *d* is easily converted to *r* (and vice versa) by using Table 35.2. This table also serves as a ready reference to compare effect sizes expressed as *r* with those given as Cohen's *d*.

■ Step 4: Calculating effect sizes for each study

A standard measure of effect size should be calculated for each of the relationships between the variables for each study reviewed. Our chosen measure of effect size is the Pearson correlation coefficient or *r*. Some studies may report this value or some other measure of effect size, but usually they do not. Where effect sizes are not reported they need to be calculated by the meta-analyst.

It is usually possible to use the test of significance reported in the original analysis to calculate the effect size *r*. Table 35.3 gives this conversion for common tests of significance. We have already seen some of these in Chapter 34.

Table 35.2 Equivalent effect sizes expressed as Cohen's *d* and Pearson correlation coefficient

Pearson *r*	Cohen's *d*	Pearson *r*	Cohen's *d*	Pearson *r*	Cohen's *d*	Pearson *r*	Cohen's *d*	Pearson *r*	Cohen's *d*
0.00	0.00	0.20	0.41	0.40	0.87	0.60	1.50	0.80	2.67
0.01	0.02	0.21	0.43	0.41	0.90	0.61	1.54	0.81	2.76
0.02	0.04	0.22	0.45	0.42	0.93	0.62	1.58	0.82	2.87
0.03	0.06	0.23	0.47	0.43	0.95	0.63	1.62	0.83	2.98
0.04	0.08	0.24	0.49	0.44	0.98	0.64	1.67	0.84	3.10
0.05	0.10	0.25	0.52	0.45	1.01	0.65	1.71	0.85	3.23
0.06	0.12	0.26	0.54	0.46	1.04	0.66	1.76	0.86	3.37
0.07	0.14	0.27	0.56	0.47	1.06	0.67	1.81	0.87	3.53
0.08	0.16	0.28	0.58	0.48	1.09	0.68	1.85	0.88	3.71
0.09	0.18	0.29	0.61	0.49	1.12	0.69	1.91	0.89	3.90
0.10	0.20	0.30	0.63	0.50	1.15	0.70	1.96	0.90	4.13
0.11	0.22	0.31	0.65	0.51	1.19	0.71	2.02	0.91	4.39
0.12	0.24	0.32	0.68	0.52	1.22	0.72	2.08	0.92	4.69
0.13	0.26	0.33	0.70	0.53	1.25	0.73	2.14	0.93	5.06
0.14	0.28	0.34	0.72	0.54	1.28	0.74	2.20	0.94	5.51
0.15	0.30	0.35	0.75	0.55	1.32	0.75	2.27	0.95	6.08
0.16	0.32	0.36	0.77	0.56	1.35	0.76	2.34	0.96	6.86
0.17	0.35	0.37	0.80	0.57	1.39	0.77	2.31	0.97	7.98
0.18	0.37	0.38	0.82	0.58	1.42	0.78	2.49	0.98	9.85
0.19	0.39	0.39	0.85	0.59	1.46	0.79	2.58	0.99	14.04

Table 35.3 Converting various tests of significance to a correlation coefficient

Statistic	Formula for converting to Pearson correlation	Notes
t-test	$r_{bis} = \sqrt{\dfrac{t^2}{t^2 + df}}$	Can be used for a related or unrelated *t*-test
Chi-square	$r = \sqrt{\dfrac{chi\text{-}square}{N}}$	Only use this formula for a 2×2 chi-square
Cohen's *d*	Convert to *r* using Table 35.2	Useful if no source of data from a study is available other than another meta-analysis
Nonparametric test	$r = \dfrac{z}{\sqrt{N}}$	Alternatively convert to parametric equivalent and substitute this value in formula (see section 34.5 on p. 424)
Pearson correlation coefficient and variants	No conversion necessary	These are already the value of the effect size
Most common tests of significance and when only significance level and sample size given	$r = \dfrac{z}{\sqrt{N}}$	Convert the significance level to *z* using Table 35.4. Then divide by the square root of the sample size involved

However, sometimes this information is missing from the primary source. If you know the sample size and the significance level, then the following formula can be used to approximate the effect size irrespective of the particular test of significance involved. The significance levels should be converted to their one-tailed equivalents if they are given as two-tailed probabilities because the absolute value of z refers to one tail of the standard normal distribution. The sign of the z score needs to be noted.

$$r = \frac{z}{\sqrt{N}}$$

The value of z for the significance level is obtained by consulting Table 35.4. So, if the significance level for a particular study is 0.7% (i.e. the probability is 0.007), then the value of z obtained from Table 35.4 is 2.32. Assuming that the one-tailed significance level is based on 40 participants, the effect size is:

$$r = \frac{2.44}{\sqrt{40}} = \frac{2.44}{6.325} = 0.39$$

Table 35.4		z-distribution for converting one-tailed probability levels to z-scores								
p	**z**	**p**	**z**	**p**	**z**	**p**	**z**	**p**	**z**	
0.000 01	4.265	0.19	0.878	0.40	0.253	0.61	−0.279	0.82	−0.915	
0.0001	3.719	0.20	0.842	0.41	0.228	0.62	−0.306	0.83	−0.954	
0.001	3.090	0.21	0.806	0.42	0.202	0.63	−0.332	0.84	−0.995	
0.01	2.326	0.22	0.772	0.43	0.176	0.64	−0.359	0.85	−1.036	
0.02	2.054	0.23	0.739	0.44	0.151	0.65	−0.385	0.86	−1.080	
0.03	1.881	0.24	0.706	0.45	0.126	0.66	−0.413	0.87	−1.126	
0.04	1.751	0.25	0.675	0.46	0.100	0.67	−0.440	0.88	−1.175	
0.05	1.645	0.26	0.643	0.47	0.075	0.68	−0.468	0.89	−1.227	
0.06	1.555	0.27	0.613	0.48	0.050	0.69	−0.496	0.90	−1.282	
0.07	1.476	0.28	0.583	0.49	0.025	0.70	−0.524	0.91	−1.341	
0.08	1.405	0.29	0.553	0.50	0.000	0.71	−0.553	0.92	−1.405	
0.09	1.341	0.30	0.524	0.51	−0.025	0.72	−0.583	0.93	−1.476	
0.10	1.282	0.31	0.496	0.52	−0.050	0.73	−0.613	0.94	−1.555	
0.11	1.227	0.32	0.468	0.53	−0.075	0.74	−0.643	0.95	−1.645	
0.12	1.175	0.33	0.440	0.54	−0.100	0.75	−0.675	0.96	−1.751	
0.13	1.126	0.34	0.413	0.55	−0.126	0.76	−0.706	0.97	−1.881	
0.14	1.080	0.35	0.385	0.56	−0.151	0.77	−0.739	0.98	−2.054	
0.15	1.036	0.36	0.359	0.57	−0.176	0.78	−0.772	0.99	−2.326	
0.16	0.995	0.37	0.332	0.58	−0.202	0.79	−0.806			
0.17	0.954	0.38	0.306	0.59	−0.228	0.80	−0.842			
0.18	0.915	0.39	0.279	0.60	−0.253	0.81	−0.878			

Find the appropriate significance or probability level p value from the table, the required z-score is adjacent to the *right*.
Reverse this process if you wish to convert your z-score back to a significance or probability level.
Remember that a probability needs to be multiplied by 100% to get the percentage probability.

This is a good approximation given the limited information required. The formula has obvious advantages for use with uncommon tests of significance or those for which a conversion formula to *r* is not available. It can also be used to convert *non*parametric significance levels to effect sizes. Of course, significance levels are not always reported very precisely which may cause problems especially when the findings are *not* significant at the 5% level. Just what is the effect size for this? Some authors report it as an effect size of zero though clearly this is not likely to be the case. Others take it as the 50% or 0.5 level of significance. In these circumstances, it would be better to estimate the effect size from the formulae in Table 35.3 if at all possible.

At the end of this step, you should have values or estimated values of the effect size for each of the studies you are using in your meta-analysis. If you are unable to give an effect size because of incomplete information in the original report of a study or because the report was unobtainable, it will have to be omitted. This omission should be reported in your report of your meta-analysis.

■ Step 5: Combining effect sizes over a number of studies

One aim of meta-analysis is to combine the findings of several studies (or a selected sub-set of studies such as those involving female participants) into a single composite effect size. The obvious way of doing this is to average the effect sizes. However, the simple numerical average of the effect sizes can give a distorted value, particularly when some of the values of the correlation coefficients are large. Instead, we average the effect sizes by converting each *r* into a *z*-score (z_r) for the correlation coefficient using Table 35.5. This table is of the correlation coefficient expressed as a normal distribution. It is different from the *z*-distribution so take care. You need the purple columns to find your value of the correlation coefficient *r* and the required value of z_r is to the right of this in the blue column. The several values of z_r are then summed and averaged by dividing by the number of values. This average can then be turned back into the combined effect size by using Table 35.5 in the reverse mode. (That is, you look for your value of the combined z_r in the right-hand side (blue) of the pairs of columns and find the value of *r* to the left of this (purple).)

Thus if we wish to calculate the average effect size from three studies with the following effect sizes:

study A: *r* = 0.3

study B: *r* = 0.7

study C: *r* = 0.5

we convert each to their z_r by using Table 35.5. These values are 0.310, 0.867 and 0.549, respectively. The numerical average of these is (0.310 + 0.867 + 0.549)/3 = 0.575. We can then reconvert this value to an overall effect size by using Table 35.5 in reverse. The effect size *r* for the three studies combined is therefore 0.52.

It is possible that a particular study has findings in the reverse direction from those of the majority. In this case, its effect size is given a negative value. Thus the overall effect size will be reduced.

■ Step 6: The significance of the combined studies

The significance level of the combined studies can also be assessed. Once again, the simple numerical average of the probability levels is misleading. Intuitively we may appreciate that this simple average makes no allowance for the greatly increased sample size obtained by combining studies. There are numerous different ways of combining

Table 35.5		Extended table of Fisher's z_r transformation of the correlation coefficient

r	z_r	r	z_r	r	z_r	r	z_r	r	z_r	r	z_r	r	z_r
0.01	0.10	0.41	0.436	0.801	1.101	0.841	1.225	0.881	1.380	0.921	1.596	0.961	1.959
0.02	0.020	0.42	0.448	0.802	1.104	0.842	1.228	0.882	1.385	0.922	1.602	0.962	1.972
0.03	0.030	0.43	0.460	0.803	1.107	0.843	1.231	0.883	1.389	0.923	1.609	0.963	1.986
0.04	0.040	0.44	0.472	0.804	1.110	0.844	1.235	0.884	1.394	0.924	1.616	0.964	2.000
0.05	0.050	0.45	0.485	0.805	1.113	0.845	1.238	0.885	1.398	0.925	1.623	0.965	2.014
0.06	0.060	0.46	0.497	0.806	1.116	0.846	1.242	0.886	1.403	0.926	1.630	0.966	2.029
0.07	0.070	0.47	0.510	0.807	1.118	0.847	1.245	0.887	1.408	0.927	1.637	0.967	2.044
0.08	0.080	0.48	0.523	0.808	1.121	0.848	1.249	0.888	1.412	0.928	1.644	0.968	2.060
0.09	0.090	0.49	0.536	0.809	1.124	0.849	1.253	0.889	1.417	0.929	1.651	0.969	2.076
0.10	0.100	0.50	0.549	0.810	1.127	0.850	1.256	0.890	1.422	0.930	1.658	0.970	2.092
0.11	0.110	0.51	0.563	0.811	1.130	0.851	1.260	0.891	1.427	0.931	1.666	0.971	2.110
0.12	0.121	0.52	0.576	0.812	1.133	0.852	1.263	0.892	1.432	0.932	1.673	0.972	2.127
0.13	0.131	0.53	0.590	0.813	1.136	0.853	1.267	0.893	1.437	0.933	1.681	0.973	2.146
0.14	0.141	0.54	0.604	0.814	1.139	0.854	1.271	0.894	1.442	0.934	1.689	0.974	2.165
0.15	0.151	0.55	0.618	0.815	1.142	0.855	1.274	0.895	1.447	0.935	1.697	0.975	2.185
0.16	0.161	0.56	0.633	0.816	1.145	0.856	1.278	0.896	1.452	0.936	1.705	0.976	2.205
0.17	0.172	0.57	0.648	0.817	1.148	0.857	1.282	0.897	1.457	0.937	1.713	0.977	2.227
0.18	0.182	0.58	0.663	0.818	1.151	0.858	1.286	0.898	1.462	0.938	1.721	0.978	2.249
0.19	0.192	0.59	0.678	0.819	1.154	0.859	1.290	0.899	1.467	0.939	1.730	0.979	2.273
0.20	0.203	0.60	0.693	0.820	1.157	0.860	1.293	0.900	1.472	0.940	1.738	0.980	2.298
0.21	0.213	0.61	0.709	0.821	1.160	0.861	1.297	0.901	1.478	0.941	1.747	0.981	2.323
0.22	0.224	0.62	0.725	0.822	1.163	0.862	1.301	0.902	1.483	0.942	1.756	0.982	2.351
0.23	0.234	0.63	0.741	0.823	1.166	0.863	1.305	0.903	1.488	0.943	1.764	0.983	2.380
0.24	0.245	0.64	0.758	0.824	1.169	0.864	1.309	0.904	1.494	0.944	1.774	0.984	2.410
0.25	0.255	0.65	0.775	0.825	1.172	0.865	1.313	0.905	1.499	0.945	1.783	0.985	2.443
0.26	0.266	0.66	0.793	0.826	1.175	0.866	1.317	0.906	1.505	0.946	1.792	0.986	2.477
0.27	0.277	0.67	0.811	0.827	1.179	0.867	1.321	0.907	1.510	0.947	1.802	0.987	2.515
0.28	0.288	0.68	0.829	0.828	1.182	0.868	1.325	0.908	1.516	0.948	1.812	0.988	2.555
0.29	0.299	0.69	0.848	0.829	1.185	0.869	1.329	0.909	1.522	0.949	1.822	0.989	2.599
0.30	0.310	0.70	0.867	0.830	1.188	0.870	1.333	0.910	1.528	0.950	1.832	0.990	2.647
0.31	0.321	0.71	0.887	0.831	1.191	0.871	1.337	0.911	1.533	0.951	1.842	0.991	2.700
0.32	0.332	0.72	0.908	0.832	1.195	0.872	1.341	0.912	1.539	0.952	1.853	0.992	2.759
0.33	0.343	0.73	0.929	0.833	1.198	0.873	1.346	0.913	1.545	0.953	1.863	0.993	2.826
0.34	0.354	0.74	0.951	0.834	1.201	0.874	1.350	0.914	1.551	0.954	1.875	0.994	2.903
0.35	0.365	0.75	0.973	0.835	1.204	0.875	1.354	0.915	1.557	0.955	1.886	0.995	2.995
0.36	0.377	0.76	0.996	0.836	1.208	0.876	1.358	0.916	1.564	0.956	1.897	0.996	3.106
0.37	0.388	0.77	1.020	0.837	1.211	0.877	1.363	0.917	1.570	0.957	1.909	0.997	3.250
0.38	0.400	0.78	1.045	0.838	1.214	0.878	1.367	0.918	1.576	0.958	1.921	0.998	3.453
0.39	0.412	0.79	1.071	0.839	1.218	0.879	1.371	0.919	1.583	0.959	1.933	0.999	3.800
0.40	0.424	0.80	1.098	0.840	1.221	0.880	1.376	0.920	1.589	0.960	1.946		

significance levels from a range of studies to give an overall significance level, each having different advantages or disadvantages. The simplest and one of the most satisfactory methods is to convert each significance level into a z-score using Table 35.4. Rather than divide by the number of z-scores to obtain the average, the sum of the z-scores is divided by the square root of the number of z-scores:

$$z = \frac{\sum z}{\sqrt{N}}$$

Thus if the significance levels from a set of studies are 0.08, 0.15 and 0.02, each of these is converted to a z-score using Table 35.4. This gives us z-scores of 1.405, 1.036 and 2.054, respectively. These z-scores are summed and divided by the square root of the number of z-scores:

$$z = \frac{1.405 + 1.036 + 2.054}{\sqrt{3}} = \frac{4.495}{1.732} = 2.595$$

This average z is converted back into a significance level using Table 35.4. In this case, this gives a combined significance level of 0.001 (or 1.0%).

Note that if the findings of a study are in the *reverse* direction from those of the majority, the corresponding z-score is given a negative sign. Once again, this tends to reduce the overall significance level.

■ Step 7: Comparing effect sizes from studies with different characteristics

Finally, what if one wished to compare effect sizes between studies with different characteristics? For example, what if one wanted to know whether studies involving female participants differed from those involving male participants in terms of their effect size? The easiest way of doing this is to turn your data into a table like Table 35.6. In this table, the effect sizes for the male and female studies are listed in separate columns. It is then a relatively simple matter to compare these two sets of effect-size 'scores' using the Mann–Whitney U-test (Calculation 18.3) or the t-test (Calculation 13.1). This is an approximate procedure in the eyes of some experts since all studies are considered equal although they may differ in terms of the sample size. Despite criticisms of such an approach, it uses familiar statistics and may well be sufficiently powerful for most purposes.

There is a significant difference between these two groups as assessed by either the Mann–Whitney U-test or the unrelated t-test. Thus the effect sizes are greater in studies which involved female participants than in studies involving male participants. If you

Table 35.6	Illustrating the comparison of effect sizes for different study characteristics	
Effect sizes of studies of males		**Effect sizes of studies of females**
0.27		0.41
0.15		0.52
0.22		0.43
0.29		0.47
Mean = 0.23		**Mean = 0.45**

choose the *t*-test, it might be advantageous to convert your effect sizes to z_r values since this will reduce the undue influence of extreme values a little.

35.6   Illustrative example

There is evidence that men's physiological responses to sexually explicit pictures may differentiate sex offenders from non-offenders and non-sex offenders. Physiological response in these studies is assessed by plethysmographs which measure either changes in the volume of the penis or changes in the circumference of the penis. The latter measure is generally not well regarded. The data reported are fictitious but help to illustrate the processes involved in meta-analysis.

■ Step 1: Define the variables of interest to you

In this case, the researchers wished to review the available studies which might indicate whether physiological responses to sexual images could be used to differentiate sex offenders from other men. Consequently the independent variable was sex offender versus non-offender or non-sex offender and the dependent variable was measured by scores on a plethysmograph assessment of the men's response to erotic pictures.

■ Step 2: Plan your database search

The researchers searched the psychological abstract database (PsycINFO – this database is discussed in Chapter 5 of the companion research methods book – see the end of the chapter) and also the medical science database using the keywords plethysmograph, sex offender, rapist, paedophile and molester. Furthermore, as the field is relatively small, the researchers were able to write to one hundred researchers in the field requesting relevant research reports, either published or unpublished.

■ Step 3: Obtain research reports

The researchers found nine studies from their database search to be obtained from their own or other university libraries. These are listed in column 1 of Table 35.7 but they also received two additional unpublished studies from their request to key researchers. Table 35.7 also includes information relevant to calculating the effect size gleaned from these reports and information about possible study variables.

■ Step 4: Calculating an effect size for each study

Table 35.7 lists the information obtained from each study relevant to calculating the effect size. The formula (or table) used is mentioned and the final column provides effect sizes expressed as *r* for each of the studies. Edwards's study, however, is so lacking in the statistical detail provided that it has been deleted by the meta-analysts.

■ Step 5: Combining effect sizes over a number of studies

The meta-analyst combined the effect sizes for all of the studies by converting each effect *r* into a z_r, averaging these and finally converting back to an effect size. This involves turning each effect size correlation into a Fisher z_r using Table 35.5. The effect sizes in order are 0.24, 0.54, 0.52, 0.37, 0.19, 0.34, 0.49, 0.34, 0.22, 0.50 according to Table 35.7.

Table 35.7 Illustrative summary of studies and the conversion of statistics to effect sizes

Study (fictitious)	Effect-size information	Significance	Plethysmograph measure	Control group	Effect-size formula	Effect size r
Brown (1976)	chi-square value given as 4.06 with 1 degree of freedom based on N of 73 cases	0.05	circumference	prisoners	$r = \sqrt{\dfrac{\text{chi-square}}{N}}$	0.24
Grey (1998)	gives effect size as $r = 0.54$	?	volume	prisoners	none needed	0.54
Black (1983)	F given as significant at 0.01 with 20 cases	0.01	circumference	prisoners	$r = \dfrac{z}{\sqrt{N}}$	0.52
White (1995)	t-value given as 2.31 with 34 cases (i.e. $df = 32$)	0.025	volume	non-prisoners	$r_{bis} = \sqrt{\dfrac{t^2}{t^2 + df}}$	0.37
Jones (1966)	t-test reported as 1.45, $df = 54$	0.10	circumference	non-prisoners	$r_{bis} = \sqrt{\dfrac{t^2}{t^2 + df}}$	0.19
Williams (1987)	Mann–Whitney U significant at 1% level based on 47 cases	0.01	circumference	non-prisoners	$r = \dfrac{z}{\sqrt{N}}$	0.34
Parton (unpublished)	related $t = 2.53$, $df = 10$, this was a matched design in which prisoners served as own control	0.025	volume	prisoners	$r_{bis} = \sqrt{\dfrac{t^2}{t^2 + df}}$ (This formula works with related t-tests)	0.49
Carter (unpublished)	$t = 1.67$ with total $N = 23$	0.075	circumference	prisoners	$r_{bis} = \sqrt{\dfrac{t^2}{t^2 + df}}$	0.34
Elliot (1999)	Cohen's d given as 0.45	0.001	circumference	prisoners	convert to r with Table 35.2	0.22
Smith (1989)	F reported as significant at 0.03 with $df = 1, 54$ (i.e. $N = 56$)	0.03	volume	non-prisoners	$r = \dfrac{z}{\sqrt{N}}$	0.50
Edwards (1953)	t-value not reported. Findings not significant at 5% level with sample size = 14	> 0.05 or set at $p = 0.50$	circumference	prisoners	use of formula too crude because of uncertainty about exact significance and no other statistics (alternatively r could be set at 0.00)	study ignored

Remember that the final study has been discarded from the analysis. The average of the corresponding z_r is:

average z_r

$$= \frac{0.245 + 0.604 + 0.576 + 0.388 + 0.192 + 0.354 + 0.536 + 0.354 + 0.224 + 0.549}{10}$$

$$= \frac{4.022}{10} = 0.4022$$

This value of z_r according to Table 35.5 corresponds to an average of the effect sizes of 0.38 (this is obtained by looking for the average z_r of 0.4022 in the body of Table 35.5 and reading off the value of r which corresponds to this value of the averaged z_r).

This process could be repeated to obtain, say, the overall effect size of the volume measure and the circumference measure separately.

■ Step 6: The significance of the combined studies

The overall significance of the combined studies is obtained by turning each significance level into the corresponding z-score using Table 35.4. The various z-scores are then summed and divided by the square root of the number (N) of significance levels employed. Note that for two studies the significance level is not reported or is not precise enough. Thus the calculation is based on just nine studies. The formula for z is:

$$z = \frac{\sum z}{\sqrt{N}}$$

This gives:

$$= \frac{1.645 + 2.326 + 1.960 + 1.281 + 2.326 + 1.960 + 1.440 + 3.090 + 1.880}{\sqrt{9}}$$

$$= \frac{17.908}{3} = 5.97$$

Remember that this is the value of z which has to be converted back to a significance level using Table 35.4. Thus the combined significance level is 0.000 01 or 0.001%.

■ Step 7: Comparing effect sizes from studies with different characteristics

Because there is some question whether the circumference measure is as good as the volume measure, the overall effect sizes were calculated for the circumference measure studies and the volume measure studies separately. This yielded the data in Table 35.8.

Comparing these overall effect sizes, it would seem that there are some grounds for thinking that circumference studies produce the smallest effect size, implying that they are inferior at identifying sex offenders from other men. This comparison is significant at only the 0.067 level with a Mann–Whitney test but significant at 0.04 with the unrelated *t*-test. Using z_r instead of the effect size made no substantial difference to the outcome. This seems reasonably strong evidence that the volume measure tends to produce greater effects than the circumference measures.

A similar analysis comparing the effect of having a prisoner versus a non-prisoner control group showed no significant difference in terms of effect size using the same tests of significance.

Table 35.8	Effect size data for volume measures and circumference penile measures compared
Effect sizes of studies involving volume measure	**Effect sizes of studies involving circumference measure**
0.54	0.24
0.37	0.52
0.49	0.19
0.50	0.34
	0.34
	0.22
Mean = 0.48	**Mean = 0.31**

35.7   Comparing a study with a previous study

Meta-analysis is useful when you are replicating another researcher's study as it provides a method of combining the results of the two studies. Furthermore, you can test to see if your effect size is significantly different from that found in the previous research. The formula involves converting each effect size to z_r using Table 35.5 and then subtracting one from the other and making other calculations involving N (the sample sizes) as in the following formula:

$$z = \frac{r_1 - r_2}{\sqrt{\dfrac{1}{N_1 - 3} + \dfrac{1}{N_2 - 3}}}$$

Thus if the effect sizes under consideration are 0.43 (with $N = 25$) and 0.62 (with $N = 47$) then these are first converted to z_r using Table 35.5. This gives us values of 0.460 and 0.725. The calculation is then:

$$z = \frac{0.460 - 0.725}{\sqrt{\dfrac{1}{25 - 3} + \dfrac{1}{47 - 3}}}$$

$$= \frac{-0.265}{\sqrt{\dfrac{1}{22} + \dfrac{1}{44}}}$$

$$= \frac{-0.265}{\sqrt{0.0455 + 0.0227}}$$

$$= \frac{-0.265}{\sqrt{0.0682}}$$

$$= \frac{-0.265}{0.261}$$

$$= -1.015$$

This value of z (*not* z_r) is turned into a significance level by using Table 35.4. This gives a probability value of 0.15 (or 15%) which is not statistically significant. Our conclusion in this case would be that the effect sizes of the two studies are similar and certainly not significantly different from each other. We could go on to report the effect size of the combined studies and the combined significance levels using the methods described above.

Of course, this formula can be used to compare any two correlation coefficients with each other to see whether they are significantly different.

35.8   Reporting the results

Meta-analytic studies are almost always substantial research studies in their own right. Consequently, many of the requirements of reporting a meta-analytic study are the very same requirements that one would require when writing a substantial report such as a journal article. You may find the detailed account of writing psychological reports in the authors' companion volume (Dennis Howitt and Duncan Cramer (2011), *Introduction to Research Methods in Psychology*, Harlow: Pearson) invaluable in reporting a meta-analysis as a consequence. Because there may be details of a large number of studies to tabulate, then special care may be required in generating the tables using, say, Excel or Word. SPSS Statistics would not be particularly helpful in this regard. Since any meta-analysis needs to make reference to previous relevant meta-analytic studies, often there is a model already available for one to consult to get an idea of style.

None of this should be a deterrent to using meta-analytic techniques as part of the literature review, say, for any study you are writing up. As we have seen, many of the calculations are relatively simple and straightforward by hand. It is perfectly feasible to, say, add in effect sizes for the findings of relevant previous research as you report them. Not only would this be good practice but it would also change the emphasis from statistical significance to that of effect size.

Key points

- This account of meta-analysis should convince you of the importance of reporting effect sizes for all studies you carry out. The most useful effect size formula is simply the Pearson's correlation coefficient between two variables.

- When carrying out a literature review, it is a positive advantage to report the effect sizes for all of the important studies. This is more important than reporting statistical significance alone.

- Experience will show that the difference between significant and non-significant findings can be very small indeed when their effect sizes are compared. Consequently, you need to consider near-significant results carefully when evaluating the research literature.

COMPUTER ANALYSIS

The basic calculations for meta-analysis are essentially straightforward and well within the capabilities of anyone prepared to give this chapter careful study. Although some of the calculations can benefit from computer assistance, the common statistical computer packages will only be of occasional help with a meta-analysis. SPSS Statistics does NOT deal with meta-analysis. Generally speaking, this program provides no particular help in relation to meta-analysis. There are a number of commercial software options available to help with meta-analysis though these may or may not be available to you at your university or college, for example.

Of more immediate practical help may be the following free meta-analytic software:

- *Meta-Analyst* is documented and available for download at http://tuftscaes.org/meta_analyst/

- *Meta-Stat – A Tool for the Meta-Analysis of Research Studies* by Lawrence M. Rudner, Gene V. Glass, David L. Evartt and Patrick J. Emery. This is documented and can be downloaded at http://echo.edres.org:8080/meta/metastat.htm

- *Statistics Software for Meta-Analysis* by Ralf Schwarzer. This is documented and can be downloaded at http://userpage.fu-berlin.de/health/meta_e.htm

- *The meta analysis calculator*. This can be used as an applet at http://www.lyonsmorris.com/lyons/metaAnalysis/index.cfm

- *The MIX program* for meta-analysis which uses Microsoft's Excel spreadsheet. Details and downloads are available at http://www.mix-for-meta-analysis.info/about/index.html

Of course, a search of the Internet will find others. Chapter 56 of Dennis Howitt and Duncan Cramer (2011) *Introduction to SPSS Statistics in Psychology: For version 19 and earlier*, Harlow: Pearson gives detailed steps for using the meta analysis calculator.

Recommended further reading

Howitt, D. and Cramer, D. (2011), *Introduction to Research Methods in Psychology*, Harlow: Pearson, Chapter 5.

Rosenthal, R. (1991), *Meta-analytic Procedures for Social Research*, Newbury Park, CA: Sage, especially Chapters 1–4.

CHAPTER 36

Reliability in scales and measurement

Consistency and agreement

Overview

- Reliability as discussed in this chapter is about the consistency of a psychological scale or similar measurements. That is, are all components of the scale measuring similar things?

- One of the conventional ways of achieving internal consistency is to ensure that all items correlate with the sum of the items on the scale. This is known as item analysis. A typical method is item–whole or, more clearly, item–total analysis. Any item which does not correlate significantly with the total (of all of the items) is deleted because it is not measuring the same thing as the total score.

- Split-half reliability is little more than the correlation between the total of one half of the items and the total of the other half of the items. If the two halves are measuring the same thing then they should correlate highly. Sometimes the sum of the odd-numbered items is correlated with the sum of the even-numbered items.

- Alpha reliability is the average of every possible split-half reliability that could be calculated on a scale. This overcomes the influence of the particular selection of items chosen for each half can have on split-half reliability.

- Kappa is a measurement of the agreement between raters or observers. That is, it assesses inter-rater or inter-observer agreement.

Preparation

The concept of correlation (Chapter 7) is an essential prerequisite to understanding the assessment of reliability. Chapter 21 on the correlated scores analysis of variance and Chapter 30 on factor analysis may also help with particular sections of this chapter.

36.1 Introduction

An important role for statistics is in assessing the adequacy of psychological scales and measures. Usually in psychology, but not always, measures consist of several different components added together to give a total score on that measure. Thus many attitude and personality tests consist of a large number of questionnaire items which are combined to give a total score on some dimension of attitude or personality. Although the analysis of such scales using factor analysis (Chapter 30) is an important and necessary part of modern psychological test and measure construction, factor analysis is not the only approach to understanding the structure of a test or measure. In many circumstances, a researcher may be concerned simply to obtain a fairly general measure of a particular psychological variable. In these circumstances, relatively simple checks on the structure of the measure may suffice. So, for example, a questionnaire designed to measure 'love' for one's partner might consist of several different questions. The researcher might wish to know the extent to which the items measure much the same thing. Generally speaking, if the items measure aspects of love then we would expect that they would intercorrelate with each other to a modest level at least. However, since it is the overall or total score on the measure of love which matters then for a good scale we would expect:

1. That scores on each item correlate with the total score (this is item–total or item–whole correlation).

2. That a score based on half of the items of the scale would correlate with scores based on the remainder of the scale (this is called split-half reliability which can be elaborated into Cronbach's coefficient alpha).

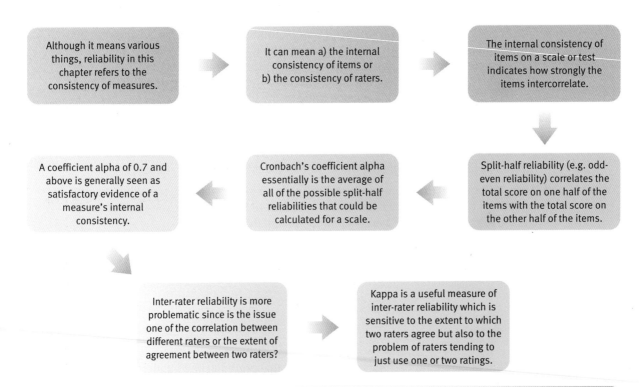

FIGURE 36.1   Conceptual steps for understanding reliability

The procedures described in this chapter are about the *internal consistency* of psychological measures. Internal consistency is the extent to which all of the items constituting a measure are measuring much the same thing. If they are measuring similar things, each item should correlate with the other items in the measure. Although this is referred to as reliability, it is a very different matter from reliability between two different points in time, for example. Figure 36.1 gives the key steps in understanding reliability.

36.2   Item-analysis using item–total correlation

Look at Table 36.1. It contains scores on four different items for ten different participants. There is also a total score given in the total column consisting of the scores on each of item 1, item 2, item 3 and item 4. So the second participant has a total score of 2 + 1 + 1 + 2 = 6. The correlations between the scores of the ten participants for item 1 and the total score can be calculated with the Pearson correlation formula (Calculation 7.1) or using a computer package, of course. The value of the correlation is 0.74 which suggests that item 1, for example, is a fairly good measure of what the total score on the measure is measuring.

Generally speaking, we would be happy with this scale given the relatively high item–total or item–whole correlation.

Notice that when an item is excluded from the total score, its correlation with this adjusted total score is reduced. Thus, in Table 36.2 the correlation of item 1 with the total score (based on summing items 2, 3 and 4) is 0.49 as opposed to a correlation of 0.74 when all items are included. This more refined analysis does nothing to revise our opinion of the scale. Generally speaking, the items which seem to be the poorest are items 1 and 4 which have the lowest item–total correlations.

Of course, four-item scales are unusual in psychological research. Normally we have many items. If we had a lot more items, we might be inclined to try to shorten the scale a little, perhaps to make it more appealing to participants. The technique for doing this is simple. Delete the low-correlating items and re-do the analysis based on the shortened scale. Although our example is a short scale, if we wanted to reduce its length then we

Table 36.1	Data from ten cases from a four-item questionnaire				
Person	**Item 1**	**Item 2**	**Item 3**	**Item 4**	**Total score**
1	1	3	5	6	15
2	2	1	1	2	6
3	1	1	1	1	4
4	5	2	4	2	13
5	6	4	3	2	15
6	5	4	5	6	20
7	4	5	3	2	14
8	2	1	2	1	6
9	1	2	1	1	5
10	1	1	2	2	6

Table 36.2	Correlations of items with the total score on the scale	
	Correlation with total score	**Correlation with total score excluding item in question**
Item 1	0.74	0.49
Item 2	0.84	0.71
Item 3	0.91	0.84
Item 4	0.76	0.55

Table 36.3	Correlations of shortened-scale items with the total score on that scale	
	Correlation with total score	**Correlation with total score excluding item in question**
Item 2	0.77	0.56
Item 3	0.94	0.87
Item 4	0.90	0.73

would probably wish to delete item 1 since it has the lowest correlation with the total score.

Table 36.3 gives the outcome of shortening the scale in this way. You will see that compared to the correlations in Table 36.2, the shortened scale has increased item–total correlations. In this sense, a better scale has been achieved by shortening it. The difficulty is that we can carry on deleting items and improving the internal consistency of the items but this may result in a shorter scale than we want. Usually it is best to exclude only the poorest of items. By doing so we leave a scale which covers a wide range of the aspects of the thing being measured. The appropriate scale length involves a degree of judgement.

A standard statistical package such as SPSS Statistics reduces the work in calculating item–total (item–whole) correlations of various sorts and makes shortening the number of items in the scale easy.

The results of this analysis can be written up as follows: 'An item–whole analysis was carried out on the items on the scale. As can be seen from Table 36.2, each item had a satisfactory correlation with the total score on all of the items combined. After the item–whole correlations had been recalculated with the item removed from the total score, there was a decline in the item–whole correlations. However, the relationships remained substantial and it was decided not to shorten the scale given that it consists of just four items.'

36.3   Split-half reliability

A computationally less demanding way of assessing the internal structure of a questionnaire is split-half reliability. Remember that internal reliability refers to the extent to which all of the items in a questionnaire (or similar measure) are assessing much the same thing. Split-half reliability simply involves computing scores based on half of the items and scores based on the other half of the items. The correlation between the scores for these two halves is the split-half reliability (more or less, but read on).

There are no rules for deciding which of the items should be in which half. There are common practices, however. Odd–even reliability is based on taking the odd-numbered items (1, 3, 5, etc.) as one set and the even-numbered items (2, 4, 6, etc.) as the other set. Alternatively, the first half of the items could be correlated with the second half. But there would be nothing against selecting the halves at random.

Calculation 36.1

Split-half reliability

Taking the data in Table 36.1, we could sum items 1 and 2 for the total of the first half and sum items 3 and 4 for the total of the second half. The correlation between the two halves is 0.477.

There is a further step. The difficulty is that we are correlating a scale half the length of our original scale with another scale half the length of our scale. Because of this, the reliability will be lower than for the full-length scale. Fortunately, it is quite easy to compute the reliability of a full scale from the reliability of half of the scale using the following formula:

$$\text{full scale reliability} = \frac{n \times \text{known reliability}}{1 + [(n-1) \times \text{known reliability}]}$$

where n is the ratio by which the number of items is to be increased or decreased.
Since we know the reliability of the half scale (r_{hh}) is 0.477, the full scale reliability is:

$$\text{full scale reliability} = \frac{2 \times 0.4771}{1 + 0.477} = \frac{0.954}{1.477} = 0.65$$

Thus the value of the split-half reliability is 0.65 when corrected to the full scale length. Standard computer statistics packages such as SPSS Statistics can do most of the hard work for you.

Reporting the results The results of this analysis may be written up as follows: 'The split-half reliability of the scale was found to be 0.65. This is a somewhat low value but given the exploratory nature of this research, the scale was nevertheless employed.' (As a rule of thumb, a value of about 0.7 or above would generally be seen as adequate evidence of reliability for general use.)

36.4 Alpha reliability

There is a problem with split-half reliability – its value will depend on which items are selected for each half. The odd–even reliability will not be the same as that found by comparing the first half of the items with the second half, for example. There is an obvious solution: calculate every possible split-half reliability having every possible combination of items in each half and then simply take the average of these. The average of all possible split-half reliabilities from a scale is known as *coefficient alpha*. We

Table 36.4	Scores for all possible split-halves from four items					
Person	Split-half version 1		Split-half version 2		Split-half version 3	
	Items 1 + 2	Items 3 + 4	Items 1 + 3	Items 2 + 4	Items 1 + 4	Items 2 + 3
1	4	11	6	9	7	8
2	3	3	3	3	4	2
3	2	2	2	2	2	2
4	7	6	9	4	7	6
5	10	5	9	6	8	7
6	9	11	10	10	11	9
7	9	5	7	7	6	8
8	3	3	4	2	3	3
9	3	2	2	3	2	3
10	2	4	3	3	3	3

Table 36.5	Correlations between split-halves and with corrections for shortened length	
	Pearson correlation	Corrected for scale length
Items 1 + 2 with items 3 + 4	0.477	0.642
Items 1 + 3 with items 2 + 4	0.730	0.844
Items 1 + 4 with items 2 + 3	0.898	0.946

will calculate this from first principles and an alternative approach based on the analysis of variance.

Table 36.4 contains all of the possible ways of splitting four items into two halves. There are only three different ways of doing this with our short scale:

1. The total of items 1 and 2 compared with the total of items 3 and 4.

2. The total of items 1 and 3 compared with the total of items 2 and 4.

3. The total of items 1 and 4 compared with the total of items 2 and 3.

The reliability coefficients for these three different possibilities are to be found in Table 36.5. The average of the split-half coefficients corrected (adjusted) for length is coefficient alpha. So the average of 0.642 + 0.844 + 0.946 (or coefficient alpha) is 0.81. It is generally accepted that a coefficient alpha of 0.7 or above is satisfactory for psychological research.

This calculation may be feasible with a short scale of four items and a sample of ten individuals, but what, say, if the scale consisted of 100 items? The number of ways of sorting these 100 items into two separate sets of 50 is huge. Obviously the conceptually correct approach given so far would take too much computation time. The alternative hand-computation method is not quite so cumbersome but still time-consuming. Basically it involves carrying out one-way analysis of variance for correlated scores on the data on each of the items. Thus the data would look like Table 36.6. Following through

Table 36.6	Data on four-item questionnaire for ten cases arranged as for correlated one-way ANOVA			
Person	**Item 1**	**Item 2**	**Item 3**	**Item 4**
1	1	3	5	6
2	2	1	1	2
3	1	1	1	1
4	5	2	4	2
5	6	4	3	2
6	5	4	5	6
7	4	5	3	2
8	2	1	2	1
9	1	2	1	1
10	1	1	2	2
Cell mean	2.8	2.4	2.7	2.5

Table 36.7	ANOVA summary table on four-item questionnaire data				
Source of variation	**Sum of squares**	**Degrees of freedom**	**Mean square (or variance estimate)**	**F-ratio**	**Significance**
Between treatments (i.e. between items)	1.00	3	not needed	not needed	not needed
Between people (i.e. individual differences)	70.60	9	7.84		
Error (i.e. residual)	40.00	27	1.48		

the procedure described in Calculation 21.1 would lead to the ANOVA summary table presented in Table 36.7. Values from this table are then substituted in the following computational formula for coefficient alpha:

$$\text{coefficient alpha} = \frac{\text{between-people variance} - \text{error variance}}{\text{between-people variance}}$$

$$= \frac{7.84 - 1.48}{7.84} = \frac{6.36}{7.84} = 0.81$$

This would be generally accepted as evidence of a satisfactory level of internal consistency since coefficients alpha above 0.7 are regarded as sufficient. The results of this analysis may be written up as follows: 'Coefficient alpha was calculated for the scale and found to be 0.81 which is generally accepted to be satisfactory.'

It should be fairly obvious that the hand calculation of coefficient alpha even with this ANOVA method has little to recommend it. It might be useful to anyone who has access to a computer program for the correlated ANOVA but not to one which computes coefficient alpha directly. It need hardly be said that the use of a computer package such as SPSS Statistics which includes coefficient alpha is highly recommended.

36.5   Agreement between raters

Not all research involves psychological scales. Some research involves ratings by a pair of judges or even a panel of judges or assessors. Sometimes rating is used because it is felt that self-completion questionnaires might be inappropriate. Let us take the concept of dangerousness, i.e. the risk posed to members of the public by the release of sex offenders or psychiatric hospital patients. One might be very unhappy about using self-completion questionnaires in these circumstances. It might be considered preferable to have expert clinical psychologists, forensic psychologists and psychiatrists interview the sex offenders or patients to assess the dangerousness of these people on release into the community. Let us assume that we have one clinical psychologist, one forensic psychologist and one psychiatrist who are used in a study of 12 sex offenders. Having interviewed each offender, read all case notes and obtained any further information they required, each of the three professionals rates each offender on a three-point dangerousness index:

- a rating of 1 means that there is no risk to the public
- a rating of 2 means that there is a moderate risk to the public
- a rating of 3 means that there is a high risk to the public.

Their ratings of the 12 offenders are shown in Table 36.8.

Table 36.9 shows the Pearson correlations between the ratings of the three professionals. The figures seem to suggest a very high level of relationship between the forensic psychologist's and the psychiatrist's ratings. A correlation of 0.83 is, after all, a very strong relationship. The difficulty with this only becomes apparent when we examine Table 36.10 which gives agreements between the forensic psychologist and the psychiatrist. This is constructed by tabulating the forensic psychologist's ratings against those of the psychiatrist. The frequencies in the diagonal represent agreements, all other frequencies represent a degree of disagreement.

Table 36.8	The data from the three professionals for each of the 12 sex offenders		
	Clinical psychologist	**Forensic psychologist**	**Psychiatrist**
Offender 1	2	3	3
Offender 2	3	3	3
Offender 3	3	3	3
Offender 4	1	1	1
Offender 5	2	1	2
Offender 6	3	3	3
Offender 7	1	2	3
Offender 8	1	3	3
Offender 9	2	2	3
Offender 10	3	3	3
Offender 11	3	3	3
Offender 12	2	3	3

Table 36.9	Correlations between the ratings of various professions	
	Forensic psychologist	**Psychiatrist**
Clinical psychologist	0.55	0.44
Forensic psychologist	–	0.83

Table 36.10	Agreements and disagreements between the forensic psychologist and the psychiatrist on ratings of sex offenders		
Forensic psychologist's ratings	**Psychiatrist's ratings**		
	1	**2**	**3**
1	1	1	0
2	0	0	2
3	0	0	8

At first sight it still might appear that there is strong agreement between the two sets of ratings. A total of 9 out of the 12 ratings suggest perfect agreement. So what is the problem? A closer examination of Table 36.10 suggests that virtually all of the agreement occurs when the two experts rate the sex offender as a high risk to the public (rating 3). For the other two ratings they agree only one time out of four. This is a much lower level of agreement. Of course, if the experts rated all of the offenders as a high risk to the public then the agreement would be perfect – although they would not appear to be discriminating between levels of risk. If it were decided to release only sex offenders rated as a low risk to the public, only one sex offender would be released on the basis of the combined ratings of the psychiatrist and forensic psychologist. In other words, correlation coefficients are not very helpful when the exact agreement of raters is required.

The index of agreement between raters needs to have the following characteristics:

1. It provides an index of the extent of overlap of ratings.

2. It should be sensitive to the problem that agreement is rather meaningless if both raters are using only one rating and do not vary their ratings.

Kappa is a useful index of agreement between a pair of raters since it is responsive to both of these things.

The kappa coefficient is calculated from the following formula:

$$\text{kappa} = \frac{\text{total frequency of agreement} - \text{expected total frequency of agreement by chance}}{\text{number of things rated} - \text{expected total frequency of agreement by chance}}$$

Kappa can take negative values if the raters agree at less than chance level. It is zero if there is no agreement greater or lesser than chance. Coefficients approaching +1.00 indicate very good agreement between the raters.

Calculation 36.2

Kappa coefficient

The above data on the ratings of the forensic psychologist and the psychiatrist will be used to calculate kappa for their ratings.

Step 1   Draw up a crosstabulation table of the data for the two raters and insert the marginal totals (i.e. the sum of frequencies for each row, the sum of frequencies for each column and the overall sum). This is shown in Table 36.11.

Table 36.11	Agreements and disagreements between the forensic psychologist and the psychiatrist on ratings of sex offenders with marginal totals added				
	Forensic psychologist's ratings	**Psychiatrist's ratings**			**Marginal totals**
		1	2	3	
	1	1	1	0	2
	2	0	0	2	2
	3	0	0	8	8
Marginal totals		1	1	10	Total = 12

Step 2   Calculate the frequencies of agreement. These are the frequencies in the diagonal of Table 36.11. They have been given in **bold**. So the frequency of agreements is $1 + 0 + 8 = 9$.

Step 3   Calculate the expected frequency of agreement by firstly calculating the following for each of the diagonals:

$$\text{expected frequency} = \frac{\text{column total} \times \text{row total}}{\text{total}}$$

Thus the expected frequency of agreement for ratings of 3 is the product of the column total of 10 and the row total of 8 divided by the overall total of 12. This is 80/12 or 6.667. Table 36.12 contains the results of these calculations.

Step 4   The expected total frequency of agreement by chance is therefore $0.167 + 0.167 + 6.667 = 7.001$.

Table 36.12	Expected frequencies for agreement					
	Forensic psychologist's ratings	Psychiatrist's ratings			Marginal totals	
		1	2	3		
	1	0.167			2	
	2		0.167		2	
	3			6.667	8	
Marginal totals		1	1	10	Total = 12	

Step 5 We can then substitute the values in the formula:

$$kappa = \frac{\text{total frequency of agreement} - \text{expected total frequency of agreement by chance}}{\text{number of things rated} - \text{expected total frequency of agreement by chance}}$$

$$= \frac{9 - 7.001}{12 - 7.001} = \frac{1.999}{4.999} = 0.40$$

Interpreting the results Notice that although the actual agreement seems high at 9 of the 12 ratings, coefficient kappa implies fairly low agreement. This reflects the relative lack of variability in the expert's ratings and the tendency for both to rate the offenders as 3 rather than any other value. Consequently, we can appreciate that coefficient kappa is superior to the simple proportion of agreement in assessing the reliability of ratings.

Reporting the results The results of this analysis can be written up as follows: 'Coefficient kappa was calculated on the relationship between the forensic psychologist's and the psychiatrist's ratings of dangerousness. Despite there being a high level of agreement overall, it was found that kappa was only 0.40, suggesting that much of the apparent agreement was in fact due to both professionals using the highest dangerousness rating much of the time.'

Key points

- Although the methods employed in calculating internal reliability are straightforward, great care is needed to differentiate between internal reliability as assessed by the methods described in this chapter and measures of external reliability which are very different. External reliability includes the correlation between scores on a measure at two different points in time (i.e. test–retest reliability).

- The difference between a correlation between scores and agreement between scores is very important. Remember that there can be a strong correlation between two variables with absolutely no match in the scores.

COMPUTER ANALYSIS

The SPSS Statistics instruction book to this text is Dennis Howitt and Duncan Cramer (2011), *Introduction to SPSS Statistics in Psychology: For version 19 and earlier*, Harlow: Pearson. Chapter 31 in that book gives detailed step-by-step procedures for the statistics described in this chapter together with advice on how to report the results. Figure 36.2 shows the SPSS Statistics steps for Cronbach's alpha internal reliability and kappa.

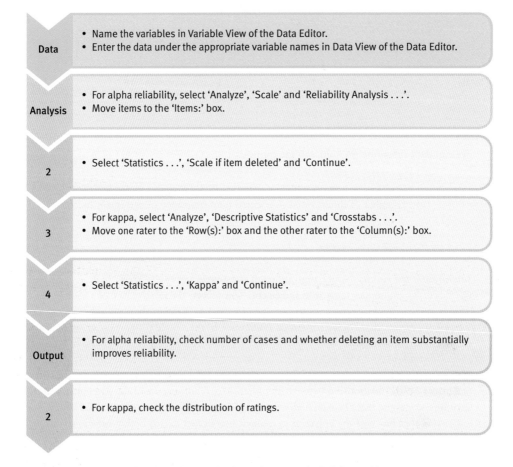

Data
- Name the variables in Variable View of the Data Editor.
- Enter the data under the appropriate variable names in Data View of the Data Editor.

Analysis
- For alpha reliability, select 'Analyze', 'Scale' and 'Reliability Analysis . . .'.
- Move items to the 'Items:' box.

2
- Select 'Statistics . . .', 'Scale if item deleted' and 'Continue'.

3
- For kappa, select 'Analyze', 'Descriptive Statistics' and 'Crosstabs . . .'.
- Move one rater to the 'Row(s):' box and the other rater to the 'Column(s):' box.

4
- Select 'Statistics . . .', 'Kappa' and 'Continue'.

Output
- For alpha reliability, check number of cases and whether deleting an item substantially improves reliability.

2
- For kappa, check the distribution of ratings.

FIGURE 36.2 SPSS Statistics steps for Cronbach's alpha internal reliability and kappa

Recommended further reading

Tinsley, H.E.A. and Weiss, D.J. (1975), 'Interrater reliability and agreement of subjective judgments', *Journal of Counseling Psychology*, **22**, 358–76.

CHAPTER 37

Confidence intervals

Overview

- Confidence intervals are an alternative way of conceptualising inferential statistics that stresses the uncertainty of statistical data. They have in recent years received some enthusiastic support.

- A confidence interval is essentially a range (of means, differences between means, correlations, etc.) within which the population value (based on our data) is most likely to lie. That is, instead of estimating the population value as a single point value (such as the population mean equals 6.0), the confidence interval approach estimates that the population mean will lie between 4.5 and 7.5 based on the characteristics of the sample.

- The confidence interval is usually calculated as the 95% confidence interval. This is the interval between the largest and the smallest values which cut off the most extreme 2.5% of values in either direction. In other words, the 95% confidence interval covers the most central 95% of values.

- The calculation of the confidence interval involves the calculation of the standard error. Since for any given sample size, tables of the t-distribution are available which indicate how many standard errors embrace the middle 95% of values, the 95% confidence interval is easily found.

Preparation

Read the previous discussions of confidence intervals in Chapters 8 and 9. Revise the concepts of standard error and sampling distributions from Chapters 11 and 13.

37.1 Introduction

The concept of confidence intervals was described briefly in earlier chapters. Although confidence intervals have been used in psychological statistics for many years, their greater use has been advocated strongly in recent years. More radically, it has been proposed that confidence intervals should replace statistical significance testing. Whatever the merits of the argument for this, both confidence intervals and significance testing based on point estimates are informative approaches to statistical analysis and likely to coexist for a good many years. This chapter provides some information on the computation of confidence intervals for a variety of statistics already discussed. Despite the fact that any measure based on a sample has a confidence interval in theory, methods of calculating confidence intervals are not readily available for many statistical procedures. However, the availability of bootstrapping methods (Box 18.1) makes such calculations much easier.

Confidence intervals concern the estimates of population characteristics (parameters) based on a sample or samples taken from that population. The characteristics of samples tend to vary somewhat from the characteristics of the population from which they came – and from each other (Chapter 13). Consequently, estimates of the characteristics of a population based on a sample drawn from that population are unlikely to be exact. Nevertheless, they remain the best estimates we can have when ignorant of the exact details of the population. In previous chapters, we have used *point estimates* of population parameters based on sample statistics. A point estimate is merely a single figure estimate as opposed to a range. Thus if the mean of a sample is 5.3 then the point estimate of the mean of the population is 5.3. Since this point estimate is only our best guess from the characteristics of the sample, usually it only approximates the true population mean at best.

The alternative to point estimates, the *confidence interval* approach, acknowledges the approximate nature of the point estimates more directly. Confidence intervals give the range of values likely to include the population value. This range of likely values is called the confidence interval since it reflects the range of values likely to include the true population mean (if we only knew this). Thus, instead of saying that our estimate of the population mean is 5.3, we say that the population mean is likely to be in the range 4.0–6.6. By expressing our inference or estimate in this way, we reinforce the notion of uncertainty as to the precise value. So a confidence interval is simply the range of values of a statistic such as the mean or correlation which is likely to contain the true population mean or correlation. The size of the confidence interval will depend on the variability of scores. The more variable the scores in a sample, the larger the confidence interval has to be for any level of confidence.

There is an obvious problem with confidence intervals. We can never be absolutely certain how different a sample mean is from the mean of the population from which it was drawn (if we are basing our estimate on a sample). Consequently, the following strategy is adopted. We state the range of sample means that includes (usually) the most likely 95% of sample means drawn at random from the population. In other words, the 95% confidence interval is the range of values we are 95% certain includes the 'true' population mean.

Chapter 13 explained how we take the characteristics of a sample to infer the most likely characteristics of the population from which that sample was taken. Furthermore, we can even calculate the distributions of samples taken from that inferred population. Remember that the *standard error* is the usual index of the amount of variability in sample means drawn at random from a population. Standard error is simply the standard deviation of sample means. The calculation of standard error is a crucial phase in estimating confidence intervals for all parametric tests.

Normal distribution theory (Chapter 11) tells us that for *large* samples, 95% of sample means lie within plus or minus 1.96 standard deviations from the population mean.

Thus if the standard error for samples has been calculated as 2.6, then 95% of sample means lie between −5.096 and +5.096 (1.96 × 2.6 = 5.096) of the mean of our sample (i.e. the estimate of the population mean). If the sample mean is 10.00 then the confidence interval is 10.00 ± 5.096. That is, the confidence interval is between 4.904 and 15.096. Since this covers 95% of the most likely sample means, it is known as the 95% confidence interval. In other words, the 95% confidence interval is 4.90 to 15.10. However, this is approximate where the sample size is small.

Confidence intervals can be set at other levels such as 99%. The more stringent 99% confidence interval involves multiplying the standard error by 2.576 = 2.576 × 2.6 = 6.698. The resulting 99% confidence interval would be 10.00 (the sample mean) ± 6.698, or 3.30 to 16.70. So the more confident we want to be, the larger the confidence interval is. We can use tables of the z-distribution to work out other confidence intervals, but the 95% and 99% are fairly conventional.

However, with small samples the z-distribution does not work perfectly. It is more usual to use the distribution of t (which is identical to that of z for large samples). With small samples, the value of t corresponding to our chosen confidence interval would be obtained from Table 37.1. This is distributed by the degrees of freedom. Thus if the degrees of freedom for a particular sample were 25, then the value of t for 95% confidence is 2.06 (from Table 37.1). So the confidence interval would be 2.06 × 2.6 on either side of the estimated population mean. That is, the 95% confidence interval would be 4.64 to 15.36. The degrees of freedom will vary according to the statistical estimate in question.

Sometimes the concept *confidence limits* is used. Confidence limits are merely the extreme values of the *confidence interval*. In the above example, the 95% confidence limits are 4.64 and 15.36.

While this introduction explains confidence intervals in principle, their calculation varies from this pattern for some statistics. Figure 37.1 gives the key steps to consider in understanding confidence intervals.

 Conventionally, estimates of statistics such as means and so forth have been given as a single figure. However, this approach has its problems. In particular, it tends to suggest a precision about statistical estimates which is not warranted. The confidence interval approach indicates the range of values within which the value of the population value is most likely to lie.

Some confidence intervals are notoriously difficult to calculate, though bootstrapping methods as now available on SPSS Statistics greatly simplify the task. Computer packages such as SPSS Statistics report many confidence intervals routinely, though sometimes you may have to select an appropriate option. Usually this is expressed as the 95% confidence interval though the use of 99% confidence intervals is not uncommon. The latter is a bigger interval, of course.

Statistically significant values are those which are NOT within the confidence interval. The use of confidence intervals either alone or in combination with the more conventionally used point estimates is increasingly common practice among modern researchers.

FIGURE 37.1   Conceptual steps for understanding confidence intervals

Table 37.1	Table of *t*-values for 95% and 99% confidence intervals	
Degrees of freedom	***t* for 95% confidence**	***t* for 99% confidence**
1	12.71	63.66
2	4.30	9.93
3	3.18	5.84
4	2.78	4.60
5	2.57	4.03
6	2.45	3.71
7	2.37	3.50
8	2.31	3.36
9	2.26	3.25
10	2.23	3.17
11	2.20	3.11
12	2.18	3.06
13	2.16	3.01
14	2.15	2.98
15	2.13	2.95
16	2.12	2.92
17	2.11	2.90
18	2.10	2.88
19	2.09	2.86
20	2.09	2.85
25	2.06	2.79
30	2.04	2.75
35	2.03	2.72
40	2.02	2.70
45	2.01	2.69
50	2.01	2.68
60	2.00	2.66
70	1.99	2.65
80	1.99	2.64
90	1.99	2.63
100	1.98	2.63
∞	1.96	2.58

Note: If the required number of degrees of freedom is missing, take the nearest lower number.

37.2 | The relationship between significance and confidence intervals

At first sight, statistical significance and confidence intervals appear dissimilar concepts. This is incorrect since they are both based on much the same inferential process. Remember that in significance testing we usually test the null hypothesis of no relationship between two variables. This usually boils down to a zero (or near-zero) correlation or to a difference of zero (or near-zero) between sample means. If the confidence interval does not contain this zero value then the obtained sample mean is statistically significant at 100% minus the confidence level. So if the 95% confidence interval is 2.30 to 8.16 but the null hypothesis would predict the population value of the statistic to be 0.00, then the null hypothesis is rejected at the 5% level of significance. In other words, confidence intervals contain enough information to judge statistical significance. However, statistical significance alone does not contain enough information to calculate confidence intervals.

Calculation 37.1

Confidence intervals for a population mean based on a single sample

Step 1 Calculate the standard error of the scores in the sample. The stages in doing this are given in Calculation 11.1. You will also need to calculate the mean of the sample and the degrees of freedom (i.e. sample size − 1).

Step 2 For the data in Table 11.1, the standard error is 0.58, the estimated population mean (the sample mean) is 5.00, and the degrees of freedom are 6 − 1 = 5 degrees of freedom.

Step 3 Decide what confidence level you require. We will use the 95% level. This is the minimum value of confidence in general use. If it was especially important that your confidence interval included the true population mean than you could use the 99% level or even the 99.9% level.

Step 4 Use Table 37.1 to find the value of t corresponding to the 95% confidence level. You need the row for the appropriate number of degrees of freedom (i.e. $N − 1 = 5$). This value of t is 2.57. Table 37.1 is merely a version of the table of the t-distribution that appears elsewhere in the book. It is included as some will find it initially less confusing to be able to look up the values directly.

Step 5 Calculate the confidence interval. It is the sample mean ± (t × the standard error). Therefore, the 95% confidence interval for the population mean is 5.00 ± (2.57 × 0.58). This gives us a 95% confidence interval of 3.51 to 6.49.

Reporting the results The results of this analysis may be written up as follows: 'The 95% confidence interval for the population mean was 3.51 to 6.49. As this interval does not include 0.00 then the null hypothesis that the sample comes from a population with a mean of 0.00 can be rejected at the 5% level of significance.'

Calculation 37.2

Confidence intervals for the unrelated *t*-test

Step 1   As most of the major steps in calculating the confidence interval involve steps in the calculation of the unrelated *t*-test, use Calculation 13.1 to calculate the necessary values.

Step 2   Make a note of the difference between the two sample means, the degrees of freedom ($N + N - 2$), and the standard error of the difference between two sample means. For the example in Calculation 13.1 (Table 13.9), the difference between the sample means = 3.917, the degrees of freedom = 20 and the standard error = 1.392.

Step 3   Decide what level of confidence you require. This time we will use the 99% level of confidence.

Step 4   From Table 37.1, the *t*-value for 99% confidence with 20 degrees of freedom = 2.85.

Step 5   The confidence interval is obtained by taking the difference between the two sample means ± ($t \times$ the standard error). Thus the 99% confidence interval for the population of differences between sample means = 3.917 ± (2.85 × 1.392). Therefore the 99% confidence interval is 3.917 ± 3.97, which gives a 99% confidence interval of −0.05 to 7.89.

Reporting the results The results of this analysis can be written up as follows: 'The 99% confidence interval for the difference in emotionality scores in two-parent and lone-parent families is −0.05 to 7.89. Since the null hypothesis holds that this difference is 0.00 then we can accept the null hypothesis at the 1% level of significance since the confidence interval includes the value 0.00. The hypothesis that emotionality is different in two-parent and lone-parent families is not supported at the 1% level of significance.'

Calculation 37.3

Confidence intervals for the related *t*-test

Step 1   Follow the calculation of the related *t*-test as described in Calculation 12.1. We will use these data to obtain the 95% confidence interval for the difference between the means.

Step 2   Make a note of the difference between the sample means, the degrees of freedom and the standard error for your data. Calculation 12.1 yields a value of the difference between the sample means of −1.50, a standard error of the difference of 0.756 with 7 degrees of freedom.

Step 3   Decide what level of confidence you require. This time we are using the 95% level of confidence.

→

Step 4 From Table 37.1, the *t*-value for 95% confidence with 7 degrees of freedom = 2.37.

Step 5 The confidence interval is obtained by taking the difference between the two sample means ± the (*t*-value × the standard error); i.e.

$$-1.50 \pm (2.37 \times 0.756) = -1.10 \pm 1.79$$
$$= -3.29 \text{ to } 0.29$$

Step 6 Thus the 95% confidence interval for the population of differences between sample means is −1.94 to 1.64.

Reporting the results The results of this analysis can be written up as follows: 'The 95% confidence interval for the difference in eye contact at six months and nine months was −3.29 to 0.29. According to the null hypothesis, this difference should be 0.00. Consequently, as this value is included in the 95% confidence interval then the null hypothesis is supported and the alternative hypothesis that eye contact is related to age is rejected.'

Calculation 37.4

Confidence interval for the Pearson correlation coefficient

Step 1 The calculation of the Pearson correlation coefficient is described in Calculation 7.1. Work through these steps for your data or compute the value of *r* using a computer.

Step 2 Make a note of the value of the correlation coefficient and the sample size. For the data in Table 7.1, the value of the correlation coefficient is −0.90 and the sample size is 10. We do *not* require the degrees of freedom for calculating the confidence interval for a Pearson correlation coefficient.

Step 3 To calculate the confidence interval, it is necessary to convert the correlation coefficient to its z_r using Table 35.5. Note that z_r is the Fisher normalised correlation coefficient. This table gives a value of z_r for a correlation of −0.90 as −1.472. The negative sign is added because the correlation is negative.

Step 4 The standard deviation of z_r is obtained using the formula:

$$\text{standard deviation of } z = \frac{1}{\sqrt{N-3}}$$

Given that in our example the sample size *N* is 10, the standard deviation according to this formula is:

$$\text{standard deviation of } z = \frac{1}{\sqrt{10-3}} \frac{1}{\sqrt{7}} = \frac{1}{2.646} = 0.378$$

→

This standard deviation is distributed as for z so that the 95% confidence interval is $1.96 \times$ the standard deviation. Thus the 95% confidence interval of z_r is the value of z_r for the correlation coefficient $\pm 1.96 \times 0.378$. That is, in our example, -1.472 ± 0.741. Therefore the 95% confidence interval for z_r is -0.731 to -2.213.

Step 5   The above is the confidence interval for z_r rather than for the original correlation coefficient. We can use Table 35.5 to convert this z_r back to the range of correlation coefficients. Thus the 95% confidence interval for the correlation coefficient is -0.62 to -0.97.

Interpreting the results You will notice that this confidence interval is *not* symmetrical around the sample correlation of -0.90. The correlation coefficient is not a linear variable so it cannot be added and divided as if it were. Hence the transformation to z_r which has linear characteristics.

Reporting the results The results of this analyis can be written up as follows: 'The 95% confidence interval for the Pearson correlation between musical and mathematical ability was -0.62 to -0.97. The null hypothesis suggests that this relationship will be 0.00. Since the value under the null hypothesis was not included in the confidence interval, the null hypothesis of no relationship between musical and mathematical ability was rejected in favour of the alternative hypothesis that there is a negative correlation between mathematical and musical ability.'

37.3   Regression

There are several confidence intervals for even a simple regression analysis since regression involves several estimates of population parameters – the slope of the regression line, the cut-point for the vertical axis and the predicted score from scores on the X variable.

Calculation 37.5

Confidence intervals for a predicted score

Step 1   Carry out the simple regression analysis according to Calculation 8.1. This will give the slope and the intercept (cut-point) of the regression line. These can be used to calculate the most likely value of variable Y from a particular value of variable X. For a value of $X = 8$, the best prediction of Y is 3.37 for the data in Table 8.2.

Step 2   Calculate the Pearson correlation between variable X and variable Y in Table 8.2 using Calculation 7.1. This gives r as -0.90.

Step 3   Calculate the standard deviation of the Y variable scores using Calculation 5.1. The standard deviation of the Y scores is 1.75.

Step 4 Using the information calculated in the previous three steps, the standard error of the estimate of Y from a particular value of X is given by the following formula:

$$\text{standard error of estimate of } Y = SD \text{ of } Y \times \sqrt{\frac{N(1 - r^2)}{N - 2}}$$

$$= 1.75 \times \sqrt{\frac{10(1 - 0.90^2)}{10 - 2}}$$

$$= 1.75 \times \sqrt{\frac{10(1 - 0.81)}{8}}$$

$$= 1.75 \times \sqrt{\frac{1.90}{8}}$$

$$= 1.75 \times \sqrt{0.2375}$$

$$= 1.75 \times 0.4873$$

$$= 0.853$$

Step 5 This standard error can be converted to the confidence interval by multiplying the value of the standard error by the appropriate value of t. The degrees of freedom for this are $N - 2$. Table 37.1 indicates that the t-value for $N - 2$ or 3 degrees of freedom is 3.18 for the 95% confidence interval. This gives us a value of the confidence interval around the predicted Y score of 3.37 of $\pm 0.85 \times 3.18 = \pm 2.70$. Thus we can be 95% sure that the population value of Y predicted from X is within the range of 0.67 to 6.07.

Interpreting the results Of course, the confidence interval will vary numerically according to which X score is being used to predict Y. The size of the interval between the upper and lower confidence limits though does not vary. This is because the standard error is an average for all estimated Y scores.

Reporting the results The results of this analysis can be written up as follows: 'The 95% confidence interval for predicting musical ability from maths score was 0.89 to 5.85 for a point-prediction of 3.37.'

37.4   Other confidence intervals

In theory, any statistic (i.e. characteristic of a sample) will have a sampling distribution and, hence, a confidence interval. In practice, however, these can be obscure or unavailable though bootstrap statistics may make their estimation possible.

Key points

- Confidence intervals for many statistical estimates are not easily obtained. Do not expect to find unusual confidence intervals explained in other than relatively difficult sources.

- Standard statistical packages routinely calculate standard errors from which confidence intervals are relatively easy to derive.

COMPUTER ANALYSIS

The SPSS Statistics instruction book to this text is Dennis Howitt and Duncan Cramer (2011), *Introduction to SPSS Statistics in Psychology: For version 19 and earlier*, Harlow: Pearson. This book gives detailed step-by-step procedures for the statistics described in this chapter together with advice on how to report the results. SPSS Statistics gives many confidence interval statistics for many tests. They frequently appear alongside the point estimates in SPSS Statistics output. These are covered in Chapter 15 of the SPSS Statistics book.

CHAPTER 38

The influence of moderator variables on relationships between two variables

Overview

- A moderator effect is where the size of the relationship between one variable and another variable is different for the values of a third variable. The moderating effect is also known as an interaction effect.

- Where all of the variables are score variables then the recommendation is that hierarchical multiple regression is used to identify interactions which indicate moderator effects. This method makes full use of the information contained in the scores.

- The interaction term is created by multiplying the two predictors together. It is recommended that the means of the two predictors should be made to be zero by the predictors being centred or standardised. One reason for this is to reduce the size of the correlations between the predictors and the interaction.

- The two predictors are entered in the first step (block 1) of the hierarchical multiple regression and the interaction in the second step (block 2). There is a moderator effect if the interaction explains a significant proportion of the variance in the criterion.

- To interpret the interaction, values of the criterion are predicted for widely separated values of the two predictors such as their mean and one standard deviation above and below their mean.

- Whether these regression coefficients differ significantly from zero can be determined but not whether the slopes differ significantly from each other.

→

● Moderator effects of categorical variables on a continuous or score variable can be tested with the analysis of variance (ANOVA). If an interaction is found between the independent and moderator variables then this indicates a moderator effect, but it remains important to determine which group means differ significantly from each other and the direction of these differences.

Preparation

You should have a working knowledge of z-scores (Chapter 5), simple regression (Chapter 8), two-way analysis of variance (Chapter 22) and multiple regression (Chapter 31).

38.1   Introduction

There are various circumstances in which a relationship between two variables is in some way affected by a third variable. Two types of third variables are mediator variables and moderator variables. We have discussed mediating variables in Chapters 29 and 32. But it is worthwhile reminding ourselves of what a mediator variable is. Take a look at Figure 38.1. It indicates that there is a relationship between the level of stress experienced by an individual and how depressed they feel. The more stress, the more depression. A mediating variable is a third variable which is responsible for the relationship between the main variables – stress and depression in this case. One reason why stress might lead to depression is that stress reduces one's available time to engage in close social relationships with friends and family and that it is the absence of close relationships which leads to depression shown in Figure 38.2. In other words, stress in our example does not directly lead to depression but it causes changes in a third variable (social relationships) which then affects depression. In this case, social relationships would be a mediator variable for the relationship between stress and depression.

This chapter deals with another type of third variable – moderator variables. These are conceptually quite distinct from mediator variables though a variable which is a moderator variable may also be a mediating variable in another context. How do you know whether a variable is a moderator variable? Quite simply, if the main relationship you are interested in is different for different levels of the third variable then this third variable is having a moderating effect – and so it is a moderator variable. A simple

FIGURE 38.1   Stress and depression

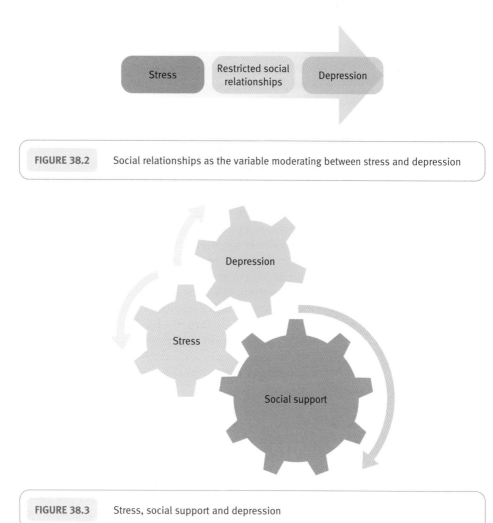

FIGURE 38.2   Social relationships as the variable moderating between stress and depression

FIGURE 38.3   Stress, social support and depression

example of a moderator might be gender *if* it were found to be the case, say, that there is no relationship between stress and depression in women but a strong relationship between the two in men. Gender is having a moderating effect on the relationship between stress and depression. Male and female are different levels of the variable gender. So we would say that gender is a moderator variable in this case.

Another possible moderator variable for the relationship between stress and depression might be the variable social support – this refers to the extent to which an individual has family and friends which provide them with a warm, supportive social environment. Figure 38.3 illustrates the interrelationships between stress and depression and social support. Stress, depression and social support, we shall assume, have each been measured using a psychological scale so each variable consists of scores.

But just what is the nature of the relationships involved? There are several possible options:

- stress leads directly to depression

- depression leads to stress

- both the above are true

- stress leads the individual to be more isolated (lack social support) and this lack of social support leads to depression

- depression leads the individual to be more isolated (lack social support) which makes them susceptible to stress.

It is very difficult to decide which of the first three might be the case. However, the last two options are examples of *mediating* variables – that is, the reason why stress leads to depression is because stress affects social support which then leads to depression. Or a similar argument might apply in which depression affects social support which then leaves the individual susceptible to stress. Partial correlation (Chapter 29) and other statistical techniques (Chapter 32) can help you decide whether social support is mediating the relationship between stress and depression.

However, remember that *moderator* variables are very different from mediating variables though they are easily confused semantically unless one is very careful. One would say that social support is a moderating variable if the extent of the relationship between stress and depression is not the same for people with excellent social support networks, people with moderate social support networks and people whose social support networks are poor – they have few friends and family who they can turn to in time of difficulty. This is illustrated in Figure 38.4. As you can see, for that group of individuals who have poor social support there is a strong relationship between stress and depression. If social support is moderate or excellent, then there is little or no relationship between stress and depression. In other words, then, the relationship between stress and depression depends on the level of social support (excellent, moderate or poor) experienced by participants in the study. In this example, individuals who lack social support seem to be vulnerable to depression when under stress. Those who have moderate or excellent social support networks seem not to be vulnerable to depression when they are stressed. That is, social support has a sort of cushioning effect preventing stress leading to depression. This is perfectly sensible since social support is there to help with problems and prevent difficulties from getting worse. So social support as a moderating variable in the relationship between stress and depression would seem to make good psychological sense.

Another way of visualising this situation is in terms of Table 38.1. What this table indicates that where there is a high level of stress but poor social support then the mean of the depression score is very high. In all other cells the level of depression is much the same. In other words, only where social support is poor do high levels of stress lead to high levels of depression. Of course, the outcome could be more complex than this. Nevertheless, this is the basic situation which leads to the suggestion that there is a

MAIN RELATIONSHIP Stress leads to depression?	POSSIBLE MODERATOR VARIABLE: social support	SIZE OF RELATIONSHIP AT DIFFERENT LEVELS OF THE MODERATOR VARIABLE
STRESS	Excellent social support	Little or no relationship
	Moderate social support	Little or no relationship
DEPRESSION	Low social support	Strong relationship

FIGURE 38.4   Social support as a moderator variable in the relationship between stress and depression

Table 38.1	Mean depression scores for groups formed on the basis of level of social support and level of stress		
	Poor social support	**Moderate social support**	**Excellent social support**
Low level of stress	6.20	5.60	5.65
Medium level of stress	6.10	4.60	5.30
High level of stress	12.25	5.60	6.25

moderator variable, social support, different levels of which lead to different relationships between stress and depression. In this example, there is no relationship between stress and depression except in circumstances in which social support is poor.

Of course, there may well be other potential moderator variables which could be included in the analysis – we simply need to work out what they may be, measure them and then establish that they do play this sort of role. But this does rely on the researcher having bright ideas about likely moderator variables. We may also look for moderator variables (interactions) in circumstances where we expect variable *A* to be related to variable *B* but nevertheless find that in reality the relationship between the two variables is weak. It is appropriate in these circumstances to think of the sorts of reasons why we would expect a stronger relation than the one we found. We have mentioned simple instances of this, but gender, age group, occupational group and so forth might be considered. What is a possibility really depends on what is being studied – and perhaps some insight on the part of the researcher. Figure 38.5 gives the key steps to consider in understanding moderator variables.

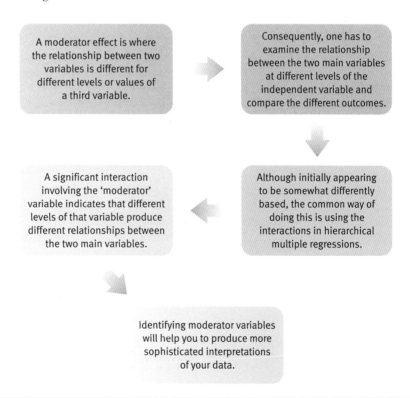

A moderator effect is where the relationship between two variables is different for different levels or values of a third variable.

Consequently, one has to examine the relationship between the two main variables at different levels of the independent variable and compare the different outcomes.

A significant interaction involving the 'moderator' variable indicates that different levels of that variable produce different relationships between the two main variables.

Although initially appearing to be somewhat differently based, the common way of doing this is using the interactions in hierarchical multiple regressions.

Identifying moderator variables will help you to produce more sophisticated interpretations of your data.

FIGURE 38.5   Conceptual steps for understanding moderator variables

38.2 Statistical approaches to finding moderator effects

You may have spotted something – that is, surely what is being referred to as a moderator variable here is part of what we called an interaction in analysis of variance (ANOVA). This is absolutely correct. It also suggests one way of examining one's data to see if there is a moderator variable – that is, simply carry out a two-way analysis of variance on the data of a sort which resulted in Table 38.1. If there is a significant interaction then there is a moderator effect. Chapter 22 discusses two-way independent samples ANOVA design which corresponds to Table 38.1. However, it should be noted that if the stress and social support categories are based on score data, then there is information in the data which is being lost by simply classifying the scores into high, medium and low categories. (That is to say, for example, that although the people in the high category would have different scores, this information about order is lost when they have been classified into the high social support category.) This is bad form in statistical analysis. However, if the study had involved variables measured in terms of nominal categories rather than scores, then the ANOVA approach is the accepted approach. Since the data which psychologists collect are usually in the form of scores rather than nominal categories, then a different form of analysis would be preferred in most cases. The alternative method – the one used where the independent variable (e.g. stress) and the moderator variable (social support) are score variables – is based on hierarchical multiple regression which is presented in Chapter 32. In other words, both the ANOVA approach and the hierarchical multiple regression approaches are very substantially the same analyses discussed in other chapters. The big difference is that the way in which we are conceptualising the analysis is somewhat different.

To summarise:

● If all of your variables are score variables then the best way to look for moderator effects is to use the hierarchical multiple regression approach.

● If your predictor and moderator variables are measured using a nominal (i.e. category or categorical) classification scheme but your dependent variable is a score, then you can use the ANOVA approach.

However, you might wish to take note of the following:

● Sometimes researchers use the ANOVA approach where all of their variables are scores. They merely categorise the moderator and the independent variables into high, medium and low categories. You may find this approach intuitively more appealing.

● You might be wondering what you can do if all of your variables are nominal category ones. Well you can't apply the two approaches described in this data for the obvious reason that the dependent variable is also a nominal category. Though you might wish to check out Chapter 40 on Log-linear analysis since this can help you deal with these circumstances.

So we will discuss the hierarchical multiple regression approach first and then go on to the ANOVA method.

38.3 The hierarchical multiple regression approach to identifying moderator effects (or interactions)

The multiple regression approach to identifying moderator variables involves many of the ideas that were discussed in Chapter 31 on 'Multiple regression and multiple correlation' and, to a lesser extent, Chapter 32 on 'Path analysis'. So if you have read those chapters then there should be few nasty surprises in what follows. However, there are new things in this section, particularly a) the use of standardisation of variables and b) the introduction of a new predictor variable – the interaction. The interaction is where the moderator effect is found. So standardisation and interaction are given extra attention in the following discussion.

We did not standardise variables for the multiple regressions described in Chapters 31 and 32. So why do we need to now? Standardisation usually means in statistics turning scores into z-scores and this applies in this case. That is, for each of our variables each score is turned into a z-score (using the methods described in Chapter 5, though we will describe the process again in this chapter). There is a technical reason for this standardisation which boils down to the fact that if this is not done, then the chances of detecting a moderator effect where one exists are reduced. A more detailed explanation depends on understanding how the regression calculation is actually done. So read the following explanation at your peril. In multiple regression where there are two or more predictors, the regression weights or regression coefficients are calculated setting the value of the other predictor variable at 0. For the raw scores, depending on what is being measured, the value of 0 could be anywhere in the distribution – i.e. it could represent a very big, a medium or a very low score. So it makes sense to involve the more typical scores in the middle of the distribution. So if we have ensured that a score of 0 is equivalent to the middle value of the distribution of scores by using z-scores where the middle of the distribution is 0, then we have ensured that the value of the 'other' variable is set at the mid-point of the distribution.

The other new thing in this chapter is the use of the interaction term in multiple regression. Although interactions have been discussed in Chapter 22 in relation to the analysis of variance (ANOVA), we have not previously discussed them in relation to multiple regression. It has to be said that there is a far closer relationship between ANOVA and multiple regression than appears on the surface. And if you understood interaction in terms of ANOVA then this should help you with it in relation to multiple regression. Essentially, the interaction term is created as a new computed variable simply by multiplying the score on one variable (stress) and the score on the moderator variable (social support). The interaction is really a new variable and is treated as such in multiple regression.

In order to understand why we standardise in this context, it is informative to compare the correlations between the three predictor variables (independent, moderator and interaction) in their unstandardised and standardised forms. Table 38.2 gives the correlations between the three raw variables involved in the multiple regression and then, separately, between the three standardised versions of the same variables for our data. It can be seen that the correlations between the two predictor variables and the interaction of the two predictor variables are larger for the raw scores than for the standardised versions of the same variables and their interaction. The correlation between stress and social support for the raw scores is −0.26 and exactly the same for the standardised scores. This is not surprising since these correlations are based on exactly the same data

Table 38.2	Correlations between the variables and their interaction in raw scores and in standardised form			
	Raw Scores		**Standardised Scores**	
	Social support	Stress	Social support	Stress
Stress	−0.26		−0.26	
Interaction	0.29	0.83	−0.00	0.02

apart from the fact that they have been standardised in one case. What is more interesting is that the correlations between the interaction and the predictor variable change from the raw scores to the standardised scores. The correlations with the interactions are much lower for the standardised scores than for the raw scores. This means that the problem of multicollinearity has been virtually eliminated by using standardised scores compared to the original unstandardised raw scores. The correlations of social support and stress with the interaction are 0.29 and 0.83 for the raw data, but in the standardised scores these correlations decline to −0.00 and −0.02 – essentially zero correlations in both cases. The reduction in multicollinearity means that the interaction of the two predictor variables (which indicates a moderator effect) is more likely to be identified.

In hierarchical multiple regression, as with any form of regression, the basic task is to assess the extent to which a set of predictor variables (independent variables if you prefer) is related to the criterion (or dependent variable). In our example, stress and social support would be independent or predictor variables and depression would be the dependent or criterion variable. Although social support is believed to be a moderator variable in this research, it is also a predictor variable for the purposes of the hierarchical multiple regression. The interaction, as we have seen, is obtained quite simply by multiplying the scores for the two independent variables (stress and social support). An interaction would normally be indicated by the term stress × social support or whatever is appropriate. The interaction term is essentially treated as an additional predictor variable – which is precisely what it is. However, in the multiple regression the interaction is dealt with after the effects of the independent and moderator variables acting independently have been taken into account.

The hierarchical multiple regression procedure is essentially as illustrated in Figure 38.6. The basic principles of the hierarchical multiple regression process are as follows:

- The independent or predictor variables are entered in blocks.

- The first block is used in the analysis first and the second, third etc. in strict order following that. In our example, there are only two blocks.

- There has to be a minimum of one independent variable in each block.

In other words, there are priorities in hierarchical multiple regression which are determined by the order of blocks of variables. Each block may have just one independent variable in it, but it may have more according to the researcher's purpose. As Figure 38.6 indicates, the first block includes both the stress and the social support variables. The second block involves the interaction of the two variables – that is, the interaction term or, in other words, a predictor variable which is created from the multiplication of the stress and social support scores. By multiplying stress and social support together we get a new variable which is normally referred to as the interaction of stress with social support. If the interaction is statistically significant in the multiple regression analysis then we have a moderator effect; if not then there is no moderator effect.

To reiterate, in our example, the first block comprises both the stress and the social support variables. This stage of the analysis seeks to find out what influence stress and

FIGURE 38.6   Structure of a hierarchical multiple regression to test for interactions (moderator variables)

social support, acting separately, have on the dependent variable – i.e. depression. By analysing these in the first block, their influence on the interaction term is taken into account just as the main effects are taken into account first in ANOVA. The second block is the interaction of stress and social support. This is calculated by multiplying each individual's score on the stress variable by their score on the social support variable. In our example, we have just one potential moderator variable, but we could have two or three if we so wished. The problem with multiple moderators is that there are multiple interactions in this case since the number of potential interactions increases disproportionately the more potential moderator variables we have. This is reminiscent of what happens in ANOVA when you have too many independent variables. In a phrase, the result is information overload. So be parsimonious in terms of the number of moderator variables you include in your analysis.

If the hierarchical multiple regression does produce a significant interaction then this is indicative of a moderator effect. Unfortunately, it does not tell us just what the moderator effect is. To see what the form of the interaction is, it is necessary to carry out further analyses. It is suggested by some statisticians that this is done by predicting the scores on the dependent or criterion variable (i.e. depression) for low, medium and high scores on the independent variable and the moderator variable using the unstandardised regression coefficients (Aiken and West, 1991). The advantage of this method is that it takes into account particular scores when determining the significance of the interaction term (i.e. moderator effect) and does not bundle together participants into somewhat arbitrarily defined groups.

Multiple regression assumes that the relationship between the criterion and the interaction can be represented by a straight line although nonlinear relations can sometimes be tested if an appropriate transformation method is available for turning the nonlinear relationships into linear ones (Aiken and West, 1991). However, this is beyond the scope of this chapter and you should consult Aiken and West if you need more information.

Box 38.1	Key concepts

Interaction in multiple regression

Interaction can be seen as a multiplicative effect in multiple regression. That is, different levels of the predictor variables have an effect on the scores which is greater than can be understood in terms of the individual effects of the predictor variables. This is much as we described interactions in ANOVA in Chapter 22. The individual predictor variables have an additive effect on the dependent variable – that is, each predictor variable has a certain influence on the dependent variable and their combined influence is simply the sum of their separate influences. Of course, it is possible that the relationship between two variables is not a simple linear (and therefore additive) one. So sometimes, but rarely, you will find other relationships explored – the square of the scores on one variable in relation to the scores on another variable, for example.

However, it is possible that the influence of the predictor variable is not simply additive (or even based on a squared or quadrupled relationship) but multiplicative instead. That is, the effects of the predictor variables are multiplied together and not simply added together. As a consequence, when we seek to understand the influence of the predictor variables on the dependent variable in multiple regression, we look for the additive effects and also the multiplicative or interaction effects. That is why, quite simply, to get the interaction in multiple regression we multiply the scores on the independent variables together. Of course, the interaction is partly predictable from the independent variables which went to make up the interaction, but not entirely so. So if the simple effects of the independent variables are removed first, then we have the 'pure' multiplicative effect. This is precisely what happens in the calculations – the main effects of the variables acting individually are removed which leaves a 'pure' interaction effect.

Calculation 38.1

Identifying moderator variables using the hierarchical multiple regression approach

The amount of data needed to study moderator variables is large. So instead of presenting the data in a table we have provided an SPSS Statistics file of the data on the website for this book. The steps in hierarchical multiple regression for moderator variables are summarised in Figure 38.7.

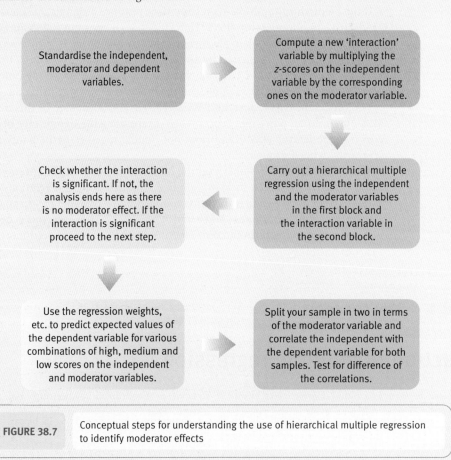

Standardise the independent, moderator and dependent variables.

Compute a new 'interaction' variable by multiplying the z-scores on the independent variable by the corresponding ones on the moderator variable.

Check whether the interaction is significant. If not, the analysis ends here as there is no moderator effect. If the interaction is significant proceed to the next step.

Carry out a hierarchical multiple regression using the independent and the moderator variables in the first block and the interaction variable in the second block.

Use the regression weights, etc. to predict expected values of the dependent variable for various combinations of high, medium and low scores on the independent and moderator variables.

Split your sample in two in terms of the moderator variable and correlate the independent with the dependent variable for both samples. Test for difference of the correlations.

FIGURE 38.7   Conceptual steps for understanding the use of hierarchical multiple regression to identify moderator effects

Step 1   When using hierarchical multiple regression to identify moderator variables, the usual practice is to standardise each of the variables (the independent variable, the dependent variable and the moderator variable). The interaction is based on the standardised independent and moderator variables. Multi-collinearity problems are likely to occur if one uses the raw scores to calculate the interaction term and these are likely to reduce the statistical significance of the interaction and risk making it non-significant. In general, it is less likely that a moderator effect will be detected if there are multicollinearity problems.

In the approach to moderating variables used in this chapter, use standard scores to eliminate collinearity influences, but there are two approaches:

1. Instead of using the raw scores, the scores are 'centred' to make 0 the mean value of the variables. This can be done simply by taking the mean score on the variable away from each score. This needs to be carried out for both the moderator and the independent variables, but it is not necessary for the dependent variable. The formula for this is as follows:

   centred score = individual score − mean score

2. The alternative to this uses standardised scores (i.e. z-scores). This ensures that the mean score on each variable is 0.00, just as the previous method. This is regarded as the preferred approach (e.g. Aiken and West, 1991) and we use it in this chapter. Essentially the standard scores approach adds an extra stage to the calculation in that each centred score is divided by the standard deviation of the scores. This gives us the standardised score or z-score. We calculated z-scores in Chapter 5 so you may wish to read through that again to remind yourself what z-scores are. Thus to standardise scores on each variable we simply apply the following formula to obtain the standardised values:

$$z\text{-score} - \frac{\text{individual score} - \text{mean score}}{\text{standard deviation of scores}}$$

Scores standardised in this way will always have a mean of 0.00 and a standard deviation of 1.00 (this is always true of z-scores as explained in Chapter 5). The criterion or dependent variable should also be standardised if the z-score method is employed rather than the centring approach (e.g. Aiken & West, 1991).

Although it is easy to turn a score into a z-score by a hand calculation, there are many such calculations to be done so a computer package is essential. Turning scores into standard scores is easy with a computer program like SPSS Statistics – it merely requires ticking a box in the 'Descriptive' analysis routine. The new variable based on z-scores will appear as a new column in the data with a slightly different variable name.

Step 2   It is equally easy to calculate the interaction variable by multiplying each z-score for the moderator variable by the corresponding z-score for the independent variable. On SPSS Statistics the 'Compute' procedure will do this for you. Once again, the outcome of doing this will appear as a new variable in the data spreadsheet, though this time you will have provided the name for the variable yourself. The interaction variable will appear as a new variable on the data spreadsheet.

Step 3   So, at this stage we have three standardised variables – the independent variable, the moderator variable and the dependent variable – plus the interaction term which is essentially a variable created by multiplying the first two variables together. The next step is to carry out a hierarchical multiple regression on these variables. The structure of this analysis is summarised in Figure 38.6. In hierarchical multiple regression different sets of variables are entered into the analysis in blocks. The variables in block 1 will be dealt with together and before variables in block 2. There is a minimum of one variable in each block. The point of this is that the interaction term needs to be analysed after the two independent variables have been dealt with since the interaction is essentially what is left over after the effects of the two independent variables have been 'removed'.

Given the general advice that a large sample size is needed when looking for moderator effects it is probably wise to use a computer package to do this calculation too.

Step 4   Table 38.3 summarises the outcome of running a hierarchical multiple regression analysis on the data. From this table you can obtain values for the intercept, the regression weights for each variable and their statistical significance. Since we are mainly interested in moderator effects, the significance level of the interaction term in Table 38.3 is most important since this tells us whether or not we have a significant

→

Table 38.3	Regression summary table		
	B (regression weight)	*t*	**Sig.**
Intercept (constant)	−0.05	0.69	0.49
Stress (standardised)	0.21	2.86	0.01
Social Support (standardised)	−0.21	2.87	0.01
Interaction	−0.19	2.86	0.01

* The dependent variable is depression

moderator effect. However, the table also has the values of the regression weights that we need for identifying just what the nature of the moderator effect is. It is clear that all of the regression weights are statistically significant.

The most important thing in Table 38.3 is the significance or otherwise of the interaction. The interaction is what indicates the presence or not of a moderator effect. If the interaction is not statistically significant, then there is no moderator effect – i.e. social support is not a moderator variable for these data. However, if there is a significant interaction then you do have a moderator effect. Unfortunately, this does not tell us precisely what the nature of this moderator effect is. (This is analogous to the situation in ANOVA where a significant ANOVA does not tell you just where the differences between the cell means lie.) So there is another step that needs to be carried out.

Step 5   The problem at this point is that the output from the hierarchical multiple regression merely gives us regression weights and their significance levels. What it does not tell us is just what parts of the data show markedly different trends from the other parts of the data differentiated by different levels of the moderator variable. The solution adopted is to choose a high score, a medium score and a low score on both the independent variable (stress) and the moderator variable (social support). This gives us nine possible combinations of high, medium and low stress and high, medium and low social support. So in other words, some fairly arbitrary values for the high, medium and low scores are chosen. The high, medium and low scores are defined simply as the score one standard deviation above the mean, a score at the mean and a score one standard deviation below the mean. Of course, expressed as standard scores (*z*-scores) these are +1, 0, and −1, respectively. Don't forget that scores on the independent, dependent and moderator variables have been turned into *z*-scores at an earlier stage. So the score corresponding to a high score is already +1, a medium score is already 0 and a low score is already −1.

What happens next is the regression weights shown in Table 38.3 are used to predict the most likely score on the dependent variable, depression, for each of the nine combinations of high, medium and low stress scores with high, medium and low social support scores. We will look at the formula for calculating the estimated depression scores in the next paragraph. However, it is important to understand that these nine predicted depression scores can be examined to find out just where the interaction effect is. That is, one is looking for just where exceptionally large or small predicted scores are to be found. Having found these, then one has identified the location of the moderator effect – that is, what combination of high, medium or low scores on stress and high, medium and low predicted scores on social support are associated with these exceptionally high or low predicted scores on depression?

In order to predict the depression score from the independent variable (*X*), the moderator variable (*M*) and the interaction (*XM*), we simply apply the following formula (which is an extension of what we saw in Chapter 31):

$$\hat{Y} = a + b_1X + b_2M + b_3XM$$

That is, we multiply the relevant X, M and XM scores by the relevant regression weight from Table 38.3 plus the constant or intercept and this gives us the best prediction of the depression score based on our predictors.

The following lists the elements of the above formula for clarity:

$\hat{Y}$ = the predicted score on the dependent variable

a = the intercept (cut-point) for the regression line – it is a constant for any particular analysis so is the same in every case

b_1 = the regression weight for the predictor (independent variable)

X = the score (z-score) on the predictor variable (i.e. +1, 0 or –1)

b_2 = the regression weight for the moderator variable

M = the score (z-score) on the moderator variable (i.e. +1, 0 or –1)

b_3 = the regression weight for the interaction

XM = the interaction of the independent and moderator variables – this is not a z-score though it is the product of the two z-scores

So, in order to work out the predicted value of the dependent variable for each of the nine combinations of high, medium and low scores for the two variables, we calculate the above equation nine times which gives nine estimated scores on the dependent variable (depression) for each of the possible combinations of the high, medium and low scores for the independent variable (stress) and the moderator variable (social support).

Well, that is what we do in theory, but there is a problem using the above formula. The problem basically is that we do not know precisely what the interaction term means. We do not know which scores it is made up from. For example, for a particular interaction value – say 2.00 – there are many different values of the moderator and the independent variable which multiplied together would give a value of 2.00. So it could be, for example, 1 on the moderator variable and 2 on the independent variable – but equally it could be 2 on the moderator variable and 1 on the independent variable. Both of these gives a value of 2.00. Fortunately, it is possible to rewrite the equation so that it does not involve the use of the interaction term. The formula for regression given above can be rearranged (by anyone clever enough) to yield the following version of that original formula:

$$a + (b_1 + b_3M)X + b_2M$$

This formula is the one which is actually used in the calculation as you can see in Table 38.4.

The nine calculations are illustrated in the nine cells of Table 38.4. As you can see:

● The prediction formula is the same in each cell, of course.

● The constant or intercept a is the same throughout for this particular analysis (it is –0.05).

● The various regression weights are the same throughout.

● Only M (the value of the moderator variable) and X (the value of the independent variable) vary in the formulae. They will be +1, 0 or –1 according to the particular cell in question. The scores to be entered depend on the column and row of the cell that we are considering. The value that goes into the calculation can be found at the top of the relevant row and the top of the relevant column.

→

Table 38.4	Illustrating the three levels of the predictor and moderator variable and the calculation of the expected mean on the dependent variable		
High score on predictor variable (X) (i.e. score at +1 standard deviation)	$a + (b_1 + b_3M)X + b_2M$ $= -0.05 + (0.21$ $+ -0.19 \times 1) \times 1$ $+ -0.21 \times 1$ $= -.14$	$a + (b_1 + b_3M)X + b_2M$ $= -0.05 + (0.21$ $+ -0.19 \times 0) \times 1$ $+ -0.21 \times 0$ $= -.26$	$a + (b_1 + b_3M)X + b_2M$ $= -0.05 + (0.21$ $+ -0.19 \times -1) \times 1$ $+ -0.21 \times -1$ $= .66$
Medium score on predictor variable (X) (i.e. score at mean)	$a + (b_1 + b_3M)X + b_2M$ $= -0.05 + (0.21$ $+ -0.19 \times 1) \times 0$ $+ -0.21 \times 1$ $= -.16$	$a + (b_1 + b_3M)X + b_2M$ $= -0.05 + (0.21$ $+ -0.19 \times 0) \times 0$ $+ -0.21 \times 0$ $= .05$	$a + (b_1 + b_3Z)X + b_2M$ $= -0.05 + (0.21$ $+ -0.19 \times -1) \times 0$ $+ -0.21 \times -1$ $= -.26$
Low score on predictor variable (X) (i.e. score at −1 standard deviation)	$a + (b_1 + b_3M)X + b_2M$ $= -0.05 + (0.21$ $+ -0.19 \times 1) \times -1$ $+ -0.21 \times 1$ $= -.18$	$a + (b_1 + b_3M)X + b_2M$ $= -0.05 + (0.21$ $+ -0.19 \times 0) \times -1$ $+ -0.21 \times 0$ $= -.16$	$a + (b_1 + b_3M)X + b_2M$ $= -0.05 + (0.21$ $+ -0.19 \times -1) \times -1$ $+ -0.21 \times -1$ $= -.14$

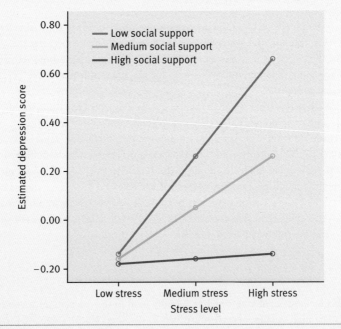

FIGURE 38.8   Plot of predicted depression scores based on output from hierarchical multiple regression

The predicted mean depression scores can be plotted onto a graph (Figure 38.8) in order to illustrate the predicted score's relationship to different levels of stress and social support. It is quite obvious that the slopes in Figure 38.8 are very different. The blue slope for low social support is quite steep whereas the red slope for high social support is quite flat. It is clear that the chart indicates that for individuals with high levels of social support, the level of stress made no difference to the level of depression. On the other hand, for those who have low social support, it is clear that as stress levels increase then so does depression. The lines are straight lines because they represent a linear (straight line) relationship between stress and depression. Although it is possible to calculate a numerical value for each slope, unfortunately there is no statistical test to establish whether the slopes of these lines differ significantly. In order to carry the analysis further then we adopt the procedure described in Step 6. However, it is important to point out that what our eyes see in Figure 38.8 about the slopes, in this example, should convince us that the interaction or moderator effect is largely to do with low levels of social support.

Step 6

So while one might expect to be able to test statistically whether the slopes in Figure 38.8 differ from each other, actually there are no available statistical techniques which identify differences between slopes expressed as coefficients (e.g. Cohen *et al.*, 2003). Hence we did not calculate these coefficients. One solution to this problem involves dividing the sample into two approximately equal sized groups in terms of the moderator variable. So there is a high (above the mean) and low (below the mean) group on the moderator variable. Basically the idea is to see whether the correlations between the independent variable and the dependent variable are different for the high and low groups. In Chapter 35, Section 35.7, we discuss how to test for significant differences between correlations. So it is, first of all, simply a matter of dividing your data into two groups on the basis of being high or low on the moderator variable (social support). This can be done on SPSS Statistics by using the Recode procedure to divide the social support scores into two groups. The correlation between the independent variable and the dependent variable is then calculated for the high group followed by the low group. Finally, the formula for the significance of the difference between two correlation coefficients can be applied. This is not available on SPSS Statistics though applets for doing the calculation are available on the web.

However, it is not too complicated to calculate the significance of the difference between two correlation coefficients. The test is a variant of the *z*-test and it is also discussed in Chapter 35. While the usual advice is to divide the sample to give equal sized groups, you might wish to modify this if you think that the moderator effect occurs towards the higher end or the lower end of the moderator variable. In this case, you might wish to adjust the split point. Using the mid-point of the social support variable resulting in the following Pearson correlations between stress and depression:

- for the high social support group the correlation is 0.002 (sig. = .989, N = 84)

- for the low social support group the correlation is 0.375 (sig = 0.001, N = 96)

These two correlations have to be transformed into standardised (*z*) correlations using Table 35.5. The formula for the test of the difference between the two correlation coefficients is as follows:

$$z = \frac{z_{r_1} - z_{r_2}}{\sqrt{\dfrac{1}{N_1 - 3} + \dfrac{1}{N_2 - 3}}}$$

In this equation, z_{r_1} and z_{r_2} are the two standardised correlation coefficients obtained by using Table 35.5. The standardised value of $r = 0.002$ is 0.000 and for $r = 0.375$ the standardised value is 0.400. These can be substituted in the formula along with the relevant sample sizes ($N_1 = 84$, $N_2 = 96$):

$$z = \frac{0.000 - 0.400}{\sqrt{\dfrac{1}{84 - 3} + \dfrac{1}{96 - 3}}}$$

$$= \frac{-0.400}{\sqrt{\dfrac{1}{81} + \dfrac{1}{93}}}$$

→

$$= \frac{-0.400}{\sqrt{0.012 + 0.011}}$$

$$= \frac{-0.400}{\sqrt{0.023}}$$

$$= \frac{-0.400}{0.152}$$

$$= -2.63$$

Interpreting the results z must equal ±1.96 or more to be statistically significant at the 0.05 level with a two-tailed test of significance (1.65 or more for the one-tailed test of significance). In other words, this analysis confirms that there is a significant difference between the correlations for high scorers on social support and low scorers on social support. The low social support group shows a strong correlation between stress and depression whereas there is a virtually zero correlation for the group high on social support.

One disadvantage of this method is that it involves dividing the sample into two smaller samples which means that the correlations and the difference between them are less likely to be statistically significant. Of course, if you wanted a quick assessment of your data in terms of possible moderator effects, the approach taken in this step would give you a good indication of any moderator effects though it is not as powerful as going through the full process including the hierarchical multiple regression.

Reporting the results One way of reporting the multiple regression results is as follows. 'Baron and Kenny (1986) have suggested that a moderator effect is most appropriately tested with multiple regression. Such an effect is indicated if the interaction of the two predictor variables explains a significant increment in the variance of the criterion variable while the two predictor variables are controlled. Aiken and West (1991) recommended that the criterion and the two predictor variables be standardised. Following these recommendations, a significant proportion of the variance in relationship satisfaction was accounted for by the interaction of stress and social support after the individual variables comprising the interaction were controlled, R^2 change $= .04$, $p < .01$. To interpret the significant interaction three separate unstandardised regression lines were plotted between standardised stress, standardised social support and the standardised level of depression at the mean and at one standard deviation above and below the mean of standardised stress and standardised social support. The relation between relationship stress and depression was strongest at low levels of social support.'

38.4 The ANOVA approach to identifying moderator effects (i.e. interactions)

The ANOVA approach is used where the independent variable and the moderator variable are in the form of nominal categories. Sometimes it is used to analyse data which have been collected in the form of scores. In this case, the scores have to be divided into three separate groups indicating high, medium and low scores for both the independent variable and the moderator variable. It is best to use three groups of scores since nonlinear relationships can be identified whereas they can't with only two groups. This grouping system can be seen in Table 38.1 which is simply a table of mean scores on depression for high, medium and low scoring groups of the independent and moderator variables. Generally speaking, it is best not to do this since information is lost from the data by doing so. On the other hand, the ANOVA approach does have some advantages in terms of being clearer and less complex.

Calculation 38.2

Identifying moderator effects using the ANOVA approach for nominal independent and moderator variables

Step 1   This calculation is based on the example already discussed in the previous section. However, the essential features of the analysis of this study can be seen in Table 38.1. Unless one or more of your predictor variables is qualitative in nature – that is, a nominal/category variable – then you need to categorise the scores on your variable as being in the high, medium and low categories in terms of their size. Although you could use just two categories – such as high and low scores – this is inadvisable if you have a substantial sample size though you may need to try it if not. It is possible to use the Recode procedure on SPSS Statistics to categorise a score variable into groups.

Step 2   The next step is to run the ANOVA calculation. We have a 3×3 ANOVA design of the sort described in Chapter 22. Chapter 2 includes an explanation of the procedure and instructions on how to carry out the analysis by hand. However, we will not repeat these instructions for this particular example. Instead, we will present the results of a computer analysis as outlined in Figure 38.9 since testing for moderator effects tends to involve substantial sample sizes.

Step 3   The mean scores for each of the cells of the ANOVA analysis can be found in Table 38.1. However, it is generally easier to interpret the meaning of the mean scores in a significant interaction by plotting them in a graph where the dependent variable is represented by the vertical axis: one of the predictors is indicated by relatively widely separated points on the horizontal axis and the other predictor is shown by different types of lines. This kind of graph is shown in Figure 38.9 where the horizontal axis represents the three levels of stress and the separate lines represent the three levels of social support. Figure 38.9 plots the mean depression scores of the nine groups formed on the basis of the three levels of stress and the three levels of social support. What seems clear from this plot is that there is one group – high stress and poor social support – which has a particularly high mean score on depression. The other eight groups, although their means do vary a little, have similar means. To anyone familiar with ANOVA, this pattern is very suggestive of a strong interaction between stress and social support. It does not seem to be the case that differences in stress level alone and differences in social support level alone have much bearing on depression since, in general, the depression level is more or less the same for each of the stress and each of the social support groups. The exception, as we have seen, is the one group with high stress but poor social support. In other words, Figure 38.9 demonstrates a clear moderator effect.

→

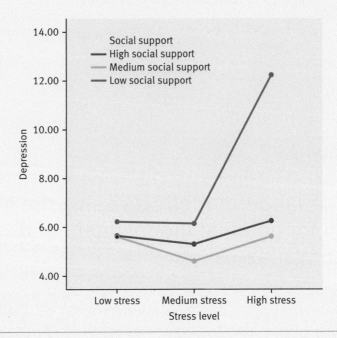

FIGURE 38.9   Plot of means of depression scores for the stress and social support groups

Step 4   You also need to check out the analysis of variance (ANOVA) summary table based on this analysis (Table 38.5). The significance levels for the variables stress and social support and the interaction between them are all statistically significant. However, it is the interaction which is the most important in terms of assessing whether or not there is a moderator effect. A significant interaction effect indicates the presence of a moderator effect. You will see that the row for the interaction of stress and social support is statistically significant at the 0.00 level which indicates strongly the presence of a moderator effect. In this case, this is clear and unproblematic. However, note that the main effects for stress and social support are also both statistically significant. On the face of things, this seems to suggest that stress and social support, acting separately, each have an effect. This is a case where one should be somewhat cautious in the light of what Figure 38.9 suggests about the group means in general – that most of the means are about the same with the one exception. It is important to remember that ANOVA adopts a particular model for analysing data in which main effects such as stress and social support take precedence in the analysis to any interactions. So what is happening here is that some of the variation due to the interaction is being misleadingly allocated to the main effects. Despite this, in this particular case there is no doubt that there is a significant moderator effect which is what you need to know. A problem would arise if the main effects had been significant and the interaction non-significant – the plot of means as in Figure 38.9 is clearly the key to identifying the risk of assuming erroneously that there is no interaction and, hence, no moderator effect. The way in which ANOVA favours main effects was explained in Chapter 22.

Table 38.5	ANOVA summary table giving significance levels for the effects of stress and social support on depression				
Source of variance	Sum of squares	Degrees of freedom	Mean square	F ratio	Sig.
Stress	248.74	2	124.37	13.67	0.00
Social Support	294.54	2	147.27	16.19	0.00
Interaction	270.06	4	67.51	7.42	0.00
Error	1555.65	171	9.10		

Step 5 One relatively simple way of checking whether there truly are main effects is to compare appropriate pairs of cells in the ANOVA table. Remember that a main effect should apply to all pairs of cells in Table 38.1. So *if* there is a main effect of stress, then the group with excellent social support should have significantly different depression in the low stress condition from the medium stress condition and so forth. That is, the main effect of stress should apply at each different level of social support. Table 38.6 illustrates this. The vertical arrows indicate the cells which should be different from each other if there is a main effect by stress. The horizontal arrows indicate the cells which should be different from each other if there is a main effect of social support. Of course, this is the perfect scenario and, of course, in reality things will not be so perfect. One quick and simple way of checking is to run a *post hoc* multiple comparison test such as the Scheffé test on all of the cells. To do this, you need to turn the ANOVA into a one-way ANOVA with, in this case, nine separate cells. On a computer, one could simply add another column indicating which of the nine groups each score of the dependent variable (depression) belonged to. That is, a code of 1 to 9 is added to the data to indicate which of the nine groups the data belong to. When this analysis is carried out on this data, the outcome is simple. None of the cell means differ from each other except for the high level of stress with poor social support. The mean of this cell is significantly higher than *all* other means in the table, just as we would expect from the plots in Figure 38.9. In other words, there are no main effects – just the interaction demonstrating that social support is, indeed, a moderator variable. This is exactly what one would expect from the pattern of means. Of course, this is, in part, a matter of judgement about the data, but ANOVA analyses can need interpretation if misleading conclusions are to be avoided.

Reporting the results One way of reporting the ANOVA results is as follows. 'ANOVA was used to seek for moderator effects in the data. A moderator effect is indicated by a significant interaction in the ANOVA. The 3 × 3 ANOVA on the data indicated main effects on Depression for Stress, $F(2, 171) = 13.67$, $p < .001$, $\eta^2 = .14$, and Social Support, $F(2, 171) = 16.19$, $p < .001$, $\eta^2 = .16$, were statistically significant. However, more importantly in this context, it was found that the interaction of stress and social support was also statistically significant, $F(4, 171) = 67.51$, $p < .001$, $\eta^2 = .15$. This interaction effect indicates that Social Support moderates the relationship between Stress and Depression. In order to identify more precisely the nature of the moderator effect, multiple comparison tests were made between the means of the nine groups. It became clear that the relationship between stress and depression was strong only for participants who lacked social support.'

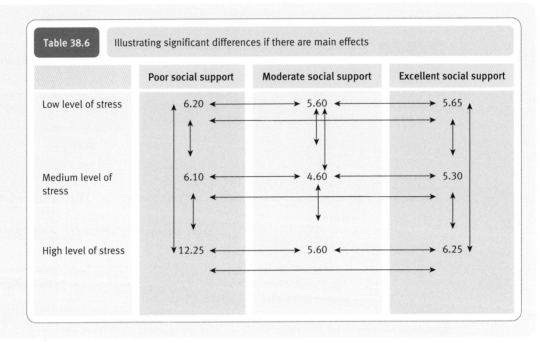

Table 38.6   Illustrating significant differences if there are main effects

	Poor social support	Moderate social support	Excellent social support
Low level of stress	6.20	5.60	5.65
Medium level of stress	6.10	4.60	5.30
High level of stress	12.25	5.60	6.25

Key points

- The most appropriate way of determining whether there is a moderating or interaction effect between two continuous (score) variables is a hierarchical multiple regression.

- This analysis involves the standardisation of the measures into *z*-scores which overcomes some technical problems raised by using raw data.

- Another name for moderator effect is interaction, and the assessment of moderator effects is based on the identification of interactions through either multiple regression or ANOVA.

- It is not possible to do the calculations in their entirety just using a standard computer package such as SPSS Statistics. There is a certain amount of hand calculations to do or doing computations on SPSS Statistics using the Compute procedure, for example.

- To interpret the interaction from a multiple regression, it is recommended that the slope or regression coefficient of the criterion on one of the predictors is calculated for three widely separated values of the other predictor such as its mean and one standard deviation above and below the mean.

COMPUTER ANALYSIS

The SPSS Statistics instruction book to this text is Dennis Howitt and Duncan Cramer (2011), *Introduction to SPSS Statistics in Psychology: For version 19 and earlier*. Harlow: Pearson. Chapter 7 in that book gives detailed step-by-step procedures for standardising variables, Chapters 43 and 44 for computing a new variable, Chapter 36 for hierarchical multiple regression and Chapter 23 for a two-way analysis of variance. These will enable you to carry out a moderator analysis.

Recommended further reading

Aiken, L.S. and West, S.G. (1991). *Multiple Regression: Testing and Interpreting Interactions*. Newbury Park, CA: Sage.

Cohen, J., Cohen, P., West, S.G. and Aiken, L.S. (2003). *Applied Multiple Regression/Correlation Analysis for the Behavioral Sciences*, 3rd edition, Hillsdale, NJ: Lawrence Erlbaum Associates.

CHAPTER 39

Statistical power analysis: Getting the sample size right

Overview

- The main purpose of statistical power analysis is to guide the planning of research. In particular, it seeks to optimise the sample size(s) used such that it is neither so small that significant results are impossible nor so large that time and other resources are used unnecessarily.

- Statistical power is the likelihood that the research study will detect an effect (i.e. trend, correlation or difference) in the sample(s) selected when one exists in reality (in the statistical population).

- The probability of deciding that there is an effect when in reality there is none is known as the Type I error and it is usually given the symbol alpha (α). Statistical significance testing gives α a low probability figure – usually 0.05 – to keep the risk of Type II errors minimal.

- The probability of failing to detect an effect when one exists is known as the Type II error. It is usually designated as beta β.

- Statistical power is, therefore, simply $1 - \beta$. Usually a figure of 0.80 is regarded as very satisfactory.

- Statistical power is interrelated with three things: (a) the standardised effect size (such as Cohen's d or the correlation coefficient), (b) the alpha (α) or significance level and (c) the sample(s) size involved in the study. The larger that any of these values is, the more power there is in the study. It is possible, though a little complex, to calculate statistical power if the other three things are known or can be estimated rationally. Furthermore, and often more usually, the researcher will calculate the required sample size(s) based on the required or estimated statistical power, the effect size and the significance level required. These calculations are best carried out using programs available on the web for ease.

→

- Statistical power calculations carried out before the main study is conducted are regarded as valuable. Questions have been asked, however, about using statistical power calculations after the data have been analysed. That is, statistical power analysis is uncontroversial in terms of planning a study but controversial as part of the analysis of the data.

- Conceptually, statistical power analysis is quite sophisticated and relies on a mature understanding of decision-making in research and the applicability of research findings. It requires the researcher to shed some faith in the significance testing model in favour of understanding decision-making in research and its application.

Preparation

This is a relatively advanced technique which can only be built on a thorough understanding of the use of statistics in research. You need a thorough understanding of the statistical tests that you will use in your research together with knowledge of sampling distributions and sampling error.

39.1 Introduction

One of the commonest questions asked by students planning research is 'What sample size do I need? Would 25 be enough?' Such questions are probably motivated by a number of factors:

- Keeping the amount of work on data collection to a minimum since time is at a premium and collecting data is not always a speedy matter.

- Giving themselves a reasonable chance of obtaining statistical significance which always feels like the preferred option when it comes to writing up a research report or submitting a dissertation. (Of course, this is an emotional rather than a logical matter.)

Now these are perfectly understandable reasons for asking the sample size question. However, unlike many topics in statistics, this is a question unlikely to provoke a completely satisfactory answer from psychologists. Amongst the likely answers are the following:

- Get as big a sample as you can.

- You can probably get away with 50 (or some other number) participants.

- It is impossible to say – depends on too many things.

Each of these is less than satisfactory but for different reasons. We can take them in turn:

- *Get as big sample as you can*: The suggestion that a researcher should get the largest possible sample is wasteful at best. Although student research generally has mainly time costs, research in general is a surprisingly costly activity and, with some types of study, the financial cost of each additional participant may run to several hundred pounds or dollars. The researcher's time is expensive, in the first place, but there may well be substantial additional costs in terms of things like travel, transcription, equipment usage and so forth. Such expenditure is justifiable if the money is being well-spent, but what if it is not?

Imagine that you were the chair of a research committee allocating research funds to eager researchers then you would have many responsibilities. While you need to be satisfied that the research is feasible and of potential value, that the research design, etc. is optimal and so forth, it is also important that the research is not unnecessarily expensive. Hence you would want a reasoned explanation for the researcher's chosen sample size so as not to waste money. Ideally, the sample size should be as big as necessary to answer the research question. This optimum is dependent on various factors including the size of the effect in the study. Ordinary statistics such as the correlation coefficient and the *t*-test are indicative of the size of the effect – we are talking about the size of the correlation coefficient and the value of the *t*-test here *not* their statistical significance. But it is also dependent on the extent to which we are prepared to risk Type I and Type II errors (Chapter 10). A Type I error is accepting the hypothesis when it is, in fact, false and a Type II error is rejecting the hypothesis when it is, in fact, true. These are dealt with in Figure 39.1. The concept of power (as in the title of this chapter) simply refers to the probability of *not* making a Type II error – if there is actually a trend or difference in reality. But we will return to that later in this chapter.

There is another reason why simply going for the largest sample size possible, irrespective of resources, is regarded as unsatisfactory. This is because with very large sample sizes, the slightest relationship or trend in the data is likely to be statistically significant. Now if statistical significance is a researcher's sole criterion of importance then this means that extremely unimpressive trends (effects) in the data will be elevated to a level of importance which they do not warrant. For example, although a correlation of 0.70 is needed to be significant at the 5% level with a sample of ten, it only takes a correlation of 0.20 to be significant with 100 participants and a correlation of 0.06 to be significant with 1000 participants. In other words, a very small relationship in the data may achieve the status of statistical significance and all that entails *if* the sample size is sufficiently large. Of course, a good researcher will modify their interpretation of their analysis in the light of such considerations. It is probably worth mentioning at this stage that there is a view among statisticians that

Type I Errors
- A Type I error is where a trend is detected in the data due to chance. There is no such trend in reality.
- Statistical significance refers to the chance of a trend being the result of chance. This is usually expressed in the phrase 'The findings were statistically significant at the .05 (or .01) level.'

Type II Errors
- A Type II error is where in reality there is a trend but the study fails to detect the trend.
- It is NOT simply the opposite of statistical significance.
- Power is related to Type II errors since power is the probability of NOT making a Type II error.

FIGURE 39.1   Type I and Type II errors

the null hypothesis is unlikely to be exactly true ever so a study with an extremely large sample size is very likely to produce a statistically significant trend. Obviously, such statistically significant but relatively minuscule trends are unlikely to be of much real interest to researchers.

- *You can probably get away with 50 (or some other number) participants*: What about the second suggestion that there is a sample size which is likely to 'do the trick'? This has some merit in that it implies that there is a sample size likely to detect 'statistically significant effects' where they exist and that it does not demand that the researcher samples beyond what is necessary. However, just where has the proposed sample size come from? If it is based on considerable experience in the particular area of research in question then it is probably of some value as it is based on useful knowledge about what sample size 'works' in a particular field of research. For example, a student who is carrying out a research project in a field of research in which their supervisor is expert might well get useful advice on sample size from them. Similarly, if a student is carrying out research which is very similar to that already published then there may be a case for considering using a similar sample size. It may be a little rough and ready but, failing anything else, it is informative. The trouble is that it is only worth considering if it is based on relevant experience. The problem is that the optimum sample size which is just big enough to meet the requirements of (a) being big enough to potentially produce statistical significant outcomes and (b) not being unnecessarily large depends on quite sophisticated statistical ideas which do not readily lend themselves to 'plucking' numbers out of the air. Of course, such suggestions about sample size may be based on rather different considerations – the idea that a certain sample size demonstrates that the student or researcher has put in sufficient effort to achieve satisfactory outcomes. This, of course, is not a rational but an emotional approach which is, therefore, difficult to justify in this context.

- *It is impossible to say – depends on too many things*: Turning to the final suggestion that optimum sample size depends on too many factors, many of which are unknown to the researcher, and so cannot be estimated. This runs counter to everything that you will learn about in this chapter. While the general idea that the estimation of appropriate sample size is not as common among psychologists as it perhaps ought to be, it is not too difficult to estimate this despite the estimation involving some of the sort of intelligent guesswork (i.e. inference and estimation) for which statistics is infamous.

The reason why you need to know about statistical power analysis is that it is increasingly expected in terms of professional level research. For one thing, journals are increasingly demanding that researchers include power as part of the statistical analyses submitted for publication. For another, those funding research are also increasingly likely to ask for estimates of the optimum sample size based on power calculations for reasons of economy and viability of a study. There are other reasons too. If a researcher is carrying out research into the effectiveness of a particular form of psychotherapy using a control group, this means that some people participating in the research will *not* receive the treatment because they have been allocated to the control group. So using a sample size which is unnecessarily big will mean that if the treatment is shown to be effective then the excess of people in the control group will not get treatment. As a consequence, they may suffer a distressing condition for much longer than they need to.

Statistical power is simply the likelihood that a study will detect a trend (or effect) in the data in circumstances in which, in reality, there is a trend. The concept of power is reviewed in Box 39.1. Remember that research deals with samples so reality, in this case, refers to the actual trend in the population which can be regarded as the baseline of truth or reality. Of course, this is largely an abstract concept since the researcher only knows about their sample(s) of data not what is actually happening in the population. So we

	In reality (which is unknown to the researcher), there is NO trend in the data (i.e. H_0, the null hypothesis, is correct).	In reality (which is unknown to the researcher), there is a trend in the data (i.e. H_1, the hypothesis, is correct).
The researcher decides that there is a trend in the data (i.e. H_1, the hypothesis, is correct).	This is a TYPE I ERROR. The researcher's decision is incorrect. This is the situation that significance testing tries to avoid. The probability of this is alpha (α).	The researcher's decision is correct. This is the situation that statistical power concentrates on. The probability of this is $1 - \beta$ (see cell below).
The researcher decides that there is NO trend in the data (i.e. H_0, the null hypothesis, is correct).	The researcher's decision is correct. The probability of this is $1 - \alpha$.	This is a TYPE II ERROR. The researcher's decision is incorrect. Statistical power analysis tries to keep Type II errors to a minimum. The probability of a Type II error is beta (β).

FIGURE 39.2   The possible correct and incorrect (errors) decisions that a researcher can make based on their data

are talking estimation and inference. There are two risks in research. The most familiar is the idea that the sample(s) of data collected for the study will show a trend or a relationship when in reality there is no trend or relationship in the population from which the data were collected. This is known as a Type I error and is illustrated in Figure 39.2. Significance testing tries to minimise the risk of the Type I error by imposing the .05 or .01 significance criteria which refer to the risk of a Type I error that the researcher is prepared to take. But by this stage you should be very familiar with all of this. The Type I error is involved in power analysis because power depends partly on the significance level you choose for your study. The other risk is that of making a Type II error. This is the risk of failing to find a trend or relationship in the study when in reality there is a trend or relationship. The Type II error is illustrated in Figure 39.2 also.

This is a somewhat formal account which makes reference to H_0 which is the null hypothesis and H_1 which is the alternative hypothesis. You can regard the null hypothesis and alternative hypothesis in the way that they are discussed in experimental design, but they are simply the situation in which there is no trend at all in the data and the situation where there is a trend in the data. Type I error should be very familiar by now as you have implicitly considered it every time you have carried out a test of statistical significance. On the other hand, Type II error is likely to be much less familiar – indeed, this chapter is probably the first occasion when understanding it is of crucial importance. The concept of statistical power is essentially the opposite of that of the Type II error. Thus statistical power is the probability of *not* making Type II error if there is a trend or relationship in the data. Thus, if the probability of making a Type II error is 0.15 then the power of the analysis (or the probability of *not* making a Type II error) is $1.00 - 0.15 = 0.85$.

Notice that these probabilities are calculated on the basis that the hypothesis (H_1) is true which only concerns the circumstances in which it is assumed that there is a relationship or trend in the population. So this is just another way of saying that statistical power is the likelihood of detecting a trend or relationship in a study in circumstances in which there is in reality a trend or a relationship exists. Much the same applies for the Type I error – the probabilities are in terms of the likelihood of making an error if in reality the null hypothesis is true.

Box 39.1   Key concept

Statistical power?

The concept of statistical power is not quite what it seems. It is very much a conceptual matter which can only be understood if the basic concepts of statistical testing are understood. If you have reached this chapter then probably you have mastered at least some of the essential basic ideas. So be warned that statistical power is not a commonsense notion in itself. Nor is it possible to suggest that the more power there is the better. Research is essentially about finding trends in whatever the researcher's field of interest is. It is traditional in psychology to conduct research by measuring the size of a correlation between two variables or the size of a difference between group means, for example. Then the researcher calculates the likelihood that a trend of this particular size could be obtained as a result of sampling fluctuations. If this is unlikely, the researcher will declare that their results are statistically significant. Usually a relatively arbitrary probability level of .05 or .01 is used to assess statistical significance. Sometimes this is expressed as the 5% level of significance or the 1% level of significance. This is little other than the likelihood that the researcher has selected a sample(s) which appears to show a trend or relationship which does not represent the true situation – that is, there is no correlation or difference in the population from which the sample(s) was selected though there does appear to be one in the sample being studied. The level of significance (.05, .01) simply represents the extreme uncharacteristic samples which will be found due to sampling fluctuations despite the reality that there is no correlation or difference. Certain things might be mentioned in respect of significance testing:

● Discussion of the concept of Type I error is fairly commonplace in analyses of research data though this is usually in terms of statistical significance. A Type I error is where the researcher accepts that there is a trend (correlation or difference) based on what can be seen in their data though this is an erroneous decision. The .05 and .01 levels of significance are probabilities that the researcher may have made a Type I error – if there is in reality no correlation or difference. If the researcher chooses the .01 level of significance then this means that there is *less* chance of making a Type I error than if they had chosen the .05 level of significance. In

this sense, the .01 level of significance can be seen as more stringent than the .05 level of significance. But it is only one part of the picture despite statistical significance being used as if it were the gold standard in research.

● Every psychology student will know that statistical significance is related to such things as sample size (the bigger the sample size the more likely a trend in the data is to be statistically significant – all other things being equal) and the size of the correlation or difference (the bigger the trend in the data the more likely one is to obtain statistical significance – all other things being equal).

All of this is likely to be very familiar. Nevertheless, it is not what power is about. Statistical power is more about a part of decision-making in research which is commonly taught but tends to be overlooked in the quest to achieve the status of statistical significance.

So although psychologists have probably heard about the concept of the Type II error, it is probably not actively considered when making decisions based on their research. The Type II error is the likelihood that a researcher has collected data which suggest that there is *not* a trend when in reality there is a trend. Sampling error is responsible for Type II errors just as it is for Type I errors. However, it is the sampling distribution of the population in which their is a real trend i.e. not of the hypothetical population distribution of the null hypothesis of no trends. So a Type II error is where the sample(s) on which a research study was based do not seem to show the trend which actually exists in reality.

Now both Type I and Type II errors are bad news in research for very different but viable reasons. The concentration on Type I errors is unfortunate, but statistics is a complex discipline and inevitably things will get simplified if their importance is not understood. Research is largely about establishing that there are trends and relationships in whatever is being studied rather than showing that there are no trends and relationships. Rarely do researchers set out to establish that there is no trend or relationship in their data. Quite the reverse – they are usually keen to establish trends and relationships in their data. If you make a Type II error you are essentially claiming that there is no relationship when there is one. Given that this is simply not what researchers want (no matter how objective and dispassionate some claim to be), then greater clarity about the implications of Type II errors seems to be essential.

Statistical power is essentially the opposite side of the coin from the Type II error. Statistical power concerns the ability of a research study to detect a relationship when there is indeed, in reality, a relationship. A Type II error is, in contrast, the likelihood of failing to detect a relationship where one exists in reality. So statistical power is really the extent to which the researcher is likely *not* to be making a Type II error – but remember that the phrase 'if the hypothesis that there is a relationship in reality' always needs to be appended to the definitions of both power and Type II errors. So statistical power = 1 – the probability of making a Type II error. If the probability of making a Type II error in a particular study is .20, the power of the study to detect a real trend or difference is $1.00 - 0.20 = 0.80$. Remember that 1.00 in probability theory (Chapter 15) refers to a single event or instance. So in this case the 1.00 refers to a single instance of a researcher's decision to decide either that there is a trend or that there is not a trend in the data. The 0.80, therefore, is the probability that this decision has been in favour of concluding that there is a trend or difference when one actually exists in reality outside of the researcher's study.

The Type II error and power both depend on the distribution of samples taken at random from the population in which there is a trend or difference. Some of these samples will depart quite markedly from what is happening in the population from which the samples were taken. Any of these samples which are in the range of the non-statistically significant samples according to the null hypothesis of zero differences or correlations would be erroneously identified as coming from the population where the null hypothesis is true. The amount of overlap between the two sampling distributions will obviously affect the size of the Type II error and the statistical power. This can be seen in Figure 39.3.

What this all boils down to is that statistical power reflects the risk that the researcher will fail to show the relationship or difference which was the real purpose of the research. Imagine that the researcher was searching for a cure for cancer – accepting the null hypothesis erroneously might lead to the abandonment of this line of research which had essentially discovered the cure for cancer. This would be an extremely serious consequence – some might say much more serious than mistakenly thinking that one had found a potential cure for cancer when, in truth, your treatment did not work. These are clearly complex arguments which are far more socially important than dry discussions of Type I and Type II errors.

Statistical power is affected by other aspects of the research, most of which should be very familiar to you by now. You might find it easier to think about the factors which will change adversely the likelihood of making a Type II error and consequently increase the power of the analysis. These factors can all be seen in Figure 39.3 which lists things which will affect statistical power (and the risk of making a Type II error). Most of these you could probably guess were involved anyway:

- The bigger the sample size then the greater the power of your study (and the less likely it is that a Type II error will be made) all other things being equal. This makes intuitive sense since a study with bigger samples is more likely to detect trends or relationships where they exist than one using smaller samples. One reason is that the bigger the sample then the smaller the sampling error (or spread of sample means taken from the population).

- The bigger the significance level (i.e. alpha or α) you choose for your test of significance, the greater the power of your study (and once again the less likely it is that you will make a Type II error) all other things being equal. Now alpha is the significance level that you choose when assessing the statistical significance of the trend or relationship in your data. If you select an alpha of .05 then this is bigger than an alpha of .01. Thus an analysis using the .05 level of significance has more power than one using the .01 level of significance – all other things being equal. It is important, though, to remember that the significance level does not have to be .05 and can

EFFECT SIZE	ALPHA LEVEL
The size of the trend in the data usually expressed as a correlation coefficient or Cohen's *d*.	The statistical probability of wrongly accepting the hypothesis on the basis of chance. Usually .05 or .01 is chosen by the researcher.

The components of statistical power analysis

SAMPLE SIZE	POWER
The numbers of participants, cases, etc. in the study. Too small a sample and the null hypothesis cannot be rejected, too large a sample and uninterestingly small trends in the data may be detected.	The likelihood that a study will detect an effect when there really is one. So power is 1 minus the probability of rejecting the hypothesis when it is true in reality. Often a somewhat arbitrary criterion of .80 is set for satisfactory power.

FIGURE 39.3   The components of statistical power calculations

vary depending on a range of circumstances associated with the research, although it is a sound fallback choice. Also remember that the significance level is the probability of identifying a trend or relationship in the data when there is no trend or relationship in reality due to sampling fluctuations (i.e. the risk of a Type I error). It is fairly obvious that where the researcher accepts a greater risk of making a Type I error (finding a trend where there isn't one) then the risk of Type II error will be lower as a consequence. But we will return to this shortly.

● The bigger the size of the effect in a study (i.e. the stronger the relationship or the greater the trend or the bigger the difference between the mean scores for each group) then the greater the power your study has (and the lower the risk of making a Type II error) – all other things being equal. If you consider that the size of the effect in a study is indicated by the size of the correlation or the size of the *t*-statistic, for example, then once again this should not surprise you. A correlation of .6 is more likely to be statistically significant than one of .3, for example, for a given sample size. This means that the researcher is more likely to accept that there is a relationship or trend in the data. Since power is the likelihood of identifying a trend or relationship in a study when one exists in reality, it is not surprising that sample size relates to power. It is usual in power calculations to use a standardised measure of effect size and usually Cohen's *d*, but sometimes a correlation coefficient is used as this is standardised too. See Box 39.2 for a more detailed discussion of measures of effect size.

Other things influence power, in particular the variability in the data:

● The greater the variability in the data, however, the *lower* the power in the study. This is because increased variability reduces the chance that your findings will be statistically significant. Remember that power is the likelihood of detecting a relationship or trend in your study when there is one in reality. Thus if the possibility of significant findings is reduced because of higher variability in the data then the power is reduced because the trend or relationship will not be detected even though in reality there is one. However, this is not necessarily an important feature of power calculations since the standardised measures of effect size (e.g. the Pearson correlation coefficient and Cohen's *d*) which are used in power analysis take this into account in their calculation. Nevertheless, the variability in the data is something which the researcher can often do something about – anything that can be done to reduce this variability increases the power of the analysis. For example, the researcher can standardise their

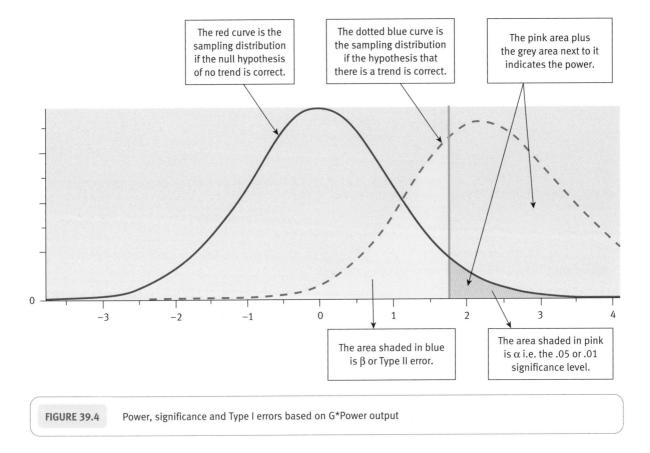

The red curve is the sampling distribution if the null hypothesis of no trend is correct.

The dotted blue curve is the sampling distribution if the hypothesis that there is a trend is correct.

The pink area plus the grey area next to it indicates the power.

The area shaded in blue is β or Type II error.

The area shaded in pink is α i.e. the .05 or .01 significance level.

FIGURE 39.4   Power, significance and Type I errors based on G*Power output

methods of conducting the research and also use well constructed tests and other measures as both these things will reduce variability and hence increase power. That is, reduce, if they can, any unwanted source of variability in the study.

All of these aspects intertwine in a study to produce the power of your analysis. Furthermore, the analysis is different for different statistical procedures (tests of significance), which means that the calculation of statistical power can be a little complex. There are two main ways to deal with this and make statistical power accessible to researchers: (a) produce tables for every test of significance which results in numerous tables to consult and (b) use computer programs in which the researcher enters key aspects of their study (sample size, effect size, and the significance level [i.e. alpha level] involved) and the calculation is left to the computer. Of course, alternative (c) is to do the calculations yourself by hand though this is not a particularly helpful option.

Figure 39.4 is important. It shows the (theoretical) distribution of samples taken from the population. The curve on the left, in red, is the distribution of differences between sample means (of a given size) if the null hypothesis that there is no trend in the data is correct. It is therefore the sampling distribution according to the null hypothesis:

● Notice that the mean or midpoint of this curve is 0.0 as you would expect if the null hypothesis is true since there should be no difference between the samples except that due to sampling error.

● The pink area is the portion of this curve selected to be the significance level for testing the hypothesis. The pink area is bigger for a .05 significance test than for a .01 significance test. That is, the vertical green line will be further to the left for .05 significance than for .01 significance.

The curve with the dotted blue line is not so familiar. It is the distribution of differences between sample means if the hypothesis is true – that is, if in reality there is a trend in the data. The mean of the dotted blue curve is about 2.3; that is, the effect of being in one group compared to the other. If this is standardised then it is an effect size.

There are a number of things that may be obvious from Figure 39.4:

- The part of the blue dotted curve which is shaded in blue to the left of the pink shaded area indicates the extent of Type II error in this particular study. The power of this particular study is indicated by the remainder of the blue dotted curve. This includes the area of statistical significance for the red curve.

- If the size of the effect of the study is increased (i.e. by mentally moving the blue dotted curve to the right) the power would increase as there would be less of the blue dotted curve to the left of the pink alpha area. Move the curve to the left and the power would decrease.

- If variability in the study were to be reduced, then the curves would have less spread and power would increase as a consequence.

- If the significance level changes then the pink alpha area will be bigger or smaller. It is smaller if the significance level is .01 which will have the effect of increasing the Type II error and so decreasing the power of the analysis. It is larger if the significance level is .05 which means that the Type II error will be smaller and the power greater, as a consequence.

What cannot be seen from Figure 39.4 is the influence of sample size on power. However, if you remember from Chapter 9 that the sampling distribution for larger samples is smaller than for smaller samples then it can be understood why sample size influences power by reducing the spread of the sampling distribution, all other things being equal.

Box 39.2   Key concept

Effect size

An effect size is the extent of the trend demonstrated by a study. Effect is a slightly odd word in the context of most research since it implies the influence or impact of one variable on another variable. However, effect size is really about the relationship between two variables rather than anything to do with cause and effect. It refers essentially to two things:

- *The size of the relationship (i.e. correlation) between two variables* The most familiar measure of this is the Pearson correlation coefficient which can be used as a measure of the effect size. In Chapter 35 the Pearson correlation coefficient is used as the measure of effect size for meta-analysis as we are very familiar with it. The

Pearson correlation coefficient is a standardised measure of the relationship between two variables. That is, one can meaningfully compare correlation coefficients even when they are taken from different studies. The bigger the correlation between two variables the bigger the effect size.

- *The difference between the mean scores of different groups of scores* For example, this could be the difference between the mean of the experimental and control group. Although such differences do indicate the actual effect, it is not used as a measure of effect size because it is dependent on the variation in the data. In other words, differences in themselves are not standardised measures.

If the difference between two means is to be used as a measure of effect size then that difference needs to be standardised so that differences in means may be compared from study to study. You should be familiar with some forms of standardisation by now. They basically involve adjusting by the variability in the data. The commonest way of doing this is to use Cohen's d as a measure of effect size. Cohen's d is simply the difference between the two mean scores $(\bar{X}_1 - \bar{X}_2)$ divided by the standard deviation of the population:

$$\text{Cohen's } d = \frac{\bar{X}_1 - \bar{X}_2}{\text{standard deviation of population}}$$

Cohen originally suggested dividing by the standard deviation based on one or other group of scores. The assumption was that the two standard deviations should be equal. But, of course, they are likely to be different to some extent in practice. Consequently, it is more usual to pool (combine together) the two standard deviations when calculating Cohen's d, much as it is when calculating the value of t for a t-test. But this actually leads to a situation in which there are various formulae for combining the two standard deviations since there is more than one way of doing this. The commonest formula for Cohen's d which involves pooling standard deviations is as follows:

$$\frac{\bar{X}_1 - \bar{X}_2}{\sqrt{\dfrac{(n_1 - 1)s_1^2 + (n_2 - 1)s_2^2}{n_1 + n_2}}}$$

The two standard deviations are listed as s_1 and s_2 in the above and their respective sample sizes are given as n_1 and n_2.

Table 39.1	Equivalent effect sizes expressed as Cohen's d and Pearson correlation coefficient								
Pearson r	Cohen's d	Pearson r	Cohen's d	Pearson r	Cohen's d	Pearson r	Cohen's d	Pearson r	Cohen's d
0.00 ↔ 0.00		0.20 ↔ 0.41		0.40 ↔ 0.87		0.60 ↔ 1.50		0.80 ↔ 2.67	
0.01	0.02	0.21	0.43	0.41	0.90	0.61	1.54	0.81	2.76
0.02	0.04	0.22	0.45	0.42	0.93	0.62	1.58	0.82	2.87
0.03	0.06	0.23	0.47	0.43	0.95	0.63	1.62	0.83	2.98
0.04	0.08	0.24	0.49	0.44	0.98	0.64	1.67	0.84	3.10
0.05	0.10	0.25	0.52	0.45	1.01	0.65	1.71	0.85	3.23
0.06	0.12	0.26	0.54	0.46	1.04	0.66	1.76	0.86	3.37
0.07	0.14	0.27	0.56	0.47	1.06	0.67	1.81	0.87	3.53
0.08	0.16	0.28	0.58	0.48	1.09	0.68	1.85	0.88	3.71
0.09	0.18	0.29	0.61	0.49	1.12	0.69	1.91	0.89	3.90
0.10	0.20	0.30	0.63	0.50	1.15	0.70	1.96	0.90	4.13
0.11	0.22	0.31	0.65	0.51	1.19	0.71	2.02	0.91	4.39
0.12	0.24	0.32	0.68	0.52	1.22	0.72	2.08	0.92	4.69
0.13	0.26	0.33	0.70	0.53	1.25	0.73	2.14	0.93	5.06
0.14	0.28	0.34	0.72	0.54	1.28	0.74	2.20	0.94	5.51
0.15	0.30	0.35	0.75	0.55	1.32	0.75	2.27	0.95	6.08
0.16	0.32	0.36	0.77	0.56	1.35	0.76	2.34	0.96	6.86
0.17	0.35	0.37	0.80	0.57	1.39	0.77	2.31	0.97	7.98
0.18	0.37	0.38	0.82	0.58	1.42	0.78	2.49	0.98	9.85
0.19	0.39	0.39	0.85	0.59	1.46	0.79	2.58	0.99	14.04

→

Should you wish to calculate the effects size for your study then there a number of effect size calculators available free on the Web which involve entering some information based on your data following which the effect size is given. Simply type the words 'effect size calculator' into your favourite search engine and make your selection from the sites that this generates. G*Power which is used in this chapter to calculate power will also calculate the appropriate measure of effect size for the particular test of significance that you are using. The information required is readily available from the output of the *t*-test on programs such as SPSS Statistics. Alternatively, you could calculate the effect size as a correlation coefficient (using SPSS Statistics or any other statistics program) – or by hand using the procedures described in Chapter 35). The dependent variable of the study is one variable in the calculation and the other variable is the group to which the participant in question belongs which is coded 1 for the control group and coded 2 for the experimental group, etc. If you want the effect size as a value of Cohen's *d* then Table 39.1 could be used to convert the resulting correlation coefficient to the equivalent value of Cohen's *d* as explained in the next paragraph.

There is a close relationship between Cohen's *d* and the Pearson correlation coefficient. This is to be seen in Table 39.1. This allows a value of Cohen's *d* effect size to be converted to a Pearson correlation coefficient and vice versa. In Table 39.1 the purple shaded columns contain values of the Pearson correlation coefficient (Pearson *r*) and the blue shaded columns contain the values of Cohen's *d*. If you wish to find the equivalent Cohen's *d* for a Pearson *r* of 0.40, simply find the 0.40 in the purple columns and look to its right in the blue column. You will find that a Pearson *r* of 0.40 corresponds to a Cohen's *d* of 0.87. If you have a Cohen's *d* of 2.20 then you look at the purple column to the left of this where you will find that the corresponding Pearson *r* value is 0.74. If you have values which go to more than two decimal places then you will need to round down to two decimal places before you use the table. If the precise value is not in the table then use the nearest value instead. Such a conversion from Cohen's *d* to a correlation coefficient is useful if you are not very familiar with Cohen's *d*. In these circumstances the Pearson *r* will almost certainly be more meaningful to you.

There are other measures of effect size when comparing two groups (Glass's Δ and Hedge's *g*) though Cohen's *d* tends to be the most commonly used. There are also other measures of effect size to deal with analysis of variance (ANOVA) designs.

39.2 Types of statistical power analysis and their limitations

There are a number of ways in which statistical power is used in research. These divide into (a) the prospective (*a priori*) use which is part of the planning of a research study and (b) the retrospective (*post hoc*) use where statistical power is calculated as part of the analysis of the data. These are illustrated in Figure 39.5. It should be quickly pointed out that opinion is divided on the value of different aspects of power analysis. Most statisticians acknowledge that the prospective uses of statistical power are of value when planning substantial research projects. On the other hand, some question the value of retrospective power analyses. Some of the arguments are quite vehement.

The argument for the prospective use of power analysis as part of the planning of a research study has largely been made earlier in this chapter. However, one argument might be particularly difficult for those trained in psychological research. Psychologists tend to stress the importance of finding statistically significant differences or relationships, often forgetting other considerations. In brief, it is good to get statistically significant results. Certainly, there is a view that significant research findings are easier to get published. Statistical power analysis puts a very different gloss on the research and basically argues that only relationships or differences of a certain magnitude are important and worthy of consideration and that sample size, in particular, should be geared to making it likely that significant trends will be found in the data where they exist in reality. In other words, for a particular area of research or a particular research study, what is the

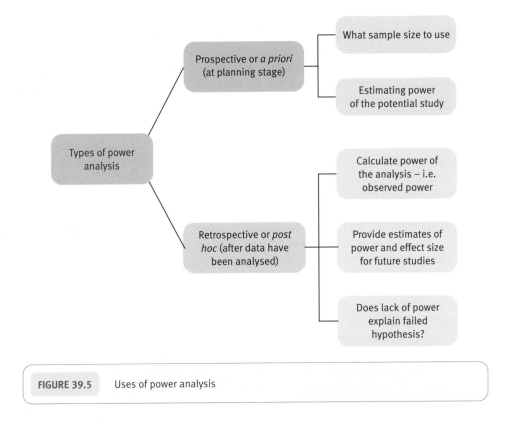

FIGURE 39.5   Uses of power analysis

size of effect which the researcher is warranted in searching for? And, given this, what is the size of sample(s) which can detect an effect of this magnitude? If a researcher's sole criterion for effective research is that statistically significant findings are obtained then very large sample sizes should normally do the trick. What emerges, though, is likely to be of trivial or no value. There is an argument in the statistical literature that null hypotheses are never (or hardly ever) true – take a large enough sample and a statistically significant difference or correlation will be found even if it involves sampling thousands of cases. Unfortunately, this is a fairly accurate caricature of some research in psychology though it is essentially mindless. Of course, statistics textbooks often inadvertently and unintentionally reinforce the view that statistical significance is a holy grail in research. Planning research should be a much more thoughtful process than this implies.

Another prospective use of power analysis is where a pilot study has been carried out on a relatively modest number of participants in order to make sure that the procedures of the study work well enough to encourage the researcher to consider a later larger scale study. It is likely to be possible to use the basic information from this pilot study concerning effect size to allow an intelligent approach to deciding an optimal sample size for the subsequent large-scale study. This is a thoughtful intelligent approach to planning research which should be encouraged.

The argument about the retrospective use of statistical power analysis is, as mentioned, somewhat more controversial and acrimoniously presented. It boils down to the question of what value such retrospective power analyses are to the researcher. This retrospective power analysis is known as *observed power* and is calculated as part of some of the statistical routines on SPSS Statistics, for example. Quite obviously, if your study produces statistically significant findings then the study had sufficient statistical power for the particular sample size used – otherwise you would not have obtained statistically significant results. It might also be of some interest to quantify the power of your study when considering the effect size. For example, you might find that your study had a very large power value. This suggests that you may have used a far too large sample size given the effect size. In other words, any future studies could involve a smaller sample size which brings consequent economies to the research. Power analysis could tell you the size of sample that future similar studies require. This, though, is rather like the case of using pilot studies discussed above and amounts to good practice for much the same reasons.

Where there is controversy is because retrospective power analysis has been used to make a rather different sort of argument. Some researchers have argued that if a study fails to obtain significant findings, that a power analysis can be used to help decide what is going on in the data as a sort of data analysis method. Imagine that the power analysis suggests that the study involves adequate statistical power yet the findings are not statistically significant. Basic statistics courses tell us that in these circumstances where we have not obtained statistical significance we reject the hypothesis and accept the null hypothesis of no difference or no relationship. Now retrospective power analysis (observed power) is sometimes used to suggest that where (a) there is no evidence in support of the hypothesis and, consequently, (b) the null hypothesis should be accepted then if the observed power is low then this suggests that the evidence in support of the null hypothesis should be regarded as weak. That is, the argument goes that the study was incapable of rejecting the null hypothesis because of its low power. The problem with this argument is that there is a direct relationship between the observed power and the probability (significance) level found using a test of significance. In other words, discussing observed power is a long-winded way of saying things which the significance level already indicates. One further criticism of using observed power (erroneously) in this way is that there are acceptable methods of testing the strength of the null hypothesis. For example, it is possible to test whether two group means are statistically equivalent rather than simply 'not significantly different' as in the case of conventional significance testing (Hoenig and Heisey, 2001). The controversy, in summary, is about whether observed power statistics add anything to the interpretation of non-significant research findings. Nevertheless, psychology journals are increasingly likely to require the reporting of observed power statistics.

The message from this seems to be clear. Power analysis as part of the planning process for a research study is generally regarded favourably by both researchers and statisticians as an important tool. It helps ensure clarity about what is an adequate effect size for a particular study but also encourages consideration of what would be an adequate sample size. In contrast, however, retrospective power analysis should be used with great caution because it is only of very limited value and is not a tool for data analysis as such. Indeed, the retrospective use of power analysis is most acceptable in circumstances where it potentially contributes to the planning of further research studies – but that is the case for prospective power analysis.

39.3 Doing power analysis

It must be understood that the following are interdependent:

- statistical power
- sample size
- effect size
- statistical significance

If three of these four things are known for a particular test of significance then it is possible to work out the fourth. Usually it is statistical power or sample size which is calculated from the other three using power analysis programs. Although it is feasible to do these calculations without the aid of a computer, there is little point in spending time on this when one has better things to do with one's time. Type the words power analysis calculator into your preferred Internet search engine and any number of resources for doing particular aspects of power analysis will be listed. Mostly they will do what you need though some have a more specialised function than others. You can download a program known as G*Power from the web and that is our preferred program, but there are others available. The authors of this have kindly allowed us to include it on the book's website so you should have access to it permanently. Some other programs are in the form of applets on web pages so you do the calculation on screen but the program is not downloaded on your computer.

You will probably have noticed a stumbling block. What is the value for statistical power, effect size and statistical significance if I want to use statistical power analysis to calculate the appropriate sample size? Where can I find these? The answer is, in general, that you can't find them but you will have to rationally decide what the appropriate values for each of these are. Let us go through the different aspects of the power calculation in turn:

- The level of statistical significance is traditionally set at .05 in psychology. This is often described as an arbitrary value and it is. There is no logic in choosing it except that it stipulates a pretty low value of probability that the researcher will choose to accept the hypothesis erroneously when the null hypothesis of no trend is in reality true. That is, there is only a one in twenty chance (5%) of accepting the hypothesis when it is, in fact, false in reality. But is this value always an adequate criterion? What if the research was about a cure for hay fever and a decision whether or not to spend a very large amount of money on research and development rested on the outcome of the study? In these circumstances, would it not be wiser to adopt a more stringent significance level (e.g. .01) in place of .05? The answer is probably yes. On the other hand, if the planned research is more exploratory and in a field where there is little previous research, then maybe a less stringent significance level of 0.10 might be adopted. For example, if the study was being carried out on a shoestring for purposes with no such immediate consequence as the spending of huge sums of money, then surely the risk of prematurely abandoning research on this topic (because the study fails to obtain significant results) might be more serious than the consequences of reaching by chance the erroneous conclusion that the hypothesis was true. Quite clearly, these are not really statistical decisions but ones, nevertheless, of some importance to the researcher.

  Of course, it is possible to explore the effect on sample size of the various possible levels of significance to see if it makes any practical difference to your research. (It should be added that it is possible to calculate significance against not the usual zero effect model of the null hypothesis but against a low level size of effect which is of no practical interest to the researcher – that is, a size of effect which, although tangible, is so small that it is not worthwhile when making decisions based on the outcome of the research. For example, if it is known that an inexpensive drug such as aspirin has a particular size of effect then this effect might be set as the baseline against which to evaluate a new much more expensive drug. Such procedures are discussed in Murphy and Myors (2004).)

- The required level of the effect size must be estimated for your proposed study. This can be based on one of several sources of information:

  (a) If there have been similar studies using the measures that you are planning to use in your study, then the effect sizes from these previous studies may be used.

Obviously the more similar the other study(ies) to yours the better this estimate is likely to be.

(b) Alternatively, a more general approach could be used. For example, Lipsey and Wilson (1993) collated effect sizes from a range of different sizes of study. They found that treatment programs for juvenile delinquents in terms of future delinquency, worksite anti-smoking programs in terms of rates of quitting smoking and small versus large school class sizes in terms of measures of achievement typically had small effect sizes of Cohen's *d*s of .20 or less. On the other hand, behaviour therapy compared to placebo controls on various outcome measures and enrichment programs for gifted children in terms of cognitive, creativity and affective outcomes had effect sizes of .5 or so – that is medium size effect sizes. Finally, psychotherapy in terms of various outcomes and positive reinforcement in the classroom had effect sizes of .85 or more – that is, large effect sizes. Cohen (1988) stipulated a small effect as a Cohen's *d* of .20, a medium effect as a Cohen's *d* of .50 and a large effect as a Cohen's *d* of .80. So if a particular type of research is known to generally produce a particular effect size then this could be used.

(c) One could simply look at the consequences of using Cohen's three levels of effect size in terms of sample size. It may be that each of them indicates a sample size which is feasible in terms of the proposed research. Otherwise, the conservative approach would be to take a Cohen's *d* of .20 (the smallest of his effect sizes) as the basis for the sample size calculation.

● The level of power required needs to be at a minimum .50 – otherwise the study is likely not to reject the null hypothesis. There is, of course, very little point in designing a study which is more than likely to support the null hypothesis. It is conventional – and no more than that – to regard a power of .80 or greater as adequate. This means that if there is truly a trend or difference in the data that it has an 80% chance of being identified by the researcher using a particular significance level and sample size(s). There is no reason why a higher level of power cannot be chosen, if this is considered appropriate by the researcher.

39.4 Calculating power

Since one cannot use SPSS Statistics to carry out most aspects of statistical power analysis we will use G*Power which is a free-to-download and flexible program which carries out a variety of statistical power analysis calculations. Of course, SPSS Statistics output does contain relevant information to be entered into these additional programs. The SPSS company does have a power analysis program SamplePower® 2.0, but this is not generally available at universities, etc. in the way SPSS Statistics is and it is quite expensive to purchase. So it is just as well to turn to other software which is available in some variety. Many of the programs have to be purchased and so it makes sense to opt for the free resources available on the web. G*Power is a serious competitor for commercially available software and it is well-regarded. It is also flexible in terms of the number of different research designs that it can deal with. For this reason, we have adopted G*Power as our primary resource for this chapter. Figure 39.6 illustrates the active interface of G*Power, but expect slight variations according to circumstances.

G*Power does a wide variety of power analyses for a variety of statistical tests which are organised into 'Test families' such as those based on the *t*-test and those based on the *F*-distribution. The term 'Test family' can be seen immediately under the big white

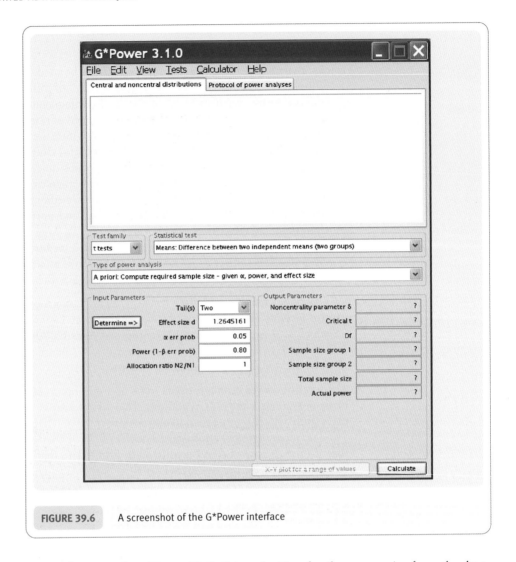

FIGURE 39.6   A screenshot of the G*Power interface

box in the screenshot (Figure 39.6). Select the Test family you require from the drop-down list which appears when you hover your mouse cursor over this box. Then select the 'Statistical test' you require from the dropdown menu. Finally select the 'Type of power analysis' again from a dropdown menu. Since these dropdown menus each offer a variety of options, it is worthwhile checking out what is available by trying out a number of these options. So, as you can see in Figure 39.6, the following have been selected but, of course, the choices made depend on the design of the study:

- Test family: *t*-test

- Statistical test: Means: difference between two independent means (two-groups)

- Type of power analysis: *A priori*: Compute required sample size – given α, power and effect size

These particular selections indicate the following: The analysis corresponds to an unrelated *t*-test comparing the difference between two means. The power analysis is intended for planning a new study (i.e. *A priori*) and it is required that the optimum sample size is computed based on the significance level (α), required level of power and the effect size. This would be a reasonable standard option for statistical power analysis when comparing, say, an experimental group with a control group. Or for comparing the means of any two groups, for that matter.

FIGURE 39.7   Effect size calculator side-menu on G*Power3

It is obvious that you then need to enter (overwrite) the Input Parameters in the white boxes. We will return to the question of just what you need to enter into each of the input boxes a little later, but we need to concentrate on the box labelled Effect size first of all as this is the most complex. There are various different measures of effect size to deal with different research designs. However, once you have selected the Test family, Statistical test and Type of power analysis, G*Power indicates what measure of Effect size is to be used. If you have relevant data, Effect size can be calculated from this. G*Power will calculate the relevant type of Effect size for you if you ask it to do so. However, this calculation is not based on the raw data but on things like the sample means and standard deviations (depending on the research design that you are dealing with). Consequently, this information needs to be calculated by you before you can enter it into G*Power. Figure 39.7 is the side-menu or drawer revealed on screen when you click on the 'Determine=>' button next to 'Effect size d'. In this screenshot, the information has already been entered into the appropriate boxes. Notice, however, that you need to select different options according to whether your sample sizes are equal or different. Although the calculation of these figures could be carried out by hand, it is probably more convenient to obtain them using SPSS Statistics or some other statistical analysis program. For example, to calculate the effect size for two independent groups using Cohen's d, you need to enter the means and standard deviations for the two samples into G*Power. These are part of the output of SPSS Statistics for the unrelated t-test. The means and standard deviations (SD) have been entered using SPSS Statistics t-test output. You probably will wish to click on the 'Calculate and transfer to the main window' button as it saves you copying it yourself into the 'Input Parameters'.

Of course, it is more likely that you have no data from which to calculate Effect size unless you have conducted a pilot study. Consequently, you might be well advised to examine previous research studies to see if a typical Effect size can be identified. Meta-analyses are particularly useful in this regard. Failing that, you may wish to use the 'standard' high, medium and low Effect sizes which have been recommended by Cohen (1988) and others. When you hover your mouse cursor over the 'Effect size' box in G*Power these standard sizes will appear on screen.

So that is one important Input Parameter dealt with. The following are suggestions as to what goes into the input boxes seen in Figure 39.6. The calculation is based on the study we used to illustrate the unrelated t-test in Chapter 13. If the researcher has no strong basis for predicting the direction of the outcome of the research, a two-tail test is selected. One could select a one-tail test if this were appropriate.

- The effect size has been entered as a Cohen's d of 1.2645161 in Figure 39.6. This is a calculated value based on the data in the study that we are using. If no such calculation is possible then you could enter other values according to whether you expect a small (0.2), medium (0.5) or large effect (0.8). Alternatively, if this were possible, the Effect size could be based on data such as when a pilot study has been carried out or the typical Effect size for similar research.

- The significance level ('α err prob') is the conventional significance level of 0.05 though, of course, another value could be selected if there were reasons to be more or less stringent about avoiding rejecting the null hypothesis.

- The required power has been set at 0.80 which is a realistic but nevertheless high requirement and difficult to exceed in practice in psychological research. Consequently it is generally accepted as a reasonable level to choose. Of course it could be lower but not below 0.50 as explained earlier.

- The 'Allocation ratio' is simply the ratio of the two sample sizes. If you want these to be equal then the allocation ratio is 1. But, say, you wanted one group bigger than the other then you would have to juggle with this ratio. Probably there is little point in doing so for most research though sometimes researchers prefer to have small control groups relative to the experimental group.

Once your Input Parameters have been inserted in the relevant boxes, then press the 'Calculate' button. The interface will change to something like you see in the screenshot at Figure 39.8. The interface also includes a graphical representation of the power analysis. We discussed a similar graphical representation earlier (Figure 39.4) so refer to this discussion if you need clarification (p. 494).

Remember that Figure 39.8 refers to the t-test analysis reported in Calculation 13.1 in Chapter 13. The most important thing is that it suggests that a sample size of 22 could generate the 0.80 level of power that we stipulated. That is, eleven in each group. The 'Actual power' simply is the consequence of turning the sample sizes into whole numbers whereas the calculation would produce decimals. So the Actual power is the power based on a total sample size of 22 rather than the Input Parameters which we entered which can result in fractions for the sample sizes. One of the main reasons why the required sample size is quite low at 22 (11 in each group) is because the Effect size (Cohen's $d = 1.26$) is so large. It corresponds to a correlation of 0.53 between the independent and dependent variable. Now if this really were a pilot study then the implications are obviously very clear – however, this is data made up for the purpose of demonstrating the unrelated t-test so we should not get too excited. Pretending that it was a real pilot study then the researcher could be excused for feeling delighted. The effect is a very strong one requiring a sample size of only 22 in total to detect it with a power requirement of .80. This is about as good as it gets. Even if we increased the required power to .95 and made the significance level more stringent at .01, then G*Power tells us that a total sample size of only 50 is needed. That is to say, with just about the most demanding criteria for a power analysis, the required sample size is relatively small in this case. Try for yourself the effects of a low effect size of, say, 0.2

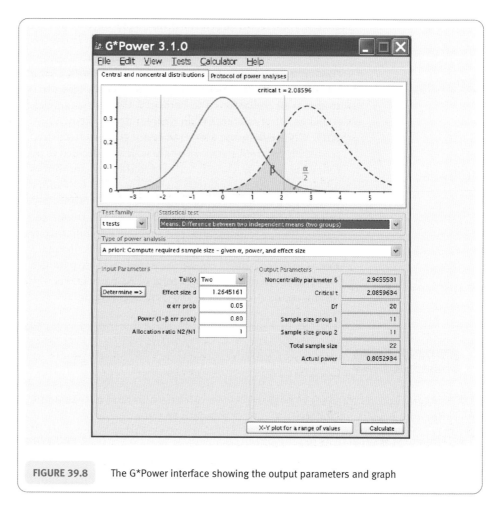

FIGURE 39.8   The G*Power interface showing the output parameters and graph

on the required sample size. You will find that the required sample size is massive to obtain the statistical significance at the required power.

Power analysis encourages more careful thought in planning research and how it requires the researcher to evaluate what sorts of research outcomes have practical implications for decision-making following the completion of the proposed study. This is a very different sort of approach to relying solely on significance testing as the holy grail of research. Obviously, power analysis forces the researcher into considering the bigger picture of research, especially when important decisions about social interventions, therapy and so forth are contingent on the outcome of the research.

39.5   Reporting the results

As might be expected, reporting the outcomes of a power analysis depends on what sort of analysis it is. If one simply wishes to indicate the power of a statistical analysis that you have carried out, you could add immediately after you have reported statistical significance something like: The observed power of this analysis was 0.7. Especially if the power was low, you might wish to comment on the size of the observed power. On the other hand, if you have carried out a power analysis in advance of the study, then the appropriate place to discuss this is where you discuss your samples in the Methods section of your report. The following might serve as a template for what you write in these circumstances:

'Power analysis was used to estimate the appropriate sample size(s) for the study. An examination of the research literature suggests that the typical effect size in similar studies is of the order of Cohen's $d = 0.5$. For example, Smith and Lawson (2007) found an effect size of 0.47 in their study and Brown (2010) reports an effect size of 0.63. While Edwinston (2002) does not give an effect size, it can be calculated as 0.53 from their reported statistical analysis. It was decided to adopt the power level of 0.80 following what is considered satisfactory by authorities in the field (e.g. Cohen, 1988). The conventional 0.05 significance level was adopted as it was not considered that Type I errors were an important consideration, especially given that previous research had consistently detected significant trends in this sort of research (e.g. Green, 2006; Kirkham, 2002). A one-tailed significance test was used given the clear evidence from previous research that the experimental condition produces higher means than the control condition. Based on these parameters, the optimal sample size was 102 (51 in each group). A total of 55 participants were, in fact, run in the experimental condition and 53 in the control condition.'

Key points

- Statistical power analysis is best used to inform the planning of research studies. It is less useful after data have been collected as part of the data analysis.

- Different statistical tests require power calculations to be done differently. In particular, the measure of (standardised) effect size will differ.

- Statistical power analysis includes assumptions and estimates which cannot be standardised for all circumstances as this would defeat its purpose. So reporting a power analysis may involve justifying the estimates and decisions that you have taken.

COMPUTER ANALYSIS

SPSS Statistics does compute some power values, but it is not very helpful for the bulk of the analyses outlined in this chapter.

Exceptionally, this chapter contains a detailed illustration of using G*Power to calculate statistical power. Nevertheless, you may find the quick summary in Figure 39.9 a useful memory aid. Please check the following link for updates on G*Power and further documentation: http://www.psycho.uni-duesseldorf.de/abteilungen/aap/gpower3/download-and-register. Although G*Power is free, its authors would appreciate that you cite one or both of the following papers in any published papers you produce using it in your research:

- Faul, F., Erdfelder, E., Buchner, A., & Lang, A.-G. (2009), 'Statistical power analyses using G*Power 3.1: Tests for correlation and regression analyses', *Behavior Research Methods*, **41**, 1149–1160.

- Faul, F., Erdfelder, E., Lang, A.-G., & Buchner, A. (2007), 'G*Power 3: A flexible statistical power analysis program for the social, behavioral, and biomedical sciences', *Behavior Research Methods*, **39**, 175–191.

Chapter 55 of Dennis Howitt and Duncan Cramer (2011), *Introduction to SPSS Statistics in Psychology: For version 19 and earlier*, Harlow: Pearson, gives detailed step-by-step procedures for using G*Power 3.

Program	• Install G*Power 3. on your computer. It can be found on the Web, or Companion website.
Data	• Decide what effect size to use if you are carrying out an a priori analysis. Otherwise G*Power will help you with this for your data.
2	• What significance level will you or have you used? 0.05 is a likely one, but it may vary. Also decide whether a one- or two-tail test is appropriate.
3	• What power do you require? A conventional choice is 0.80, but do not go below 0.50.
Analysis	• Start G*Power: Figure 39.6 gives a screenshot.
2	• Select the Test family, Statistical test and Type of power analysis in that order from their drop down menus.
3	• Insert whether one- or two-tail test, the significance level (α err prob), power required and change the Allocation ratio if you want different relative sizes of samples.
4	• Click the Determine$\Rightarrow$ button to calculate Effect size from data. Otherwise enter the Effect size you wish to use – small, medium or large.
Output	• Click the Calculate button to obtain the output parameters for your analysis – in particular the sample sizes needed.

FIGURE 39.9 Computer steps for power analysis using G*Power

PART 6

Advanced qualitative or nominal techniques

CHAPTER 40

Log-linear methods

The analysis of complex contingency tables

Overview

- The analysis of nominal (category) data using chi-square is severely limited by the fact that a maximum of only two variables can be used in any one analysis.

- Log-linear can be conceived as an extension of chi-square to cover greater numbers of variables.

- Log-linear uses the likelihood ratio chi-square (rather than the Pearson chi-square we are familiar with from Chapter 14). This involves natural or Napierian logarithms.

- The analysis essentially examines the adequacy of the various possible models. The simplest model merely involves the overall mean frequency – that is, the model does not involve any influence of the variables either acting individually or interactively in combination. The most complex models involve in addition the individual effects of the variables (main effects) as well as all levels of interactions between variables. If there are three variables, there would be three main effects, plus several two-way interactions plus one three-way interaction.

- A saturated model is the most complex model and involves all of the possible components. As a consequence, the saturated model always explains the data completely, but at the price of not being the simplest model to fit the actual data. It is essentially a conceptual and computational device.

Preparation

If you are hazy about contingency tables then look back to the discussion in Chapter 6. Also revise chi-square (Chapter 14) since it is involved in log-linear analyses. Log-linear shares concepts such as main effect and interaction with ANOVA which ought to be reviewed as general preparation (especially Chapter 22).

40.1 Introduction

In essence, log-linear methods are used for the analysis of complex contingency (or crosstabulation) tables. Data in Chapter 14 which were analysed using chi-square could be subjected to log-linear procedures although with no particular benefits. Log-linear goes further than this and comes into its own when dealing with three or more variables. Log-linear analysis identifies how the variables acting alone or in combination influence the frequencies in the cells of the contingency table. The frequencies can be regarded as if they are the dependent variable.

Some basic concepts need to be introduced:

1. *Interactions* Like analysis of variance (ANOVA), log-linear analysis uses the concept of interactions between two or more variables. The concept is a little difficult to understand at first. It refers to the effects of the variables that cannot be explained by the effects of these variables acting separately. Much of this chapter is devoted to explaining the concept in more detail.

2. *Models* A model in log-linear analysis is a statement (which can be expressed as a formula) which explains how the variables such as gender, age and social class result in the cell frequencies found in the contingency table. For example, one model might suggest that the pattern of frequencies in the contingency table is the result of the independent influences of the variable gender and the variable age. There are probably other contending models for all but the simplest cases. An alternative model for this example is that the data are the result of the influence of variable social class plus the influence of variable gender *plus* the combined influence of variable gender interacting with the variable age. Table 40.1 gives the components of models for different numbers of variables in the contingency table. We will return to this later, but notice how the components include a constant (or the average frequency) *plus* the main effects of the variables *plus* interactive effects of the variables. Log-linear analysis helps a researcher to decide which of the possible models (i.e. which selection of the components in Table 40.1) is the best for the actual data. These different components will become clearer as we progress through this chapter. Model building can serve different purposes. Unless you have theoretical reasons for being interested in a particular model, then log-linear methods allow you to build up the model purely empirically.

3. *Goodness-of-fit* This is simply the degree of match between the actual data and those values predicted on the basis of the model. Chi-square is a common measure of goodness-of-fit. Chi-square is zero if the observed data are exactly the same as the expected (or predicted) data. The bigger the value of chi-square, the greater the *misfit* between obtained and expected values. In Chapter 14, a significant value of chi-square caused us to reject the 'model' specified by the null hypothesis. A good-fitting model would have a chi-square value approximating zero whereas a badly fitting model would have a large chi-square value.

4. *Pearson chi-square* This is the version of chi-square used in Chapter 14 although common practice is simply to call it chi-square. The formula for the Pearson chi-square is:

$$\text{Pearson chi-square} = \sum \frac{(\text{observed} - \text{expected})^2}{\text{expected}}$$

The Pearson chi-square is used in log-linear analysis but it is not essential.

Table 40.1	Possible model components for different sizes of contingency table				
Component of model	**1**	**2**	**3**	**4**	**5**
Overall mean (equal frequencies)	yes	yes	yes	yes	yes
Main effects	A	A + B	A + B + C	A + B + C + D	A + B + C + D + E
Two-way interactions	—	A * B	A * B	A * B	A * B
			A * C	A * C	A * C
			B * C	A * D	A * D
				B * C	A * E
				B * D	B * C
				C * D	B * D
					B * E
					C * D
					C * E
Three-way interactions			A × B × C	A * B * C	A * B * C
				A * B * D	A * B * D
				A * C * D	A * B * E
				B * C * D	A * C * D
					A * C * E
					A * D * E
					B * C * D
					B * C * E
					B * D * E
					C * D * E
Four-way interactions				A * B * C * D	A * B * C * D
					A * B * C * E
					A * B * D * E
					B * C * D * E

5. *Likelihood ratio chi-square* This is the more common formula when doing log-linear analysis:

$$\text{Likelihood ratio chi-square} = 2 \times \sum \text{observed frequency} \times \ln \text{ of } \frac{\text{observed frequency}}{\text{expected frequency}}$$

The term ln is a symbol for *natural logarithm*. Don't worry if you know nothing about natural logarithms. Although tables of natural logarithms are available, it is easier to obtain them from a scientific calculator (or the calculator built into Windows, for instance). Observed frequency refers to the obtained data and expected frequency refers to the values expected according to the particular model being tested.

6. *Differences between Pearson and likelihood ratio chi-square* The formulae give slightly different values of chi-square for small sample sizes but converge as the sample sizes get large. Both formulae are often computed as measures of goodness-of-fit by computer programs for log-linear analysis. Nevertheless, it is best to concentrate on likelihood ratio chi-square in log-linear analysis because of its *additive* properties. This means that different components of chi-square can be added together to give the combined effects of different components of the chosen model. The Pearson chi-square does not act additively so cannot be used in this way, hence its comparative unimportance in log-linear analysis.

40.2   A two-variable example

The distinctive approach of log-linear analysis can take a little time to absorb. Its characteristic logic is probably best explained by re-analysing an example from Chapter 14. The study of favourite types of television programme of males and females (Calculation 14.1) will be presented using the log-linear perspective. The data are given in Table 40.2, but they are exactly the same as the data in Table 14.8 in Chapter 14. The two variables were gender and favourite type of programme. In the (Pearson) chi-square analysis (Calculation 14.1) there is a gender difference in favourite type of television programme. Another way of putting this is that there is an interaction between a person's gender and their favourite type of television programme. (In Chapter 14, it was found that gender and favourite type of programme acting separately were insufficient to account for the data. The expected frequencies in that chapter are the frequencies expected on the basis of gender and programme effects having separate and unrelated effects. In Chapter 14, a significant value of chi-square meant that the distribution of cell frequencies could not be explained on the basis of this independent influence of gender and favourite programme type. The different genders had different preferences. This would be an interaction in terms of log-linear analysis.)

A log-linear analysis of the data in Table 40.2 would examine possible underlying models (combinations of the variables) which might predict the obtained data. Theoretically, there are a number of possibilities according to log-linear analysis:

1. *Equal frequencies model* This suggests that the observed cell frequencies are merely the total of cell frequencies divided equally between the cells. Since there are 119 observations in Table 40.2 and six cells then we would *expect* a frequency of 119/6 = 19.833 in each cell. Obviously this model, even if it fits the data best, is virtually a non-model.

2. *Main effects model* This suggests that the observed cell frequencies are the consequence of the separate effects of the variables. While this might seem an important possibility if you recall main effects for ANOVA, in log-linear analysis, main effects

Table 40.2	Data to be modelled using log-linear analysis		
	Soap opera	**Crime drama**	**Neither**
Males	observed = 27	observed = 14	observed = 19
Females	observed = 17	observed = 33	observed = 9

are often trivial. The object of log-linear analysis is to account for the pattern of observed frequencies in the data. In Table 40.2 note that there are slightly unequal numbers of males and females (60 males and 59 females) but, more importantly, the choices of the different programme types are unequal. That is, the different values of gender (male and female) and favourite television programme (soap opera, crime drama and neither) are not equally represented. For the main effect of gender, the inequality is small (60 males versus 59 females), but it is somewhat larger for the main effect of favourite television programme (44 choosing soap operas, 47 choosing crime dramas and 28 choosing neither). The main effects merely refer to these inequalities which may be uninteresting in terms of the primary purpose of the analysis. In our example, a researcher is likely not to be particularly interested in these main effects but much more interested if the interaction between gender and favourite programme type explains the data. In order for there to be *no* main effects, each of the categories of each of the variables would have to have the same frequency. This is rare in research.

3. *The interaction(s)* An interaction is the effect of the interrelationship between the variables. In the present example, because we have only two variables, there is just one interaction which could be termed gender × favourite TV programme interaction. You will see from Table 40.1 that had there been more variables there would be more interactions to investigate. The number of interactions escalates with increasing numbers of variables (much as it does for ANOVA). Interactions interest researchers because they indicate the associations or correlations between variables.

The interactions and main effects are combined in log-linear analysis in order to see what main effects and what interactions are necessary to best account for (fit with) the observed data.

Log-linear analysis for this simple example involves the consideration of several different models.

■ Step 1: The equal frequencies model

In a manner of speaking, this is the no-model model. It tests the idea that the cell frequencies require no explanation since they are equally distributed. This is *not* the same as the null hypothesis predictions made in Chapter 14 since these predicted not equal frequencies but *proportionate* frequencies according to the marginal totals. The equal frequencies model simply assumes that all of the cells of the contingency table have equal frequencies. Since we have a total frequency of 119 in the 6 cells of our analysis, the equal frequencies model predicts (expects) that there should be 119/6 or 19.833 in each cell as shown in Table 40.3. The likelihood ratio chi-square applied to this table is

Table 40.3	Contingency table for testing the equal frequencies model, i.e. the expected frequencies			
	Soap opera	**Crime drama**	**Neither**	**Total**
Males	observed = 27	observed = 14	observed = 19	
	expected = 19.833	expected = 19.833	expected = 19.833	
Females	observed = 17	observed = 33	observed = 9	
	expected = 19.833	expected = 19.833	expected = 19.833	
Total				119

Table 40.4	Calculation of the fit of the equal frequencies model			
Observed frequency	Expected frequency according to equal frequencies model	Observed + expected	Natural logarithm of observed + expected	Observed frequency × natural logarithm of observed + expected
27	19.833	1.361	0.308	8.329
14	19.833	0.857	−0.154	−2.620
19	19.833	0.706	−0.348	−4.876
17	19.833	1.664	0.509	16.802
33	19.833	0.958	−0.043	−0.815
9	19.933	0.454	0.857	−7.111
				Total = 9.709
Likelihood ratio chi-square = 2 × total = 2 × 9.709 = 19.418				

calculated in Table 40.4. Remember that the natural logarithms are obtained from a scientific calculator or one you find as a program on your computer. The use of natural logarithms is only important for understanding the basic calculation of log-linear.

The fit of the equal frequencies model to the data is poor. The likelihood ratio chi-square is 19.418. This is the amount of misfit of that particular model to the data. (It is also the amount by which the main effects and the interactions can increase the fit of the best model to the data.)

The differences between the values expected according to the model and what is actually found in the data are known as the *residuals*. The residuals can be used to assess the fit of the model to the data in addition to the likelihood ratio chi-squares. Often, residuals are standardised so that comparisons can be made easily between the different cells, in which case they are known as standardised or adjusted residuals. The smaller the residuals the better the fit of the model to the data.

■ Step 2: The saturated model

The log-linear analysis of these data could be carried out in a number of ways since there are a variety of different models that could be tested. In general, we will concentrate on the procedures which would commonly be employed when using computer programs such as SPSS Statistics. Often these compute the *saturated model* for you. A saturated model is one which includes all of the possible components as shown in Table 40.1 which, consequently, accounts perfectly for the data. That is, the values predicted by the saturated model are exactly the same as the data. Any model based on all of the components by definition accounts for the data perfectly. Since there is always a perfect correspondence or fit between the observed data and the predictions based on the likelihood ratio chi-square for the saturated model, this chi-square is always zero for the saturated model.

Table 40.5 gives the data and the expected frequencies for the saturated model. Notice, as we have already indicated, that the observed and expected frequencies for any cell of the contingency table are identical for this model. We will not bother to do this calculation. It is worth noting that computer programs often routinely increase the observed values by 0.5. This is done to avoid undesirable divisions by zero in the calculation while making very little difference to the calculation otherwise.

Table 40.5	Contingency table for testing the saturated model			
	Soap opera	**Crime drama**	**Neither**	**Total**
Males	observed = 27	observed = 14	observed = 19	
	expected = 27.000	expected = 14.000	expected = 19.000	
Females	observed = 17	observed = 33	observed = 9	
	expected = 17.000	expected = 33.000	expected = 9.000	
Total				119

Step 3: Preparing to test for the main effects components of the model

The perfectly fitting model of the data (the saturated model) involves all possible components. It is not quite as impressive as the perfect fit suggests. We do not know what it is about our model which caused such a good fit. It could be the effects of gender, the effects of the type of programme, or the effects of the interaction of gender with type of programme, or any combination of these three possibilities. It could even mean that the equal frequencies model is correct if we had not already rejected that possibility. Further exploration is necessary to assess which of these components are contributing to the goodness-of-fit of the data to that predicted by the model. Any component of the model which does not increase the goodness-of-fit of the model to the data is superfluous since it does nothing to explain the data. (To anticipate a common practice in log-linear analysis, the corollary of this is also true: components are only retained if they *decrease* the fit of the model when they are *removed*.)

(Usually in the initial stages of log-linear analyses using a computer, similar components of the model are dealt with collectively. That is, the main effects of gender and favourite programme type are dealt with as if they were a unit of analysis. Had there been more than one interaction, these would also be dealt with collectively. At a later stage, it is usual to extend the analysis to deal with the combined components individually. That is, the data are explored in more detail in order to assess what main effects are actually influencing the data.)

To reiterate what we have already achieved we can say that we have examined two extremes of the model-building process: the saturated model and the equal frequencies model. We have established that the equal frequencies model is a poor fit to the data on this occasion (the saturated model is always a perfect fit). The misfit of the equal frequencies model to the data (likelihood ratio chi-square = 19.418) is the amount of improvement in fit achieved by the saturated model.

Step 4: TV programme type main effect

Main effects are one level of components in the saturated model. Understanding their calculation is fairly simple. Let us take the main effect of programme type. In order to predict the frequencies in the data based solely on the effects of the different programme type we simply replace each cell by the average of the frequencies in cells referring to that programme type. This in effect means that for our example we combine the data frequencies for the males and females who prefer soap operas and average this total by the number of cells involved (i.e. 2 cells). Twenty-seven males and 17 females claim to prefer soap operas so the total is 44 which is divided between the two cells involved in

Table 40.6	Table of data and expected frequencies based solely on the main effect of programme type			
	Soap opera	**Crime drama**	**Neither**	**Total**
Males	observed = 27	observed = 14	observed = 19	
	expected = 22.000	expected = 23.500	expected = 14.000	
Females	observed = 17	observed = 33	observed = 9	
	expected = 22.000	expected = 23.500	expected = 14.000	
Total	**44**	**47**	**28**	**119**

this case. This gives us a predicted frequency on the basis of the main effects model for programme type of 22.00 in each of the soap opera cells. This is shown in Table 40.6. The predicted value for crime drama is 14 + 33 divided by 2 which equals 23.50. The predicted value for the neither category is 19 + 9 divided by 2 = 14.00. Again these can be seen in Table 40.6.

Now one can calculate the goodness-of-fit of this model simply by calculating the likelihood ratio chi-square for the data in Table 40.6. Just follow the model of the calculation in Table 40.4. The value of the likelihood ratio chi-square is 13.849. Compare this with the misfit based on the equal frequencies model (likelihood ratio chi-square = 19.418). It seems that there has been an improvement of 19.418 − 13.849 = 5.569 in the fit due to the programme main effect. (Remember that the bigger the likelihood ratio chi-square then the poorer the fit of the model to the data). Because the likelihood ratio chi-square has additive properties, this difference of 5.569 is the contribution of the main effect of programme type.

■ Step 5: Gender main effect

Because the frequencies of males and females in the data are nearly equal, there clearly is a minimal main effect due to the variable gender in this case. Nevertheless, this minimal value needs to be calculated. A similar procedure is adopted to calculate the main effects of gender. This time we need to sum the frequencies over the three different programme types for each gender separately and average this total frequency by the three programme types. Thus the sum of the observed frequencies for males in each of the three different programme type conditions is (27 + 14 + 19)/3 = 60/3 = 20. This gives a predicted value per male cell of 20. This is entered in Table 40.7. Similarly, the calculation for females is to sum the three observed frequencies and divide by the number of female cells. This is (17 + 33 + 9)/3 = 59/3 = 19.667. Again these values are entered in Table 40.7.

Table 40.7	Table of data and expected frequencies based on the main effect of gender type			
	Soap opera	**Crime drama**	**Neither**	**Total**
Males	observed = 27	observed = 14	observed = 19	60
	expected = 20.000	expected = 20.000	expected = 20.000	
Females	observed = 17	observed = 33	observed = 9	59
	expected = 19.667	expected = 19.667	expected = 19.667	
Total				**119**

The likelihood ratio chi-square for the main effect of gender in Table 40.7 is 19.405. Compared with the value of 19.418 for the equal frequencies model, there is virtually no change, indicating the smallness of the gender difference in row frequencies. The improvement in fit due to gender alone is only 0.013.

■ Step 6: The main effects of programme type plus gender

This can now be obtained. It involves taking each cell in turn and working out the effect on the frequencies of the programme type and the gender concerned. This is done relative to the frequencies from the equal frequencies model (that is, 119/6 = 19.833 in every case). So, looking at Table 40.6, the expected frequency for soap operas is 22.000. This means that being a soap opera cell increases the frequency by 22.000 − 19.833 = 2.167 as shown in Table 40.8. It may sound banal, but in order to add in the effect of being a soap opera cell we have to add 2.167 to the expected frequencies under the equal frequencies model. Similarly, being a crime drama cell increases the frequency to 23.500 from our baseline equal frequencies expectation of 19.833. Being a crime drama cell increases the frequency by 23.500 − 19.833 = 3.667.

In contrast, being in the neither category tends to decrease the frequencies in the cell compared with the equal frequencies expectation of 19.833. From Table 40.6 we can see that the expected frequencies in the neither column due to programme type are 14.000, which is below the equal frequencies expectation of 19.833 as shown in Table 40.8. Thus, being a neither cell changes frequencies by 14.000 − 19.833 = −5.833. That is, being neither decreases frequencies by −5.833. In order to adjust the equal frequencies expectations for the programme type main effect, we have to add 2.167 to the soap opera cells, add 3.667 to the crime drama cells and subtract 5.833 from (that is add −5.833 to) the neither cells. This can be seen in Table 40.8.

We also need to make similar adjustments for the main effect of gender although these are much smaller. Compared with the equal frequencies value of 19.833, the male cells have an expected frequency of 20.000 which is an increase of 0.167. In order to adjust the equal frequencies baseline of 19.833 for a cell being male we therefore have to add 0.167. This can be seen in Table 40.8. For female cells, the expected frequency is 19.667, a reduction of 0.166. In short, we add −0.166 for a cell being female. This is also shown in Table 40.8. (Of course, the additions and subtractions for the males and females should be identical, which they are within the limits of calculation rounding.)

Table 40.8	Table of expected (predicted) frequencies based on adding the main effects of programme type and gender to the equal frequencies expectation			
	Soap opera	**Crime drama**	**Neither**	**Total**
Males	observed = 27	observed = 14	observed = 19	60
	expected = 19.833 + 2.167 + 0.167 = 22.167[a]	expected = 19.833 + 3.667 + 0.167 = 23.667[a]	expected = 19.833 + −5.833 + 0.167 = 14.167[a]	
Females	observed = 17	observed = 33	observed = 9	59
	expected = 19.833 + 2.167 + −0.166 = 21.834[a]	expected = 19.883 + 3.667 + −0.166 = 23.334[a]	expected = 19.883 + −5.833 + −0.166 = 13.834[a]	
Total				119

[a] These hand-calculated values are very approximate and do not correspond to the best values for reasons discussed in the text.

At this point there is a big problem. That is, the values of the expected frequencies based on the main effects model gives the wrong answers according to computer output. For that matter, it does not give the same expected frequencies as given in the equivalent Pearson chi-square calculation we did in Chapter 14. Actually, the computer prints our expected frequencies which are the same as those calculated in Chapter 14. The problem is that we are not actually doing what the computer is doing. Think back to the two-way analysis of variance. These calculations worked as long as you have equal numbers of scores in each of the cells. Once you have unequal numbers, then the calculations have to be done a different way (and best of all by computer). This is because you are not adding effects proportionately once you have different cell frequencies. In log-linear analysis, the problem arises because the marginal totals are usually unequal for each variable. This inequality means that simple linear additions and subtractions of main effects such as we have just done do not give the best estimates. That is in essence why a computer program is vital in log-linear analysis. Better estimates of expected frequencies are made using an iterative process. This means that an approximation is calculated but then refined by re-entering the approximation in recalculations. This is done repeatedly until a minimum criterion of change is found between calculations (i.e. between iterations). Computer programs allow you to decide on the size of this change and even the maximum number of iterations.

Now that we have some idea of how the adjustments are made for the main effects, even though we must rely on the computer for a bit of finesse, we will use the computer-generated values to finish off our explanation. Table 40.9 contains the observed and expected values due to the influence of the main effects as calculated by the computer's iterative process.

The value of the likelihood ratio chi-square for the data in Table 40.9 is, according to the computer, 13.841 (which is significant at 0.001 with $df = 2$). At this point, we can obtain the value of the gender*programme type interaction. We now know the following:

1. The fit of the saturated model which includes main effects plus the interaction is 0.000.

2. The fit of the model based on the two main effects is 13.841.

3. The fit of the model based on the equal frequencies model is 19.418.

It becomes a simple matter of subtraction to work out the improvement in fit due to the different components. Thus:

1. The increase in fit due to the two main effects = 19.418 − 13.841 = 5.577.

2. The increase in fit due to the interaction = 13.841 − 0.000 = 13.841.

Table 40.9	Table of expected (predicted) frequencies based on adding the main effects of programme type and gender to the equal frequencies expectation as obtained by the iterative computer process			
	Soap opera	**Crime drama**	**Neither**	**Total**
Males	observed = 27 expected = 22.18	observed = 14 expected = 23.70	observed = 19 expected = 14.72	60
Females	observed = 17 expected = 21.82	observed = 33 expected = 23.30	observed = 9 expected = 13.88	59
Total	**44**	**47**	**28**	**119**

These numerical values are likelihood ratio chi-squares. Only the interaction is statistically significant out of these major components. The main effect of programme type taken on its own would be statistically significant as it includes fewer degrees of freedom and has nearly the same likelihood ratio chi-square value. This is of no real interest as it merely shows that different proportions of people were choosing the different programme types as their favourites. In short, the interesting part of the model is the interaction which is statistically significant. Formally, this model is expressed simply as:

constant (i.e. equal frequency cell mean) + programme main effect + A*B interaction

As the interaction is fairly simple, it is readily interpreted with the help of Table 40.8. So we can conclude that in order to model the data effectively we need the two-variable interaction. This we did in essence in Chapter 14 when interpreting the Pearson chi-square analysis of those data. Remember that the interaction is based on the residuals in that table (i.e. the differences between the observed and expected frequencies). As can be clearly seen, males are less inclined to choose crime dramas than women but are more inclined to choose soap operas.

40.3   A three-variable example

Interactions when the data have three or more variables become a little more difficult to understand. In any case, only when there are three or more variables does log-linear analysis achieve much more than the Pearson chi-square described in Chapter 14. Consequently it is important to study one of these more complex examples. Even though log-linear analysis usually requires the use of a computer using the iterative procedures, quite a lot can be achieved by trying to understand approximately what the computer is doing when it is calculating several second-order and higher-order interactions.

Table 40.1 gives the possible model components of any log-linear analysis for one to five variables. It is very unlikely that anyone would wish to use log-linear analysis when they have just one variable, but it is useful to start from there just so that the patterns build up more clearly in the table. Computer programs can handle more variables than five, but we are constrained by space and, moreover, log-linear analyses of ten variables are both atypical of psychological research designs and call for a great deal of statistical sophistication – especially experience with simpler log-linear analyses.

Basically, the more variables you have the more components there will be to the model. All models consist of main effects plus interactions. The variables involved in model-building are those which might possibly cause differences between the frequencies in the different cells. These variables have to be measurable by the researcher too for them to be in the analysis. Also note that the more variables in a model, the more complex the interactions.

Our example involves three variables. If you look in the column for three variables in Table 40.1 you will find listed all of the possible components of the model for these data. In this column there are three main effects (one for each of the variables), three two-way interactions between all possible distinct pairs taken from the three variables and one three-way interaction. The analysis is much the same as for our earlier two-variable example, but there are more components to add in. In particular, the meaning of the interactions needs to be clarified as there are now four of them rather than just one. Remember that it is usual to take similar levels of the model together for the initial model fitting. Thus all the main effects are combined; all of the second-order interactions (two-variable interactions) together; all of the third-order (three-variable interactions)

Table 40.10	A three-way contingency showing the relationship between gender, sexual abuse and physical abuse in a sample of psychiatric hospital patients				
Variable B	**Variable C**	**Variable A Gender**			**Margin totals**
Sexual abuse	**Physical abuse**	**Female**	**Male**		
Sexually abused	Physical abuse	45	55		100
	No physical	40	60		100
Not sexually abused	Physical abuse	55	45		100
	No physical	80	20		100
Margin totals		220	180		400

together and so forth. Only when this analysis is done is it usual to see precisely which combinations at which levels of the model are having an effect.

Our example involves the relationship between gender, sexual abuse and physical abuse in a sample of psychiatric patients. The data are to be found in Table 40.10 which gives the three-way crosstabulation or contingency table for our example. The numbers in the cells are *frequencies*. Each of the variables has been coded as a dichotomy: (a) female or male, (b) sexually abused or not and (c) physically abused or not. (Variables could have more than two categories, but this is not the case for these particular data.) The researchers are interested in explaining the frequencies in the table on the basis of the three *variables* – gender, sexual abuse and physical abuse – acting individually (main effects) or in combination (interactions). This would be described as a three-way contingency table because it involves *three variables*. It is worthwhile remembering that the more variables and the more categories of each variable the greater the sample size needs to be in order to have sufficient frequencies in each cell.

Two of the possible models are easily tested. They are the equal frequencies and the saturated models which are the extreme possibilities in log-linear analyses. The equal frequencies model simply involves the first row of Table 40.10 and no other influences. The saturated model includes all sources of influence in the table for the column for three variables.

■ Step 1: The equal frequencies model

The equal frequencies model is, in a sense, the worst-fit scenario for a model. It is what the data would look like if none of the variables in isolation or combination were needed to explain the data. The equal frequencies model merely describes what the data would look like if the frequencies were equally distributed through the cells of the table. As there are eight cells and a total of 400 observations, under the equal frequencies model it would be expected that each cell contains 400/8 = 50 cases. This model and the calculation of its fit with the observed data for which we are developing a model are shown in Table 40.11.

Just a reminder – the likelihood ratio chi-square is zero if the model fits the data exactly and increasingly bigger with greater amounts of misfit between the data and the data as predicted by the model. The chi-square value for the equal frequencies model is an indication of how much the variables and their interaction have to explain. The value of 44.58 obtained for the likelihood ratio chi-square on the equal frequencies model indicates that the data are poorly explained by that model. That is, there is a lot of variation in the frequencies which remains to be explained by models other than the

Table 40.11	The calculation of the likelihood ratio chi-square for the equal frequencies model

Observed frequency	Expected frequency according to the equal frequencies model	Observed + expected	Natural logarithm of observed + expected	Observed frequency × natural logarithm of observed + expected
45	50.0	0.90	−0.1054	−4.743
40	50.0	0.80	−0.2231	−8.924
55	50.0	1.10	0.0953	5.242
80	50.0	1.60	0.4700	37.600
55	50.0	1.10	0.0953	5.242
60	50.0	1.20	0.1823	10.938
45	50.0	0.90	−0.1054	−4.741
20	50.0	0.40	−0.9163	−18.326
				Total = 22.290

Likelihood ratio chi-square = 2 × sum of final column = 2 × 22.290 = 44.580

equal frequencies model. Notice that the equal frequencies model only contains the mean frequency which is one of the potential components of all models. The equal frequencies value is sometimes called the constant. If it is zero or nearly zero then the equal frequencies model fits the model well. Do not get too excited if the equal frequencies model fits badly since the variation in frequencies between the cells might be explained by the main effects. To reiterate, main effects in the log-linear analysis are often of very little interest to psychologists. Only rarely will real-life data have no main effects in log-linear analysis since main effects occur when the categories of a variable are unequally distributed. In our data in Table 40.10, the marginal totals for physical abuse and sexual abuse are the same since equal numbers had been abused as had not been abused. Nevertheless, there is a possible main effect for gender since there are more females in the study than males. Whether or not this gender difference is significant has yet to be tested. So whatever the final model we select, it has already been clearly established that there is plenty of variation in the cell means to be explained by the main effects acting independently and the two-way interactions of pairs of these variables plus the three-way interaction of all of the variables.

■ Step 2: The saturated model

This model involves all of the possible variables acting separately and in combination. It includes all components given in Table 40.1 for a given number of variables. For a three-way contingency table the saturated model includes the mean frequency per cell (i.e. constant) plus the main effects plus the three two-variable interactions plus the three-variable interaction. Predictions based on the saturated model are exactly the same as the data themselves – they have to be since the saturated model includes every possible component of the model and so there is no other possible source of variation.

It is hardly worth computing the saturated model as it has to be a perfect fit to the data thus giving a likelihood ratio chi-square of 0.000. A zero value like this indicates a perfect fit between the observed data and the expectations (predictions) based on the model. Remember that for the saturated model, most computer programs will automatically add 0.5 to the observed frequencies to avoid divisions by zero which are unhelpful mathematically. This addition of 0.5 to each of the frequencies is not always necessary so some computer programs will give you the choice of not using it. Its influence is so negligible that the analysis is hardly affected.

■ Step 3: Building up the main-effects model

The process of building up a model in log-linear analysis is fairly straightforward once the basic principles are understood, as we have seen. The stumbling block is the calculation of expected frequencies when marginal frequencies are unequal. They are unequal most of the time in real data. In these circumstances, only an approximate explanation can be given of what the computer is doing. Fortunately, as we have already seen, we can go a long way using simple maths.

Table 40.12 contains the expected frequencies based on different components of the model. Remember that the expected frequencies are those based on a particular model or component of the model. The first column contains the data (which are exactly the same as the predictions based on the saturated model already discussed). The fourth column gives the expected frequencies based on the equal frequencies model. This has already been discussed – the frequencies are merely the total frequencies averaged over the number of cells.

The next three cells have the major heading 'Main effects', and there are separate columns for the main effect of gender, the main effect of sexual abuse and the main effect of physical abuse. The fourth column headed 'All' is for the added effect of these three main effects. How are these expected (predicted) values calculated? They are simply the averages of the appropriate cells. Thus for females, the four cells in Table 40.12 are 45, 40, 55 and 80 which totals 220. Thus if the cells in the female column reflect only the effects of being female then we would expect all four female cells to contain 220/4 = 55.00 cases. In Table 40.12, the expected frequencies under gender for the four female cells are all 55.00. Similarly for the four remaining cells in that column which all involve males, the total male frequency is 180 so we would expect 180/4 or 45.00 in each of the male cells.

Exactly the same process is applied to the sexual abuse column. Two hundred of the cases were sexually abused in childhood whereas 200 were not. Thus we average the 200 sexually abused cases over the four cells in Table 40.12 which involve sexually abused individuals (i.e. 200/4 = 50.00). Then we average the 200 non-sexually abused individuals over the four cells containing non-sexually abused individuals (i.e. 200/4 = 50.00). Because there are equal numbers of sexually and non-sexually abused individuals, no main effect of sexual abuse is present and all of the values in the sexual abuse column are 50.00.

Given that there are also 200 physically abused and 200 non-physically abused cases, it is not surprising to find that all of the expected frequencies are 50.00 in the physical abuse column too. The reasoning is exactly the same as for sexual abuse in the previous paragraph.

The combined main effects column labelled 'All' is easily computed for our example. It is simply the combined individual effects of the three separate main effects. So it is the effect of gender plus sexual abuse plus physical abuse. Thus being female adds a frequency of five compared with the equal frequencies model figure of 50.00, being sexually abused adds zero and being physically abused adds zero. For example, for the first row which consists of 45 females who had been sexually abused and physically abused, we take the equal frequencies frequency of 50.00 and add 5 for being female, + 0 for being sexually abused and + 0 for being physically abused. This gives the expected figure of 55.00 under the all main effects column.

To give another example, take the fifth row down where the data give a frequency of 55. This row refers to males who had been sexually abused and physically abused. Being male

Table 40.12 The expected (or predicted) frequencies based on separate components of the model

Data	Details of cell			Equal frequencies model	Main effects				Two-way interactions			
	Gender	Sexual abuse	Physical abuse		Gender	Sexual	Physical	All	Gender* Sexual	Gender* Physical	Sexual* Physical	All
45	female	yes	yes	50.00	55.00	50.00	50.00	55.00	42.50	50.00	50.00	37.23
40	female	yes	no	50.00	55.00	50.00	50.00	55.00	42.50	60.00	50.00	47.77
55	female	no	yes	50.00	55.00	50.00	50.00	55.00	67.50	50.00	50.00	62.77
80	female	no	no	50.00	55.00	50.00	50.00	55.00	67.50	60.00	50.00	72.33
55	male	yes	yes	50.00	45.00	50.00	50.00	45.00	57.50	50.00	50.00	62.77
60	male	yes	no	50.00	45.00	50.00	50.00	45.00	57.50	40.00	50.00	52.23
45	male	no	yes	50.00	45.00	50.00	50.00	45.00	32.50	50.00	50.00	37.23
20	male	no	no	50.00	45.00	50.00	50.00	45.00	32.50	40.00	50.00	27.77

* between two or more variable names is one way of indicating interactions.

subtracts 5.00 from the equal frequency value, being sexually abused adds nothing and being physically abused also adds nothing. So our expected value is $50 - 5 + 0 + 0 = 45$, the expected value for all of the main effects added together.

■ Step 4: The two-variable interactions

The two-way interactions are not difficult to estimate either. The two-way interaction for gender*sexual abuse is obtained by combining together the physical abuse categories. In our example, there are some who have been physically abused and some who have not among the females who had been sexually abused. Of these sexually abused females, 45 had been physically abused and 40 had not been physically abused. Combining these two frequencies and averaging them across the two relevant cells gives us:

$$\frac{45 + 40}{2} = \frac{85}{2} = 42.5$$

This is the value that you see under the gender*sexual abuse interaction for the first two rows.

If you need another example, take the last two rows which have values in the data column of 45 and 20. These rows consist of the males who had not been sexually abused. One row is those who had been physically abused and the other those who had not been physically abused. The two-way interaction of gender*sexual abuse is obtained by adding together the two different physical abuse categories and entering the average of these into the last two rows. So the frequencies are 45 and 20 which equals 65, which divided between the two relevant cells gives us 32.5. This is the value that you see for the gender*sexual abuse interaction for the final two rows.

What about the next interaction – gender*physical abuse? The calculation is basically the same. The only difficulty is that the rows corresponding to the cells we are interested in are physically further apart in the table. The gender*physical abuse interaction is obtained by combining the sexual abuse categories (i.e. the sexually abused and non-sexually abused). Let us take the females who had not been physically abused. These are the second and fourth rows. If we look at the observed values in the data these are frequencies of 40 and 80. The average of these is 60, and this is the value you find in the second and fourth rows of the gender*physical abuse interaction.

The sexual abuse*physical abuse interaction is calculated in a similar way – this time we combine the male and female groups for each of the four sexual abuse*physical abuse combinations. Take the sexually *and* physically abused individuals. These are to be found in rows 1 and 5. The data (observed) values for these rows are 45 and 55. This averages at 50.00 – the value of the entry for this two-way interaction in the first and fifth rows. (Actually all of the rows for this particular column have the same value indicating a lack of a sexual abuse*physical abuse interaction.)

The combined effects of the three two-way interactions cannot be seen directly from the table. This is because the values are based on an iterative process which involves several computational stages which are best done by the computer. The values in the last column of Table 40.12 are taken from SPSS Statistics computer output. Although we will not be showing this calculation here because of its complexity, we can show the essential logic although, as you will see, it gives slightly the wrong answers. All effects in log-linear analysis are additive so we should be able to combine the three two-way interactions in order to obtain the sum of the three two-way interactions.

This is quite simple. Compared with the equal frequencies mean frequency of 50.00 for each cell, what is the effect of each interaction? Taking the first row, we can see that the gender*sexual abuse interaction changes the score by −7.50 (i.e. 42.5 − 50.00), the gender*physical abuse interaction changes the score by 0.00 (i.e. 50.00 − 50.00) and the sexual abuse*physical abuse interaction changes the score by 0.00 (50.00 − 50.00). Adding these separate effects to the equal frequencies mean frequency of 50.00 we get:

$$50.00 + (−7.50) + 0.00 + 0.00 = 42.50$$

This at first sight is the wrong answer since it is nowhere near the 37.23 obtained from the computer.

What we have not allowed for is the fact that these interactions also include the effect of the main effects. The main effects for this row combined to give a prediction of 55.00 compared with the equal frequencies mean of 50.00. That is to say, the main effects are increasing the prediction for this row by 5.00. This would have to be taken away from the prediction based on the interaction to leave the pure effects of the two-way interactions. So our value 42.50 contains 5.00 due to the main effects; getting rid of the main effects gives us the prediction of 37.50 based on the two-way interactions. This is pretty close to the 37.23 predicted by the model but not sufficiently so. The unequal marginal totals necessitate the adjustments made automatically by the iterative computer program. Had our marginal totals been a lot more unequal then our fit to the computer's value would have been much poorer. Simple methods are only suitable as ways of understanding the basics of the process.

If you would like another example of how the entries are computed, look at the final row of Table 40.12. The predicted values based on all the two-way interactions is 27.77. How is that value achieved? Notice that the two-way gender*sexual abuse interaction prediction is 32.50 which is 17.50 less than that according to the equal frequencies model prediction of 50.00; the gender*physical abuse prediction is 40.00, which is 10.00 less and the sexual abuse*physical abuse prediction is 50.00, exactly the same. So to get the prediction based on the three two-way interactions together, the calculation is the equal frequencies mean (50.00) + (−17.50) + (−10.00) + 0.00 = 22.50, but then we need to take away the influence of all the main effects which involves adding 5.00 this time. Thus we end up with a prediction of 27.50. Again this is not precisely the computer predicted value but it is close enough for purposes of explanation. Remember, it is only close because the main effects are small or zero.

What is the normal output of a computer program such as SPSS Statistics? The important point to remember is that it is usual to explore the model first of all as combined effects – the sum of the interactions, the sum of the main effects – rather than the individual components in the first analysis. For the data in Table 40.10 we obtained the information in Tables 40.13 and 40.14 from the computer by stipulating a saturated model.

Table 40.13	Tests of the increase in fit for the main effects and higher-order effects			
Level of effects	**Types of effect involved**	**Degrees of freedom**	**Likelihood ratio chi-square**	**Probability**
3	three-way interaction	1	10.713	0.0011
2 (and above)	all the two-way interactions + the three-way interaction	4	40.573	0.0000
1 (and above)	all the main effects + the two-way interaction + the three-way interaction only	7	44.579	0.0000

Table 40.14	Tests that the levels of effect are zero			
Level of effects	**Types of effect involved**	**Degrees of freedom**	**Likelihood ratio chi-square**	**Probability**
1	all the main effects only	3	4.007	0.2607
2	all the two-way interactions only	3	29.860	0.0000
3	three-way interaction only	1	10.713	0.0011

What do Tables 40.13 and 40.14 tell us? Remember that when we assessed the fit of the data based on the equal frequencies model we obtained a likelihood ratio chi-square value of 44.580. This large value indicates a large misfit of the model to the data. (The smaller the size of chi-square the better the fit.) Notice that this value of chi-square is exactly the same (within the errors of rounding) as the chi-square value in Table 40.13 for the contribution of the main effects, two-way interactions and the three-way interactions. Thus 44.580 is the improvement in the fit of the model created by including the three different levels of effect *together*.

If we take just the two-way and three-way interactions (omitting the main effects from the model), the improvement is a little less at 40.573 according to Table 40.13. Remember that the likelihood ratio chi-square is linear, so you can add and subtract values. Consequently, the improvement in fit due to the main effects is 44.579 – 40.573 = 4.006. Within the limits of rounding error, this is the same value as for the sum of all of the main effects in Table 40.14 (i.e. 4.007).

If we take only the three-way interaction in Table 40.13 (i.e. omitting the two-way interaction and main effects from the model), we get a value of 10.713 for the amount of misfit. This is the value given in Table 40.14.

Where does the value for the two-way interactions come from? We have just found that the value for the main effect is 4.006 and the value for the three-way interaction is 10.713. If we take these away from the chi-square of 44.580 we get 44.580 – 4.006 – 10.713 = 29.861 for the contribution of the two-way interactions to the fit (exactly as can be found in Table 40.14 within the limits of rounding error).

It looks as if a good model for the data can exclude the main effects which are failing to contribute significantly to the goodness-of-fit even though the value of the likelihood ratio chi-square is 4.007. Thus a model based on the two-way and three-way interactions accounts for the data well.

■ Step 5: Which components account for the data?

This analysis has demonstrated the substantial contributions of the two-way and three-way interactions to the model's fit to the data. Since there is only one three-way interaction in this case, then there is no question what interaction is causing this three-way effect. There are three different two-way interactions for this model, not all of which may be contributing to the fit to the data. The way of checking for the relative influence of the different two-way interactions is to repeat the analysis but omitting one of the two-way interactions. This is easy to do on most computer programs. Doing this for the data in Table 40.10, we obtain the following:

● Based solely on gender*sexual abuse: chi-square = 15.036, $df = 4$, $p = 0.005$.

● Based solely on gender*physical abuse: chi-square = 36.525, $df = 4$, $p = 0.000$.

● Based solely on sexual abuse*physical abuse: chi-square = 44.579, $df = 4$, $p = 0.000$.

Working backwards, compared with the value of 44.580 for the misfit between the data and the equal frequencies model, there is no improvement in the fit by adding in the sexual abuse*physical abuse interaction since the value of likelihood ratio chi-square does not change (significantly) from that value 44.580. This means that the sexual abuse*physical abuse interaction contributes nothing to the model fit and can be dropped from the model.

Considering solely the gender*physical abuse interaction, there is a moderate improvement in fit. The maximum misfit of 44.580 as assessed by the likelihood ratio chi-square reduces to 36.526 when the gender*physical abuse interaction is included. This suggests that this interaction is quite important in the model and should be retained.

Finally, using solely the gender*sexual abuse interaction, the likelihood ratio chi-square value declines to 15.036 from the maximum of 44.579, suggesting that the gender*sexual abuse interaction has a substantial influence and improves the fit of the model substantially.

It should be remembered that there is a main effect for gender in all of the above two-way interactions except for the sexual abuse*physical abuse interaction where it is not present. (Check the marginal totals for the expected frequencies to see this.) In order to understand just how much change in fit is due to the two-way interaction, we need to adjust for the main effect of gender which we have already calculated as a likelihood ratio chi-square of 4.007. So to calculate the likelihood ratio chi-square of the gender*physical abuse interaction we have to take 36.525 from 44.580 which gives a value for the improvement in fit of 8.054. This value is the improvement in fit due to the gender main effect and the gender*physical abuse interaction. So for the improvement in fit due to the gender*physical abuse interaction only, we take 8.055 and subtract 4.007 to give a value of 4.048. This value is only roughly correct because of the unequal marginals involved which means that a better approximation will be achieved through an iterative process.

Box 40.1   Focus on

Degrees of freedom

Using the computer means that you never need to actually calculate the degrees of freedom. However, if you understand their calculation from chi-square in Chapter 14, then you should have few problems with their calculation for log-linear. When reading degrees of freedom in tables, they will often include extra degrees of freedom for lower-level interactions or main effects. Adjustments may have to be made. Here are a few examples:

1. Total degrees of freedom are always the number of cells − 1.

2. Degrees of freedom for the equal frequencies model = 1.

3. Degrees of freedom for a main effect

$$= \frac{\text{total degrees of freedom}}{\text{number of different categories of the main effect}}$$

4. Degrees of freedom for the saturated model = 0.

Remember that the degrees of freedom for *all* of the main effects, for example, is not the same as the degrees of freedom for any of the main effects taken separately.

Table 40.15	The amounts of fit due to different components of the model			
Model	Likelihood ratio chi-square	Degrees of freedom	Prob.	Chi-square change
Saturated	0.000			–
All two-way interactions + all main effects (i.e. minus three-way interaction)	10.713	1	0.001	10.713[a]
Previous row less gender*sexual abuse	36.525	2	0.000	25.812[a]
Previous row less sexual abuse*physical abuse	36.525	3	0.000	0.000
Previous row less gender*physical abuse	40.573	4	0.000	4.048
Previous row less sexual abuse	40.573	5	0.000	0.000
Previous row less gender	44.579	6	0.000	4.006
Previous row less physical abuse	44.579	7	0.000	0.000

[a] Change significant at the 5% level.

Table 40.15 gives the results of an analysis starting with the saturated model and gradually removing components. If a removed component is having an effect on the fit there will be a non-zero value for the chi-square change for that row which needs to be tested for significance. The saturated model is a perfect fit (i.e. chi-square = 0.000), but taking away the three-way interaction increases the misfit to 10.713. This change (10.713 − 0.000) is the influence of the three-way interaction on the degree of fit. Taking away the interaction of gender*sexual abuse gives a chi-square change of 25.812 which indicates that the gender*sexual abuse interaction is having a big effect on the fit of the model.

When we take away sexual abuse*physical abuse there is a 0.000 chi-square change. This indicates that this interaction is doing nothing to improve the fit of the model. Thus the sexual abuse*physical abuse interaction may be dropped from the model.

Similarly, the row of Table 40.15 where the main effect of sexual abuse is dropped has a zero likelihood ratio chi-square, indicating that the main effect of sexual abuse can be dropped from the model. Also the final row where the main effect of physical abuse is dropped also shows no change, implying that this main effect can be dropped from the model. Actually, only two of the components are statistically significant at the 5% level so that the model could be built on these solely. Our model then becomes:

mean frequency (i.e. equal frequencies mean) + gender*sexual abuse interaction + gender*sexual abuse*physical abuse interaction.

■ Step 6: More on the interpretation of log-linear analysis

By this stage, it should be possible to attempt fitting a log-linear model. Of course, a little practice will be necessary with your chosen computer in order to familiarise yourself with its procedures. This is not too technical in practice with careful organisation and the creation of systematic tables to record the computer output. If these things are not done, the sheer quantity of frequently redundant computer output will cause confusion.

Specifying the best-fitting model using likelihood ratio chi-squares is *not* a complete interpretation of the model. This is much as the value of Pearson chi-square in Chapter 14 is insufficient without careful examination of the data. An important concept in this respect is that of residuals. A residual is merely the difference between the data and the data predicted on the basis of the model. These can be expressed merely as the data value minus the modelled value. So residuals may take positive or negative values and there is one residual per cell. Not only this, since in a log-linear analysis you may be comparing one or more components of the model with the data then several sets of residuals will have to be computed, and so you may be calculating different residuals for different components of the model or different models. Residuals can be standardised so that values are more easily compared one with another.

The good news is twofold. There is no difficulty in calculating simple residuals, and computers generally do it for you anyway as part of calculating the model fit. If you look back to Table 40.12, you can easily calculate the residuals by subtracting any of the predicted model values from the actual data. The residuals for the saturated model are all zero, of course, indicating a perfect fit. The residuals for the equal frequencies model are −5.00, −10.00, 5.00, 30.00, 5.00, 10.00, −5.00 and −30.00; that is, the value of the frequency for that cell in the data −50.000 in each case.

The other helpful thing when interpreting log-linear models is the estimated cell frequencies based on different components of the model. Remember that not only can you calculate these fairly directly but they are usually generated for you by the computer. The important thing about these estimated cell frequencies is that they tell you the trends in the data caused by, say, the interactions. For example, look at Table 40.12 and the column for the gender*sexual abuse interaction. You can see there that there are relatively few females who had been sexually abused and relatively more males who had been sexually abused in these data. It is best to compare these frequencies with the ones for the effects of the three main effects since the interaction figures actually include the effects of the main effects. Thus this comparison removes the main effects from the interaction. Figure 40.1 gives the key steps in log-linear analysis.

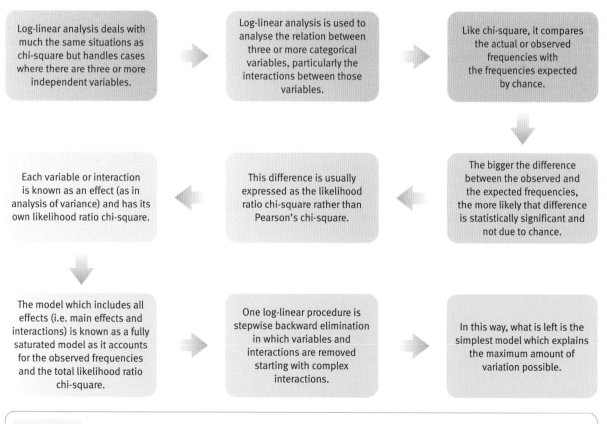

Log-linear analysis deals with much the same situations as chi-square but handles cases where there are three or more independent variables.	Log-linear analysis is used to analyse the relation between three or more categorical variables, particularly the interactions between those variables.	Like chi-square, it compares the actual or observed frequencies with the frequencies expected by chance.
Each variable or interaction is known as an effect (as in analysis of variance) and has its own likelihood ratio chi-square.	This difference is usually expressed as the likelihood ratio chi-square rather than Pearson's chi-square.	The bigger the difference between the observed and the expected frequencies, the more likely that difference is statistically significant and not due to chance.
The model which includes all effects (i.e. main effects and interactions) is known as a fully saturated model as it accounts for the observed frequencies and the total likelihood ratio chi-square.	One log-linear procedure is stepwise backward elimination in which variables and interactions are removed starting with complex interactions.	In this way, what is left is the simplest model which explains the maximum amount of variation possible.

FIGURE 40.1   Conceptual steps for log-linear analysis

40.4   Reporting the results

With something as complex as a log-linear analysis, you might expect that writing up the results of the analysis will be complex. Indeed it can be, and expect to write much more about your analysis than you would, for example, writing up the results of a correlation coefficient or a t-test. The purposes of log-linear analysis can be very varied, stretching from a fairly empirical examination of the data of the sort described earlier to testing the fit of a theoretical model to the actual data. Obviously there is no single sentence that can be usefully employed for describing the outcome of a log-linear analysis. Nevertheless certain things are very important. They are:

1. A table giving the data and the residuals for each of the models that you examine. Without this, the reader cannot assess precisely the form of the fit of the models to the data. Table 40.12 would be a useful format for doing this.

2. A table giving indications of the improvement in fit due to each component of the model. This will almost invariably be the likelihood ratio chi-square. Table 40.15 could be adapted to your particular data.

The text should discuss the final model which you have selected on the basis of your log-linear analysis. These could be expressed in terms of the components of the model which contribute significantly to the fit or, alternatively, as the lambda values mentioned in the panel. Earlier in this chapter we indicated the models for our two examples in a simple form.

Box 40.2   Focus on

Lambda and hierarchical models

Lambda

Often in log-linear analysis, the models are specified in terms of lambda (λ). This is simply the natural log of the influence of each of the different sorts of component of the cell frequencies. Thus a model may be built up from a succession of lambdas. These are given superscripts to denote what type of effect is involved: λ^A is the main effect of variable A and λ^{A*B} is the effect of the interaction of variables A and B. So an equation involving these and other components might be:

$$\text{Model} = \lambda + \lambda^A + \lambda^B + \lambda^{A*B}$$

This simply means that we add to the natural logarithm of the equal-cell mean or constant (λ), the natural logarithm of the main effects of the variable A (remember that this has positive and negative values), the natural logarithm of the main effects of the variable B and the natural logarithm of the interaction of the variables $A*B$.

Hierarchical models

Hierarchical models imply lower-order components and do not specify what these lower-order components are. Thus a hierarchical model may specify a four-variable interaction $A*B*C*D$. Any component involving A, B, C and D is assumed to be a component of that model. So the main effects A, B, C and D, the two-way interactions $A*B$, $A*C$, $A*D$, $B*C$, $B*D$ and $C*D$, and the three-way interactions $A*B*C$, $A*B*D$, $A*C*D$ and $B*C*D$ are automatically specified as possible components in a hierarchical model. Notice that our examples employ a hierarchical approach.

Key points

- It is recommended that before analysing your own data with log-linear, you reproduce our analyses in order to become familiar with the characteristics of your chosen computer program.

- Confine yourself to small numbers of variables when first using log-linear analysis. Although computers may handle, say, ten variables, you may find it difficult without a lot of experience.

- Log-linear analysis can include score variables if these are treated as frequencies.

- Log-linear analysis is not as commonly used in psychological research as it is in other disciplines. The reason is the preference of psychologists for using score variables.

COMPUTER ANALYSIS

The SPSS Statistics instruction book to this text is Dennis Howitt and Duncan Cramer (2011), *Introduction to SPSS Statistics in Psychology*: *For version 19 and earlier*, Harlow: Pearson. Chapter 37 in that book gives detailed step-by-step procedures for the statistics described in this chapter together with advice on how to report the results. Figure 40.2 shows the SPSS Statistics steps for a log-linear analysis.

Data	• Name the variables in Variable View of the Data Editor. • Enter the data under the appropriate variable names in Data View of the Data Editor.
Analysis	• Select 'Analyze', 'Log linear' and 'Model Selection . . .'.
2	• Move variables to the 'Factor(s):' box.
3	• Select 'Define Range' and define range for each variable.
Output	• In the 'Step Summary' table note the best-fitting model which is presented last and which should not be significant.

FIGURE 40.2 SPSS Statistics steps for log-linear analysis

Recommended further reading

Agresti, A. (1996), *An Introduction to Categorical Data Analysis*, New York: Wiley, Chapters 1–4.

Anderson, E.B. (1997), *Introduction to the Statistical Analysis of Categorical Data*, Berlin: Springer, Chapters 2–4.

CHAPTER 41

Multinomial logistic regression

Distinguishing between several different categories or groups

Overview

- Multinomial logistic regression is a form of multiple regression in which a number of predictors are used to predict values of a single nominal dependent or criterion variable.

- There may be any number of values (categories) of the dependent variable with a minimum of 3. It can be used with just two categories but binomial multiple regression (Chapter 42) would be more appropriate in these circumstances.

- It is used to assess the most likely group (category) to which a case belongs on the basis of a number of predictor variables. That is, the objective is to find the pattern of predictor variables that identify of which category an individual is most likely to be a member.

- Multinomial logistic regression uses nominal or category variables as the criterion or dependent variable. The independent or predictor variables may be score variables or nominal (dichotomised) variables. In this chapter we concentrate on nominal variables as predictors.

- The concept of dummy variable is crucial in multinomial logistic regression. A dummy variable is a way of dichotomising a nominal category variable with three or more different values. A new variable is computed for each category (just one!) and participants coded as having that characteristic or not. The code for belonging to the category is normally 1 and the code for belonging to any of the other categories is normally 0.

→

● Multinomial logistic regression produces *B*-weights and constants just as in the case of other forms of regression. However, the complication is that these are applied to the logit. This is the natural (or Napierian) logarithm of the odds ratio (a close relative of probability). This allows the computation of the likelihood that an individual is in a particular category of the dependent or criterion variable given his or her pattern on the predictor variables.

● A classification table is produced which basically describes the accuracy of the predictors in placing participants correctly in the category or group to which they belong.

Preparation

Make sure you are familiar with Chapter 14 on chi-square and Chapters 8 and 31 on regression.

41.1   Introduction

A simple example should clarify the purpose of multinomial logistic regression. Professionals who work with sex offenders would find it helpful to identify the patterns of characteristics which differentiate between three types – rapists, incestuous child abusers and paedophiles. The key variable would be type of sex offence, and rapists, incestuous child abusers and paedophiles would be the three different values (categories) of this nominal (category) variable. In a regression, type of sex offender would be called the dependent variable or the criterion or the predicted variable. Just what is different between the three groups of offenders – that is, what differentiates the groups defined by the different values of the dependent variable? The researcher would collect a number of measures (variables) from each of the participants in the study in addition to their offence type. These measures are really predictor variables since we want to know whether it is possible to assess which sort of offender an individual is on the basis of information about aspects of their background. Such predictors are also known as independent variables in regression.

Imagine the researcher has information on the following independent variables (predictor variables). They are all nominal/category variables in this example, but it is possible to use score variables or a mixture of score and nominal/category variables as predictors. The dependent variable has to be a nominal/category variable (see Box 41.1):

● age of offender (younger versus older; i.e. 30 plus)

● physically abused when a child

● sexually abused when a child

● depression (low depression versus high depression) measured on the DASS (Depression Anxiety Stress Scale)

● offender spent a period of childhood in children's homes

Table 41.1	An example of how the offender groups could be compared on the predictors		
	Rapists	Incestuous offender	Paedophile
Father hostile to offender as a child	30	50	40
Father not hostile to offender	40	30	10

- mother's hostility as assessed by a family experiences scale (mother not hostile versus mother hostile)

- father's hostility as assessed by a family experiences scale (father not hostile versus father hostile).

These data could be analysed in a number of ways. One very obvious choice would be to carry out a succession of chi-square tests. The type of offender could be one of the variables and any of the variables in the above list could be the predictor variable. An example of this is shown in Table 41.1. Examining the table, these data seem to suggest that if the offender had a hostile father then he is unlikely to be a rapist, more likely to be an incestuous offender, but most likely to be a paedophile. Similar analyses could be carried out for each of the predictor variables in the list.

There is not a great deal wrong with this approach – it would readily identify the specific variables on which the three offender groups differ (and those on which they did not differ). One could also examine how the three offender groups differed from the others on any of the predictor variables. Since the analysis is based on chi-square, then partitioning would help to test which groups differ from the others (Chapter 14) in terms of any of the predictors.

The obvious problem with the chi-square approach is that it handles a set of predictors one by one. This is fine if we only have one predictor, but we have *several* predictor variables. A method of handling all of the predictor variables at the same time would have obvious advantages. Predictor variables are often correlated and this overlap also needs to be taken into account (as it is with multiple regression – see Chapters 31 and 32). That is, ideally the *pattern* of variables that best predicts group membership should be identified.

In many ways, multinomial logistic regression is the more general case of binomial logistic regression described in Chapter 42. The dependent variable in multinomial logistic regression can have one of several (not just two) nominal values. Nevertheless the two forms of logistic regression share many essential characteristics. For example, the dependent variable is membership of a category (e.g. group) in both cases. Like binomial logistic regression, multinomial logistic regression uses nominal (category) variables. However, not all of the sophisticated regression procedures which are available for binomial logistic regression can be used in multinomial logistic regression. Because of this, multinomial logistic regression is actually easier than binomial logistic regression. Nevertheless, there is a disadvantage for the more advanced user since there are few model-building options (no stepwise, no forward selection, no backward selection). This makes multinomial logistic regression simpler. Sometimes multinomial logistic regression is described as being rather like doing two or more binomial logistic regressions on the data. It could replace binomial logistic regression for the dichotomous category case – that is, when the dependent variable consists of just two categories.

Box 41.1 Focus on

Using score variables in logistic regression

Although we concentrate on nominal or category variables as the independent or predictor variables in logistic regression in this chapter, this is because it is conceptually harder to deal with them than score variables as independent variables. So for pedagogic reasons, we have not considered score variables directly in this chapter. However, score variables can be used as the independent or predictor variables and can be mixed with nominal/category variables in logistic regression. Conceptually, you should have no difficulty going on to using score variables in this way once you have mastered the material in this chapter and Chapter 42. You may have more difficulty running the analyses on SPSS Statistics since it uses somewhat idiosyncratic terminology to refer to the two types of variable and it is not even consistent between the binomial logistic regression and multinomial logistic regression. If you consult the companion *Introduction to SPSS Statistics in Psychology: For version 19 and earlier* what to do should be clear as should the SPSS Statistics steps provided at the end of this chapter.

41.2 Dummy variables

A key to understanding multinomial logistic regression lies in the concept of dummy variables. In our example, there are three values of the dependent variable, category *A*, category *B* and category *C*. These three values could be converted into *two* dichotomous variables and these dichotomous variables are known as dummy variables:

1. *Dummy variable 1* Category *A* versus categories *B* and *C*

2. *Dummy variable 2* Category *B* versus categories *A* and *C*

Dummy variables are as simple as that. The two values of each dummy variable are normally coded 1 and 0.

What about the comparison of category *C* with categories *A* and *B*? Well, no such dummy variable is used. The reason is simple. All of the information that distinguishes category *C* from categories *A* and *B* has already been provided by the first two dummy variables. The first dummy variable explains how to distinguish category *C* from category *A*, and the second dummy variable explains how to distinguish category *C* from category *B*. The third dummy variable is not used because it would overlap completely with the variation explained by the first two dummy variables. This would cause something called multicollinearity which means that some predictors intercorrelate highly with each other. So, in our example, only two of the dummy variables can be used. Multicollinearity should be avoided in any form of regression as it is the cause of a great deal of confusion in the interpretation of the findings.

The choice of which dummy variable to omit in dummy coding is arbitrary. The outcome is the same in terms of prediction and classification whatever value is omitted.

If you are struggling with dummy variables and collinearity consider the following. Imagine the variable gender which consists of just two values – male and female. Try to change gender into dummy variables. One dummy variable would be 'male or not' and the other dummy variable would be 'female or not'. There would be a perfect negative correlation between these two dummy variables – they are simply different ways of measuring the same thing. So one dummy variable has to be dropped since it has already been accounted for by the other dummy variable. If there are more than two dummy variables then the same logic applies although the dropped dummy variable is accounted for by several dummy variables, not just one.

41.3 What can multinomial logistic regression do?

Multinomial logistic regression can help:

1. Identify a small number of variables which effectively distinguish between groups or categories of the dependent variable.

2. Identify the other variables which are ineffective in terms of distinguishing between groups or categories of the dependent variable.

3. Make actual predictions of which group an individual will be a member (i.e. what category of the dependent variable) on the basis of their known values on the predictor variables.

What are we hoping to achieve with our multinomial logistic regression? The main things are:

1. Whether our predictors actually predict the offence categories at better than the chance level.

2. The constants and regression weights that need to be applied to the predictors to optimally allocate the offenders to the actual offending group.

3. A classification table that indicates how accurately the classification is based on the predictors compared to the known category of offence.

4. To identify the pattern of predictor variables which classifies the offenders into their offence category most accurately.

This list is more or less the same as would be applied to any form of regression.

Some researchers would use a different technique (discriminant analysis or discriminant function analysis) to analyse our data (see Box 41.2). However, multinomial logistic regression does an arguably better job since it makes fewer (unattainable?) assumptions about the characteristics of the data. More often than not, there will be little difference between the two in terms of your findings. In those rare circumstances when substantially different outcomes emerge, the multinomial logistic regression is preferred because of its relative lack of restrictive assumptions about the data. In other words, there is no advantage in using discriminant function analysis but there are disadvantages.

Figure 41.1 outlines the key steps in multinomial logistic regression.

Box 41.2 Key concepts

The difference between discriminant function analysis and logistic regression

Discriminant function analysis is very similar in its application to multinomial logistic regression. There is no particular advantage of discriminant function analysis which is in some circumstances inferior to multinomial logistic regression. It could be used for the data in this chapter on different types of sex offenders. However, it is more characteristically used when the independent variables are score variables. It would help us to find what the really important factors are in differentiating between the three groups of sex offenders. The dependent variable in discriminant function analysis consists of the various categories or groups which we want to differentiate.

The discriminant function is a weighted combination of predictors which maximise the differentation between the various groups which make up the dependent variable. So the formula for a discriminant function might be as follows:

Discriminant (function) score
$$= \text{constant} + b_1x_1 + b_2x_2 + b_3x_3 + b_4x_4 + b_5x_5 + b_6x_6$$

The statistic Wilks' lambda indicates the contribution of each of the predictor variables to distinguishing the groups. A small value of lambda indicates the greater the power of the predictor variable to differentiate groups. The bs in the formula above are merely regression weights (just like in multiple regression) and x_1, etc. are an individual's scores on each of the predictor variables. As with multiple regressions, regression weights may be expressed in unstandardised or standardised form. When expressed in standardised form, the relative impact of the different predictors is more accurately indicated. In our example,

there will be two discriminant functions because there are three groups to differentiate. The number of discriminant functions is generally one less than the number of groups. However, if the number of predictors is less than the number of discriminant functions, the number of discriminant functions may be reduced.

The *centroid* is the average score on the discriminant function of a person who is classified as belonging to one of the groups. If the analysis involves just two groups, there are two centroids. For a two-group discriminant function analysis there are two centroids. Cut-off points are provided which help the researcher identify to which group an individual belongs. This cut-off point lies halfway between the two centroids if both groups are equal in size. The cut-off point is weighted towards one of the centroids in the case of unequal group size. A classification table (in this context also known as a confusion matrix or prediction table) indicates how good the discrimination between the groups is in practice. Such a table gives the known distribution of groups compared to how the discriminant function analysis categorises the individuals. Chapter 27 covers discriminant function analysis in relation to MANOVA.

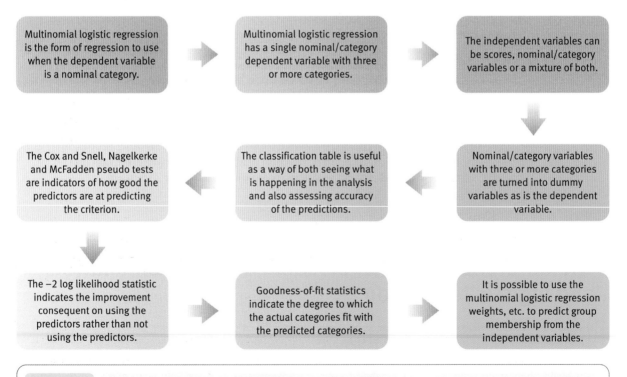

FIGURE 41.1   Conceptual steps for understanding multinomial logistic regression

41.4   Worked example

The data used are shown in Table 41.2. To make the output realistic, these 20 cases have been entered ten times to give a total sample of 200 cases. This is strictly improper as a statistical technique, of course, but helpful for pedagogic reasons.

It is not feasible to calculate multinomial logistic regression by hand. Inevitably a computer program has to be used. Consequently, the discussion refers to a computer analysis rather than to computational steps to be followed. Figure 41.2 reminds us of the basic task in multinomial logistic regression. The predictors are scores and/or nominal variables. The criterion being predicted is always a nominal variable but one with more than two categories or values. Since nominal variables have no underlying scale by definition, the several nominal categories are essentially re-coded individually as present or absent. In this way, each value is compared with *all* of the other values. It does not matter which comparison is left out and, of course, computer programs largely make the choices for you. Figure 41.3 takes the basic structure and applies it directly to our study of offenders in order to make things concrete. Remember that one dummy variable is not used in the analysis.

Table 41.2	The data for the multinomial logistic regression						
	Age	**DASS**	**Mother hostile**	**Father hostile**	**Children's home**	**Physical abuse**	**Sexual abuse**	**Type of offence**
1	younger	low	high	low	no	yes	no	rapist
2	younger	low	high	low	no	yes	yes	rapist
3	older	low	high	low	no	yes	yes	rapist
4	older	high	high	high	yes	no	no	incest
5	older	high	high	high	yes	yes	yes	rapist
6	younger	low	high	low	no	no	no	rapist
7	older	high	low	high	no	yes	yes	rapist
8	older	high	low	high	yes	no	no	incest
9	younger	low	low	high	yes	no	yes	incest
10	older	high	high	low	no	yes	yes	incest
11	older	high	low	low	yes	no	yes	incest
12	younger	high	low	high	no	yes	no	rapist
13	older	high	low	high	yes	no	yes	incest
14	older	high	high	low	yes	yes	yes	incest
15	older	low	high	high	no	yes	yes	incest
16	younger	high	high	low	yes	no	no	paedophile
17	older	high	low	high	yes	no	yes	paedophile
18	older	low	high	high	no	no	yes	paedophile
19	younger	high	low	high	yes	yes	yes	paedophile
20	older	low	low	high	yes	no	no	paedophile
etc.								

Predictor variables
Nominal variables
(though score
variables may be
covariates or
dichotomised)

Categories of nominal
'criterion' variable
which have been
turned into a number
of dummy variables

FIGURE 41.2   Multinomial logistic regression

Nominal predictor variables
Age of offender
Depression on DAS scale
Mother's hostility
Father's hostility
Spent time in children's home
Physically abused when a child
Sexually abused when a child

**Dummy variables for
categories – one of
nominal/category variable
'type of offence'**
Dummy 1: Rapist versus not
Dummy 2: Incestuous child
abuser versus not
Dummy 3: NOT USED

FIGURE 41.3   The structure of the example

Our list of independent or predictor variables actually only includes two-value variables (binary or dichotomous variables). We could use more complex nominal variables as predictors. However, they would have to be made into several dummy variables just as the dependent variable is turned into several dummy variables.

Remember that the dependent variable in this case is the type of offence. There are three different types, categories or values of sex offender in the study. Hence there are two dummy variables listed (out of the maximum of three possible). Dummy variable 1 is rapist versus not (not implies the offender is an incestuous child abuser or a paedophile). Dummy variable 2 is incestuous child abuser versus not (not implies the offender is a rapist or a paedophile). The choice of which dummy variable to leave out of the analysis is purely arbitrary, makes no difference to the outcome and, typically, is automatically chosen by the computer program.

41.5   Accuracy of the prediction

Once the analysis has been run through an appropriate computer program, a useful starting point is the classification table (that is, an accuracy assessment). Sometimes this is an option that you will have to select rather than something automatically produced by the program. The classification table is a crosstabulation (or contingency) table which compares the predicted allocation of the offenders to the three offender groups to which they are known to belong. Usually, such tables include percentage figures to indicate the degree of accuracy of the prediction. Classification tables make a lot of sense intuitively and help clarify what the analysis is achieving. Table 41.3 is such a classification table for our data. We have yet to look at the calculation steps that allow this table to be generated. This comes later.

Table 41.3	Predicted versus actual offence category of offenders			
Observed	Predicted to be rapist offender	Predicted to be incestuous	Predicted to be a paedophile	Percentage correct for row
Actually a rapist	60	10	0	85.7%
Actually an incestuous offender	20	50	10	62.5%
Actually a paedophile	0	30	20	40.0%
Column percentage	40.0%	45.0%	15.0%	Overall percentage correct = 65%

For the rapists, the analysis is rather accurate. Indeed, the overwhelming majority of rapists have been correctly identified as being rapists. Hence the row percentage correctly classified for rapists is 85.7%. This calculation is simply the number of correctly identified rapists (60) expressed as a percentage of the number of rapists in total (70). So the accuracy for the prediction for rapists is $60/70 \times 100\% = 0.857 \times 100\% = 85.7\%$. None of the rapists were predicted to be paedophiles though some were predicted to be incestuous offenders. The other two categories of offender could not be differentiated to the same level of accuracy. For the incestuous offenders, 62.5% were correctly identified as being incestuous offenders. The paedophiles were relatively poorly predicted – only 40% of paedophiles were correctly identified. Interestingly, the paedophiles are only ever wrongly classified as being incestuous offenders, they are never wrongly classified as rapists.

So it would appear that the model (pattern of predictors of offence category) is reasonably successful at distinguishing the offender types. Nevertheless, the identification of incestuous offenders and paedophiles is not particularly good. Obviously, if we were to persist in our research then we would seek to include further predictor variables that were better at differentiating the incestuous and paedophile groups.

41.6   How good are the predictors?

Calculating multinomial logistic regression using a computer program generates a variety of statistical analyses apart from the classification table discussed so far. We need to turn to other aspects of this multinomial logistic regression output in order to identify just how successful each predictor is and what predictors should be included in the model. The classification table gives no indication of this since it does not deal with the individual predictor variables.

Is the prediction better than chance? At some point in the analysis, there should be a table or tables including output referring to, say, 'Cox and Snell' or 'Nagelkerke' or 'McFadden' or to several of these. These may be described as pseudo *r*-square statistics. They refer to the amount of variation in the dependent variable which is predicted by the predictor variables collectively. The maximum value of this, in theory, is 1.00 if the relationship is perfect; it will be 0.00 if there is no relationship. They are pseudo-statistics because they appear to be like *r*-square (which is the square of the multiple correlation between the independent and dependent variable – see p. 388) but they are only actually analogous to it. One simply cannot compute a Pearson correlation involving a nominal variable with more than two values (categories). The nearer the pseudo-statistic is to a

Table 41.4	Pseudo *r*-square statistics

	Pseudo-statistic
Cox and Snell	0.546
Nagelkerke	0.617
McFadden	0.365

Table 41.5	Model fitting information indicating whether the prediction actually changes significantly from the values if the predictors were not used

Model components	−2 log likelihood statistic*	Chi-square for change	Degrees of freedom	Significance
Intercept (i.e. constant) only	407.957			
Final model	248.734	159.224	14	0.001

*See Box 41.3 for a discussion of this statistic.

perfect relationship of 1.00 the better the prediction (just as it would with a proper *r*-square). The value for 'Cox and Snell' is 0.546, the value for Nagelkerke is 0.617 and the value for McFadden is 0.365. So the relationship between the predictors and the criterion is moderate (see Table 41.4). We would interpret these values more or less as if they were analogous to a squared Pearson correlation coefficient.

Another table will be found in the computer output to indicate how well the model improves fit over using *no* model at all (Table 41.5). This is also an indication of whether the set of predictors actually contributes to the classification process over and above what random allocation would achieve. This is known as the model fit (but really is whether the modelled predictions are different from purely random predictions). This involves a statistic called −2 log likelihood which is discussed in Box 41.3. Often the value for the intercept is given (remember this is a regression so there is a constant of some fixed value). Table 41.5 illustrates this aspect of the output. The chi-square value is calculated using the −2 log likelihood statistic. This amounts to a measure of the amount of change due to using the predictors versus not using the predictors. As can be seen, there is a significant change, so it is worthwhile using the model. (It is significant at the 0.001 level. That is, it is a change in predictive power which is significant at better than the 5% level or 0.05 level.)

There is yet another statistic that is worth considering – the goodness-of-fit of the model to the data. The model is not merely intended to be better than no model at all but, ideally, it will fit or predict the actual data fairly precisely. A chi-square test can be performed comparing the fit of the predicted data to the actual data. In this case, of course, the ideal outcome is no significant difference between the actual data and those predicted from the model. This would indicate that it is pointless searching for additional predictors to fit the model – assuming that the sample is fairly large so sampling fluctuations may not be too much of a problem. In this example, the model makes predictions which are significantly different from the obtained classification of the offender. The incomplete match between the data and the predicted data is not surprising given the classification table (Table 41.3). This does not mean that the model is no good, merely that it could be better. Table 41.6 gives the goodness-of-fit statistics. Probably in

Table 41.6	Goodness-of-fit of the actual offence category to the predicted offence category		
	Chi-square	Degrees of freedom	Significance
Pearson goodness-of-fit statistic	228.010	22	0.001

psychology and the social sciences, it is unrealistic to expect any model to predict the actual data perfectly. Moderate levels of fit would be acceptable.

Box 41.3 Key concepts

Change in the −2 log likelihood

Logistic regression uses a statistic called −2 log likelihood. This statistic is used to indicate (a) how well both the model (the pattern of predictors) actually fits the obtained data, (b) the change in fit of the model to data if a predictor is removed from the model and (c) the extent to which using the model is an improvement on *not* using the model. These uses are different although the same statistic is used in assessing them.

There is a similarity, however. All of them involve the closeness of fit between different versions of the classification table. Earlier in studying statistics, we would have used chi-square in order to assess the significance of these discrepancies between one classification table and another. Actually that is more or less what we are doing when we use the −2 log likelihood statistic. This statistic is distributed like the chi-square statistic. Hence, you will find reference to chi-square values close to where the −2 log likelihood statistic is reported. The −2 is there because it ensures that the log likelihood is distributed according to the chi-square distribution. It is merely a pragmatic adjustment.

Just like chi-square, then, a 0 value of the −2 log likelihood is indicative that the two contingency tables involved fit each other perfectly. That is, the model fits the data perfectly, dropping a predictor makes no difference to the predictive power of the analysis, or the model is no different from a purely chance pattern. All of these are more similar than they might at first appear. Similarly, the bigger the value of the −2 log likelihood statistic, the more likely is there to be a significant difference between the versions of the contingency table. That is, the model is less than perfect in that it does not reproduce the data exactly (though it may be a fairly useful model); the variable which has been dropped from the model should not be dropped since it makes a useful contribution to understanding the data; or the model is better than a chance distribution – that is, makes a useful contribution to understanding the pattern of the data on the dependent variable.

The statistic usually reported is the *change* in the −2 log likelihood. The calculation of the degrees of freedom is a little less straightforward than for chi-square. It is dependent on the change in the number of predictors associated with the change in the −2 log likelihood.

So which are the best predictors? It was clear from Table 41.4 that the predictors improve the accuracy of the classification. However, this is for *all* of the predictors. It does not tell us which predictors (components of the model) are actually responsible for this improvement. To address that issue, it is necessary to examine the outcomes of a number of likelihood ratio tests. Once again these use the −2 log likelihood calculation, but the strategy is different. There is a succession of such tests that examine the effect of removing *one* predictor from the model (set of potential predictors). The change in the −2 log likelihood statistic consequent on doing this is distributed like the chi-square distribution. Table 41.7 shows such a set of calculations for our data. Notice that in general

Table 41.7	Likelihood ratio tests			
Predictor	−2 log likelihood of reduced model; i.e. without the predictor to the left	Chi-square	Degrees of freedom	Significance
Intercept (constant)	248.734			
Age	267.272	18.538	2	0.000
DASS	249.454	0.721	2	0.697
Mother's hostility	248.932	0.199	2	0.905
Father's hostility	256.089	7.355	2	0.025
Children's home	259.677	10.943	2	0.004
Physical abuse	287.304	38.571	2	0.000
Sexual abuse	263.914	15.181	2	0.001

little changes (i.e. the chi-square values are small) in a number of cases – DASS anxiety and hostility of the mother. Removing these variables one at a time makes *no* difference of any importance in the model's ability to predict. In other words, neither DASS anxiety nor hostility of the mother are useful predictors.

Other predictors can be seen to be effective predictors simply because removing them individually makes a significant difference to the power of the model. That is, the model with any of these predictors taken away is a worse fit to the data than when the predictor is included (i.e. the full model). While we have identified the good predictors, this is not the end of the story since we cannot say what each of the good predictors is good at predicting – remember that we have several (two in this example) dummy variables to predict. The predictors may be good for some of the dummy variables but not for others.

41.7   The prediction

So how do we predict to which group an offender is likely to belong given his particular pattern on the predictor variables? This is very much the same question as asking which of the predictor variables have predictive power. It is done in exactly the same way that we would make the prediction in any sort of regression. That is we multiply each of the 'scores' by its regression weight, add up all of these products and, finally, add the intercept (i.e. constant) (see Chapter 31 for this sort of calculation). In logistic regression we are actually predicting category membership or, in other words, which value of the dependent or criterion variable the offender has. Is he a rapist, incestuous offender or paedophile? This is done mathematically by calculating something known as 'the logit' (see also Chapter 42 on binomial logistic regression). The logit is the natural logarithm of something known as the odds ratio. The odds ratio relates very closely and simply to the probability that an offender is in one category rather than the others. A key thing to note is that multinomial logistic regression, like multiple regression (Chapter 31), actually calculates a set of regression weights (*B*) which are applied to the logit. It also calculates a constant or cut-point as in any other form of regression.

Table 41.8 gives the regression values calculated for our data. There are a number of things to bear in mind:

Table 41.8	Constants and regression weights for predictors used					
Category	Predictor	B	Standard error	Wald	Degrees of freedom	Sig.
Rapist – not	Intercept	−0.260	1.158	0.050	1	0.822
	Age (younger)	−0.159	0.678	0.055	1	0.814
	Age (older)	0			0	
	DASS (lower)	0.575	0.735	0.612	1	0.434
	DASS (higher)	0			0	
	Mother's hostility (lower)	−0.328	0.791	0.171	1	0.679
	Mother's hostility (higher)	0			0	
	Father's hostility (lower)	0.838	0.863	0.943	1	0.332
	Father's hostility (higher)	0			0	
	Children's home (yes)	−1.576	0.815	3.739	1	0.053*
	Children's home (no)	0			0	
	Physically abused (yes)	20.540	0.713	830.866	1	0.000*
	Physically abused (no)	0			0	
	Sexually abused (yes)	−18.570	0.000	∞	1	
	Sexually abused (no)	0			0	
Incestuous child abuser – not	Intercept	−0.314	0.813	0.150	1	0.699
	Age (younger)	−1.970	0.542	13.187	1	0.000*
	Age (older)	0			0	
	DASS (lower)	0.086	0.562	0.024	1	0.878
	DASS (higher)	0			0	
	Mother's hostility (lower)	−0.014	0.505	0.01	1	0.977
	Mother's hostility (higher)	0			0	
	Father's hostility (lower)	1.486	0.615	5.836	1	0.016*
	Father's hostility (higher)	0			0	
	Children's home (yes)	0.479	0.704	0.463	1	0.496
	Children's home (no)	0			0	
	Physically abused (yes)	0.652	0.582	1.255	1	0.263
	Physically abused (no)	0			0	
	Sexually abused (yes)	0.498	0.498	1.003	1	0.317
	Sexually abused (no)	0			0	

* Wald test is significant at better than the 0.05 level.

1. The table is in two parts because there is more than one dependent variable to predict – that is, there are two dummy variables. If there were three dummy variables then this table would be in three parts and so forth.

2. The dichotomous variables are each given a regression weight (B) value for each value. The value coded 1 has a numerical value which may be positive or negative. The other value is given a regression weight of 0 every time. That is, by multiplying

the numerical value by 0 we are always going to get 0. In other words, one of the values of a dichotomous predictor has no effect on the calculation.

3. There is a statistic called the Wald statistic in Table 41.8. This statistic is based on the ratio between the B-weight and the standard error. Thus for the first dummy variable it is 0.055. This is not statistically significant ($p = 0.814$). Sometimes the output will be a little misleading since if the standard error is 0.00 then it is not possible to calculate the Wald statistic as it is an infinitely large value. Any value divided by 0 is infinitely large. An infinitely large value is statistically significant, but its significance value cannot be calculated. The significance values of the Wald statistic indicate which of our predictors is statistically significant.

41.8 What have we found?

It is fairly self-evident that the features which distinguish the three groups of offenders are as follows:

1. Rapists (as opposed to incestuous and paedophile offenders) are less likely to have been in a children's home ($B = -1.576$, the minus sign means that the reverse of spending some time in a children's home is true). This is significant at 0.053 which is just about significant. The rapists were also more likely to have been physically abused ($B = 20.540$ and the sign is positive). This is much more statistically significant and the best predictor of all. Finally, the rapists were less likely to have been sexually abused. There is no significance level reported for this because the standard error is 0.000 which makes the Wald statistic infinitely large. Hence a significance level cannot be calculated but really it is extremely statistically significant.

2. Incestuous abusers (as opposed to rapists and paedophile offenders) are more likely to be in the young group and to have a father low on hostility.

The findings are presented in Table 41.9. There were two dummy variables so there are two dimensions to the table. This table probably will help you to understand why only two dummy variables are needed to account for the differences between three groups.

Table 41.9	Differentiating characteristics of the three offender types	
	Younger age group: Father not hostile	Older age group: Father hostile
Children's home: Not physically abused, but sexually abused	incestuous abuser	paedophile
Never in children's home: Physically abused, but not sexually abused		rapist

41.9 Reporting the results

As with some other more advanced statistical procedures, there is no standard way of presenting the outcome of a multinomial logistic regression. One way of reporting the broad findings of the analysis would be as follows: 'A multinomial logistic regression was conducted using six dichotomous predictors to predict classification on the multinomial dependent variable offence type (paedophile, incestuous offender, rapist). The predictors were capable of identifying the offender group at better than the chance level. Two regression patterns were identified – one for rapists versus the other two groups, the second for incestuous offenders versus the other two groups). The pseudo-r^2 (Cox and Snell) was 0.55 indicating a moderate fit between the total model and data although the fit was less than perfect. Rapists were differentiated from the other two groups by not having spent time in a children's home, being physically abused but not being sexually abused. Incestuous offenders were significantly differentiated from the other two groups by being in the younger age group and their father not being hostile to them as children. Rapists were correctly identified with a high degree of accuracy (85.7% correct). Incestuous offenders were less accurately identified (62.5% correct). Paedophiles were more likely to be wrongly classified (accuracy 40.0% correct) but as incestuous offenders rather than rapists. The regression weights are to be found in Table 41.8.'

Key points

- The power of multinomial logistic regression to help identify differences among psychologically interesting – but different – groups of individuals means that it has far greater scope within psychological research than has yet been fully appreciated by researchers.

- The unfamiliarity of some of the concepts should not be regarded as a deterrent. The key features of the analysis are accessible to any researcher no matter how statistically unskilled.

COMPUTER ANALYSIS

The SPSS Statistics instruction book to this text is Dennis Howitt and Duncan Cramer (2011), *Introduction to SPSS Statistics in Psychology: For version 19 and earlier*, Harlow: Pearson. Chapter 38 in that book gives detailed step-by-step procedures for the statistics described in this chapter together with advice on how to report the results. Figure 41.4 shows the SPSS Statistics steps for a multinomial logistic regression.

Data	• Name the variables in Variable View of the Data Editor. • Enter the data under the appropriate variable names in Data View of the Data Editor.
Analysis	• Select 'Analyze', 'Regression' and 'Multinominal Logistic . . .'. • Move the dependent variable to the 'Dependent:' box and the independent variable to the 'Factor(s):' box.
2	• Select 'Model', 'Main effects' and 'Continue'.
3	• Select 'Statistics . . .', 'Cell probabilities', 'Classification table', 'Goodness of fit', 'Continue' and 'OK'.
Output	• Check the way the dependent variable has been coded in the 'Dependent Variable Encoding' table.
2	• The 'Parameter Estimates' table gives the regression weights for the predictors together with their statistical significance.

FIGURE 41.4 SPSS Statistics steps for binomial logistic regression

CHAPTER 42

Binomial logistic regression

- Binomial (or binary) logistic regression is a form of multiple regression which is applied when the dependent variable is dichotomous – that is, has only two different possible values.

- A set of predictors is identified which assesses the most likely of the two nominal categories a particular case falls into.

- The predictor variables may be any type of variable including scores. However, in this chapter we concentrate on using dichotomous predictor variables.

- As in multiple regression, different ways of entering predictor variables are available. What is appropriate is determined partly by the purpose of the analysis. Blocks may be used in order to control for, or partial out, demographic variables for example.

- Classification tables compare the actual distribution on the dependent variable with that predicted on the basis on the independent variables.

- Like other forms of regression, logistic regression generates *B*-weights (or slope) and a constant. However, these are used to calculate something known as the logit rather than scores. The logit is the natural logarithm of odds for the category. The percentage predicted in each category of the dependent variable can be calculated from this and compared with the actual percentage.

- As in all multivariate forms of regression, the final regression calculation provides information about the significant predictors among those being employed.

Preparation

Look back at Chapter 8 on simple regression, Chapter 14 on chi-square and Chapter 31 on multiple regression. Chapter 41 on multinomial logistic regression may be helpful in consolidating understanding of the material in this chapter.

42.1 Introduction

Binomial (or binary) logistic regression may be used to:

1. Determine a small group of variables which characterise the two different groups or categories of cases.

2. Identify which other variables are ineffective in differentiating these two groups or categories of cases.

3. Make actual predictions about which of the two groups a particular individual is likely to be a member given that individual's pattern on the other variables.

A simple way to understand binomial logistic regression is to regard it as a variant of linear multiple regression (Chapter 31). Binomial logistic regression, however, uses a dependent variable which is nominal and consists of just two nominal categories. By employing a weighted pattern of predictor variables, binary logistic regression assesses a person's most likely classification on this binary dependent variable. This prediction is expressed as a probability or using some related concept. Other examples of possible binomial dependent variables include:

- success or failure in an exam

- suffering schizophrenia or not

- going to university or not.

If the dependent variable has three or more nominal categories, then multinomial logistic regression should be used (Chapter 41). In other words, if there are three or more groups or categories, multinomial logistic regression is the appropriate approach. Often, but not necessarily, the independent variables are also binary nominal category variables. So gender and age group could be used as the predictor variables to estimate whether a person will own a mobile phone or not, for example.

Because the dependent variable is nominal data, regression weights are calculated which help calculate the probability that a particular individual will be in category *A* rather than category *B* of the dependent variable. More precisely:

1. The regression weights and constant are used to calculate the logit.

2. This in its turn is the natural logarithm of something called the odds.

3. Odds are not very different from probability and are turned into probabilities using a simple formula.

This is a little daunting at first, but it is not that difficult in practice – especially given that one rarely would need to calculate anything by hand!

You may find it helpful to turn to Box 42.1 on simple logistic regression. Studying this will introduce you to most of the concepts in binomial logistic regression without too much confusing detail and complexity. Simple logistic regression would not normally be calculated since it achieves nothing computationally which is not more simply done in other ways. Box 42.2 explains natural logarithms.

Box 42.1   Focus on

Simple logistic regression

In this chapter we are looking at binomial logistic regression and applying it to predicting recidivism (re-offending by prisoners). We will take a simple example of this which uses one independent variable (whether the prisoner has previous convictions) and one dependent variable (whether or not prisoners re-offend). Table 42.1 illustrates such data. The table clearly shows that *prisoners who have previous convictions* are much more likely to re-offend than prisoners who have *not got previous convictions* (i.e. first-time offenders). If a prisoner has previous convictions, the odds are 40 to 10 that they will re-offend. This equates to a percentage of 80% (i.e. 40/(40 + 10) × 100%). If a prisoner has *no* previous convictions then the odds are 15 to 30 that they will re-offend. This equates to a percentage of 33.33% (i.e. 15/(15 + 30) × 100%).

It would be a simple matter of predicting recidivism from these figures. Basically if a prisoner has previous convictions then they are very likely to re-offend (80% likelihood), but if they have no previous convictions then they are unlikely to re-offend (33% likelihood). Table 42.2 illustrates what we would expect on the basis of the data in Table 42.1. There is virtually no difference between the two tables – we have merely added the percentage of correct predictions for each row, that is, how easy the

prediction is in this simple case. Notice we are more accurate at predicting re-offending in those with previous convictions than we are at predicting no re-offending in those with no previous convictions. That is how simple the prediction is with just a single predictor variable.

In logistic regression, simply for mathematical computation reasons, calculations are carried out using odds rather than probabilities. However, odds and probability are closely related. The odds of re-offending *if the prisoner has previous convictions* is simply the numbers re-offending divided by the numbers not re-offending. That is, the odds of re-offending *if the prisoner has prior convictions* are 40/10 = 4.0. On the other hand, *if the prisoner has no previous convictions*, the odds for re-offending are 15/30 = 0.50.

A simple formula links probability and odds so it is very easy to convert odds into probabilities (and vice versa if necessary):

$$\text{probability (of re-offending)} = \text{odds}/(1 + \text{odds})$$
$$= 4.0/(1 + 4.0)$$
$$= 4.0/0.5$$
$$= 0.80$$
$$(= 80\% \text{ as a percentage})$$

Table 42.1	Tabulation of previous convictions against re-offending	
	Re-offends	**No re-offending**
Previous conviction	40	10
First offender	15	30

Table 42.2	Classification table including percentage of correct predictions		
	Re-offends	**No re-offending**	**Row correct**
Previous conviction	40	10	80.0%
No previous conviction	15	30	66.7%

→

It should be stressed that in reality things are even easier since, apart from explanations of logistic regression such as this, all of the calculations are done by the computer program.

The concept of *odds ratio* occurs frequently in discussions of logistic regression. An *odds ratio* is simply the ratio of two sets of odds. Hence the odds ratio for *has previous offences* against *not having previous offences* is simply 4.0/0.50 = 8.0. This means that *if a prisoner has previous convictions* he is eight times more likely to re-offend than *a prisoner who has no previous convictions*. Of course, there are other odds ratios. For example, if the prisoner *has no previous convictions* he is 0.50/4.0 = 0.125 times as likely to re-offend than *if he has previous convictions*. An odds ratio of 0.125 seems hard to decipher, but it is merely the decimal value of the fraction 1/8. That seems more intuitively obvious to understand than the decimal. All that is being said is that there is eight times more chance of having outcome A than outcome B – which is the same thing as saying that there is an eighth of a chance of have outcome B rather than outcome A.

The actual calculations in logistic regression revolve around a concept known as the logit. This is simply odds or odds ratios expressed as their equivalent value expressed as natural logarithms (see Box 42.2 for an explanation of natural logarithms). So a logit is the natural logarithm of the odds (or odds ratio). Natural logarithms are explained in a separate panel. For a short table of natural logarithms see Table 42.3. Most scientific calcula-

tors will provide the natural logarithm of any number – they are also known as Napierian logarithms.

If we run the data from Table 42.1 through the logistic regression program, a number of tables are generated. One of the most important tables will contain a *B*-weight and a constant. These are somewhat analogous to the *b*-weight and the constant that are obtained in linear regression (Chapter 8) and multiple regression. For our data the *B* is 2.079 and the constant is −0.693. (If you try to reproduce this calculation using a computer program such as SPSS Statistics be very careful since programs sometimes impose different values for the cells from those you may be expecting.) The constant and *B*-weight are applied to the *values of the dependent variable* in order to indicate the likelihood of each of the two values occurring in offenders with previous convictions. Remember that the dependent variable is coded either 1 (if the offender has previous convictions) or 0 (if the offender has *no* previous convictions). The result of this calculation then gives us the logit from which a probability of either outcome may be calculated, though normally there is no need to do so.

So, if we wish to know the likelihood of re-offending, the dependent variable in our example variable has a value of 1 if the offender re-offends after release from prison. The logit (of the odds that the offender will re-offend) is calculated as

$$\text{constant} + (1 \times B) = -0.693 + (1 \times 2.079)$$
$$= -0.693 + 2.079 = 1.386$$

Table 42.3	Some odds and their corresponding natural logarithm values		
Odds (or odds ratio)	**Natural logarithm (logit)**	**Odds (or odds ratio)**	**Natural logarithm (logit)**
0.10	−2.30	1.50	0.41
0.20	−1.61	2.00	0.69
0.25	−1.39	3.00	1.10
0.30	−1.20	4.00	1.39
0.40	−0.92	5.00	1.61
0.50	−0.69	6.00	1.79
0.60	−0.51	7.00	1.95
0.70	−0.36	8.00	2.08
0.80	−0.22	9.00	2.20
0.90	−0.11	10.00	2.30
1.00	0.00	100.00	4.61

→

This value of the logit can be turned into odds using the table of natural logarithms (Table 42.3). The odds for a logit of 1.386 is 4.00. This is no surprise as we calculated the odds for re-offending earlier in this box using very simple methods. Expressed as a probability, this is 4.00/(1 + 4.00) = 4.00/5.00 = 0.80 = 80% as a percentage.

On the other hand, if the predictor variable has a value of 0 (i.e. the offender does not re-offend after leaving prison) then the calculation of the logit is as follows:

$$logit = constant + (0 \times B) = -0.693 + (0 \times 2.079)$$
$$= -0.693 + 0 = -0.693$$

Again Table 42.3 can be consulted to convert this logit (natural logarithm of the odds) into the odds. We find that the odds for a logit of 0.693 is 0.50. Remember what this means. We have calculated the odds that a prisoner who has *no* previous offences will re-offend on release to be 0.50. We can express this as a probability by applying the earlier formula. This is 0.50/(1 + 0.50) = 0.50/1.50 = 0.33 or 33% as a percentage.

Thus, the probability of re-offending (if the prisoner has previous convictions) is 0.67 (or 67%) and the probability of *not* re-offending is 0.33 or 33%.

Unfortunately, binomial multiple regression is not quite that simple but only because it employs several predictor (independent variables) which may well be to a degree associated. Consequently, the prediction becomes much more complex and cannot be done without the help of a computer program because it is incredibly computationally intensive. But the main difference in practical terms is not great since the user rarely has to do even the most basic calculation. Instead of one *B*-weight, several regression weights may be produced – one for each predictor variable. This merely extends the calculation a little as you will see in the main text for this chapter.

| Box 42.2 | Key concepts |

Natural logarithms

We do not really need to know about natural logarithms to use logistic regression, but the following may be helpful to those who want to dig a little deeper. Natural logarithms are also known as Napierian logarithms. A logarithm is simply the exponential power to which a particular base number (that can be any number) has to be raised in order to give the number for which the logarithm is required. Let us assume, for example, that the base number is 2.00 and we want to find the logarithm for the number 4.00. We simply have to calculate e (the exponential or power) in the following formula:

$$2.00^e = 4.00$$

It is probably obvious that in order to get 4.00, we have to square 2.00 (i.e. raise to the power of 2). So the logarithm to the base 2.00 for the number 4.00 is 2. Similarly, the logarithm of 8 to the base 2.00 is 3 and the logarithm of 16 is 4. Natural logarithms have as their base 2.71828. Table 42.3 gives some natural logarithms for a selection of numbers.

Natural logarithms are vital to the calculation of logistic regression because it is based on the Poisson distribution. Poisson distributions are largely used to calculate probabilities of rare occurrences in large populations. Multiple regression is based on the normal distribution, logistic regression is based on the Poisson distribution. One feature of logarithms is that they can be applied to any numerical measures in order to compact the distribution by making the large values relatively much smaller without affecting the small values so much. This can be seen in Table 42.3. Notice that if we take the odds ratios for 1 through to 100, the logit values only increase from 0 to 4.61. Also noteworthy is that the natural log of 1.00 (the point at which both outcomes are equally probable) is 0.0. In terms of the calculations, the main consequence of this is that the logistic regression *B*-weights have a greater influence when applied to a logit close to the mid-point (i.e. log of the odds ratio of 1.00) than it does higher on the natural logarithm scale.

42.2 Typical example

A typical use of binomial logistic regression would be in the assessment of the likelihood of re-offending if a prisoner is released from prison. This re-offending (i.e. recidivism) could be assessed as a binomial (i.e. dichotomous) variable. In this case, the variable re-offending simply takes one of two values – the prisoner re-offends or the prisoner does *not* re-offend (Table 42.4). (If one, for example, *counted* the number of times each prisoner re-offended in that period then regular multiple regression (Chapter 31) would be more appropriate since this would amount to a numerical score.) Decision-making about prisoner release is improved by knowing which of a set of variables are most associated with re-offending. Such variables (i.e. independent variables) might include:

- age (over 30 years versus 29 and under)

- whether they had previously been in prison

- whether they received treatment (therapy) in prison

- whether they express contrition (regret) for their offence

- whether they are married

- type of offender (sex offender or not).

Data on these variables plus re-offending (recidivism) are to be found in Table 42.5. There are only 19 different cases listed, but they have been reproduced five times to give a 'sample' of 95 cases. This helps make the output of the analysis more realistic for pedagogic purposes though statistically and methodologically it is otherwise totally unjustified. Nevertheless, readers may find it easier to duplicate our analysis on the computer because one block of data can be copied several times. The basic structure of our data for this regression analysis is shown in Figure 42.1.

Although we have selected binary (i.e. dichotomous) variables as the predictors in our example, score variables could also be used as predictors in binomial logistic regression. Equally, one could use nominal variables with three or more values though these have to be turned into dummy variables for the purpose of the analysis (see Chapter 41, section 41.2). A dummy variable is a binary variable taking the values of 0 or 1. Any nominal (category) variable having three or more values may be converted into several dummy variables. More than one type of variable can be used in any analysis. That is, the choice of types of predictor variables is very flexible. One thing is not flexible – the dependent variable can only be dichotomous; i.e. only two alternative values of the dependent variable are possible.

As with any sort of regression, we work with known data from a sample of individuals. The relationships are calculated between the independent variables and the dependent variable using the data from this sample. The relationships (usually expressed as

Table 42.4	Step 1 classification table			
		Predicted recidivist	Predicted non-recidivist	Percentage row correct
Actually re-offends		40	5	88.9%
Actually does not re-offend		5	45	90.0%

| | Table 42.5 | Data for the study of recidivism – the data from 19 cases is reproduced five times to give realistic sample sizes but only to facilitate explanation |

	Recidivism	Age	Previous prison term	Treatment	Contrite	Married	Sex offender
1	yes	younger	yes	no	no	no	yes
2	yes	older	yes	no	no	no	yes
3	yes	older	yes	yes	no	no	yes
4	yes	older	yes	yes	no	yes	no
5	yes	younger	yes	no	no	no	no
6	yes	younger	no	yes	yes	no	no
7	yes	older	no	yes	yes	yes	yes
8	yes	younger	yes	no	no	no	yes
9	yes	younger	no	no	no	yes	yes
10	yes	older	no	no	no	no	no
11	no	younger	no	yes	yes	no	no
12	no	older	no	yes	yes	no	no
13	no	older	yes	yes	yes	yes	yes
14	no	younger	no	yes	yes	yes	yes
15	no	younger	no	yes	yes	no	yes
16	no	younger	no	no	yes	yes	no
17	no	older	no	no	no	yes	no
18	no	older	yes	yes	yes	no	no
19	no	older	yes	yes	yes	no	no
etc.	yes	younger	yes	no	no	no	yes

Nominal predictor variables
Age of offender
Previous imprisonment
Therapy
Contrition
Married
Sex offender

Binary dependent variable
Recidivism

| **FIGURE 42.1** | Structure of an example |

B-weights) between the independent and dependent variables are sometimes generalised to further individuals who were not part of the original sample. In our example, knowing the characteristics of prisoners who re-offend, we would be less likely to release a particular prisoner showing the pattern of characteristics which is associated with re-offending.

The terms independent and dependent variable are frequently used in regression. The thing being 'predicted' in regression is often termed the dependent variable. It is

Table 42.6	Data from Table 42.5 coded in binary fashion as 0 and 1 for each variable					
	Recidivism	Age	Previous prison term	Treatment	Contrite	Married	Sex offender
1	1	0	1	0	0	0	1
2	1	1	1	0	0	0	1
3	1	1	1	1	0	0	1
4	1	1	1	1	0	1	0
5	1	0	1	0	0	0	0
6	1	0	0	1	1	0	0
7	1	1	0	1	1	1	1
8	1	0	1	0	0	0	1
9	1	0	0	0	0	1	1
10	1	1	0	0	0	0	0
11	0	0	0	1	1	0	0
12	0	1	0	1	1	0	0
13	0	1	1	1	1	1	1
14	0	0	0	1	1	1	1
15	0	0	0	1	1	0	1
16	0	0	0	0	1	1	0
17	0	1	0	0	0	1	0
18	0	1	1	1	1	0	0
19	0	1	1	1	1	0	0
etc.	1	0	1	0	0	0	1

important not to confuse this with cause-and-effect sequences. Variations in the independent variables are not assumed to *cause* the variations in the dependent variable. There might be a causal relationship, but not necessarily so. All that is sought is an association. To anticipate a potential source of confusion, it should be mentioned that researchers sometimes use a particular variable as both an independent and a dependent variable at different stages of an analysis.

The data in Table 42.5 could be prepared for analysis by coding the presence of a feature as 1 and the absence of a feature as 0. In a sense, it does not matter which category of the two is coded 1. However, the category coded 1 will be regarded as the category having influence or being influenced. In other words, if recidivism is coded 1 then the analysis is about predicting recidivism. If non-recidivism is coded 1 then the analysis is about predicting non-recidivism. You just need to make a note of what values you have coded 1 in order that you can later understand what the analysis means. If you do not use codes 0 and 1 then the computer program often will impose them (SPSS Statistics does this, for example) and you will need to consult the output to find out what codings have been used for each of the values. The coding of our data is shown in Table 42.6.

Box 42.3   Focus on

Score variables as predictors in logistic regression

It is important to realise that score variables can be used as the independent or predictor variables in binomial logistic regression. In this chapter, we concentrate on nominal (category) variables as independent/predictor variables to avoid cluttering the chapter overly. Score variables used in this way can be interpreted more or less as a binomial category/nominal variable would be, so do not add any real complexity. The difficulties come in relation to using a program such as SPSS Statistics to carry out the analysis when the user has to specify which predictor variables are score variables and which are category/nominal variables (see also Box 41.1 on p. 538).

42.3   Applying the logistic regression procedure

Logistic binary regression is only ever calculated using computers. The key steps involved are outlined in Figure 42.2. The output largely consists of three aspects:

1. Regression calculations involving a constant and *B*-weights as for any form of regression. Table 42.7 gives the constant and *B*-weights for our calculation.

2. Classification tables which show how well cases are classified by the regression calculation. These are to be found in Table 42.8.

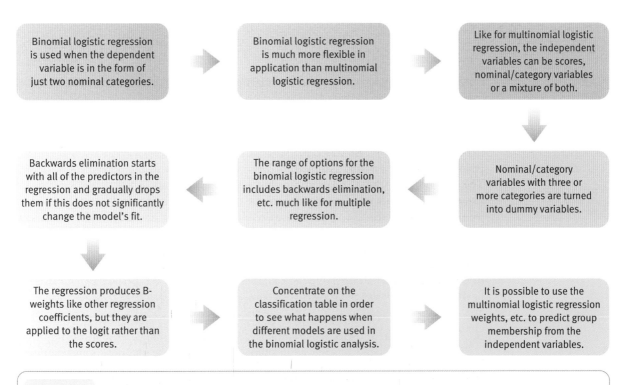

FIGURE 42.2   Conceptual steps for understanding binomial logistic regression

Table 42.7	Regression models for step 1 and step 2				
	B	Standard error	Wald	Degrees of freedom	Significance
Step 1					
Age (younger)	−2.726	0.736	13.702	1	0.000
Previous convictions – yes	−1.086	0.730	2.215	1	0.137
Treatment – no	19.362	8901.292	0.000	1	0.998
Contrite – no	41.459	11325.913	0.000	1	0.997
Married – no	−0.307	0.674	0.208	1	0.648
Sex offender – no	−20.641	7003.92	0.000	1	0.998
Constant	23.802	7003.92	0.000	1	0.997
Step 2					
Age (younger)	−2.699	0.731	13.625	1	0.000
Previous convictions – yes	−1.153	0.708	2.648	1	0.104
Treatment – no	19.428	8895.914	0.000	1	0.998
Contrite – no	−41.375	11337.365	0.000	1	0.997
Sex offender – no	−20.475	7028.411	0.000	1	0.998
Constant	23.542	7020.411	0.000	1	0.997

Table 42.8	Classification tables having eliminated worst predictor		
	Not predicted recidivist	Predicted recidivist	Percentage correct
Step 1: *includes all predictor variables – age, previous imprisonment, treatment, contrition, married and sex offender*			
Not recidivist	45	5	90.0%
Recidivist	5	40	88.9%
			Overall correct 89.5%
Step 2: *married is dropped at this stage so age, previous imprisonment, contrition and sex offender remain in the analysis*			
Not recidivist	45	5	90.0%
Recidivist	5	40	88.9%
			Overall correct 89.5%
The analysis terminated at this stage.			

3. Goodness-of-fit statistics which indicate, among other things, how much improvement (or worsening) is achieved in successive stages of the analysis. Some examples of these are presented in the text. Examples of these are in Table 42.9.

As with most forms of multiple regression, it is possible to stipulate any of a number of methods of doing the analysis. Entering all of the independent variables at one time

Table 42.9	Omnibus tests of model coefficients		
	Chi-square	**Degrees of freedom**	**Significance**
Step 1			
Step	70.953	6	0.000
Block	70.953	6	0.000
Model	70.953	6	0.000
Step 2			
Step	−0.210	1	0.647
Block	70.743	5	0.000
Model	70.743	5	0.000

Table 42.10	Classification table based solely on distribution of re-offending – the step 0 classification table		
	Best prediction: re-offends	**Best prediction: does not re-offend**	**% accuracy**
Actually re-offends	0	45	0%
Actually no re-offending	0	50	100%
			Overall accuracy = 52.6%

is merely one of these options. Entering all predictors at the same time generally produces the simplest-looking computer output. Some of the alternatives to this method are discussed in Box 41.2 on discriminant function analysis on pp. 539–40 as they apply to many different forms of regression. To illustrate one of the possibilities, we will carry out *backwards elimination analysis* as our approach to the analysis of the data. There are several types of backwards elimination. Our choice is to use backwards stepwise conditional which is one of the options readily available on SPSS Statistics. The precise mechanics of this form of analysis are really beyond a book of this nature.

In backwards elimination there is a minimum of three steps:

1. Step 0 includes no predictors. Since we know the distribution of values on the *dependent* variable – in this case recidivism – then this would help us make an intelligent guess or prediction as to whether prisoners are likely to re-offend. Our study involves a sample of 95 prisoners. It emerged that 45 of them re-offended whereas the other 50 stayed on the straight and narrow. Hence, if we were to make a prediction in the absence of any other information, it would be that a prisoner will *not* re-offend since this is the commonest outcome. This is shown in Table 42.10. Such a classification table indicates the accuracy of the prediction. If we predict that no prisoner will re-offend, then we are 100% correct for those who do not re-offend, and 0% correct (totally wrong) for those who do re-offend. The overall accuracy for the classification table (Table 42.8) is 52.6%. This is calculated from the total of correct predictions as a percentage of all predictions. That is, $50/95 \times 100\% = 0.526 \times 100\% = 52.6\%$.

2. Step 1 (in backwards elimination) includes all of the predictors. That is, they are all entered at the same time. This step is to be found in Tables 42.7 and 42.8. This is a perfectly sound regression analysis in its own right. It is the simplest approach in order to maximise the classificatory power of the predictors.

3. Step 2 involves the first stage of the backwards elimination. We obtain step 2 simply by eliminating the predictor which, if dropped from the step 1 model, makes no appreciable difference to the fit between the data and the predicted data (i.e. married – no). If omitting this predictor makes no difference to the outcome, it may be safely removed from the analysis. This is also illustrated in Tables 42.7 and 42.8. Dropping a variable means that the other values all have to be recalculated.

4. There may be further steps if it is possible to drop further ineffective predictors. The elimination of predictor variables in backwards elimination is not absolute. Instead, a predictor variable may be allowed back into the set of predictors at a later stage when other predictors have been eliminated. The reason for this is that the predictors are generally somewhat inter-correlated. As a consequence, the elimination of one predictor variable requires the recalculation of the predictive power associated with the other predictor variables. This means that sometimes a predictor which has previously been dropped from the analysis will return to the analysis at a later stage. There are no examples of the re-entry of variables previously dropped in our analysis – actually the analysis is now complete using our chosen method. Other methods of backwards elimination may involve more steps. There are criteria for the re-entry and dropping of predictors built into the statistical routine – the values of these may be varied.

The steps (step 0, step 1, step 2, etc.) could also be referred to as 'models'. A model is simply a (mathematical) statement describing the relationship of a set of predictors with what is being predicted. There are usually several ways of combining all or some of the predictor variables. What is the best model depends partly on the data but equally on the researcher's requirements. Often the ideal is a model that includes the minimum set of predictors that are correlated with (or predict) the dependent (predicted) variable.

Table 42.9 gives the goodness-of-fit statistics for the step 1 and step 2 models to the step 0 model. The significant value of chi-square indicates that the step 1 model is very different from the step 0 model. However, there is very little difference between the step 1 and step 2 models. Dropping the variable marital status from step 1 to give the step 2 model makes very little difference to the value of the chi-square – certainly not a significant difference. The computer output can be consulted to see the change if a particular predictor is removed though we have not reproduced such a table here. At step 2, having removed marital status makes a very small and non-significant change in fit. Indeed, marital status is selected for elimination because removing it produces the least change to the predictive power of the model. The chi-square value is −0.210 (the difference in the chi-square values) which indicates that the model is slightly less different from the step 0 model, but this chi-square is not significant (the probability is 0.647). Hence marital status was dropped from the model in step 2 because it makes little difference to the fit, whether included or not. The computer program then assesses the effect of dropping each of the predictors at step 2. Briefly no further predictors could be dropped without significantly affecting the fit of the model to the data. So there is no step 3 to report in this example.

Table 42.8 gives the classification tables for steps 1 and 2. (Step 0 can be seen in Table 42.10.) At the step 1 stage, all of the predictors are entered. Comparing the step 0 and step 1 classification tables reveals that step 1 appears to be a marked improvement over the step 0 model. That is, the predictor variables in combination improve the prediction quite considerably. There are only 10 (i.e. 5 + 5) misclassifications and 85

(40 + 45) correct predictions using the step 1 model – an overall correct prediction rate of 85/95 × 100% = 89.5%. If we released early, say, those prisoners predicted not to re-offend on the basis of our predictors then, overwhelmingly, they will not re-offend. At step 2, the classification table is exactly the same as for step 1. While the underlying model is clearly slightly different (see Table 42.7), in practical terms this is making no tangible difference in this case.

There is just one more useful statistic to be pulled from the computer output. This is known as the 'pseudo r^2' (see Chapter 41, section 41.6, pp. 543–4). It is roughly analogous to the multiple r^2 statistic used in multiple regression. It is a single indicator of how well the set of predictors predict. There are a number of such pseudo r^2. The Cox and Snell R-square and the Nagelkerke R-square are common ones. Several different ones may be given in the computer output. Although this is not shown in any of the tables, the value for the Cox and Snell R-square at step 2 is 0.525. This suggests a reasonably good level of prediction but there is clearly the possibility of finding further predictors to increase predictive power.

42.4 The regression formula

For most purposes, the above is sufficient. That is, we have generated reasonably powerful models for predicting the pattern of our data. The only really important task is making predictions about individuals based on their pattern on the predictor variables. If your work does not require individual predictions then there is no need for the following. Although we talk of prediction in relation to regression, this is often not the researcher's objective. Most typically, they are simply keen to identify the pattern of variables most closely associated with another variable (the dependent variable).

The predictor variables in our example are as follows:

- age – younger and older
- previous prison sentence or none
- treatment for offence or none
- contrition over offence or not
- marital status – married or not
- sex offender or not.

The dependent variable is recidivism (or not) following discharge from prison.

It is important to recall that all of the variables were coded in binary fashion using the following. That is:

1. The variables were coded as 1 if the characteristic is present.

2. The variables were coded as 0 if the characteristic is absent.

By using these values, the predictors act as weights. It is important to note that multiplying by 0 means that we had nothing when we multiply values of 0 by their logistic regression weights. Computer programs such as SPSS statistics usually recode binary variables for you in this way though care needs to be taken to check the output to find out just how the recoding has been done.

The basic formula for the prediction is:

predicted logit = constant + $(B_1 \times X_1) + (B_2 \times X_2)$ + etc.

That is, the formula predicts the logarithm of the odds of re-offending (recidivism) for an individual showing a particular pattern on the independent variables. X refers to the 'score' on a predictor variable (1 or 0 for a binary variable) which has to be multiplied by the appropriate regression weight (B). There is also a constant. It should be emphasised that this formula gives the predicted logit for a particular pattern of values on the independent variables. In other words, it is part of the calculation of the likelihood that a particular individual will re-offend though the predicted logit must be turned into odds and then probabilities before the likelihoods are known. It should be very clear from our step 2 model (Table 42.7) that the risk of re-offending is greater if the prisoner is young, has previous convictions, is undergoing treatment, is not contrite and is not a sex offender.

Just what is the likelihood that an individual with a particular pattern on the predictor variables will re-offend? Let us take a concrete example – an individual whose pattern is that he is young, has previously been in prison, has undergone treatment, is not contrite and is not a sex offender. The first four of these are coded 1 if that characteristic is present. Not being a sex offender is coded 0. The formula for the predicted logit then is:

$$\text{logit} = -12.732 + (1 \times 2.699) + (1 \times 1.153) + (1 \times -9.428) + (1 \times 21.375) + (0 \times 10.475)$$

$$= -12.732 + (2.699) + (1.153) + (-9.428) + (21.375) + (0)$$

$$= 3.067$$

This value for the logit of 3.067 translates approximately to odds of 21.5 of being in the re-offender rather than non-re-offender group with that pattern on the predictor variable. (That is, the natural logarithm of 21.5 is 4.067.) An odds ratio of 21.5 gives a probability of $21.5/(1 + 21.5) = 21.5/22.5 = 0.96$ or 96%. This is rather approximate as the calculation has been subject to a rounding error. So a person with this particular pattern on the predictor variables is extremely likely to re-offend.

42.5 Reporting the results

The reporting of any regression is somewhat dependent on the purpose of the analysis. Consequently, only the broad outlines can be given here. The final model has been chosen though there would be reason to choose some of the others in some circumstances. The following may be helpful as a structure for reporting one's findings. 'A binomial logistic regression was conducted in order to find the set of predictors which best distinguish between the offending and re-offending group. All the predictor variables were binary coded as was the criterion variable, offender group. The analysis employed backwards elimination of variables. The final model to emerge included five predictors of recidivism – being young, having previously been in prison, having undergone treatment, not being contrite and not being a sex offender. This model had a pseudo r-square of 0.53 using the Cox and Snell statistic which indicates that the fit of the model to the data possibly could be improved with the addition of further predictors. The success rate of the model was 90.0% for predicting non-re-offending and 88.9% for predicting re-offending.'

Key points

- Given the power of binomial logistic regression to find the pattern of variables which are best able to differentiate two different groups of individuals in terms of their psychological characteristics, it might be regarded as a fundamental technique for any study comparing the characteristics of two groups of individuals. In other words, it is much more effective to use logistic regression than to carry out numerous *t*-tests on individual variables.

- Binomial logistic regression has great flexibility in the variety of variables used so long as the groups being compared are just two in number.

COMPUTER ANALYSIS

The SPSS Statistics instruction book to this text is Dennis Howitt and Duncan Cramer (2011), *Introduction to SPSS Statistics in Psychology: For version 19 and earlier*, Harlow: Pearson. Chapter 39 in that book gives detailed step-by-step procedures for the statistics described in this chapter together with advice on how to report the results. Figure 42.3 shows the SPSS Statistics steps for a binomial logistic regression.

Data
- Name the variables in Variable View of the Data Editor.
- Enter the data under the appropriate variable names in Data View of the Data Editor.

Analysis
- Select 'Analyze', 'Regression' and 'Binary Logistic . . .'.
- Move the dependent variable to the 'Dependent:' box, the predictors to the 'Covariate(s):' box and select 'Categorical . . .'.

2
- Move the categorical predictors to the 'Categorical Covariate(s):' box and select 'Continue'.

3
- Select the 'Method:' of entry from the dropdown menu next to this option (e.g. 'Backward conditional') and 'OK'.

Output
- Check the way the dependent variable has been coded in the 'Dependent Variable Encoding' table.

2
- Note the predictors in the 'Variables in the Equation' table for the final model and the direction of the association for the regression weights.

3
- Note the percentage of cases correctly identified in the 'Classification Table' for this model.

FIGURE 42.3 SPSS Statistics steps for binomial logistic regression

Testing for excessively skewed distributions

The use of nonparametric tests (Mann–Whitney U-test, Wilcoxon matched pairs test) rather than parametric tests (unrelated t-test, related t-test) is conventionally recommended by some textbooks when the distribution of scores on a variable is significantly skewed (Chapter 18). There are a number of difficulties with this advice, particularly just how one knows that there is too much skew. It is possible to test for significant skewness. One simply computes skewness and then divides this by the standard error of the skewness. If the resulting value equals or exceeds 1.96 then your skewness is significant at the 5% level (two-tailed test) and the null hypothesis that your sample comes from a symmetrical population should be rejected.

A.1 Skewness

The formula for skewness is:

$$\text{skewness} = \frac{\left(\sum d^3\right)N}{\text{SD}^3 \times (N - 1) \times (N - 2)}$$

Notice that much of the formula is familiar: N is the number of scores, d is the deviation of each score from the mean of the sample and SD is the estimated standard deviation of the scores (i.e. you use $N - 1$ in the formula for standard deviation as described in Chapter 11). What is different is the use of cubing. To cube a number you multiply it by itself twice. Thus the cube of 3 is $3 \times 3 \times 3 \times 27$. A negative number cubed gives a negative number. Thus the cube of -4 is $(-4) \times (-4) \times (-4) = -64$.

We will take the data from Table 5.1 in Chapter 5 to illustrate the calculation of skewness. For simplicity's sake we will be using a definitional formula which involves the calculation of the sample mean. Table A.1 gives the data in column 1 as well as the calculation steps to be followed. The number of scores N equals 9.

Table A.1	Steps in the calculation of skewness		
Column 1 **Age (years)**	**Column 2** **Scores – sample mean**	**Column 3** **Square values in column 2**	**Column 4** **Cube values in column 2**
20	$20 - 23 = -3$	9	-27
25	$25 - 23 = 2$	4	8
19	$19 - 23 = -4$	16	-64
35	$35 - 23 = 12$	144	1728
19	$19 - 23 = -4$	16	-64
17	$17 - 23 = -6$	36	-216
15	$15 - 23 = -8$	64	-512
30	$30 - 23 = 7$	49	343
27	$27 - 23 = 4$	16	64
ΣX = sum of scores = 207		$\Sigma d^2 = 354$	$\Sigma d^3 = 1260$
$\bar{X}$ = mean score = 23			

For Table A.1,

$$\text{estimated standard deviation (SD)} = \sqrt{\frac{\sum d^2}{N - 1}}$$

$$= 6.652$$

Substituting this value and the values from the table in the formula for skewness we get:

$$\text{skewness} = \frac{1260 \times 9}{6.652^3 \times (9 - 1) \times (9 - 2)}$$

$$= \frac{11\ 340}{16\ 483.332}$$

$$= 0.688$$

(Skewness could have a negative value.)

A.2   Standard error of skewness

The standard error of skewness involves calculating the value of the following formula for our particular sample size ($N = 9$):

$$\text{standard error of skewness} = \sqrt{\frac{6 \times N \times (N - 1)}{(N - 2) \times (N + 1) \times (N + 3)}}$$

$$= \sqrt{\frac{432}{840}}$$

$$= \sqrt{0.514}$$

$$= 0.717$$

The significance of skewness involves a z-score:

$$z = \frac{\text{skewness}}{\text{standard error of skewness}}$$

$$= \frac{0.688}{0.717}$$

$$= 0.96$$

This value of z is lower than the minimum value of z (1.96) required to be statistically significant at the 5% level with a two-tailed test. Thus the scores are *not* extremely skewed. This implies that you may use parametric tests rather than nonparametric tests for comparisons involving this variable. Obviously you need to do the skewness test for the other variables involved.

For the related t-test, it is the skewness of the *differences* between the two sets of scores which needs to be examined, not the skewnesses of the two different sets of scores.

Large-sample formulae for the nonparametric tests

Sometimes you may wish to do a nonparametric test when the sample sizes exceed the tabulated values of the significance tables in Chapter 18. In these circumstances, we would recommend using a computer. The reason is that ranking large numbers of scores is extremely time-consuming and you risk making errors. However, if a computer is not available to do the analyses, you can make use of the following large-sample formulae for nonparametric tests.

B1.1 Mann–Whitney U-test

$$z = \frac{U - \dfrac{n_1 n_2}{2}}{\sqrt{\left(\dfrac{n_1 n_2}{N(N-1)}\right)\left(\dfrac{N^3 - N}{12} - \sum \dfrac{t^3 - 1}{12}\right)}}$$

U is as calculated in Chapter 18, n_1 and n_2 are the sizes of the two samples and N is the sum of n_1 and n_2. t is a new symbol in this context: the number of scores tied at a particular value. Thus if you have three scores of 6 in your data, $t = 3$ for the score 6.

Notice that $\sum$ precedes the part of the formula involving t. This indicates that for every score which has ties you need to do the calculation for the number of ties involved *and* sum all of these separate calculations. Where there are no ties, this part of the formula reduces to zero.

The calculated value of z must equal or exceed 1.96 to be statistically significant with a two-tailed test.

B1.2 Wilcoxon matched pairs test

$$z = \frac{T - \dfrac{N(N+1)}{4}}{\sqrt{\dfrac{N(N+1)(2N+1)}{24}}}$$

T is the value of the Wilcoxon matched pairs statistic as calculated in Chapter 18. N is the number of pairs of scores in that calculation.

As before, z must equal or exceed 1.96 to be statistically significant with a two-tailed test.

Nonparametric tests for three or more groups

Several nonparametric tests were described in Chapter 18. However, these dealt with circumstances in which only two sets of scores were compared. If you have three or more sets of scores, there are other tests of significance which can be used. These are nowhere near so flexible and powerful as the analyses of variance described in Chapters 20–25.

B2.1 The Kruskal–Wallis three or more unrelated conditions test

The Kruskal–Wallis test is used in circumstances where there are *more than two* groups of independent or unrelated scores. All of the scores are *ranked* from lowest to highest irrespective of which group they belong to. The average rank in each group is examined. If the null hypothesis is true, then all groups should have more or less the same average rank.

Imagine that the reading abilities of children are compared under three conditions: (1) high motivation, (2) medium motivation and (3) low motivation. The data might be as in Table B2.1. Different children are used in each condition so the data are unrelated. The scores on the dependent variable are on a standard reading test.

The scores are ranked from lowest to highest, ignoring the particular group they are in. Tied scores are given the average of the ranks they would have been given if they were different (Chapter 18). The results of this would look like Table B2.2, which also includes:

● Row A: the mean rank in each condition

● Row B: the square of the sum of the ranks in each condition

● Row C: the square of the sum of ranks from row B divided by the number of scores in each condition

● Row D: R which equals the sum of the squares of the sums of ranks divided by the sample size, i.e. the sum of the figures in row C.

Table B2.1	Reading scores under three different levels of motivation

High motivation	Medium motivation	Low motivation
17	10	3
14	11	9
19	8	2
16	12	5
18	9	1
20	11	7
23	8	6
21	12	
18	9	
	10	

Table B2.2	Scores in Table B2.1 ranked from smallest to largest

Row	High motivation	Medium motivation	Low motivation
	20	12.5	3
	18	14.5	10
	23	7.5	2
	19	16.5	4
	21.5	10	1
	24	14.5	6
	26	7.5	5
	25	16.5	
	21.5	10	
		12.5	
A	Mean ranks $= \dfrac{198}{9} = 22.00$	Mean ranks $= \dfrac{122}{10} = 12.20$	Mean ranks $= \dfrac{31}{7} = 4.43$
B	Sum of ranks$^2 = 198^2 = 39\ 204$	Sum of ranks$^2 = 122^2 = 14\ 884$	Sum of ranks$^2 = 31^2 = 961$
C	Mean ranks$^2 = \dfrac{39\ 204}{9} = 4356$	Mean ranks$^2 = \dfrac{14\ 884}{10} = 1488.40$	Mean ranks$^2 = \dfrac{961}{7} = 137.29$
D	$R =$ sum of calculations in row $C = 4356.00 + 1488.40 + 137.29 = 5981.69$		

The statistic H is calculated next using the following formula:

$$H = \frac{12R}{N(N+1)} - 3(N+1)$$

where R is the sum of the mean rank squared in Row D in Table B2.2 and N is the number of scores ranked. Substituting,

$$H = \frac{12 \times 5981.69}{26(26 + 1)} - 3(26 + 1)$$

$$= \frac{71\ 780.28}{702} - 81$$

$$= 102.251 - 81$$

$$= 21.25$$

The distribution of H approximates that of chi-square. The degrees of freedom are the number of different groups of scores minus one. Thus the significance of H can be assessed against Significance Table 14.1 which tells us that our value of H needs to equal or exceed 6.0 to be significant at the 5% level (two-tailed test). Thus we reject our null hypothesis that reading was unaffected by levels of motivation.

B2.2 The Friedman three or more related samples test

This test is used in circumstances in which you have three or more *related* samples of scores. The scores for each participant in the research are ranked from smallest to largest separately. In other words the scores for Joe Bloggs are ranked from 1 to 3 (or however many conditions there are), the scores for Jenny Bloggs are also ranged from 1 to 3 and so forth for the rest. The test essentially examines whether the average ranks in the several conditions of the experiment are more or less equal, as they should be if the null hypothesis is true.

Table B2.3 gives the scores in an experiment to test the recall of pairs of nonsense syllables under three conditions – high, medium and low distraction. The same participants were used in all conditions of the experiment.

Table B2.4 shows the scores ranked from smallest to largest for each participant in the research separately. Ties are given the average of the ranks that they would have otherwise been given.

- Row A gives the sums of the ranks for each condition or level of distraction.
- Row B gives the square of each sum of ranks for each condition.
- Row C gives the total, R, of the squared sums of ranks from row B.

Table B2.3	Scores on memory ability under three different levels of distraction		
	Low distraction	**Medium distraction**	**High distraction**
John	9	6	7
Mary	15	7	2
Shaun	12	9	5
Edmund	16	8	2
Sanjit	22	15	6
Ann	8	3	4

Table B2.4	Scores ranked separately for each participant		
	Low distraction	**Medium distraction**	**High distraction**
John	3	1	2
Mary	3	2	1
Shaun	3	2	1
Edmund	3	2	1
Sanjit	3	2	1
Ann	3	1	2
Row A	Sum of ranks = 18	Sum of ranks = 10	Sum of ranks = 8
Row B	Square = 18^2 = 324	Square = 10^2 = 100	Square = 8^2 = 64
Row C	R = sum of above squares = 324 + 100 + 64 = 488		

The value of R is entered in the following formula:

$$\chi_r^2 = \frac{12R}{nK(K + 1)} - 3n(K + 1)$$

where n is the number of participants (i.e. of rows of scores) = 6 and K is the number of columns of data (i.e. of different conditions) = 3. Therefore,

$$\chi_r^2 = \frac{12 \times 488}{6 \times 3 \times (3 + 1)} - 3 \times 6 \times (3 + 1)$$

$$= \frac{5856}{72} - 72$$

$$= 9.33$$

The statistical significance of χ_r^2 is assessed using the chi-square table (Significance Table 14.1). The degrees of freedom are the number of conditions − 1 = 3 − 1 = 2. This table tells us that a value of 6.0 or more is needed to be statistically significant at the 5% level (two-tailed test). Thus, it appears that the null hypothesis that the conditions have no effect should be rejected in favour of the hypothesis that levels of distraction influence memory.

COMPUTER ANALYSIS

The SPSS Statistics instruction book to this text is Dennis Howitt and Duncan Cramer (2011), *Introduction to SPSS Statistics in Psychology: For version 19 and earlier*, Harlow: Pearson. Chapter 19 in that book gives detailed step-by-step procedures for the statistics described in this appendix together with advice on how to report the results. Figure B2.1 shows the SPSS Statistics steps for the Kruskal–Wallis unrelated and Friedman related nonparametric tests.

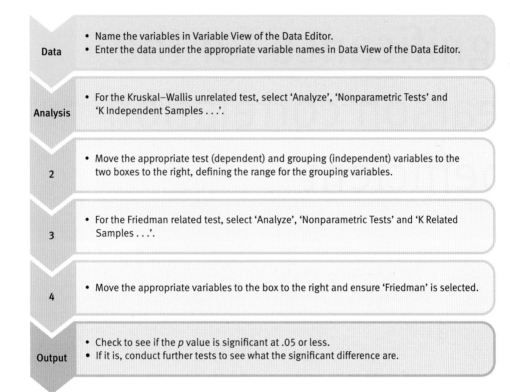

Data
- Name the variables in Variable View of the Data Editor.
- Enter the data under the appropriate variable names in Data View of the Data Editor.

Analysis
- For the Kruskal–Wallis unrelated test, select 'Analyze', 'Nonparametric Tests' and 'K Independent Samples . . .'.

2
- Move the appropriate test (dependent) and grouping (independent) variables to the two boxes to the right, defining the range for the grouping variables.

3
- For the Friedman related test, select 'Analyze', 'Nonparametric Tests' and 'K Related Samples . . .'.

4
- Move the appropriate variables to the box to the right and ensure 'Friedman' is selected.

Output
- Check to see if the *p* value is significant at .05 or less.
- If it is, conduct further tests to see what the significant difference are.

FIGURE B2.1 SPSS Statistics steps for the Kruskal–Wallis and Friedman nonparametric tests

Extended table of significance for the Pearson correlation coefficient

The following table gives both two-tailed and one-tailed values for the significance of the Pearson correlation coefficient. Ignoring the sign of the correlation coefficient obtained, your value has to be equal to, or be larger than, the value in the table in order to be statistically significant at the level of significance stipulated in the column heading.

Sample size	Two-tailed: 10% One-tailed: 5%	Two-tailed: 5% One-tailed: 2.5%	Two-tailed: 2% One-tailed: 1%	Two-tailed: 1% One-tailed: 0.5%
3	0.988	0.997	1.000	1.000
4	0.900	0.950	0.980	0.990
5	0.805	0.878	0.934	0.959
6	0.729	0.811	0.882	0.917
7	0.669	0.754	0.833	0.875
8	0.621	0.707	0.808	0.834
9	0.582	0.666	0.750	0.798
10	0.549	0.632	0.715	0.765
11	0.521	0.602	0.685	0.735
12	0.497	0.576	0.658	0.708
13	0.476	0.553	0.634	0.684
14	0.458	0.532	0.612	0.661
15	0.441	0.514	0.592	0.641

Sample size	Two-tailed: 10% One-tailed: 5%	Two-tailed: 5% One-tailed: 2.5%	Two-tailed: 2% One-tailed: 1%	Two-tailed: 1% One-tailed: 0.5%
16	0.426	0.497	0.574	0.623
17	0.412	0.482	0.558	0.606
18	0.400	0.468	0.543	0.590
19	0.389	0.456	0.529	0.575
20	0.378	0.444	0.516	0.561
21	0.369	0.433	0.503	0.549
22	0.360	0.423	0.492	0.537
23	0.352	0.413	0.482	0.526
24	0.344	0.404	0.472	0.515
25	0.337	0.396	0.462	0.505
26	0.330	0.388	0.453	0.496
27	0.323	0.382	0.445	0.487
28	0.317	0.374	0.437	0.479
29	0.311	0.367	0.430	0.471
30	0.306	0.361	0.423	0.463
31	0.301	0.355	0.416	0.456
32	0.296	0.349	0.409	0.449
33	0.291	0.344	0.403	0.442
34	0.287	0.339	0.397	0.436
35	0.283	0.334	0.392	0.430
36	0.279	0.329	0.386	0.424
37	0.275	0.325	0.381	0.418
38	0.271	0.320	0.376	0.413
39	0.267	0.316	0.371	0.408
40	0.264	0.312	0.367	0.403
41	0.260	0.308	0.362	0.398
42	0.257	0.304	0.358	0.393
43	0.254	0.301	0.354	0.389
44	0.251	0.297	0.350	0.384
45	0.248	0.294	0.346	0.380
46	0.246	0.291	0.342	0.376
47	0.243	0.288	0.338	0.372
48	0.240	0.285	0.335	0.368
49	0.238	0.282	0.331	0.365
50	0.235	0.279	0.328	0.361
51	0.233	0.276	0.325	0.358
52	0.231	0.273	0.322	0.354
53	0.228	0.271	0.319	0.351

Sample size	Two-tailed: 10% One-tailed: 5%	Two-tailed: 5% One-tailed: 2.5%	Two-tailed: 2% One-tailed: 1%	Two-tailed: 1% One-tailed: 0.5%
54	0.226	0.268	0.316	0.348
55	0.224	0.266	0.313	0.345
56	0.222	0.263	0.310	0.341
57	0.220	0.261	0.307	0.339
58	0.218	0.259	0.305	0.336
59	0.216	0.256	0.302	0.333
60	0.214	0.254	0.300	0.330
61	0.213	0.252	0.297	0.327
62	0.211	0.250	0.295	0.325
63	0.209	0.248	0.293	0.322
64	0.207	0.246	0.290	0.320
65	0.206	0.244	0.288	0.317
66	0.204	0.242	0.286	0.315
67	0.203	0.240	0.284	0.313
68	0.201	0.239	0.282	0.310
69	0.200	0.237	0.280	0.308
70	0.198	0.235	0.278	0.306
71	0.197	0.234	0.276	0.304
72	0.195	0.232	0.274	0.302
73	0.194	0.230	0.272	0.300
74	0.193	0.229	0.270	0.298
75	0.191	0.227	0.268	0.296
76	0.190	0.226	0.266	0.294
77	0.189	0.224	0.265	0.292
78	0.188	0.223	0.263	0.290
79	0.186	0.221	0.261	0.288
80	0.185	0.220	0.260	0.286
81	0.184	0.219	0.258	0.285
82	0.183	0.217	0.257	0.283
83	0.182	0.216	0.255	0.281
84	0.181	0.215	0.253	0.280
85	0.180	0.213	0.252	0.278
86	0.179	0.212	0.251	0.276
87	0.178	0.211	0.249	0.275
88	0.176	0.210	0.248	0.273
89	0.175	0.208	0.246	0.272
90	0.174	0.207	0.245	0.270
91	0.174	0.206	0.244	0.269

Sample size	Two-tailed: 10% One-tailed: 5%	Two-tailed: 5% One-tailed: 2.5%	Two-tailed: 2% One-tailed: 1%	Two-tailed: 1% One-tailed: 0.5%
92	0.173	0.205	0.242	0.267
93	0.172	0.204	0.241	0.266
94	0.171	0.203	0.240	0.264
95	0.170	0.202	0.238	0.263
96	0.169	0.201	0.237	0.262
97	0.168	0.200	0.236	0.260
98	0.167	0.199	0.235	0.259
99	0.166	0.198	0.234	0.258
100	0.165	0.197	0.232	0.256
200	0.117	0.139	0.164	0.182
300	0.095	0.113	0.134	0.149
400	0.082	0.098	0.116	0.129
500	0.074	0.088	0.104	0.115
1000	0.052	0.062	0.074	0.081

APPENDIX D

Table of significance for the Spearman correlation coefficient

The following table gives both two-tailed and one-tailed values for the significance of the Spearman correlation coefficient. Ignoring the sign of the correlation coefficient obtained, your value has to equal or be larger than the value in the table in order to be statistically significant at the level of significance stipulated in the column heading. Do not use the following table if you used the Pearson correlation coefficient approach described in Calculation 7.2. It is in most applications an approximation. The following table should only be used when the calculation has used the formula described in Calculation 7.3 and there are ties.

Sample size	Two-tailed: 10% One-tailed: 5%	Two-tailed: 5% One-tailed: 2.5%	Two-tailed: 2% One-tailed: 1%	Two-tailed: 1% One-tailed: 0.5%
5	0.900	–	–	–
6	0.829	0.886	0.943	–
7	0.714	0.786	0.893	–
8	0.643	0.738	0.833	0.881
9	0.600	0.683	0.783	0.833
10	0.564	0.648	0.745	0.858
11	0.520	0.620	0.737	0.814
12	0.496	0.591	0.703	0.776
13	0.475	0.566	0.673	0.743
14	0.456	0.544	0.646	0.714
15	0.440	0.524	0.623	0.688
16	0.425	0.506	0.602	0.665
17	0.411	0.490	0.583	0.644

Sample size	Two-tailed: 10% One-tailed: 5%	Two-tailed: 5% One-tailed: 2.5%	Two-tailed: 2% One-tailed: 1%	Two-tailed: 1% One-tailed: 0.5%
18	0.399	0.475	0.565	0.625
19	0.388	0.462	0.549	0.607
20	0.377	0.450	0.535	0.591
21	0.368	0.438	0.521	0.576
22	0.359	0.428	0.508	0.562
23	0.351	0.418	0.497	0.549
24	0.343	0.409	0.486	0.537
25	0.336	0.400	0.476	0.526
26	0.329	0.392	0.466	0.515
27	0.323	0.384	0.457	0.505
28	0.317	0.377	0.448	0.496
29	0.311	0.370	0.440	0.487
30	0.305	0.364	0.433	0.478
31	0.300	0.358	0.425	0.470
32	0.295	0.352	0.418	0.462
33	0.291	0.346	0.412	0.455
34	0.286	0.341	0.406	0.448
35	0.282	0.336	0.400	0.442
36	0.278	0.331	0.394	0.435
37	0.274	0.327	0.388	0.429
38	0.270	0.322	0.383	0.423
39	0.267	0.318	0.378	0.418
40	0.263	0.314	0.373	0.412
41	0.260	0.310	0.368	0.407
42	0.257	0.306	0.364	0.402
43	0.254	0.302	0.360	0.397
44	0.251	0.299	0.355	0.393
45	0.248	0.295	0.351	0.388
46	0.245	0.292	0.347	0.384
47	0.243	0.289	0.344	0.380
48	0.240	0.286	0.340	0.376
49	0.237	0.283	0.336	0.372
50	0.235	0.280	0.333	0.368
51	0.233	0.277	0.330	0.364
52	0.230	0.274	0.326	0.361
53	0.228	0.272	0.323	0.357
54	0.226	0.269	0.320	0.354
55	0.224	0.267	0.317	0.350

→

Sample size	Two-tailed: 10% One-tailed: 5%	Two-tailed: 5% One-tailed: 2.5%	Two-tailed: 2% One-tailed: 1%	Two-tailed: 1% One-tailed: 0.5%
56	0.222	0.264	0.314	0.347
57	0.220	0.262	0.311	0.344
58	0.218	0.260	0.309	0.341
59	0.216	0.257	0.306	0.338
60	0.214	0.255	0.303	0.335
61	0.212	0.253	0.301	0.332
62	0.211	0.251	0.298	0.330
63	0.209	0.249	0.296	0.327
64	0.207	0.247	0.294	0.324
65	0.206	0.245	0.291	0.322
66	0.204	0.243	0.289	0.319
67	0.202	0.241	0.287	0.317
68	0.201	0.239	0.285	0.315
69	0.199	0.238	0.283	0.312
70	0.198	0.236	0.280	0.310
71	0.197	0.234	0.278	0.308
72	0.195	0.233	0.277	0.306
73	0.194	0.231	0.275	0.303
74	0.193	0.229	0.273	0.301
75	0.191	0.228	0.271	0.299
76	0.190	0.226	0.269	0.297
77	0.189	0.225	0.267	0.295
78	0.187	0.223	0.266	0.293
79	0.186	0.222	0.264	0.292
80	0.185	0.221	0.262	0.290
81	0.184	0.219	0.261	0.288
82	0.183	0.218	0.259	0.286
83	0.182	0.216	0.257	0.284
84	0.181	0.215	0.256	0.283
85	0.179	0.214	0.254	0.281
86	0.178	0.213	0.253	0.279
87	0.177	0.211	0.251	0.278
88	0.176	0.210	0.250	0.276
89	0.175	0.209	0.248	0.274
90	0.174	0.208	0.247	0.273
91	0.173	0.207	0.246	0.271
92	0.172	0.205	0.244	0.270
93	0.172	0.204	0.243	0.268

Sample size	Two-tailed: 10% One-tailed: 5%	Two-tailed: 5% One-tailed: 2.5%	Two-tailed: 2% One-tailed: 1%	Two-tailed: 1% One-tailed: 0.5%
94	0.171	0.203	0.242	0.267
95	0.170	0.202	0.240	0.266
96	0.169	0.201	0.239	0.264
97	0.168	0.200	0.238	0.263
98	0.167	0.199	0.237	0.261
99	0.166	0.198	0.235	0.260
100	0.165	0.197	0.234	0.259
200	0.117	0.139	0.165	0.183
300	0.095	0.113	0.135	0.149
400	0.082	0.098	0.117	0.129
500	0.074	0.088	0.104	0.115
1000	0.052	0.062	0.074	0.081

APPENDIX E

Extended table of significance for the *t*-test

The following table gives two-tailed and one-tailed significance values for the *t*-test. The value of *t* which you obtain (ignoring sign) in your calculation has to equal or be larger than the listed value in order to be statistically significant at the level of significance given in each column heading.

For the related *t*-test the degrees of freedom are the *number of pairs* of scores – 1.

For the unrelated *t*-test the degrees of freedom are the number of scores – 2.

Degrees of freedom	Two-tailed: 10% One-tailed: 5%	Two-tailed: 5% One-tailed: 2.5%	Two-tailed: 2% One-tailed: 1%	Two-tailed: 1% One-tailed: 0.5%
1	6.314	12.706	31.820	63.657
2	2.920	4.303	6.965	9.925
3	2.353	3.182	4.541	5.841
4	2.132	2.776	3.747	4.604
5	2.015	2.571	3.365	4.032
6	1.943	2.447	3.365	3.708
7	1.895	2.365	2.998	3.500
8	1.860	2.306	2.897	3.355
9	1.833	2.262	2.821	3.250
10	1.813	2.228	2.764	3.169
11	1.796	2.201	2.718	3.106
12	1.782	2.179	2.681	3.055
13	1.771	2.160	2.650	3.012

Degrees of freedom	Two-tailed: 10% One-tailed: 5%	Two-tailed: 5% One-tailed: 2.5%	Two-tailed: 2% One-tailed: 1%	Two-tailed: 1% One-tailed: 0.5%
14	1.761	2.145	2.625	2.977
15	1.753	2.132	2.603	2.947
16	1.746	2.120	2.583	2.921
17	1.740	2.110	2.567	2.898
18	1.734	2.101	2.552	2.878
19	1.729	2.093	2.539	2.861
20	1.725	2.086	2.528	2.845
21	1.721	2.080	2.518	2.831
22	1.717	2.074	2.508	2.819
23	1.714	2.069	2.500	2.807
24	1.711	2.064	2.492	2.797
25	1.708	2.064	2.485	2.787
26	1.706	2.055	2.479	2.779
27	1.703	2.052	2.473	2.771
28	1.701	2.048	2.467	2.763
29	1.699	2.045	2.462	2.756
30	1.697	2.042	2.457	2.750
31	1.696	2.039	2.453	2.744
32	1.694	2.037	2.449	2.739
33	1.692	2.035	2.445	2.733
34	1.691	2.032	2.441	2.728
35	1.690	2.030	2.438	2.724
36	1.688	2.028	2.434	2.720
37	1.687	2.026	2.431	2.715
38	1.686	2.024	2.429	2.712
39	1.685	2.023	2.426	2.708
40	1.684	2.021	2.423	2.704
41	1.683	2.020	2.421	2.701
42	1.682	2.018	2.418	2.698
43	1.681	2.017	2.416	2.695
44	1.680	2.017	2.414	2.692
45	1.679	2.014	2.412	2.690
46	1.679	2.013	2.410	2.687
47	1.678	2.012	2.408	2.685
48	1.677	2.011	2.408	2.682
49	1.677	2.010	2.405	2.680
50	1.676	2.009	2.403	2.678
51	1.675	2.008	2.402	2.676

Degrees of freedom	Two-tailed: 10% One-tailed: 5%	Two-tailed: 5% One-tailed: 2.5%	Two-tailed: 2% One-tailed: 1%	Two-tailed: 1% One-tailed: 0.5%
52	1.675	2.007	2.400	2.674
53	1.674	2.006	2.399	2.672
54	1.674	2.005	2.397	2.670
55	1.673	2.004	2.396	2.668
56	1.672	2.003	2.395	2.667
57	1.672	2.002	2.394	2.665
58	1.672	2.002	2.392	2.663
59	1.671	2.001	2.391	2.662
60	1.671	2.000	2.390	2.660
61	1.670	2.000	2.389	2.659
62	1.670	1.999	2.388	2.658
63	1.669	1.998	2.387	2.656
64	1.669	1.998	2.386	2.655
65	1.669	1.997	2.385	2.654
66	1.668	1.997	2.384	2.652
67	1.668	1.996	2.383	2.651
68	1.668	1.995	2.383	2.650
69	1.667	1.995	2.382	2.649
70	1.667	1.994	2.381	2.648
71	1.667	1.994	2.380	2.647
72	1.666	1.994	2.379	2.646
73	1.666	1.993	2.379	2.645
74	1.666	1.993	2.378	2.644
75	1.665	1.992	2.377	2.643
76	1.665	1.992	2.376	2.642
77	1.665	1.991	2.376	2.641
78	1.665	1.991	2.375	2.640
79	1.664	1.990	2.375	2.640
80	1.664	1.990	2.374	2.639
81	1.664	1.990	2.373	2.638
82	1.664	1.989	2.373	2.637
83	1.663	1.989	2.372	2.636
84	1.663	1.989	2.372	2.636
85	1.663	1.988	2.371	2.635
86	1.663	1.988	2.370	2.634
87	1.663	1.988	2.370	2.634
88	1.662	1.987	2.369	2.633
89	1.662	1.987	2.369	2.632

Degrees of freedom	Two-tailed: 10% One-tailed: 5%	Two-tailed: 5% One-tailed: 2.5%	Two-tailed: 2% One-tailed: 1%	Two-tailed: 1% One-tailed: 0.5%
90	1.662	1.987	2.369	2.632
91	1.662	1.986	2.368	2.631
92	1.662	1.986	2.368	2.630
93	1.661	1.986	2.367	2.630
94	1.661	1.986	2.367	2.629
95	1.661	1.985	2.366	2.629
96	1.661	1.985	2.366	2.628
97	1.661	1.985	2.365	2.627
98	1.661	1.984	2.365	2.627
99	1.660	1.984	2.365	2.626
100	1.660	1.984	2.364	2.626
200	1.653	1.972	2.345	2.601
300	1.650	1.968	2.339	2.592
400	1.649	1.966	2.336	2.588
500	1.648	1.965	2.334	2.586
1000	1.646	1.962	2.330	2.581
∞	1.645	1.960	2.326	2.576

Table of significance for chi-square

The following table gives one-tailed and two-tailed significance values for chi-square. The obtained value of chi-square has to equal or exceed the listed value to be statistically significant at the level in the column heading.

Degrees of freedom	5%	1%
1 (1-tailed)[a]	2.705	5.412
1 (2-tailed)	3.841	6.635
2 (2-tailed)	5.992	9.210
3 (2-tailed)	7.815	11.345
4 (2-tailed)	9.488	13.277
5 (2-tailed)	11.070	15.086
6 (2-tailed)	12.592	16.812
7 (2-tailed)	14.067	18.475
8 (2-tailed)	15.507	20.090
9 (2-tailed)	16.919	21.666
10 (2-tailed)	18.307	23.209
11 (2-tailed)	19.675	24.725
12 (2-tailed)	21.026	26.217

[a] It is correct to carry out a one-tailed chi-square only when there is just one degree of freedom.

Extended table of significance for the sign test

Your value must be smaller than or equal to the listed value to be significant at the level stipulated in the column heading.

N	Two-tailed: 5% One-tailed: 2.5%	Two-tailed: 2% One-tailed: 1%	Two-tailed: 1% One-tailed: 0.5%
5	0		
6	0	0	
7	0	0	
8	1	0	0
9	1	1	0
10	1	1	0
11	2	1	0
12	2	2	1
13	3	2	1
14	3	2	1
15	3	3	2
16	4	3	2
17	4	4	2
18	5	4	3
19	5	4	3
20	5	5	3
21	6	5	4
22	6	5	4
23	7	6	5
24	7	6	5

N	Two-tailed: 5% One-tailed: 2.5%	Two-tailed: 2% One-tailed: 1%	Two-tailed: 1% One-tailed: 0.5%
25	7	7	5
26	8	8	6
27	9	8	6
28	9	8	7
29	10	9	7
30	10	9	7
31	10	10	8
32	11	10	8
33	11	10	9
34	12	11	9
35	12	11	9
36	13	12	10
37	13	12	10
38	13	12	11
39	14	13	11
40	14	13	11
41	15	14	12
42	15	14	12
43	16	15	13
44	16	15	13
45	16	15	13
46	17	16	14
47	17	16	14
48	18	17	15
49	18	17	15
50	19	18	15
51	19	18	16
52	20	18	16
53	20	19	17
54	20	19	17
55	21	20	17
56	21	20	18
57	22	21	18
58	22	21	19
59	23	21	19
60	23	22	19
61	24	22	20
62	24	23	20
63	24	23	21
64	25	24	21
65	25	24	22

→

N	Two-tailed: 5% One-tailed: 2.5%	Two-tailed: 2% One-tailed: 1%	Two-tailed: 1% One-tailed: 0.5%
66	26	25	22
67	26	25	22
68	27	25	23
69	27	26	23
70	28	26	24
71	28	27	24
72	28	27	24
73	29	28	25
74	29	28	25
75	30	29	26
76	30	29	26
77	31	29	27
78	31	30	27
79	32	30	27
80	32	31	28
81	33	31	28
82	33	32	29
83	33	32	29
84	34	32	30
85	34	33	30
86	35	33	30
87	35	34	31
88	36	34	31
89	36	35	32
90	37	35	32
91	37	36	33
92	38	36	33
93	38	36	34
94	38	37	34
95	39	37	34
96	39	38	35
97	40	38	35
98	40	39	36
99	41	39	36
100	41	40	37
200	88	86	81
300	135	132	127
400	183	180	174
500	231	228	221
1000	473	468	459

Table of significance for the Wilcoxon matched pairs test

Your value must be smaller than or equal to the listed value to be significant at the level stipulated in the column heading.

Number of pairs of scores	Two-tailed: 10% One-tailed: 5%	Two-tailed: 5% One-tailed: 2.5%	Two-tailed: 1% One-tailed: 0.5%
6	2	0	–
7	4	2	–
8	6	4	0
9	8	6	2
10	11	8	3
11	14	11	5
12	17	14	7
13	21	17	10
14	26	21	13
15	31	25	16
16	36	30	20
17	42	35	24
18	47	40	28
19	54	46	33
20	60	52	37
21	68	59	42
22	76	66	47
23	84	74	54

Number of pairs of scores	Two-tailed: 10% One-tailed: 5%	Two-tailed: 5% One-tailed: 2.5%	Two-tailed: 1% One-tailed: 0.5%
24	92	81	60
25	101	90	67
26	111	98	74
27	121	107	82
28	131	117	90
29	141	127	99
30	153	137	108
31	164	148	117
32	176	159	127
33	188	171	137
34	201	183	147
35	215	195	158
36	228	208	169
37	242	222	181
38	257	235	193
39	272	250	206
40	288	264	219
41	304	279	232
42	320	295	246
43	337	311	260
44	354	327	275
45	372	344	290
46	390	361	305
47	409	379	321
48	428	397	337
49	447	415	354
50	467	434	371
51	488	454	389
52	508	474	407
53	530	494	425
54	551	515	444
55	574	536	463
56	596	558	483
57	619	580	503
58	643	602	524
59	667	625	545
60	692	649	566
61	716	673	588

→

Number of pairs of scores	Two-tailed: 10% One-tailed: 5%	Two-tailed: 5% One-tailed: 2.5%	Two-tailed: 1% One-tailed: 0.5%
62	742	697	610
63	768	722	633
64	794	747	656
65	821	773	679
66	848	799	703
67	876	825	728
68	904	852	752
69	932	880	778
70	961	908	803
71	991	936	29
72	1021	965	856
73	1051	994	883
74	1082	1024	910
75	1113	1054	938
76	1145	1084	967
77	1178	1115	995
78	1210	1147	1025
79	1243	1179	1054
80	1277	1211	1084
81	1311	1244	1115
82	1346	1278	1146
83	1381	1311	1177
84	1416	1346	1209
85	1452	1380	1241
86	1488	1415	1274
87	1525	1451	1307
88	1563	1487	1340
89	1600	1523	1374
90	1639	1560	1409
91	1677	1598	1444
92	1717	1636	1479
93	1756	1674	1515
94	1796	1713	1551
95	1837	1752	1588
96	1878	1792	1625
97	1919	1832	1662
98	1961	1872	1700
99	2004	1913	1739

→

Number of pairs of scores	Two-tailed: 10% One-tailed: 5%	Two-tailed: 5% One-tailed: 2.5%	Two-tailed: 1% One-tailed: 0.5%
100	2047	1955	1778
200	8702	8444	7944
300	20 101	19 628	18 710
400	36 294	35 565	34 154
500	57 308	56 290	54 318
1000	235 222	232 344	226 772

Table of significance for the Mann–Whitney *U*-test

Table I.1	5% significant values level for the Mann–Whitney *U*-statistic (one-tailed test)

See Table I.1 opposite: Your value must be in the listed ranges for your sample sizes to be significant at the 5% level; i.e. to accept the hypothesis. In addition, you should have predicted which group would have the smaller sum of ranks.

Table I.2	1% significant values level for the Mann–Whitney *U*-statistic (two-tailed test)

See Table I.2 on page 598: Your value must be in the listed ranges for your sample sizes to be significant at the 1% level; i.e. to accept the hypothesis at the 1% level.

Table I.1 5% significant values level for the Mann–Whitney *U*-statistic (one-tailed test)

Sample size for larger group

Sample size for smaller group		5	6	7	8	9	10	11	12	13	14	20
5	0–4	0–5	0–6	0–8	0–9	0–11	0–12	0–13	0–15	0–16	0–18	0–25
21–25	25–30	29–35	32–40	36–45	39–50	43–55	47–60	50–65	54–70	57–75	75–100	
6	0–5	0–7	0–8	0–10	0–12	0–14	0–16	0–17	0–19	0–21	0–23	0–32
25–30	29–36	34–42	38–48	42–54	46–60	50–66	55–72	59–78	61–82	67–90	88–120	
7	0–6	0–8	0–10	0–13	0–15	0–17	0–19	0–21	0–24	0–26	0–28	0–39
29–35	34–42	38–49	43–56	48–63	53–70	58–77	63–84	67–91	72–98	77–105	101–140	
8	0–8	0–10	0–13	0–15	0–18	0–20	0–23	0–26	0–28	0–31	0–33	0–47
32–40	38–48	43–56	49–64	54–72	60–80	65–88	70–96	76–104	81–112	87–120	113–160	
9	0–9	0–12	0–15	0–18	0–21	0–24	0–27	0–30	0–33	0–36	0–39	0–54
36–45	42–54	48–63	54–72	60–81	66–90	72–99	78–108	84–117	90–126	96–135	126–180	
10	0–11	0–14	0–17	0–20	0–24	0–27	0–31	0–34	0–37	4–41	0–44	0–62
39–50	46–60	53–70	60–80	65–88	72–99	78–108	86–120	93–130	99–140	106–150	138–200	
11	0–12	0–16	0–19	0–23	0–27	0–31	0–34	0–38	0–42	0–46	0–50	0–69
43–55	50–66	58–77	66–90	73–100	79–110	86–120	93–130	101–143	108–154	115–165	163–240	
12	0–13	0–17	0–21	0–26	0–30	0–34	0–38	0–42	0–47	0–51	0–55	0–77
47–60	55–72	63–84	72–99	79–110	87–121	94–132	101–143	108–154	115–165	125–180	151–220	
13	0–15	0–19	0–24	0–28	0–33	0–37	0–42	0–47	0–51	0–56	0–61	0–84
50–65	59–78	67–91	76–104	86–120	94–132	102–144	109–156	117–168	125–180	134–195	176–260	
14	0–16	0–21	0–26	0–31	0–36	0–41	0–46	0–51	0–56	0–61	0–66	0–92
54–70	61–82	72–98	81–112	90–126	99–140	108–154	109–168	126–182	135–196	144–210	188–280	
15	0–18	0–23	0–28	0–33	0–39	0–44	0–50	0–55	0–61	0–66	0–72	0–100
57–75	67–90	77–105	87–120	96–135	106–150	115–165	125–180	144–210	153–225	200–300		
20	0–25	0–32	0–39	0–47	0–54	0–62	0–69	0–77	0–84	0–92	0–100	0–138
75–100	88–120	101–140	126–180	138–200	151–220	163–240	200–260	188–280	200–300	262–400		

Source: The above table has been adapted from Table I of *Fundamentals of Behavioral Statistics*, The McGraw Hill Companies Inc. (Runyon, R.P. and Haber, A., 1989), with permission.

Table I.2   1% significant values level for the Mann–Whitney *U*-statistic (two-tailed test)

Sample size for smaller group				Sample size for larger group								
	5	6	7	8	9	10	11	12	13	14	15	20
5	0	0–1	0–1	0–2	0–3	0–4	0–5	0–6	0–7	0–7	0–8	0–13
25	29–30	34–35	38–40	42–45	46–50	50–55	54–60	58–65	67–70	67–75	87–100	
6	0–1	0–2	0–3	0–4	0–5	0–6	0–7	0–9	0–10	0–11	0–12	0–18
29–30	34–36	39–42	44–48	49–54	54–60	59–66	63–72	68–78	71–82	78–90	102–120	
7	0–1	0–3	0–4	0–6	0–7	0–9	0–10	0–12	0–13	0–15	0–16	0–24
34–35	39–42	45–49	50–56	56–63	61–70	67–77	72–84	78–91	83–98	89–105	116–140	
8	0–2	0–4	0–6	0–7	0–9	0–11	0–13	0–15	0–17	0–18	0–20	0–30
38–40	44–48	50–56	57–64	63–72	69–80	75–88	81–96	87–104	94–112	100–120	130–160	
9	0–3	0–5	0–7	0–9	0–11	0–13	0–16	0–18	0–20	0–22	0–24	0–36
42–45	49–54	56–63	63–72	70–81	77–90	81–99	90–108	89–117	104–126	101–135	144–180	
10	0–4	0–6	0–9	0–11	0–13	0–16	0–18	0–21	0–24	0–26	0–29	0–42
46–50	54–60	61–70	69–80	77–90	84–100	92–110	99–120	97–130	114–140	111–150	158–200	
11	0–5	0–7	0–10	0–13	0–16	0–18	0–21	0–24	0–27	0–30	0–33	0–48
50–55	59–66	67–77	75–88	83–99	92–110	90–111	108–132	106–143	124–154	132–165	172–220	
12	0–6	0–9	0–12	0–15	0–18	0–21	0–24	0–27	0–31	0–34	0–37	0–54
54–60	63–72	72–84	81–96	90–108	99–120	108–132	117–144	115–156	134–168	143–180	186–240	
13	0–7	0–10	0–13	0–17	0–20	0–24	0–27	0–31	0–34	0–38	0–42	0–60
58–65	68–78	78–91	87–104	97–117	106–130	116–143	125–156	135–169	144–182	153–195	200–260	
14	0–7	0–11	0–15	0–18	0–22	0–26	0–30	0–34	0–38	0–42	0–46	0–67
63–70	71–82	83–98	94–112	104–126	114–140	124–154	134–168	144–182	154–196	164–210	213–280	
15	0–8	0–12	0–16	0–20	0–24	0–29	0–33	0–37	0–42	0–46	0–51	0–73
67–75	78–90	89–105	100–120	111–135	121–150	132–165	143–180	153–195	164–210	174–225	227–300	
20	0–13	0–18	0–24	0–30	0–36	0–42	0–48	0–54	0–60	0–67	0–73	0–105
87–100	102–120	116–140	130–160	144–180	158–200	172–220	186–240	200–260	213–280	227–300	295–400	

Source: The above table has been adapted from Table I of *Fundamentals of Behavioral Statistics*, The McGraw Hill Companies Inc. (Runyon, R.P. and Haber, A., 1989), with permission.

Table of significance values for the *F*-distribution

Your value has to equal or be larger than the tabled value to be significant at the 5% level for an effect to be significant.

Degrees of freedom for error or within-cells mean square (or variance estimate)	Degrees of freedom for between-treatments mean square (or variance estimate)					
	1	2	3	4	5	∞
1	161.448	199.500	215.707	224.583	230.162	254.314
2	18.513	19.000	19.165	19.247	19.297	19.496
3	10.128	9.553	9.277	9.118	9.014	8.527
4	7.709	6.945	6.592	6.389	6.257	5.628
5	6.608	5.787	5.410	5.193	5.051	4.365
6	5.988	5.144	4.758	4.534	4.388	3.669
7	5.592	4.738	4.347	4.121	3.972	3.230
8	5.318	4.459	4.067	3.838	3.688	2.928
9	5.118	4.257	3.863	3.634	3.482	2.707
10	4.965	4.103	3.709	3.479	3.326	2.538
13	4.668	3.806	3.411	3.180	3.026	2.207
15	4.544	3.683	3.288	3.056	2.902	2.066
20	4.352	3.493	3.099	2.867	2.711	1.844
30	4.171	3.316	2.923	2.690	2.534	1.623
60	4.002	3.151	2.759	2.526	2.369	1.390
∞	3.842	2.996	2.605	2.372	2.215	1.000

J.2   1% significant values of the *F*-distribution (one-tailed test)

Your value has to equal or be larger than the tabled value to be significant at the 1% level for an effect to be significant.

Degrees of freedom for error or within-cells mean square (or variance estimate)	Degrees of freedom for between-treatments mean square (or variance estimate)					
	1	2	3	4	5	∞
1	4052.180	4999.500	5403.350	5624.580	5763.650	6365.860
2	98.503	99.000	99.167	99.250	99.300	99.500
3	34.117	30.817	29.457	28.710	28.238	26.126
4	21.198	18.000	16.695	15.977	15.522	13.464
5	16.259	13.274	12.060	11.392	10.967	9.021
6	13.745	10.925	9.780	9.149	8.746	6.880
7	12.247	9.547	8.452	7.847	7.461	5.650
8	11.259	8.650	7.591	7.007	6.632	4.859
9	10.562	8.022	6.992	6.423	6.057	4.311
10	10.045	7.560	6.553	5.995	5.637	3.909
13	9.074	6.701	5.740	5.206	4.862	3.166
15	8.684	6.359	5.417	4.894	4.556	2.869
20	8.096	5.849	4.939	4.431	4.103	2.422
30	7.563	5.391	4.510	4.018	3.699	2.007
60	7.078	4.978	4.126	3.650	3.339	1.607
∞	6.635	4.606	3.782	3.320	3.018	1.000

J.3 10% significance levels for the *F*-distribution for testing differences between two groups (one-tailed test)

This table is only to be used for determining whether an *F* value which is not significant at the 5% level for two groups is significant at the 10% level which is the equivalent to a one-tailed *t*-test. You should only do this if you have good grounds for predicting the direction of the difference between the two means. Your value has to equal or be larger than the tabled value to be significant at the one-tailed 5% level for the *t*-test.

Degrees of freedom for error or within-cells mean square (or variance estimate)	Degrees of freedom for between-treatments mean square (or variance estimate)
	1
1	39.864
2	8.527
3	5.539
4	4.545
5	4.061
6	3.776
7	3.590
8	3.458
9	3.361
10	3.285
13	3.137
15	3.074
20	2.975
30	2.881
60	2.792
∞	2.706

APPENDIX K

Table of significant values of *t* when making multiple *t*-tests

The following table gives the 5% significance values for two-tailed *t*-tests when you are making up to ten unplanned comparisons. The number of comparisons you decide to make is up to you and does not have to be the maximum possible. This table can be used in any circumstances where you have multiple *t*-tests.

Degrees of freedom	Number of comparisons being made									
	1	2	3	4	5	6	7	8	9	10
1	12.706	25.452	38.188	50.923	63.657	76.390	89.124	101.856	114.589	127.321
2	4.303	6.205	7.649	8.860	9.925	10.886	11.769	12.590	13.360	14.089
3	3.182	4.177	4.857	5.392	5.841	6.231	6.580	6.895	7.185	7.453
4	2.776	3.495	3.961	4.315	4.604	4.851	5.067	5.261	5.437	5.598
5	2.571	3.163	3.534	3.810	4.032	4.219	4.382	4.526	4.655	4.773
6	2.447	2.969	3.288	3.521	3.708	3.863	3.997	4.115	4.221	4.317
7	2.365	2.841	3.128	3.335	3.500	3.636	3.753	3.855	3.947	4.029
8	2.306	2.752	3.016	3.206	3.355	3.479	3.584	3.677	3.759	3.833
9	2.262	2.685	2.933	3.111	3.250	3.364	3.462	3.547	3.622	3.690
10	2.228	2.634	2.870	3.038	3.169	3.277	3.368	3.448	3.518	3.581
11	2.201	2.593	2.820	2.981	3.106	3.208	3.295	3.370	3.437	3.497
12	2.179	2.560	2.780	2.934	3.055	3.153	3.236	3.308	3.371	3.428
13	2.160	2.533	2.746	2.896	3.012	3.107	3.187	3.257	3.318	3.373
14	2.145	2.510	2.718	2.864	2.977	3.069	3.146	3.213	3.273	3.326
15	2.132	2.490	2.694	2.837	2.947	3.036	3.112	3.177	3.235	3.286
16	2.120	2.473	2.673	2.813	2.921	3.008	3.082	3.146	3.202	3.252

Degrees of freedom	Number of comparisons being made									
	1	2	3	4	5	6	7	8	9	10
17	2.110	2.458	2.655	2.793	2.898	2.984	3.056	3.119	3.174	3.222
18	2.101	2.445	2.639	2.774	2.878	2.963	3.034	3.095	3.149	3.197
19	2.093	2.433	2.625	2.759	2.861	2.944	3.014	3.074	3.127	3.174
20	2.086	2.423	2.613	2.744	2.845	2.927	2.996	3.055	3.107	3.153
21	2.080	2.414	2.601	2.732	2.831	2.912	2.980	3.038	3.090	3.135
22	2.074	2.406	2.591	2.720	2.819	2.898	2.966	3.023	3.074	3.119
23	2.069	2.398	2.582	2.710	2.807	2.886	2.953	3.010	3.059	3.104
24	2.064	2.391	2.574	2.700	2.797	2.875	2.941	2.997	3.047	3.091
25	2.064	2.385	2.566	2.692	2.787	2.865	2.930	2.986	3.035	3.078
26	2.055	2.379	2.559	2.684	2.779	2.856	2.920	2.975	3.024	3.067
27	2.052	2.373	2.553	2.676	2.771	2.847	2.911	2.966	3.014	3.057
28	2.048	2.369	2.547	2.670	2.763	2.839	2.902	2.957	3.005	3.047
29	2.045	2.364	2.541	2.663	2.756	2.832	2.894	2.949	2.996	3.038
30	2.042	2.360	2.536	2.657	2.750	2.825	2.887	2.941	2.988	3.030
31	2.039	2.356	2.531	2.652	2.744	2.818	2.880	2.934	2.981	3.022
32	2.037	2.352	2.526	2.647	2.739	2.812	2.874	2.927	2.974	3.015
33	2.035	2.348	2.522	2.642	2.733	2.807	2.868	2.921	2.967	3.008
34	2.032	2.345	2.518	2.638	2.728	2.801	2.863	2.915	2.961	3.002
35	2.030	2.342	2.515	2.633	2.724	2.797	2.857	2.910	2.955	2.996
36	2.028	2.339	2.511	2.630	2.720	2.792	2.853	2.905	2.950	2.990
37	2.026	2.336	2.508	2.626	2.715	2.788	2.848	2.900	2.945	2.985
38	2.024	2.334	2.505	2.622	2.712	2.784	2.844	2.895	2.940	2.980
39	2.023	2.331	2.502	2.619	2.708	2.780	2.839	2.891	2.936	2.976
40	2.021	2.329	2.499	2.616	2.704	2.776	2.836	2.887	2.931	2.971
41	2.020	2.327	2.496	2.613	2.701	2.772	2.832	2.883	2.927	2.967
42	2.018	2.325	2.494	2.610	2.698	2.769	2.828	2.879	2.923	2.963
43	2.017	2.323	2.491	2.607	2.695	2.766	2.825	2.875	2.920	2.959
44	2.017	2.321	2.489	2.605	2.692	2.763	2.822	2.872	2.916	2.955
45	2.014	2.319	2.487	2.602	2.690	2.760	2.819	2.869	2.913	2.952
46	2.013	2.317	2.485	2.600	2.687	2.757	2.816	2.866	2.910	2.949
47	2.012	2.316	2.483	2.598	2.685	2.755	2.813	2.863	2.907	2.946
48	2.011	2.314	2.481	2.595	2.682	2.752	2.810	2.860	2.904	2.943
49	2.010	2.312	2.479	2.593	2.680	2.750	2.808	2.857	2.901	2.940
50	2.009	2.311	2.477	2.591	2.678	2.747	2.805	2.855	2.898	2.937
51	2.008	2.309	2.476	2.589	2.676	2.745	2.803	2.853	2.896	2.934
52	2.007	2.308	2.474	2.588	2.674	2.743	2.801	2.850	2.893	2.932
53	2.006	2.307	2.472	2.586	2.672	2.741	2.798	2.848	2.891	2.929

→

Degrees of freedom	Number of comparisons being made									
	1	2	3	4	5	6	7	8	9	10
54	2.005	2.306	2.471	2.584	2.670	2.739	2.797	2.846	2.889	2.927
55	2.004	2.304	2.469	2.583	2.668	2.737	2.795	2.844	2.887	2.925
56	2.003	2.303	2.468	2.581	2.667	2.735	2.793	2.842	2.885	2.922
57	2.002	2.302	2.467	2.579	2.665	2.734	2.791	2.840	2.882	2.920
58	2.002	2.301	2.465	2.578	2.663	2.732	2.789	2.838	2.881	2.918
59	2.001	2.300	2.464	2.577	2.662	2.730	2.787	2.836	2.879	2.916
60	2.000	2.299	2.463	2.575	2.660	2.729	2.786	2.834	2.877	2.915
61	2.000	2.298	2.462	2.574	2.659	2.727	2.784	2.833	2.875	2.913
62	1.999	2.297	2.461	2.573	2.658	2.726	2.782	2.831	2.873	2.911
63	1.998	2.296	2.460	2.571	2.656	2.724	2.781	2.829	2.872	2.909
64	1.998	2.295	2.459	2.570	2.655	2.723	2.779	2.828	2.870	2.908
65	1.997	2.295	2.458	2.569	2.654	2.721	2.778	2.826	2.869	2.906
66	1.997	2.294	2.457	2.568	2.652	2.720	2.777	2.825	2.867	2.905
67	1.996	2.293	2.456	2.567	2.651	2.719	2.775	2.824	2.866	2.903
68	1.995	2.292	2.455	2.566	2.650	2.718	2.774	2.822	2.864	2.902
69	1.995	2.291	2.454	2.565	2.649	2.716	2.773	2.821	2.863	2.900
70	1.994	2.291	2.453	2.564	2.648	2.715	2.772	2.820	2.862	2.899
71	1.994	2.290	2.452	2.563	2.647	2.714	2.770	2.818	2.860	2.898
72	1.994	2.289	2.451	2.562	2.646	2.713	2.769	2.817	2.859	2.896
73	1.993	2.289	2.450	2.561	2.645	2.712	2.768	2.816	2.858	2.895
74	1.993	2.288	2.450	2.560	2.644	2.711	2.767	2.815	2.857	2.894
75	1.992	2.287	2.449	2.559	2.643	2.710	2.766	2.814	2.856	2.893
76	1.992	2.287	2.448	2.559	2.642	2.709	2.765	2.813	2.854	2.891
77	1.991	2.286	2.447	2.558	2.641	2.708	2.764	2.812	2.853	2.890
78	1.991	2.285	2.447	2.557	2.640	2.707	2.763	2.811	2.852	2.889
79	1.990	2.285	2.446	2.556	2.640	2.706	2.762	2.810	2.851	2.888
80	1.990	2.284	2.445	2.555	2.639	2.705	2.761	2.809	2.850	2.887
81	1.990	2.284	2.445	2.555	2.638	2.705	2.760	2.808	2.849	2.886
82	1.989	2.283	2.444	2.554	2.637	2.704	2.759	2.807	2.848	2.885
83	1.989	2.283	2.444	2.553	2.636	2.703	2.759	2.806	2.847	2.884
84	1.989	2.282	2.443	2.553	2.636	2.702	2.758	2.805	2.846	2.883
85	1.988	2.282	2.442	2.552	2.635	2.701	2.757	2.804	2.845	2.882
86	1.988	2.281	2.442	2.551	2.634	2.701	2.756	2.803	2.845	2.881
87	1.988	2.281	2.441	2.551	2.634	2.700	2.755	2.803	2.844	2.880
88	1.987	2.280	2.441	2.550	2.633	2.699	2.755	2.802	2.843	2.880
89	1.987	2.280	2.440	2.550	2.632	2.699	2.754	2.801	2.842	2.879
90	1.987	2.280	2.440	2.549	2.632	2.698	2.753	2.800	2.841	2.878

Degrees of freedom	Number of comparisons being made									
	1	2	3	4	5	6	7	8	9	10
91	1.986	2.279	2.439	2.548	2.631	2.697	2.752	2.800	2.841	2.877
92	1.986	2.279	2.439	2.548	2.630	2.696	2.752	2.799	2.840	2.876
93	1.986	2.278	2.438	2.547	2.630	2.696	2.751	2.798	2.839	2.876
94	1.986	2.278	2.438	2.547	2.629	2.695	2.750	2.797	2.838	2.875
95	1.985	2.277	2.437	2.546	2.629	2.695	2.750	2.797	2.838	2.874
96	1.985	2.277	2.437	2.546	2.628	2.694	2.749	2.796	2.837	2.873
97	1.985	2.277	2.436	2.545	2.627	2.694	2.748	2.795	2.836	2.873
98	1.984	2.276	2.436	2.545	2.627	2.693	2.748	2.795	2.836	2.872
99	1.984	2.276	2.435	2.544	2.626	2.692	2.747	2.794	2.835	2.871
100	1.984	2.276	2.435	2.544	2.626	2.692	2.747	2.793	2.834	2.871
∞	1.960	2.241	2.394	2.498	2.576	2.638	2.690	2.734	2.773	2.807

GLOSSARY

−2 log likelihood (ratio) test: Used in logistic regression, it is a form of chi-square test which compares the goodness-of-fit of two models where one model is a part of (i.e. nested or a subset of) the other model. The chi-square is the difference in the −2 log likelihood values for the two models.

A priori **test:** A test of the difference between two groups of scores when this comparison has been planned ignorant of the actual data. This contrasts with a *post hoc* test which is carried out after the data have been collected and which has no particularly strong expectations about the outcome.

Adjusted mean: A mean score when the influence of one or more covariates has been removed especially in analysis of covariance.

Alpha level: The level of risk that the researcher is prepared to mistakenly accept the hypothesis on the basis of the available data. Typically this is set at a maximum of 5% or .05 and is, of course, otherwise referred to as the level of significance.

Analysis of covariance (ANCOVA): A variant of the analysis of variance (ANOVA) in which scores on the dependent variable are adjusted to take into account (control) a covariate(s). For example, differences between conditions of an experiment at pre-test can be controlled for.

Analysis of variance (ANOVA): An extensive group of tests of significance which compare means on a dependent variable. There may be one or more independent (grouping) variables or factors. ANOVA is essential in the analysis of most laboratory experiments.

Association: A relationship between two variables.

Bar chart: A picture in which frequencies are represented by the height of a set of bars. It should be the areas of a set of bars, but SPSS Statistics ignores this and settles for height.

Bartlett's test of sphericity: A test used in MANOVA of whether the correlations between the variables differ significantly from zero.

Beta level: The risk that we are prepared to accept of rejecting the null hypothesis when it is in fact true.

Beta weight: The standardised regression weight in multiple regression. It corresponds to the correlation coefficient in simple regression.

Between-groups design: Basically a design where different participants are allocated to different groups or conditions.

Between-subjects design: *see* Between-groups design.

Bimodal: A frequency distribution with two modes.

Bivariate: Involving two variables as opposed to univariate which involves just one variable.

Bivariate correlation: A correlation between two variables.

Block: A subset of variables which will be analysed together in a sequence of blocks.

Bonferroni adjustment: A method of adjusting significance levels for the fact that many statistical analyses have been carried out on the data.

Bootstrapping: A method of creating sampling distributions from the basic sample which is reproduced numerous times to approximate the 'population'. This allows repeated sampling and hence the calculation of sampling distributions for all sorts of statistics.

Boxplot: A diagram indicating the distribution of scores on a variable. It gives the median in a box, the left and right hand sides of which are the lower and upper values of the interquartile range. Lines at each side of the box identify the largest and smallest scores.

Box's M: A statistical test which partly establishes whether the data meet the requirements for a MANOVA analysis. It examines the extent to which the covariances of the dependent variables are similar for each of the groups in the analysis. Ideally, then, Box's M should not be significant. The test is used in MANOVA though its interpretation is complex.

Case: The basic unit of analysis on which data are collected such as individuals or organisations.

Categorical variable: A nominal or category variable.

Category variable: A variable which consists of categories rather than numerical scores. The categories have no particular quantitative order. However, usually on SPSS Statistics they will be coded as numbers.

Cell: The intersection of one category of a variable with another category of one or more other variables. So if a variable has categories A, B and C and the other variable has categories X, Y and Z, then the cells are A with X, A with Y, A with Z, B with X, B with Y, etc. It is a term frequently used in ANOVA as well as with chi-square tables (i.e. crosstabulation and contingency tables).

Chart: A graphical or pictorial representation of the characteristics of one's data.

Chart Editor window: In SPSS Statistics it is a window which can be opened up to refine a chart.

Chi-square distribution: A set of theoretical probability distributions which vary according to the degrees of freedom and which are used to determine the statistical significance of a chi-square test.

Chi-square test, Pearson's: A test of goodness-of-fit or association for frequency data. It compares the observed data with the estimated (or actual) population distribution (this is usually based on combining two or more samples).

Cluster analysis: A variety of techniques which identify the patterns of variables or cases which tend to be similar to each other. No cluster analysis techniques are dealt with in this book as they are uncommon in psychology. Often factor analysis, which is in this book, does a similar job.

Cochran's Q test: A test of whether the frequencies of a dichotomous variable differ significantly for more than two related samples or groups.

Coefficient of determination: The square of Pearson's correlation coefficient. So a correlation of 0.4 has a coefficient of determination of 0.16. It is useful especially since it gives a numerically more accurate representation of the relative importance of different correlation coefficients than the correlation coefficients themselves do.

Common variance: The variance that two or more variables share.

Communality: The variance that a particular variable in an analysis shares with other variables. It is distinct from error variance and specific variance (which is confined to a particular variable). It mainly appears in factor analysis.

Component matrix: A table showing the correlations between components and variables in factor analysis.

Compute: In SPSS Statistics, this procedure allows the researcher to derive new variables from the original variables. For example, it would be possible to sum the scores for each participant on several variables.

Condition: One of the groups in ANOVA or the t-test.

Confidence interval: A more realistic way of presenting the outcomes of statistical analysis than, for example, the mean or the standard deviation would be. It gives the range within which 95% or 99% of the most common means, standard deviations, etc. would lie. Thus instead of saying that the mean is 6.7 we would say that the 95% confidence interval for the mean is 5.2 to 8.2.

Confirmatory factor analysis: A test of whether a particular model or factor structure fits a set of data satisfactorily.

Confounding variable: Any variable which clouds the interpretation of a correlation or any other statistical relationship. Once the effects of the confounding variable are removed, the remaining relationship presents a truer picture of what is going on in reality.

Contingency table: A frequency table giving the frequencies in all of the categories of two or more nominal (category) variables tabulated together.

Correlation coefficient: An index which gives the extent and the direction of the linear association between two variables.

Correlation matrix: A matrix of the correlations of pairs of variables.

Count: The number of times (frequency) a particular observation (score or category, for example) occurs.

Counterbalancing: If some participants take part in condition A of a study first, followed by condition B later, then to counterbalance any time or sequence effects other participants should take part in condition B first followed by condition A second.

Covariance: The variance which two or more score variables have in common (i.e. share). It is basically calculated like variance, but instead of squaring each score's deviation from the mean the deviation of variable X from its mean is multiplied by the deviation of variable Y from its mean.

Covariate: A variable which correlates with the variables that are the researcher's main focus of interest. In the analysis of covariance, it is the undesired influence of the covariate which is controlled for.

Cox and Snell's R^2: The amount of variance in the criterion variable accounted for by the predictor variables. It is used in logistic regression.

Cramer's V: Also known as Cramer's phi, this correlation coefficient is usually applied to a contingency or crosstabulation table greater than 2 rows × 2 columns.

Critical value: Used when calculating statistical significance with statistical tables such as those in the back of this book. It is the minimum value of the statistical calculation which is statistically significant (i.e. which rejects the null hypothesis).

Cronbach's alpha: A measure of the extent to which cases respond in a similar or consistent way on all the variables that go to make up a scale.

Data Editor window: The data spreadsheet in which data items are entered in SPSS Statistics.

Data handling: The various techniques to deal with data from a study excluding its statistical analysis. It would include data entry into the spreadsheet, the search for errors in data entry, recoding variables into new values, computing new variables and so forth.

Data View: The window in SPSS Statistics which allows you to see the data spreadsheet.

Degrees of freedom: The number of components of the data that can vary while still yielding a given population value for characteristics such as mean scores. All other things being equal, the bigger the degrees of freedom the more likely it is that the research findings will be statistically significant.

Dependent variable: A variable which potentially may be affected or predicted by other variables in the analysis. It is sometimes known as the criterion or outcome variable.

Descriptive statistics: Indices which describe the major characteristics of variables or the relationships between variables. It includes measures of central tendency (mean, median and mode for example) and measures of spread (range, variance, etc.).

Deviation: Usually the difference between a score and the mean of the set of scores.

Dialog box: A rectangular picture in SPSS Statistics which allows the user to select various procedures.

Dichotomous: A nominal (category) variable with just two categories. Gender (male/female) is an obvious example.

Direct Oblimin: A rotation procedure for making factors in a factor analysis more meaningful or interpretable. Its essential characteristic is that the factors are not required to be uncorrelated (independent) of each other.

Discriminant (function) analysis: A statistical technique for score variables which maximises the difference(s) between two or more groups of participants on a set of variables. It generates a set of 'weights' which are applied to these variables.

Discriminant function: Found mainly in discriminant (function) analysis. A derived variable based on combining a set of variables in such a way that groups are as different as possible on the discriminant function. More than one discriminant function may emerge, but each discriminant function is uncorrelated with the others.

Discriminant score: An individual's score on a discriminant function.

Dummy coding: Used when analysing nominal (category) data to allow such variables to be used analogously to scores. Each category of the nominal (category) variable is made into a separate dummy variable. If the nominal (category) variable has three categories A, B and C then two new variables, say A versus not A and B versus not B, are created. The categories may be coded with the value 1 and 0. It would not be used where a variable has only two different categories.

Dummy variable: A variable created by dummy coding.

Effect size: A measure of the strength of the relationship between two variables. Most commonly used in meta-analysis. The Pearson correlation coefficient is a very familiar measure of effect size. Also commonly used is Cohen's d. The correlation coefficient is recommended as the most user-friendly measure of effect size as it is very familiar to most of us and easily understood.

Eigenvalue: The variance accounted for by a factor. It is simply the sum of the squared factor loadings. The concept is also used for discriminant functions.

Endogenous variable: Any variable in path analysis that can be explained on the basis of one or more variables in that analysis.

Eta: A measure of association for non-linear (curved) relationships.

Exact significance: The precise significance level at and beyond which a result is statistically significant.

Exogenous variable: A variable in path analysis which is not accounted for by any other variable in that analysis.

Exploratory factor analysis: The common form of factor analysis which finds the major dimensions of a correlation matrix using weighted combinations of the variables in the study. It identifies combinations of variables which can be described as one or more superordinate variables or factors.

Exponent or power: A number with an exponent or power superscript is multiplied by itself by that number of times. Thus 3^2 means 3×3 whereas 4^3 means $4 \times 4 \times 4$.

Extraction: The process of obtaining factors in factor analysis.

F-ratio: The ratio of two variances. It can be used to test whether these two variances differ significantly using the F-distribution. It can be used on its own but is also part of the t-test and ANOVA.

Factor matrix: A table showing the correlations between factors and the variables.

Factor scores: Standardised scores for a factor. They provide a way of calculating an individual's score on a factor which precisely reflects that factor.

Factor, factor analysis: A variable derived by combining other variables in a weighted combination. A factor seeks to synthesise the variance shared by variables into a more general variable to which the variables relate.

Factor, in analysis of variance: An independent or subject variable but is best regarded as a variable on which groups of participants are formed. The variances of these groups are then compared using ANOVA. A factor should consist of a nominal (category) variable with a small number of categories.

Factorial ANOVA: An analysis of variance with two or more independent or subject variables.

Family error rate: The probability or significance level for a finding when a family or number of tests or comparisons are being made on the same data.

Fisher test: Tests of significance (or association) for 2×2 and 2×3 contingency tables.

Frequency: The number of times a particular category occurs.

Frequency distribution: A table or diagram giving the frequencies of values of a variable.

Friedman's test: A nonparametric test for determining whether the mean ranks of three or more related samples or groups differ significantly.

Goodness-of-fit index: A measure of the extent to which a particular model (or pattern of variables) designed to describe a set of data actually matches the data.

Graph: A diagram for illustrating the values of one or more variables.

Grouping variable: A variable which forms the groups or conditions which are to be compared.

Harmonic mean: The number of scores, divided by the sum of the reciprocal ($1/x$) of each score.

Help: A facility in software with a graphical interface such as SPSS Statistics which provides information about its features.

Hierarchical agglomerative clustering: A form of cluster analysis, at each step of which a variable or cluster is paired with the most similar variable or cluster until one cluster remains.

Hierarchical or sequential entry: A variant of regression in which the order in which the independent (predictor) variables are entered into the analysis is decided by the analyst rather than mathematical criteria.

Hierarchical regression: *see* Hierarchical or sequential entry.

Histogram: A chart which represents the frequency of particular scores or ranges of scores in terms of a set of bars. The height of the bar represents the frequency of this score or range of scores in the data.

Homogeneity of regression slope: The similarity of the regression slope of the covariate on the criterion variable in the different groups of the predictor variable.

Homogeneity of variance: The similarity of the variance of the scores in the groups of the predictor variable.

Homoscedasticity: The similarity of the scatter or spread of the data points around the regression line of best fit in different parts of that line.

Hypothesis: A statement expressing the expected or predicted relationship between two or more variables.

Icicle plot: A graphical representation of the results of a cluster analysis in which *x*s are used to indicate which variables or clusters are paired at which stage.

Identification: The extent to which the parameters of a structural equation model can be estimated from the original data.

Independence: Events or variables being unrelated to each other.

Independent groups design: A design in which different cases are assigned to different conditions or groups.

Independent *t*-test: A parametric test for determining whether the means of two unrelated or independent groups differ significantly.

Independent variable: A variable which may affect (predict) the values of another variable(s). It is used to form the groups in experimental designs, but it is also used in regression for the variables used to predict the dependent variable.

Inferential statistics: Statistical techniques which help predict the population characteristics from the sample characteristics.

Interaction: This describes outcomes in research which cannot be accounted for on the basis of the separate influences of two or more variables. So, for example, an interaction occurs when two variables have a significant influence when combined.

Interaction graph: A graph showing the relationship of the means of two or more variables.

Interquartile range: The range of the middle 50% of a distribution. By ignoring the extreme quarter in each direction from the mean, the interquartile range is less affected by extreme scores.

Interval data: Data making up a scale in which the distance or interval between adjacent points is assumed to be the same or equal but where there is no meaningful zero point.

Just-identified model: A structural equation model in which the data are just sufficient to estimate its parameters.

Kaiser or Kaiser–Guttman criterion: A statistical criterion in factor analysis for determining the number of factors or components for consideration and possible rotation in which factors or components with eigenvalues of one or less are ignored.

Kendall's tau (τ): An index of the linear association between two ordinal variables. A correlation coefficient for non-parametric data in other words.

Kolmogorov–Smirnov test for two samples: A nonparametric test for determining whether the distributions of scores on an ordinal variable differ significantly for two unrelated samples.

Kruskal–Wallis test: A nonparametric test for determining whether the mean ranked scores for three or more unrelated samples differ significantly.

Kurtosis: The extent to which the shape of a bell-shaped curve is flatter or more elongated than a normal distribution.

Latent variable: An unobserved variable that is measured by one or more manifest variables or indicators.

Level: Used in analysis of variance to describe the different conditions of an independent variable (or factor). The term has its origins in agricultural research where levels of treatment would correspond to, say, different amounts of fertiliser being applied to crops.

Levels of measurement: A four-fold hierarchical distinction proposed for measures comprising nominal, ordinal, equal interval and ratio.

Levene's test: An analysis of variance on absolute differences to determine whether the variances of two or more unrelated groups differ significantly.

Likelihood ratio chi-square test: A form of chi-square which involves natural logarithms. It is primarily associated with log-linear analysis.

Line graph: A diagram in which lines are used to indicate the frequency of a variable.

Linear association or relationship: This occurs when there is a straight line relationship between two sets of scores. The scattergram for these data will be represented best by a straight line rather than a curved line.

Linear model: A model which assumes a linear relationship between the variables.

LISREL: The name of a particular software designed to carry out *li*near *s*tructural *rel*ationship analysis also known as structural equation modelling.

Loading: An index of the size and direction of the association of a variable with a factor or discriminant function of which it is part. A loading is simply the correlation between a variable and the factor or discriminant function.

Log likelihood: An index based on the difference between the frequencies for a category variable(s) and what is predicted on the basis of the predictors (i.e. the modelled data). The bigger the log likelihood the poorer the fit of the model to the data.

Log-linear analysis: A statistical technique for nominal (category) data which is essentially an extension of chi-square where there are three or more independent variables.

Logarithm: The amount to which a given base number (e.g. 10) has to be multiplied by itself to obtain a particular number. So in the expression 3^2, 2 would be the logarithm for the base 3 which makes 9. Sometimes it is recommended that scores are converted to their logarithms if this results in the data fitting the requirements of the statistical procedure better.

Logistic or logit regression: A version of multiple regression in which the dependent, criterion or outcome variable takes the form of a nominal (category) variable. Any mixture of scores and nominal (category) variables can act as predictors. The procedure uses dummy variables extensively.

Main effect: The effect of an independent or predictor variable on a dependent or criterion variable.

Manifest variable: A variable which directly reflects the measure used to assess it.

Mann–Whitney Test: A nonparametric test for seeing whether the number of times scores from one sample are ranked significantly higher than scores from another unrelated sample.

Marginal totals: The marginal totals are the row and column total frequencies in crosstabulation and contingency tables.

Matched-subjects design: A related design in which participants are matched in pairs on a covariate or where participants serve as their own control. In other words, a repeated or related measures design.

Matrix: A rectangular array of rows and columns of data.

Mauchly's test: A test for determining whether the assumption that the variance–covariance matrix in a repeated measures analysis of variance is spherical or circular.

Maximum likelihood method: A method for finding estimates of the population parameters of a model which are most likely to give rise to the pattern of observations in the sample data.

McNemar test: A test for assessing whether there has been a significant change in the frequencies of two categories on two occasions in the same or similar cases.

Mean: The everyday numerical average score. Thus the mean of 2 and 3 is 2.5.

Mean square: A term for variance estimate used in analysis of variance.

Measure of dispersion: A measure of the variation in the scores such as the variance, range, interquartile range and standard error.

Median: The score which is halfway in the scores ordered from smallest to largest.

Mediating variable: One which is responsible for the relationship between two other variables.

Mixed ANOVA: An ANOVA in which at least one independent variable consists of related scores and at least one other variable consists of uncorrelated scores.

Mixed design: *see* Mixed ANOVA.

Mode: The most commonly occurring score or category.

Moderating or moderator effect: A relationship between two variables which differs according to a third variable. For example, the correlation between age and income may be moderated by a variable such as gender. In other words,

the correlation for men and the correlation for women between age and income is different.

Multicollinearity: When two or more independent or predictor variables are highly correlated.

Multimodal: A frequency distribution having three or more modes.

Multiple correlation or R: A form of correlation coefficient which correlates a single score (A) with two or more other scores (B + C) in combination. Used particularly in multiple regression to denote the correlation of a set of predictor variables with the dependent (or outcome) variable.

Multiple regression: A parametric test to determine what pattern of two or more predictor (independent) variables is associated with scores on the dependent variable. It takes into account the associations (correlations) between the predictor variables. If desired, interactions between predictor variables may be included.

Multivariate: Involving more than two variables.

Multivariate analysis of variance (MANOVA): A variant of analysis of variance in which there are two or more *dependent* variables combined. MANOVA identifies differences between groups in terms of the combined dependent variable.

Nagelkerke's R^2: The amount of variance in the criterion variable accounted for by the predictor variables.

Natural or Napierian logarithm: The logarithms calculated using 2.718 as the base number.

Nested model: A model which is a simpler subset of another model and which can be derived from that model.

Nonparametric test: A statistical test of significance which requires fewer assumptions about the distribution of values in a sample than a parametric test.

Normal distribution: A mathematical distribution with very important characteristics. However, it is easier to regard it as a bell-shaped frequency curve. The tails of the curve should stretch to infinity in both directions but this, in the end, is of little practical importance.

Numeric variables: Variables for which the data are collected in the form of scores which indicate quantity.

Oblique factors: In factor analysis, oblique factors are ones which, during rotation, are allowed to correlate with each other. This may be more realistic than orthogonal rotations. One way of looking at this is to consider height and weight. These are distinct variables, but they correlate to some degree. Oblique factors are distinct, but they can correlate.

Odds: Obtained by dividing the probability of something occurring by the probability of it not occurring.

Odds ratio: The number by which the odds of something occurring must be multiplied for a one unit change in a predictor variable.

One-tailed test: A version of significance testing in which a strong prediction is made as to the direction of the relationship. This should be theoretically and empirically well founded on previous research. The prediction should be made prior to examination of the data.

Ordinal data: Numbers for which little can be said other than the numbers give the rank order of cases on the variable from smallest to largest.

Orthogonal: Essentially means at right angles.

Orthogonal factors: In factor analysis, orthogonal factors are factors which do not correlate with each other.

Outcome variable: A word used especially in medical statistics to denote the dependent variable. It is also the criterion variable. It is the variable which is expected to vary with variation in the independent variable(s).

Outlier: A score or data point which differs substantially from the other scores or data points. It is an extremely unusual or infrequent score or data point.

Output window: The window of computer software which displays the results of an analysis.

Over-identified model: A structural equation model in which the number of data points is greater than the number of parameters to be estimated, enabling the fit of the model to the data to be determined.

Paired comparisons: The process of comparing each variable mean with every (or most) other variable mean in pairs.

Parameter: A characteristic such as the mean or standard deviation which is based on the population of scores. In contrast, a statistic is a characteristic which is based on a sample of scores.

Parametric: To do with the characteristics of the population.

Parametric test: A statistical test which assumes that the scores used come from a population of scores which is normally distributed.

Part or semi-partial correlation: The correlation between a criterion and a predictor when the predictor's correlation with other predictors is partialled out.

Partial correlation: The correlation between a criterion and a predictor when the criterion's and the predictor's correlation with other predictors have been partialled out.

Participant: Someone who takes part in research. A more appropriate term than the archaic and misleading 'subject'.

PASW Statistics: The name for SPSS Statistics in 2008–9.

Path diagram: A diagram in which the relationships (actual or hypothetical) between variables are presented.

Pathway: A line in a path diagram depicting a relationship between two variables.

Phi: A measure of association between two binomial or dichotomous variables.

Pivot table: A table in SPSS Statistics which can be edited.

Planned comparisons: Testing whether a difference between two groups is significant when there are strong grounds for expecting such a difference.

Point-biserial correlation: A correlation between a score variable and a binomial (dichotomous) variable – i.e. one with two categories.

Population: All of the scores from which a sample is taken. It is erroneous in statistics to think of the population as people since it is the population of scores on a variable.

Post hoc **test:** A test to see whether two groups differ significantly when the researcher has no strong grounds for predicting or expecting that they will. Essentially they are unplanned tests which were not stipulated prior to the collection of data.

Power: In statistics, the ability of a test to reject the null hypothesis when it is false.

Principal component analysis: Primarily a form of factor analysis in which the variance of each variable is set at the maximum value of 1 as no adjustment has been made for communalities. Probably best reserved for instances in which the correlation matrix tends to have high values which is not common in psychological research.

Probability distribution: The distribution of outcomes expected by chance.

Promax: A method of oblique rotation in factor analysis.

Quantitative research: Research which at the very least involves counting the frequency of categories in the main variable of interest.

Quartimax: A method of orthogonal rotation in factor analysis.

Randomisation: The assignment of cases to conditions using some method of assigning by chance.

Range: The difference between the largest and smallest score of a variable.

Ratio data: A measure for which it is possible to say that a score is a multiple of another score such as 20 being twice 10. Also there should be a zero point on the measure. This is a holy grail of statistical theory which psychologists will never find unless variables such as time and distance are considered.

Recode: Giving a value, or set of values, another value such as recoding age into ranges of age.

Regression coefficient: The weight which is applied to a predictor variable to give the value of the dependent variable.

Related design: A design in which participants provide data in more than one condition of the experiment. This is where participants serve as their own controls. More rarely, if samples are matched on a pairwise basis to be as similar as possible on a matching variable then this also constitutes a related design if the matching variable correlates with the dependent variable.

Related factorial design: A design in which there are two or more independent or predictor variables which have the same or similar cases in them.

Reliability: Internal reliability is the extent to which items which make up a scale or measure are internally consistent. It is usually calculated either using a form of split-half reliability in which the score for half the items is correlated with the score for the other half of the items (with anadjustment for the shortened length of the scale) or using Cronbach's alpha (which is the average of all possible split-half reliabilities). A distinct form of reliability is test–retest reliability which measures consistency over time.

Repeated measures design: A design in which the groups of the independent variables have the same or similar cases in them.

Repeated-measures ANOVA: An analysis of variance which is based on one or more related factors having the same or similar cases in them.

Residual: The difference between an observed and expected score.

Residual sum of squares: The sum of squares that are left over after other sources of variance have been removed.

Rotation: *see* Rotation of factors.

Rotation of factors: This adjusts the factors (axes) of a factor analysis in order to make the factors more interpretable. To do so, the numbers of high and low factor loadings are maximised whereas the numbers of middle-sized factor loadings are made minimal. Originally it involved plotting the axes (factors) on graph paper and rotating them physically on the page, leaving the factor loadings in the same points on the graph paper. As a consequence, the factor loadings change since these have not moved but the axes have.

Sample: A selection or subset of scores on a variable. Samples cannot be guaranteed to be representative of the population, but if they are selected at random then there will be no systematic difference between the samples and the population.

Sampling distribution: The theoretical distribution of a particular size of sample which would result if samples of that size were repeatedly taken from that population.

Saturated model: A model (set of variables) which fully accounts for the data. It is a concept used in log-linear analysis.

Scattergram: *see* Scatterplot.

Scatterplot: A diagram or chart which shows the relationship between two score variables. It consists of a horizontal and a vertical scale which are used to plot the scores of each individual on both variables.

Scheffé test: A *post hoc* test used in analysis of variance to test whether two group means differ significantly from each other.

Score statistic: A measure of association in logistic regression.

Scree test: A graph of the eigenvalues of successive factors in a factor analysis. It is used to help determine the 'significant' number of factors prior to rotation. The point at which the curve becomes flat and 'straight' determines the number of 'significant' factors.

Select cases: The name of an SPSS Statistics procedure for selecting subsamples of cases based on one or more criteria such as the gender of participants.

Sign test: A nonparametric test which determines whether the number of positive and negative differences between the scores in two conditions with the same or similar cases differ significantly.

Significance level: The probability level at and below which an outcome is assumed to be unlikely to be due to chance.

Simple regression: A test for describing the size and direction of the association between a predictor variable and a criterion variable.

Skew: A description given to a frequency distribution in which the scores tend to be in one tail of the distribution. In other words, it is a lop-sided frequency distribution compared to a normal (bell-shaped) curve.

Sort cases: The name of an SPSS Statistics procedure for ordering cases in the data file according to the values of one or more variables.

Spearman's correlation coefficient: A measure of the size and direction of the association between two variables rank ordered in size.

Sphericity: Similarity of the correlations between the dependent variable in the different conditions.

Split-half reliability: The correlation between the two halves of a scale adjusted for the number of variables in each scale.

SPSS: A statistical computer package which in 2008–9 was renamed PASW Statistics. In 2010 it was renamed SPSS Statistics.

Squared Euclidean distance: The sum of the squared differences between the scores on two variables for the sample.

Standard deviation: Conceptually, the average amount by which the scores differ from the mean.

Standard error: Conceptually, the average amount by which the means of samples differ from the mean of the population.

Standard or direct entry: A form of multiple regression in which all of the predictor variables are entered into the analysis at the same time.

Standardised coefficients or weights: The coefficients or weights of the predictors in an equation are expressed in terms of their standardised scores.

Stepwise entry: A form of multiple regression in which variables are entered into the analysis one step at a time. In this way, the most predictive predictor is chosen first, then the second most predictive predictor is chosen second having dealt with the variance due to the first predictor, and so forth.

Sum of squares: The total obtained by adding up the squared differences between each score and the mean of that set of scores. The 'average' of this is the variance.

Syntax: Statements or commands for carrying out various procedures in computer software.

Test–retest reliability: The correlation of a measure taken at one point in time with the same (or very similar) measure taken at a different point in time.

Transformation: Ways of adjusting the data to meet the requirements for the data for a particular statistical technique. For example, the data could be changed by taking the square root of each score, turning each score into a logarithm and so forth. Trial and error may be required to find an appropriate transformation.

Two-tailed test: A test which assesses the statistical significance of a relationship or difference in either direction.

Type I error: Accepting the hypothesis when it is actually false.

Type II error: Rejecting the hypothesis when it is actually true.

Under-identified model: A structural equation model in which there are not enough data points to estimate its parameters.

Unique variance: Variance of a variable which is not shared with other variables in the analysis.

Univariate: Involving one variable.

Unplanned comparisons: Comparisons between groups which were not stipulated before the data were collected but after its collection.

Unstandardised coefficients or weights: The coefficients or weights which are applied to scores (as opposed to standardised scores).

Value label: The name or label given to the value of a variable such as 'Female' for '1'.

Variable label: The name or label given to a variable.

Variable name: The name of a variable.

Variable View: The window in SPSS Statistics Data Editor which shows the names of variables and their specification.

Variance: The mean of the sum of the squared difference between each score and the mean of the set of scores. It constitutes a measure of the variability or dispersion of scores on a quantitative variable.

Variance ratio: The ratio between two variances, commonly referred to in ANOVA (analysis of variance).

Variance–covariance matrix: A matrix containing the variance of the variables (in the diagonal) and the covariances between pairs of variables in the rest of the table.

Variance estimate: The variance of the population of scores calculated from the variance of a sample of scores from that population.

Varimax: In factor analysis, a procedure for rotating the factors to simplify understanding of the factors which maintains the zero correlation between all of the factors.

Wald statistic: The ratio of the beta coefficient to its standard error. Used in logistic regression.

Weights: An adjustment made to reflect the size of a variable or sample.

Wilcoxon signed-rank test: A nonparametric test for assessing whether the scores from two samples that come from the same or similar cases differ significantly.

Wilks' lambda: A measure, involving the ratio of the within-groups to the total sum of squares, used to determine if the means of variables differ significantly across groups.

Within-subjects design: A correlated or repeated measures design.

Yates's continuity correction: An outmoded adjustment to a 2×2 chi-square test held to improve the fit of the test to the chi-square distribution.

z-score: A score expressed as the number of standard deviations a score is from the mean of the set of scores.

REFERENCES

Aiken, L.S. and West, S.G. (1991), *Multiple Regression: Testing and Interpreting Interactions*. Newbury Park, CA: Sage.

Baron, R.M. and Kenny, D.A. (1986), 'The moderator-mediator variable distinction in social psychological research: Conceptual, strategic, and statistical considerations', *Journal of Personality and Social Psychology*, **51**, 1173–82.

Baron, L. and Straus, M. (1989), *Four Theories of Rape: A State-Level Analysis*, New Haven, CT: Yale University Press.

Blalock, H.M. (1972), *Social Statistics*, New York: McGraw-Hill.

Butler, C. (1995a), 'Teachers' qualities, resources and involvement of special needs children in mainstream classrooms', unpublished thesis, Department of Social Sciences, Loughborough University.

Butler, R. (1995b), 'Motivational and informational functions and consequences of children's attention to peers' work', *Journal of Educational Psychology*, **87**(3), 347–60.

Cohen, J. (1988). *Statistical Power Analysis for the Behavioural Sciences*, 2nd edition, Hillsdale, NJ: Lawrence Erlbaum Associates.

Cohen, J., Cohen, P., West, S.G. and Aiken, L.S. (2003), *Applied Multiple Regression/Correlation Analysis for the Behavioral Sciences*, 3rd edition, Hillsdale, NJ: Lawrence Erlbaum Associates.

Cramer, D. (1992), *Personality and Psychotherapy*, Milton Keynes: Open University Press.

Crighton, D. and Towl, G. (1994), 'The selection and recruitment of prison officers', *Forensic Update: A Newsletter for Forensic Psychologists*, **39**, 4–7.

Donnerstein, E. (1980), 'Aggressive erotica and violence against women', *Journal of Personality and Social Psychology*, **39**(2), 269–77.

Gillis, J.S. (1980), *Child Anxiety Scale Manual*, Champaign, IL: Institute of Personality and Ability Testing.

Glantz, S.A. and Slinker, B.K. (1990), *Primer of Applied Regression and Analysis of Variance*, New York: McGraw-Hill.

Hoenig, J.M. and Heisey, D.M. (2001), 'The abuse of power: The pervasive fallacy of power calculations for data analysis', *The American Statistician*, **55**(1), 19–24.

Howell, D. (2010), *Statistical Methods for Psychology*, 7th edition, Belmont, CA: Duxbury Press.

Howitt, D. and Cumberbatch, G. (1990), *Pornography: Impacts and Influences*, London: Home Office Research and Planning Unit.

Huitema, B.E. (1980), *The Analysis of Covariance and its Alternatives*, New York: Wiley.

Johnston, F.A. and Johnston, S.A. (1986), 'Differences between human figure drawings of child molesters and control groups', *Journal of Clinical Psychology*, **42**(4), 638–47.

Kerlinger, F.N. (1986), *Foundations of Behavioral Research*, New York: Holt, Rinehart & Winston.

Lipsey, M.W. and Wilson, D.B. (1993), 'The efficacy of psychological, educational, and behavioral treatment: Confirmation from meta-analysis', *American Psychologist*, **48**(12), 1181–1209.

Munford, M.B. (1994), 'Relationship of gender, self-esteem, social class and racial identity to depression in blacks', *Journal of Black Psychology*, **20**, 157–74.

Murphy, K.R. and Myors, B. (2004), *Statistical Power Analysis: A simple and general model for traditional and modern hypothesis tests*, 2nd edition, Mahwah, NJ: Lawrence Erlbaum Associates.

Rosenthal, J.A. (1988), 'Patterns of reported child abuse and neglect', *Child Abuse and Neglect*, **12**, 263–71.

Szostak, H. (1995), 'Competitive performance, anxiety and perceptions of parental pressure in young tennis players', unpublished thesis, Department of Social Sciences, Loughborough University.

Wagner, U. and Zick, A. (1995), 'The relation of formal education to ethnic prejudice: its reliability, validity and explanation', *European Journal of Social Psychology*, **25**, 41–56.

INDEX